BOOKS BY MICHAEL BESCHLOSS

Taking Charge: The Johnson White House Tapes, 1963–1964 (1997)

The Crisis Years: Kennedy and Khrushchev, 1960–1963 (1991)

Mayday: Eisenhower, Khrushchev, and the U-2 Affair (1986)

Kennedy and Roosevelt: The Uneasy Alliance (1980)

At the Highest Levels: The Inside Story of the End of the Cold War (1993)
(WITH STROBE TALBOTT)

REACHING FOR GLORY

*Lyndon Johnson's Secret
White House Tapes,
1964–1965*

EDITED AND WITH COMMENTARY BY

MICHAEL BESCHLOSS

SIMON & SCHUSTER
New York   London   Toronto   Sydney   Singapore

SIMON & SCHUSTER
Rockefeller Center
1230 Avenue of the Americas
New York, NY 10020

For information regarding special discounts for bulk purchases,
please contact Simon & Schuster Special Sales at
1-800-456-6798 or business@simonandschuster.com

Designed by Leslie Phillips
Manufactured in the United States of America

1   3   5   7   9   10   8   6   4   2

Library of Congress Cataloging-in-Publication Data is available.

ISBN 0-684-80408-5

For James MacGregor Burns

CONTENTS

REACHING
FOR GLORY

Prologue

"JACKIE, I LOVE YOU!"

Give Caroline and John-John a hug for me. . . . Tell them I'd like to be their daddy!

LBJ *to* Jacqueline Kennedy, *December 7, 1963*

Most of Lyndon Johnson's secretly recorded tapes of his conversations with Jacqueline Kennedy in 1963 and 1964 were absent from the first volume of this trilogy, *Taking Charge*. Noting her mother's zeal for privacy, Caroline Kennedy had persuaded Johnson Library officials to keep them closed. But since then, she has agreed to the unsealing of her mother's taped conversations, which appear in this prologue.

Toward his Vice President, John Kennedy felt a mixture of respect, empathy, amusement, and annoyance. Attorney General Robert Kennedy detested the man his brother had put on the 1960 Democratic ticket. Not Jackie. Johnson scarcely met her standards of stylishness, but she had always felt comfortable with older men. (LBJ was twenty-one years her senior.) She empathized with his predicament—one moment dominating the Senate, then suffering through a very peripheral role in her husband's administration. Johnson responded to her with a courtly flirtatiousness.

In the summer of 1963, the Vice President sold some LBJ Ranch cattle and used the proceeds to buy an 1861 Abraham Lincoln appointments book for Jackie's White House collection. He drafted a joking letter to her saying, "Never before has Texas beef found a market of such quality as in winding up on Mrs. Kennedy's bookshelves between the covers of Mr. Lincoln's records. Too bad it couldn't be on Mr. Lincoln's bookshelves between the . . . well, never mind."[1] But when he finally read his letter, he thought it was too risqué and refused to send it.

Then, on November 22, 1963, Lyndon Johnson and Jacqueline Kennedy became the two chief survivors of one of the searing dramas of American history.

---

1. The unsent letter is in the Lyndon Baines Johnson Library in Austin, Texas, hereafter referred to as LBJL.

11

The day after John Kennedy's funeral, Jackie wrote the new President from the White House that "the greatest act of a gentleman" that she had "seen on this earth" was how LBJ, who was Majority Leader when Jack "came to the Senate as just another little freshman," could serve as Vice President for "a man who had served under you and been taught by you." She added, "It was so strange last night. I was wandering through this house. . . . In the library I showed Bobby the Lincoln Record book you gave."[1]

On Sunday, December 1, LBJ scrawled to Jackie, "You have been magnificent and have won a warm place in the heart of history. I only wish things could be different—that I didn't have to be here. . . . You have for now and for *always* our warm, warm *love*."[2]

JACQUELINE BOUVIER KENNEDY

Monday, December 2, 1963, 2:42 P.M.

> From the Oval Office, LBJ calls Jackie, who is still staying with her children in the Executive Mansion. A bundle of raw nerve endings, she sounds tranquilized, emotional, tinny, breathy, girlish, otherworldly, on the verge of weeping. With her ardor for privacy, she would no doubt be horrified to know that Johnson is surreptitiously taping their conversation.

JACQUELINE: Mr. President?
LBJ: I just wanted you to know you were loved and by so many and so much and—
JACQUELINE: Oh, Mr. President!
LBJ: —I'm one of them.
JACQUELINE: I tried. I didn't *dare* bother you again, but I got Kenny O'Donnell[3] over here to give you a message if he ever saw you. Did he give it to you yet?
LBJ: No.
JACQUELINE: About my letter? That was waiting for me last night?
LBJ: Listen, sweetie. Now, first thing you've got to learn—you've got some things to learn, and one of them is that you don't bother me. You give me strength.
JACQUELINE: But I wasn't going to send you in one more letter. I was so scared you'd *answer*.
LBJ: Don't send me anything, don't send me anything! You just come on over and put your *arm* around me. That's all you do. When you haven't got anything

---

1. Jacqueline Kennedy to Lyndon Johnson, November 26, 1963, LBJL.
2. Lyndon Johnson to Jacqueline Kennedy, December 1, 1963, LBJL.
3. JFK's appointments secretary, now remaining on Johnson's staff.

else to do, let's take a *walk*. Let's walk around the back *yard* and just let me tell you how much you *mean* to all of us and how we can carry on if you give us a little *strength!*

JACQUELINE: But you know what I wanted to say to you about that *letter?* I *know* how rare a letter is in a President's handwriting. Do you know that I've got more [*voice quivers, near tears*] in your handwriting than I do in Jack's now?[1]

LBJ: Well—

JACQUELINE: And for you to write it at this time, and then to send me that thing today of, you know, your Cape announcement[2] and everything—

LBJ: I want you to just know this, that I told my mama a lon-ng time ago, when everybody else gave up about my election in '48[3]—

JACQUELINE: Yes?

LBJ: My mother and my wife and my sisters and you females got a lot of courage that we men don't *have*. And so we *have* to rely on you and depend on you, and you've got something to do. You've got the President *relying* on you. And this is not the *first* one you've had! So there're not many women, you know, running around with a good many Presidents. So you just bear that in mind. You've got the biggest job of your life!

JACQUELINE: [*laughs*] "She ran around with two Presidents." That's what they'll say about me!

LBJ: [*quietly chortles*]

JACQUELINE: Okay! Anytime!

LBJ: Goodbye, darling.

JACQUELINE: Thank you for calling, Mr. President. Goodbye.

LBJ: Bye, sweetie. Do come by.

JACQUELINE: [*warmly:*] I will.

"The man had incredible warmth, didn't he?" Jackie recalled in a 1974 oral history interview for the Johnson Presidential Library. "I almost felt sorry for him because I knew he felt sorry for me. . . . I think the situation gave him pain and he tried to do the best he could. And . . . I was really touched by that generosity of spirit. . . . I always felt that way about him."[4]

---

1. This was not literally true.

2. In response to Jacqueline's request that he do something to honor JFK's stewardship of the American space program, Johnson had announced that Cape Canaveral would be renamed Cape Kennedy. Years later the decision was reversed on grounds that Canaveral was one of the oldest place names in North America. Jacqueline said in her 1974 LBJL oral history interview that by then she realized that it was "so wrong" to rename the site: "If I'd known Cape Canaveral was the name from the time of Columbus, it would be the last thing Jack would have wanted."

3. To the U.S. Senate, when LBJ prevailed with his famous 87-vote margin.

4. Jacqueline Kennedy Onassis 1974 oral history, LBJL.

JACQUELINE BOUVIER KENNEDY

Saturday, December 7, 1963, 5:20 P.M.

Today Jackie and her children have moved out of the White House and into the Georgetown house of JFK's Under Secretary of State W. Averell Harriman. When LBJ calls Jackie, he is straining to comfort the distraught widow but also to ensure that she remains friendly with him. He is justifiably worried that Robert Kennedy, whom she adores, might turn her against him.

Johnson knows that many Americans view him as an interloper thrust into the office of a hero who was killed in his home state. To help establish his legitimacy, LBJ wants the public to see him on close terms with Jackie and her children. He wants her to be photographed by his side at White House state dinners and ceremonies. He hopes to encourage Caroline and John to treat him as a kind of surrogate father. In this call, LBJ prods the widow to visit him at the White House. But for Jackie, the idea is torture. These days she asks her Secret Service driver to avoid streets from which she might glimpse the old mansion.[1] Johnson has the recorder turned on after this conversation begins.

JACQUELINE: —tonight, will it[2] be in the news?

LBJ: It might be. I don't know. . . . I just had them come in the office, and they just sat around while I was drinking coffee. I don't know whether they even took TV of it, or not. I guess they did. . . .

JACQUELINE: Oh, listen. Oh, good, because I thought it might have been one of those things that went on while you were doing it.[3]

LBJ: Did it keep you busy all day?

JACQUELINE: Oh, listen, I'm just collapsed. I haven't gotten out of bed.

LBJ: Your picture was *gorgeous*. Now you had that chin up and that chest out and you looked so pretty marching in the front page of the *New York Daily News*[4] today, and I think they had the same picture in Washington. Little John-John[5] and Caroline, they were wonderful, too. Have you seen the *Daily News*?

JACQUELINE: No, but I haven't seen anything today except the [*Washington*] *Post* 'cause I just sort of collapsed, but they're all downstairs.

LBJ: Well . . . I'm looking at it now, and I just came, sat in my desk and started signing a lot of long things, and I decided I wanted to flirt with you a little bit.

JACQUELINE: How *sweet!* And I read— Will you sleep in the White House tonight?

---

1. Jacqueline Kennedy Onassis 1974 oral history, LBJL.
2. LBJ had that day given his first press conference—an informal session in the Oval Office.
3. Meaning that she thought the conference might have been televised live.
4 Jacqueline was shown walking Caroline and John out of the White House.
5. Johnson does not realize that Jackie loathes this nickname, which was largely a media creation.

LBJ. [*laughs*] I guess so. I'm paid to.

JACQUELINE: Oh! . . . You all three[1] sleep in the same room, because it's the *worst* time, your first night.

LBJ: Darling, you know what I said to the Congress—I'd give anything in the world if I wasn't here today.[2] [*laughs*]

JACQUELINE: Well, listen, oh, it's going to be funny because the rooms are all so *big*. You'll all get *lost*, but anyway—

LBJ: You going to come back and see me?

JACQUELINE: [*chuckles*]

LBJ: Hmm?

JACQUELINE: *Some* day I will.

LBJ: *Some* day?

JACQUELINE: [*changes subject*] But anyway, take a big sleeping pill.

LBJ: Aren't you going to bring— You know what they do with me, they just keep my, they're just like taking a hypo, they just stimulate me and I just get every idea out of every head in my life comes back and I start thinking new things and new roads to conquer.[3]

JACQUELINE: [*not quite convincingly*] Yeah? Great.

LBJ: So I can't. Sleeping pill won't put me to sleep. It just wakes me up.

JACQUELINE: Oh.

LBJ: But if I know that you are going to come back to see me some morning when you are bringing your—

JACQUELINE: I will.

LBJ: —kid to school,[4] and first time you do, *please* come and walk and let me walk down to the seesaw with you like old times.[5]

JACQUELINE: I will, Mr. President.

LBJ: Okay. Give Caroline and John-John a hug for me.

JACQUELINE: I will.

LBJ: Tell them I'd like to be their daddy!

JACQUELINE: I will.

---

1. Lynda Bird, the Johnsons' nineteen-year-old elder daughter, had returned to the University of Texas.

2. In his speech to a Joint Session of Congress three days after JFK's funeral, Johnson had said, "All I have I would have given gladly not to be standing here today."

3. Exhilaration is not the most sensitive thing LBJ could express to the widow. Nor does it jibe with his refrain that he wishes he didn't have to be President.

4. Caroline's school would continue to meet in the third-floor White House Solarium until Christmas.

5. While Vice President, Johnson walked on the White House South Grounds with Mrs. Kennedy while Caroline and John played.

JACQUELINE BOUVIER KENNEDY

Saturday, December 21, 1963, 6:55 P.M.

Jackie and her children have gone to Palm Beach for Christmas. The previous Tuesday, before leaving Washington, she sent LBJ a note saying that when she came to the White House to see Caroline's kindergarten play, she had planned to say "goodbye" to him and give him his Christmas present. Then she learned that Johnson was to be in New York that day: "I felt so stupid." She promised, on her return, to "watch your schedule for what looks like a not too busy day. Then I will come and say hello to you as you suggested."[1] Jackie's offer to punish herself by returning to the White House is testimony to her respect for her public role and her appreciation for the Johnsons' kindnesses after the assassination.

LBJ: Jackie?

JACQUELINE: Mr. President?

LBJ: I *love* you!

JACQUELINE: Aren't you sweet? Where are you?

LBJ: You just skipped away from this town. I ought to have had you arrested!

JACQUELINE: But I was so mad at myself.

LBJ: Well, you *ought* to be mad. You almost made me mad at you leaving without coming by and hugging me and telling me goodbye.

JACQUELINE: Yeah, but did you get my note?

LBJ: Yes, I did. And I—

JACQUELINE: . . . I felt so stupid.

LBJ: Well, I miss you, and I'm thinking of you and I know your Christmas won't be what it ought to be. But I wish that I could make it happier.

JACQUELINE: Oh, well, you're so nice. And you know something, sending Luci Baines[2] was so sweet when she brought those presents over.

LBJ: Well—

JACQUELINE: He[3] just rode that fire engine around for two hours and broke all the Harrimans' furniture.

LBJ: [*laughs*] Well, you're mighty sweet. And I appreciate my book so much. Here's a little girl that wants to tell you hello.

JACQUELINE: Okay.

LADY BIRD: Jackie?

JACQUELINE: Oh, Lady Bird?

LADY BIRD: Yes!

---

1. Jacqueline Kennedy to Lyndon Johnson, December 17, 1963, LBJL.
2. LBJ's sixteen-year-old younger daughter.
3. John F. Kennedy, Jr.

JACQUELINE: How are you?

LADY BIRD: Oh, knee-deep in all sorts of decisions and unpacking and things, and the recalcitrant Congress, but also ready to go home and see kinfolks and sit by the fire and tell tales.

JACQUELINE: Oh, and you go home when?

LADY BIRD: Well, we were going home tomorrow night, immediately after lighting the Christmas tree, but now it's uncertain.[1]

JACQUELINE: I see. Oh, poor Lady Bird, with everything else you have, you just hit that place at Christmastime, too.

LADY BIRD: [laughs] Just in front of Mr. Erhard.[2] I hope that you have, that the children are gay and happy, and that the weather is beautiful and that you get some rest.

JACQUELINE: Oh, you're so nice, Lady Bird. You're so thoughtful to think of me, and I know you've been calling Jayne Wrightsman,[3] and you're just so sweet it makes me cry.

LADY BIRD: Not at all. I've just got to get to work and learn a lot. Lyndon wants to say another word, and lots of love to you.

JACQUELINE: Oh, same to you and all your family.

LBJ: When I got ready to go to home for my Christmas, the Congress just said they'd spank me and hit me right in the face and wouldn't let me go, and that's the way I am going to do you next time if you don't tell me goodbye.

JACQUELINE: Oh, listen, as soon as you get back, I'll come and get a vitamin B shot from Dr. Travell.[4]

LBJ: Won't you do that?

JACQUELINE: Yes.

LBJ: Thank you, honey. . . . Merry Christmas.

JACQUELINE: Merry Christmas, Mr. President.

LBJ: Give that little girl a hug for me.

JACQUELINE: I will.

JACQUELINE BOUVIER KENNEDY

Monday, December 23, 1963, 7:18 P.M.

This time, LBJ overplays his hand. During an interview with four woman reporters in the Cabinet Room, he once again calls Jackie in Palm Beach. Without informing

---

1. Congressional troubles have delayed the Johnsons' departure for the LBJ Ranch.

2. German Chancellor Ludwig Erhard is about to visit the Johnsons at their ranch—an official visit that was originally to have been hosted by the Kennedys, including a state dinner on November 25, 1963, which turned out to be the day of John Kennedy's funeral.

3. Of New York and Palm Beach, one of Jacqueline's closest friends.

4. Janet Travell, one of JFK's official doctors, remained on the White House staff.

her, he lets the newswomen eavesdrop on his end of the conversation to show off how close he is to JFK's widow and children. Jackie's guarded responses suggest that she realizes something strange is going on. Why else would Johnson call her again, after having wished her goodbye and Merry Christmas just two days earlier?

JACQUELINE: Mr. President?

LBJ: I hope that you're doing all right.

JACQUELINE: Oh, I'm doing fine, thank you.

LBJ: Well, this Congress is getting pretty rough up here and I may have to send for you before it gets through.

JACQUELINE: I hope you get home for Christmas. Will you?

LBJ: I don't know.

JACQUELINE: You're so nice to call me, Mr. President. You must be out of your mind with work piled up.

LBJ: I have a few things to do, but not anything that I enjoy more than what I'm doing now.

JACQUELINE: You're nice.

LBJ: How's my little girl?

JACQUELINE: She's fine, and John just set off this awful jet plane, so it's noisy here in the background.

LBJ: [*laughs*] Well, tell him hello, and I wish all of you a Merry Christmas, and I wished I could do something to make it happier for you.

JACQUELINE: Oh, no, you are so nice, and you've done everything you could. . . . Thank you so much. . . .

LBJ: You know how much we love you?

JACQUELINE: Oh, well, you're awfully nice.

LBJ: You *don't* know?

JACQUELINE: [*embarrassed:*] Well, no, I don't—well, yes, I do—you know.

LBJ: You *better* know! All the 180 million love you, dear.

JACQUELINE: Oh, thanks, Mr. President.

LBJ: And all the world, and I'll see you after Christmas, I hope. And if you ever come back here again and don't come to see me, why, there's going to be trouble.

JACQUELINE: All right.

LBJ: You don't realize I have the FBI at my disposal, do you?[1]

JACQUELINE: [*chuckles*] No, I promise I will.

LBJ: I'm going to send for you if you don't come by.

JACQUELINE: Good.

---

1. Here LBJ uses the same line he used to get Senator Richard Russell to join the Warren Commission. (See Michael Beschloss, ed., *Taking Charge,* Simon & Schuster, 1997, p. 67.)

LBJ: Or someday they're going to create a traffic jam out there in Georgetown.[1]
JACQUELINE: Okay, well, that would be great.
LBJ: You have a good Christmas, dear.
JACQUELINE: Thank you. The same to you.

Exhilarated by his performance, with his recorder still running, Johnson next calls Pierre Salinger, the press secretary he has inherited from JFK. He says, "This is screwy, but can you hold on to your chair? . . . Would it be just terrible to offer to ask Miz Kennedy to be Ambassador to Mexico? . . . God Almighty! . . . It'd electrify the Western Hemisphere. . . . She'd just walk out on that balcony and look down on 'em, and they'd just pee all over themselves every day."

Salinger thinks it is a "great idea" but wants to sleep on it. LBJ asks, "You think they'd think we were trying to use her or something?" Salinger replies, "That's really what I'm concerned about."

"This is just something that came to me," Johnson goes on. "I talked to her a while ago, and she just oohed and aahed over the phone, and she's just the sweetest thing. And she was always nicer to me than anybody in the Kennedy family. . . . She just made me feel like I was a human being." Johnson says that if he gave the job to Jackie, "her husband up there in heaven would look down and say, 'By God, *he* saw she had it just like *I* did!' "[2]

Later that evening, at 9:45, Salinger warns the President that Frances Lewine of the Associated Press has filed "a very lengthy story" about LBJ's talk with Jackie, showing that the President allowed Lewine and other reporters to eavesdrop without Mrs. Kennedy's knowledge. Indignant, Johnson snaps, "I see nothing wrong with the President calling Miz Kennedy and the children and wishing them a Merry Christmas. . . . I want to be as nice and affectionate and considerate and thoughtful of Miz Kennedy as I can during these days. And I just think that's good politics."[3]

Worried, Johnson calls Lewine: "I got some kickback from the family and I don't want to get hurt, honey. . . . I just don't want to be carrying on my private conversations in public and have her think I'm using her or something."[4]

JACQUELINE BOUVIER KENNEDY
Wednesday, January 1, 1964, 6:10 P.M.

From the LBJ ranch, after taking a nap, Johnson calls Jackie in Palm Beach.

---

1. Meaning that Johnson will arrive at her home with a presidential motorcade.
2. This conversation between Johnson and Salinger, in LBJL, was previously sealed under the same terms as the Jackie-LBJ conversations.
3. Beschloss, *Taking Charge*, pp. 125–26.
4. *Ibid.*, pp. 127–28.

LBJ: Happy New Year!

JACQUELINE: Oh, happy New Year, Mr. President!

LBJ: How are you doing?

JACQUELINE: Oh, I'm doing fine. . . .

LBJ: You getting some sunshine?

JACQUELINE: [*chuckles*] It's pouring rain today.

LBJ: We have a beautiful day here.

JACQUELINE: Oh, I see. All of Texas— It looks so successful, the Erhard thing.[1] That really went off beautifully, didn't it?

LBJ: Yes, we had a good meeting. He's a pretty good fellow.

JACQUELINE: Gosh, I thought you'd get some rest when you went home, but you did more than you do at the White House! . . . You should go to bed.

LBJ: Well, I did this afternoon. I just waked up. I'm still in bed and I just waked up thinking about you and wondering how you were getting along and what you did during the holidays. Did Santa Claus come see the kiddos?

JACQUELINE: Oh, yes. You've been so nice to me.

LBJ: *I* haven't been nice to you. I just, I want to see you. When are you coming back to Washington?

JACQUELINE: Ahhh—Sunday.

LBJ: Sunday?

JACQUELINE: Yes.

LBJ: Well, I'll probably come back Sunday, too. I haven't made up my mind, but that's pretty persuasive.

JACQUELINE: [*chuckles*] Oh, but I will come to see you. . . . I'll let you know.

LBJ: Anytime, anytime! You just quit being so modest now. Did you have any fun at all? Did you get out on the water any?

JACQUELINE: Oh, I did. I went swimming every day—And your *present!* Gosh, that Fairfax letter![2] . . . That's a treasure!

LBJ: Well, you're sweet, you're sweet.

JACQUELINE: You know, I grew up in Fairfax County.[3]

LBJ: Well, bless your heart. They did a good job on you. Tell me, does John like his automobile?[4]

---

1. The visit by West German Chancellor Erhard.

2. In response to the Johnsons' Christmas gift, a letter by Lord Fairfax, Jackie wrote Lady Bird, "How can I ever thank you for the most precious Fairfax letter? . . . And your thoughtfulness at this exhausting and confused time in your life means so much to me too" (Jacqueline Kennedy to Lady Bird Johnson, December 31, 1963, LBJL).

3. Jacqueline's mother and stepfather, Janet and Hugh Auchincloss, lived in a large house in McLean, Virginia.

4. Another gift from the Johnsons, brought by their daughter Luci.

JACQUELINE: Oh, he loves that so. That ladder! We have to take it down to the beach, up again . . . down to the living room.

LBJ: [*chuckles*]

JACQUELINE: He's *so* mad about it.

LBJ: I'm going to come see him when he gets back to Washington.

JACQUELINE: She's so cute, Luci is.

LBJ: Well, she was up to see the Navy game today. Lynda had mixed emotions. Her boyfriend was a Navy man and she was going to Texas.

JACQUELINE: Oh, who won? . . . The Secret Service all were betting on it.

LBJ: Twenty-eight to six Navy. I mean Texas, Texas! Twenty-eight to six Texas.

JACQUELINE: Oh, that's the Cotton Bowl.

LBJ: Yeah, that's right.

JACQUELINE: I remember.[1]

LBJ: You sound cheerful. I hope you are.

JACQUELINE: I'm getting so much better. It's always tough . . .

LBJ: I think you are a pretty great girl, myself. . . . I just wanted to hear your voice and wish you a happy New Year, and I'll see you next week.

JACQUELINE: Great, Mr. President. You know, I'm so touched by [*inaudible*] with all you've got to do.

LBJ: Well, I've got a lot to do with you yet, dear.

JACQUELINE: Oh, I'd just do anything for you, because you've been so nice to me.

LBJ: Goodbye, darling.

JACQUELINE BOUVIER KENNEDY

Thursday, January 9, 1964, 11:30 A.M.

> Returned to the White House, LBJ calls Jackie, back in Georgetown, to renew his request for a White House visit. By now she has summoned the fortitude to tell him that she cannot return to the mansion. He begins recording in midconversation.

JACQUELINE: [*laughs*]

LBJ: I'll *resign!* [*laughs*] Yeah, listen, I don't like these ten o'clock nights—lights still burning over here—and these early morning breakfast appointments.

---

1. On November 22, 1963, the Kennedys and Johnsons were to have flown from Dallas to Bergstrom Air Force Base in Austin, where JFK would receive an autographed football from the University of Texas head coach. (See William Manchester, *The Death of a President*, Harper, 1967, p. 107.)

JACQUELINE: Will you please start to take a nap after lunch?

LBJ: I'm going to.

JACQUELINE: It changed Jack's whole life.

LBJ: I'm going to.

JACQUELINE: He was always sick. And when we got to the White House, he did it every day, even if you can't sleep. And you know, Churchill did that. And you just, now that you've got your State of the Union over, you just *can't* tear around.

LBJ: I'll start it the day you come down here to see me, and if you don't, I'm going to come out there to see you.

JACQUELINE: Oh, Mr. President—

LBJ: And I will just have all those motor-sickle cops around your house, and it will cause you all kinds of trouble, and—

JACQUELINE: I *can't* come down there. I wanted to tell you. I've really gotten ahold of myself. You know, I would do anything for you. I'll talk to you on the phone. I'm so scared I'll start to cry again.

LBJ: Oh, you never cried—honey, I never saw anyone as brave as you.

JACQUELINE: But I, you know—

LBJ: Or as great.

JACQUELINE: I just *can't*.

LBJ: You know how great we think you are?

JACQUELINE: [*embarrassed:*] Well, you know. I'll talk to you. I'll do anything I can. But *don't* make me come down there again.

LBJ: Well, I've got to see you before long. I've got to see you.

JACQUELINE: Well, any time you say is great.

LBJ: All right.

JACQUELINE: Thanks.

LBJ: I'll call you sometime and come by.

JACQUELINE: Okay.

Jacqueline Kennedy never again set foot in the Johnson White House.[1] She turned down LBJ's repeated invitations to state dinners and to appoint her as Ambassador to Mexico or France. Robert Kennedy warned her not to let Johnson exploit her. After one of LBJ's telephone calls, or so Jackie's friend Franklin Roosevelt, Jr., re-

---

1. Before her death in 1994, Jacqueline returned to the mansion only once—in 1971, with her children, to dine privately with Richard and Pat Nixon and view the recently acquired official portraits of herself and JFK. Before agreeing to the visit, she won the Nixons' assurance that there would be no photographers and no announcement until she and her children had departed the White House.

called, who fumed about Johnson's overfamiliarity and the "pressure" he put on her to return to the White House. According to Roosevelt, when he warned Johnson about Jackie's attitude, LBJ "drew himself up to his full height" and sputtered, "I've bent over backwards for that woman. I've done cartwheels and deep knee squats, and all I get is criticism."[1]

The main reason for Jacqueline's growing distance from LBJ was her determination to start a new life out of politics. In the fall of 1964, she fled Georgetown, where tourists had gaped into her bedroom windows, for a Fifth Avenue apartment in New York, where Robert Kennedy was launching his campaign for the Senate. Jackie did not plan to cast any vote for President that fall, because that vote would have been for her murdered husband. Knowing LBJ's hypersensitivity, she worried that his feelings would be hurt when he found out.[2]

Although they grew more distant from each other, neither Lyndon Johnson nor Jacqueline Kennedy lost the sense of their historical kinship that grew out of Dallas. "You and I have been through a lot together," she wrote the President late in 1964. LBJ replied, "Time goes by too swiftly, my dear Jackie. . . . But the day never goes by without some tremor of a memory or some edge of a feeling that reminds me of all that you and I went through together."[3]

———————

1. Quoted in C. David Heymann, *A Woman Named Jackie* (Lyle Stuart, 1989), p. 424.

2. Jacqueline Kennedy Onassis 1974 oral history, LBJL.

3. Jacqueline Kennedy to Lyndon Johnson, December 10, 1964; and Lyndon Johnson to Jacqueline Kennedy, December 15, 1964, LBJL.

Chapter One

MUDSLINGING CAMPAIGN

This Goldwater, talking about morality! If we wanted to deal in morality, what we could show on that guy! ... He's lined up with every one of these gambler thugs. ... Had them in his home. ... Just unthinkable! ... We haven't brought any of that out. And I hope we don't have to.

LBJ to WILLIAM S. WHITE, *September 5, 1964*

JUANITA ROBERTS

Personal Secretary to the President
Tuesday, September 1, 1964, 5:45 P.M.

A week from now, Johnson will begin his campaign for a full term as President against Barry Goldwater. Although the polls show him poised to defeat the hard-right Arizona Senator by a historic landslide, he is exhausted and apprehensive. As Majority Leader, he had worked amiably with Goldwater in the Senate. But in 1960, when LBJ took second place on John Kennedy's ticket, Goldwater told Johnson that he was "nauseated" that he would run with a liberal whose views he did not share.[1] Now, LBJ fears that the only way Goldwater will believe he can win is by defaming Johnson's character. Today, when the President's chief secretary calls him in his bedroom, she finds him in bad humor.

ROBERTS: We have two bills here. . . . May I send them right over to you?
LBJ: No! I'm trying to take a nap. I've *got* to. I'm going to let them go, come hell or high water. . . . I've been fighting all day to get them, and I'm just not going to do it now. I just got undressed and got in bed.
ROBERTS: Uh-huh.

---

1. Quoted in Rowland Evans and Robert Novak, *Lyndon B. Johnson: The Exercise of Power* (New American Library, 1966), p. 287n.

LBJ: . . . It'll wait an hour. If it doesn't, why, I'll just have to suffer the consequences!

GEORGE REEDY

Press Secretary to the President
Thursday, September 3, 1964, 11:39 A.M.

Robert Kennedy was scheduled to arrive at the Oval Office at eleven-thirty to formally tender his resignation as LBJ's Attorney General to run for the U.S. Senate from New York, but he is late. Johnson feels compelled to help his rival's campaign but is worried that the Senate will give Kennedy a national platform from which to oppose him.

LBJ: Do you think we ought to necessarily have a man to take pictures of me and Bobby?
REEDY: Yes, I do.
LBJ: . . . It'll be kind of hypocritical of both of us.
REEDY: It would be, sir, but . . . this . . . is a case where the picture doesn't mean so much, but the lack of a picture becomes a story.
LBJ: I don't have pictures when everybody comes in.
REEDY: No, but this is an occasion I think they would make something out of the fact that there wasn't a picture. . . .
LBJ: All right. What about the letter? I guess he gives me a letter and I give him one in reply?
REEDY: Right. They will have to be released, I think. I certainly hope his letter is a good one.[1]

ROBERT KENNEDY

Attorney General
Thursday, September 3, 1964, 11:58 A.M.

Now Kennedy is sitting on an Oval Office sofa, with LBJ in a rocking chair. RFK wants Johnson to give him money from the national Democratic treasury. He argues that much of the money had been raised from New York—and that there is a precedent: in 1962, at President Kennedy's request, the national party had helped finance Robert Morgenthau's Senate campaign from New York. LBJ refuses.

---

1. In his formal resignation letter, the best praise RFK could offer Johnson was to say that under LBJ's leadership, President Kennedy's accomplishments had been "consolidated." Johnson reciprocated with cool acknowledgment of RFK's "very vital role in the conduct of public affairs" (September 3, 1964, LBJL).

RFK: Did they talk to you about the problem that I have? This is going to cost me . . . easily a million dollars. . . . I don't mind going into debt five or six hundred thousand dollars. But I can't raise, quite frankly, more than three hundred thousand dollars. . . . To get started up there, I need right now four hundred and fifty. . . . And I'm going to need more money later on. . . . If I go to Arthur Krim[1] or ask any of them for money, they say, "We're giving to President Johnson." . . . They were all closely identified with President Kennedy and they're friends of mine. . . . They'd all like to see you win and see me win, but I don't want to get that all screwed up or competing. . . . I can raise *some* money. . . . I can get some perhaps from Massachusetts. . . . The assessment is that perhaps we can get three hundred thousand bucks. To get through to November, I need a million.

LBJ: [*mildly belligerent:*] Well, I don't know where you're gonna get any of it out of the *national* fund. We need *fifteen* million. . . . We've got the drain of all the big states. . . . I'm scared to death we're not going to raise any money in Ohio. . . . You've just got to go in there and make those folks and everybody you can in New York contribute.

RFK: [*irritated and plaintive:*] I *can't* do that, Mr. President. . . .

LBJ: I don't have the money. I haven't got it! . . . So far as the Democratic National Committee being committed to finance a separate race in New York for the Senate . . . I'm not going to make any commitment.

RFK: I understand, but I'm suggesting a commitment *was* made, Mr. President— prior to the time you became President.[2]

*   *   *

LBJ: [*growing shrill:*] I haven't got it! . . . The money's not here. . . .

RFK: Mr. President, it's a different situation in New York than those other states.

LBJ: *I* don't know how it's different!

RICHARD MAGUIRE

Treasurer, Democratic National Committee
Thursday, September 3, 1964, 1:05 P.M.

> As soon as RFK is out of his office, a nervous LBJ calls his chief fund-raiser, a onetime Kennedy man who is now loyal to Johnson, to ensure that Kennedy cannot encroach on his New York funding sources.

LBJ: The Attorney General came in. We had quite a discussion and some little heat generated. He said his campaign's going to cost a million and a half. . . . That

---

1. Democratic fund-raiser and President of United Artists.
2. Here RFK refers to the 1962 help to Morgenthau.

he could raise about three hundred thousand on his own. That he could borrow about half a million. But that would just take about half of it. And he felt like we had a commitment to take care of the rest of it for him. I told him that . . . but that *I* had made no commitment to spending several hundred thousand in any single senatorial campaign. . . . If I did in New York . . . how could I avoid it in California? . . .

MAGUIRE: . . . As far as I'm concerned, I know of absolutely *no such commitment.* . . . Steve Smith[1] has approached two or three fellows up there—Abe Feinberg,[2] Arthur Krim—to ask them to really help. Each one of them has . . . told him that they are working 100 percent for you. . . .

LBJ: Well, I think you better get them down here. . . . Let's talk to them tomorrow . . . so we don't have a misunderstanding. . . . You better get the top four or five of them and have them in here tomorrow or the next day. . . . Just tell them . . . we've got a little crisis I want to talk over with them. Then we've got to tell them that we've got this $15 million that we've got to raise. . . .

MAGUIRE: . . . If I may say in bold terms of Arthur Krim and Abe Feinberg, sir . . . they are clear as crystal, sir, that . . . all of their efforts are 100 percent on your behalf. . . . They are getting to know you more and more and . . . of course, Mr. Goldwater—he scares the devil out of a lot of those people. . . . I anticipated this was coming, sir, and all the hatches are battened down.

LBJ: All right. Now I want to see where our money is coming from . . . so the first time you get a chance, you get your figures together and come back over here.

ANATOLY DOBRYNIN

Soviet Ambassador to the United States
Friday, September 4, 1964, 2:00 P.M.

Dobrynin calls with a private message from his chief, Nikita Khrushchev.

DOBRYNIN: Mr. President, several days ago I spoke with Chairman Khrushchev.
LBJ: Yes? How is he getting along?
DOBRYNIN: . . . He is in good health. On his trip going around the Soviet Union, he saw the harvest all over the country. . . .
LBJ: . . . When you get out and see the folks, you feel better.
DOBRYNIN: Yes, and he asked me to give you personally, Mr. President, his regards and best wishes. . . . Now, the Chairman frankly thinks, of course, that

---

1. Kennedy's brother-in-law and campaign manager.
2. Feinberg was a New York businessman and large Democratic donor.

Tonkin Gulf, Cyprus, or the Congo [1] do not necessarily, in his words, "decorate the U.S. policy." . . . He added that . . . during the election campaign, some unfortunate things occur. . . . The Chairman asked me . . . to tell you, Mr. President, that he, Khrushchev, votes for you, so to speak, although . . . we are not going to . . . interfere in the American election campaign. . . .[2]

LBJ: Fine. Well, I think that you understand our situation here. It's better to leave the election matters up to the American people themselves. . . . We can never tell . . . how they'll vote. And it may look good in September and be bad in November. But we'll just have to wait and see, and we hope everything works out, and I appreciate your bringing me the Chairman's good wishes.

WILLIAM S. WHITE

Syndicated Columnist
Saturday, September 5, 1964, 11:50 A.M.

From the Oval Office, LBJ calls his friend White, perhaps the most reliably pro-Johnson columnist and author of an admiring Johnson biography.[3] The thin-skinned President is already smarting from attacks by Goldwater and his running mate, Congressman William Miller of Lockport, New York, against LBJ's patriotism, his "morality," and scandal-tainted Johnson associates such as Billy Sol Estes and Bobby Baker. Miller cried, "You've got Bobby Baker and Billy Sol Estes and Lyndon Johnson has the colossal nerve to say, 'Let us continue!' "[4] Convinced that the best defense is a good offense, LBJ provides White and other friendly journalists with damaging confidential information against Goldwater and Miller.

---

1. This refers to the U.S. attack on North Vietnam after the Tonkin Gulf incident of August 1964 as well as the American role in conflicts in Cyprus and the Congo.
2. The relentlessly activist Khrushchev did not like to let an American presidential campaign unfold without some kind of personal intervention. In 1960, his then-Ambassador, Mikhail Menshikov, privately told Adlai Stevenson that Khrushchev supported him and asked what the Soviets could do to help (Michael Beschloss, *The Crisis Years,* Harper, 1991, pp. 32–33). Khrushchev told John Kennedy in Vienna that he had "voted" for him in his heart (Nikita S. Khrushchev, *Khrushchev Remembers,* trans. and ed. by Strobe Talbott, Little, Brown, 1970, p. 458).
3. *The Professional: Lyndon B. Johnson* (Houghton Mifflin, 1964). Before leaving office in 1969, Johnson gave White a Presidential Medal of Freedom.
4. Estes was a fertilizer speculator and swindler from Pecos, Texas, accused of abusing his relationship with Vice President Johnson to get government favors. He was ultimately sentenced to fifteen years in federal prison for mail fraud and conspiracy. The FBI has told LBJ of a rumor that Goldwater has offered Estes a presidential pardon and/or a million dollars if he will go on television and tell everything about his history with Johnson (Goldwater file, FBI). Baker, who as secretary of the Senate had been LBJ's close aide, is under investigation by the Senate Rules Committee for abusing his official position for private gain. He had been accused by a Maryland insurance agent, Don Reynolds, of demanding that Reynolds give kickbacks to LBJ, including a hi-fi set and purchase of advertising time on the Johnson radio station, when LBJ, at Baker's urging, bought life insurance from Reynolds. (See Beschloss, *Taking Charge,* pp. 92–93.) "Let us continue" was a reference to LBJ's speech to Congress on November 27, 1963, after the Kennedy assassination.

LBJ: Here is a man [Goldwater] that is going to be Commander-in-Chief. . . . He called everybody in the United States Army a bunch of misfits yesterday.

WHITE: [*laughing*] He did? . . .

LBJ: Yeah! Well, wait a minute, let me read. . . . Here is the ticker. . . . "The GOP presidential aspirant questioned the Texas National Guard serving barbecue to Johnson." Sixty thousand "misfits" in the Army!"[1] [*chortles and snorts*] . . . Just imagine now! Here is de Gaulle and Erhard,[2] Khrushchev—all these guys—saying here is a man who's Commander-in-Chief of a bunch of "misfits!" . . . Those mamas. I bet *they* don't agree with him! . . . It's an *insult* to our servicemen to say that the Army has taken sixty thousand misfits. . . . What the Senator seems unable to understand is the program is designed to find ways of increasing the number of men who qualify for military service.

WHITE: . . . I've done for Monday a very tough piece about Goldwater's opening speech, in which I think I pretty well nailed him in on his irresponsibility about the draft.[3] Walter[4] mentioned this business about Miller. . . . I have no hesitation about taking this on. I don't know whether it's effective twice in a row. What do you think?

LBJ: Oh, I'd just be shocked. I would say that . . . you hope Goldwater doesn't stoop to . . . guilt by association. We cannot have character assassination. We had that in the McCarthy days.[5] . . . I'd just take the high line—that is, we just cannot deteriorate and degenerate. That's fine for a fellow that's against the nuclear treaty.[6] . . . And if he's for giving the commanders in the field the authority to handle the weapons,[7] let's debate it out. . . . I would take both of them's

---

1. Goldwater said that under the Democrats, there were "sixty thousand misfits in the Army" and that they had "turned the Army into a C.C.C. camp" (*Phoenix Gazette,* September 5, 1964). He was referring to a new Johnson program to admit for trial enlistments volunteers who normally would not meet minimum standards and to help draft rejectees qualify for either voluntary service or civilian jobs. The Civilian Conversation Corps was Franklin Roosevelt's New Deal relief measure to enroll jobless young men in work camps under Army supervision.

2. French President Charles de Gaulle and West German Chancellor Ludwig Erhard.

3. In his column White denounced Goldwater's promise in his speech to "end" the military draft (*Atlanta Constitution,* September 9, 1964).

4. Johnson's chief aide, Walter Jenkins.

5. In his opening speech, in Prescott, Arizona, Goldwater had gasconaded against the alleged moral decline in America embodied by the Johnson circle. Referring to the controversy over LBJ's old Senate aide Bobby Baker, Goldwater had said, "The shadow of scandal falls, unlighted yet by full answers, across the White House itself." At the same event, Miller had complained, "There is a grave sickness of our nation's spirit at the knowledge of corruption in high places" (*New York Times,* September 4, 1964). By "the McCarthy days," LBJ refers to Senator Joseph McCarthy's 1950s campaign to root hidden Communists out of American society.

6. Goldwater had opposed the Partial Nuclear Test Ban Treaty signed by John Kennedy in 1963.

7. In his first speech of the 1964 campaign, Goldwater had said he favored giving the Supreme Allied Commander in Europe, General Lyman Lemnitzer, authority to fire nuclear weapons without asking the White House (*New York Times,* January 8, 1964).

opening, and I would take my opening . . . in Detroit [1]   I'm not going to talk politics.

WHITE: That's good. I think that's wonderful.

LBJ: But I'd just take my speech and Miller's and contrast them and say now here is one speech that tries to unite the country. There is no reason why we can't have a pro-and-con election. . . . There's no reason why we can't have Democrat-Republican. But the business of being traitors, or treasonable, or their morals or something else—that's another thing. Nobody thinks Hubert Humphrey [2] has been controlled by any force except the force of the people and forces of compassion. And to try to leave the impression otherwise is a reflection on the Grand Old Party and it's a reflection on Goldwater. And Goldwater said he wasn't going to deal in personalities.

WHITE: Yeah, that's right, but he sure did, didn't he?

LBJ: [*voice growing more shrill:*] He still is! And . . . he said "phony" [3] and he got such a reaction to it. But he got right back and said he is not going to deal in [personalities]. But he can't deal on them through this guy [4] either. This guy was so lowly held up there [5] that he couldn't even be reelected to Congress. . . . He's pretty *scummy*, this fellow is!

WHITE: Yeah. I agree.

LBJ: We caught him—just between us, I don't want to get you this, but I want to prove it to you. He sold a bowling alley up there. He's tied in with a bunch of these coin machine operators around, and he had a $58,000 markup in a bowling alley. The son of a bitch didn't even report it.

WHITE: . . . I'm so pleased you are taking that tone in Detroit. . . .

LBJ: . . . That's what I want to do and I want you to do that. . . . We don't run but once. . . . Already the first quarter of the game is gone. [6] . . . We've been on the sidelines, and we've got to get in there before the half. We've got to win. And if you just look at the Lippmanns and the Restons and the Alsops and the Rowland Evanses on Kennedy around here in 1960, and . . . the Joe Krafts, and the rest of them, I think the Johnsons had a real minimum of personal treat-

---

1. Johnson refers to Goldwater's and Miller's opening speeches for the fall campaign and his own—in Cadillac Square, Detroit, where Democratic presidential nominees usually launched their campaigns, on September 7.

2. Johnson's vice presidential candidate.

3. On July 15, the day Republicans nominated him for President, Goldwater had called Johnson "the biggest faker in the United States" and "the phoniest individual who ever came around" because he had "opposed civil rights until this year." (This was not true.) That same day Goldwater told reporters that he would not wage a campaign of personal attack (*New York Times,* July 16, 1964).

4. Miller.

5. In his home district.

6. Meaning that the presidential campaign is already partly over.

ment.[1] Now, when *I* get some of it, it's bad, but when other people get it, it's par for the course.

WHITE: I don't want you to misunderstand. I haven't the slightest hesitation about this.

LBJ: Well, we've got a bunch of goddamned thugs here taking us on. Now, this Goldwater, talking about morality! If we wanted to deal in morality, what we could show on *that* guy! I've got the record in front of me, where his eighty-nine-year-old mother is drawing a tax deduction from the Goldwater stores, that are owned by Associated Dry Goods, for forty-nine hundred a year. And she's too damned old to even *get* to the store![2] And when they raised hell, he agreed to reduce it to twelve hundred. So just let them take a tax deduction pension of a hundred.

WHITE: [*laughs*] Yeah? I'll be damned!

LBJ: And then they talk to me about *morality!* . . . He's lined up with every one of these gambler thugs. This . . . outfit flew him back and forth to Nevada. Played with them all the time, had them in his home, all that kind of stuff.[3] Just *unthinkable!* But *we* haven't brought any of *that* out. And I hope we don't *have* to. But I'm tired of them talking to *me* about *morality!*

BILL MOYERS

Special Assistant to the President
Saturday, September 5, 1964, 4:20 P.M.

Relaxing upstairs in the mansion, LBJ ponders his opening speech of the fall campaign, set for Monday, September 7, in Detroit. He has just spoken by telephone with Walter Reuther, president of the United Auto Workers, who will be on the

---

1. Johnson is indignant that he does not get what he considers to be the adulation he believes JFK received from journalists like Walter Lippmann, James Reston, Joseph and Stewart Alsop, Rowland Evans, and Joseph Kraft.

2. The Goldwater department stores, which the family had sold, were the source of Goldwater's fortune. Like other Presidents, from Franklin Roosevelt through Richard Nixon, LBJ used his access to confidential FBI, Internal Revenue Service, Pentagon, and other official archives against foes like Goldwater. (On other presidential abuses, see Arthur Schlesinger, *The Imperial Presidency*, Houghton Mifflin, 1973, and Victor Lasky, *It Didn't Start with Watergate*, Dial, 1977.)

3. LBJ is severely exaggerating fragmentary material in Goldwater's FBI file suggesting links with organized crime (see Goldwater file, FBI). The file says, for instance, that he was "an associate of Willie Bioff, the racketeer who was killed when a bomb blew up his truck on 11-4-55 in Phoenix, Arizona. Goldwater reportedly had been trying to help Bioff get a Presidential pardon." The file also noted that in 1963 a book called *The Green Felt Jungle*, by Ed Reid and Ovid Demaris (Trident Press), alleged that Goldwater had ties to organized crime figures in Phoenix and Las Vegas. In a news conference after the book's publication, Goldwater denied wrongdoing. In his autobiography Goldwater decried suggestions that he obtained favors from Nevada gambling operations, adding that some "were a crude attempt to embarrass me as a Jew. It was claimed that Phoenix had a Jewish Mafia that was closely linked to the Nevada underworld and other vice" (*Goldwater,* Doubleday, 1988, pp. 103–5).

platform. In a drowsy voice, he asks Moyers to draft a succinct statement of his basic purposes that Americans can easily remember.

LBJ: Walter Reuther is going to say that "I'm . . . for Johnson because he's for a poverty program, and because he's for education, and he's for taking care of the sick." He wants a real strong sentence on medical care. I assume there is a sentence on medical care in here, and on education in here.

MOYERS: Yes, sir, and poverty.

LBJ: But I want one paragraph . . . along the line . . . of . . . "We have a right to *wish* what we want to, *think* what we want to, *worship* where we want to, *sleep* where we want to." Everything like the basic fundamentals. . . . Child's mind to be trained, a church to pray in, a home to sleep in, a job to work in. Let's get education, religion, free speech, free press. Read what he pleases. That'll round [the child] out as a well-balanced, tolerant, understanding individual, right? Instead of one of these kooks. . . .

MOYERS: Got you.

LBJ: I want that one paragraph . . . you can quote . . . the rest of our life . . . "I have a vision of a land where a child can have a home to live in . . . and read what he wants to, can wish what he wants to, and can dream what he wants to." . . . Let's get a little of this Holy Roller populist stuff. . . . A land where every child can have training to fit his abilities. A home to protect him from the elements. A church to kneel in. And throw at least two biblical quotations in . . . that every one of them have heard. . . . These auto mechanics. It's what you Baptists just pour to them all the time![1]

MOYERS: [*laughs*] All right.

LBJ: Simple. . . . Go back and get me one of the Commandments. These Baptist preachers don't get on that adultery one. [*chuckles*] Get some of these "Thou Shalt Not Lie on Thy Brother!"

DREW PEARSON

Syndicated Columnist
Saturday, September 5, 1964, 6:42 P.M.

Here LBJ promises to have aides give the muckraking columnist damaging confidential information against Goldwater and Miller. A week later, drawing from White House leaks of FBI and other files, Pearson and his partner, Jack Anderson, will publish an exposé revealing that Miller had once offered a House colleague monthly payments of $400 to $500 to help him block development of the power industry in Niagara Falls.

---

1. Moyers was an ordained Baptist minister.

LBJ: They'll have Goldwater apologizing on this draft thing when two or three million mothers get after him because he's saying that they've got a bunch of "misfits." That's not very good psychology for a prospective Commander-in-Chief to tell the Germans and the Italians and the Russians and the French that all of his Army's made up of "misfits." . . . Little boys are going through Vietnam. Eighteen thousand of 'em out there. Little boys in Korea and those that are walking along that barbed-wire fence in Berlin. They don't think *they're* misfits! Just because some general gets two stars on his shoulder and comes into an air-conditioned Senate Office Building for a forty-five-minute lecture and then gets to fly on a jet plane for free,[1] that's no reason why they're misfits. . . . There are more misfit generals than there are GIs! . . . You better warm up here the next six or seven weeks and expose this thing.

PEARSON: You're damned right.

LBJ: They've got nothing really, except the Klan and the kooks.[2] . . . He voted against the civil rights bill to try to sew up the South,[3] and he's gonna do it. But that's *all* he's going to have. . . .

PEARSON: . . . I'll take off the gloves. . . .

LBJ: . . . You can call [Mike Feldman][4] and give him ideas anytime and he'll give you some leaks. I told Walter Jenkins[5]—he's the most faithful man I've got . . . to give you some of this stuff that they could verify. Now I'll give you one thing. . . . Some of these . . . [riots] in some of these Northern cities—the evidence looks pretty close to Mr. Lamar Hunt of Dallas, Texas.[6]

PEARSON: Oh, among the Negroes.

LBJ: Some of the folding money—to finance that. Now would you know where I get my information?[7]

PEARSON: Yeah, I would.

LBJ: . . . Now don't use Hoover.[8] . . . You better just . . . say, "I want to send a warning to some of these oil millionaires that are putting their dough in some of this rioting. . . . They're going to get themselves into deep trouble and they're going to hurt their country. Are you listening, Mr. Lamar Hunt?"

---

1. LBJ refers to Goldwater, who was a Major General in the Air Force Reserve.

2. Johnson's way of saying that Goldwater's strongest supporters are the Ku Klux Klan and conservative radicals.

3. Goldwater had indeed voted against Johnson's Civil Rights Act of 1964, claiming that it was not Constitutional.

4. Myer Feldman, a Kennedy holdover, was deputy White House counsel.

5. Johnson's closest aide.

6. The FBI had given LBJ evidence that the radical Texas oil mogul H. L. Hunt may have financed black rioters in Harlem or Newark in order to generate a white backlash against the civil rights revolution. (See Beschloss, *Taking Charge,* p. 467.)

7. Meaning the FBI.

8. FBI Director J. Edgar Hoover.

LADY BIRD JOHNSON

Monday, September 7, 1964, Tape-recorded Diary

> Dictating into her tape recorder to create her daily private diary, Lady Bird recounts the launching of LBJ's presidential campaign with his Detroit speech before a hundred thousand people.

LADY BIRD: There was a fantastic-sized crowd. . . . In Cadillac Square, now renamed Kennedy Square, like so many things across the face of the country, there were . . . acres of humanity. . . . One little girl fainted because she was so excited. . . . I plucked a yellow rose from my bouquet and handed it to her. . . . Miracle of this age, we arrived back at the White House about 3:15 [P.M.]. . . . Luci came in. I am . . . a little startled to discover that she thinks it was a good idea that her daddy did, at times, use corporal punishment. . . . He used it on Lynda and not on her—ever—but she says it had a good effect on her nonetheless![1] . . . She has told me over and over how grateful she is that I trust her and . . . Lynda and therefore they are bound not to do anything disgraceful. . . . At one point, she said, "Oh, I could never get mad at you. You're too passive for that." Which did indeed make me feel like a small, gray mouse in the corner, with my hands folded neatly. . . . The end of the day was long and lazy. . . . Lyndon and I had dinner on our trays in his bed. We listened to the hi-fi, read magazines, and talked.

McGEORGE BUNDY

Special Assistant to the President for National Security Affairs
Tuesday, September 8, 1964, 6:40 P.M.

> A month after the Gulf of Tonkin attack, Republicans are complaining that Johnson and his people are being evasive about their plans for Vietnam. To stop the criticism, LBJ asks Bundy to have his Ambassador to Saigon, General Maxwell Taylor, who is back in Washington, meet with key congressional committees.

LBJ: I would have all the Armed Services people and Foreign Relations.[2]
BUNDY: Probably get the same people we had for the Gulf of Tonkin.[3] . . .

---

1. By this, Luci meant that the spankings helped to discipline Lynda, who helped to discipline her (author's interview with Luci Johnson, April 3, 2001).
2. Committees of the House and Senate.
3. Incident. (See Beschloss, *Taking Charge,* pp. 506–8.)

LBJ: And I wouldn't build it up as anything. . . . Let Max tell them what's happened out there, particularly the last ten days.[1]

BUNDY: The only risk I see in it is the additional noise level on a subject that isn't our favorite topic. Do you think it helps cool it off in the long pull?

LBJ: No, but I think it's an answer to the question that they don't know what's going on. . . . They'll say the country doesn't know, and we won't tell them. . . . Taylor . . . can say, "What the hell would you do?"

BUNDY: Exactly.

LBJ: [*laughs darkly*] I mean, if they can't protect themselves, if you have a government that can't protect itself from the kids in the streets, what the hell can you do about an invading army?[2]

LADY BIRD JOHNSON

Tuesday, September 8, 1964, Tape-recorded Diary

LADY BIRD: It was well over 10:00 [P.M.] before Lyndon sat down to the table. His strong perseverance with his exercises is not being matched by his willingness to give up second helpings and ignore desserts. So he is several pounds heavier than he ought to be.

LADY BIRD JOHNSON

Thursday, September 10, 1964, Tape-recorded Diary

LADY BIRD: I [changed] my clothes to something elegant to go with Lyndon to a fund-raising dinner in Harrisburg, Pennsylvania. . . . The number of applauses was enough to kill the heart of any Republican. . . . I've never seen Ken O'Donnell[3] so relaxed, friendly, and almost enthusiastic. I expect it would be impossible for him to feel close to us, but in a purely professional way he was very much impressed. . . . Lyndon was drenched with sweat when we emerged. He changed his

---

1. In Saigon, rioters and coup plotters were threatening a caretaker government headed by rival South Vietnamese generals. Taylor ultimately reported to the Senate Foreign Relations Committee on September 10.

2. That day Johnson had received a Special National Intelligence Estimate saying that "at present the odds are against the emergence of a stable government capable of effectively prosecuting the war in South Vietnam." *Foreign Relations of the United States, 1964–1968: Vietnam,* vols. 1, 2, and 3 (U.S. Government Printing Office, 1992), hereafter referred to as *FRUS.* Vol. 1, p. 742.

3. LBJ had kept on JFK's close aide, who was now working at the Democratic National Committee, but did not trust him. See below.

shirt in a little trailer set up right outside the hall We shook hands with the crowd and were engulfed by the seas of humanity. . . . He really has an electric, magnetic quality. And so does the office![1]

ROBERT McNAMARA

Secretary of Defense
Friday, September 18, 1964, 10:18 A.M.

> In the Gulf of Tonkin off North Vietnam, where it is nighttime, the destroyers *Morton* and *Edwards* have reported that they are under possible attack. It is six weeks after the Gulf of Tonkin incident, in which, while McNamara was assessing ambiguous evidence about whether the North Vietnamese had attacked an American ship, a press leak spurred LBJ to bomb North Vietnam in order to avoid election-year charges that he was being too soft.[2]

McNAMARA: I think the most important question we have to answer is—is there an attack under way, and is there evidence it was an intentional action by the government of North Vietnam? There is beginning to appear evidence that there *is* an attack under way, and it *was* intentional. I just talked to Oley Sharp.[3] . . . The latest information he has is that there appear to be four PT boats attacking our two destroyers. The two destroyers are firing all guns, and they think they may have hit one PT boat. Now the problem, it seems to me, is not to hit the PT boats, or destroy them. The problem is—if it is an intentional attack, what additional action do we take? I've got the Chiefs[4] thinking about that now.
LBJ: Okay.

ROBERT McNAMARA

Friday, September 18, 1964, 11:46 A.M.

> Johnson is still feeling uneasy about the August Tonkin Gulf incident, in which, he believes, he was forced to attack North Vietnam on the basis of a report that might have been false. He also knows that whatever attack on American vessels occurred in August was probably in response to American covert actions against North Vietnam that he could not reveal to the public.[5] Johnson is determined to keep Vietnam on the back burner, if possible, until after Election Day.

---

1. Of President.
2. See Beschloss, *Taking Charge,* pp. 493–510.
3. General Ulysses S. Grant Sharp, Jr., American commander for the Pacific.
4. Joint Chiefs of Staff.
5. See Beschloss, *Taking Charge,* pp. 493–510.

These instincts, plus his long congressional experience on military issues, make him extremely skeptical of McNamara's report. Several hours after the following conversation, LBJ will tell McNamara and Bundy that he is "deeply annoyed" that—as in the August Tonkin Gulf case—Pentagon leaks are generating pressure for presidential action. He will say he is "not interested in rapid escalation on so frail evidence and with a very fragile government in South Vietnam." LBJ's instincts are excellent: the Pentagon will find no definite proof of a premeditated torpedo boat attack.[1]

LBJ: Now, Bob, I have found over the years that we see and we hear and we imagine a lot of things in the form of attacks and shots—

McNAMARA: Yeah.

LBJ: —and people running at us, and I think it would . . . make us very vulnerable if we conclude that these people were attacking us and we were merely responding and it develops that that just wasn't true at all. And I think we ought to check that very, very carefully. And I don't know why in the hell, some time or other, they can't be sure that they are being attacked. It looks like to me they would hear a shot or see a shot, or do something before they just get worked up and start pulling a LeMay on us.[2] I think that if we have this kind of response and then it develops that we just started [it] with our own destroyers that people are going to conclude . . . that we're just playing cops, trying to get a lot of attention, and trying to show how tough we are. I want to be tough where we . . . are justified in being tough. . . . But I sure want more caution on the part of these admirals and these destroyer commanders . . . about whether they are being fired on or not.

McNAMARA: Yeah.

LBJ: I don't want them just being some change-o'-life woman running up and saying that, by God, she was being *raped* just because a man walks in the *room!* And that looks like to me that's what happens in the thirty years that I've been watching them. A man gets enough braid on him, and he walks in a room, and he just immediately concludes that he's being attacked. And that's the basic argument between you and Goldwater.

McNAMARA: That's exactly right.

LBJ: Now, let's don't get sucked in on his side of it.

McNAMARA: Right, and that's what we are trying to probe here. This is the reason why I have—

LBJ: Take the best military man you have, though, and just tell him that I've been watching and listening to these stories for thirty years before the Armed Services

---

1. Quoted in Bundy memorandum for the record, September 20, 1964, in *FRUS,* vol. 1, pp. 778–80.

2. Here LBJ refers to Air Force Chief of Staff General Curtis LeMay, known for his quickness on the trigger.

Committee, and we are always sure we've been attacked. Then in a day or two, we are *not* so damned sure. And then in a day or two more, we're sure it didn't happen at *all!*

McNAMARA: Yeah, yeah.

LBJ: Just say that you want to be sure . . . that we *were* fired upon. Because you just came in . . . a few weeks ago[1] and said that—"Damn, they are launching an attack on us—they are firing on us." When we got through with all the firing, we concluded maybe they hadn't fired at all.

McNAMARA: . . . We've got a number of messages here now and considerable evidence that, as I say, there was either an intentional attack or a substantial engagement. I differentiate one from the other.

LBJ: Well, what is a substantial engagement? Mean that *we* could have started it and they just *responded?*

McNAMARA: But they stayed there for an hour or so. The first—

LBJ: They would be justified in staying, though, if we started shooting at them.

McNAMARA: . . . We shot a warning shot across their bows, so the messages say, and instead of turning around, they kept coming toward the destroyers. And they split up and passed on either side of them, which is what you would do if you were closing for an attack instead of breaking off. But in any case . . . the question you raise is the basic question, and this is what we have been trying to develop evidence on.

C. RICHARD WEST

Editorial Page Editor, Dallas Morning News
Monday, September 21, 1964

> During an Oval Office conversation with the conservative editor, LBJ rants with rising anger against his opponent.

LBJ: Goldwater is a nervous man. An impulsive man. A childish man. . . . You want the real questions answered, don't you? Goldwater has had two serious nervous breakdowns. Had to be taken off, taken out of the country, hospitalized. His wife wrote about it in full in *Good Housekeeping.*[2] . . . He said that I was the greatest phony and faker in the country. That afternoon, he said he wouldn't get personal at all.[3] He'd forgotten he'd said it that morning. He'll do one thing one

---

1. The Tonkin Gulf incident was actually six weeks ago.

2. In a May 1964 *Good Housekeeping* interview (perhaps designed to get the potentially damaging information out in a casual way), Peggy Goldwater mentioned that her husband had twice suffered from nervous exhaustion.

3. See William S. White conversation above, September 5, 1964.

morning and in the afternoon say the same thing. He'll say "small conventional weapons"[1] in the morning, and then he'll say, "Oh, I didn't mean that." He went and made his campaign all through New Hampshire on repealing Social Security and making it voluntary.[2] Now he says he didn't mean that. . . . He's not a stable person. . . . I think I'm stable. I measure my words carefully before I make them. I wait twelve hours, twenty-four hours to think a thing through. But Don Yarborough doesn't and Ralph Yarborough doesn't.[3] . . . Goldwater is the same type of person. . . . I just treated him like I treat a nineteen-year-old boy when he came to see me after he was nominated.[4] . . . He's got an image of being a terrible, protective, conservative politician of the nation's purse. . . . The budget has been increasing $5 billion a year. But I was the first President that ever cut it down. Even Eisenhower was going up all the time. . . . When I came in, Kennedy had a budget of a hundred and three billion. . . . I cut the son of a bitch down to ninety-seven nine. . . . Now I've got a growing population, I've got growing needs, I got a country that's getting more children in it. More schools, more roads, more everything. And I'm operating a billion and one under what *he* did!

ROBERT McNAMARA

Thursday, September 24, 1964, 8:39 P.M.

Goldwater has begun referring to the Vietnam conflict as "Johnson's War."

LBJ: Looks like to me you . . . transferred this from "McNamara's War" to "Johnson's War."

McNAMARA: [*laughs jovially*] By God, it's the first time he hasn't attacked *me!* I think he's finally getting some *sense,* Mr. President. I think it was a serious political error for him to run against me, instead of you!

LBJ: I have been reading about all these coups out there, all the problems with Khanh.[5] . . . Now tell me, what's your evaluation of this stuff we are getting from Taylor tonight?[6] . . . It doesn't look very good.

---

1. Referring to Goldwater's January proposal to let the Supreme Commander in Europe fire tactical atomic weapons without approval from higher authority.

2. In a *New York Times Magazine* interview (November 24, 1963) and on January 7, 1964, his first day campaigning in the New Hampshire primary, Goldwater had said that he wished to make Social Security voluntary. He later modified his position. (*The New York Times: The Road to the White House,* McGraw-Hill, 1965, p. 24.)

3. The Texas Democrats Don Yarborough and Senator Ralph Yarborough (no relation) were two of Johnson's political adversaries.

4. See Beschloss, *Taking Charge,* p. 472.

5. Nguyen Khanh, chief of the Saigon regime, had survived still another coup on September 13.

6. Ambassador Taylor had sent a cable from Saigon stressing the shakiness of Khanh's government: "All elements are present for major disorders which could degenerate into anarchy and chaos if not controlled" (*FRUS,* vol. 1, pp. 789–92).

McNAMARA: It *doesn't* look good, Mr. President. . . . I think the odds are we can squeeze through between now and the next several weeks.[1] But it certainly is a weak situation. . . . But neither do I think it's going to completely collapse during that period. Afterwards, though, after the election, we've got a real problem on our hands.

*   *   *

LBJ: Now, are you going out to SAC with us?[2]

McNAMARA: Oh, yes, surely, I'd like to very much. I didn't know that you had finally decided to go.

LBJ: Yeah, I think we ought to, and I think we ought to . . . milk it for all it's worth. . . . I'm looking to you-all to give me some initiatives these days, because it's getting pretty blue over here. All I read is just the criticism.

McNAMARA: Oh, come on now.

LBJ: . . . And it's no longer "McNamara's War"! I kind of enjoyed hearing Goldwater talk about McNamara, but when he started talking about *Johnson,* I said, "Well, wait a minute!"

CLINTON ANDERSON

Democratic Senator from New Mexico
Thursday, September 24, 1964, 8:50 P.M.

> Senator Anderson reports that Wilbur Mills, Chairman of the House Ways and Means Committee, has reneged on a deal to support LBJ's Medicare bill. Johnson reacts with a salty anecdote.

LBJ: Clint, they tell me that we had kind of a disaster up there this afternoon.

ANDERSON: We had an awful bad day. Wilbur just didn't stand up to what he talked about at all. . . .

LBJ: Did you ever hear about the fellow that is bending over, holding his ankles? The fellow that captured him tied his hands to his ankles. And he was bending over holding his ankles. And a fellow came in and looked at him. Kind of sized him up and started pulling his zipper down. And the fellow said, "Oh, my God!" Said, "*Ple-e-ease* don't do this to me! Goddamn, I've got enough hell. You see what they've done to me? *Ple-e-ease* just have mercy on me!" And the fellow looked at him and said, "I'm afraid, pardner, this just *ain't your day!*"

ANDERSON: [*laughs*]

---

1. Until Election Day.
2. Johnson was planning to tour the underground Strategic Air Command headquarters in Omaha on September 29, to help refute Goldwater's accusations that as Commander-in-Chief he was not stalwart enough.

LBJ: [*guffaws*] That's the way I feel about this one. As far as I'm concerned, it just *ain't my day!*

McGEORGE BUNDY

Saturday, September 26, 1964, 11:17 A.M.

> Johnson is relaxing at the LBJ Ranch after having spoken the previous day to cheering crowds in El Paso with the Mexican President, Adolfo López Mateos, at his side. While eating breakfast in the kitchen, Johnson calls Bundy in response to his urgent cable requesting permission to "shore up" the Saigon government with a naval patrol by South Vietnamese PT boats sixty miles north of the North Vietnamese boundary.

BUNDY: I hear it was terrific at El Paso.

LBJ: We had good meetings, I thought. Pretty good.[1]

BUNDY: Fantastic crowds, the way my people told it to me.

LBJ: It was. On this—

BUNDY: Patrol.

LBJ: . . . Looks like intelligence out there doesn't look good.

BUNDY: That checklist[2] is a shade—we almost didn't send it to you because I thought myself that it was a shade blue, not quite a balanced account. They are a little bit covering their flanks over in the Agency[3] and making sure that they are the ones that are giving the gloomy news first. . . .

LBJ: What about this rumoring of another coup?

BUNDY: They have moved additional troops into Saigon, and there does appear to be some kind of threat to Khanh from the younger officers who protected him in the September affair to the effect that he's got to clean out some of the deadwood by about the third week of October. I think it's the 25th of October or else.[4]

LBJ: Isn't there some way that we can . . . get them to move up their target date a little bit?[5] Why do we have to have all these troubles the last week?

BUNDY: [*laughs*] I couldn't agree more! We have a standing telegram of instructions to Taylor[6] that doesn't exactly put it in that form of a date but makes the general proposition pretty clear. You're coming back tomorrow, aren't you?

---

1. Referring to his meetings with the Mexican President.

2. The President's Intelligence Checklist was the daily intelligence bulletin that LBJ read.

3. Central Intelligence Agency.

4. A Defense Department paper the day before reported that the situation in Saigon was "deteriorating rapidly," with General Khanh and his partners squabbling over how to achieve a permanent government by late October. (*FRUS*, vol. 1, pp. 793–94.)

5. Johnson means he wishes that the crunch in Saigon will not come so close to the election.

6. Ambassador Maxwell Taylor in Saigon, who has been told to consider how to extend the deadline if the government breaks down before late October. (See *FRUS*, vol. 1, p. 793.)

LBJ: Oh, yeah, coming back tomorrow night.

BUNDY: Because there will be one or two things that need to be settled before you go off to New England[1] . . . There is one decision that needs to be taken. I'm a little hesitant to talk about it on the phone. . . . You—or, if not you, then the Secretary of State—should call attention to what we now estimate is a real possibility that the Chinese may do a nuclear test on their anniversary, which is the first of October.[2]

LBJ: Hmm.

HUBERT HUMPHREY

Democratic Senator from Minnesota and Vice Presidential Nominee
Thursday, October 1, 1964, 9:46 P.M.

> Johnson talks to his running mate, who is campaigning in Seattle. LBJ had hoped that Congress would recess and then, after the election, pass Medicare, his audacious plan to provide older Americans with government-sponsored health insurance. But on September 30, when Majority Leader Mike Mansfield raised the idea on the Senate floor, his Republican counterpart, Everett Dirksen, refused to endorse a postelection session. Instead the 88th Congress will adjourn for good.

LBJ: Goddamn if Mike didn't walk right in and tell Dirksen on the floor. . . . He got the damnedest fight started. And now they haven't got the votes to recess.[3]

HUMPHREY: Oh, no!

LBJ: And didn't do anything but get his name in the paper. Now, I guess we will have to adjourn.

HUMPHREY: Oh, God!

LBJ: And that means Medicare— I don't know whether we can pass it next year or not.

HUMPHREY: . . . He made another statement today about the President and the Vice Presidential candidates walking into the crowd. . . . Every press conference, they wanted to know what I think about that.[4]

---

1. A campaign swing through all of the New England states was planned for Monday, September 28.

2. October 1 would be the fifteenth anniversary of Mao Tse-tung's 1949 revolution. American intelligence had discovered that Mao's China was about to go nuclear. As it happened, the Chinese did not perform their first nuclear test until mid-October.

3. Instead of adjourn.

4. Mansfield had issued a statement saying that the presidential and vice presidential candidates owed it to the nation to avoid "exposing themselves unnecessarily" to assassination. That day LBJ had walked three blocks through an unruly crowd in Baltimore.

LBJ: Just tell them that the Secret Service has never had the slightest concern or anybody else . . . that knows anything about it. That's the way to cut him.

HUMPHREY: Well, what I—

LBJ: [*disgusted:*] For shaking hands with high school kids that are American citizens! What they need is to cover the route that a candidate follows. The buildings and the cowards that lurk in the dark. There is not any problem with getting out and shaking hands. Kennedy shook hands with three or four groups.[1] That wasn't what killed Kennedy. No President has ever been assassinated by shaking hands with somebody or being in a crowd.[2] They are assassinated when they go to a theater, or when they drive down the street and somebody can hide.

HUMPHREY: That's right. . . . I've just simply said that the President of the United States is a man of the people . . . and that possibly the most dangerous part of his trip is after he leaves the crowd and goes to the airport, not while he's with the people of the United States. . . . Mr. President . . . I just wanted to report to you that . . . the people are very strong for you. . . . The South we need to firm up simply for their good—not for your good.

LBJ: If you've got any friends in the House—any of the Blatniks, or anybody else who are really your friends—there is one little boy from California named Edwards[3] that got up today and demanded that Miller tell him why he got this two hundred thousand in retainers for ten years.[4] Somebody ought to get up and demand that they throw this felt man, the head of this corporation, off of . . . Miller's plane. . . . The newspapers [should] ask him what function *he's* performing. And are we going to turn over the Vice Presidency to the Lockport Felt Company?[5]

HUMPHREY: Yes, sir. . . . I'll call John Blatnik right away.

LBJ: Just tell him to get you three or four to stay after this guy . . . because that takes the heat off *us*. . . . We're going to have enough Billy Sol Esteses and Bobby Bakers. And they're just up every day talking about our Communism and soft on it.

HUMPHREY: . . . Oh brother, that one really is a dilly. . . . I just want to report one other thing out here in California since Mr. Nixon has gotten in the act. I just

---

1. Along his Dallas motorcade route.

2. Johnson was ignoring how Presidents Garfield and McKinley had been murdered.

3. LBJ refers to Democratic Congressmen John Blatnik of Minnesota and Don Edwards of California.

4. Edwards had done so that day on the House floor.

5. On September 20, the New York State Democratic chairman charged Miller with "blatant conflict of interest" by making speeches on the House floor on behalf of the Lockport Felt Company, which he served as assistant secretary and director and from which he took large fees (*New York Times,* September 21, 1964). Miller responded by charging that the Johnson administration was using "Gestapo-style methods"—leaking confidential government information against him to "certain favored columnists" to discredit him (*New York Times,* September 23, 1964). As the conversations above show, Miller was not wrong.

got a full review on Nixon's statements on Goldwater.[1] And when Salinger and
Humphrey go up the valley on the train, which we are going to do, we're going to
have a little debate . . . between Goldwater and Nixon.[2] The two of us are just
going to read those statements.

LBJ: That's good.

HUMPHREY: And then after we are through with that one, why, we'll take on
the Rockefeller-Goldwater statements, and then . . . take on the Scranton and the
Romney. . . . We thought we would just keep that show going for a little while.[3]

LBJ: Now . . . NBC gives California to the Republicans. And Gallup this week—
he's the best pollster we've got—shows that we dropped 3 percent last week and
he gained 3. That's not good. It's *psychologically* bad.

HUMPHREY: Yeah, that's right. . . . Mr. President . . . these people are highly
organized. . . . They're very rude. They're very mean.[4] They're at every airport
with their signs. . . . They really try their damnedest to embarrass everybody. But
. . . when these people see you, when you start taking this tour,[5] this is going to
break their back, because Mr. Goldwater, I think, is within two degrees of blowing
his stack right now. . . . This trip that you are about to take is very timely.

LBJ: Well, now, we're going to do it, but . . . if you've got any friends on that
plane, tell them to ask Goldwater how he justifies his eighty-nine-year-old mother
being on the payroll at forty-nine hundred a year.

HUMPHREY: Uh-huh.

LBJ: [*bitterly:*] He talks to us about Bobby Baker, but he's been deducting that
from his taxes. . . . And we've found now that Bobby Baker gave Dirksen five
thousand in hundred-dollar bills. So it's not going to be too bad if they really want
to get rough.[6] But I think if you just told them that you don't want to be quoted, but

---

1. Former Vice President Richard Nixon, now campaigning for Goldwater, had on June 9 made an
eleventh-hour effort to block Goldwater's nomination by publicly listing various of the Arizonan's
hard-line views that should be "challenged and repudiated."

2. Humphrey was to campaign in California's San Joaquin Valley with Pierre Salinger, former
press secretary to JFK and LBJ, who had been appointed U.S. Senator from California to fill a vacancy
by death after winning the Democratic primary. The two Senators planned to read out statements by
Goldwater and Nixon to show the size of the ideological gulf between the 1960 and 1964 Republican
nominees.

3. Governors Nelson Rockefeller of New York and William Scranton of Pennsylvania, defeated by
Goldwater for the nomination, had also spoken out against his extremism, as had Michigan Governor
George Romney. On July 12, during the Republican convention, Scranton had fired off a public letter
to Goldwater warning that "Goldwaterism has come to stand for a whole crazy-quilt collection of ab-
surd and dangerous positions."

4. During his California tour, Humphrey had been confronted by demonstrators organized by the
John Birch Society and other hard-right organizations.

5. After campaigning in the Midwest and South, LBJ was scheduled to visit San Francisco on October 11.

6. With the Senate Republican leader susceptible to blackmail over his own involvement with
Baker, LBJ knows that Republicans are unlikely to push the scandal to the hilt.

you heard . . . that [Goldwater's] mother doesn't need any Medicare. He's been paying her out of the corporation and deducting it as a business expense. Forty-nine hundred dollars! Now the truth of it is the Internal Revenue caught him and he backed up and he's reduced it to twelve hundred. But she's ninety years old and still getting twelve hundred, and the government is paying 52 percent of it.

HUMPHREY: [*laughs*] All right, we'll do our damnedest. . . .

LBJ: I would just call them in and say now while they are talking, while they are doing a little investigation here on Miller, and he's talking about covenants and so forth, that you just think it might be a good thing.[1]

DEAN RUSK

Secretary of State
Friday, October 2, 1964, 4:10 P.M.

RUSK: You were very good today.[2]

LBJ: No, I'm not.

RUSK: We've had many comments about it at my luncheon for these same people.

LBJ: You heard the story, didn't you, about the young city district attorney that came out and said he made the greatest speech of his life. They said, "Yeah, what was it?" He said, "Before the jury, this client of mine—this Nigro—had been charged with rape. . . . I just had them all in tears. The greatest speech I ever made." They said, "What did the jury do?" And he said, "They *hung* the son of a bitch!" [*laughs*] So, all these good things I'm doing? Looks like I'm going bad to *worse!*

WILLARD WIRTZ

Secretary of Labor
Monday, October 5, 1964, 10:15 A.M.

Wirtz is encouraging the President to boast in public of the Kennedy-Johnson efforts to eliminate nuclear testing. But LBJ is reluctant. He recalls the frenzy of criticism in September that followed his campaign's airing of the notorious "daisy girl" commercial, which unsubtly suggested that electing Goldwater might risk a

---

1. On September 15, Miller had revealed that Johnson had once bought and sold lots in Austin, Texas, that had restrictive covenants against blacks. Nine days later, Miller was forced to concede that in 1958 he had purchased a house in Bethesda, Maryland, with a racial covenant (*New York Times,* September 25, 1964).

2. LBJ had spoken to a group of visitors at the White House.

nuclear war. Aired during NBC's *Saturday Night at the Movies* on September 7, the spot showed a girl plucking a daisy, then a nuclear countdown and blast, with LBJ's voice crying, "These are the stakes. . . . We must either love each other, or we must die." Then the announcer: "Vote for President Johnson on November third. The stakes are too high for you to stay home." Denounced as heavy-handed, the ad was canceled.

LBJ: Now, let's be sure that we don't get into something like we did on that spot thing—that we're overdoing it. You remember the little girl pulling the petals out on the spot and the Bomb going up?

WIRTZ: Yes.

LBJ: . . . I just don't want them to think that I'm overdoing it.

LADY BIRD JOHNSON
LYNDA BIRD JOHNSON

Wednesday, October 7, 1964, 9:40 P.M.

At the end of a long campaign day, LBJ is lying on the massage table in the Presidential Suite of the O'Hare Inn outside Chicago. His wife and daughters are spending the night in Charleston, South Carolina, during their four-day "Lady Bird Special" railroad tour of Southern states that are furious at Johnson over civil rights. Lynda is a twenty-year-old student at George Washington University. Luci is a seventeen-year-old student at the National Cathedral School.

LADY BIRD: Tell me about your day.

LBJ: . . . We had the biggest crowd I ever saw in Des Moines. . . . We're in Chicago now. I'm getting rubbed, getting ready to eat a sandwich with Vicky and Marie.[1] . . . My throat's held up pretty good. Didn't see the television tonight, did you?

LADY BIRD: No, darling, I didn't. . . .

LBJ: [*irritated:*] Well, I was on, you know, nationwide. The first nationwide television, at nine-thirty Washington time.[2] . . . Didn't you know about it?

LADY BIRD: Yes, I knew about it, but I didn't know the timing on it, darling.

LBJ: Why in the hell don't you find out?

LADY BIRD: What, dear?

LBJ: Why don't you find one of those eighty women you got with you to find out?

---

1. The President's secretaries Vicky McCammon and Marie Fehmer.
2. LBJ had taped his address at the White House the day before.

LADY BIRD: I guess because all I'm doing is running from one thing to the other . . .

LBJ: Now, is tomorrow your last day?

LADY BIRD: No, two more days.

LBJ: What states are you in tomorrow?

LADY BIRD: Georgia and Florida. And the next day, Florida, Alabama, Mississippi . . . Don't let anybody talk you into doing anything on Saturday or until late Sunday.

LBJ: Sam Fore[1] wants us to come to the peanut festival in Floresville.

LADY BIRD: If you do, I will just come and *slap* you!

LBJ: *Slap* me! Don't ever slap me!

LADY BIRD: Because, darling, I want you to live a long time. . . . You've known Sam Fore for about thirty years now, and you can get by without the peanut festival. . . . I'm very worried about you and I love you so much. And don't you love me?

LBJ: Ver-ry, ver-ry much.

*   *   *

LYNDA: Hi, Daddy!

LBJ: They tell me you're the star of the ball.

LYNDA: . . . Well, I *was* pretty good!

LBJ: You were?

LYNDA: Yes, sir!

LBJ: You think we're going to carry the South?

LYNDA: I think we're going to carry the South. I'm not too sure about South Carolina. . . . Tonight Mother, Luci, and myself—we're just all done smiling and saying nice things. We'll just attack.

LBJ: Cuss 'em out! Senator Johnston?[2]

LYNDA: He did. . . . The Congressman[3] and lots of people did.

LBJ: What did the Congressman say?

LYNDA: He just gave them hell. . . . He [told them] several times [that] they weren't showing very good manners. . . . We did this very, very big shopping center. They took a vote of all the people who had stores there, and all but one voted against letting us [speak]. The man who owns it is a good Democrat, so he let us do it. . . . We'll get a lot of sympathy reports because these people were bad. . . .

LBJ: Okay, I love you. Be a good girl and don't run out with the Marines too much.[4]

---

1. Old Johnson friend and publisher of the Floresville, Texas, *Journal*.
2. Olin Johnston, Democrat of South Carolina.
3. Democrat Mendel Rivers of Charleston, whose endorsement of Johnson and Humphrey was his first support of a Democratic ticket in twenty years.
4. Referring to Lynda's boyfriends.

LYNDA: I love you too, Daddy. . . .

LBJ: You tell them to get you in by . . . four o'clock, anyway. [*chuckles*]

LYNDA: Daddy, this is my problem—there's no plane out of here until tomorrow afternoon. . . .

LBJ: Why do you have to get back at all?

LYNDA: Because I have to go to school, Daddy.

LBJ: . . . Okay, I love you. Good night. Let me talk to Luci.

LYNDA: She's not here, Daddy.

LBJ: Don't tell me she's out with a man.

LYNDA: Just one of her friends, Daddy.

LBJ: My goodness alive! That girl, I don't know what's going to happen to her.

LYNDA: Nothing's going to happen to her, except she's going to be happy.

LBJ: Okay, good night. Let me talk to your mama.

LYNDA: . . . You know you're loved. . . .

LADY BIRD: Darling?

LBJ: This little Mary Pakenham writes some mean stories in the [*Chicago*] *Tribune*. You know her?

LADY BIRD: [*chuckles*] Yes, I know her. She wouldn't have a job with the *Chicago Tribune*[1] if she didn't write these stories, would she?

LBJ: [*reads aloud from* Chicago Tribune *story saying that Lynda had sung her father's anthem "Hello, Lyndon!" in an "off-key girlish soprano"*]

LYNDA: So what, Daddy? That'll just get me the sympathy vote of all of those people who can't sing on-key. . . .

LBJ: Why don't you learn to sing on-key? Take some lessons! [*reads further from story, noting his unpopularity in the South*]

LYNDA: . . . Daddy, she's just talking. . . .

LBJ: How many people did you have in Charleston tonight?

LYNDA: . . . About twenty thousand. Pretty good crowds. . . .

LBJ: How many hecklers did you have?

LYNDA: Oh, I don't know. Forty, fifty. . . . I love you. . . . Want to talk to Mommy? . . . [*hands telephone to her mother*]

LBJ: Just to tell you I love you and I'll see you on Friday.

LADY BIRD: Okay, darling.

---

1. Which endorsed Goldwater in 1964.

WALTER JENKINS

Special Assistant to the President
Saturday, October 10, 1964, 10:38 A.M.

Resting at the LBJ Ranch, Johnson is lying in bed with Lady Bird, reading the morning newspapers. Both are back from their campaign trips. Johnson's closest aide, who has worked for him since 1939, calls him from Washington about the latest polls.

JENKINS: I thought maybe that you might want Lou Harris's latest figures. . . .
LBJ: Son of a bitch! Looks to me, he's working for [Goldwater]. He keeps saying how he's "lunging." . . . His adjectives just scare me to death. What are they?
JENKINS: . . . New York. Sixty-six [Johnson]. Twenty-seven [Goldwater]. And seven [undecided]. . . . That's down a little bit. . . . He said Bobby Kennedy is slipping and is down to fifty-fifty. He's destroying himself every day by invoking his brother and talking about nobody but him, and taking John-John [1] out to rallies.

*   *   *

LBJ: Now tell Humphrey, and tell the Cabinet, . . . "When you are referring to the President, never refer to him as 'Lyndon' or 'Lyndon Johnson.' Refer to him as 'the President.' " It has so much more prestige. . . . Humphrey is just like a gigolo. He jumps up every day, saying, "They're hitting Lyndon Johnson." . . . But he ought to be saying, "They're hitting our dear President." Or "our great President."

GEORGE REEDY

Saturday, October 10, 1964, 12:25 P.M.

From the ranch, LBJ asks his press secretary what he is hearing about the speech he gave the previous evening at a New Orleans fund-raising dinner. Defending his battle for civil rights, Johnson cited the Southern Senator who once noted that his state hadn't heard a Democratic speech in thirty years and exclaimed, "All they ever hear at election time is nigger, nigger, nigger!" [2] Mary McGrory wrote in the *Washington Star* that LBJ had given "the most moving speech of his campaign."

---

1. John Kennedy, Jr.
2. Expurgated versions of the speech did not include the word "nigger," but LBJ's aide Jack Valenti, among others, insists that Johnson used it. (Jack Valenti, *A Very Human President,* Norton, 1975, p. 207.)

LBJ: Kay Graham[1] told me that it's the greatest speech she's ever heard in her life. Mary McGrory told me about the same thing.

REEDY: It was, sir.

LBJ: Is Mary McGrory there?

REEDY: ... I don't know that she went back or not last night. ...

LBJ: If it doesn't get me in trouble, I wouldn't mind flirting with her out here. Just tell her ... if she didn't mind having a date with me, I wouldn't mind her coming out here and resting with me. It wouldn't make her mad with Miz Johnson out here, would it?

REEDY: I don't think so, just as long as she doesn't get anything on the record. ...

LBJ: See if she's there and tell her that ... Lady Bird and I are out here, and Liz[2] is going to be out here. I would just like to philosophize with her a little bit. Just visit with her. If she doesn't have anything else to do, I'll have her come out in a helicopter.[3]

JOHN CONNALLY

Democratic Governor of Texas
Saturday, October 10, 1964, 1:21 P.M.

> Johnson asks for campaign help from his old friend and onetime aide, who was wounded the previous November in the car in which John Kennedy was shot to death in Dallas. Although all the polls show that LBJ would trounce Goldwater, Johnson's eternal dread of apocalypse just around the corner causes him to fear that some unexpected event late in the campaign might jeopardize his victory.

LBJ: I think we've got a cinch if they just don't take it away from us the last three weeks. ... Keep your engagements just to a minimum so you can come in there. ... I want to do it for *your* good, too. I don't want a Bobby Kennedy thing.[4] ... But I want you definitely speaking and to be identified with this campaign as my counselor and confidant for a lot of reasons. And it may cost you some-

---

1. Katharine Graham was president of the Washington Post Company and widow of LBJ's late friend Philip Graham. In December 1963, while pressing her to publish editorials against the recalcitrant Congress, he charmingly complained that he never got to see her: "I just hear that sweet voice ... and I'd like to break out of here and be like one of these young animals down on my ranch. Jump a fence." (Beschloss, *Taking Charge*, p. 81.)

2. Liz Carpenter was Mrs. Johnson's press secretary and staff director.

3. McGrory did not come to the ranch then, although she did several weeks later, when Johnson renewed the invitation.

4. A relationship as close as RFK's to his brother John.

thing down here, but it's not going to cost you anything in America ten years from now.[1]

CONNALLY: All right, sir.

LBJ: . . . Now, go on and take care of your [Southern] governors.[2]

CONNALLY: All right. Incidentally, all the [Southern] governors . . . Sanders, all of them are extremely encouraged. So is Albertis Harrison. So is Don Russell.[3]

LBJ: I told two or three of them, for your own good and mine, to tell you that you were indispensable. . . . I thought that it would be a good thing if they were begging you to go, and if they thought you were the man with the fuzzy balls.[4] I mean, it would be good for you, in your relationship with them.

CONNALLY: I appreciate that.

LBJ: So go on and do it now . . . because we've got [to work] twenty-four hours a day.

WALTER JENKINS

Saturday, October 10, 1964, 8:21 P.M.

> After dinner at the ranch, LBJ talks again to Jenkins in Washington. Johnson has asked Jenkins to funnel money into the campaign of former Delaware Governor Elbert Carvel to defeat Senator John J. Williams, the leader of Senate Republicans probing LBJ's involvement in the Bobby Baker scandal.

JENKINS: Dick Maguire[5] said he would call Carvel and work it out to help him.

LBJ: I really want labor and Nigras in on that, too. . . . Get Stanton[6] to send you three or four copies of that transcript on the [John] Birch Society.[7] . . . And we got to get some of the editors like Palmer Hoyt[8] to make AP and UP write features about it and ask him [Goldwater] questions about it.

JENKINS: All right.

---

1. By "cost you something," LBJ means that Texans who resent his stand for civil rights might take it out on Connally. Johnson is hinting that he may help Connally to run for President himself a decade hence. (As it happened, 1974 indeed found Connally planning to run for President—but as a Nixon Republican.)

2. Johnson wants Connally to help keep Southern Democratic governors on his side.

3. Carl Sanders, Albertis Harrison, and Donald Russell were governors, respectively, of Georgia, Virginia, and South Carolina.

4. "The man with the fuzzy balls" is Johnson's way of describing a man with power.

5. Democratic National Committee treasurer.

6. CBS President Frank Stanton was LBJ's close friend.

7. A CBS News broadcast in 1962, called *Thunder on the Right,* had reported on Goldwater's connections to the John Birch Society and other extremist groups.

8. Editor and publisher of the *Denver Post,* an LBJ friend.

LBJ: If we don't get a few things like this . . . going, he [Goldwater] is going to have *us* answering all the time. . . .

JENKINS: Ken O'Donnell said he would send you some reports [on the progress of the Johnson campaign], and he's sorry he hasn't.

LBJ: . . . He just defies the boss, huh?[1]

JENKINS: More or less. He just said . . . he would write some up tonight.

LBJ: [*irritated:*] I have no idea what's happening anywhere unless he tells me. Tell him I don't want to be in a vacuum. . . . Tell him *you* report to me every day, and I want *him* to report to me every day.

---

1. LBJ presumes that the Kennedy loyalist, who is close to Robert Kennedy, is thumbing his nose at the President.

Chapter Two

SEX SCANDAL IN THE
THRONE ROOM

*I wouldn't say anything! I just wouldn't be available . . . it's not something
for you to get involved in now. . . . Don't create any more problems than I've
got! . . . You just can't do that to the Presidency, honey!*

LBJ *to* LADY BIRD, *October 15, 1964*

ABE FORTAS

Partner, Arnold, Fortas & Porter
Wednesday, October 14, 1964, 3:56 P.M.

Johnson has long feared that the Goldwater campaign would pin some calumny on
him in the last weeks of the campaign. Now his nightmare seems to be coming to
pass. Abe Fortas, his personal lawyer, troubleshooter, and confidant, calls to break
the news that late on October 7, his closest aide, Walter Jenkins, whom LBJ once
called "my vice president in charge of everything," was arrested in a pay toilet
stall in the basement men's room of the YMCA a few blocks from the White
House while performing oral sex on another man.[1]

Jenkins had forfeited fifty dollars in collateral and returned to work without
telling the President what had happened. But now the news is spreading through
Washington. As Fortas relates, he and Johnson's other personal lawyer, Clark Clifford, have been struggling to keep it out of the newspapers. LBJ has just awoken
from a nap in Suite 35-A of the Waldorf Towers in New York City, where he has
been campaigning. He is hoarse from a cold. He cannot believe what he is hearing.

LBJ: Hello?

FORTAS: Mr. President, this is Abe. And Clark is sitting here with me. We have

---

1. The other man was a sixty-two-year-old, Hungarian-born retired Army sergeant and timekeeper
at the Army-Navy Club named Andy Choka, who lived in the Old Soldiers' Home in Washington.
Jenkins and Choka were under surveillance by two plainclothes policemen who watched them
through a transom from a padlocked shower room.

54

had a very serious problem that came up today. Walter came over to see me this morning, and he got involved in a quite serious situation. We hope that we have it under control. The net-net of it is this: Walter's doctor was over here just a little while ago. And Walter is, on doctor's orders, going into George Washington Hospital for hypertension and acute nervous exhaustion, and he'll be in there for some days. Now, because of a . . . situation that we'll have to explain to you in detail, we have to handle it this way. Walter's secretary has been authorized to tell people that call in that Walter has been put in the hospital for hypertension and nervous exhaustion. We believe that unpleasant publicity—*very* unpleasant publicity— . . . has been averted.

I think that if you're asked about it, you should say only that you have heard that Walter Jenkins is in the hospital on doctor's orders and that you are sorry to hear it, and that you hope to get more details. And that's all. Clark, do you agree? [*pauses to consult Clifford, then:*] Clark says, "That's right, and don't say anything more." . . . It would be a mistake . . . to make a big play about Walter having worked himself into a state of exhaustion. . . . I know that this sounds strange, Mr. President, but it's a weird situation, and we want to fill you in on it at the first moment that you say. And I guess, Clark and I are the only ones that know all the details.

LBJ: Well, is it—

FORTAS: Have I gotten this across at all to you?

LBJ: No.

FORTAS: Well, is it all right to talk on this phone?

LBJ: Yes, I think so.

FORTAS: About a week ago, Walter went to a party and, after the party, was picked up by the police and booked. This morning . . . he came over and saw me and told me that the [*Washington*] *Star* man had called Liz Carpenter[1] and that the *Star* had the story—that it was a morals charge and that they were going to publish it. So I got ahold of Clark, and we went over and saw . . . Noyes[2] . . . and the *Star* says . . . they won't publish it. . . . The [*Washington*] *News* had the story too. Went over and saw John O'Rourke,[3] with the same result. And we believe that the [*Washington*] *Post* will take the same position.[4] Under the circumstances . . . the only thing to do was . . . we got the doctor over here and . . . he had Walter go into the hospital for hypertension and nervous exhaustion. We've got a lot of problems.

LBJ: I can't hear you. Talk a little louder!

FORTAS: I say we've got a lot of problems, obviously, as a consequence of this. . . . Clark and I, of course, are available and will do anything in the world that we

---

1. Press Secretary and Staff Director to Mrs. Johnson.
2. Newbold Noyes was editor of the *Washington Evening Star.*
3. Editor of the *Washington Daily News.*
4. They had also called the *Post*'s editor, J. Russell Wiggins.

can do. We think we've got the situation in as good shape now as we can. Would you like to say a word to Clark about it?

LBJ: [*more tense:*] No, just tell me—could this be *true?*

FORTAS: Mr. President, I'm afraid so.

LBJ: Well, who was *involved?*

FORTAS: Just some bum. It happened at the YMCA.

LBJ: I can't hear you!

FORTAS: I said just a case of a fellow going off his rocker for long enough to get involved in that kind of thing and the police broke in and picked them both up. . . .

LBJ: Now, what's the—what do you say—these other people, what'd you explain to them?

FORTAS: . . . I told them that Walter came over to see me this morning and that he has a complete blackout about the period involved, that he did go to this party, and he had a couple of martinis, exhausted . . . and he doesn't remember anything. . . . And that whether this story is justified or not justified, why, it shouldn't be printed. It has nothing to do with the charges of public responsibility. Finally, the people at the *Star* agreed they had a wonderful scoop, but that it wouldn't be a decent thing to do. . . . We are waiting for the *Post.* We are both quite hopeful that they will take the same position. But the problem is . . . you can never tell how far these things go. And we thought, in the circumstances, that certainly Walter ought not to be around the White House, and that the best way to handle it was for him to go to the hospital . . . with instructions that no phone calls, no visitors, no nothing. And he'll be kept there. . . .

LBJ: Does his wife know about this?

FORTAS: We haven't been able to reach her yet. We didn't want to reach her until after the doctor was here. The doctor's their family doctor, a very able, fine man and very operational. And we're not going to ever tell her anything, except that he was exhausted and in the hospital.

LBJ: Now, did Walter talk to you frankly?

FORTAS: Yes, sir. Yes, sir.

LBJ: I just can't *believe* this!

FORTAS: Sir?

LBJ: I just can't *believe* this!

FORTAS: I couldn't either, Mr. President. It's the most fantastic thing I've heard in all my life. I thought I had heard everything. But, you know, you never know.

LBJ: Ever been any of this before? Any history of it?

FORTAS: He told me no. But the *Star* had a record of an arrest in 1959. Walter told me no. . . . Since [then] I found out about the arrest in 1959, you know. And then we came back to the house and [have] been with Walter all day long. I just didn't have the heart to ask him about that 1959 thing, which we'll have to do one of these days. But the *Star* says that he was photographed by the police in '59. They took a mug shot of him. . . . What we've done is just to work as hard as we can . . . all day long, trying to get ahold of the situation. I think it's in as good a shape as it can be.

LBJ: Well, you don't foresee that you can keep this lid on for three weeks, do you?

FORTAS: No, sir. I think that, however, if we can keep it out of the news stories that it won't assume a great deal of dignity. And I think that Walter ought to stay in the hospital awhile, and then be sent off somewhere . . . to recuperate. But I think we wouldn't be very sensible if we didn't assume that the Republican National Committee has it or will have it. How they use it is another problem. I think that if we just keep it out of the news stories, we can still keep it in the atmosphere of malicious gossip and general accusation.

LBJ: What are they going to do with the charge?

FORTAS: Well, he put up fifty dollars collateral . . . and, apparently on the suggestion of the police chief, said that he'd forfeit the collateral. The charges—they're on the books and no contest is what forfeiting the collateral amounts to. . . . Deke[1] called and I talked with him, and he's going to look into the question of the police blotter—what if anything can be done.[2] He offered to do that. I didn't suggest it. . . . I never heard of it, of course, until this morning, and Walter explained that nothing had happened. The cop had told him that nothing would be known on it, which of course wasn't true.

LBJ: What did he say to you?

FORTAS: Well, it happened. He told me that it happened. . . . I think he was exhausted, had a couple of drinks, and was sort of out of his mind. . . . His version of it is that he blacked out. He doesn't remember anything. . . .

LBJ: Abe, Mary Lasker and these folks, and various people at times have been seeing him every day until the last few days, and you ought to talk to him and to Mildred, so that what his situation is goes over to you.[3]

FORTAS: So that what?

---

1. Cartha "Deke" DeLoach was Assistant Director of the FBI and J. Edgar Hoover's liaison to LBJ.

2. Presumably whether Jenkins's name could be expunged. DeLoach had sent two agents to talk to the Metropolitan Police (see Cartha DeLoach, *Hoover's FBI,* Regnery, 1995, pp. 384–87).

3. Mary Lasker was a New York philanthropist who had a flirtatious relationship with LBJ (see Beschloss, *Taking Charge,* pp. 170–72). This presumably refers to her efforts, in those days before campaign finance disclosure laws, to help quietly finance the Johnson presidential campaign, working through Walter Jenkins and his trusted confidential assistant, Mildred Stegall. Jenkins had been LBJ's liaison to the FBI. Johnson is intensely concerned that Jenkins's safe, which contains potentially embarrassing FBI and other information on the private lives of LBJ (see Chapter 4), administration appointees, Goldwater, Miller, and other political friends and enemies—and perhaps cash and records of secret donations—is kept in safe and friendly hands. The President particularly wants to keep the material away from FBI Director J. Edgar Hoover, who might use it against him.

LBJ: What he has goes over to you. Do you follow me?

FORTAS: Yes, sir.

LBJ: Mary Lasker and some of them—a . . . good many folks have been talking to him. Clark has. Tell Clark about it so that you can go talk to Mildred about it.

FORTAS: Clark and I will handle it.

*   *   *

LBJ: All right, is there anything else?

FORTAS: No, sir. Do you want us to come up and meet you, or see you, or do anything? You know, anything in the world.

LBJ: No, I don't know.

FORTAS: . . . The doctor is going to take calls and say that Walter had hypertension for a year, he's been telling him he's going to kill himself, and that today Walter had the shakes and felt like the top of his head was going to blow off, and that no alternative, if the man wanted to live, but to put him in the hospital.

LBJ: You know, Abe, I swear, I just can't *believe* this!

FORTAS: Isn't it fantastic? I would have believed it of my own brother or myself. I mean, this of all things. It's just *incredible, incredible!*

LBJ: What's this going to *do?*

FORTAS: . . . I don't think the other side will be able to make much of it. We should just keep it out of the news. . . .

LBJ: Do you reckon this was a frame deal?[1]

FORTAS: No, sir. I have to tell you that I don't think it was. Just think the man went off his rocker.

LBJ: How did he locate him though?[2] . . .

FORTAS: He went over to the YMCA, where there's dozens of them around there.[3] . . . The place is just full of that kind of fellow and also of undercover cops. But he was involved here with [another man, who] was arrested the other day too, you see.

LBJ: And they both admitted it?

FORTAS: Yes.

LBJ: Had they known each other before?

FORTAS: No, sir. It was pure pickup.

LBJ: Was a *fee* involved?

FORTAS: No, sir.

LBJ: What's his explanation?

---

1. LBJ immediately suspects that the Jenkins arrest was a frame-up to embarrass the President and cost him the election.

2. Meaning how did Jenkins locate Choka.

3. The men's room of the YMCA was known locally as a homosexual trysting place.

FORTAS: Well, he doesn't have any. He was drunk and sick. . . . Just went off his rocker. . . . Drunk. . . . You know, psychiatric problem that he's managed to handle all these years. But it's there. . . .

LBJ: What time?

FORTAS: I haven't got the exact time, but it must have been around nine o'clock at night. . . . It was a cocktail party given for the opening of the new offices of *Newsweek*. He and Marjorie[1] went over to that, and Marjorie left because she had a dinner engagement. Walter stayed a little longer. Says he had three martinis. And then Walter went over to the YMCA. Then this thing happened. . . . Now Clark telephoned Mrs. Johnson.[2] Just told her that Walter was in the hospital for hypertension. Told her there was some other aspects of it but that she ought to be filled in later. . . . We were worried about either you or her being too fulsome at this time . . . saying things about the strain of the office. . . . Thought we'd play it down now. But definitely [say] that he's in the hospital, don't know anything about it.

LBJ: Who told me that he was?

FORTAS: Well, Mildred could have told you. . . . She knows, and she is telling people.

LBJ: Does she know the facts?

FORTAS: Well, she was the one who first got the word from Liz. Liz called her first and told her it was a ridiculous accusation. And then . . . the *Evening Star* man called Liz. Liz called Mildred and Mildred told her to talk to Walter. And then she talked to Walter. So Mildred knows something. But . . . she doesn't know whether it's true or not.

LBJ: What does this do to your Baker angle?[3]

FORTAS: Well, it all depends on how boldly this thing is played by the other side.[4] If we can keep it in the area of speculation, it's hard for them to handle. It's kind of an accusation. . . . But [as part of a] general attack on moral standards? . . . I don't know what else we can do . . . at this time. I think that if there is any break about the blotter entry on the police record, Walter won't be available. . . . But I think that our immediate objective . . . is to try to, first, keep it out of the news stories, and second, to try to set the stage for the future. Which meant, first, getting Walter out of the White House on some plausible basis and, second, to get him to a place where we can protect him . . . and where there'll be a certain appeal to sympathy.

LBJ: I think you better tell Bird and Marjorie the truth.

FORTAS: Not Marjorie, I don't think. The doctor, who knows her very well,

---

1. Mrs. Jenkins.
2. Lady Bird.
3. LBJ had charged Fortas with ensuring that the Bobby Baker scandal did not blow up before Election Day.
4. The Goldwater campaign.

doesn't think so. . . . She's not a very sturdy girl. . . . What you don't know about her is she has problems.

LBJ: I didn't know that.

FORTAS: . . . I think maybe a little more with Bird might be advisable. Don't you think so?

LBJ: Uh-huh.

FORTAS: But I don't think Marjorie. . . . It might knock her off her rocker.

LBJ: I think that you ought to— Will you be seeing [Walter] at all?

FORTAS: I can. I can make sure to.

LBJ: [*almost croaking:*] I think you ought to . . . ask him where he has these materials,[1] so that you can be positive of that right away.

FORTAS: Where he has the what?

LBJ: This Mary stuff—Mary Lasker stuff.[2]

FORTAS: Yeah. I'll see him and find out where that is and get it.

LBJ: Yes. Because it's going to be used this next week in television and everything.

FORTAS: I see.

LBJ: You better do that, though, right away.

ABE FORTAS
CLARK CLIFFORD

Partner, Clifford & Miller
Wednesday, October 14, 1964, 8:02 P.M.

> Reeling from Fortas's call, Johnson has gone, along with Robert Kennedy, to see Jacqueline Kennedy at her new Fifth Avenue apartment. He will later tell Jackie that here he was with one of the most "sweet and beautiful creatures" of his life[3] and all he could think of was Jenkins in jail down in Washington. RFK has told Johnson that the Jenkins story is breaking in the press. Back in his bedroom at the Waldorf, LBJ calls Clifford and Fortas in Washington.

LBJ: [*croaking quietly:*] Clark, I can't talk very loud. I'm having trouble with my voice. Everybody up here knows this story in detail and in all of its gruesome aspects. Bobby Kennedy just told me about it, and I went over to see Jackie. UP told George Reedy—and they go back into . . . 1959, where they say they got it from a

---

1. Jenkins's private files.
2. Presumably referring to cash and/or records of donations from Mrs. Lasker.
3. See March 25, 1965, conversation with Jacqueline Kennedy, below.

Supreme Court reporter.[1] It seems to me that the Presidency is at stake. It's not important what happens to me or Walter. I don't believe that we can know this and sit around on it and do nothing. I think that we just build it up that way.

CLIFFORD: I think we must wait and see how it's treated.[2] . . . Then I think we'll know better what steps to take. . . . It is at least conceivable in my mind that this . . . might warrant a special appearance by you at an appropriate time on nationwide TV. I don't know. . . . The fact is that we have to be awfully careful that we don't rush it too soon—as though we have known it all along. Which we have not. So I believe we can watch it and see . . . how big a play it gets. . . . It would be unwise for you or anyone on your behalf to say anything about it—or until we have had time to get a good full reading on it tomorrow. . . .

LBJ: Well, my judgment is all you know about it will be in the papers. UP told George Reedy about what you-all told me. . . . Isn't it better for us . . . to take prompt action and accept his resignation than to dillydally around and let it build up and let it look like we are forced to do it? . . . I don't think he can be ever saved from it, and I don't think I can be—or the Presidency can be—if we . . . have knowledge of it, and don't act decisively and promptly.

CLIFFORD: What I'd still like to do is to see the treatment in the morning.

LBJ: Well, but hell, whatever the treatment is, we know the *facts!* The facts are that he's got to get out of the White House. . . . But we've got to *say* that he's out. Now, what conceivably could you hear in the morning that would change our position? . . . He's out. And I don't see any way in the world we can ever bring him back, do you?

CLIFFORD: No. . . . There's another little factor about somebody who's now been put in the hospital with nervous exhaustion. . . . I was wondering . . . whether . . . instead of some statement coming from you, it might come from him.

LBJ: That's what I thought.

CLIFFORD: I hate to have to ask you or anybody on your behalf to handle it, because then it brings it in under the White House roof.

LBJ: You don't *need* to bring it in! It's *in* there!

CLIFFORD: . . . I'm just so anxious that you not have to make a statement right away. . . .

LBJ: What do the [*Washington*] *Post* people say?

CLIFFORD: . . . Their inclination is to run the story. What we are doing now is checking with the *New York Times* to see what the *Times* is going to do with it. Some of the papers indicated that all they are going to carry is the release about his

---

1. That evening United Press International had released a report, including a reference to Jenkins's 1959 arrest.
2. By the press and the Goldwater campaign.

illness. I've already checked with the doctor, and the doctor gave out a statement about his nervous exhaustion that put him in the hospital. . . .

LBJ: . . . My judgment is that [Abe] ought to say to the active boy there on duty at the White House press [room] that his doctor hospitalized him indefinitely and that he's resigning, and they ought to put that out.

CLIFFORD: . . . I would be completely in favor of that. . . .

LBJ: Now, what's his attitude? What did Walter say?

CLIFFORD: Walter feels the same way. Walter feels terrible regret, disservice to the country. . . . This morning we were a little concerned because his reaction was such that he didn't see how he could go on living. But we got him over that. Walter will do anything that you suggest . . . to lessen the damage that he has done. . . .

LBJ: . . . I think if you blow it up, I wait and deliberate and debate— We know he can't come back. And I think the quicker he acts and we act—don't cover it up, don't try to hide it—why, the better off we are. The whole question is whether he's going to [go on medical] leave or whether he would resign. I don't see how you can [go on] leave when you've got that '59 record, and I think you ought to talk to him about that. You and Abe. . . . That's something that I think adds fuel to the fire.

CLIFFORD: Yes, all right. . . . I'm leaving here and going over to the White House. . . . I will move on this with him. . . . We ought to see if we can get to Walter tonight.

LBJ: I think you ought to go on that same story. And you can see it's on the wires. . . . They're all talking it out on the streets here in New York. . . .

CLIFFORD: All right. . . . Statement to be given out by the White House that you have been contacted by Jenkins and informed that his resignation has been accepted.

LBJ: Sure think that ought to be done right away. Now, let me talk to Abe a minute. . . .

FORTAS: [*gets on line*] Hello?

LBJ: Yes, Abe. . . . Did you take care of that thing I told you to? Have you been by Walter's office?

FORTAS: Yes, sir.

LBJ: Did you get that material?

FORTAS: It's all taken care of. I don't have the material, but it's all in order. I know where it is and everything about it.

LBJ: Well, I sure hope that you can get it over to your place.

FORTAS: All right, sir.

LBJ: I think that's important. . . . You ought to go by there this evening, pack up the papers in your briefcase, get Mildred to meet you there.

FORTAS: All right, sir, I will do that.

LBJ: Now, everybody up here knows it. They are running really crazy for copy. . . . *Chicago Tribune* has been calling about it.

FORTAS: *Chicago Tribune* is not going to publish it. That's definite. . . . I was just in on a conversation with Walter Trohan.[1] Says he's not going to write it, and he won't let anybody on his staff write it.

LBJ: What's his reaction?

FORTAS: He said that he can't bring himself to write a story like this about a man who has got six children. . . .

LBJ: I think what I ought to do—and I feel awfully strong about this—I think that we've crossed the bridge. We can't ever come back on it. I think the Presidency is something we've got to protect and you can't protect it by procrastinating.

FORTAS: Yes, sir.

LBJ: I think that [Walter] ought to say to Kilduff,[2] George Reedy's assistant, that his doctor has advised him that he'll be away indefinitely and therefore cannot return to his duties, and this is his resignation. Kilduff ought to say that he has resigned, and we appointed Bill Moyers in his place.

FORTAS: All right.

LBJ: Now, what's your reaction to that? . . .

FORTAS: . . . Well, he's under pretty heavy sedation now. We could do it and he would validate it. I don't know that we could get anything out of him now. We could try. But if you wanted it done, I know we could do it.

LBJ: Well, don't you think it ought to be done? Everybody I talked to thinks that if I'm covering up some more, and I'm trying to hide, and I'm prolonging it, I'm procrastinating about it, [then] I've been watching this thing since '59. And by God . . . I never heard of it! But I just don't think that the President should be put in the position of sitting and not acting.

FORTAS: Uh-huh.

LBJ: Eddie [Weisl][3] didn't think we ought to use the word "resign" because that convicts him. But I don't know what else to use. I think if you don't resign, they put the stuff on you. Then you've had it because you are trying to keep him. . . .

FORTAS: Well, how about . . . the arrest?

LBJ: . . . Say . . . we've been looking into this— If you've ever had any problems in your family . . . everybody has problems, and I regret it very much. All of us have problems. Some of us have mentally retarded brothers. Some of us have alcoholic brothers.[4] Somebody is wrong in every family. Kind of a sympathetic statement.

---

1. The *Tribune*'s Washington bureau chief.
2. Malcolm Kilduff.
3. Edwin Weisl, Sr., a New York lawyer and close Johnson adviser, was now with him at the Waldorf.
4. The public did not know that LBJ's own brother, Sam Houston Johnson, was one.

ABE FORTAS

Wednesday, October 14, 1964, 8:32 P.M.

> Johnson has moved to the Waldorf living room, where he is huddled with Weisl, George Reedy, and Special Assistant Jack Valenti.

LBJ: [*very tense:*] Yes?

FORTAS: The story is on the UPI ticker.

LBJ: Yeah?

FORTAS: In complete detail. . . .

LBJ: They tell me they are making a big play that this is a foreigner, and national security secrets are involved.

FORTAS: Oh, no, there is nothing to that. This fellow is a timekeeper . . . the other fellow.

LBJ: Well, Burch has got a big statement. The Republican National Committee is saying the White House is trying to suppress—highest national security.[1]

FORTAS: That's probably just because—don't you suppose just because of the general idea that fellows who engage in this kind of thing are a danger to the national security?[2]

LBJ: Republican National Committee has called every newspaper in town.

FORTAS: . . . Is Kilduff at the White House?

LBJ: [*turns to Reedy*] Is Kilduff at the White House? Who do you have at the White House that can issue a statement? What about these— Well, are they there? What about the boys that you brought over from the State Department? [*angrily at Reedy:*] He oughtn't be on a campaign trip. I don't give a *damn!* You get him *back* here! And don't you *ever* put him on a campaign trip! . . . Never let him get out of that damned office!

FORTAS: Well, do you want us to get up a statement and telephone it to George?

LBJ: I guess so. [*confers with Reedy, then:*] George has come up with a new theory. . . . George thinks we ought not do anything. I think he's wrong as he can be. . . . I think you ought to get up a statement . . . and call me as soon as I get through with this speech.

FORTAS: Do you want me to clear it with Walter?

LBJ: Yeah, see what he thinks. I don't see, first, that he can ever come back.

---

1. Republican National Committee Chairman Dean Burch had issued a statement at about 6:00 P.M. charging that the White House was "desperately trying to suppress a major news story affecting the national security."

2. Fortas refers to the presumption of the time that secret homosexuals in government were security risks.

FORTAS: No, we have been clear on that for a long time.

LBJ: ... When you know something and you don't act on it, the President is properly criticizable. And I know it, and I've got the proof. ... If you act on it, then it's behind you. ... We've got 3 million people,[1] and we do have mistakes made by people ... [and] we have to act on it. But all I can do is just further destroy him, and I think destroy myself, and I think destroy the Presidency. Which is the real thing. If a President knows something like this and doesn't take prompt action, what the goddamn hell confidence are they going to have in the Presidency? Pussyfooting and procrastinating.

FORTAS: Yeah. All right, sir, we'll go ahead and clear it.

LBJ: What's the *Post* going to do? ...

FORTAS: ... I think with the UPI story, they will probably run it.

LBJ: What did the UPI say?

FORTAS: UPI's got the whole thing. I have it here in front of me: "Walter Jenkins, Special Assistant to President Johnson, was arrested October 7th on a disorderly charge involving indecent gestures and elected to forfeit fifty dollars' collateral. ... D.C. police records revealed the incident today after rumors flooded Washington that Jenkins had been arrested by officers of the D.C. Morals Division. The record shows that Jenkins, forty-six, was picked up at the YMCA by two plainclothesmen of the Morals Division ... on charges of disorderly conduct and indecent gestures. ... The record showed that [a resident of] the Soldiers' Home here was arrested at the same time by the same officers. ... Jenkins has been admitted to the hospital." And the doctor's statement. ... Then reference to the Bobby Baker case. ...

LBJ: What does it say about Bobby?

FORTAS: Just says that Jenkins is one of the men Republicans want summoned as a witness in the resumption of the Bobby Baker investigation by the Senate Rules Committee. ...

LBJ: What's your best judgment?

FORTAS: ... I think that the only thing left is the resignation. ...

LBJ: Eddie doesn't want to use the word "resignation" because he thinks that confirms the guilt. He says just say that he was informed by his doctors that he cannot return to duty. That he had a complete collapse.

FORTAS: We'll do that. Now, the doctor has, in a fresh statement, said [Walter] had to be in the hospital four or five days at least, and that's created a little awkwardness for us today. Now, actually there have been cardiograms, blood pressure tests, and Walter's been in pretty difficult shape. But the four or five days statement makes it pretty difficult.

---

1. In the Executive Branch.

LBJ: . . . I'll be at this dinner. I have to go about nine-thirty.

FORTAS: We'll write something up, and then I will go out and see Walter and tell him that it's tentative, but we may decide to go ahead with it if it's all right with you.

LBJ: I would try to go see him right quick . . . before he goes to bed. Write it up later, but—

FORTAS: Clark [Clifford] will work on the draft while I go over to see Walter.

LBJ: That's right. You don't neglect that other mission either.[1]

FORTAS: No, sir. What time do we call you back?

LBJ: Well, I will be here until nine-thirty, quarter of ten. Then I'll be speaking, I guess, for an hour. I'll call you as soon as I get back from my speech. But we're going to miss all the papers, I'm afraid. . . . You-all think you can talk to him on the phone?

FORTAS: I can't get through. I have to get the doctor. I've got Clark working on the doctor right now trying to get him to isolate him. And I will do it as fast as I can.

LBJ: Okay.

JOHN CONNALLY

Wednesday, October 14, 1964, 8:45 P.M.

> When the Texas Governor calls from Austin about a Dallas political problem, it takes him a moment to realize how serious the Jenkins scandal really is.

CONNALLY: Mr. President, how are you?

LBJ: Oh, I've got a bad throat, John, and lots of problems.

CONNALLY: I understand Walter is under the weather.

LBJ: Blood and heart. But he had a police arrest a week ago on a morals charge, and they picked him up once before in '59, according to the information we're just now getting. And the Republican National Committee and Goldwater's people called every reporter in town. UPI is running a big story on it. . . .

CONNALLY: *Walter?* God Almighty! They've *got* him?

LBJ: Yeah. It's on the ticker now. You'll see it, I imagine, on the ten o'clock news.

CONNALLY: [*not comprehending the gravity of the Jenkins problem, changes subject to a scheduled campaign dinner for LBJ in Dallas*] . . . I don't want to add to your troubles. I know you've got lots of them. . . . They sold $113,000 worth of tickets. . . . But I understand you just said you're not going to go.

---

1. Ensuring that the contents of Jenkins's safe and files are in reliable hands.

LBJ: . . . They came in here and said we are having a fund-raising dinner in Fort Worth or . . . Dallas—and I said, . . . "We cannot look like that we killed Kennedy in Dallas, and I'm going down and they're going to give me a lot of money." Everybody I talked to thinks it would be revolting. Most of them think I made a terrible mistake [to consider] going back to Dallas. But I think you've got to go back sometime. I think that you ought to go back with your chin up and march in and show them that you don't believe that they are all thugs. But when I do it for a consideration[1] . . . it'll be bad for Dallas and it'll be bad for me. . . . I just caught hell the last two days for [considering] going to Dallas at all. And they'll think I'm bringing up all the memories and I'm retracing the same steps. They had me going to Fort Worth first and then over to Dallas. Just like Kennedy did. . . . I want to do some things for those people that help me. I want to do them in December.[2] And I don't want to do them for a consideration.

CONNALLY: . . . I think I better go up there and talk to them and explain as best I can why it's being called off. . . . We've got support in Dallas that you've never had in all your political history,[3] and I don't want to see it go down the drain. . . .

LBJ: Why don't you get on that plane tonight or tomorrow and come on up here? You sure are needed, my friend.

CONNALLY: God, it's so close.[4] We've got so many problems here. I thought I would just wait and visit with you Saturday and see what I can do to be helpful.

LBJ: Don't you think this thing[5] is a bombshell?

CONNALLY: [*misunderstanding*] . . . I think there is some element of danger in it. . . . As you know, I didn't know it had been set up until—

LBJ: No, I mean the Walter thing.

CONNALLY: Oh, yes, yes, yes, yes, I do. I sure do.

LBJ: Could you believe it?

CONNALLY: . . . It's damn hard to believe.

LBJ: Did you ever have any indication of it?

CONNALLY: [*tentatively:*] No, no, I would have to say not. . . .

LBJ: You sound like you might have had some intuition.

CONNALLY: No . . . I can't say that. There have been some times—oh, very fleeting times—when I detected some gestures and some mannerisms[6] that might have indicated it. But . . . I must say I'm very surprised.

LBJ: Now, I don't think I have any choice, once I know the facts, but to have him resign, do you?

---

1. Raising campaign money.
2. After the election, when such a visit cannot damage him politically.
3. Dallas conservatives had never been Johnson's natural constituency.
4. The Johnson-Goldwater contest in Texas.
5. The Jenkins scandal.
6. By Jenkins.

CONNALLY: None whatever.

LBJ: And I ought to do it tonight, don't you think?

CONNALLY: Yes, sir. . . . You have no choice.

LBJ: . . . Suppose we *don't* say he's resigned.

CONNALLY: Oh, I think you are going to have to say that. I don't think you can cover it up. Hell, if the facts are out, you don't have any choice. It's just one of those tragic things. . . .

LBJ: What's the political effect of it on top of [Bobby] Baker?

CONNALLY: It'll be harmful, but not appreciably so. . . . Now they will be digging up the Summer Welles thing[1]—at least in their private conversations, you know—and talking about Communists and homos and everything else that infiltrated the government . . . and tying [it] in to the morals business.[2] . . . I think your only answer to it is to be swift and decisive in your actions. . . .

LBJ: . . . I haven't got any throat left.

CONNALLY: Well, don't talk to me, God Almighty! . . . I know what you are going through . . . because we went through it in '41, we went through it in '48,[3] and they are all tough. . . . You've got two weeks left. . . . The only place you are vulnerable at all is on . . . the moral thing, the character thing.[4] . . . The only way you answer that is not directly, but in your demeanor. . . . I would very strongly suggest that you think . . . about making Mrs. Johnson go with you and the girls go with you wherever you go. . . . Leave the impression now that there are not all four of you out running in every direction just grabbing votes—I'm putting it crudely to make a point—but that you are consolidating. You are a family. You are a husband—and your wife, and your two daughters. You are an American family. . . .

LBJ: Well, she's going to do it, except on one engagement in Pennsylvania and a day in Texas. She's going to be with me in . . . all the other travels. Luci's got— They booked her each weekend. . . .

CONNALLY: . . . I know you've got a speech tonight. . . . But I think this is the greatest answer you can give. . . . You draw your family as close to you as you can. You travel together as a unit. . . . You photograph together as a unit. . . . You're way ahead. And what you've got to do now is be damn sure you don't make a mistake.

LBJ: Okay.

---

1. FDR had reluctantly fired Under Secretary of State Sumner Welles after rumors of Welles's homosexual behavior spread through Washington.

2. Goldwater's criticism of LBJ's lack of "morality."

3. As a Johnson friend and aide, Connally had helped LBJ weather his hairbreadth loss for the U.S. Senate in 1941 and his contested eighty-seven-vote Senate victory in 1948.

4. Meaning that morality and character is the only issue on which Goldwater might win the election.

CARTHA "DEKE" DeLOACH

Assistant Director, Federal Bureau of Investigation, and Liaison to the President
Wednesday, October 14, 1964, 9:00 P.M.

DeLoach is Jenkins's regular contact at the FBI, a friend and fellow devout Catholic. He reports on his mission to the Washington Police Department. By their immediate cooperation in trying to suppress the Jenkins scandal, Hoover and De-Loach show their confidence that LBJ will win the election and that they had better stay on his good side.

LBJ: Deke . . . what are the facts on this '59 charge?

DeLOACH: He was arrested on January 15, 1959 . . . and at that time was making indecent gestures. The charge on the blotter was for suspicion. . . . But it was also in the basement in the men's room of the YMCA here in Washington. At that time he was fingerprinted and booked, and a photograph taken by the police. But there was no copulation—no acts going through it with another person. He was simply loitering, apparently, at that time.

LBJ: Well, was he with anyone?

DeLOACH: No, sir, he was not with anyone.

LBJ: Well, why would they pick up a guy if he was just by himself?

DeLOACH: Apparently he was hanging around in the basement, in the men's room there at the YMCA, and according to the . . . police report, he must have pulled down his zipper or something like that, Mr. President. . . .

LBJ: Pulled down his zipper by himself?

DeLOACH: I don't know that, sir. I don't know that to be the truth. But the *Evening Star* did have that information today. So they claimed.

LBJ: Well, now, have you checked the police record?

DeLOACH: . . . I had an agent go over there and discreetly check it this afternoon, and they came up with the 1959 arrest, plus the one a week ago. . . .

LBJ: Was he investigated when he came to the White House?

DeLOACH: He was investigated in 1958, sir, but not since then. We didn't feel there was any need to because we knew him real well, of course, and everything was fine.

LBJ: Has everybody else been checked there?

DeLOACH: . . . For the most part, I believe they have, yes, sir. But I will check to make sure.

LBJ: When I came in, I gave instructions that everybody that would get on the White House payroll had to have an FBI.[1] Well, see what happened to it.

---

1. When LBJ became President, he had asked for FBI checks on all top appointees.

DeLOACH: Yes, sir.

LBJ: Folks like Bill Moyers—have you got an FBI on him?

DeLOACH: I'll check in the morning to make certain we do, Mr. President.

LBJ: Have we got one on Jack Valenti?

DeLOACH: Yes, sir, we do have one on him. I'll check to make certain that everybody on your staff has had that check.

LBJ: . . . [Walter's] record with us was a very fine one. He had no secrets that I know of. Anything wrong with this fellow that he was with?

DeLOACH: He's sixty-two years old. He's a retired Army sergeant. . . . We're checking him out at the present time. Now, Mr. President . . . don't you think it would be a good idea if I were to go to Walter and—with his doctor's permission, of course—and take a signed statement from him just to make sure we have his side of the story?

LBJ: I expect so. . . . [Abe Fortas] is on his way out there, and I think you ought to get on over there and tell him. He told me nothing happened before this, but you better tell him what the record shows on him in '59. I think the quicker you get over there to see him, the better off we are.

DeLOACH: Get over to the hospital?

LBJ: Yes. I think a very thorough investigation. . . . And I have standing instructions to investigate everybody working [in the White House], and I wish you would sure see that it's done. . . . I don't know how we can justify not doing it originally. How do you think we can?

DeLOACH: Well, Mr. President, he was investigated in 1958 . . . at your instructions. . . . And there was nothing at that time that showed up. So I think, frankly, if the question is asked, that you have a perfect right to say that this man had been investigated in the past and nothing showed up of this nature. It would be my opinion, sir, for what it's worth, the less said, the better off we'll be. I think the Republicans are going to try to push it. There is no doubt about that. But I think it's going to die pretty fast because of the nature of the matter.

LBJ: What makes you think that?

DeLOACH: Well, these things in Washington have come up quite often before, of a morals nature, and they always get hit pretty fast. . . .

LBJ: You think he could have been framed?

DeLOACH: . . . Yes, sir, he could have been framed. It's entirely possible.

LBJ: How would these three policemen be peeking through the door and know he was there if they hadn't had some indication?

DeLOACH: Well, now, they do hang around Lafayette Park, and they hang around places like the men's room in the basement of the YMCA, because this a place where known homosexuals hang out.

LBJ: Where did they see him?

DeLOACH: . . . They claimed they saw it through the transom of the men's room.

LBJ: . . . Was this happening in the men's room?

DeLOACH: Yes, sir, so they claim. But it's entirely possible that they could have been bribed. It's entirely possible they're lying about it. But we can certainly check it out and find out and make a very thorough investigation into the matter.

LBJ: Who is supposed to have been working on who?

DeLOACH: Walter was supposed to be the active one, Mr. President. In other words, this sixty-two-year-old man was letting Walter have it, and Walter was taking it, according to the police officer. Which is pretty hard to believe.

LBJ: Sure is. Is it odd that it would be just confined to '59 and '64? Nothing in five years or twenty-five years?

DeLOACH: Yes, sir. . . . It's entirely possible that the boy could have just broken down, and what he said today that he could have had lapses of memory as to what he was doing.

LBJ: Has he shown any indication of that around you?

DeLOACH: No, sir, none whatsoever. We've played golf at least fifty times. He allowed both of us to go to Camp David[1] together. We've had many walks together. There has never been the slightest inclination of homosexuality. Nothing. I have been to church with him on numerous occasions. We've been to the altar rail together for communion. And there has been nothing that would reflect that.

LBJ: Well, you better get out there and tell him what '59 shows, right quick.[2]

MILDRED STEGALL

Assistant to Walter Jenkins

ABE FORTAS
CLARK CLIFFORD
EDWIN WEISL, SR.

Partner, Simpson, Thacher & Bartlett, New York
Wednesday, October 14, 1964, 9:36 P.M.

In Jenkins's White House office, Mildred Stegall, his confidential assistant, and Abe Fortas are joined by Clark Clifford. Speaking from the Waldorf, LBJ is anxious for Fortas to seize the contents of Jenkins's private safe and files, which include material that Johnson fears could be used to damage him. He worries that if Fortas does not grab it first, the FBI might impound it. He is at the Waldorf with his close, longtime adviser Edwin Weisl.

---

1. The presidential retreat.
2. Worried that Jenkins might dig in his heels and refuse to resign, pleading a single lapse and/or a frame-up, LBJ wants Jenkins informed that he knows about the 1959 arrest.

LBJ: Lady Bird is going to call you. Has she already called you?

STEGALL: Yes, sir. She's coming over here in a few minutes.

LBJ: Well, before you leave there, you see that Abe Fortas comes by.

STEGALL: He's here now, Mr. President, and Deke [DeLoach] is on his way over.

LBJ: Well, you see that Abe gets all your material.

STEGALL: Yes, sir. Everything?

LBJ: Yup.

STEGALL: All right, sir. Anything you want to tell him? Because he's right here.

LBJ: No, I just wanted to— I was afraid you'd leave.

STEGALL: No, sir. Don't worry about that.

LBJ: Well, I want you to go out there with Marjorie, though.

STEGALL: Well, I'm going to send Willie Day[1] because Clark Clifford is coming too, and they wanted me to help them here.

LBJ: . . . All right, let me talk to Abe now. . . .

FORTAS: [*gets on line*] Hello?

LBJ: . . . Lady Bird said she's going to ask Mildred to go out to Walter's, and I didn't want her to leave until you got there. That's what I was calling her for, because I'm fearful that Deke's boys . . . might be coming over there [to] look at confidential papers and other things . . . and . . . I wanted to be sure that you got in there and got all that material.

FORTAS: Yes, sir. I will do that. Now . . . I've been up to see Walter, and that's okay. He's submitted his resignation. . . . I'm trying to get Marjorie Jenkins to go to my house, but she won't do it. We're just going to send Willie Day out there. She doesn't want that either.

LBJ: Have you told her?

FORTAS: She heard it on the radio—and her son. . . . There's relatives that have called. . . . She thinks it's all a put-up job and a lie, and I'm going to tell her it is a lie, put-up job and entrapment. We've got to help that woman.

LBJ: Did you go into the '59 thing with him?

FORTAS: With Walter?

LBJ: Yeah.

FORTAS: He said he was picked up once before. He doesn't think it was '59. He thinks he was much younger—more likely '54. But you know, that's enough. There was another incident.

LBJ: Who gave you the '59 record?

FORTAS: We were told '59 by the people at the *Star*. Now, Deke has those police records and he's coming over here. . . .

LBJ: Why didn't Walter tell you that this morning?

---

1. Willie Day Taylor had long cared for the Johnson children.

FORTAS: Mr. President, he was pretty well off his rocker this morning. I really can't blame him for it. He's in a hell of a fix. . . .

LBJ: Has he ever had any other experiences[1] besides those two?

FORTAS: He says not. . . . You know, there probably were other instances. It's going to take a little time and some very loving care to get it out.

LBJ: Is there any chance that anybody could have been getting any secrets[2] from him?

FORTAS: Oh, no, sir. Not a chance.

LBJ: The Burch thing indicated that because he had security stuff.

FORTAS: Well, I think that's just because this kind of incident is considered a security risk. . . . This kind of thing is the product of excessive fatigue and a fellow that's got that kind of propensity. . . . Now, do you want me to take everything that Mildred's got here?

LBJ: Yeah.

FORTAS: Everything. All right, sir.

LBJ: Take it to your safe.

FORTAS: Yes, sir, I will do it.

LBJ: Now, but do it before somebody moves in there.

FORTAS: It's going to be done tonight.

*   *   *

LBJ: Now what do you think we are going to say on this other statement?

CLIFFORD: The one . . . that I've just phoned up there is "Walter W. Jenkins submitted his resignation this evening as Special Assistant to the President. The resignation was accepted and the President has appointed Bill D. Moyers to succeed him." Now, that's in line with your thought that the resignation should be included in the story that will come out in the morning. I think that if we attempt to explain the resignation, if we attempt to attribute it to health or one thing or another like that, it makes us a little vulnerable. . . .

LBJ: Eddie Weisl feels very strongly against using the word "resignation." . . . You prove what they say when you say "resignation," according to Weisl.

CLIFFORD: . . . I think we have to expect that, because that's proved. What I think that we must refrain from doing is to get into a contest or controversy over whether or not that the charge was a proper one. . . . We're going to lose that fight, and I think it just has a tendency to dramatize it and inflate—

LBJ: Wait a minute, I want you to tell him that I agree with you. . . .

WEISL: [*gets on line*] Hello, Clark?

CLIFFORD: Ed, the President thought I ought to mention this to you—the facts

---

1. Homosexual experiences.
2. National security secrets.

and the record are all dead against him. . . . He himself, although he's hazy about some of the details, does not deny that the incident took place. A statement of one of the arresting officers . . . is very bad about the activity which was going on when the officer sprung on them suddenly.

WEISL: But . . . the officer may have been bought anyhow.[1]

CLIFFORD: . . . Walter says that some activity was taking place. . . . The other man was apprehended. Very likely he's available. . . . And then also this exceedingly damaging record back in 1959 . . . involving Walter.

WEISL: . . . He admits that?

CLIFFORD: . . . Walter admits there was a prior incident. . . . They have the record of the prior offense, and I said, "That's a very common name. That could be anybody." Oh, no, they said, they took his picture at the time and his picture was there . . . in the Washington police records. . . .

WEISL: Well . . . he may be guilty of this offense. . . . But I think it's possible that this fellow . . . was bought by the Goldwater people.

CLIFFORD: . . . I would like very much to believe it, but Walter says that he went to this cocktail party and had drinks, and he concedes being tired and all that he may have had too many drinks. . . . The man picked him up. Walter voluntarily walked from a cocktail party for about two blocks until he got to the YMCA. . . . So I don't know how it could be a kind of a plant. . . . [Walter] didn't know that he would end up in the YMCA. . . .

LBJ: [*back on line:*] Clark, I would change this statement one way here. I would say Walter "submitted his resignation this evening as Special Assistant. . . . The President has appointed Bill D. Moyers to succeed him." Be sure that's all right with Bill.

CLIFFORD: All right. . . .

LBJ: Now what do we say tomorrow? . . . George is thinking of saying for background that we heard about it just as I went to Miz Kennedy's this evening. I came back, I got on the phone, and we were informed that he resigned and I appointed Moyers. Now, we don't know anything about the facts.

CLIFFORD: . . . I think that's exactly right. . . .

LBJ: Now, is there something we can say that's good, like—off the record—"if none of you have never had anything like this in your family, why, you wouldn't understand it, but nearly every family has had some problem and we regret it very much, but we don't think we can add anything to it."

CLIFFORD: No. . . . Every family has problems, but they don't happen to have *this* kind. And I believe it would not be wise to attempt to deprecate it. I think that

---

1. Like LBJ, Weisl suspects that the Republicans framed Jenkins.

might would play into their hands. I think that this is clean and clear cut, and I believe, by God, it's about all that can be said.

LBJ: Bobby Baker's was clean and clear-cut, you know. He resigned forthwith.[1]

CLIFFORD: Yeah, that's right. . . . But I just think that just to say something without being absolutely sure ahead of time just what we're going to say would constitute a mistake.

LBJ: . . . You can imagine they're hounding us at every stop.[2] . . . All radio and television.

CLIFFORD: Yeah, but the fact is, you see, you just don't *have* any facts about it. You've been away, you got it by phone, you just don't know what this *is*. . . .

LBJ: Somebody better take some precautions on him and Marjorie, too, because he may do something rash, and she might do something rash.[3]

CLIFFORD: Yes, all right. We will give attention to that.

LBJ: I told Lady Bird that she ought to go out there, but maybe you ought to make Tommy[4] go out. They are good Catholics together. Reason with her.

CLIFFORD: Yes. But it's got to be somebody else, because—

LBJ: A priest or Tommy or somebody.

CLIFFORD: Somebody like that, but it can't be Bird.[5]

LBJ: Okay.

ABE FORTAS

Thursday, October 15, 1964, 12:02 A.M.

Halting and morose, LBJ has delivered a speech to the Alfred E. Smith Memorial Dinner downstairs, cutting his text in half. A tearful George Reedy has announced Jenkins's resignation to the press. Now Johnson is back in his Waldorf suite, eating a sandwich and drinking consommé as he plots his way out of the Jenkins scandal with his aides. He calls Fortas in Washington.

LBJ: I just wanted to see if you knew anything else.

FORTAS: No. . . . Everything here has proceeded according to order, and Deke

---

1. In October 1963, Baker resigned as secretary of the Senate, which was about to investigate him, rather than take a leave of absence.

2. By now, the press was assaulting George Reedy with questions.

3. LBJ was worried that if the Jenkinses were angry about the forced resignation, they might say something embarrassing to the press.

4. The Washington lawyer-lobbyist Thomas Corcoran had been a close ally of LBJ's since he was a top White House aide to FDR and Johnson a New Deal Congressman in the late 1930s. Corcoran was also a close friend of Jenkins.

5. Clifford was worried that if Lady Bird were photographed calling on Mrs. Jenkins at home, it would tie the President further into the scandal.

was over here and they're going ahead tomorrow with the interviews.[1] And I have that material[2] in boxes and I'm taking it with me. . . .

LBJ: Now, what date did you find out this other incident?

FORTAS: Well, the official record is January 1959. . . . And [Walter's] last FBI security check was 1958, so they didn't make any subsequent security check. . . .

LBJ: [*angry:*] Oh . . . you can't believe them, by God, on oath! That's the first order I issued when I went in there—have everyone that came forth for me checked—and [DeLoach] told me that they were. I asked him tonight why not. Why, he said, he played golf with him fifty times. . . . Well, I don't give a damn if he's my *wife!* I want him *checked*—and I told him that for the record! . . . Say I asked them to do this when I first came in here, and now, please, get it done for every human being. Including me! They always manage to weasel out themselves. . . . I wonder what the record would show about [Walter's] military service. What checks they made to make him a lieutenant colonel.[3]

FORTAS: I don't know.

LBJ: I think one of the things working in our favor is that . . . he was in this reserve unit in the Army under Goldwater. He was his commanding officer for many years, and he didn't do anything but have the highest respect for him.[4]

FORTAS: . . . I think that's very good. All right, sir, well, I hope you get some rest.

LBJ: What do you see flowing from this now?

FORTAS: . . . I really don't think that it's going to be of any substantial lasting effect. I think we're going to have a very unpleasant few days. Did you see the statement that White made—of the Republican committee?[5]

LBJ: No.

FORTAS: . . . It's not as mean a statement as expected, but I suppose the meaner ones will come along. . . .

LBJ: Now you-all, you and Clark both, leave word when you leave your of-

---

1. At LBJ's order, DeLoach is investigating the circumstances of Jenkins's arrest.

2. Jenkins's private files.

3. LBJ was relieved to be reminded that Jenkins had served in an Air Force Reserve squadron on Capitol Hill under General Barry Goldwater, who had signed glowing testimonials to Jenkins's performance. These, Johnson thought, would keep Goldwater from exploiting the scandal too energetically.

4. Around 7:00 P.M., McNamara had asked his assistant, Joseph Califano, to have Jenkins's military file photocopied immediately. By Califano's account, McNamara then read aloud by telephone to LBJ from Goldwater's glowing testimonials to Jenkins's fitness. With this ace in the hole, Johnson said he would ensure that Goldwater was reminded of them: "I know he wouldn't want to embarrass himself by making any damned-fool statements." (Califano, *The Triumph and Tragedy of Lyndon Johnson,* Simon & Schuster, 1992, pp. 19–20.)

5. F. Clifton White, National Director of Citizens for Goldwater-Miller, had declared that while "compassion" for Jenkins was warranted, his predicament was more than a "personal tragedy" and might harm America both domestically and internationally.

fice . . . because I don't want to wait an hour just trying to search for you and nobody having any idea in God's world where you are.

FORTAS: Yes, sir. I'm going to stay right close.

LBJ: . . . You got any more trips planned between now and the next two and a
half weeks?

FORTAS: . . . I'll just cancel everything and be right here.

LBJ: Okay.

ABE FORTAS

Thursday, October 15, 1964, 1:13 A.M.

Johnson is agitated about the first wave of publicity about Jenkins.

LBJ: They are playing this security angle very big—that here is a man that sat in
the highest councils, privy to everything, and who else might he have had something to do with, and what secrets might have been given away. Kind of the
Burgess-Maclean thing.[1] Now, I told Deke DeLoach to go on a thorough investigation immediately.

FORTAS: Yes, sir.

LBJ: I don't know whether that's going to be enough to satisfy people or not. It's
got to be quick and it's got to be thorough, and it's got to cover every possible
angle. . . . They are just flooding us with calls—the whole country—and . . . the
question is whether we ought to go further and have a commission.

FORTAS: I wouldn't. No, sir, at least not at this juncture, because I don't know
what it would investigate. . . . Your saying that you ordered a complete FBI investigation of all aspects of the matter ought to take care of it.

LBJ: Well, I thought that would take care of it on some of these other things, but
it doesn't. Like the McCloskey stuff.[2]

FORTAS: . . . It doesn't seem to me that a commission would be appropriate
here. . . . There is really no security angle. . . . What the Republicans are talking
about is the assumption [that] any person who has this kind of a tendency can be
blackmailed. . . .

---

1. Guy Burgess and Donald Maclean were British diplomats who disappeared in 1951 and surfaced
in Moscow in 1956 in one of the Cold War's most famous espionage cases.

2. Charges made by Don Reynolds before the Senate Rules Committee that LBJ and Bobby Baker
peddled influence on behalf of the Philadelphia contractor and Democratic fund-raiser Matthew
McCloskey.

LBJ: That's right. Every farmer in the country is upset about it. City folks not so much, but they're upset, too. . . . It could mean, as I told you, the ball game.[1]

FORTAS: . . . It's going to be tough to handle. Deke . . . thinks the whole thing sounds kind of fishy. In terms of three morals officers looking over the transom. . . .

LBJ: You'll have investigating committees of the House and Senate, you see.

FORTAS: Of course, those really can't get into action soon enough, anyway.

LBJ: I would imagine Goldwater will be having John Stennis[2] convene tomorrow.

FORTAS: I don't know . . . how they're going to be able to deploy that to any advantage . . . I just talked with Jim Rowe,[3] and he said that he's going to get some of his people pretty far away from the official family to get out the line that the Republicans ought to understand about nervous breakdowns because, after all, Goldwater has had two of them.[4] And that's pretty good, I think. . . . A lot will depend on what Deke comes up with on the basis of the FBI interview of this fellow tomorrow. . . .

LBJ: . . . Hoover[5] ought to announce early in the morning that early this evening . . . I asked him to make a thorough check immediately, and that he's interviewing all the people he can. He'll make a report at the earliest possible date. . . . I think he ought to talk to Nick [Katzenbach],[6] if he could tonight, so that he knows about it. I would call him, but I'm just afraid my voice would be to where I can't talk at all in the morning. I have been on this damn phone all afternoon. But Attorney General[7] . . . thinks we ought to talk to Katzenbach, who has a lot of experience in this field and a good background and good judgment, and get him in on it and guiding them. . . . And I think you ought to ask Bundy what security might be involved, what meetings he's attended.[8] Look up his files and . . . see what they show. . . .

FORTAS: Yes, sir. . . .

LBJ: Make your record of it, though.[9] . . . As I recall it, I called [Deke] . . . and

---

1. Meaning the outcome of the election.

2. The Mississippi Democrat was Chairman of the Senate Select Committee on Standards and Conduct.

3. The Washington lawyer James Rowe was an alumnus of the FDR White House, a close Johnson ally, and a law partner of Thomas Corcoran.

4. See September 21, 1964, above.

5. J. Edgar Hoover.

6. As Acting Attorney General since RFK's resignation, Nicholas Katzenbach was (at least nominally) Hoover's boss.

7. LBJ still refers to RFK by his old title.

8. Johnson wants McGeorge Bundy to assess Jenkins's exposure to confidential national security matters.

9. Worried that the FBI might protect itself from the Jenkins scandal at his expense, Johnson is adamant that his people keep a record that will show his own reaction to the problem to have been exemplary.

told him to immediately proceed. . . . You just tell him you've got to have a report in a week. I can't go too long.[1]

FORTAS: You ought to have it sooner than that.

LBJ: . . . Any possibility this guy[2] might be an agent of anybody?

FORTAS: Deke is going to get to the bottom of that, but reviewing it tonight, we just didn't think so. The whole circumstances are too casual. You mean, of a foreign agent?

LBJ: Yeah.

FORTAS: Oh, no. That, I was afraid of because of his name. . . . We're pretty sure this was a one-time meeting, number one, and number two, this fellow, despite his name, has lived here most of his life. . . .

LBJ: I think that's pretty important. Was he born here?

FORTAS: I don't know. . . . They've sent for his Army records, which should be here in the morning. . . .

LBJ: Did you get any information that's helpful from Walter tonight?

FORTAS: . . . No, sir. You know, I went over there to get him to—

LBJ: Yeah, but I thought maybe you might be talking to him and you might find out [if it] looks like there is any claim of any frame-up.[3]

FORTAS: When I talked to him, what he's told me indicates that . . . he just . . . started out for a walk and then ended up over there, which would negative—really negative—the idea of a plant.

LBJ: . . . Nobody suggested to him to go over there?

FORTAS: That's right. He went all alone.

LBJ: Where from?

FORTAS: From the *Newsweek* cocktail party. He and Marjorie went over to a cocktail party Kay Graham[4] had for the opening of the new offices of *Newsweek*. . . . I'm beginning to believe that he had quite a lot to drink—not just three drinks, as he told me—because he told me tonight that he took Marjorie down to the car and then he went back up to get his overcoat and stayed and had some more drinks. . . . And . . . after he stayed there awhile, he began to feel sick, and he went out for a walk and ended up at the YMCA. So, it's pretty terrible. I'm going back over to visit with him tomorrow morning, try and get a little more. . . .

LBJ: Can you think of anything else we ought to do?

FORTAS: No, sir. Hubert [Humphrey] called me this evening. . . . What he's

---

1. Johnson wants a quick FBI report that will close off the matter and keep it from spreading through the end of the campaign.

2. Andy Choka.

3. Bolstering his suspicions of a frame-up, LBJ had been told that the waiters at the *Newsweek* party who had plied Jenkins with drinks had been hired by the Republican National Committee.

4. Katharine Graham was chief of the Washington Post Company, which owned *Newsweek*.

going to do is to keep calling attention to [Jenkins's] Catholic religion and wife and six children.

THOMAS CORCORAN

Partner, Corcoran, Youngman & Rowe
Thursday, October 15, 1964, 1:30 A.M.

> Drawing on his old Dutch uncle relationship with LBJ, which started when Corcoran, a New Deal lion, did favors for the greenhorn Congressman Johnson in the late 1930s, Corcoran is one of the very few who call the President by his first name. In a purring voice, he beseeches LBJ, at Marjorie Jenkins's behest, not to fire her husband, hinting that Catholic voters might resent Johnson's cavalier treatment of a Catholic loyalist.

CORCORAN: Lyndon, this is Tommy. . . . I suppose you are just terribly tired, and I suppose you are terribly hurt.
LBJ: Yeah.
CORCORAN: . . . I have an uneasy feeling. . . . These fellows[1] are probably giving up a little more easily than a real pro like yourself would. All I hope is [that we don't] just admit everything and throw an old retainer overboard too easily. Particularly a Catholic retainer. . . . You know the way Eisenhower botched the U-2 thing by talking too much too soon.[2] . . .
LBJ: Did you talk to Marjorie?
CORCORAN: I went up to see her. Lady Bird suggested that I should. . . . And of course, what I'd love to get around here somewhere is the feeling that this could have been a great frame-up. A big lie by a bunch of fascists and Nazis who, up at the San Francisco convention,[3] showed that they were capable of a big lie. . . . Marjorie . . . said to me, "Don't you think I ought to go and stay in the hospital with Walter?" And I said, "Yes, I think the idea of the loyal wife being with the husband at a time like this is a very good image." But, of course, she said that it's a frame. . . . That Walter never even as much as thirsted [for] vice. . . . All I'm concerned is that the master's touch be on this and not just a bunch of amateurs like me, or amateurs like Clark [Clifford] or Abe [Fortas]. . . . Where are you going to be tomorrow, Lyndon?

---

1. Fortas and Clifford.
2. When the Soviets downed an American U-2 plane in 1960, the Eisenhower administration announced that it had been conducting weather surveillance. Then Nikita Khrushchev revealed to the world that the Americans had lied. The Kremlin used the pilot and his equipment, which had survived the crash, to show that the U-2 had actually been spying on their territory—a major embarrassment to the United States.
3. The hard-line Republicans who had nominated Goldwater in July.

LBJ: I'm going to be in Buffalo and, oh, I forgot, upstate somewhere.
CORCORAN: I'm sure nobody will think they see any signs of distress in your face about it. I'm sure that the impression they'll get is the true impression that you're a leader to whom even a blow like this doesn't hurt.[1] . . . This is very, very important. . . .
LBJ: Okay.

NICHOLAS KATZENBACH

Acting Attorney General
Thursday, October 15, 1964, 7:26 A.M.

> After a harrowing night, Johnson awakens in the Waldorf Towers and asks his Acting Attorney General to supervise the issuance of an official report declaring that Jenkins has not endangered national security. He shows his suspicions that the Republicans will broaden the scandal to launch a new attack on Johnson for his connection to scandals involving Billy Sol Estes and Bobby Baker.

LBJ: I don't know how quick we can get this report, but we ought to get one just as quick as we humanly can. . . . I don't know where this thing may lead. Abe [Fortas] tells me that there's no indication that there's any security involved at all.
KATZENBACH: I would think not.
LBJ: . . . Abe thinks that [Choka] is just a professional and this is a one-time incident. Never heard of each other before. . . . I would just as soon believe you and Lady Bird has been living together every night!
                              *   *   *
LBJ: He[2] and Deke DeLoach are just about as close as two men could be intimately associated. . . . He handled everything that Deke brought over [to the White House]. Every report that he had. So you ought to get him to really put every man he's got in town on it, because it's going to be nothing but a debate until it is. . . . I don't think there's any question that this will be a bombshell and be an issue in this campaign. . . . In the meantime, we've got to leak everything we know. No connection with security. Just a question of a sick man. Very sick. . . . It just shocks me as much as it does as if my daughter committed treason.
KATZENBACH: Yeah. . . .
LBJ: We've got to protect the office of the Presidency. . . . This thing's just got two weeks.[3] . . . We're going to have to be a little careful on the Baker

---

1. Honed over decades, this was Corcoran's manner of advising politicians.
2. Jenkins.
3. Meaning that the campaign has two weeks to go.

thing.[1] . . . I think this emphasizes that a little more. . . . I don't know . . . how closely Internal Revenue is working with you, but we have an acting man there. . . . Be sure that all personnel that he's got is turned loose on this Suburban Trust outfit. . . . What's important is after this guy deposited his money into Suburban Trust in October, find out how he got any money or what sources he could have gotten it to pay this $25,000.[2]

KATZENBACH: I've got a bunch of people working now.

*   *   *

LBJ: Anybody looking into this felt company outfit?[3]

KATZENBACH: No, Mr. President . . . there really isn't any violation of law that any of the facts would indicate here.

LBJ: . . . His law partner was on the payroll. . . . Fourteen thousand. And he was having contacts with the Federal Trade Commission on their matters. Now, that is a violation, isn't it?

KATZENBACH: . . . The law partner doing it is not a violation, unless that money went to Miller at the same time.

LBJ: . . . I'd put men over at that Federal Trade Commission and see who had the contacts over there. . . .

KATZENBACH: . . . Mr. President, you want to avoid creating the impression you're turning the whole FBI loose on the Congress. . . .

LBJ: Oh, there's no question about that. But I think if [Drew] Pearson is charging this . . . you're on notice.[4] . . . I'd have as my objective some kind of [report] Sunday night. . . . I would establish an all-time record of real promptness here, because we can't be a Harding.[5] . . . Your instructions are now that you forget [whether] this is Democrat or Republican or Catholic or Jew, an employee of the President or anything else. The President has instructed you to turn the whole resources of that Bu-

---

1. Don Reynolds, Johnson's accuser in the Bobby Baker scandal, testified against him before the Senate Rules Committee on October 1 and 2.

2. Here Johnson is turning the Internal Revenue Service against Reynolds, who had given Senator John Williams a written statement charging that he and Baker had arranged for Baker to funnel an illegal $25,000 payment to the 1960 Kennedy-Johnson campaign fund from the Democratic treasurer and Philadelphia contractor Matthew McCloskey, a Reynolds client, to help McCloskey obtain a performance bond for construction of the District of Columbia Stadium (*Congressional Record, U.S. Senate,* September 1, 1964). Reynolds's bank was the Suburban Trust Company of Silver Spring, Maryland. (See *Hearings Before the Committee on Rules and Administration, U.S. Senate,* October 1 and 2, 1964, U.S. Government Printing Office, 1964, p. 188.)

3. Now Johnson is asking if the FBI has turned up anything new on William Miller's relationship with the Lockport Felt Company that can be used to damage Goldwater's running mate (see Chapter 1).

4. LBJ knows full well that the reason Pearson is casting aspersions on Miller and the felt company is the FBI information he ordered leaked to the columnist (see Chapter 1).

5. LBJ is worried that he will be made into another Warren Harding—a President known to history mainly for the corruption around him.

reau[1] over to this case so the American people can feel that . . . the interest of the United States is not jeopardized. . . . Beginning with the President himself, and the President's wife. . . . They ought to just get those damn statements . . . because . . . you'll be damn lucky if you're not a witness between now and the election. Do you have that same concern that I do, or am I overplaying this?

KATZENBACH: I don't think the Congress will try to get him[2] as a witness. I think Mr. Goldwater will be playing it in the press.

LBJ: They've been trying to get him every day as a witness on the other matter.[3] . . . They asked Walter . . . what he knew about the details of this thing. He told them he had no knowledge of the details of it. . . . That didn't mean that he didn't know he was advertising. . . . He just meant that he didn't work them out. That's a stretch, though. What it looks like is perjury. I'm not sure that that wouldn't be a thing that you ought to ask about while you're talking to him over to the hospital. . . .

KATZENBACH: Yeah.

LBJ: Now, I expect a Billy Sol Estes bombshell before this thing is over, because I'm told that Goldwater had him aboard his plane,[4] . . . I'm told that they told him they'd pardon him. Desperate man. He's doing anything in the world he can to keep going to feed his family. . . . Yarborough[5] was his intimate. The fellow took a lie detector test that claimed that he gave Yarborough fifty thousand. . . . Now, my own judgment is Yarborough is a damn fool. But he's the last man in the world I would think would be a crook. I think he did take money. As all of us do.[6] But they're going to bring that up. . . . This Negro and this convict . . . told . . . the *Dallas [Morning] News* . . . that they gave him fifty thousand in bills.[7] . . . The lie detector is going to show that they were telling the truth. I don't believe those lie detectors.

KATZENBACH: . . . They've told their story, [but] they're so inconsistent all throughout, Mr. President.

LBJ: . . . The important thing here is you're going to have these historians writing about the Hardings. I'm not important. . . . The Presidency is awfully important. . . . I would certainly get the Internal Revenue man over there as quick as I could this morning. Tell him that I'm damned tired of them messing around.

---

1. The FBI.

2. Jenkins.

3. The Baker scandal. Jenkins was asked about his role in arranging kickbacks to LBJ from Don Reynolds in exchange for buying insurance from him.

4. Referring to the rumor LBJ had heard that Goldwater, if elected, would pardon Estes in exchange for dirt against Johnson (see Goldwater file, FBI).

5. Texas Democratic Senator Ralph Yarborough.

6. LBJ here concedes that he accepts cash payments, perhaps for campaign purposes.

7. Two men had claimed they saw Estes hand Yarborough an envelope containing $50,000 in 1960. One later admitted that his story was false. (See *New York Times,* May 2, 1964.)

They've had one year. . . . I want them working nights . . . so that when they get up before that committee[1] they can say that I ordered them to put everybody they could to see where this . . . $25,000 went.

KATZENBACH: All right.

LBJ: . . . The only instruction you have from the President is to guarantee equal and exact justice . . . and let the chips fall where they may, from the President and First Lady on down. And if we all wind up in the penitentiary tomorrow, I want that record to be clear.

LADY BIRD JOHNSON

Thursday, October 15, 1964, 9:12 A.M.

> Johnson is aboard *Air Force One* at New York's La Guardia Airport. He is about to take off for an upstate campaign tour with Ethel and Robert Kennedy when Lady Bird calls to advise him to treat Jenkins gently. She wants her husband to be viewed as compassionate and loyal to an aide of long standing.

LBJ: Hello?

LADY BIRD: Darling?

LBJ: Louder, honey, I can't hear!

LADY BIRD: Can you hear me now?

LBJ: No, no, I can't. You'll just have to talk real loud.

LADY BIRD: [*loudly into telephone:*] All right. I would like to do two things about Walter. I would like to offer him the number two job at KTBC.[2] . . .

LBJ: I wouldn't do anything along that line now. I'll just let them know generally through Tom [Corcoran] that they have no problem in that connection. Go ahead—next!

LADY BIRD: I don't think that's right. Second, when questioned—and I will be questioned—I'm going to say that this is incredible for a man that I've known all these years, a devout Catholic, the father of six children, a happily married husband. It can only be a small period of nervous breakdown balanced against—

LBJ: I wouldn't say anything! I just wouldn't be available . . . because it's not something for you to get involved in now. We are trying to work that out with the best minds that we have. . . . Eddie Weisl is on the way down there today. Whatever you do, don't do anything until I talk to Eddie and Clark and Abe.[3] I feel it

---

1. The Senate Rules Committee.
2. The Johnson station in Austin, for which Jenkins had worked while also working on LBJ's Senate staff.
3. Weisl, Clifford, and Fortas.

stronger than you do. But I don't want you to hurt him more than he's hurt, and when we move into it, we do that. We blow it up more. . . .

LADY BIRD: All right, I think if we don't express some support to him . . . we will lose the entire love and devotion of all the people who have been with us, or so drain them—

LBJ: Well, you get ahold of Clark and Abe and them. . . . You'll see what advice I'm getting. I'm late now, and I'm going to make three speeches,[1] and you can imagine what shape I'm in to do it. So don't create any more problems than I've got! Talk to them about it. Anything you can get them to approve, let me know.

LADY BIRD: All right. Abe approves of the job offer. . . . Abe approves of such a statement when questioned.

LBJ: Well, talk to Clark.

LADY BIRD: I must say that Clark does not approve of the latter.

LBJ: . . . I don't see any reason [for you to speak] publicly, because then . . . you confirm it, you prove that you're a part of it. You just can't do that to the Presidency, honey! . . . I would try to get Abe and Clark to let me talk to Miz Jenkins. . . .

LADY BIRD: All right, she's called me this morning, honey, . . . She is so hysterical and so bitter that . . . it's dreadful. She feels that her life is ruined, that their life is ruined, and it's all been laid on the altar of working for us.

LBJ: Is she angry at us?

LADY BIRD: Yes. You see, she doesn't believe any of this. She believes it's a framed, put-up job.

LBJ: Well, I think somebody better go talk to her and tell her the *facts*.[2] . . .

LADY BIRD: Well . . . I will try to be discreet, but it is my strong feeling that a gesture of support to Walter on our part is best.

LBJ: I'd make all the gestures I could, but I don't think that I would put myself in a position of defending what we say in the public in a situation like this. . . . The average farmer just can't understand your knowing it and approving it or condoning it, any more than he can [Dean] Acheson not turning his back [on Alger Hiss].[3]

LADY BIRD: Are you unalterably opposed to the job offer?

LBJ: I am publicly. I am not unalterably opposed to giving him anything and everything we have. All of us. And let him know it through Tom and through Abe and through you, but I see no reason . . . to . . . blow it up [so that it] makes the headlines. . . . I don't think that you'd have a license five minutes with a station

---

1. With RFK at his side, LBJ was to speak in Rochester, Buffalo, and Brooklyn, then address a Liberal party rally in Madison Square Garden.

2. Of Jenkins's two arrests on morals charges.

3. When Alger Hiss of the Roosevelt-Truman State Department was accused of espionage, Under Secretary of State Dean Acheson incurred public fury by saying that he would not turn his back on his old colleague.

being operated by someone like that. . . . I don't think the job is the important thing. . . . The finance is the minimum thing, honey.

LADY BIRD: I think a gesture of support on some of our part is necessary to hold our own forces together.

LBJ: Well, talk to Abe and Clark about it.

LADY BIRD: My poor darling, my heart breaks for you, too.

LBJ: I know, honey, and—

LADY BIRD: And I suppose I will let you go now. But if I get questioned, what I'm going to say is that I cannot believe this picture that's put before me, this man whom I've known all these years. . . .

LBJ: Does she[1] know that he walked in after he left the *Newsweek* party voluntarily in the YMCA?

LADY BIRD: . . . I'm not sure that she does.

LBJ: Don't you think Tom ought to tell her, or Abe, right quick? . . . They were all afraid to tell her . . . and I think they ought to tell her what happened there. That's the first thing that's got to be done so she can understand. The second thing that's got to be done—they've got to tell her whatever we have, they have.[2] Let's ride this thing out for two weeks. . . . Does she doubt that we are [on their side]?

LADY BIRD: Yes. . . . She just said, "You ruined my life and you ruined my husband's life, and what am I going to tell my children?"

LBJ: Well, how did we *ruin* it?

LADY BIRD: Honey, she just sees her life being ruined around her, and she's got to reach out and lash at somebody. She thinks it was overwork and overstrain, and that caused him to do whatever he did.

LBJ: Well . . . I think that's likely. But *I* didn't take him to the cocktail party and *I* didn't get him tired . . . and *I* never asked him to work anytime that he didn't want to. Somebody's got to give her the other side. . . . That's why I said you ought to go out last night. They wouldn't allow that. . . . So Abe, Eddie Weisl, some of them better go see her this morning, because if we don't, she will be talking to the papers.

LADY BIRD: . . . If you don't mind me going to see her, if I can get the company of somebody like Ed Weisl or Tom Corcoran or anybody, I will.

LBJ: . . . I don't think you realize the First Lady can't be doing it. I've got to go. They're holding the plane with the Mayor[3] and everybody on it. We are an hour late now.

LADY BIRD: My love, my love. I pray for you, along with Walter. Goodbye.

---

1. Marjorie Jenkins.
2. In other words, the Johnsons will be financially generous to the Jenkinses.
3. New York Mayor Robert Wagner.

LBJ: . . . Have Abe go see her, if he could. Or have a priest go talk to her.

LADY BIRD: All right. You are a brave, good guy, and if you read where I've said some things in Walter's support, they will be along the line that I have just said to you.

LBJ: You think I ought to call her?

LADY BIRD: Uh, yes, I do. I think we ought to offer support in any way we can.

LBJ: Well, why don't you talk to them and try to call her. Tell her I'm on the plane, but I . . . asked you to call her . . . and tell her anything we have, they have. We can't put him with the [television] station with the [need to have the government renew the station's] license.[1] Do you understand that?

LADY BIRD: I hear you when you say it. But I would just almost rather make an offer to do it, and then let the license go down the drain.

LBJ: Well, that doesn't do anybody any good, does it? Offer him something else—running the ranch.[2]

LADY BIRD: All right, okay. . . . Goodbye, my beloved.[3]

BILLY GRAHAM

Evangelist
Tuesday, October 20, 1964, 5:00 P.M.

> Terrified that the Jenkins scandal would damage his national popularity, LBJ had asked his private pollster, Oliver Quayle, to conduct a flash poll on its impact. Quayle reported that Americans did not seem to care. Johnson also enjoyed some luck. Within forty-eight hours of the Jenkins revelation, the press and the nation were distracted by the first Chinese nuclear test, Nikita Khrushchev's ouster as Soviet leader, and the defeat of the British Conservative government, not to mention the World Series. On hearing about the Jenkins scandal, many Republicans thought it might win them the Presidency. But Goldwater did not stress the issue. Privately he told reporters, "What a way to win an election—Communists and cocksuckers!"[4]
>
> Johnson felt he had another fire wall against the Jenkins scandal. He confided to Deke DeLoach that, from his Air Force Reserve service with Goldwater, Jenkins had learned of Goldwater's use of prostitutes and a paternity suit by a Houston woman.[5] An opponent with such weaknesses in his own private life was unlikely

---

1. Johnson argues that for KTBC to hire a twice-arrested man would jeopardize the station's Federal Communications Commission license.

2. The LBJ Ranch.

3. Lady Bird issued a statement starting, "My heart is aching today for someone who has reached the end point of exhaustion in dedicated service to his country."

4. Quoted in Robert Dallek, *Flawed Giant* (Oxford, 1998), p. 181.

5. DeLoach to Hoover, in Goldwater file, FBI. A Johnson family member, interviewed by the current author, also heard LBJ privately mention the Goldwater paternity rumor in the fall of 1964.

to encourage a war of all against all. Now, almost a week after the scandal broke, LBJ has had Bill Moyers call the nation's most famous evangelist to ask him to spend the night with the Johnsons at the White House.

LBJ: Hello, Billy. How are you, my friend?

GRAHAM: Well, God bless you. I was telling Bill [Moyers] that last night I couldn't sleep, and I got on my knees and prayed for you that the Lord would just give you strength.

LBJ: I told my sweet wife last night we've got mental telepathy. . . . I said, "Please, dear Lord, I need you more than I ever did in my life. I've got the Russians on one side of me. . . . The Chinese are dropping bombs around, contaminating the atmosphere,[1] and the best man I ever knew had a stroke, and disease hit him.[2] And I've been tied in here with my Cabinet all day and I'd [like to] have him, just make him come down and spend Sunday with me."

GRAHAM: Well, bless your heart. I would be glad to. I told Bill that there were two things. One was I just felt terribly impressed to tell you to slow down a little bit. I have been awfully worried about you physically. . . . You've got this election, in my opinion, wrapped up, and you've got it wrapped up big. . . . You know, when Jesus dealt with people with moral problems, like dear Walter had—and I was telling Bill I wanted to send my love and sympathy to him—

LBJ: Thank you.

GRAHAM: —he always dealt tenderly. Always. . . . I know the weaknesses of men, and the Bible says we're all sinners . . . and I just hope if you have any contact with him, you'll just give him my love and understanding.

LBJ: Well, that'll mean more than anything. Come down here Saturday evening and have dinner with us, and let's have a quiet visit, and maybe have a little service Sunday morning in the White House itself.

GRAHAM: Well, I will be very happy to. I told Bill that my wife couldn't come, because she's in bed sick with the flu.

LBJ: Oh, gosh, I'm sorry.

GRAHAM: I'm in Maine, and I'm traveling all over New England in different towns, preaching every night in a different town.

LBJ: Oh, wonderful, wonderful.

---

1. LBJ refers to the ouster of Nikita Khrushchev and the Chinese nuclear test.
2. Johnson means Jenkins's blood pressure and hypertension problems, for which he had ostensibly been hospitalized.

CARTHA "DEKE" DeLOACH

Friday, October 23, 1964, 10:51 A.M.

The previous evening the FBI had issued its report on the Jenkins case. As part of the investigation, two FBI agents outraged Goldwater by calling on him at 6:30 A.M., while he was shaving, at a Chicago hotel to ask about his own relationship with Jenkins and Jenkins's "personal habits." It would have been natural for Goldwater to wonder whether the FBI inquisition, on October 17, was intended to intimidate him from using the scandal against Johnson. Goldwater fired off an angry letter to Hoover, saying it was "curious" that "not one but two agents" arrived at an hour that was "unusual and reflected apparent urgency." When Hoover sent DeLoach to apologize in person, Goldwater complained that in the Jenkins investigation, Johnson was abusing the FBI "for political purposes."[1]

Drawing on five hundred interviews, the FBI report concluded that Jenkins had not jeopardized national security. When interviewed on October 18, it said, Jenkins "admitted having engaged in the indecent acts for which he was arrested in 1959 and 1964" and had "had limited association with . . . sex deviates." LBJ has been told that Jenkins and his wife are irate at the report's publication. Jenkins is threatening to disavow his FBI interview and publicly charge that the Bureau coerced him into confessing misconduct. Johnson is in the White House family quarters, where he has just discussed the problem with Clark Clifford, Abe Fortas, and Ed Weisl. Now he calls his FBI liaison to make sure that he and Hoover are in line.

LBJ: Problem this morning. It's all under control, though. And as I told you the other night, you're dealing with not the same individual at all. . . . It's totally beyond the comprehension almost.

DeLOACH: Yes, sir. Mr. President, he wasn't himself.

LBJ: No, not at all. I'm going to get the Boss[2] and tell him, after I get through this funeral[3] today . . . what a real thorough, dependable, and intelligent job he did. . . . And this thing—You just have to consider the same thing happened the other night,[4] and neither one of us can do anything about it. . . . Don't you let it get your blood pressure up. You're just doing a fine job and you just continue to do it. Forget it all.

DeLOACH: Well, thank you, sir. I was quite hurt this morning.

LBJ: Well, don't do that, because you are about the best friend [Walter's] got, and he knows that. He's told me that many, many times. He's strong for you for

---

1. Goldwater to Hoover, and DeLoach memorandum, both October 19, 1964, in Goldwater file, FBI.

2. Hoover.

3. LBJ was to lay a wreath at the coffin of former President Herbert Hoover, lying in state in the Capitol Rotunda.

4. Jenkins had once again lost his temper and flailed at those he thought had failed him.

Pope,[1] and that's the highest job in his outfit that there is, and he's told me that not once but twenty-five times. It's just a condition. If your wife goes crazy, your daddy goes crazy . . . you can't help it.

DeLOACH: I'll still stand by him, though.

LBJ: Got to. Thank you, my friend.

J. EDGAR HOOVER

Director, Federal Bureau of Investigation
Friday, October 23, 1964, 6:00 P.M.

> Johnson thanks Hoover for his report. In the course of the investigation, Hoover warned him that the Republicans were planning to use evidence that George Reedy had been a socialist connected to "Trotskyites" while a University of Chicago undergraduate.[2] LBJ brushed it off. Now he consoles Hoover about Jenkins's diatribes against the FBI and public criticism of Hoover for sending Jenkins flowers after his hospitalization with a get-well card from "J. Edgar Hoover and Associates."

LBJ: I thought that you did a very thorough and very fine job. . . . I told Deke to tell you, but I didn't want to let it go by without my saying so myself. . . . I don't think that this poor person that you think so much of—and I do too—is in his normal faculties, and both of us are suffering from it. But . . . at least I'm very grateful for your thoroughness and your patriotism and the way you have handled it, as I am everything else you have ever done.

HOOVER: Of course, I realize the spot that you have been in and the terrible other burdens that you've had, and it's awful bad this thing happened. But I think we handled it with compassion.

LBJ: You handled it with thoroughness and with diligence and with compassion. . . . And he just got off on this quirk. . . . He doesn't feel unkind. I guess the best friend he's got is Deke, and he knows that—the church relationship and all that stuff. And I think the person he admires as much as any Cabinet member—or more than any of them that he's close to—is you. He had this feeling that he didn't intend to . . . admit that he knew . . . sex deviates.[3] . . . He says he does not remember these two acts.[4] He's not denying them, but that he doesn't want to admit that he knew what he was doing. . . .

HOOVER: Plus he had admitted to the police at the police station when he was down there, and he, of course, admitted to our two agents . . . that there were other

---

1. Johnson's way of saying that someone is admired.
2. George Reedy file, FBI.
3. The part of Jenkins's FBI statement that he wished to disavow.
4. Which led to his 1959 and 1964 arrests.

acts, but . . . that he must, as he said, have been drunk or terribly tired and fatigued, and therefore had no recollection of it, that he had indulged in these acts on very rare occasions. I think the man is a desperately ill man.

LBJ: Yes . . . I doubt he will pull out of it. . . . I sure do thank you, Edgar. You've been a soldier. . . .

HOOVER: Well, I had a long talk with Fortas this morning. He was on his way to the hospital to see him[1] then. I told Fortas that I thought it would be very wise to see the superintendent at the hospital and get orders issued to the switchboard so that no incoming calls should be . . . put through to his room.

LBJ: I agree with that.

HOOVER: His wife, you see, was the one that told him all about this last night that set him off.

LBJ: Well, both of them are *really* off-balance right now.

HOOVER: Indeed they are. . . . I got, I guess, twenty to thirty telegrams today— some of them from pretty prominent publishers—asking whether it was true that I had sent flowers. I replied back to them that I had, and that he was a friend, and that they had been sent to him before you had ordered me to make the investigation of it. . . . Of course, there are so damn many hypocrites, you know. . . . Particularly in the press in the country. They are just like vultures.

LBJ: That's right.

HOOVER: And I was as stunned as anyone else was, because I had looked upon him in the highest regard, and still do. I think he's a desperately sick man.

LBJ: No question.

HOOVER: . . . I think that there might, some thought be given to getting him into Walter Reed,[2] which has a psychiatric ward. . . . They would have better control over people going in to see him. What I'm fearful of is some of these newspaper people will get in to him and talk to him in one of these periods where he has this kind of flighty idea he wants to have a press conference.

LBJ: [*chuckles*] He's not going to have any of that! You just remember, my friend, you have done your duty as you have been doing all your life, and I'm proud of it. And I'm prouder of you now than I have ever been before. I've known for thirty years that there's nobody like you. That's why I told him months ago that as long as I'm around here, he's got to stay pretty close [to you].

HOOVER: Well, that's mighty nice of you, Mr. President. . . .

LBJ: And Deke's the same way. Now, don't you think that boy hasn't done his duty! And it's a shame for Walter and him to have a quarrel, but he listened to it as long as he ought to have, and then he did what he ought to have done. . . .

---

1. Jenkins.
2. Walter Reed Army Hospital.

HOOVER: Well, I think this thing will gradually quiet down. You see, the thing about it is, these things are generally ten-day wonders. And on this last poll I saw, instead of you going down, you have gone up after these things had happened.

LBJ: [*laughs*] That's right! That's right! . . . I'll tell you another thing. I think the psychiatrists and all them agree that it's a pretty good thing for some of us to send him flowers or write him something. . . . They all tell me that the odds were ninety-five to five that he would kill himself the first day if he didn't have a little encouragement . . . and I don't think anybody criticized you.

HOOVER: Well, I don't care whether they do or not. I've got a pretty powerful hide on that. I've listened to it so long.

LBJ: [*laughs*] You did your duty and I'm proud of you. And as long as your Commander-in-Chief feels that way about you—

HOOVER: That's all I care.

LBJ: —that's okay, my friend.

GEORGE REEDY

Friday, October 23, 1964, 6:24 P.M.

> Johnson's press secretary informs him of a report, passed to him by a friend in the press, that the Republicans have photographs of LBJ *in flagrante* with a Louisiana woman.

REEDY: Mr. President, Jack Horner [1]—just as a friendly friend—came in today. And he tells me the Republicans are now claiming that they have a picture of you taken some time late in 1960 or early in 1961, with a woman named Wanda DuBonier in a compromising situation. He says they haven't produced the picture, but they are pushing this one around town. She is supposed to be a whore from Louisiana that Bobby Baker produced for you. And she's supposed to be back in Louisiana now.

LBJ: No, I never heard of her.

REEDY: I don't think that we need to worry about this one because— But nevertheless—

LBJ: No, I don't know her.

REEDY: —I talked to Abe [Fortas] about it, and Abe thought I should tell you.

LBJ: No, I never heard of it, and I don't know the name, but you might—

REEDY: Should I tell Deke [DeLoach] to look into it?

---

1. Garrett Horner was the *Washington Star* White House correspondent.

LBJ: I would call the principal, Bobby,[1] and ask him—
REEDY: Right.
LBJ: —what he knows about it, and then I would ask Deke to look into it.

ROBERT KENNEDY

Democratic Candidate for U.S. Senate from New York
Monday, October 26, 1964, 11:45 P.M.

Robert Kennedy, whose campaign against Kenneth Keating, incumbent Senator from New York, has been stalling, swallows his pride to call Johnson for help. LBJ has been campaigning that day in Florida, Georgia, and South Carolina.

LBJ: Been in South Carolina.
KENNEDY: How was that?
LBJ: Not too good. We're . . . going to lose Georgia, I'm pretty sure. And I think we have maybe a forty-five, fifty-five chance in Florida. Nobody is doing any work down there. George Smathers and [Spessard] Holland[2]—everybody is looking out after themselves. South Carolina, we had a good meeting—Olin Johnston[3] and all the fellows. But we got a good chance to lose in those three states. . . . I don't think it's critical, but I would like to have them. . . . How are you getting along?
KENNEDY: Well, fine. I didn't know whether on this, you know—and I know how hard you have been going—but it would make a—be a big help, I think, in Long Island. You know, the day that you are coming in, I think, is the thirty-first. If perhaps you could come in a couple of hours early and we could take a trip through—you know, arrive at the airport out on Long Island and take a trip through Nassau County. They think they can get a couple hundred thousand people out.
LBJ: Well, if it's not already blocked out, it will be done, period. . . . I speak that night at Madison Square Garden.[4]
KENNEDY: Yeah, and if you could come in so that you could maybe arrive at one of those fields out on Long Island and then just take a motorcade in through.
LBJ: Say at three o'clock or four, something?

---

1. Bobby Baker, whom Fortas had represented until he gave up the case when LBJ became President.
2. The two Democratic Senators from Florida.
3. Democratic Senator from South Carolina.
4. A Democratic rally was scheduled featuring Kirk Douglas, Gregory Peck, Jill St. John, Connie Francis, and other stars.

KENNEDY: Yeah.

LBJ: [*after consulting Jack Valenti*] . . . I'll give you three hours.

KENNEDY: And I'll get the people there.

LBJ: . . . You just do it quietly and call on anybody in the federal government that you need.[1] But do it where they don't catch you! . . .

KENNEDY: Thanks a lot.

LBJ: Now, is there anything else I can do?

KENNEDY: No, that's terrific.

LBJ: When you turn over there tonight and put that Ethel [Kennedy] on your arm, give her a hug for me, will you?

KENNEDY: I'll do that.

CARTHA "DEKE" DeLOACH

Tuesday, October 27, 1964, 1:45 P.M.

Reaching his FBI liaison at lunch, LBJ checks on Jenkins's current mental state and explores his suspicion that the Jenkins arrest was a Republican frame-up. A week earlier he told DeLoach that Republican operatives might have inspired the waiters at the *Newsweek* party to get Jenkins drunk.[2]

LBJ: Are you working for me or Hoover? Where are you?

DeLOACH: Well, I'm working for you. I'm at the Army-Navy City Club having lunch with the [American] Legion heads.

LBJ: Oh, well, I'm sorry I bothered you over there. . . . I got to go to Boston, Pittsburgh, Evansville, Indiana, and Albuquerque. . . . That's a pretty long trip for one afternoon, isn't it?

DeLOACH: It is, sir, but I'm sure you will knock them dead, just like you've been doing.

LBJ: We are doing our best. Have you seen Walter?

DeLOACH: I haven't seen him . . . since last week.

LBJ: Have you had any report on him?

DeLOACH: I've talked on the phone to him Sunday night. Talked at great length.

LBJ: Is that since he blew up?

DeLOACH: Yes, sir.

LBJ: Does he seem any better?

DeLOACH: Yes, sir. . . . What he said he wanted to do was to get this as a matter of record his disavowal of the statements he made to the [FBI] agents. I said, . . .

---

1. To arrange the event.
2. DeLoach to Hoover, October 20, 1964, in Goldwater file, FBI.

"It's all taken care of." . . . He said, "Well, that sets my mind at ease. . . . I won't bring up the subject again."

LBJ: . . . I never was convinced that you-all completed what you ought to complete on this Choka.[1] . . . Is there nothing else we ought to do?

DeLOACH: No, sir. . . . I don't think he was part of any frame-up. This man has been arrested three times previously on morals charges, and he was known in the Army as a homosexual. So I think frankly that this man was just hanging around in the same place, hoping to pick up someone. . . .

LBJ: You reckon there is any way in the world, though, that we could pursue him further, ask him, give him a list of names and ask him which ones of these he knows? Ask him if he ever saw Grenier, or ask him if he ever saw Burch?[2] . . . I got a report that was very distressing to me from [Drew] Pearson. . . . Pearson says that one of our friends . . . tipped him off four or five days ahead of time. . . . The reporters had it on the plane four days before I knew it.[3]

DeLOACH: Yes, sir.

LBJ: I've always thought that that former park policeman and the present park policeman offered some problems there.[4] And if you do have positive evidence that he was not in the park that evening . . . it seems to me that we ought to ask a grand jury to have that fellow called before them, and ask him . . . if anybody had talked to him about it. Not for the purpose of convicting anybody but for the purpose of really trying to see what all entered into this situation. Now Pearson may be crazy . . . but I hate to think that he'd break something that we know nothing about.

DeLOACH: I would, too, very much so.

LBJ: . . . He says that several days before this happened, a fellow named Goelet, who Dick Berlin[5] referred to us too— You maybe ought to talk to Dick Berlin and ask him what his information is about Goelet coming down here.

DeLOACH: I've already done that, Mr. President. . . . He is a man that has been established by the Republican National Committee to handle strictly the Jenkins case for the rest of the campaign. And he has been the one that's been issuing these smears by the hour on this thing, and also these other rumors about various other White House personnel.

---

1. Andy Choka, with whom Jenkins was arrested at the YMCA.

2. LBJ wanted Choka interrogated to find out whether he had been in touch with influential Republicans like John Grenier and Dean Burch, both of the Republican National Committee.

3. Johnson refers to rumors that Jenkins had been framed and the fact that Republicans knew of his arrest before LBJ did.

4. Johnson wanted officers who were in Lafayette Park at the time Jenkins allegedly picked up Choka to testify to what they had seen. One park policeman was saying that Jenkins had tried to proposition him in the park.

5. Richard Berlin, chief of the Hearst publishing combine, was an LBJ ally.

LBJ: Well, now, that was the word that Dick gave us. But now Pearson says that he told a fellow . . . that he had this thing set up.

DeLOACH: . . . Mr. President, what I'd like to do first, rather than the grand jury routine . . . is to go to Bill Moyers and tell Moyers to call Stewart Udall[1] and tell Udall to call this man in and really put the pressure to him and say he has got to re-lease all facts in his possession concerning this matter. Now, this man has been thumbing his nose at the FBI, even after pressure was put on him in the first place.

LBJ: Well, Udall did that, and he said to "screw you." . . .

DeLOACH: [*turning to the story that LBJ had been photographed* in flagrante *with a Louisiana woman*] I ran that down thoroughly, and there was no truth what-soever to the fact that [you and she] got together in New Orleans. . . . We traced it to the White Citizens' Council[2] head there. . . . We have gone so far back to trace it down to this fellow Leander Perez,[3] who was talking to the head of the White Citizens' Council. We're not sure that Perez instituted all of this, but we do know that he and the head of the White Citizens' Council are very close friends. But the man said that he got it as a result of an anonymous call, and he gave it to the Asso-ciated Press. . . . We then went to Dallas and checked out [*name deleted*][4] there, and he had two arrests—both for driving while intoxicated. Now, Henry Wade[5] had the [*name deleted*] file over in his office and was keeping it under lock and key, and we didn't ask Henry to let us see it, but we know that that file does not concern any immoral activity. . . .

LBJ: Right. . . . Now . . . are you proceeding with the rest of the people here?[6]

DeLOACH: Yes, sir.

LBJ: Why, now, that's good. Now, on this Hoover thing, I think you ought to spend a little time with him. And I think it was very unfortunate that they indicated that any flowers went. But I think that's only unfortunate for two or three vicious, vile people. . . . I get a message from Mr. Khrushchev and flowers on our anniver-sary here, or if I get sick—and he's dedicated to bury us! He . . . sent these flowers . . . before I called him and ordered the investigation.[7] . . . It would be a normal thing to send flowers. . . . It didn't impair the investigation. It *helped* the investi-gation. It made [Walter] feel that he ought to talk and tell everything he knew. . . . Let him know that his boss thinks he did exactly the right thing. . . . In my judg-ment, history will record he's a bigger man for having done it. And even if he did

---

1. Secretary of the Interior, who oversaw the National Park Service officers present in Lafayette Park.

2. White Citizens Councils opposed "race-mixing."

3. Perez was a rabid New Orleans segregationist.

4. Under National Archives regulations, the Johnson Library has the right to delete names from the LBJ tapes for privacy reasons.

5. Dallas County district attorney.

6. LBJ refers to his request that the FBI newly investigate his top appointees.

7. Of Jenkins.

it without any affection, by God, it served his purpose. Because he got a two hour interview out of this guy that didn't need to tell him anything. So, just tell him that I feel that way . . . and that nobody is ever going to reflect [badly] on him as long as I'm around here.

DeLOACH: Mr. President, . . . I know how busy you are, but this is so humorous, I felt like I just had to tell you. We got a rumor that—in fact, Bill Moyers knew about it and asked me to check it out—that [*a member of the Johnson staff*][1] was involved in a homosexual incident down in Houston, Texas.

LBJ: I believe anything now, so check them all out.

DeLOACH: We checked it out very thoroughly, but we found out that his reputation down there was exactly to the contrary!

LBJ: [*laughs and snorts*] Well, he's a man around town, I'll tell you that. Don't check too hard on those things, because you might get some confirmations!

DeLOACH: Yes, sir.

LBJ: [*Name deleted*] is a very active fellow. I've found that out.

RICHARD GOODWIN

Presidential Speechwriter
Tuesday, October 27, 1964, 2:59 P.M.

LBJ: I'm going to make Mac Bundy and Bob McNamara try to get you twelve headlines between now and next Tuesday. Which will be six in six of the morning papers, and six afternoon. So I just don't have to say, "I'm glad to be here, it's wonderful to see you, you've got a beautiful town and a lot of smiling faces." Because they get tired of that. And I've got to where *I* vomit when I say it.

GOODWIN: All right.

LBJ: So we are going to write Khrushchev or Kosygin[2] or somebody a letter, by God, and recommend they raise the price of eggs, and that will get on the front page. What I used to do when I was a congressional secretary when I wanted to make a headline . . . was I would write a Cabinet officer . . . and just as soon as it was delivered, I would issue it, and I got . . . a Cabinet name. But these fellows— we don't know how to do that around here. The last good piece of news I've had, I guess, was . . . the Chinese Bomb.

---

1. The staff member's name has been deleted by the LBJ Library.
2. Alexei Kosygin had succeeded to Khrushchev's position as Soviet Prime Minister.

NICHOLAS KATZENBACH

Wednesday, October 28, 1964, 11:43 P.M.

> Campaigning in the West, Johnson calls Katzenbach from the Hotel Utah in Salt Lake City. Earlier that evening in San Diego, as the President departed *Air Force One*, a radio reporter had asked him about his administration's "morality" problems. Overtired, LBJ had blurted out, "Practically every administration has them. . . . President Eisenhower had the same type of problem." Johnson recalled the case of Arthur Vandenberg, Jr., son of the Michigan Republican Senator who cast aside his isolationism to help Truman enact his Cold War strategy. As Johnson had read in FBI files, Eisenhower had revoked the younger Vandenberg's selection for his staff as appointments secretary after hearing reports that Vandenberg was a homosexual. "The only difference," LBJ told reporters, "is we Democrats felt sorry for him and thought it was a case of sickness and disease and didn't try to capitalize on a man's misfortune." Now that his comments are being publicized, Johnson wants to make sure that he can back up what he said in case Vandenberg sues him for slander. He also fears that he might have angered President Eisenhower by dredging up an embarrassing old incident.

LBJ: What do we have on Arthur Vandenberg? . . . I read a report in the last month showing that he had some sex problems, and they had to let him go. . . .
KATZENBACH: . . . Yes, that's right.
LBJ: Now . . . a local radio boy in San Diego [asked me], "What about the sex deviates in the administration?" Mr. Jenkins and so on. . . . I said that every administration has these problems. . . . Now the press plays it up pretty big, as if I indicted Eisenhower as having a pervert as his appointments secretary. . . . I did not intend to do that. . . . My thought was that every President I'd known [had such problems]. From Hoover when he had Andrew Mellon[1] . . . to Roosevelt with Sumner Welles, to Harry Truman with Matt Connelly and with Harry Dexter White,[2] Eisenhower with Vandenberg. . . .
KATZENBACH: Uh-huh.
LBJ: And Kennedy had Jim Landis or he had Fred Korth.[3] . . . And we'll have them from time to time. . . . Now the question is, Did I slander somebody and can

---

1. Secretary of the Treasury under Harding, Coolidge, and Hoover. Mellon's 1931 tax returns were questioned, but he was exonerated.
2. Connelly was a Truman aide who went to prison for tax evasion, White a Roosevelt-Truman Treasury official suspected of being a Soviet spy.
3. Landis, former Harvard Law School Dean and Kennedy family retainer, was convicted of tax evasion after appointment to JFK's White House staff. JFK fired Korth, his Secretary of the Navy, for using official stationery and other resources to aid his Fort Worth bank.

they have a suit against me for slander? The press is trying to play it up as a pretty big fight. . . . Maybe they think . . . that I am guilty of McCarthy-type character assassination . . . because I did specify that Ike had this problem with his appointments secretary. So, my problem is . . . to immediately identify the appointments secretary in my own mind—not for public use, but to be sure that I'm on safe ground. . . .

KATZENBACH: One reaction to the general statement, Mr. President, is that it's perfectly true. It always happens. . . .

LBJ: . . . Well, Mr. Attorney General, you're my lawyer, so in the morning— I hate to call you so late, but it's going to be a big play, I imagine, for the next two or three days. It might be right into the election, as a blooper, and so we better get the facts on . . . Arthur Vandenberg, Jr. . . . They're going to be mobbing me.

NICHOLAS KATZENBACH

Thursday, October 29, 1964, 7:52 A.M.

KATZENBACH: Vandenberg—he was active in the Eisenhower campaign and was publicly announced to be appointments secretary. At that point there came out rumors as to homosexuality. . . . They did find that he as a bachelor had been taking in young men to live with him. And these young men were homosexuals, or many of them, or were known associates of homosexuals.

LBJ: Right, right.

KATZENBACH: At that point, President Eisenhower decided that, at the very least, he'd exercised bad judgment. . . . So it was announced that he had ulcers, and for that reason, he never actually took the job . . . and he went on down to teach at a university, from which he subsequently left for reasons of ill health.

LBJ: . . . Okay. . . . It would have been better if it hadn't have been said, but we will try to keep them from making anything out of it.

DEAN RUSK

Friday, October 30, 1964, 6:24 P.M.

During a talk with his Secretary of State, LBJ mentions that J. Edgar Hoover has passed along a Drew Pearson report that the Republicans might drop a "bombshell" against some Johnson administration official on Halloween—three days before Election Day.

LBJ: How're things going?

RUSK: Things are generally a little calm at the moment, except in Cambodia.[1] I thought we ought to begin trickling some of our dependents out of there, seeing as how it's getting pretty crazy. . . . No great surprises out of the Soviet Union. . . . Are you getting questions on your trip about foreign policy matters? . . .

LBJ: Well, we are talking foreign policy most of the time and peace generally. . . . They are supposed to drop the big bombshell tomorrow.

RUSK: Uh-huh. I was talking to Bill Moyers for about fifteen minutes about that. . . .

LBJ: . . . Yeah, he said that Hoover[2] told him that they told Drew [Pearson] that it was a member of the Cabinet. Now, what do you think we ought to do about it?

RUSK: I think we ought to try to find out a little more, if we can . . . who it could be. I think Bill called me because of the remark I made the other day that I was always accompanied by a chaperone, armed with a pistol, so I don't think they got anything on me.[3] But one of my colleagues in a Cabinet meeting the other day advised everybody to be sure they're traveling with other people all the time . . . because he thought we were being followed.[4] . . .

LBJ: . . . What do you think about your calling [the Cabinet] together in the morning, telling [them about] the report you've heard from Hoover? See if they have been followed or if they have anything suspicious. . . . Ask them if they've got an FBI report on . . . every officer that has to be confirmed.

RUSK: . . . I guess I better have those that are in town drop by here, rather than over at the White House.[5] . . .

LBJ: . . . You might want to even talk to them on the phone.

* * *

LBJ: How do things appear to you? . . . Do you see any chance for this fellow . . . Goldwater? I don't, but I may be too close to [the situation].

RUSK: No, I think . . . this tremendous effort you're making now is really more relevant to the Senate and congressional races than it is to your own. But I can see why you want to keep going. Just not to take any chances.

LBJ: Well, we'll be through tomorrow.

---

1. On October 24, Cambodia had downed an American transport plane.

2. The FBI Director.

3. LBJ had said that he was so closely watched, he couldn't have committed any offense without being immediately exposed.

4. LBJ was worried that if Jenkins had been the victim of a frame-up, the Republicans would try again.

5. Rusk means at the State Department. He does not wish to call attention to such a meeting.

J. EDGAR HOOVER

Saturday, October 31, 1964, 10:35 A.M.

Today is Halloween, the day that the Republicans were supposed to have exploded their bombshell. From the White House, LBJ calls Hoover to ask if he has heard anything. In the course of the conversation, despite longtime rumors that he is himself involved with his housemate, Deputy FBI Director Clyde Tolson, Hoover lectures on how to spot a secret homosexual.

LBJ: What do you know this morning?

HOOVER: Well, I haven't heard anything more than that rumor that we got yesterday.

LBJ: . . . I've been out speaking, but I'm just getting ready to go to New York. Do you have any idea who that might be?

HOOVER: No. . . . They always refer to a Cabinet officer. But I do know that over in the Defense Department, the Navy have had under surveillance this fellow . . . that works for an assistant secretary by the name of BeLieu[1] . . . in connection with some deviation. . . . We took over that investigation yesterday. . . . They said that this particular man had been under surveillance and that they were going to explode this bomb today. Now, the only person I know of who has been under surveillance by any agency has been this man over in the Navy Department. . . .

LBJ: . . . They raised the question of the way he combed his hair and the way he did something else, but they had no act of his. . . .

HOOVER: It's just . . . that his mannerisms . . . were suspicious.

LBJ: Yeah, he worked for me for four or five years, but he wasn't even suspicious to me. I guess you are going to have to teach me something about this stuff.[2] . . . I swear I can't recognize them. I don't know anything about them.

HOOVER: It's a thing that you just can't tell sometimes. Just like in the case of the poor fellow Jenkins. . . . There are some people who walk kind of funny. That you might kind of think a little bit off or maybe queer. But there was no indication of that in the Jenkins case.

*   *   *

HOOVER: [*on the Drew Pearson report that Jenkins had been framed by Republicans*] We got an affidavit from that source saying that it was absolutely untrue. It was just said as a gag. . . . It's not a very funny gag. But, I mean, that's the kind of dirt and rumors that are going around. . . . As we get nearer to next Tues-

---

1. Assistant Secretary of the Navy Kenneth BeLieu, who had worked for LBJ in the Senate.
2. LBJ knew full well the rumors that Hoover was a secret homosexual.

day[1] . . . there's likelihood of a lot of this rumoring . . . that they can't prove. . . . Of course . . . one of these dirty columnists is very apt to carry something in a column. So far I haven't been able to get any more detail than was given to me yesterday. Namely, that this man was a Cabinet officer and it would be exposed today. . . . None of them raise any suspicion in my mind.

LBJ: None in mine. . . . If [we win] on Tuesday . . . you and Deke give a little thought to it from my standpoint. Kind of representing me. I don't want to run you crazy over there. But I rather think that you ought to protect everybody. From me, right on down.

---

1. Election Day.

Chapter Three

A LANDSLIDE CAN'T BUY HAPPINESS

I got the biggest vote anybody ever got before. I had the greatest affection that had ever been demonstrated. . . . But . . . the Bobby Kennedy group . . . put out this stuff that nobody loves Johnson. . . . That I was just the lesser of two evils, and that people didn't care.

LBJ *to* EDWIN WEISL, SR., *November 4, 1964*

DEAN RUSK

Tuesday, November 3, 1964, Afternoon

During earlier campaigns, the anxious, depleted Johnson had suffered physical and emotional breakdowns. Two days before his first election to Congress in 1937, he collapsed with appendicitis. In 1941, after learning that the popular Texas Governor W. Lee "Pappy" O'Daniel would oppose him for the Senate, he took to bed "depressed," Lady Bird recalled, "and it was bad." With his illness variously described as pneumonia and nervous exhaustion, he was put into a clinic, with LBJ insisting that his doctors keep it secret.[1] After declaring for the Senate in 1948, he was hospitalized with kidney stones.

Even though he is expecting to win by a landslide, on Election Day 1964, Johnson is suffering various body aches and an emotional letdown from the intensity of the campaign. He has spent most of the day at the ranch lying in bed with Lady Bird. The first returns are about to come in.

LBJ: I've just got a sore back. Sore hip been hurting me. And sore head. I've had a headache all day, and I've been in bed all day. I just kind of came off the mountain, you know. I've been kind of keyed up and I'm just kind of feeling punch-drunk.

---

1. Quoted in Robert Caro, *The Years of Lyndon Johnson: The Path to Power* (Knopf, 1982), pp. 703–4. O'Daniel won.

RUSK: You need to get rest. Get it, if you possibly can, in the next few days.

LBJ: Weren't you awfully nice to bring the Cabinet over yesterday?[1] . . .

RUSK: They were thrilled to have a chance to . . . see you off. I called Hubert [Humphrey] this morning to tell him how much everybody appreciated the job he did in the campaign.

LBJ: Well, he's wonderful. I just wanted to check in with you to see if we had any problem in Vietnam.

RUSK: . . . We've got a problem, of course.[2] I did see Dobrynin[3] today, and he raised the Cambodian incident along the border.[4] . . . [I] told him that after today was over, I wanted to have very serious talks with him about Southeast Asia.

BILL MOYERS

Tuesday, November 3, 1964, 6:41 P.M.

> At the ranch house, listening to early election results on television, LBJ consults Moyers at the White House.

MOYERS: Mr. President, Olin Johnston[5] said we're going to lose South Carolina by 46 to 53. . . . And he said the civil rights backlash[6] did it.

LBJ: Yeah? . . . Okay.

MOYERS: Sorry to give you that. It looks like we're going to carry Young in Ohio.[7]

LBJ: I hope so. . . . How much we carrying Ohio by?

MOYERS: At last count it was 54 percent.

LBJ: Well, they told me *60* on television.

---

1. Rusk had led a gaggle of Cabinet members to see LBJ's helicopter take off from the White House grounds, starting the trip to Texas.

2. Two days earlier the Vietcong had staged a large attack on the U.S. air base at Bien Hoa. See November 5, 1964, below.

3. The Soviet Ambassador.

4. On October 24, an unarmed American C-123 transport was downed in Cambodia, killing eight Americans. The United States said the plane had "accidentally" penetrated Cambodian airspace but conceded that Americans and South Vietnamese had that week struck at least five times against Cambodian targets.

5. Democratic Senator from South Carolina, who had gallantly escorted Mrs. Johnson on the "Lady Bird Special."

6. The backlash against LBJ's championship of the Civil Rights Act of 1964, passed the previous summer.

7. Moyers refers to Democratic Senator Stephen Young. He was wrong.

BILL MOYERS

Tuesday, November 3, 1964, 9:01 P.M.

Johnson and Lady Bird are now settled in the Jim Hogg Suite of the Driskill Hotel in Austin. Watching television from a chair, LBJ greets family and friends and makes calls. At one point in the evening he says, "God, I hate for it to be over, because the hell starts then."[1] Now, with the sound of television in the background, Moyers reports new figures.

MOYERS: You are going to carry New York 62 percent . . . or more, and Kennedy is going to carry it 59 percent.[2]

LBJ: Sixty-two and 59? God, I—

MOYERS: But wait just a minute. Steve Smith[3] says that their polls show you're going to carry it by 71 percent—3 million votes. And Oliver Quayle[4] thinks it will be up above 69 or 70.

*   *   *

LBJ: What did I lose? Alabama and South Carolina and—

MOYERS: Mississippi and Louisiana.

LBJ: . . . What about Arizona?[5]

MOYERS: Arizona you're ahead right now. . . . He predicts you'll get 49.3 percent.

LBJ: And he'll carry it?

MOYERS: Yes, sir.[6] . . .

LBJ: Well, what did we lose? Six states?

MOYERS: . . . No, four states, plus Arizona. Five. . . .

LBJ: What do those electoral votes add up to? . . .

MOYERS: . . . That's forty votes. . . . Harris[7] says he will not budge from his 64 percent figure.

*   *   *

LBJ: Are we picking up any Senators and any Congressmen?

MOYERS: Right now Blatt[8] is ahead, and Bobby is winning. So we're picking

---

1. President's Daily Diary, November 3, 1964, LBJL.
2. Robert Kennedy was defeating incumbent Senator Kenneth Keating.
3. Kennedy's brother-in-law and campaign manager.
4. Johnson's pollster.
5. LBJ was very eager to take Goldwater's home state, where he had made a brief campaign stop to attend church and tacitly taunt his opponent.
6. Quayle was wrong. In the end, Goldwater took Arizona by less than 1 percent of the vote.
7. Pollster Louis Harris.
8. Judge Genevieve Blatt was running against Republican Hugh Scott for the Senate from Pennsylvania. Johnson was eager to defeat Scott, one of his antagonists on the Bobby Baker scandal. He ultimately failed.

up two there, as of right now. Taft[1] is winning, so we're losing one there. . . . I haven't heard the latest on Harris[2] in Oklahoma. But it looks like maybe . . . three or four we are picking up.

LBJ: . . . Where are we picking them up?

MOYERS: . . . They think now that Salinger[3] is going to pull ahead. . . . Tydings[4] we picked up. . . . We're going to pick up Blatt, if she continues. . . .

LBJ: . . . You're going to pick up Blatt and Bobby, and you're going to lose Young and Harris.

MOYERS: That's right. So that evens out.

LBJ: . . . It would be even. Unless we can pick up Carvel.[5] *God,* I pray on that one!

ROBERT KENNEDY

Tuesday, November 3, 1964, 11:55 P.M.

Johnson has just watched New York Senator Kenneth Keating on television conceding that Robert Kennedy has defeated him. By campaigning with RFK in New York and taking the state by a landslide, Johnson has helped Kennedy win the Senate seat. After this call, as LBJ will relate in several of his later conversations, he will be angry with Kennedy for being so stingy with appreciation.

LBJ: I just listened to the old man Keating brag on you.

KENNEDY: [*jubilant:*] Listen, I pulled you through up here![6]

LBJ: Yeah? Well, by God, whenever you can get Keating to brag on you, why, I've got to watch that New York combination!

KENNEDY: [*laughs*] Good work, though, huh?

LBJ: Well, I thought so.

KENNEDY: It was terrific everywhere. What did you—just lost three states?

LBJ: Oh, no, we'll lose eight or ten.

KENNEDY: No, no, no.

LBJ: Yeah, we're going to lose Alabama and Mississippi and Louisiana and South Carolina, and Georgia, and Arizona. That's six. And we'll probably lose South Dakota and maybe Wyoming. We may lose two or three more.

KENNEDY: What about the Senators? Wyoming?

---

1. Robert Taft, Jr., who was beating Senator Young in Ohio.
2. Senate candidate Fred Harris, who finally won.
3. Pierre Salinger of California, running to fill a Senate vacancy to which he had been appointed.
4. Senate candidate Joseph Tydings of Maryland.
5. Senate candidate Elbert Carvel of Delaware, who was running against John Williams, another Senator who had dogged LBJ about Bobby Baker. Carvel ultimately lost.
6. Kennedy is joking about the fact that LBJ, whose margin was 2 million votes larger than his, had helped pull him into office.

LBJ: It's close. We think we'll win it. God damn it, we could have won the Delaware one that we ought to have won. We could have won Pennsylvania. We had a candidate, and they . . . got to fighting, and we had a close race there. But Scott's[1] going to win.

KENNEDY: Pierre Salinger's close, isn't it?

LBJ: Yes, and it looks bad to me. . . . He was desperate last night. I was flying, and they said to please call him or wire him immediately. . . . I couldn't get him on the phone. And they said it was monitored[2]—I oughtn't to do it. So I sent him a wire to read on his program. . . . I feel awfully bad about it. It's good about Tydings, though.

KENNEDY: Yeah, that one—

LBJ: And it's good about Montoya.[3] We picked up New Mexico. . . . That's two, but we'll lose Salinger and we'll lose Young, so we lose two. And then we'll have to stand off. That damn Taft! I hate to see him win.

KENNEDY: I hate to see him win.

LBJ: We could have won if we'd had a candidate.[4]

KENNEDY: Yeah, John Glenn was.[5]

LBJ: We've just got to go out and find young people. Now, you just go to looking for them after you get your little old staff set up. . . . Let's go to talent hunting and try to find some damn good, young, able people to bring into government.

KENNEDY: . . . God, we certainly need them up here.

LBJ: Teddy[6] called me, and I tried to answer it. I guess I've got a bunch of communications switchboards down here, and they're not worth a damn. But they say his line's busy. If you talk to him, tell him I'm mighty proud of him. Massachusetts was wonderful.[7]

KENNEDY: Yeah, it really was good, wasn't it?

LBJ: Oh, it's just out of this world. I thought everything went better than we had a right to expect.

KENNEDY: Yeah, it really was terrific. You did a great job.

LBJ: We've got a lot to be thankful for, Bobby. And give our love to Ethel.

KENNEDY: Yes, sir.

LBJ: And let's stay as close together as he'd[8] want us to.

---

1. Senator Hugh Scott.
2. Vulnerable to interception by a third party.
3. Joseph Montoya, the Senate winner in New Mexico.
4. Meaning a candidate of quality.
5. The first American to orbit the earth was a Kennedy family friend. Glenn had pulled out of the race after a bathroom fall.
6. Kennedy, who had just been reelected Senator from Massachusetts in a landslide.
7. Massachusetts had voted 76.2 percent for Johnson.
8. President Kennedy.

KENNEDY: That'd be fine, Mr. President. Congratulations.

LBJ: Tell all that staff of yours: ain't nobody going to divide us. And I'll tell mine the same way, and we'll—

KENNEDY: That's right.

LBJ: —we'll move ahead. There's plenty in life for all of us.

KENNEDY: That's right.

LBJ: I'm proud of you.

KENNEDY: Thanks very much. Thanks for your help.

LBJ: Thank you for calling.

KENNEDY: Made a hell of a difference.

LBJ: Bye.

EDWARD KENNEDY

Democratic Senator from Massachusetts
Wednesday, November 4, 1964, 12:04 A.M.

> Campaigning from his Boston hospital bed after nearly being killed in a June air crash, the late President's younger brother has been resoundingly reelected.

LBJ: Sorry I missed you, Teddy. . . .

KENNEDY: Oh, no. . . . You were up in that helicopter. I want to congratulate you. It's many hours overdue, but—

LBJ: If you don't mind, I'd like you to take all these other forty-nine states and bring them in like you do Massachusetts. If you can stay in the hospital and do 'em that way, why, we're all right.

KENNEDY: That's a great, great tribute to you. . . . You certainly have won the support and the hearts and loyalty and the affection of all the people. You must be very proud. It's certainly well deserved. And I just join all those other millions of people that today are saluting your victory. . . .

LBJ: Mighty proud of you and Joan [1]—and very happy for Bobby. I just talked to him about ten minutes ago in New York. I'm sorry for Pierre [Salinger], but maybe he can pull through.

KENNEDY: I guess that looks like he's out of luck out there now. . . .

LBJ: I don't understand that, do you?

KENNEDY: . . . I just don't. . . .

LBJ: . . . Tell Joan we sure do appreciate all she did. . . . I want to work with you and help you any way in the world that I possibly can.

---

1. Kennedy's then-wife.

KENNEDY: That's very kind. Your words up here were very well received, and I appreciated them. . . .

LBJ: Well, we . . . thought you had Boston in good shape. We didn't think we needed to come up there and find out how *you* stood. But I wanted them to know how *I* stood.

KENNEDY: . . . Well, you won a lot of friends.

LBJ: Thank you, Ted.

JOHN CONNALLY

Wednesday, November 4, 1964, 12:11 A.M.

> In a call to the Driskill, the Texas Governor encourages LBJ to come to the Municipal Auditorium, where he is to deliver his victory speech. This is the same hall where, on the evening of November 22, 1963, after flying in from Dallas, Johnson and Connally had been scheduled to welcome President Kennedy at a banquet of Texas Democrats.

CONNALLY: Mr. President, I don't want to tell you how to run your business, but out here . . . you've got a magnificent setup. You've got five rooms. It's quiet. It's sumptuous. You've got a bedroom. You've got a tier of three television cameras. If you came out—I don't know what your plans are—but just your mere appearance out here would absolutely cut in all these networks.[1] . . .

LBJ: All right. I had been trying to talk to the people that I needed to, like Teddy and Bobby,[2] that had been calling me. . . . I'm afraid I'll get out there with two or three thousand [people] that . . . and I don't really know . . . whether I ought to be saying anything until he[3] concedes. What's your judgment?

CONNALLY: He's not going to concede until in the morning. . . . I don't think you ought to yet claim victory until he concedes, but I think you can say all but that you're claiming victory.

LBJ: Why do you think the son of a bitch wouldn't concede with this—

CONNALLY: I knew he wouldn't. He just wants to make it embarrassing for you by not conceding tonight. He doesn't want you to get this tremendous play tonight with this television audience. He wants to do it in the morning, when everybody's at work.

---

1. Television networks.
2. Kennedy.
3. Goldwater.

LAWRENCE O'BRIEN

Special Assistant to the President for Congressional Relations
Wednesday, November 4, 1964, 2:24 A.M.

After traveling by motorcade to the Municipal Auditorium, the Johnsons walked onstage at 1:40 A.M. Introduced by Governor Connally, the newly elected President told the nation, "Tonight our purpose must be to bind up our wounds, to heal our history, and to make this nation whole." Now the First Family is back in their crowded Driskill suite. LBJ eyes the television screens, offers "loot" (presidential pens and medallions) to the children present and, in a sleepy voice, makes thank-you calls.

LBJ: I want to tell you how proud I was of you, and what a good job you did, and how much you meant to us all.

O'BRIEN: Well, I want to congratulate *you,* Mr. President. I was just watching you on television a few minutes ago. It was marvelous.

LBJ: [When] I was talking about all those folks at every precinct, I was talking about you.

O'BRIEN: Well, gosh, I'm telling you, it's just a great, great night. . . . The American people have placed their confidence in you like it's never been placed in a man in history. . . .

LBJ: What happened to us on the Senate? Did it about break even?

O'BRIEN: Yeah, it looks like we'll break even or possibly be one up. . . . Some of those fellows will thank you for the rest of their lives.

LBJ: They picked up about twenty in the House, didn't they?

O'BRIEN: . . . We might do slightly better. We had three or four close ones that we weren't counting as ours. . . . [1]

LBJ: I think I got rid of both Republicans in Texas.[2]

O'BRIEN: Yeah, both of them are gone. You cleared the House out down there.

LBJ: They're son of a bitches, too! . . . You go get you some rest, Larry. . . . And you tell me what you think we ought to do. . . . How do you like that New York vote? Four million seventy-seven thousand to a million nine!

O'BRIEN: [*laughs*] The old saying that they will weigh them instead of count them applied there!

LBJ: We carried it over 2 million. And the record was 1 million!

O'BRIEN: Oh, God, listen, remember we were talking about a million and a half a month or so ago? And both of us were smiling, if you remember.

---

1. O'Brien's predictions proved unduly cautious.
2. Congressmen Bruce Alger of Dallas and Edgar Foreman of Odessa.

LBJ: Now, look at this—Goddamn Scott beat [Blatt] 65,000. We ought to have beat him. And I guess Williams was elected.[1]

O'BRIEN: Yeah . . . but that was worth the shot you made there. . . . We had a couple of disappointments . . . and a couple of pleasant surprises. So it evened out pretty well. . . . When you said it's a mandate, it's a mandate. . . .

LBJ: Was my statement all right?

O'BRIEN: . . . I had tears in my eyes here watching it—and the family. . . .

LBJ: Hope you will tell your wife how much I appreciate the sacrifice she's made, letting you stay down there every night and call and raise hell and travel all the time.

BILL MOYERS
McGEORGE BUNDY

Wednesday, November 4, 1964, 9:56 A.M.

Heavy rains have flooded the roads around the LBJ ranch, forcing the Johnsons to make the short trip back home by Jetstar, with the President napping in his seat. On landing, he woke up and drove a golf cart to the ranch house, where he took a rub-down and went back to sleep.

Now, in the burst of morning, the victor has awakened in his bedroom, with Lady Bird at his side. Lyndon Baines Johnson has won the greatest presidential landslide of modern times—61 percent of the popular vote. He has won 486 electoral votes and forty-four states, and the largest congressional majority since Franklin Roosevelt's in 1936—68 Democrats in the Senate (a net gain of 2) and 295 Democrats in the House (a net gain of 37). Despite this decisive judgment, Goldwater still has not conceded defeat. Yawning, LBJ talks to Moyers and Bundy at the White House.

LBJ: Bill?

MOYERS: Yes, sir!

LBJ: Well, you talk mighty chipper!

MOYERS: Well, I'm feeling pretty good. Mac Bundy and I here are just—

LBJ: What did you get so far off on your polls for?[2]

MOYERS: . . . I just was taking them as they came.

LBJ: I just wanted you to know that you are mighty trusted and mighty valued and mighty loved. And I wanted to take time when I didn't have forty people around to tell you that. . . . I don't think any thirty-year-old in the history of the nation ever had so much to do with so many so well.

---

1. Republican Senators Hugh Scott of Pennsylvania and John Williams of Delaware.
2. Referring to their conversations of last night.

MOYERS: You are very generous.

LBJ: No, I'm not. I'm just telling you what the facts are. And I hope you get a good rest. And I hope you don't let something happen to you like Walter,[1] because if you break down, why, everything in the world would go to hell. . . . I thought I had gone under yesterday. I just stayed in bed all day. I had the damnedest headache, and my hip was hurting. . . . But I'd shaken, I bet, fifty thousand hands in Austin the night before. . . . [2]

MOYERS: . . . We're all proud of you. I don't see any way it could have been improved on. . . . You campaigned well, you carried the election, you made the right decisions. . . . You're the one we have to worry about from the standpoint of weariness.

*   *   *

LBJ: Now are you leaving today?

MOYERS: No. . . . I'm leaving in the morning.[3]

LBJ: . . . Who are going to be our bastions of strength there?

MOYERS: Well, you've got the Honorable McGeorge Bundy, who's here, and he just got on the line, in fact.

LBJ: Ask him if he will take over the domestic operations, too!

BUNDY: [*laughs*] With pleasure! You can be sure that we'll follow a policy of inactivity if you'll do the same.

LBJ: I've always regarded you as Sherman Adams[4] in every respect, except integrity.

BUNDY: You are a very amiable fibber. What a marvelous day!

LBJ: Well, it's a tribute to you, my friend, as much as it is to any human being— you and that Cabinet.

BUNDY: . . . I've collected five dollars from McNamara[5] because he said you weren't going to get 60 percent of the vote. And he never paid five dollars with more of a smile on his face.

LBJ: I hope you'll call your mother and tell her I think her two boys[6]—

BUNDY: Well, we're just so full of heart for you, Mr. President. . . . How is the weather down there?

LBJ: Oh, it's kind of rainy. We got a good rain. That helped us. We like it to rain. We're going to have a barbecue for the press today. We haven't gotten up yet. . . . My body's aching, but my hip's a lot better. I felt pretty good last night. I didn't get to bed until about five.

---

1. Jenkins, who is still on Johnson's mind.
2. At a rally in front of the State Capitol, attended by 100,000 people.
3. For a vacation in Puerto Rico.
4. Eisenhower's capable, powerful, and errant chief aide, whom he fired for influence-peddling.
5. Secretary of Defense Robert McNamara.
6. Bundy's brother William was Assistant Secretary of State for East Asia.

* * *

MOYERS: If you'll take a couple of days and fly down to the Dorado Beach [Hotel] in Puerto Rico, you can be my guest.

LBJ: [*laughs*] . . . Jack Valenti . . . is going off as somebody's guest at Palm Springs. . . . How do you think Jack's FBI[1] is working out? . . . Don't you know what Hoover[2] said? That he had no problems in *that* direction. Emphasized *that* direction.[3]

BUNDY: In the *other* direction.

LBJ: We call him a little stud!

BUNDY: . . . Mr. President, we're having a survey done of communications security, and we're not a bit sure that it's safe to talk from the ranch to the White House.[4]

LBJ: . . . I can't talk anywhere. . . . But they're bringing a bunch of corporals down here with the Army that back home they were truck drivers. I don't know why the White House can't get twenty competent girls that worked on the switchboard at Chesapeake and Potomac[5] someplace. . . .

BUNDY: [*chuckles*] There isn't any reason why you shouldn't interpret your mandate as giving you a right to speak to people, Mr. President. . . .

LBJ: What is the percentage going to be?

BUNDY: Sixty-one point three is the 7:30[6] ticker with 90 percent in. That's what Quayle said.[7]

* * *

BUNDY: CBS and IBM and Harris pooled their talents to produce this [Voter Profile Analysis] that Cronkite was using last night.[8] I don't think they missed any states . . . including one or two that wavered, like Georgia. Dean Rusk says he doesn't dare speak to you.[9]

LBJ: . . . I didn't care about the other Southern states. Louisiana's a bunch of crooks, and Mississippi's too ignorant to know any better, and Alabama's the same way.[10] But Georgia knows better. . . .

---

1. The FBI investigation LBJ ordered on all top staff and Cabinet members after the Jenkins episode.

2. J. Edgar Hoover.

3. Meaning that Valenti was not a homosexual. He had been a bachelor until the age of forty-one.

4. Meaning that presidential calls from the ranch could be intercepted.

5. The telephone company that served Washington, D.C.

6. A.M., Eastern Standard Time.

7. In the end, LBJ got exactly 61 percent of the vote.

8. The CBS news anchor Walter Cronkite, who was also Lady Bird's University of Texas schoolmate, had drawn on a system called Voter Profile Analysis to assess the results.

9. The Secretary of State was abashed that his home state had rejected LBJ.

10. All had voted for Goldwater.

MOYERS: . . . We've been sitting here for the last hour talking about staffing responsibilities. . . . I'd just like, on the phone, rather than send you a memo that you'd have to read, just [to] throw out some names that you might tuck away for possible White House service. . . .

LBJ: Well, I'm going to keep all of them that'll stay. . . . I thought I'd satisfied everybody on the New Frontier with Bobby in New York.[1] Because if I'd kept my mouth shut, he'd have been beat. . . . And very frankly, though, I thought last night it took him a long time to get around to admit the President had anything to do with it.[2] And there was a thousand people in the room. And he kept thanking County Judge So-and-So, and County Surrogate So-and-So. . . . But the guy that campaigned up there through thirty-three miles of Brooklyn . . . and carried over 2 million—he just never could find it while I was out bragging on his brother. And I just guess he can't bring himself to it. Did you-all see his victory statement?

BUNDY: No, I did not.

MOYERS: I saw it.

LBJ: Did you feel that way, Bill?

MOYERS: No, I really didn't. I thought he saved the best for last.[3]

LBJ: Everybody in the *room* just sat there, including Lady Bird, and just couldn't *believe* that he wouldn't acknowledge that the President had had *anything* to do with his landslide victory. . . . But he just couldn't *do* it. He had . . . Mayor Wagner, and . . . Averell Harriman[4] was the hero of the deal.

BUNDY: [*trying to mollify:*] Well, Mr. President, he didn't realize you weren't in that room, and all those other sons of bitches *were!*

LBJ: [*laughs*] He called me and thanked me and privately said it to me as strong as he could. But if *I* had been making the statement, I would have said, like I did in my statement, that we carried on John Kennedy's program. And I would have made a statement that I think that President Johnson and Senator Humphrey—

BUNDY: The way I heard it from their headquarters—and I haven't talked to Bob myself—but I think . . . they're *damn* grateful.

---

1. In other words, the Kennedy loyalists should be delighted with LBJ for saving RFK's candidacy by campaigning with him in New York.

2. LBJ was fuming that in his long televised victory speech, RFK had thanked him so briefly and so late.

3. Moyers and Bundy, who maintained their friendships with RFK despite working for LBJ, were continually trying to tamp down the President's suspicions about Kennedy.

4. RFK had thanked New York Mayor Robert Wagner and former New York Governor Averell Harriman, who were at his side.

EVERETT DIRKSEN

Republican Senator from Illinois and Senate Minority Leader
Wednesday, November 4, 1964, 11:22 A.M.

From his ranch bedroom LBJ calls the old friend with whom he has horse-traded for decades in the House and Senate. In Sibley Hospital in Washington, Dirksen is in traction for back trouble. Johnson knows that keeping Dirksen benign will be crucial when he tries to move his Great Society program through Congress in 1965.

DIRKSEN: Congratulations!

LBJ: Thank you, my friend.

DIRKSEN: You shouldn't have done it quite in such big style.

LBJ: How are you feeling?

DIRKSEN: [*chuckles*] I'm in the hospital, and I'm leaving here tomorrow to go to Florida.

LBJ: I just hope you get a good rest and that you come out of it all right, because we can't afford to have you on the sidelines. . . . The first thing you do is take care of yourself because we love you. . . . And if anything is emergency, urgent, I'll have a jet plane there to bring you anytime.

DIRKSEN: Fine.

LBJ: I want to work awfully close with you. I think you've got a wonderful chance now to make a great contribution to your party and to the country, too. I just hope that you take the leadership on it, because we got awful nasty down here. Just got awful nasty.[1]

JOHN CONNALLY

Wednesday, November 4, 1964, 11:28 A.M.

On his television set in the ranch bedroom, LBJ has just watched Goldwater in Phoenix finally concede defeat. The Arizona Senator has read aloud from a churlish telegram he sent his opponent, saying that Republicans will remain "the party of opposition when opposition is called for." Hearing that, Johnson sputtered, "That damn son of a bitch!"[2] Now he asks Connally to come to the ranch. Like an older brother, Johnson once again hints that he would like to build up the Texas Governor as a national figure.

LBJ: John, I came on out here last night. I didn't feel too good . . . and I slept late this morning. Just waked up for Goldwater's statement. . . . I just wondered if I

---

1. LBJ means the bitterness of the Goldwater campaign.
2. President's Daily Diary, November 4, 1964, LBJL.

couldn't have a helicopter—if you felt like it—pick it up and you come on out here and we'll stroll around and . . . get this barbecue[1] out of the way and then we'll drive off and look at our cattle.

CONNALLY: Sure. That's fine.

LBJ: . . . I thought you did a wonderful job for us last night on television.[2] I saw some of it replayed this morning and it was real good. . . . You were the best one on it. A fellow better stay off television with you!

CONNALLY: [*laughs*] I doubt that.

LBJ: . . . With the world in the shape it's in, it would be a wonderful thing if you would leave the image of [just] being my closest adviser of twenty-five years. . . . I would move around and try to get to know some of the philosophizers— the . . . *Los Angeles Times* and the *New York Times* boys, and the *Wall Street Journal*s. . . . I'd try to extend my friendships . . . to this press field. I don't want to be telling you what to do. But I think if you could do it for a couple of hours, you and Nellie,[3] that it would be—

CONNALLY: Well, we'll do it.

LBJ: —it would be pretty well national instead of just being a hell of a good Texas Governor. . . . And then they might be thinking of *you* down the road. . . .

CONNALLY: All right. How are you going to dress? Is a sport coat all right?

LBJ: Yeah, yeah, that's what I'd wear. I'd wear a pair of khaki britches, if you got them, and your boots, if you want to, or your regular shoes, and a brown shirt and a tie and a sport coat. That's what I'm going to wear. . . . Tell Nellie to wear low heels if she wants to, and just come around and show her sparkling self, because she made me feel mighty good last night, kidding me. . . . And bring anybody that you want. . . . Anybody that travels with you is welcome.

HARRY TRUMAN

33rd President of the United States
Wednesday, November 4, 1964, 11:36 A.M.

> From Independence, Missouri, Truman congratulates the victor. A Johnson friend since the 1930s, he views LBJ's Great Society as the continuation of his own Fair Deal. Suffering from a bathroom fall three weeks earlier, the eighty-year-old former President is frail.

---

1. The Johnsons were to hold a barbecue that afternoon for the White House press corps and the new Vice President–elect and Muriel Humphrey, who were flying down from Minneapolis.

2. LBJ had been introduced by Connally before giving his victory speech.

3. Mrs. Connally.

LBJ: Mr. President, I love you, as everybody in America does, and I'm just so honored that you would take the time to call me.

TRUMAN: I called you because I think you set a record that has never been equaled and never will be.

LBJ: Anybody got your record will never equal it. When you go to looking at the Truman Doctrine and NATO, and the Marshall Plan, and everything else, it makes all of us look like pygmies, and . . . I got sense enough to know it.

TRUMAN: Well, you're all right in my book. I just wanted to congratulate you. I feel just as happy about it as you do.

LBJ: I know you feel happier, because you've always been more for your party and the other folks than you've been for yourself. And I just want you to know that as long as I'm in that office, *you're* in it. And there's not a privilege of it, or a power of it, or a purpose of it that you can't share. Your bedroom's up there [at the White House] waiting for you, and your plane's standing by your side.[1]

TRUMAN: Appreciate it.

LBJ: And your doctors and anything else you want or need, why, by God—Uncle Sam will—

TRUMAN: First time I'm able to travel . . . I'd like to come and see you and just talk over old times, with nothing to do but to see Lyndon Johnson.

LBJ: . . . You bring Margaret[2] and your grandkids down. We'll have a plane pick both of you up . . . and I want to get your advice and talk to you. I think we've got a good chance, but we're in trouble on foreign things.

TRUMAN: . . . You won't have any serious trouble at all, and if there is anything I can do to help you, you know I'm available.

LBJ: Well, you've done it. I came to you when I wanted to know how to run for Vice President, and I came to you when I wanted to know how to run for President, and I think that we gave them a good mauling—just what you wanted them given—didn't we?

TRUMAN: Just exactly what they ought to have had. It's the finest thing that's happened in the history of the country.

LBJ: [We] rubbed their nose in it. . . . They were dirty. Oh-h-h-h! You don't know how dirty they were. They put out mean—

TRUMAN: Oh, I do, too. I got so damn mad I could've killed somebody.

LBJ: They put out these mean books, and they questioned my integrity and my honesty.[3]

---

1. Meaning a White House guest room and a presidential plane.
2. Truman's daughter.
3. Johnson refers particularly to *A Texan Looks at Lyndon: A Study in Illegitimate Power*, by J. Evetts Haley (Palo Duro Press, 1964). There were 7.3 million copies of the tract, promoted by the John Birch Society. Johnson was also piqued by Phyllis Schlafly's *A Choice, Not an Echo* (Pere Marquette Press, 1964) and John Stormer's *None Dare Call It Treason* (Liberty Bell Press, 1964).

TRUMAN: [*sounding fatherly:*] I know they did, but you want to forget that, because . . . the vast majority of the American people never believed a word of it.

RICHARD J. DALEY

Mayor of Chicago
Wednesday, November 4, 1964, 11:42 A.M.

> Johnson is careful to keep the country's most powerful city boss friendly. Daley is eager to demonstrate how much his Chicago machine has contributed to Johnson's victory.

LBJ: Dick, I love you!

DALEY: Mr. President, congratulations and God bless you and good health. You have all the wishes of the Daley family and their prayers.

LBJ: I've always had that.

DALEY: By God, we said we would get you seven-fifty in Chicago, and it will be closer to eight fifty or nine hundred thousand. Looks as though you'll win the state by a million. . . . You saved the Governor,[1] and you've helped the entire ticket. . . . But you conducted yourself masterfully and fine and decently. . . .

LBJ: I think you're a wonderful friend to have, and I'm proud of you first as a friend and as a confidant and a brother. But I think you're the greatest political leader we've got in America. You've just got to save yourself and try to think in national terms now, because we've got to rebuild this party and we've got to give them the kind of leadership in the nation that you give them in Chicago.

DALEY: You've been giving them wonderful leadership.

LBJ: Well, we've got to. . . . And I want your judgments and I want you to throw away that modesty and pick up that phone and call me. I count you among one of two or three that were there when the going was tough, and things were wobbly.[2] . . . I never forget how you treated me when I ran for Vice President.[3] . . . You always take care of things ten years ahead of time, Dick!

DALEY: [*cackles*] Well, we try to. But God love you, and may the Lord shower his blessings upon you and your family. And we'll be there anytime. You know it. At your side. Night and day. We are still fighting out here. . . . Every time they printed those cartoons in the paper,[4] we said to our fellows, "Go out and get him a hundred more votes per precinct!"

---

1. Governor Otto Kerner had come back to win reelection after a strong challenge by Republican Charles Percy.

2. Daley had stood by Johnson in the summer of 1964, when LBJ was worried that RFK might make trouble for him unless made Vice President. (See Beschloss, *Taking Charge,* pp. 462–64.)

3. In 1960, when JFK chose LBJ, unlike other Northern city bosses, who were worried about a Texan on the ticket, Daley had embraced Johnson and given him valuable advice.

4. The *Chicago Tribune,* which endorsed Goldwater, ran front-page cartoons ridiculing LBJ.

* * *

LBJ: Dick, you don't know how dirty these people were. It's the worst I ever saw.

DALEY: They were pretty dirty up here . . . but our fellows just battled them in the precinct.[1] . . . I went in a couple of precincts myself where they were trying to interfere with my neighbors in voting.[2]

LBJ: . . . In every Nigro [mailbox] . . . they put out that all your traffic tickets, all your violations, everything is going to be checked, and you'll be prosecuted if you vote. Just scared them to death. Made them all think they were going to the penitentiary. . . . It was the most fascist operation I've ever seen.[3] They uncovered it in Houston. . . . We got copies of it. . . . Everything that would scare a Nigro to death, they had it. It was kind of a Klan[4] operation. . . .

DALEY: We've got to rebuild all that. . . . You do it with patience and . . . forgiveness, I suppose. And you do it with the kind of attitude that you displayed— your philosophy last night with binding up the wounds and getting everyone together in a unified country.

LBJ: Did you like that statement?

DALEY: Oh, I thought it was beautiful, just masterful. . . . And the quotation on Lincoln![5] . . .

LBJ: . . . Let's get together, and you be doing some thinking for me, Dick.

EDWIN WEISL, SR.

Wednesday, November 4, 1964, 12:46 P.M.

> Although LBJ has just won by a landslide, he is anxious and resentful, seizing whatever black lining might exist within the silver cloud of victory. Searching for reassurance, he calls his longtime adviser in New York, who has powerful friends and clients among publishers and television executives. LBJ complains that television commentators are carping that he beat Goldwater only as the lesser of two evils. He also vents his spleen about RFK's failure to thank him properly for shoring up his Senate candidacy in New York.

LBJ: Eddie, I just wanted to tell you how much I loved you and what a great source of strength you'd been, and how I couldn't have made it without [you].

WEISL: Oh, Lyndon, I've never been so happy and proud of a man in my life.

---

1. Daley pronounces this "pre-sint."

2. Daley refers to reports that Republican operatives attempted to obstruct Democrats, especially African Americans, trying to vote.

3. As LBJ speaks, one can hear the determination that will lead him to propose a voting rights bill in 1965.

4. Ku Klux Klan.

5. Johnson had quoted from Lincoln's 1861 farewell address to his fellow citizens of Springfield, Illinois.

LBJ: ... We've never doubted each other. ... I'm just getting ready to go out and meet Hubert. He's going to land here in about two minutes, and we're going to have a little barbecue with the press. I thought things went about as good as we could expect.

WEISL: It was the greatest victory in the history of the United States. ...

LBJ: Eddie, you've got to do this, and you're the only one that can do it. ... The rest of them just talk about it. We don't have any propaganda machine and we don't have anybody that can get out our stuff. Now Red Mueller[1] started this story that they're just voting against Goldwater and they didn't like either one of us. And that Johnson didn't have any rapport, and he didn't have any style, and he was a buffoon, and he was full of corn. Every place I went in this campaign, and I went to forty-nine states with Lady Bird and the two girls—I was in forty-four myself—I had the biggest crowds they had ever had before and I got the biggest vote anybody ever got before. I had the greatest affection that had ever been demonstrated before. And the greatest loyalty. And more big business men and more labor men and more Nigras and more Jews and more ethnic groups. More everybody!

But they say, "Aw-w-w-w, that doesn't amount to anything." So the Bobby Kennedy group, they put out this stuff ... that nobody loves Johnson. They are going to have it built up by January that I didn't get any mandate at all. That I was just the lesser of two evils, and that people didn't care. Now ... Dick Daley says that he figured we'd run 750,000 in Chicago and now we're going to run eight-fifty to nine. And we saved the Governor and we run over a million in the state. [I'm] the greatest candidate that he's ever seen. ... I think you've got to quote him, because that's what he told me a dozen times. I think you've got to quote men like Lawrence[2] that's saying that. And you've got to sell the fact that business and labor doesn't have to hate each other. And that we have put together divergent viewpoints and united them in peace, like we always unite in war. ... And somebody's got to try to get the [*New York*] *Times* to give us a little approach, because the first thing they're going to do is going to try to make a Warren Harding out of us on account of Baker and Jenkins.[3]

WEISL: Yeah.

LBJ: Second thing they're going to do is say there's no mandate. Third thing they're going to do is try to have the Southern coalition[4] ... combine with the Republicans and not let us get anything [passed]. ... Even Roosevelt in '36 never captured the number of people and never had them jumping in the air and yelling

---

1. Merrill "Red" Mueller of NBC.
2. David Lawrence, former Governor of Pennsylvania.
3. LBJ was worried that the *New York Times* would now revive the Bobby Baker and Walter Jenkins scandals and make Johnson into another President Harding.
4. Old Southern Democrats who opposed civil rights and other liberal legislation.

and giving the loyalty that we did. Now, we've got to build that up. You're going to have to get that advertising agency that we've got there in New York and call them in. That Bill Moyers hired. Find out who they are.[1]

WEISL: All right.

LBJ: Say, "Now how in the hell do we create this image?" Here's Newhouse and here's Dick Berlin, and here's Roy Howard,[2] and here's the *Washington Post* and *Star*—they're our friends—

WEISL: And we've got *Life* and *Look* and—

LBJ: We've got all of these folks. "Now *damn* it, let's give this guy a *chance*.[3] Let's give him a chance to try to hold the country together. . . . He's got problems with de Gaulle and the Alliance[4] right now, and he doesn't want to be any hero, and he's not going to revolutionize things, and he's not going to send a program to Congress that's going to attack the Court.[5] He's going to be a moderate, temperate man." But let's say that the people . . . saw him and they liked him, and that he came, he saw, and he conquered. Now, I can't do that because I can't be that immodest. But you can just raise *hell* with them and call that agency in. . . . In Iowa, I beat five of the six Democratic congressmen.

WEISL: Yeah.

LBJ: I had twice the crowd *Eisenhower* ever had.[6] They wrote about Eisenhower for eight years, but they've never written one word about us.[7] And they've *got* to say something about the auditorium at Austin, Texas, being filled at two-thirty in the morning just waiting to see me[8]—the people that knew me best and voted for me six and eight to one in my home boxes . . . and the *love* and *affection* they had for *thirty years*. All they write about is not love and affection. They write, "The lesser of two evils. Cornpone. Southern."

WEISL: It's not quite as bad as that, but . . . I will undertake to do it. . . .

LBJ: . . . Call up the head of that agency and tell him . . . you want him to plan a campaign. . . . Then you talk to Dick [Berlin] and say, "Now God damn it, these little old half-assed editorials that you-all wrote saying, 'We are for Johnson,' but then treating them all equally." . . . It looked like to me Goldwater got better news than we did. . . .

---

1. Doyle, Dane and Bernbach, which had made Johnson's television commercials, including the controversial "daisy girl" spot.

2. The press magnates and LBJ friends Samuel Newhouse of the Newhouse newspapers, Richard Berlin of Hearst, and Roy Howard of Scripps-Howard.

3. LBJ is speaking about himself.

4. Charles de Gaulle, president of France, is threatening to withdraw from NATO's military structure.

5. Referring to FDR's polarizing Supreme Court–packing plan of 1937.

6. LBJ was thronged by 175,000 people in Des Moines on October 7.

7. Meaning that Eisenhower had more favorable press coverage than he.

8. On Election Night.

WEISL: . . . I'll get busy. I'm meeting Mr. Newhouse for dinner tonight.

LBJ: . . . You just tell Newhouse . . . that I want you-all to say that this man is *loved,* that this man has the affection of the *country,* that this man won the hearts of the *people,* that there's nothing like it ever *happened,* and let's give him a *chance,* and let's *help* him. And tell him, by God, I'll stand by his side in all of his ventures and help *him.*

WEISL: . . . I will do everything I can. . . .

LBJ: . . . Just look at the votes! Now, what did we carry New York by?

WEISL: . . . Close to two and a half million.

LBJ: All right, now, Roosevelt by a million and a half was the biggest, wasn't it?[1]

WEISL: Eisenhower by a million six was the biggest.[2]

LBJ: But here's Roosevelt, who lived there and [was] Governor and everybody loved him, and here's Eisenhower. And we increased it over a million.

WEISL: That's right. . . .

LBJ: Ohio we did the same. Pennsylvania we did the—

WEISL: New Jersey you won by almost a million.

LBJ: New Jersey, Pennsylvania, Ohio.

WEISL: Connecticut, every county. In the state of New York you carried every single county.

LBJ: Is that right?

WEISL: Every one, without exception.

LBJ: I guess we elected Bobby, didn't we?

WEISL: Oh, sure. He ran a million seven hundred thousand votes behind you, and still was elected.

LBJ: Well, let's get busy on this, Eddie, before they ruin us and make a Harding out of us. . . . And we've got to be thinking what we do about this Attorney General now.[3] We've got to get the ablest, strongest, finest, most respectable man we can get because they want to make a bunch of crooks out of us.[4]

WEISL: . . . We have to get one that has all of those qualities and is loyal.

LBJ: . . . Think hard about it because you're my daddy, and I'm depending on you. Don't turn over all this money you [get] to Bobby up there,[5] because we are going to owe about $3 million. . . . You hold some of it in your box.[6]

---

1. FDR in 1936.

2. In 1956.

3. Since RFK's resignation, Nicholas Katzenbach had been LBJ's Acting Attorney General, but Johnson is suspicious of him as a Kennedy loyalist.

4. Johnson feels that if the opposition is girding for a new assault on his integrity, he had better have an Attorney General who is a devout Johnson man to protect him.

5. Robert Kennedy in New York.

6. Johnson refers to campaign money collected by Weisl.

ABE FORTAS

Wednesday, November 4, 1964, 1:00 P.M.

On what should be the happiest day of his political life, LBJ is distracted by his political problems. Always running scared, he worries that his enemies, including Robert Kennedy, might tar him with the kind of corruption scandal that destroyed Warren Harding. That, he insists, will require a new Attorney General tough and loyal enough to protect him.

LBJ: We've got to give a lot of thought to that Attorney Generalship, because they're going to make a Harding out of us, if we're not awfully careful. . . . These people were just so vicious. They intimidated every Nigra voter down here. . . . We ought to be using some of these things so we can at least make the Dirksens[1] listen to us, because that damn Williams[2] is going to be back right at our tail.

FORTAS: Yes, sir.

LBJ: And old Scott,[3] he got reelected. . . . We'll be just dodging all the blows. . . . I wish you'd try to do some skull practice on it.

FORTAS: I have been, and we'll do some more.

LBJ: Dillon[4] wants to leave, they tell me, and I sure don't want him to, because the Treasury has the confidence of the country and the dollar. He says his daddy is worth a quarter of a billion dollars and nobody's handled it for ten or twelve years, and he's just got to do it and he can't stay after January. But we've got folks like Don Cook and Frank Stanton[5] that we might force loose. They never have been willing to yet, but I guess they might be for Cabinet. . . . We've got to bring in a lot more people. Not only the White House. Like this . . . fellow over in McNamara—

FORTAS: Califano.[6]

LBJ: Califano and some of them. But we've got to try to bring in some creative people to deal with the Ed Williams things.[7] I just don't know how to really handle that one. I've never understood why Ed Williams or Bobby or some of them didn't go on and point out that they've been ransacked and searched and harassed and in-

---

1. Meaning reasonable Republicans.
2. The just reelected John Williams of Delaware, a leader of the Senate's Bobby Baker investigation.
3. Pennsylvania Republican Senator Hugh Scott, another of LBJ's antagonists on Bobby Baker.
4. The Kennedy holdover C. Douglas Dillon, Secretary of the Treasury.
5. Both longtime LBJ cronies. Cook was President of the American Electric Power Company, Stanton President of CBS.
6. McNamara's special assistant Joseph Califano, whom LBJ will hire eight months hence as his chief domestic adviser. (See Epilogue.)
7. Referring to the Bobby Baker problems. Edward Bennett Williams had succeeded Fortas as Baker's lawyer.

timidated for a year.[1] Couldn't find any law that they ever violated. Just pull a Hoffa[2] and answer the other side, and say, "God damn it, why are you persecuting me?" . . . I guess that they can't. . . . They think that he's been guilty of treason to his country. . . . I think the Jenkins thing[3] has washed out pretty well.

FORTAS: I do, too, yes, sir.

LBJ: . . . But I'm afraid they'll be subpoenaing *him* in an hour.[4] . . .

FORTAS: . . . I think Clark [Clifford] is available to you for the AG,[5] if you want it. . . .

LBJ: I think he's wonderful, and I think that you're wonderful. But I'll be damned if I don't believe that you'd be more powerful where you're not getting shot at every second before a committee.[6]

FORTAS: [*laughs*] Maybe! . . . I think Clark would be great at this. . . . It's a spot on which you ought not take any chances.

LBJ: [*skeptical:*] Well . . . I noticed when Kennedy appointed him on that intelligence board, they said, "They just got . . . one of Truman's cronies. Just a Washington fixer that represented a few outfits and was no great legal shakes."[7] . . . I'm thinking about the Lippmanns and the Restons.[8] All of them. They're going to want a Tom Walsh type.[9] . . . They're going to say, "Well, he spent the day around here trying to keep this out of the newspapers."[10] I think the publication of that hurt us.

FORTAS: But that's one on which I wouldn't take any chances about loyalty and understanding of the total picture. I really think I'd take a little heat on that one than take a chance. Because once that's done, we have to live with it. I would take a little heat on that rather than run a risk of getting somebody who isn't entirely our man. . . .

LBJ: I agree with that, but can't you get both? . . . What about Eddie [Weisl]?

FORTAS: Eddie's fine . . . if he can take the punishment of it. You know, Eddie's

---

1. During the Senate Rules Committee's investigations of Baker.

2. Referring to Teamster President James Hoffa's tactics in facing down judicial and congressional investigations.

3. Walter Jenkins scandal.

4. LBJ worries that the Senate, which had already once tried to call Jenkins as a witness in the Baker investigation, will try again.

5. Attorney General.

6. LBJ is worried that, as the repository of decades of Johnson's secrets, Fortas might be vulnerable as Attorney General, forced to submit regularly to questioning by hostile members of Congress.

7. The *New York Times* criticized Clifford's appointment as Chairman of JFK's Foreign Intelligence Advisory Board, saying on April 29, 1963, that he was "inextricably associated with partisan politics."

8. The columnists Walter Lippmann and James Reston were supreme opinion leaders of the time.

9. FDR's first nominee for Attorney General (who died two days before the inauguration) made his name by investigating Harding's Teapot Dome scandal.

10. The efforts by Clifford and Fortas to keep Jenkins's arrest out of the press.

sixty-seven years old. . . . That's kind of a tough age at which to start that kind of a brutal job.

LBJ: Yeah. . . . I think, too, the South would accept Clark better than anybody else.[1] And I think that's going to be one of the real problems. . . . I just wonder if the Bar[2] thinks he's more than an aide to Truman.

FORTAS: . . . I don't know that he has been in court much . . . but you don't need it for that post. . . . We've just got to have our own man in there. . . . If our New York race had come out differently, I might feel differently about it.[3] I'm scared . . . because the young man that was elected in New York is certainly going to try to keep his clutches on that office.[4] . . .

LBJ: Yeah, I am, too. I thought he had a lot of trouble ever getting around to mentioning me last night.[5] Didn't you?

FORTAS: He can't. That's the terrible thing. Of course, he wouldn't have had a Chinaman's chance if it hadn't been for the tremendous votes you rolled up there.

LBJ: Two and a half million, and Eddie [Weisl] said the highest was a million six.[6]

FORTAS: . . . Fantastic. Just absolutely fantastic.

✦   ✦   ✦

LBJ: [back to his refrain:] They're going to try to point out that we are another Harding. And the Baker and the Jenkins stuff. . . . And . . . "the lesser of two evils." And Bobby is already talking a little bit about . . . "they don't have the love and affection and the style that . . . Kennedy had." . . . You've got to talk to every press man—and get Clark to, and all of our friends, and tell them that . . . Daley told me this morning there has never been a candidate in Illinois that captivated them like we did. Downstate, upstate, every damn place! I carried every single county in New York. And we've got to have some love and affection in our own right, instead of just being a part of Bobby Kennedy or somebody else. We've got to get our people to thinking and talking that way. . . . You and Clark both ought to work at that the next two or three days. Take what Daley said. . . . I carried [Illinois] by a million. In Pennsylvania, a million. In Ohio, a million. And New York two and a half million. And all the Midwest and all of New England. And Roo-

---

1. Clifford was from Missouri, a border state, and had a less liberal reputation than the others LBJ was thinking of.

2. American Bar Association.

3. In other words, if RFK had lost, he would not be a threat and hence it would not be so essential to have a Johnson loyalist to defend the President as Attorney General. Fortas here shows that he thinks Kennedy might try to exacerbate scandal charges to weaken the President. He also worries that Katzenbach might be a double agent, subverting LBJ and tattling his secrets back to RFK.

4. Meaning that RFK was trying to control the Justice Department through Katzenbach, his old deputy and friend, whom he had recommended to Johnson as his successor.

5. In RFK's victory speech.

6. Meaning the highest previous presidential margin.

sevelt couldn't even touch 'em.[1] And they said that "he's cornpone, and he didn't do this and that." But that you've been with [Johnson] since '35, and NYA,[2] and you have seen the compassion, and you've seen what he does for people, and by God, it's a combination of Roosevelt and Jackson.[3] . . .

FORTAS: . . . That's right.

LBJ: Please, we've *got* to have some folks talking that. . . . Kennedy just used to call them[4] in, and even General Clifton, his aide,[5] had to watch Roscoe Drummond[6] and somebody else. Mac Bundy's assignment was Max Freedman and Walter Lippmann and Jimmy Reston.[7] I have nobody doing that at all.[8] You and Clark, though, have got around. . . . You-all have got to say some of that stuff. Pour that into Kay Graham and say, "God damn it, you didn't endorse us, Kay,[9] but get your people now to help him and give him a chance to start off. Don't handicap him!"

FORTAS: Well, you've got it, and the people have said that. People don't vote this way—

LBJ: No, but the papers are building that up. I heard it on the television this morning, they don't know whether they were voting against Goldwater or for Johnson.

FORTAS: I don't think anybody is going to pay any attention to that.

LBJ: I think you've got to have a positive, constructive propaganda on the other side, and you just go doing some of it.

PHILIP KAZEN

Lawyer and Democratic Leader, Laredo, Texas
Wednesday, November 4, 1964, 10:33 P.M.

This political boss was said to have been present when the famous Box 13 in Jim Wells County gave LBJ his hairbreadth eighty-seven-vote margin as "Landslide Lyndon" to become Senator from Texas in 1948.[10] In this conversation, Johnson shows his ostentatious contradictions. After complaining to Mayor Daley and others about illicit tactics used to prevent blacks from voting for him, Johnson now jokes with Kazen about using similar tricks to keep whites from voting against him.

---

1. Meaning that FDR could not match LBJ's landslide.
2. Johnson's service as National Youth Administration director in Texas under Roosevelt.
3. Andrew Jackson.
4. Reporters.
5. General Chester Clifton was JFK's Army aide.
6. *New York Herald Tribune* columnist.
7. Reston's actual nickname was Scotty.
8. Once again Johnson is feeling sorry for himself about what JFK had and he doesn't.
9. The *Washington Post* publisher, despite the close friendship of her late husband, Philip, with Johnson, had stuck to the paper's nonendorsement policy. She observed that this "hurt LBJ deeply" (Katharine Graham, *Personal History,* Knopf, 1997, p. 367).
10. See, for instance, *Houston Chronicle,* November 5, 1989.

LBJ: [*laughs*] Did Charlie arrest anybody that wasn't for us? Did he make them pay any customs penalties?

KAZEN: . . . Well, we used the old Lyndon Johnson tactic.

LBJ: Oh-h-h, you don't do that! You'll go to jail if you do that! . . . You tell old Charlie and Chick . . . and all of them [1] hello for me.

KAZEN: God bless you and thank you so much.

LBJ: Tell me—wait a minute. I want to know, how did the vote go? How many did you have in Webb County?

KAZEN: . . . It was 7,639 to 1,039.

LBJ: Good God Almighty, yeah! You're going to be teaching these Nigras how to vote! [2]

KAZEN: [*laughs*] . . . Down in Zapata we had fourteen to one for you.

LBJ: Fourteen to one! God bless them!

KAZEN: I'm going to send you . . . the list.

LBJ: Send to me all of them. . . . Tell me who I can call . . . because I love them. I'd rather carry from Piedras Negras to Corpus Christi than anyplace in America.

MIKE MANSFIELD
ROSS BASS
JOSEPH MONTOYA
FRED HARRIS
ROBERT KENNEDY

Senator and Senators-Elect
Thursday, November 5, 1964, 10:37 A.M.

On front pages across the country are pictures of Johnson and Vice President–elect Hubert Humphrey on horseback at the LBJ Ranch the previous day. The President had made Humphrey don a khaki ranch suit and Stetson just like his, as if to demonstrate to the world that the Minnesotan is now a wholly owned Johnson subsidiary. That evening over dinner, Johnson twitted HHH for not having been "mean enough" during the campaign.[3] Now, in a jovial, chortling mood, sitting with Humphrey in his wood-paneled den under a portrait of himself, LBJ talks by telephone to Senate Majority Leader Mansfield and just-elected Democratic Senators Ross Bass of Tennessee, Fred Harris of Minnesota, and Robert Kennedy of New York. Once again he lampoons his new number-two man.

---

1. Kazen's political claque.

2. Some who have heard this tape think that LBJ is saying "niggers." To the author's ear, he says, "Nigras."

3. Quoted in President's Daily Diary, November 4, 1964, LBJL.

LBJ: I'm sorry I called early. . . . I had to get old Hubert up. He's been riding horses down here. And he's a pretty late sleeper. You ruined him up there in the Senate. Hell, when *I* was up there, he'd come to *work* in the morning. He doesn't get up down here now till *mid-morning*.

MANSFIELD: You ruined him during this campaign, and now you've got to make up for it!

LBJ: [*laughs*] . . . Let Hubert get on the other line and say hello to you while he's here. He's got his robe on and he's got one eye opened.

HUMPHREY: Hello, Mike!

MANSFIELD: . . . You look great in that Western outfit.[1]

LBJ: . . . Wayne Morse[2] said if he ever got on another horse, he'd never vote for him again! . . . Hubert . . . said, by God . . . he would resign . . . if there's any more horseback riding.

HUMPHREY: [*chuckles*] I told them I'd done enough for the President.

LBJ: A President can ask only so much.

* * *

LBJ: By God, Ross, how's that Goldwater country?

BASS: [*laughs*] Listen, you just absolutely slaughtered them down there, and we certainly appreciate that last trip.[3] . . . It did the trick. . . .

LBJ: We needed both of those trips, didn't we?

BASS: . . . You're a great man. . . . The greatest victory in the history of the country.

* * *

LBJ: Ross, how do you think Hubert looks on a horse?

BASS: [*laughs*] . . . That's a desecration to put him on a Tennessee Walking Horse.

LBJ: [*guffaws*] Are you desecrating *Hubert* or the *horse?*

* * *

LBJ: *José, cómo te va?* [How are you?]

MONTOYA: *Cómo está,* you-all! [How are you, you-all?]

LBJ: *Bien, usted?* [Good, you?]

MONTOYA: Oh, fine.

LBJ: God damn! You ran away from them out there, didn't you?

MONTOYA: Yes, we did, but . . . you carried the state by ninety thousand.

LBJ: . . . What did that Mechem[4] do?

MONTOYA: I beat him by thirty thousand. . . .

---

1. Referring to the photo of LBJ and HHH on horseback.
2. Democratic Senator from Oregon.
3. Johnson had campaigned in Nashville on October 9 and Chattanooga on October 24.
4. Defeated Senator Edwin Mechem.

LBJ: That's wonderful. Damn him! He ought to have quit voting with Goldwater all the time. . . . I'm awfully proud of you.

* * *

LBJ: Fred . . . you just . . . be nice to old Humphrey here, because he's liable to get ruthless in that chair[1] with all this power. He might not want to recognize an Okie!

HARRIS: [laughs]

* * *

MANSFIELD: Mr. President, I went to see Everett Dirksen yesterday in the hospital. . . . He was awfully good to us in the last couple of years when we needed him.

LBJ: . . . I talked to him yesterday. . . . I told him if we had any problems, I'd call him. We do have a hell of a lot of troubles in Vietnam. . . . They[2] came in there the other day and got some pretty strong ideas. I sent them back and told them, "Let's be careful. Let's look where we're going before we go, and take a good look at it."[3]

* * *

MANSFIELD: Bob Kennedy just came in. Okay?

LBJ: Yes, sir. Yeah.

KENNEDY: Hello?

LBJ: By God, *you* learned how to smile in this campaign![4]

KENNEDY: [laughs] I told you I did what you told me to do after you came up there!

LBJ: Yeah, yeah. I just picked up all the papers here. . . . You must think you're going to be running up there a long time! I saw you smiling and waving to a bunch of kids. They're not even registered!

KENNEDY: You know what I was doing? I was just thinking of working with you. That made me smile.

LBJ: [laughs] . . . Looks like you had a nice meeting with Teddy.[5] . . . What'd you let him get you that way for? He practically destroyed you in Massachusetts.[6]

KENNEDY: Of course he did. And he brought up the seniority system.[7]

LBJ: [laughs] By God, he's already throwing his weight around even before he gets out of the hospital!

---

1. Presiding over the Senate.
2. Johnson's military advisers.
3. LBJ is playing to the dovish Mansfield.
4. LBJ had advised Kennedy to smile more in public.
5. RFK had called on his brother Edward in his Boston hospital.
6. Meaning that Ted had been reelected with a much larger margin than Robert.
7. Although the younger brother, Edward will be senior to Robert in the Senate.

KENNEDY: I know. You know he won by almost a million up there. He ran almost as well as you.

LBJ: Isn't that wonderful? . . . How did we do in Brooklyn? Did that trip hurt us much?[1]

KENNEDY: No, no, I think it was terrific. It was really terrific. Now if you can do the Brooklyn Navy Yard, as you promised.[2]

LBJ: [*laughs*] Those goddamned Navy yards! I bet I never hear the last of them.

KENNEDY: Listen, I counted up the promises I made during the campaign. They're two hundred and twenty.

LBJ: You better promise Hubert something here, because [otherwise] . . . you may not even get recognized.[3] Hubert, get on here with him!

KENNEDY: How are you, Hubert?

HUMPHREY: Fine. I'll keep him reminded about that Navy yard.

KENNEDY: Thank you. Congratulations, though. That was terrific.

HUMPHREY: Yeah, it was wonderful. . . . Ted told me he figured that the way to get elected is to just let the women do it. He said when he worked it over real hard, he won about three hundred thousand. When he let Joanie[4] do it, why, he won by a million.[5]

LBJ: Somebody told me I ought to call you up and find out how to get them to concede early. How did you get old Keating[6] to come out there and give us that forced smile?

KENNEDY: How did you get old Senator Goldwater to run again?[7]

LBJ: Hell, he didn't! Goldwater didn't come until the next day. He waited twenty-four hours.[8]

KENNEDY: [*joking:*] Yeah, and I know, everybody was worried about who was ahead.

LBJ: . . . I lost my ratings![9]

KENNEDY: We were all concerned about it. You had a lot of sympathy.

LBJ: Well, I'm going to need a hell of a lot, I'll tell you that. . . . Meantime, if you get any solution to Vietnam, just call me direct, will you?

---

1. LBJ is unsubtly reminding RFK that his Brooklyn campaign trip may deserve the credit for Kennedy's victory.
2. Brooklyn was one of the military installations in jeopardy of being closed after the election. It was.
3. On the Senate floor.
4. Mrs. Kennedy.
5. Contrasting Kennedy's 1962 victory with the 1964 one, when Joan Kennedy carried the campaign for her bedridden husband.
6. Kennedy's opponent.
7. In his press conference, Goldwater had left the door open to a 1968 candidacy.
8. To concede.
9. Television ratings.

KENNEDY: I just talked to Bob McNamara.
LBJ: Yeah, yeah. Well, he's the best one. You can't beat him. . . . I want to talk to you. . . . I'll give you a ring.
KENNEDY: Okay.
LBJ: Give Ethel my love.

MARY LASKER

President, Albert and Mary Lasker Foundation

LADY BIRD JOHNSON

Thursday, November 5, 1964, 2:42 P.M.

> Johnson makes a thank-you call to the New York philanthropist, whose efforts for medical research he had encouraged since he was Majority Leader. He loves to flirt with her and gibe her about her dates with UN Ambassador Adlai Stevenson. Mrs. Lasker is the lavish Johnson donor whose discreet contributions LBJ had been worried would be revealed when the FBI stormed Walter Jenkins's office in October.

LASKER: Hello?
LBJ: All right, you just tell Adlai to move over. I'm coming in!
LASKER: Oh, good! You're wonderful. I've never been so thrilled in my life. Have you got Hubert there?
LBJ: No! Now quit calling down here! Every time . . . you come smelling like a rose and then you mess it all up by asking where's Adlai or Hubert. . . . I'm not going to yield you to all these youngsters.
LASKER: That makes me happy. When are you coming home?
LBJ: Next weekend. I love you a lot, and I appreciate all you did, and Hubert said this morning—he left about an hour ago—that he had to find a way to get back from Puerto Rico to make some speech for you.
LASKER: He said he would if he could.
LBJ: . . . I guess . . . you know . . . they've run a bunch of ads down here that said that your heart people said that the average life expectancy after a heart attack was ten years. I had one in July of '55, so I was supposed to just have six more allotted months.[1] . . . I understood from you that a man who just had one heart attack had a better life expectancy than a fellow that's had two nervous breakdowns.[2]
LASKER: That's right. You were right. How is your Lady Bird?
LBJ: Oh, she's running around here. She's, I guess, upstairs. . . . I'm jealous of

---

1. Republicans had run advertisements in Texas citing coronary research to suggest that Johnson, who had suffered a massive heart attack in July 1955, would not survive a full term in office.
2. LBJ again mentions Goldwater's two alleged nervous breakdowns.

her, though. I wish you would quit shunting me aside for Hubert and Lady Bird and everybody and pay a little attention to me yourself!

LASKER: But you have too much competition for me.

LBJ: I don't have *any* competition, honey!

LASKER: . . . First time I knew!

LBJ: [*turns to wife*] . . . Lady Bird, here's a girlfriend of yours that I'm in love with.

LADY BIRD: [*gets on line*] . . . I don't know whether to be outraged or to be curious, if it's who I think it is. . . .

LASKER: It's your Mary, who wants to tell you that she thinks that the two of you did the best job in the history of the country.

LBJ: . . . Mary . . . I love you and you did so much to help us, I'll never forget you. . . . Anytime you are down, come and put your arm around me.[1]

LASKER: I'll do that.

LADY BIRD: And, Mary, when I go thinking of some of the things that I would hopefully like to point my way toward doing during the next four years, I may not ever get them done. May not make a ripple on the smooth surface. But you'll be one of the people that I might be getting some advice from. . . .

LASKER: . . . There's nothing we can't do now. . . . The people of the United States want you. . . .

LADY BIRD: Well, bless you. . . . I hope we're going to stay down here for several days, and just ride around over the hills and sleep and rest.

ROBERT McNAMARA

Thursday, November 5, 1964, 2:48 P.M.

> Two days before the election, a Vietcong attack on the U.S. air base at Bien Hoa had killed five Americans, wounded seventy-six, and destroyed twenty-seven aircraft. The Joint Chiefs had demanded retaliatory air strikes on North Vietnam. LBJ refused but took the precaution of asking the pollster Louis Harris to reassure him that his restraint would not hurt him with voters. As Harris predicted, it did not. But now that the campaign is over, LBJ knows he can no longer postpone basic, perilous decisions about the war. The Joint Chiefs are pressing the war in a way that might threaten direct conflict with China.
>
> At this moment McNamara is groping for a position between the extremes. Three days after this conversation, Secretary of State Dean Rusk will inform Ambassador Maxwell Taylor that if Hanoi's behavior does not improve, "we would

---

1. LBJ here makes the same invitation he made to Jacqueline Kennedy after the assassination. (See Prologue.)

initiate in January a program of slowly graduated military actions against the North, in conjunction with negotiating moves." They would "keep alive a clear threat of additional action."[1]

LBJ: What about Vietnam?
McNAMARA: . . . It's just a worrisome problem. None of us have a pat answer that we're ready to give you yet. . . . I don't think there's any strong sentiment for trying to go in and clobber China at the moment, other than [from] a strictly military organization. I'm sure we can sit on top of that. I do think there's a general feeling that the current course is leading to some kind of a form of accommodation with the Chinese, probably through a popular front government initially, and that this is not good. And that there may be something in between the current course and this "clobber China" school that will help us strengthen our position there.

MARTIN LUTHER KING, JR.

President, Southern Christian Leadership Conference
Thursday, November 5, 1964, 3:20 P.M.

Johnson calls the civil rights leader in New York to thank him for the substantial black role in his landslide. King had tried to avert open partisanship but signaled his choice by telling crowds, "You know who to vote for, don't you?" On Election Eve, when Republicans had encouraged voters to write in King's name for President, which would have diluted the Johnson vote, King had disavowed the suggestion.

But Dr. King has just announced that he will soon lead demonstrations "based around the right to vote" in Alabama or Mississippi. Johnson is worried that King will pressure him to act faster than he wishes, to ensure black voting rights. He would prefer to let some time pass after the Civil Rights Act so that Americans can absorb the impact of desegregating public facilities. He also fears that asking Congress for more immediate action on civil rights will endanger his Great Society programs. But King will not wait. LBJ's friendly telephone call is presumably being intercepted by his own FBI, which has King under surveillance as a potential danger to the republic.[2]

LBJ: Doctor, I just wanted to tell you how mighty proud I was of a lot of folks last Tuesday. . . . I still haven't shaved or got off my bathrobe. . . . I thought I'd call a

---

1. Rusk to Taylor, November 8, 1964, *FRUS*, vol. 1, pp. 875–96. See also David Kaiser, *American Tragedy* (Harvard, 2000), pp. 354–81; Fredrik Logevall, *Choosing War* (University of California, 1999), pp. 252–99; II. R. McMasters, *Dereliction of Duty* (HarperCollins, 1997), pp. 179–96; and Robert Schulzinger, *A Time for War* (Oxford, 1997), pp.165–70.
2. See Taylor Branch, *Pillar of Fire* (Simon & Schuster, 1998), pp. 168, 195–98.

half dozen or so folks and tell them how much I appreciate their confidence and what a go-o-od job I thought they had done, and how they justified our faith, and how many more now we've got to help to get out of their bondage.

KING: Yes, well, we're certainly all very happy about the outcome. It was just such a great victory. . . . We have some bright days ahead, I think.

LBJ: It was a great tribute to the intelligence and the judgment and the patriotism of the Nigro people that they[1] couldn't mislead them and they couldn't fool them.

KING: Yes.

LBJ: Their leaders made great progress for them, and I know they all take great pride in your great honor.[2] I wired you the other day, but I was moving pretty fast, and I don't know what day it was. As a matter of fact, I don't know where I am hardly! I'm like Dr. Theodore Francis Green.[3] You know, he was at one of Miz Mesta's[4] parties one time. . . . He was about eighty-seven years old, and I said, "What are you trying to do, see where you are going from here?" And he said, "No, I'm trying to find out where I am!"

KING: [laughs] . . . Well, I know you really need some real rest. I know what you've gone through the last few days.

LBJ: We'll be back up there working on our program, and . . . we're going to spend a lot of time with Shriver on our poverty thing.[5] I wish you'd give a little thought to it. Because that offers a lot of opportunity for our young people that have been denied. We got nearly a billion dollars this year, and we ought to get it going around the first of the year. . . . Then next year we can do it a lot bigger and expand it. And it offers a lot of economic hope, too. I'll be calling on you, and we'll . . . try to get our heads together. . . . We've got to move on the next four years and make some advances. . . .

KING: Well, good. . . . Let me . . . say what a great moment we think this is for our country. It was a great victory for the forces of progress, and a defeat for the forces of retrogress. . . . We're all with you. . . . Give my best regards to the madam and your lovely daughters.

LBJ: Sure will. . . . She took on a pretty hard assignment, didn't she?[6]

KING: I'm telling you! But she did it beautifully and eloquently. We are all mighty proud of her.

LBJ: . . . I'll be calling you when we get back to Washington.

---

1. The Goldwater forces.
2. King had been chosen for the Nobel Peace Prize.
3. The elderly former Democratic Senator from Rhode Island.
4. Perle Mesta, the Washington hostess who sold her Washington house to the Johnsons when LBJ became Vice President.
5. LBJ had appointed the Kennedy brother-in-law Sargent Shriver as Director of his War on Poverty.
6. Referring to Mrs. Johnson's campaign for Southern votes aboard the "Lady Bird Special."

Chapter Four

GIRDING FOR BATTLES

They have these little parties out at Georgetown. . . . They had a party last night . . . and the Kennedy crowd decided that I had framed up to . . . put the Vietnam War on Kennedy's tomb. And that I had a conspiracy going on to show that it was Kennedy's immaturity and poor judgment that originally led us into this thing. . . . And that his execution of it had brought havoc to the country. . . . And that this was my game—to lay Vietnam off onto Kennedy's inexperience [and] immaturity.

LBJ *to* ROBERT McNAMARA, *January 13, 1965*

DOUGLAS WYNN

Mississippi Delegate to 1964 Democratic National Convention
Saturday, November 7, 1964, 8:45 A.M.

With much of the South having voted for Goldwater, LBJ is imagining how he might bring the country together. Here he calls a white moderate in Greenville, Mississippi, a Johnson family friend who was one of only three Mississippi delegates at the Democratic convention in Atlantic City pledged to support LBJ, subjecting themselves to abuse and Ku Klux Klan death threats. "You're a patriot," Johnson had told Wynn that week by telephone. "This is history and you'll always be proud of this."[1]

LBJ: We ought to be able to unite Alabama and Mississippi. . . . If the call came up, they'd be the first soldiers in there to enlist.[2] They've just got to realize that we're not going to be punitive. We've got to try to find some way to live together. . . .

WYNN: . . . Mr. President, I know I did what was right and . . . honorable, and they can't ever take that away from me.

LBJ: . . . Remember this. Lincoln went back to Springfield, Missouri, after he was President. He went down the street in a town where he lived his life. He said there wasn't one person in it that would speak to him. Not one. . . . One woman

---

1. Taped conversation, August 25, 1964, in LBJL.
2. Johnson refers to the strong military tradition in those states.

couldn't get across the street without speaking to him. She begrudgingly spoke to him. He said it made him mighty proud that he had done what he had done, and mighty sorry for those folks. Because it wasn't important whether the Lord was on his side. . . . What was important was whether he was on the Lord's side.[1] . . . We know the Lord doesn't say we're superior. The Lord tells us to help those others. . . . We've got to help them, educate them, train them, and prepare them.[2]. . . If we don't, we are . . . going to have to feed them always. . . . And we just got to educate them.

WYNN: Yes, sir.

LBJ: You can't do it by putting them off by themselves. Because that creates a juvenile problem right off the bat. . . . The sociologists say if they . . . put you in a retarded school or second-class one . . . you develop an inferiority complex and the rest of your life you're hitting at people. You think they're going to strike you, even when they are not. . . . It's going to take a lon-n-ng time. But we'll do it in four years. . . . They[3] think we're ragtags and we're crackpots, and we're wild and we're gonna blow up the country. We're not gonna do any of those things. . . . We're going to have our troubles. But we're not running from nothing. . . .

WYNN: God bless you.

LBJ: . . . And remember old Abraham Lincoln. Go get that story about him going back to Springfield. I made it in one of my speeches out in Springfield. . . . They don't ever remember many of these Presidents from Jackson to Lincoln. They don't remember many from Lincoln to Roosevelt. The ones they remember are those that stood up for human rights. . . . And if you've got any religion, why, you better quit feeling superior to other people.

RICHARD RUSSELL

Democratic Senator from Georgia and Chairman, Senate Armed Services Committee
Monday, November 9, 1964, 11:57 A.M.

One of the most important conversations LBJ ever taped was with his old Senate mentor from Georgia, "Mr. Defense," on May 27, 1964, when Russell warned him that Vietnam was "just one of those places where you can't win." If the United

---

1. Here LBJ badly distorts history. Lincoln, of course, came from Springfield, Illinois—not Missouri—and never returned there after leaving for Washington in 1861 to become President. Johnson is combining a story he told in an October 7 Springfield, Illinois, speech about Lincoln's friendlessness on arriving there at age twenty-eight with Lincoln's famous remark, which LBJ quoted in a September 23 speech, about the importance of being on God's side.
2. Meaning African Americans.
3. Southern whites.

States got involved in Vietnam in "any considerable" way, Russell said, it would be "a Korea on a much bigger scale . . . the most expensive venture this country ever went into." Johnson replied that he could "make a tremendous case for moving out." Russell suggested that one way to withdraw would be to have "a man running the government over there that told us to get out."[1]

Now, five months later, Russell sticks to his earlier advice. If Johnson's commitment to prevent a North Vietnamese victory at this moment rested merely on a fear of being called soft on Communism and damaging his efforts to pass the Great Society, he might have used Russell's offer as a means to withdraw from the war. With the towering Georgia hawk proclaiming that Vietnam was not the place to invest American blood and treasure and a new Saigon regime demanding that the Yankees go home, Johnson might have had a heat shield with which to protect himself politically. His failure to seriously entertain Russell's suggestion, however, shows how seriously he takes what he considers to be a treaty commitment, inherited from Eisenhower and Kennedy, to defend South Vietnam.

RUSSELL: Well, it was a tremendous victory. . . . You've got the majority to get anything you want. All you've got to do is keep your good judgment and your head on your shoulders.[2]

LBJ: . . . That's awfully important. . . . What are we going to do about Vietnam?

RUSSELL: I wish we could figure some way to get *out* of that, Mr. President. I think if we get in there and get messing around with those Chinese, we could be in there for the next ten years. But I don't know how we can get *out*. I told John McCone[3] he ought to get somebody to run that country [who] didn't want us in there. . . . Then . . . we could get out with good grace.[4] But he didn't take me very seriously. [It would have] been a whole lot better than putting in this Khanh and all that crowd.[5] But that is the worst problem you've got right now. . . . Give Lady Bird my love.

LBJ: Here she is. Say howdy to her.

LADY BIRD: Senator?

RUSSELL: Honey, how are you doing?

LADY BIRD: Oh . . . I'm lying in the sunshine and just enjoying it, and facing going back to the fray with not too brave a heart. But we'll soon be ready.

RUSSELL: I think you're entitled to a rest after getting out and electing a man by

---

1. Beschloss, *Taking Charge,* pp. 363–70.

2. Russell tacitly (and ruefully) acknowledges that LBJ will use his triumph to pass bills for civil rights and big government that the Senator abhors.

3. Director of Central Intelligence. Russell knew, of course, that the CIA was in the business of orchestrating such changes of government.

4. This was the strategy that some JFK acolytes later claimed would have been Kennedy's after the 1964 election, had he lived. (See, for example, Kenneth O'Donnell and David Powers, *"Johnny, We Hardly Knew Ye,"* Little, Brown, 1972, pp. 16–18.)

5. The current regime and its immediate predecessors.

such a majority as that. I want to personally apologize to you . . . about that booing down at Savannah.[1]

LADY BIRD: That didn't matter at all.

RUSSELL: . . . I heard about it with great humiliation.

LADY BIRD: We thought we better go into the worst parts.[2] . . . Anyhow, we-all got a-*plenty* ahead of us, so we'll just have to recuperate our strength and get back at it.

LEONARD CLARK

Student, San Jose State College
Tuesday, November 10, 1964, 11:15 P.M.

> Whether playing a prank or simply clueless, a California college student manages to get through to LBJ by claiming that he is the newly elected Republican Senator from California, George Murphy. Johnson is sitting in his ranch house office with his aide Marvin Watson, who quickly intervenes.

CLARK: President Johnson?

LBJ: Yes.

CLARK: My name's Leonard Clark. I'm sorry I bothered you, but I kind of felt it important to call you. Do you mind? I'm a student at San Jose State College and I called to ask you a very special favor. [*chuckles*] I'm a very good Democrat and tonight we . . . needed a little bit of help. . . . I felt that if I could get it from any-body, I could get it from Lyndon Baines Johnson. Are you there? Sir?

WATSON: [*takes receiver from Johnson*] Hello? Hello?

CLARK: Yes, sir.

WATSON: The President has gone to bed. Could we take a message?

CLARK: No, sir, I'm sorry. You can't. . . . I'd like to speak to him, please.

WATSON: That would be impossible tonight. He's already retired.[3] . . .

CLARK: . . . Sir . . . a friend of mine needs to get to Germany. . . . We [need] a special visa so he can leave at nine o'clock in the morning.

WATSON: . . . I think that's impossible. . . . The offices are all closed in Wash-ington. I thought you identified yourself as Senator-elect George Murphy.

CLARK: We did that just to get through. I'm sorry. . . . I fully voted Democrat for the first time in my life. . . . I know I'm not entitled to speak to the President. But I'm entitled to . . . just a little consideration somewhere, because my very

---

1. Mrs. Johnson had encountered a small group of hecklers in Savannah on October 8.
2. Meaning the most anti-Johnson parts of the South.
3. Actually, Johnson was still sitting with Watson in the office.

good friend was a Goldwater fan, and I tried to convince him . . . that us Democrats aren't too bad.

ABE FORTAS

Wednesday, November 11, 1964, 10:30 P.M.

> Johnson complains to his confidant that Walter Jenkins's wife is giving out news-
> paper interviews. He asks Fortas to warn Jenkins that if it doesn't stop the Presi-
> dent will not be inclined to help him create a new life for himself and his family.

LBJ: Did you read the [*New York*] *Herald Tribune,* page five? "Jenkins Home, 'Coming Along Fine.' " [by] Dom Bonafede, who is their guy that promoted the Bobby Baker story. . . . Has got Walter's big picture and a one-two-three-four-five-column headline. [*reads aloud:*] "Asked about the future, [Mrs. Jenkins] said, "We are playing it by ear." . . . She did not know whether the family would return to Texas. . . . During his weeks in the hospital, scores of Jenkins's friends stood by him and reportedly offered him many employments. . . ." Now I would tell him— as strongly and as persuasively and as effectively as I know how—to *ple-e-ase* don't make a five-column headline. . . . He didn't get any check or dividend for making that statement. Didn't *help* anything. It just reminded everybody that he was still a morals victim and he had some charges against him. . . . If he just *has* to answer the telephone, why, let *us* call him and talk to him.
FORTAS: Right. That sounds like his wife doing it.
LBJ: Yes, but . . . maybe he can cut off the phone. You told him to quit talking to these people. . . . Say now, "Bobby [Baker] didn't listen to me, and if you don't I can't help you." Just tell him. That bluntly.
FORTAS: [*laughs*] Right!
LBJ: Just say now, "I told [Bobby] to listen to me,[1] and he didn't do it. . . . If you-all can't listen to me and can't stay out of the papers, I can't help you." . . . I don't think anybody can help them when they make that kind of a headline with a big picture . . . by that criminal reporter. Because he's not trying to help him, you know.
FORTAS: He sure isn't. What I'm afraid [of is that] she talked to him once be-
fore, you know, and everybody criticized her for doing it, and we all laced into her, and I guess she did it again.
LBJ: I don't think you need to lace into her. Just . . . call him, talk to him on a money matter, and then I'd say to him, "Now, I don't want to be messing in your

---

1. Keep a low profile when he got into trouble.

business. I know you can't help a lot of things—I can't in my *own* home—but if I were you, I would cut off that phone some way."

FORTAS: . . . I'll do it, sir. . . .

LBJ: . . . I think he's on cloud nine. . . . I talked to him the other night, and he was telling me about three thousand letters he'd received. I think you ought to just say now, "We looked over everything. . . . The Los Angeles banking firm—we tried it, and they're a little bit shy.[1] Most people *are* shy. You've got to work with us. We all got to pull together here, and we just can't be giving out these interviews." . . . Show him this *Herald Tribune*. . . . Hand it to him and say, "Now, we don't want to quarrel, just don't go home and get mad, but let's just try to cut off the damn phone." . . . Because . . . the *Wall Street Journal* will be there tomorrow. The *Washington Star* will be there in the afternoon. . . . He doesn't understand it. He [thinks] he's kind of a hero as a result of this.

FORTAS: . . . Well, he's pretty mixed up.

*   *   *

FORTAS: [*changing subjects:*] [Clark Clifford] said he doesn't really think that the young man who's just been elected[2] . . . really had much potential or was much of a threat. Said . . . he was one of those fellows who always took and never gave, and that his personal relations with people were very bad, and he'd probably get chopped up. And I said the thing that bothers me is that I have the feeling this fellow may try to appear as the knight in shining armor and . . . try to make a position for himself as a Democratic Senator Williams.[3] He wouldn't give a damn about how his fellow Senators felt.

LBJ: Yeah.

FORTAS: . . . He kept reiterating that he thought the young man's potential was vastly overestimated. . . . He was pretty well bound to stub his toe because he just got so many people mad at him.

ROBERT McNAMARA

Saturday, November 14, 1964, 10:31 A.M.

During the campaign, Goldwater had excoriated LBJ's plan to lower Army admissions standards, intended in part to train and socialize young men. Now McNamara warns Johnson that Richard Russell, the Senate Armed Services chairman, is worried that the Army will become too black. LBJ suggests that Russell will en-

1. Fortas had tried to get Jenkins a job with a financial firm in Los Angeles.
2. Robert Kennedy.
3. In other words, RFK might try to enmesh LBJ in scandal.

dorse the program if persuaded that the result will be to move black youth from the South to the North.

McNAMARA: We're having a terrible time with our friend Senator Russell. . . .

LBJ: . . . I want you to steal enough money where you can teach people discipline. . . . Yesterday one of your boys [1] in the communications center of the White House came in my office, took a key out . . . of my private secretary's desk, unlocked the outfit, got himself a little loot—a few pencils and a medallion or two that we give to people that come in. . . . He's got clearance for everything. So we've got a little problem. . . . You've got to take those boys like that and give them some discipline. . . .

McNAMARA: Right.

LBJ: . . . Your people— You have the discipline built in there. . . . You get them up and wash their teeth and shave them and bathe them and get them on time. . . . You-all came out of the Army in 1946 and all of us started breeding. Now we've got eighteen-year-olds this year . . . and we've got a hell of a problem, because there are going to be . . . a million kids . . . that can't go to college. . . . They've got no room for them. And they can't go in the workforce. . . . Somebody has got to do some planning. I think you can do it better than the social scientists.

*   *   *

LBJ: Looks to me like what it would do for Russell is move all these Nigra boys that are now rejects and sent back on his community, to move them [into the Army], clean them up, prepare them to do something, and send them into Detroit. . . . You have to tell him. . . . "We'll take this Nigra boy in from Johnson City, Texas, and from Winder, Georgia,[2] and we'll get rid of the tapeworms and get the ticks off of him, and teach him to get up at daylight and work till dark and shave and to bathe. . . . We'll put some weight on him and keep him out of a charity hospital . . . and keep him from eating off the old man's relief check. And when we turn him out, we'll have him prepared at least to drive a truck or bakery wagon or stand at a gate. . . . And he's not going to want to go back to Winder after he's had this taste of life." . . . How many do you think you would take of these second-class fellows?

McNAMARA: We want to build up to take in twenty thousand a year.

LBJ: . . . That doesn't even make a dent. . . .

McNAMARA: . . . This is the way I sold the program to the department, because they don't want to be in the business of dealing with "morons." They call these "moron camps" now, inside the [Pentagon]. . . . The Army doesn't want to be thought of as a rehabilitation agency.

---

1. Meaning a military officer.
2. Russell's hometown.

ROBERT KENNEDY

Monday, November 16, 1964, 8:25 A.M.

> During a talk with the new Senator from New York, Johnson claims that in the Senate he was happier than in any job before or since.

KENNEDY: I just wanted you to know I'm back here[1] and been back here working.

LBJ: Good, good!

KENNEDY: I'm just trying to do my best for the United States, state of New York.

LBJ: Good.

KENNEDY: [*joking:*] And I just knew you would want to know that while you've been down at the ranch, I've been here.

LBJ: [*laughs*] Wonderful!

KENNEDY: How are you?

LBJ: I couldn't be better.

KENNEDY: Get a rest at all?

LBJ: No, no, I've just been trying to put these things together for the coming year, and I think we're making *some* progress on it. . . .

KENNEDY: You sounded awful busy.

LBJ: Well, we covered the waterfront pretty well. . . . Got to put this budget together, and the rest of this month will be on it, I expect. . . . I thought that was a wonderful picture of Joan,[2] didn't you?

KENNEDY: Yeah, wasn't it nice?

LBJ: . . . I saw it in all of the papers this morning.

KENNEDY: They're doing very well. That boy got almost as many votes as you did, I think.

LBJ: Tell me, when he's going to get out?[3]

KENNEDY: Supposed to get out on the eighth of December. . . .

LBJ: How do you like your new job?

KENNEDY: I don't know yet. [*chuckles*] You think I'll like it?

LBJ: I do. I was happier than in any job I ever had. It'll be pretty frustrating to you for a while, but—

KENNEDY: I'll come over and smile at you.[4]

LBJ: Wish you would!

---

1. In Washington.
2. Edward Kennedy's then-wife.
3. Of the hospital.
4. Referring to LBJ's campaign suggestion that RFK smile more.

GEORGE REEDY

Monday, November 16, 1964, 11:20 A.M.

> Irritated at bad press coverage and Reedy's fear of appointing a strong deputy, LBJ would like to fire the press secretary but is slow to dismiss such a longtime loyalist. Instead, here he is trying to goad Reedy to quit. He complains that Reedy has not done enough to combat the view that LBJ won as the "lesser of two evils." Despite the election triumph, Johnson shows his growing suspiciousness about the press, the Kennedy circle, his own staff, and enemies wiretapping his telephones.

LBJ: We've just got all kinds of bad publicity. . . . The Secretary of State, Secretary of Defense, Bundy,[1] Secretary of Labor—all of them have . . . said we've got to do something about our press office. . . . They're all of the opinion that you would prefer [to do] something else, but that you kind of hesitate to tell me. . . .
REEDY: It's not true.
LBJ: . . . But that's their feeling. . . . They say that . . . we cannot lead the world if we handle our own stuff this way. . . . Now I've tried for a year to improve it. . . . We've got to get a sizable person that can operate with you. . . . We don't think we can do it by keeping people down [and] not wanting somebody that's our equal.[2] I'm not afraid of anybody in this country, and although they may be more gifted than I am in certain ways and have more leadership than I have, I'm still willing to work with them. Whether it's *Jack* Kennedy or whether it's *Bobby* Kennedy. And that's what we've got to do here in this press office. . . . Where we don't leave the impression that we slept in our clothes the night before, or we can't catch up with the train.[3] . . . You've got to put some better people on your team. If you don't, I've got to form a *new* team. I'm going in to play the world's championship, and I'm willing to assume that you are a Mickey Mantle. . . . But . . . I've got to have . . . Babe Ruth and Lou Gehrig playing together to win this world championship. . . . I didn't have much experience in the presidency before. I've learned. . . . I just can't rely on Willie Day[4] to handle my press relations. . . . We've lost Schlesinger and Sorensen and Salinger—the three S's.[5] . . . They say the White House staff is in shambles. . . .
REEDY: . . . The staff can't be in such a shambles with that 60 to 40 [percent] vote, regardless of all the crap they throw around. . . .

---

1. National Security Adviser McGeorge Bundy.
2. Feeling threatened, Reedy had vetoed each of LBJ's suggestions for a strong deputy press secretary.
3. Here LBJ refers to Reedy's sloppiness and girth, which kept him from moving fast.
4. Willie Day Taylor was a Johnson family servant.
5. Arthur Schlesinger, Jr., Theodore Sorensen, and Pierre Salinger, of the Kennedy White House staff.

LBJ: . . . Their theory, which they've pretty well sold America on—because . . . we did nothing about it—is that "it wasn't Johnson's popularity or any efficiency. Because neither really exists. It was the hate and fear of *Goldwater.*" Now the liberal Republicans have sold that and the Kennedy people have sold that, and the country has *bought* that. . . . I think the basic reason that we [won the election] is [that in] the first ninety days, we convinced them that we would try to be President of all of the people. And a good many businesspeople . . . thought we were responsible. . . .

Now . . . they've sold [the] picture that we've got to be watched and we're corrupt . . . and we're too close to our friends. The Walter Jenkins thing has hurt us. *Substantially.* I don't care *what* you say. It's hurt us with the staff. Every one of them are taking vacations.[1] Every one of them are getting independent as hell. We've got to stay away from these cocktail parties. That destroyed him. [Walter] would never have been hurt if he hadn't gone there and gotten too many drinks that night. Just got to stay away from the lobbyists. . . . We've just got to give up our social life pretty well, outside of an intimate thing every day or two with some different correspondents. . . . They are laying for us, and they are following us, and they are tapping our phones. They're tapping McNamara's. He's caught two taps in the last month. They are watching every move that we make.

So, we've got to . . . take the initiative in these things. I couldn't get it done any other way, so I called Eddie Weisl, and I got him to have stories written saying that Johnson *was* popular and . . . he *did* have a good organization.[2] He *did* have a record of accomplishment in the Congress. . . . And it wasn't just anti-Goldwater. It was for *Johnson.* . . . I got him to put it in the Hearst papers, . . . and *Life* says they're going to do something on it. That's what we've got to have one man doing here all the time. . . . But . . . we're just a great big bear that, by God, is just getting punched at like a Mexican bullfight. They're just throwing arrows in, and we are standing there shivering and bleeding. . . . Now, if we're competent, we're going to have to show them. . . . If we don't, why, we've lost the election. . . .

REEDY: . . . I don't believe that the country is sold on the fact that you beat Goldwater only because people were afraid of Goldwater. I think that might be a theory that's being pumped around in this town.

LBJ: I think it is by two forces. By the progressive Republicans, who want to show that if they'd have been listened to, it would have been better. By the Kennedy people, who do not want to acknowledge me. And number three, by the columnists. . . .

REEDY: . . . There is kind of a clique around this town.

---

1. See Chapter 3. The exhausted Bill Moyers had gone to San Juan and the exhausted Jack Valenti to Palm Springs.

2. See Edwin Weisl conversation in Chapter 3.

LBJ: That's right. And they are circulating more, and they are more attractive . . . better dinner partners . . . and they are more exciting than we are socially.

*   *   *

REEDY: I think the big world issue is peace. . . . That is where you just have to have . . . men in whom you personally have a feeling of confidence and rapport.
LBJ: Our trouble is, George, we do not have acquaintances [like that]. . . . San Marcos[1] didn't produce them. And you haven't been able to produce them from your Chicago background. We just don't have those people.

J. EDGAR HOOVER

Tuesday, November 17, 1964, 1:37 P.M.

Johnson tries to stir up the FBI Director by reporting that Hoover's nemesis, Robert Kennedy, is campaigning to force LBJ to choose Kennedy's deputy and ally, Nicholas Katzenbach, as the permanent Attorney General.

LBJ: He's making another pitch on his friend as successor. And there are individuals who are going around that . . . you have a pretty good record on. I didn't know it, but I heard it last night, [that] Alsop[2] . . . had some problems.
HOOVER: He was caught in a homosexual situation over in Moscow.[3]
LBJ: Well . . . he's gone in and told Abe Fortas last week—just kind of laid it on the line almost—that this fellow had to [be Attorney General]. . . . Your former boss notified Alsop that . . . we . . . from the South . . . could have prejudices by moving certain folks out.[4] . . . So that's, you can see, a little inside blackmail.

LADY BIRD JOHNSON

Tuesday, November 17, 1964, Tape-recorded Diary

Mrs. Johnson tells of seeing Walter and Marjorie Jenkins off before they go home to Texas.

LADY BIRD: Walter looks surprisingly young and well. His face was no longer red. His nose had been sort of bulbous and red, with an acne type of condition.

---

1. Southwest Texas State Teachers College at San Marcos was LBJ's alma mater.
2. The columnist Joseph Alsop.
3. In 1957 the Soviets photographed Alsop *in flagrante* with another man in Moscow and confronted him with the evidence. (See Alsop file, FBI.)
4. Meaning that RFK had said that LBJ was moving Katzenbach out because he was too pro–civil rights.

Now he appeared quite rested and quite relaxed, but somehow too calm and quiet—rather like an inhabitant of Mars, looking down on us strange earth creatures . . . detached and disassociated. I cannot measure the suffering he has gone through. But for me, it's been one of the two or three most painful things in my life—more painful than the death of many close to me. . . .

I told him very simply that no army of men could take his place. . . . He said one nice thing that had come out of all this is that Walter [1] is just being a model boy and is spending hours and hours every weekend with him. . . . He said he felt like an anvil had been lifted from his chest when it was clear about ten o'clock [on Election Night] that Lyndon had certainly won.[2] . . . I told them I hoped perhaps they might go back to live in Austin, that we would give them [land], . . . and if he opened an accountant's office, we would want him to handle our private account—the ranch's and I could think of two or three other accounts to begin with. There is no estrangement between us three. None at all. But there is a complete understanding that everything has changed.[3]

RUSSELL LONG

Democratic Senator from Louisiana
Wednesday, November 18, 1964, 8:25 P.M.

> The Louisiana Senator has heard that Fort Polk, Louisiana, might be on the list, which the Pentagon will reveal the next day, of eighty military installations to be closed. He pleads with Johnson to save it.

LONG: If that base closes down . . . people are going to say, "Russell Long is a no-account faker." . . . Don't close that one. . . . I'm begging! . . .
LBJ: Russell, . . . I couldn't change it because I would have a national scandal on my hands. McNamara . . . doesn't ask me to approve [the list]. . . . He'd resign before he'd do it. . . . I will talk to him. . . . I just hope and pray it's not on that [list]. But if it's on there, ain't all hell can change it. . . . If my wife's life depended on it, I couldn't. . . .
LONG: . . . If I could tell those people [at Fort Polk], "It don't mean you," it'll sound like Russell Long and Lyndon Johnson are the most wonderful, finest men God ever invented.

---

1. Jenkins's son.
2. And that the Jenkins scandal had not reduced LBJ's margin.
3. Jenkins returned to Texas and his old occupation as a certified public accountant. When LBJ left the White House in 1969, he said he had two resolutions—to take up smoking and to throw his arms around Walter Jenkins. He kept both. (See *Hartford Courant,* December 22, 1999.)

LBJ: [*exasperated:*] . . . If it's on there, ain't all the king's horses can't change it because it will just blow right up in my face. . . .

LONG: Mr. President, when I had that vote to kill Medicare . . . that's not the attitude I took on you.[1] It's all right with me if you want to take the attitude on me, but I'll be your friend forever, and God bless you. . . .

LBJ: [*almost shouting:*] . . . Russell, you know, if we handle our bases on that basis, sweetheart, there wouldn't be any of them closed. Not a one. . . . Have *mercy* on me! Don't be cruel, and let's keep our friendship. Let's don't destroy it!

LONG: I'll love you forever, but as much as I—

LBJ: I've helped you every time I could, and I will help you every time I can, but don't ask me to help you when I can't!

LONG: . . . As much as I've come through for you, you could at least make a telephone call to see if I'm dead or not.

LBJ: I told you I would do that, Russell, as soon as I hang up here. . . . I wish *you'd* call McNamara, though, because it's not easy for me to do. . . .

LONG: . . . Hell, everybody in America is trying to get McNamara! You are the only guy that can get him on the telephone. . . . Find out if I'm dead and call me back.

LBJ: [*laughs*] Russell, I'm not going to call you back, but . . . I'll tell him what you said.

LONG: Have Bill Moyers or somebody call.

LBJ: There ain't nobody here but me. Everybody else has gone to the hospital or something.

LONG: . . . Mr. President, I'm not going to quarrel with you anymore. You're my boss, and I love you.

LBJ: I'm not anybody's boss, but I reciprocate.

CYRUS VANCE

Deputy Secretary of Defense
Wednesday, November 18, 1964, 8:40 P.M.

Unable to reach McNamara, LBJ calls his number two man.

LBJ: Senator Long has been calling . . . with tears in his eyes. . . . He's afraid I'm closing [Fort Polk]. . . .

VANCE: It's not on the list, sir.

LBJ: . . . You sure of that?

---

1. Long had helped LBJ fight for government-backed old age health insurance during the session of Congress just ended.

VANCE: Positive.

LBJ: All right. . . . Let's don't get it on any damn list. . . . I'll just call him back and tell him.

RUSSELL LONG

Wednesday, November 18, 1964, 8:45 P.M.

LBJ: Russell?

LONG: Yes, sir, Boss Man.

LBJ: Now, don't you tell anybody you called up here, and don't you quote me at all, because I got to stay away from these things. . . . But you can go back and go to sleep. I don't think you've got anything that will keep you awake.

LONG: [*exhilarated:*] Thank you, Mr. Boss Man! You can count on old Long!

LBJ: Well, I could count on him anyway, but you just go on and go to sleep. . . .

LONG: Mr. Boss Man, God bless you!

LBJ: Bye.

LONG: Love you forever!

LADY BIRD JOHNSON

Thursday, November 19, 1964, Tape-recorded Diary

At the LBJ Ranch the Johnsons dined with their friends Senator Stuart Symington of Missouri and his wife, Sylvia. After dinner, LBJ gasconaded into the night.

LADY BIRD: I wish for two reasons that he had been quieter. One, I wanted to hear Sylvia talk more and also Stuart. Besides, they'll like it better if *they* talk more. Everybody likes to hear themselves some. And second, I don't want him to spend himself so prodigally. Even his amazing energy won't hold out forever. I want him to save it for the toughest times and to pace himself more. But perhaps one can't be the person one is and change radically. Within the limits of a little moderate molding, I'll have to let him remain the person he is.

CARTHA "DEKE" DeLOACH

Friday, November 20, 1964, 4:23 P.M.

On November 18, before a small group of female reporters, J. Edgar Hoover had caused national indignation by calling Martin Luther King, Jr., "the most notorious liar in the country." This was in response to King's charge that Southern FBI agents were stalling on civil rights violations. Johnson asks DeLoach to tell Hoover not to worry. Always eager to keep Hoover friendly, he implies that he shares Hoover's views of King.

LBJ: I don't think two people out of a hundred . . . outside of some of your super-extreme shadowy groups . . . would find anything to criticize about his operation. They all have great confidence in him. I think you ought to boost him up that way. We all get to feeling sorry for ourselves once in a while, and feel like somebody is picking on us.[1] . . . And sometimes people do.

DeLOACH: He was outraged at the criticism by Martin Luther King.

LBJ: . . . But he knows Martin Luther King.[2] [*chuckles*] I mean, he knows him better than anybody in the country. . . . There's no reason why he ought to get in a fight with . . . him. . . . I invited [King] to come and see me yesterday, and he wasn't with that group.[3] And I think that's very odd when a President asks him to come in and talk about problems, if you are really interested in them, they haven't got time to come and see the President.

DeLOACH: He was down at the Bahamas at a very lavish resort place with a couple of his henchmen, supposedly writing a speech in acceptance for the Nobel Peace Prize. He claims that's why he wasn't here.[4]

ROBERT McNAMARA

Monday, November 23, 1964, 3:48 P.M.

Johnson is angry about a *Washington Post* report that his Ambassador to Saigon, General Maxwell Taylor, is demanding escalation of the war in Vietnam.

LBJ: "Taylor may seek limited bombing in the North[5] and Laos. . . . Taylor will decide on whether to keep his job, based on what position the Johnson administration takes on future conduct of the war." . . . I don't know why we try this war in the newspapers. . . .

McNAMARA: I'm just absolutely certain he didn't make any such statements. He's not that kind of a person. . . .

LBJ: That's blackmail, isn't it?

---

1. Johnson knows whereof he speaks.
2. Johnson refers to Hoover's close surveillance of King's private life.
3. King had declined an invitation for civil rights leaders to meet with Johnson.
4. Within two days of this call, DeLoach and his colleagues gave reporters and religious leaders damaging sexual and other confidential information against King. Despite Katzenbach's complaint to LBJ, the President was unwilling to antagonize Hoover and DeLoach by reprimanding them. (See Taylor Branch, *Pillar of Fire*, Simon & Schuster, 1998, pp. 531–20.)
5. North Vietnam.

McNAMARA: Yeah, but I'm just positive, Mr. President, Max would never do that. . . .

LBJ: Well . . . let's just don't be giving out these damn interviews about what we're going to recommend.

McNAMARA: The worst one of all, the one that really disturbed me . . . was the Alsop article this morning . . . [1]

LBJ: . . . He's crazy. He wrote me a two-page letter saying that we were already liquidating the United States' interest in the Pacific, and we'd move back to Hon-o-lu-lah. . . .

McNAMARA: . . . This morning, he's quoting George Ball's report, . . . of which there are only four copies. It's just a nasty article on George Ball. Implies that he doesn't know anything at all about Southeast Asia. He's European-oriented, and wants to give up the place to the Chinese.

LBJ: Why in the hell don't you call them all together and say we can't run a government if we've got to hand this stuff out? . . . I saw [Alsop] at dinner the other night . . . and he was the same going-to-hell-in-a-hack-immediately. I said, "Of course, we've got very serious problems, but you tell me we've got thirty days. . . . You walked around the garden with me first of last year and told me we had thirty days. I hope that you're as far off on this estimate as you were then." That just made him furious.

McNAMARA: The article itself was bad enough this morning, but the thing that *really* annoyed me was the *leak* . . . of the most *confidential* paper. My God! I've gone to great lengths here to try to get Dean [Rusk] and George Ball and Mac [Bundy] and Cy [Vance] and myself to really exchange . . . intimate opinions on this thing in a way that wouldn't get into the press. . . .

LBJ: Why don't you find out who he saw? I have never seen the paper. . . . I get most of my information from the government through the papers. . . . I have to rely on Alsop to give it to me! That's a disgrace! And if you would read his FBI on him[2]—have you ever read it?

McNAMARA: No, sir, I haven't.

LBJ: Well, you better read it. Because Walter Jenkins is just minor.

McNAMARA: I should have, because Tom Gates[3] told me just two sentences about it before he left. I never read it, and I will.

LBJ: He's been involved in practically every capital of the world. . . . I just read it the other night. Tell Bill Moyers you want to see it.

---

1. Joseph Alsop revealed a secret memorandum by Under Secretary of State George Ball, "whose knowledge of Asia could be comfortably contained in a fairly small thimble," asking for "a negotiated settlement with the Vietnamese Communists" (*Washington Post,* November 23, 1964).

2. Alsop's FBI file was rife with references to his homosexual activities on various continents (Joseph Alsop file, FBI).

3. Eisenhower's last Defense Secretary.

CARTHA "DEKE" DeLOACH

Thursday, December 3, 1964, 9:40 A.M.

DeLoach reports that the FBI has fulfilled the President's request that agents investigate Wanda DuBonier, the woman who, as George Reedy warned the President in October,[1] was allegedly photographed in a compromising position with him. The rumor further had it that Bobby Baker had introduced the woman to Johnson. LBJ presumes that the rumor originated with Don Reynolds, his antagonist in the Bobby Baker scandal, who is testifying in secret this week before the Senate Rules Committee on subjects including Baker's use of "party girls" to entertain Senators and business clients.[2]

DeLOACH: She termed the . . . allegations as outlandish, ridiculous. She denied everything. She said she'd never had any relationships with you of any kind. That she had met you on four occasions . . . but you would not even know her. . . . We tried to bear down to see whether it was a frame-up here[3] or not. She said . . . a Grace Johnson told her that Sarah McClendon[4] was going to try to get in touch with her. . . . And that she could name her own price if she would give Sarah her story. And Sarah did try to call her about five times, and this girl refused to talk to Sarah.

She said that she never has had sexual intercourse with Don Reynolds. That Reynolds tried to date her four or five times . . . and that she was always a little afraid of him and didn't want to date him. She says on one or two occasions, Bobby Baker asked her what she did in her spare time, and she just passed it off. She's trying to portray herself as rather a very innocent, injured little girl. But she says all these charges are absolutely ridiculous, and she's given a signed statement accordingly. Now, she admits to bad check charges, and not only in Baton Rouge but also in various other localities. She's out on bond on that at the present time. Now, that's pretty much the story, Mr. President.

LBJ: Well, that's an excellent job. . . . Now . . . as my representative, you get together in your little file . . . these other two or three or four similar stories about me.[5] . . .

DeLOACH: . . . There's been about five, all total. Walter and I have kept, as you know, a very cozy file over there with Mildred that nobody can look at.[6]

---

1. See October 23, 1964 conversation, above.
2. *New York Times*, December 2, 1964.
3. By Republicans, as LBJ suspected.
4. Outspoken White House correspondent for Texas newspapers.
5. Sexual allegations against Johnson.
6. This refers to the file in Walter Jenkins's office kept by his aide, Mildred Stegall, about whose disposition LBJ had been so worried about after Jenkins's resignation in October. (See Chapter 2.)

LBJ: Have you looked at this Billy Sol Estes thing the other day . . . where they offered him a million dollars?[1] . . . It's some file that you-all brought me the other day. Let's see, his lawyer . . . told the FBI agent [the Republicans] told him they would give him a million dollars if he'd speak for thirty minutes on the TV and tell his story.

DeLOACH: I will check into that right away.

LBJ: . . . [Get] all these supposed blackmails . . . together and keep them, so that when I ask you on a moment's notice what you can do about it, why do it. . . .

DeLOACH: Very good, sir.

LBJ: What do you reckon caused [Reynolds] to say that? He must be crazy, isn't he? Abe [Fortas] says he's a paranoid. Whatever that is. . . . [Otherwise] he wouldn't be quoting a woman and giving her name and almost her address and saying she did these things. . . . He's bound to know we'd try to confirm it.

DeLOACH: Man is psycho enough to blame anything, and why Curtis and Scott will sit up there and listen to this crap and try to back this man up is beyond me.[2]

CARTHA "DEKE" DeLOACH

Tuesday, December 8, 1964, 10:45 A.M.

> In the wake of his victory, Johnson wants the FBI to combat other accusations by Don Reynolds during a closed session of the Senate Rules Committee that might endanger his presidency. A cooperative Hoover will issue an FBI report four months hence refuting Reynolds's charges.

DeLOACH: We've made excellent progress, Mr. President. Mr. Hoover had already seen to it that 50 to 60 percent of those allegations that Abe Fortas mentioned to me on the telephone have been investigated and have been cleared up.

LBJ: What about the woman? We got that behind us. Have you got the Howard Johnson stuff and Smathers behind you?[3]

DeLOACH: . . . Yes, sir, the Howard Johnson franchises, the privilege franchises, we're working on that right now. That's one that we had not cleared up.

LBJ: All right, now what about the General Dynamics and . . . Grumman?[4]

---

1. To incriminate Johnson before the election in exchange for a pardon from Goldwater if he won.

2. Referring to the efforts by Republicans Hugh Scott and Carl Curtis of Nebraska to use Reynolds's Rules Committee testimony to embarrass Johnson.

3. More Reynolds charges involving Howard Johnson hotel and restaurant franchises and Florida Democratic Senator George Smathers.

4. Three days before LBJ became President, the Senate Permanent Investigations Subcommittee examined whether he had taken cash and used illicit influence to guide part of a government contract for the TFX fighter-bomber to General Dynamics and Grumman. (*New York Times,* November 20, 1963.)

DeLOACH: . . . Mr. Evans, the president of Grumman . . . denied it. . . . We're in good shape there.

LBJ: . . . Abe says he studies this paranoid and psychotic stuff. Said a guy [like Reynolds] reads about Walter [Jenkins] in the paper and then he immediately . . . thinks that another guy is involved with Walter. And that's where he gets the idea about . . . saying me and DuBonier or whatever it is. Says that's a mental thing. He says a guy reads in the paper about TFX . . . so he immediately sees a big satchel in connection with that. . . . Don't you-all have psychiatrists or something working for you that can analyze this kind of stuff?

DeLOACH: No, sir, we don't. We'd go beyond the realm of our authority if we had that. . . . But this man is a psychopathic liar. . . . I think he's the type . . . who wants . . . to be in the limelight all the time. . . .

LBJ: Well, what do we do about it?

DeLOACH: I think what we've got to do is to discredit him, and which is exactly what's being done. But it's long overdue. The papers thus far carried the cudgel for the Republicans, and now that facts are being presented to the [Justice] Department and the allegations are all being run down, why the man *can* be discredited.

LBJ: . . . What else have you investigated besides the woman and Evans? Have you gone through Grumman pretty carefully with a fine-tooth comb? Are you sure that they haven't paid anybody down there? . . . Be sure that McNamara is interviewed. . . . Ask him whether I ever talked to him about it. . . . Ask him if Kennedy [1] talked to him. Just go over the whole damn thing. Get a good interview from the man that you'd have to put on the stand. . . .

DeLOACH: Yes, sir. We'll have that wrapped up completely, Mr. President.

DWIGHT D. EISENHOWER

34th President of the United States
Monday, December 14, 1964, 10:15 A.M.

> Johnson calls the former President, just arrived at his winter home in Palm Desert, California. Eisenhower uses the opportunity to clear up a misunderstanding.

LBJ: Lady Bird and I . . . sure hope you could come to the inauguration. . . . Come see everything that you wanted to see, and nothing that you didn't want to see. [*chuckles*] Maybe you've had too many of them.

EISENHOWER: No, Mr. President, you are very kind, but you see, Mamie won't travel, except by train. Now to come back all the way just after we have gotten out there . . . would be quite a burden on her. . . .

---

1. President Kennedy.

LBJ: . . . There's not anything I want more than for both of you to conserve all you have so you'll be with us as long as everything. . . .

EISENHOWER: . . . While you are on the phone . . . I was out at Hershey[1] at a meeting with the Republicans during the last campaign. . . . It turned out that there was a reporter there. Now, he apparently gave to *Newsweek* or some other darn organization a statement which purported to be a quote from me in which I said . . . we had to do our best to win . . . "and throw out this Communistic form of government we have in Washington." Now, never in my life have I accused anybody or any organization in the United States of being Communist.

LBJ: [*chuckles*] I know that.

EISENHOWER: . . . I know this can't hurt *you,* but it can hurt me terribly in my own mind that . . . people could think me guilty of *saying* such a damn thing.

LBJ: Nobody thinks you guilty of anything except the very best motives. . . . As long as I'm here, there is nobody going to have more respect or really more affection than you. . . .

EISENHOWER: . . . I told them, . . . "If this man writes this statement, whatever I can do to discredit him in the public, I'm going to do it." . . .

LBJ: . . . We're in different parties, but we're for the same country. . . . I served under you eight years . . . and I found myself down there on the front row voting for your recommendations a good many times when Republican leaders were on the back row *fighting* them. . . . You can fight a good Republican fight, and I'll do my best, but we'll both be for the country when the chips are down. . . . I'm not going to drag you in to get any chestnuts out of the fire unless I really get my tail in a crack internationally. And when I do, I'm going to come running.

LADY BIRD JOHNSON

Friday, January 8, 1965, Tape-recorded Diary

LADY BIRD: Late in the evening, approaching ten, I went to Lyndon's office, hoping that I could get him to come home and eat dinner. . . . But there was phone call after phone call. I doubt that it is helpful. It is more like nagging. But it is hard to stand by wordless or even selfishly pursue my own pleasures, of which there are many, when I know that wisdom and moderation indicate that he ought to come home and eat dinner before ten-thirty. . . . Dr. Gould[2] commented on what I had told him about Lyndon being a good student and able to pick up anything he was told if he was interested, with extraordinary speed. . . . I sometimes wonder what

---

1. Pennsylvania.
2. Dr. Wilbur Gould, a New York throat specialist whom the Johnsons had consulted.

Lyndon would have been like if, instead of being exposed in his youth to Johnson City and a state teacher's college, he had been exposed to a sophisticated society of many facets and a school like Harvard.

LADY BIRD JOHNSON

Saturday, January 9, 1965, Tape-recorded Diary

LADY BIRD: I went over to Lyndon's office . . . and, to my surprise, found him in his small room covered with a blanket, the light out, and apparently asleep. . . . I think fatigue has finally begun to build up in him.

RUSSELL LONG

Tuesday, January 12, 1965, 10:40 A.M.

> Having begged LBJ to save Fort Polk, the newly elected Senate Democratic Whip now pleads to save the post office in Shreveport, which the President knows as one of the most rabidly anti-Johnson cities in the nation.

LONG: That's going to hurt me badly. And I'll have to get it back the hard way, if it has to get down to that. But all the time it would take me . . . to get a few dollars for that Shreveport post office is just time I could be spending working on your program. . . . Just let us have a million dollars or so to get started on that post office.

LBJ: God, Russell! You don't want to reward *Shreveport!* . . . I'd be run out of the whole United *States* if somebody put Shreveport in there until they behave. My God Al-*mighty!* . . . If we did that, we would be laughingstock, Russell.

LONG: That's not how you got everybody for you in Texas. You got them for you . . . by . . . wooing and pursuing those people until they finally voted for you, and you wound up getting them all. . . .

LBJ: Russell, *ple-e-ease,* my friend, I want to do anything in the world you want done. But . . . no Long . . . ever asked you to reward people that cut their throat. . . . Those are the meanest, most vicious people in the United States. . . . God Al-*mighty!* . . . I've got literature that's the worst that I ever saw. Called me a *crook!* Called me a *rapist!* Called me everything under the sun! Right out of Shreveport. . . . They would ridicule me out of that state and every other one, and ridicule you. . . .

LONG: They might ridicule you, but they gonna run me out!

LBJ: Well, they ain't going to run you out this year. . . . There ain't no election in [1965].

LONG: Mr. President, I need that the worst kind of way to build Russell Long.

LBJ: I would do anything in the world to build Russell Long. . . . Your daddy[1] would turn over in his grave. . . . He didn't reward his people that way. . . . You tell them that the first thing they've got to do is apologize for calling me a thief. . . . The second thing they've got to do is get those damn Birchites out of that newspaper[2] that called me a dirty, low-down, thieving, son of a bitch every day. . . .

LONG: Mr. President. . . . we've got some good people who own that *Times-Picayune*[3] who are hoping to buy that paper. . . . Meanwhile, it's not going to help us to have the image of trying to hurt Shreveport. . . . By the time you signed that civil rights bill you lost that area. . . . But we can build that back up. By the time you get some colored folks registered, you'll carry the area. . . .

LBJ: . . . Russell, it's a premium on *disloyalty!* . . . God Almighty! You've lost all the Long in you! . . . I will not sign *anything* connected with Shreveport until they withdraw their charges that I'm a thief and a thug. 'Cause I'm not! . . .

LONG: . . . You've got a lot of mean people up in Shreveport. I know it. . . . You've also got some damn good people up there who want to help you.

LBJ: About 15 percent.

LONG: And my mama is one of them.

LBJ: I'm for your mama! Don't tell me your mama can't ever look at anything I ever said or did since 1933 that she won't approve of, so far as the Longs are concerned. . . . I'm a populist just like [Huey Long] was, by God! I'm for the poor people. I'm going to pour the education to them. I'm going to pour the roads to them. I'm going to pour the health to them. . . . But I sure as hell ain't for that Shreveport crowd. . . . And you can't be either. . . . You have a little touch of marijuana or something this morning? . . . By God, I put out the red carpet . . . and I gave them lead pencils and souvenirs. . . . I did everything I could.[4] And then I picked up the paper, by God, and they said that "he's a notorious thief." I never *read* such stuff! . . . You just tell Shreveport you'll try to help them, but Shreveport's in deep trouble. . . .

LONG: . . . I'm not going to quarrel with you anymore. Your mind's made up. . . .

LBJ: Well, you saw what I did with them here. . . . Could a man have been nicer? Could a man have done more than I did?

LONG: Oh, I agree, I agree. But you signed that civil rights bill!

---

1. The Louisiana Governor and Senator Huey Long, one of LBJ's heroes.
2. The ultraconservative *Shreveport Times*.
3. The *New Orleans Times-Picayune*.
4. Johnson had met with *Shreveport Times* editors.

LBJ: How could I veto that? How could I veto that?[1]

LONG: . . . I'm not going to quarrel with you anymore about it. I've taken enough of your time.

LBJ: . . . It hurts me not to do anything you want to do. . . . But God Almighty, don't you pick out the cross-eyed, stuttering, bowlegged girl and bring her up and say, "Now, listen, this ought to be the beauty queen, and you name her, by God, and it's a favor to me!"

ROBERT McNAMARA

Wednesday, January 13, 1965, 3:07 P.M.

> Johnson complains to his Defense Secretary about what he considers to be the Kennedy circle in Georgetown, which he believes is a cabal against him. (He is slightly needling McNamara, a member of the circle in good standing, as well as suggesting that he plead the Johnson case with them.) LBJ goes on to display his conviction that President Kennedy intended to press the war to defend South Vietnam—and his worry that Robert Kennedy's crowd will destroy him if the President forsakes what he thinks to be JFK's Vietnam commitment.

LBJ: They're out[2] and they don't get consulted and they don't feel that great power. And you could throw all three of them on a scale at once and they wouldn't be eighty-nine pounds.[3] But they have these little parties out at Georgetown. . . . Bill Moyers tells me . . . that they had a party last night. Joe Alsop[4] called up, very excited, today and said that he and Kraft and Evans[5] . . . and the Kennedy crowd decided that I had framed up to get [the] Armed Services [Committee] in the Senate[6] to call McCone[7] to put the Vietnam War on Kennedy's tomb. And that I had a conspiracy going on to show that it was Kennedy's immaturity and poor judgment that originally led us into this thing. . . . And that his execution of it had brought havoc to the country. And that McCone had gone up and done it. And that this was my game—to lay Vietnam off onto Kennedy's inexperience [and] immaturity. . . . McCone told me he . . . didn't mention Vietnam.[8] . . . So I assumed, since McNamara was a part of the administration, that—

---

1. As often when talking with an anti–civil rights Southerner, LBJ tries a whopper, pretending that he was not really for the 1964 Civil Rights Act and had only been forced not to veto it.
2. After JFK's death.
3. In other words, they are lightweights.
4. The columnist.
5. The columnists Joseph Kraft and Rowland Evans, whose wives were cousins.
6. Meaning Chairman Richard Russell.
7. CIA Director John McCone, a Kennedy family intimate.
8. During his Armed Services testimony.

McNAMARA: And is going to be tagged with the war in any case! [*laughs*]

LBJ: . . . That since he was a part of the administration, I had assumed that he didn't resent very much what I'd said or he would have said to me . . . that it wasn't true. . . . [I told Moyers] that I considered myself responsible for every decision made by Kennedy. . . . And that whatever he did, I supported. And if they can find a more loyal man in this town to him or to his memory, I would like for them to produce him. And that I had a considerably bigger slice of the Kennedy presidential pie, making him President, than either Rowland Evans or Joe Kraft.[1] Even though they wrote a few speeches. Now, that's about the story. . . . I wanted you to know that that's what they were saying. And I assume it's an injustice to McCone too, isn't it?

McNAMARA: I think so, Mr. President. . . . I can maybe do something about this. I probably should have gone to that party last night. . . . I can get back into communication with those people and, I think, throw some light of realism onto whatever they are thinking about. Did I understand that Alsop called to report this?

LBJ: Called to report it to Bill. . . . Alsop's charging that I'm getting McCone to go up and lay the blame for Vietnam on Kennedy's tomb. Now, of course, I have never laid any blame on Kennedy. Have you ever heard me blame Kennedy for anything?

McNAMARA: No, no, absolutely not! . . . I have mentioned this to Jackie several times. I've been very impressed by your attitude on that as well as when the President was alive.

LBJ: I may not have anything else in my life, but I've got loyalty! . . . If any of this crowd [is] in your vicinity . . . what you ought to say to them is . . . that I assume full responsibility for everything and don't ask anybody else to take it. *Including* President Kennedy. And during his lifetime, whatever he did, I was *for*. And in his death, it's my *complete* responsibility. And I don't shove it off on *anybody* else.

LADY BIRD JOHNSON

Wednesday, January 13, 1965, Tape-recorded Diary

LADY BIRD: Someone mentioned to me . . . that it was Ashton's[2] birthday. Lyndon was standing by, and he heard it too. In one second, he had gone to his closet full of gifts, had gathered up pell-mell five or six items from our travels. Maybe a book, maybe a medallion, maybe an ashtray. . . . Gone up, given Ashton a kiss, marched out of the room. . . . Swift, generous deeds are typical of him, just

---

1. LBJ refers to his role in carrying Texas and other Southern states for Kennedy in 1960.
2. Lady Bird's secretary, Ashton Gonella.

as are swift, sometimes cutting words. This afternoon, he didn't get a nap at the alleged nap time. . . . The phone kept on ringing. . . . He said, "I'm too old for this job." . . . He lives in constant concern that somebody somewhere in his periphery will be mixed up, fairly or unfairly, in some shady business. I'm probably the only living person who would attest, believe, swear that he never wanted to be President. But now that he's in it, he wants history to record . . . a hardworking President, a "people-loving" President, a President who believes that man can solve his problems. I think the fear that haunts him is a sort of Harding complex. In more than thirty years, we've known so many folks . . . that somebody somewhere is going to do something wrong—or something that can be made to appear wrong—and their closeness to us would suddenly bloom and grow in the press, at least, and in the mind of the public and maybe on history's page. That is one more of the phantoms or realities that Lyndon is fighting.

MARTIN LUTHER KING, JR.

Friday, January 15, 1965, 12:06 P.M.

> At the White House one month earlier, LBJ welcomed the civil rights leader back from Oslo, where he had accepted the Nobel Peace Prize. During their brief meeting King asked him for federal legislation to ensure black voting rights in the South. As King later recalled, the President replied, "Martin, you're right about that. I'm going to do it eventually, but I can't get a voting rights bill through in this session of Congress."[1] Now, on King's thirty-sixth birthday, LBJ calls him in Selma, Alabama. King has gone there to lead blacks as they apply for whites-only jobs, integrate hotels and restaurants, and "make it clear to the nation that we are determined to vote." Johnson hopes King will not generate too much public pressure on him for a voting rights bill.

LBJ: Just got down here to meet the Prime Minister of Canada this morning . . . and I thought maybe I better try to reply to your call.
KING: . . . I don't want to take but just a minute of your time. First I want to thank you for that great State of the Union message. . . . I think we are on the way now toward the Great Society.[2]
LBJ: I'll tell you what our problem is. We've got to try with every force at our command—and I mean *every* force—to get these education bills that go to those people under two thousand dollars a year income. . . . And this poverty [bill] is a

---

1. Quoted in David Garrow, *Bearing the Cross* (Quill, 1986), p. 368.
2. In his State of the Union on January 4, LBJ had demanded "a new quest for union," a century beyond the Civil War's "terrible test of blood and fire." He outlined his vision of his Great Society and War on Poverty.

billion and a half, and this health [bill is] going to be $900 million next year. . . . We've got to get them passed before the vicious forces concentrate and get them a coalition that can block them. . . . Your people ought to be very, very diligent in looking at those committee members that come from urban areas that are friendly to you to see that those bills get reported right out. Because you have no idea—it's shocking to you—how much benefits they will get. There's $8.5 billion this year for education, compared to $700 million when I started. . . . Now, if we can get that, and we can get a Medicare—I ought to get that by February—and then we get our poverty, that will be more than double what it was last year. Then we've got to come up with the qualification of voters.[1] That will answer 70 percent of your problems.

KING: That's right.

LBJ: . . . No tests on what Chaucer said or Browning's poetry or constitutions or memorizing or anything else. And then we may have to put [voter registration] in the post office. Let the postmaster [do it]. That's a federal employee that I control. Who they can say is local. . . . If he doesn't register everybody, I can put a new one in. . . . They can all just go to the post office like they buy a stamp. . . . I talked to the Attorney General, and I've got them working on it. I don't want to start off with that any more than I do the 14 million, because we wouldn't get anything else.[2] . . .

KING: Yes, well, I remembered your message to me . . . when we met at the White House and I [was] very diligent about making this statement.[3]

LBJ: Your statement was perfect about the votes. . . . Very important. . . . I just don't see how anybody can say that a man can fight in Vietnam but he can't vote in the post office.

KING: Yes, yes. Mr. President, I tell you, the main thing I wanted to share with you really arose out of conversations I've had with all of the civil rights leaders. . . . We have a strong feeling that it would mean so much to improve the health of our whole democracy . . . to have a Negro in the Cabinet. . . . I'm sure it would give a new sense of dignity and self-respect to millions of . . . Negro youths who feel that they don't have anything to look forward to in life.

LBJ: I agree with that. I have not publicly shouted from the housetop, but . . . the first move I made was to . . . put one in charge of every bit of the information that went to all of the 120 nations.[4] . . . And I am trying my best to get the housing and

---

1. The voting rights bill that King was insisting on was not part of Johnson's State of the Union. Such a bill would eliminate the arcane tests Southern localities required of voters in order to disqualify African Americans.

2. LBJ is explaining why he wishes to delay voting rights.

3. After they met on December 18, King told reporters that LBJ was determined to help ensure voting rights.

4. Carl Rowan, ex-Ambassador to Finland, whom LBJ had appointed chief of the U.S. Information Agency.

urban and city problems—which is the number-one problem in America, as I see it—made into a Cabinet post.[1] . . . I don't want to make a commitment on it, because I don't want to get tied down in the Congress, but . . . probably it would be Weaver.[2] . . .

KING: He's an awful nice man.

LBJ: He's done a good job. . . . If we put somebody into a job and he fails, we lose three steps and we go ahead one. And I haven't had any of that. . . . We haven't had any mistakes, any corruption, or any scandals of any kind, and I've moved them in, I mean, by the wholesale. Both women and men.[3]

KING: . . . This is very encouraging. . . . It would be another great step to a Great Society.

LBJ: I have seen where they considered Whitney Young[4] for a place with a top job with Shriver.[5] . . . I have very high regard for Whitney. . . . I honestly don't feel that Roy Wilkins or with you or with Randolph,[6] or the man from CORE that meets with us[7]—I don't really think I have the moral obligation to any of them like I have to Weaver, who has been in there. It's kind of like you being assistant pastor to your church for ten years with the understanding of your deacons that you would take over . . . and then finally when the good day comes, they say, "Well, you get back and sit at the second table." I just don't feel like saying that to Weaver.

KING: Yes.

LBJ: Now, Weaver's not my man. . . . He's a Kennedy man. But I just think that there would be a pretty revolutionary feeling about him. . . .

KING: Yeah. . . . Well, we think very highly of Whitney.

LBJ: I do, too. . . . You know, he's worked very closely [with me in] equal employment.[8] . . . I think there's been substantial progress with industry on a higher level, don't you?

KING: . . . There's no doubt about it.

LBJ: Every corporation I talk to [is] looking for Negroes that can do the job. . . . Then when they get in, they can look after the ones below them. Like you're looking after your people. . . . There's not going to be anything, though, Doctor, as effective as all of them voting. That will get you a message that all the eloquence in

---

1. The Department of Housing and Urban Development was indeed established in 1966.
2. Robert Weaver was head of the Housing and Home Finance Agency.
3. African Americans.
4. Of the National Urban League.
5. Sargent Shriver, chief of the War on Poverty.
6. A. Philip Randolph of the Brotherhood of Sleeping Car Porters.
7. Presumably James Farmer.
8. One of the few jobs JFK gave LBJ as Vice President was to explore employment opportunities for blacks.

the world won't bring because the fellow will be coming to you then, instead of you calling him.

KING: It's very interesting, Mr. President, to notice that the only states you didn't carry in the South . . . have less than 40 percent of the Negroes registered to vote. . . . It's so important to get Negroes registered to vote in large numbers in the South. It would be this coalition of the Negro vote and the moderate white vote that will really make the new South.[1]

LBJ: That's exactly right. I think it's very important that we not say that we're doing this . . . because it's Negroes or whites, but we take the position that every person born in this country, when they reach a certain age, that he have a right to vote just like he has a right to fight—and that we just extend it whether it's a Negro, whether it's a Mexican or who it is.

KING: Yes, sir.

LBJ: . . . I think you can contribute a great deal by getting your leaders and you yourself—taking very simple examples of discrimination where a man's got to memorize Longfellow or whether he's got to quote the first ten amendments, or he's got to tell you what Amendment 15, 16, 17 is. . . . Some people don't have to do that. But when a Negro comes in, he's got to do it. And if we can just repeat, and repeat, and repeat. I don't want to follow Hitler, but he had an idea—

KING: Yeah.

LBJ: —that if you just take a simple thing and repeat it often enough, even if it wasn't true, why people accept it. Well, now, this is true. If you can find the worst conditions that you run into in Alabama, Mississippi, or Louisiana, or South Carolina . . . and if you just take that one illustration and get it on radio and get it on television, and get it in the pulpits, get it in the meetings, get it every place you can, pretty soon, the fellow that didn't do anything but drive a tractor will say, "That's not right. That's not fair." And then that will help us when we are going to shove through in the end.

KING: Yes, you're exactly right about that.

LBJ: And if we do that . . . it will be the greatest breakthrough of anything. . . . The greatest achievement of my administration, . . . I said to a group yesterday, was the passage of the 1964 Civil Rights Act. But I think this will be bigger, because it'll do things that even that '64 act couldn't do.

KING: That's right. . . .

LBJ: . . . Second thing is, *please* look at that labor committee in the House and Senate. *Please* look at that health committee. *Please* look at that immigration committee. And let's us try to get health, and education, and poverty through the first ninety days.

---

1. One more instance of King's gift for prophecy.

KING: Yes. . . . You can count on our absolute support.

LBJ: Whitney's group can go to talking to them, and Roy's group can, and your group can, and they ought to tell Ryan of New York [1] and they ought to tell so-and-so of Philadelphia . . . "Please get this bill reported." Because I don't think you have any conception of the proportion of assistance that comes to your people in these bills. . . . I haven't stressed it.[2] . . . You can figure out what $8 billion in education, what $1 billion in health, and what a billion and a half in poverty will do if it goes to people who earn less than two thousand dollars a year. . . . You know who earns less than two thousand, don't you?[3] [laughs]

KING: That's right. . . . We've just got to work harder.

LBJ: . . . Now I've got those messages up there. First time any President, by January 15th, has ever had a half a dozen messages before the Congress.[4] . . . And we're not just going to talk. . . . We talked the first three years of our administration.[5] We promised, and we held it up, and people were getting to be pretty disillusioned, I think, when I finally beat the Rules Committee and got civil rights out.[6]

KING: . . . That's right. Oh, that sense of disillusionment would have been serious.

LBJ: . . . So that's what we've got to do now. And you get in there and help us.

KING: I certainly will, and you know you can always count on that.

LBJ: Thank you so much.

KING: All right. God bless you.

NICHOLAS KATZENBACH

Friday, January 15, 1965, 1:38 P.M.

Johnson complains to his Acting Attorney General that the Kennedy people are annoyed that he has let JFK's old cronies David Powers and Kenneth O'Donnell leave his White House staff.[7] Since LBJ is still deciding whether Katzenbach

---

1. William Fitts Ryan, Democrat-Liberal Congressman from Manhattan and ardent civil rights champion.

2. In order to keep the bills from being viewed as mainly for blacks, which could stall them in Congress.

3. In bidding for King's support, LBJ is not being very subtle. This is the same kind of appeal he would have made to a Mayor Daley.

4. Johnson had done this to jump-start the passage of the Great Society legislation.

5. Meaning the Kennedy-Johnson administration.

6. LBJ is criticizing JFK for taking two years and five months to propose a civil rights act and complimenting himself for getting it through Congress.

7. By O'Donnell's account, when he told LBJ in the Oval Office that he was resigning to go back to Boston, "he did not wish me good luck or even say goodbye. He said only, 'Well, it's all right with me, and when you leave, take Powers with you. He's never worked for anybody around here except you and the Kennedys anyway.' " (O'Donnell and Powers, *"Johnny, We Hardly Knew Ye,"* p. 404.)

should be his Attorney General, this is also a little loyalty test to see whose side Robert Kennedy's friend is on.

LBJ: I would like to really get my inaugural over with because they're picayunish, this little cult. You've seen Rowland Evans and this crowd that runs around out there in Georgetown together. . . . They don't get invited to [my] cocktail parties. They're making a big issue about Powers and O'Donnell. . . . Dave really hasn't worked since the assassination. I've just carried him because of [his] children. And I've tried to be nice to Ken. He helped some in the campaign, but he hasn't been here since. He's down in Florida.

GERALD FORD

Congressman from Michigan and Minority Leader, House of Representatives
Tuesday, January 19, 1965, 2:29 P.M.

The day before his inauguration, Johnson calls the future thirty-eighth President, who has just deposed Charles Halleck of Indiana to become House Minority Leader.

LBJ: Jerry? . . . Congratulations! . . . I would have done it earlier, but . . . I'm not sure that I'm supposed to be messing around in you-all's intramural activities.
FORD: I understand.
LBJ: Jerry, I saw, by way of the newspaper this morning, you hadn't been briefed adequately.[1] . . . There's not anything that we know that we don't want you to know. . . . I don't want to start off fighting with you because I'm not running for reelection.[2] I'm just trying to make a good President. And I want you to help me. I told you that when I talked to you about the Warren Commission.[3]
FORD: Right.
LBJ: . . . I'd hope . . . that you could support me when you thought it was right . . . and be proud of it. I think it will get you more Republican seats than anything else if you show that you are not picayunish, and not fighting. . . . We're in a hell of a shape. . . . Rusk tells me he's called you twice and that you haven't returned either call. So, you better . . . see if there's a breakdown in your shop. . . .
FORD: I think he called me once.
LBJ: . . . I'm a Ford man. . . . We want you-all in on the takeoff. Provided you

---

1. Ford had complained on ABC's *Issues and Answers* of lack of information from the White House on foreign policy. (*Washington Post*, January 18, 1965.)

2. Johnson may be alluding to an intention not to run in 1968, or he may be saying that at this moment his business is governing, not politics.

3. Johnson had called Ford in November 1963 to appoint him to the Warren Commission investigating the JFK assassination. (See Beschloss, *Taking Charge*, pp. 64–65.)

will get in on the takeoff. . . . We . . . say, "Here are the alternatives. We can bomb the hell out of Hanoi and the hundred MiGs there, or we can go the other direction and get out completely. . . . Now, what do you think we ought to do?" . . . Halleck looks over to me and says, "Now, Mr. President, that's your responsibility as Commander-in-Chief." I said, "I know it is, Charlie. . . . I goddamn sure want . . . the record to show that you chucked it back to me." . . . I want you to know as much as the President knows. . . . Because when I get run out of Vietnam or when I get in a war with China, or if I got another stalemate for a year, there're going to be Republican boys shot just like Democrats. . . . I'm perfectly willing and anxious to admit—just like I know you would be if you wound up here in the morning by fate, like I did[1]—to know that I don't know all the answers.

FORD: . . . Your statement in the State of the Union message on our commitment to South Vietnam,[2] I wholeheartedly and unequivocally stand by. . . . But I do think that it's important that I and others on our side be kept up-to-date as well as we can. . . .

LBJ: . . . Eisenhower did that with me. . . . I said to him, "Mr. President, when I can't agree with you, I'll come tell you. I'll disagree with you with dignity and decency, and I won't talk about your dog or your boy.[3] But I'll try to offer an alternative, and then I'll try to bloody your nose." . . . I never had a quarrelsome word with Eisenhower for six years. Now, a good many times we differed. . . . I think it's the duty of the opposition to analyze and do what's best for their country. . . . I'll tell you what it did: it gave me the Senate in two years. And I kept it for six more because the people said, . . . "While he's a Democrat, he's not a mean, vicious, blind one."

FORD: . . . You can be assured, Mr. President, that . . . when we oppose, it will be on the issue and not on the personal.

LBJ: I know that. . . . Pick up this phone anytime you want to . . . and tell me frankly what you think. . . . That's the only way people can get along.

---

1. LBJ could not know that this was precisely what would happen to Ford in 1974, when he became President after the resignation of Richard Nixon.

2. In his January 4 State of the Union, Johnson vowed not to "break" the Eisenhower-Kennedy pledge to help South Vietnam "against the Communist aggression."

3. In the 1944 campaign, Republicans lampooned FDR by claiming that he had used official money to send a destroyer to Alaska to pick up his dog Fala, and that he had wangled a special wartime commission for his son Elliott.

Chapter Five

"I DON'T SEE ANY WAY OF WINNING"

Now we're off to bombing these people. We're over that hurdle. I don't think anything is going to be as bad as losing, and I don't see any way of winning.

LBJ *to* ROBERT MCNAMARA, *February 26, 1965*

RICHARD RUSSELL

Friday, January 22, 1965, 11:15 A.M.

Two days after his inauguration, LBJ has to decide whom to appoint as Attorney General, succeeding Robert Kennedy. The Acting Attorney General, Nicholas Katzenbach, has asked him to give him the full title or fire him before Congress reconvenes.[1] Johnson's first choice is Abe Fortas, the intimate who has helped him survive personal and political crises from his contested 1948 Senate victory through the Bobby Baker and Walter Jenkins scandals.

Johnson thinks Katzenbach has done an "A-plus" job but worries that he will be more loyal to RFK than to him. Fearing that the new Senator Kennedy might fan the flames of scandal against him, LBJ wants to be sure that his Attorney General will walk through fire for the President. He wonders whether Katzenbach would.

LBJ: He's Bobby's closest friend and Bobby's closest man. . . . As a consequence, most of my people are constantly shoving me, saying, "You ought to make this change." . . . The person that I *want* to be my Attorney General—the person I respect most from the legal standpoint and from the compassionate standpoint and from the integrity standpoint—is Abe Fortas. . . . I've known him since 1940, when we were both young Southerners up here running around, trying to find our way and supporting Roosevelt and the New Deal. . . . He's by far the ablest lawyer I know. . . .

---

1. Clark Clifford with Richard Holbrooke, *Counsel to the President* (Random House, 1991), p. 439.

Clark Clifford[1] is a third one. But . . . he's not quite as patient with me as you are when I'm talking to you. . . . He's a little cooler customer and a little more of a Fancy Dan. More country club. And he just doesn't [understand] us in Johnson City the way Fortas does. . . . [Fortas] is a poor boy and he knows it. . . . He's constantly trying to find ways for me to answer problems. . . . When Bobby Baker got in trouble . . . he went to see Fortas because he knew that I thought that Fortas was the ablest lawyer in the country.[2] . . . Now back in the early '40s . . . he belonged to one or two liberal outfits. At least, they had his name. He denies that he belonged to them. Lawyers Guild, I think.[3] . . . But through the last fifteen years, he's been head of, I expect, the biggest law firm here and one of the best. . . . The question that I need somebody that's frank and fatherly with me to tell me is, Do his connections and . . . reputation [cost] me more than [they] would be worth? Or should I go on and do what my judgment tells me I want to do? . . . The man I want's Fortas.

RUSSELL: . . . If I were in your shoes, I would appoint the man I wanted. . . .

LBJ: . . . He says he does not want to come. . . . He says . . . they'll say I'm putting Baker's lawyer in as Attorney General.

RUSSELL: . . . I don't think that's going to stir up any great commotion. . . . If I wanted Fortas, I would appoint Fortas.

JAMES EASTLAND

Democratic Senator from Mississippi and Chairman, Senate Judiciary Committee
Friday, January 22, 1965, 11:40 A.M.

Johnson wants to know from Eastland whether Abe Fortas might have confirmation troubles.

EASTLAND: You've got to have a man that's first loyal to you. You don't have that now.[4]

LBJ: That's right. . . . I've got to have a man kind of like my priest—that I confess to and I say, "Here are the problems. Now you tell me what the law is and tell me how to fix it." . . . I've got Katzenbach. . . . We don't snap at each other. . . . He's fair and judicious, and *apparently* friendly. Nearly every [adviser] I have . . .

---

1. The former young Truman aide, a high-priced Washington lobbyist in 1965, had engineered LBJ's effort to keep RFK off the 1964 ticket and helped Fortas guide him through the Jenkins scandal.

2. Fortas had served as Baker's lawyer until LBJ became President and Fortas resigned the case to avoid conflict of interest.

3. Founded in 1936, the National Lawyers Guild was accused of being a Communist front.

4. In other words, Katzenbach is loyal to RFK, not to LBJ.

[says] I'm President and now Bobby Kennedy is running the show—why in the hell don't I have my own Attorney General? . . .

EASTLAND: *I* feel that way!

*   *   *

LBJ: I honestly believe that the man I want is Fortas.

EASTLAND: Well, I'll cooperate. I doubt if you can get him. I think these Jewish organizations don't want a Jew Attorney General. I've heard that's the reason Ribicoff turned it down.[1]

LBJ: . . . If *you* cooperate, you can run your committee in the Senate, can't you?

EASTLAND: . . . I can't run it, but, . . . by God, I think you ought to get your own man for Attorney General now.[2]

LADY BIRD JOHNSON

Saturday, January 23, 1965, Tape-recorded Diary

> Johnson has been suddenly taken before dawn to Bethesda Naval Hospital, the same place he was rushed in 1955 with the heart attack that almost killed him. Striving to calm the public, Reedy announces that the President has a "bad cold" and tracheal inflammation. With LBJ's history of physical and emotional maladies when he is under political pressure, one must wonder whether the illness, coming so soon after the inauguration, has been aggravated by his painful awareness of the challenges he is about to face.[3] Johnson knows that he will have to make painful choices about the war in Vietnam, cope with civil rights demonstrations in the South, and pass Medicare and the other basic laws of the Great Society before the backlash he is certain will follow.[4] Lady Bird was at Camp David, resting after the inaugural events, when she was informed of her husband's hospitalization. She has talked to him by telephone.

LADY BIRD: He sounded rasping and hoarse and subdued, but not alarmed. . . . I was quite calm, not the least bit frightened, and thought maybe the Lord had laid

---

1. When approached about the possibility of being JFK's Attorney General, Abraham Ribicoff, Democratic Governor of Connecticut, had said he did not think a Jewish Attorney General should be putting black children into white Southern schools. (See Arthur Schlesinger, Jr., *A Thousand Days,* Houghton Mifflin, 1965, pp. 141–42.)

2. LBJ offered the job to Fortas, who refused. Fortas thought he was essential to his law firm, he worried that the experience of working so closely for Johnson might not be enjoyable, and he did not think he could live on a government salary. When Johnson and Fortas told Clifford that he must take the job, Clifford said he did not think that administering the Justice Department was a good use of his services. LBJ decided to give the job to Katzenbach. (Laura Kalman, *Abe Fortas,* Yale, 1990, pp. 230–32, and Clifford, *Counsel to the President,* pp. 438–40.)

3. See, for instance, Lady Bird's January 29, 1965, diary entry, below.

4. Johnson told his congressional liaison team in January 1965 that his 16-million-vote margin had already begun to slip away: "After a fight with Congress . . . I'll lose another couple of million. I could be down to 8 million in a couple of months." (Quoted in Dallek, *Flawed Giant,* p. 190.)

Lyndon low so he could get some rest. . . . My hair made me look like a poster girl for the poverty program, but I did the best I could with it, put on a hat and a smile, and drove up to the front door of Bethesda.[1] . . . I tried to look normal and walk swiftly. . . . Lyndon . . . looked just like Lyndon, lying in bed, quiet . . . I think somewhat sedated. . . . I didn't want to add an extra germ, so I just patted him and sat down and held his hand. . . . It could have been a frightening day.[2] It was a day I had expected and thought about.

LADY BIRD JOHNSON

Wednesday, January 27, 1965, Tape-recorded Diary

> Turned down by Abe Fortas and Clark Clifford, LBJ has told Nicholas Katzenbach, over drinks with their wives, that he will be Attorney General. Lady Bird fears that her husband has retained still another Kennedy holdover who may not be loyal to him.

LADY BIRD: [Katzenbach] is a Bobby Kennedy man from the beginning, and that will be a hard blow to some of the closest Johnson people. . . . I do not feel close to either one of them. We are poles apart.

HUBERT HUMPHREY

Thursday, January 28, 1965, 6:32 P.M.

> Already there are newspaper stories about LBJ's efforts to diminish his newly fledged Vice President. These are fed when Johnson's illness keeps him from attending Winston Churchill's funeral in London and he chooses Chief Justice Earl Warren, not Humphrey, to lead the American delegation.[3] "Whatever became of Hubert?" the political balladeer Tom Lehrer will sing. "Did Lyndon, recalling when he was VP, say, 'I'll do unto you as they did unto me'? Do you dream about staging a coup? Hubert, what happened to you?"
>
> With the full details of Johnson's illness concealed, Humphrey, next in the line of succession, feared that his boss might have secretly suffered another heart attack. White House aides told him simply to go about his business. "For Humphrey, it was an eye-opener," wrote his friend Dr. Edgar Berman. "He had no idea of the

---

1. Where there were many reporters and photographers.
2. Referring to the specter of another coronary.
3. Humphrey felt that the incident drove "a small wedge between Johnson and me," which was not ameliorated when LBJ later told him that he hoped HHH would not become the Administration's "number-one funeral attender." (Humphrey, *The Education of a Public Man*, Doubleday, 1976, p. 419.)

depth of LBJ's quirks, his irrational secretiveness, and his suspicions of disloyalty."[1] Now Humphrey calls the ailing Johnson, perhaps hoping for reassurance about his place in the President's circle. LBJ's voice has become almost a whisper.

HUMPHREY: I just wanted to let you know that I've been sure thinking about you all the time.
LBJ: Thank you, my friend. Thank you.
HUMPHREY: I haven't bothered you because I figured enough people were doing that.
LBJ: I've got a bad bug. I think that I'm going to get rid of it, but I still got it. . . . [*coughs painfully*]
HUMPHREY: . . . I've been talking to Jack [Valenti] and to Bill [Moyers] each day. Kind of keeping in touch with you. . . . You've got to watch it. . . . Just stay in there and stay good and warm, and don't work too hard. We'll all work a little extra for you!
LBJ: Okay, pardner.

LADY BIRD JOHNSON

Friday, January 29, 1965, Tape-recorded Diary

LADY BIRD: Lyndon still feels the washed-out, depressed way one does after a heavy dosage of antibiotics. . . . But he had dragged himself and gone to work. . . . This week's mood is not good. But how to fight it? I think by work, activity, as soon as Lyndon is once more physically able. It's sort of a slough of despond. . . . The "Valley of the Black Pig." The obstacles indeed are no shadows. They are real substance—Vietnam, the biggest. Walter [Jenkins]. The need of getting really superior people . . . and bringing them into the government. The carping of the press. . . . And someday we may really know a storm.

LADY BIRD JOHNSON

Sunday, January 31, 1965, Tape-recorded Diary

LADY BIRD: Lyndon spent most of the day in bed. . . . Such willingness to rest means he is not quite strong yet, not quite himself. . . . For a man of his temperament, it means you have time to worry. Work is his antidote to worry. . . . [Over dinner with friends] the conversation got around to George Reedy and the bad

---

1. Edgar Berman, *Hubert* (Putnam, 1979), pp. 91–92.

time the press is giving him. . . . Lyndon said, "They think a press secretary is there for them to rape." . . . We discussed Bobby Kennedy's relations with the press. Someone said he has the most instantaneously obedient portion of the press of anybody around town.

NICHOLAS KATZENBACH

Attorney General–designate
Monday, February 1, 1965, 4:12 P.M.

Katzenbach consults LBJ about the jailing of Martin Luther King, Jr., and hundreds of other civil rights marchers in Selma, Alabama.

KATZENBACH: That situation in Selma . . . got heated up today a little bit. King got himself arrested down there. You may have seen that on the ticker.
LBJ: No, I haven't.
KATZENBACH: Well, he got himself arrested, apparently for refusing to obey the police officer's order when he was holding a press conference. And there were about 260 Negroes arrested down there by the city authorities, who've been pretty decent, for parading without a permit. Then the sheriff,[1] who is a bad actor, arrested a bunch more. Some of them were schoolchildren. . . . Now John Doar[2] has been working on this, and he's been having some off-the-record discussions with the judges down there. . . . We . . . hope to get a court order on Wednesday from a fairly reluctant judge[3] . . . which would take some of the heat off the situation. . . . So I think we are going to have to ride with it for tomorrow until Wednesday.
LBJ: Okay.

NICHOLAS KATZENBACH

Friday, February 5, 1965, 3:00 P.M.

After King's jailing, his aide Andrew Young relayed three demands to the White House: Johnson must send a personal representative to Selma, declare his support for voting rights in Alabama, and take executive and congressional action to achieve those rights across the nation. But LBJ refused to make the strong statement that King was asking for. At a Tuesday morning press conference, while declaring that "all Americans should be indignant when one American is denied the

---

1. The soon-to-be-infamous Jim Clark.
2. Assistant Attorney General.
3. U.S. District Judge Daniel Thomas.

right to vote," he said that the problem in Selma was "the slow pace of voting registration for Negroes." The district judge ordered that Alabama's literacy test be suspended and that Selma speed up voter registration. After this talk with Katzenbach, King will post bond and leave jail. The next morning, the White House will announce that LBJ will send a voting rights bill to Congress before the end of 1965.

KATZENBACH: The demonstrations are still continuing down in Selma, despite that court order that we got yesterday. And about four hundred schoolkids were arrested just a little while ago for singing in front of the courthouse down there. John Doar is down there trying to work things out. . . . King is going to get out of jail, I think, later this afternoon. Doar will speak to him. He may be more reasonable. They've gotten about everything they wanted, but they're still demonstrating.

LBJ: Hmm.

KATZENBACH: And they've got these kids whipped up there, you know. They don't, I suppose, want to lose the momentum. They've lost their own judgment about it. King may be better. Maybe they'll calm down.

LBJ: I think that we ought to give a chance for the order to operate. . . . He ought to be told that "here's what I said yesterday, and that is about as strong as a man can say it.[1] . . . We've been in one court, and we'll be in others." This is what he asked for, and this is what he's got. And we expect some quid pro quos.[2] Tell him.

KATZENBACH: John will tell him, Mr. President. There's fifteen Congressmen down there now.[3] . . . Doar's got a meeting with them to try and get them to say a similar thing. . . . But these are all, you know, way on the liberal side. At least it's worth the effort. And it might even help.[4]

CYRUS VANCE

Sunday, February 7, 1965, 4:10 A.M.

The Vietcong have waged a surprise attack on South Vietnamese airfields and U.S. Army barracks in the market town of Pleiku, killing 8 and wounding 126 Americans. LBJ has retaliated with an American airstrike against three North Vietnamese targets, in concert with a South Vietnamese attack on a fourth. "Cowardice has gotten us into more wars than response has," Johnson told his ad-

---

1. At the press conference.
2. Johnson wanted King to relax his public pressure for an immediate voting rights bill.
3. To support the marchers.
4. On Tuesday, February 9, King called on LBJ at the White House and told reporters afterward that Johnson had said he would send a voting rights bill to Congress "very soon." (*Washington Post,* February 10, 1965.)

visers.[1] Now Vance interrupts the President's sleep to report on the mission. LBJ responds in a drowsy voice.

VANCE: "Many fires started in buildings. . . . Heavy [antiaircraft] fire observed from two gunboats on river north of complex." That's the only information so far, but apparently they did hit it pretty well.

LBJ: What is this heavy gunboat fire?

VANCE: That's A-A [antiaircraft] fire against our planes from two gunboats on the river. . . .

LBJ: . . . When we go in they start shooting on us?

VANCE: That's right, sir.

LBJ: I thought [they] didn't have much A-A equipment there.

VANCE: No A-A equipment on the ground of much substance, sir, but we expected some A-A fire. . . .

LBJ: . . . All right. You keep on calling me when you get anything.

CYRUS VANCE

Sunday, February 7, 1965, 4:55 A.M.

Vance reports that at least one American pilot has been downed over water.

VANCE: We know he ejected from his aircraft as it went down. . . . There is one other aircraft as yet unaccounted. . . .

LBJ: Means they've got two of them down then, probably, doesn't it?

VANCE: Probably. . . . Although the other one may not be down. He may have landed down at Danang . . . and we may not have picked him up yet. The tougher job will be getting that pilot out of the water who is fifteen miles off the shore.

CYRUS VANCE

Sunday, February 7, 1965, 5:10 A.M.

VANCE: Mr. President, all aircraft are now back safely accounted for, except for the one pilot down in the water.

LBJ: That's good news. . . . Now, when you get that boy back . . . no question but what we killed some people, you think?

---

1. Memorandum of White House meeting, February 6, 1965, in *FRUS*, vol. 2, pp. 158–60.

VANCE: I think no question about it. The in-flight report of the flight leader is that it was a successful strike. . . .

LBJ: Okay. That's good, Cy.

EMMERSON "MIKE" COOK

Lieutenant Colonel, Office of the White House Military Aide
Sunday, February 7, 1965, 8:51 P.M.

> After enduring a lecture from his doctor, George Burkley, for endangering his blood pressure by disrupting his sleep, LBJ gets a further report on the counterattack. Bad weather has prevented three targets from being struck.

COOK: We lost three U.S. aircraft. Recovered all of the pilots. Now, you remember the one we told you about that exploded on landing at Danang? The pilot was able to abandon the aircraft before it exploded, so he was saved. We have one aircraft unaccounted for at this time. . . .

LBJ: Gosh . . . that antiaircraft's better than we think it is, isn't it?

COOK: Yes, sir. Of course, one of these airplanes . . . flamed out. And a second one had mechanical failure. . . . There's one . . . that's unaccounted for. . . .

LBJ: Has he had time to get back?

COOK: Yes, sir. He should have been back well before now if he was going to make it back, but they haven't been able to locate him.

LBJ: And he would be the only human we've lost?

COOK: . . . That's correct, Mr. President.

LBJ: . . . Any substantial number of people in this target we hit?

COOK: I don't have that number, sir. I'll have to check and see if they have an estimate for us at the [Defense] Intelligence Agency.

LBJ: Okay. Much obliged.

LADY BIRD JOHNSON

Sunday, February 7, 1965, Tape-recorded Diary

LADY BIRD: In the night, we were waiting to hear how the attack had gone. It came at one o'clock, and two o'clock, and three, and again at five—the ring of the phone, the quick reach for it, and tense, quiet talk. . . . It was a tense and shadowed day, but we'll probably have to learn to live in the middle of it—for not hours or days, but years.

J. WILLIAM FULBRIGHT

Democratic Senator from Arkansas and Chairman,
Senate Foreign Relations Committee
Tuesday, February 9, 1965, 12:29 P.M.

> Johnson calls his proud, sensitive Senate friend to assure him that he did not deliberately exclude him from a White House meeting with congressional leaders on the counterattack in Vietnam. As Fulbright turns against Johnson's involvement in Vietnam, there will be few more friendly conversations like this.

LBJ: I see by the papers where you've been snubbed, and I wanted to assure you that somebody misinterpreted . . .

FULBRIGHT: They looked like they're determined to stir up trouble. Hell's bells! Doug[1] came over and explained it to me. They just asked me, . . . "Were you called down to the White House?" And I said no. . . .

LBJ: Well, I called your house, and you were not there. . . . It was something that we had to act on . . . right away . . .

FULBRIGHT: You don't need to explain. . . . Hell, I never feel snubbed! God damn it, I was so mad when I read that. . . .

LBJ: Well, I'd *love* to see you, if you've got any time. . . .

FULBRIGHT: Hell, anytime you say!

LBJ: . . . I'll send a car up there and get you, and you come right on down now. . . . I'm talking to the Governor of Puerto Rico now. . . . What entrance do you want [the driver] at, the Capitol entrance?

FULBRIGHT: I'm over at my office now. . . . Constitution and First. . . . I'll come right out that entrance on the southwest corner.

LBJ: It's where the two buildings meet nearest to the Capitol. . . . Okay.[2]

McGEORGE BUNDY

Wednesday, February 10, 1965, 10:06 A.M.

> While flying back from Saigon, Bundy wrote LBJ that "without new U.S. action," a Vietnam defeat "appears inevitable."[3] Johnson has been pondering Operation Rolling Thunder—systematic, regular American bombing of North Vietnam. But he has been wary of starting Rolling Thunder until the new Soviet Premier, Alexei Kosygin, ends a "friendship visit" to Hanoi. Now Bundy calls LBJ about a new Vietcong attack against the coastal city of Qui Nhon, causing more casualties than America has ever suffered in a single incident in Vietnam.

---

1. LBJ's aide Douglass Cater.
2. When Fulbright arrived, LBJ spent seventy minutes with him.
3. Bundy to Johnson, February 7, 1965, in LBJL.

BUNDY: Mr. President, we've had another bombing, as you may have heard.

LBJ: No.

BUNDY: A barracks in a town called Qui Nhon. . . . We don't yet have casualty reports, except twenty-one wounded. But the whole building collapsed, so the chances are there'll be something more.[1] . . . We probably ought to be very careful, [since] this is a U.S. barracks, to tie into this enterprise something Vietnamese, so that we don't get in a position that only white men get avenged. . . . McNamara and I feel very strongly about it. . . . There is an area in which we can perhaps tie them in. . . . There has been a resumption of attacks on the railroad in the South. The railroad in the North is an extremely easy target and a particularly . . . relevant one. We may . . . [recommend] that there be a retaliation that relates to the barracks and a retaliation relating to the railroad that would again be U.S. and GVN.[2] . . . [It is] well worth considering whether, within the next two or three nights, you might . . . want to do a full-dress account of this affair . . . coolly and directly to the American people.[3] . . .

LBJ: . . . I would tell Wheeler[4] to have his group . . . considering every possible angle. Not getting inflammatory or bombastic, but let's proceed—

BUNDY: Coolly.

LBJ: Coolly and thoroughly and promptly and adequately. . . . Wheeler ought to tell Westmoreland[5] right now to . . . tell his people and his carrier people—whoever he needs—to go on and start getting ready.

BUNDY: The preliminary instructions have already been issued by CINCPAC[6] and they're on alert.

LBJ: Then let's just get them to loading their stuff, and let's pick the targets and be sure we get [a] recommendation [from] all of our Joint Staff. . . . Where is Qui Nhon located? . . .

BUNDY: Northern part of South Vietnam, as I understand it.

LBJ: And it's strictly American?

BUNDY: This particular building was requisitioned for an aircraft maintenance detachment. . . .

LBJ: And what was it, mortar fire again?

BUNDY: No, it seems to have been a sabotage bomb, but they don't say for sure. . . . We heard about it about an hour ago, and you were on the phone.

LBJ: Well, call the other phone and just tell them to get the President when some-

---

1. Ultimately, twenty-three Americans were killed and more than twenty wounded.
2. Government of [South] Vietnam.
3. Meaning a television speech.
4. Earle Wheeler, Chairman, Joint Chiefs of Staff.
5. General William Westmoreland, Commander, Military Assistance Command, Vietnam.
6. General Ulysses S. Grant Sharp, Jr., was Commander-in-Chief in the Pacific.

thing like this happens. Let's don't wait an hour. I've got sergeants sitting out there all the time.

BUNDY: I could have done it. . . . I should have.

LBJ: Let's get them all ready, and let's go, if we can, today.

JOHN McCORMACK

Speaker of the House of Representatives
Wednesday, February 10, 1965, 10:25 A.M.

Johnson confidentially informs the House Speaker about the Qui Nhon attack.

LBJ: We've got between twenty, thirty dead—we don't know how many more—Americans, and we've got to meet right quick on targets.[1]

LADY BIRD JOHNSON

Wednesday, February 10, 1965, Tape-recorded Diary

LADY BIRD: More ominous news from Vietnam. An attack on barracks. . . . About six o'clock, cars began to drive in.[2] . . . Lyndon . . . is remaining curiously calm, but I know it must be at a price. . . . I emerged . . . to find the guests departed and McGeorge Bundy lingering with Lyndon. . . . He's one of the brightest men I've ever met. I suppose what I'm really looking for, for Lynda to marry, is a twenty-five-year-old McGeorge Bundy.

LADY BIRD JOHNSON

Thursday, February 11, 1965, Tape-recorded Diary

LADY BIRD: While Lyndon and Hubert were talking, I was rather startled to hear [Lyndon] say something that I had heard so often, but did not really expect to come out of his mouth in front of anyone else. "I'm not temperamentally equipped to be Commander-in-Chief," he said. They were talking about the crisis in Vietnam, the long nights with phone calls about planes going out . . . the necessity of giving orders that would produce God knows what cataclysmic results. He said, "I'm too sentimental to give the orders." Somehow I could not wish him *not* to hurt when he gives the orders.

---

1. For retaliatory attack.
2. For a briefing of congressional leaders on Vietnam by LBJ.

LADY BIRD JOHNSON

Sunday, February 14, 1965, Tape-recorded Diary

LADY BIRD: Lyndon's liking for [McNamara] is so evident that I almost fear that it might make other people gang up on him out of jealousy. He said, "If I got word that Bob had died or quit, I don't believe I could go on with this job."

DWIGHT D. EISENHOWER

Monday, February 15, 1965, 10:03 P.M.

> On February 13, Johnson gave the order to prepare the Rolling Thunder bombing campaign.[1] Anxious about upsetting the public or distracting Congress from his Great Society program, he has refused advice to deliver a major speech on this historic escalation of the Vietnam War. Now he calls the hero of World War II, in California.

LBJ: General, I want to visit with you in the next day or so on our problems out in Southeast Asia, and I just wondered what your schedule was. . . .
EISENHOWER: Well, of course, I could do anything.
LBJ: I don't want to put it up like we are in deep trouble, because I don't think it's reached that point. . . . I don't know whether you have anything you need to do back this way or not. But if you did . . . I could have a Jetstar pick you up. . . . I'm a little concerned about leaving the appearance that we've got an emergency or something.
EISENHOWER: I see. Well, I think I could manufacture something.
LBJ: Have you got anybody in New York that you need to talk to? . . .
EISENHOWER: I've always got a publisher up there, Mr. President.[2]
LBJ: Why don't you . . . come on down here and spend a day with me at the White House and let me say, for the public, that I understood that you were going to be in New York and I wanted to advise with you on general problems . . . so it doesn't look too dramatic, that we've got a real emergency. It's not that deep. But it's deep enough that I want to talk to you. I think that probably you could be more comforting to me now than anybody I know. . . . Why don't you come stay all night with me? I'll put you in Lincoln's bed.
EISENHOWER: [*chuckles*] Lincoln's bed? . . .

---

1. George Ball to Maxwell Taylor, February 13, 1965, *FRUS*, vol. 2, pp. 263–65.
2. Eisenhower was writing his memoirs for Doubleday.

LBJ: Well . . . I would love for you—I wish you would stay at the White House. I need you a little bit. I need a little Billy Graham these days. I need somebody. You know Sid is gone, and I called Milton a day or so ago, and he's gone out of the country.[1] . . . You come prepared to stay with me for a day or two. Don't be in a hurry, because I need you.

EMMERSON "MIKE" COOK

Monday, February 15, 1965, 10:16 P.M.

> Eager to keep Eisenhower on the reservation, Johnson takes personal command of logistics for his trip in a talk with Colonel Cook of the White House military aide's office.

LBJ: Send somebody that's really going to know how to take care of him. . . . I would like my Jetstar to pick him up because it doesn't attract too much attention. If you take the big *Air Force One*, I'm afraid it will get a lot of notoriety. . . . Tell Clifton[2] I tried to reach him, but he's out at some social engagement. These generals, you know.

COOK: [*laughs*] All right, sir.

LBJ: Tell him I haven't had my dinner yet. I'm working. But he and Bill Moyers and all these boys of mine—they're all out to a cocktail party!

COOK: All right, sir. . . . I'll go on out to Palm Springs and pick up General Eisenhower.

LBJ: . . . And give him the works. Be sure he's got the best food aboard, and every comfort in the world, and whoever he wants to bring.

HARRY TRUMAN

Monday, February 15, 1965, 10:35 P.M.

> Now Johnson calls the father of the American war in Korea. Despite LBJ's invitation, Truman's failing health will keep him at home, but he will issue a strong endorsement of Johnson's policies in Vietnam.

LBJ: How are you feeling?

TRUMAN: I'm feeling pretty good. How are you?

---

1. Characteristically LBJ cites two of the friends he and Eisenhower share—the late Texas oilman Sid Richardson and Eisenhower's beloved brother Milton, president of Johns Hopkins University.
2. LBJ's military aide, General Chester Clifton.

LBJ: Oh, I'm having hell.

TRUMAN: What's the trouble?

LBJ: Well, I got . . . a little bit with Indochina. The Vietnamese. . . . I just thought I'd call you and try to get a little advice and a little inspiration. I've been reading history and saw how much hell you had, and you handled it pretty good, and I just thought maybe I could learn something from you.

TRUMAN: I think you're handling it pretty good, too.

LBJ: No.

TRUMAN: . . . You know how to do it. And I know you *can* do it.

LBJ: I'm doing the best I can. My problem is kind of like what you had in Korea. I talked to Clark Clifford[1] today at lunch. We just looked back over what you did. . . . I got a letter I wrote you the day afterwards, when I was a young Senator, and I said I just think what you've done is wonderful and I wanted to tell you that I'm behind you in whatever you do.[2] That was before old Bob Taft got up on the floor and started raising hell about you ought to have had a resolution or something.[3]

TRUMAN: [*laughs*]

LBJ: I want to send you a copy of that letter tomorrow. . . . All I know to do out there is what I am doing. I think when they go in and kill your boys, you've got to hit back. And I'm not trying to spread the war and I'm not trying—

TRUMAN: You bet you have! You bust them in the nose every time you get a chance. And they understand that language better than any other kind.

LBJ: . . . And anytime you feel like it and can or want to, I would like to have you come up here and spend the night with me.

TRUMAN: All right, I'll see if I can't do that.

LBJ: You talk to Miss Bess,[4] and maybe you might come up over the weekend. . . . I'll just send a plane out for you and pick you up over the weekend, and you can all spend the weekend at the White House. We'll get Margaret and her husband down.[5] . . . You don't have to make any presentation. Don't have to raise any hell. We'll just go in there and we'll have a drink or two together, and then we'll go to church.

TRUMAN: . . . I haven't been feeling very well.

LBJ: . . . I don't want to tax you, but I always want you to know I need your counsel, and I love you.

---

1. Truman's first-term aide.

2. On June 28, 1950, the day after Truman announced the American response to the North Korean invasion, LBJ wrote him, "You have my most sincere prayers and my total confidence" (LBJL).

3. Senate Republican Leader Robert Taft of Ohio had vainly demanded that Truman seek a congressional resolution for his actions in Korea.

4. Mrs. Truman.

5. Truman's daughter and son-in-law, Margaret and Clifton Daniel.

TRUMAN: Well, that's mutual. And I'm glad to give you whatever experience I've had, although you know it as well as I do.

LBJ: No, I don't.

EVERETT DIRKSEN

Wednesday, February 17, 1965, 6:20 P.M.

> This morning Johnson has talked with Eisenhower for two and a half hours. Ike told LBJ that the time had come to shift from retaliatory strikes to a "campaign of pressure." If it took eight U.S. divisions to prevent a Communist takeover of South Vietnam, "so be it."[1] Now Johnson speaks with the Senate Republican Leader, who has just heard Democrats Frank Church of Idaho and George McGovern of South Dakota criticizing LBJ on the Senate floor.

DIRKSEN: I just listened to your friend and brother in the faith Mr. Church[2] tee off on your administration for forty-five minutes. And Mr. George McGovern of South Dakota did an hour teeing off on your Vietnamese policy. I thought you needed a little defense on the floor of the Senate, from your friend on the other side of the aisle.

LBJ: Good!

DIRKSEN: So, I wondered whether, after your session with Ike, you had anything that I needed to know before I did it.

LBJ: No, he was in hearty agreement with what we were doing. . . . The worst problem we have is not the ambushes. Is not the raids. Is not the accidents that occur to our own people. Really the worst problem that we have are the speeches that are made about negotiations.

DIRKSEN: You are right about that.

LBJ: And about pulling out. . . . The Communists take them and print them up in pamphlets, circularize them in newspapers. . . . We've had nine changes of government [in Saigon] because all of them are afraid we are going to pull out. Afraid we are going to negotiate. Now President Eisenhower said this morning, . . . "You don't negotiate until the other side must want to negotiate. . . . When you are dealing with these people, you must have a self-enforcing treaty. They do not keep their word, so whatever you agree on is of no value." . . . That we know, from Munich on, that when you give, the dictators feed on raw meat. If they take South Vietnam, they take Thailand, they take Indonesia, they take Burma, they come

---

1. Robert S. McNamara, *In Retrospect* (Times Books, 1996), pp. 172–73.
2. Dirksen loved to use such acid sarcasm, knowing that LBJ disdained Church as a maverick.

right on back to the Philippines.[1] . . . The Communists take our speeches and they quote what Mansfield says or what Church says or what de Gaulle says, what McGovern says, and they think that's the government of the United States.[2] . . . [Eisenhower] would do everything he could with the CIA to create better morale and, if necessary, to almost buy it with that government. . . . He said, "You must push South Vietnamese participation. You've got to put your own boys with them." . . . [He] said when they go on a raid like they went on the other night,[3] . . . each one of those men come back and they tell their families about what they did, instead of what the Americans did. And that makes them want to fight. . . . We've killed sixteen thousand Vietcong and we've lost about seventy-five hundred Vietnamese [during] this last twelve months. . . . And we've lost between a hundred and two hundred Americans. That's about what you lost in the airplane crash in New York the other day.[4]

DIRKSEN: Yeah.

LBJ: He says . . . he would make it clear that we are going to stay. . . . He thinks that I ought to just be guarded in my statements and "not let some damn columnist needle you." . . . He says, "You've got to let Russians and the Chi-Coms[5] know that you are not wanting to fight them. You just want to protect these folks that are in South Vietnam." . . . He says it may take a long time. . . . Thinks we are in there a long time. He said we had a long time in Korea. . . . When he came in as President, they had been negotiating in Korea for a year and a half. But we had agreed there that we wouldn't cross a certain area. And we had agreed there that we would use only a small type of weapon. And he said that they knew that if we didn't go across a certain area, and if we would only use a small type of weapon, that we never could have any settlement because we'd tied our hands.[6]

DIRKSEN: Uh-huh.

LBJ: So he said the first thing he did was call up Nehru[7] because he knew Nehru was a leak. He told Nehru that . . . if they didn't settle . . . he wasn't going to be bound by any sanctuaries . . . and he wasn't going to be bound by any weapons.[8] He said, "We made a hell of a lot of weapons. We spent a lot of money on them.

---

1. In short, the domino theory.

2. Senate Majority Leader Mike Mansfield of Montana and French President Charles de Gaulle were also skeptical of American plans to escalate the war.

3. The retaliation for Pleiku.

4. On February 8, an Eastern Air Lines DC-7 had crashed off Jones Beach, New York, killing eighty-four people.

5. Chinese Communists.

6. Truman had limited the battle area in Korea and refrained from using nuclear weapons.

7. The neutralist Indian Prime Minister, Jawaharlal Nehru.

8. Rather than via a telephone call, this message actually was transmitted by Secretary of State John Foster Dulles during a May 22, 1953, talk with Nehru. (See Dulles memorandum of conversation in *Foreign Relations of the United States; 1952–1954: Korea*, U.S. Government Printing Office, 1984, p. 1071.)

What the hell we make them for if we don't ever use them if we have to?'" He said he never intended to do anything except let that get back to them. . . . Then they came in wanting to negotiate with *him*.[1] . . .

DIRKSEN: Yeah.

LBJ: . . . Now, he said, . . . "These fellows just ought to quit talking about negotiating. . . . We have said a hundred times everywhere that if they will just get out of the country, why, we'll get out and we'll leave it alone. But they won't do that. They want a revolution." . . .

DIRKSEN: Yeah.

LBJ: . . . Mansfield[2] said he'd support us, but . . . his heart's not in this thing, as you know. Humphrey feels as we do. Every member of the Joint Chiefs . . . Taylor, Westmoreland . . . Rusk, Ball, and Harriman,[3] . . . McNamara and Vance. We're all agreed on a course of action. We do not want to go further than to say that we will continue, but . . . these actions will be measured and fitting. . . . Any day they want to keep their '54 agreement[4]— There's no use of making a new one if they don't keep the one they got. They made one in Laos in '62[5]—they are not keeping it. . . . Why do you think they would keep one in '65 when they wouldn't keep one in '62? . . . They don't *have* to have an agreement. They've just got to stay across that line.[6] And if *they* stay across it, *we'll* stay across it. But they can't come bomb *us*, kill *our* people, and expect us to go in a *cave!*

McGEORGE BUNDY

Thursday, February 18, 1965, Morning

> Johnson complains to Bundy about a speech by Hubert Humphrey in New York raising the possibility of negotiations over Vietnam. The Vice President has privately written Johnson that by escalating the war he might be making "the most fateful decisions of [his] administration." LBJ must make "a cogent, convincing case" to the American people "if we are to enjoy sustained public support."[7] Humphrey later recalled that Johnson's response to his letter was to throw him into

---

1. Meaning the North Koreans.
2. Johnson's party leader in the Senate.
3. Actually George Ball had already begun to voice his skepticism about the American commitment to Saigon.
4. The 1954 Geneva agreement on Indochina divided Vietnam at the seventeenth parallel, demanded general elections to unify Vietnam, and banned the introduction of foreign troops and arms.
5. The 1962 Geneva agreement on Laos called for a peaceful, neutral, independent, democratic Laos and removal of foreign military units.
6. The seventeenth parallel, separating North from South Vietnam.
7. Humphrey to Johnson, February 15, 1965, in LBJL.

"limbo" and keep him out of Vietnam discussions until he agreed to adopt the official line.[1]

LBJ: Get old Hubert to clear very carefully what he said in New York with you.
BUNDY: He did.
LBJ: I see he's got a good deal of negotiation in it. . . . I don't want anybody, while I'm President, talking about it until we have some indication that some of them[2] *might* be willing to. That's the first essential of a negotiation. [*reading from* Baltimore Sun:] "His remarks obviously have been cleared in advance with President Johnson. Thus it signals an American diplomatic offensive." . . . I would just as soon he stay out of the peacekeeping and negotiating field at this point. So let's just watch him very carefully.
BUNDY: I will.
LBJ: I told him the other day, . . . "You're really the last man to get into the atomic field"—because he's regarded as pretty liberal—"and if I were you, I would try to stay on some of these subjects that you're dealing with and not get into negotiating." Now, I just really feel very deeply that—God, I want to negotiate more than any man in the world! I'll *guarantee* you that.
BUNDY: I'll bet.
LBJ: But I don't think my wanting to negotiate is necessarily the best way to win the girl.
BUNDY: Exactly.

*   *   *

LBJ: We ought to set up today some way for Rusk or you to try to sit down with McGovern, who's supposed to be an administration man . . . [but] who's taking his cues from Church.[3] Now, neither one of them really fought in many wars,[4] and neither one of them are really outstanding experts in this field. But they ought to be told . . . that the thing that hurts us most is not the hitting our compound or blowing up our hotels. [It's] these goddamned speeches that the Communists blow up that show that we are about to pull out. . . . They're injuring a hell of a lot of people. . . .

---

1. Humphrey, *The Education of a Public Man,* pp. 325–29. In an unpublished draft of his presidential memoirs, LBJ insisted that Humphrey had "no serious disagreements" with him on Vietnam: "Only in the desperation of his own Presidential campaign did he disappoint me—and, more importantly, foreclose his chance of ever occupying the White House. . . . In the fall of 1968, his advisors persuaded him that the only way he could be President was to picture himself as a dissenter from the cause. Incredibly enough, he tried to do just that, in a speech in Salt Lake City. . . . It was not his best hour. He endeavored to convince me that what he was saying represented no change in his policy. But I was not fooled. Neither, I think, were the American people. I will always be convinced that that Utah speech cost Hubert the White House." (Unpublished draft of *The Vantage Point,* LBJL, courtesy of the LBJ Foundation.)
2. The North Vietnamese.
3. Senators George McGovern and Frank Church.
4. In fact, McGovern was a genuine World War II hero, flying three dozen combat missions.

BUNDY: We're supposed to have a meeting with Hubert to talk with him as soon as he gets back.

LBJ: Hubert just talks and keeps the ball in the air and jumps around. . . . I would ask [McGovern and Church] to your office . . . and . . . say, . . . "I have just returned [from Saigon] . . . and one of the biggest problems we have is stability in [the South Vietnamese] government." We've had nine of them,[1] and the thing that causes them to just pee in their pants is to read a speech by Morse[2] saying . . . we ought to run out—or [by] Mansfield. . . . Let them know that there is no greater disservice that they can render. Then if they want to do it, then they are on their own.[3] . . . [Tell Mansfield that the President] "wants peace more than you do. . . . He's the poor bastard that stays awake every night on these things. He's the guy that sends these men to die! But he doesn't know how he can negotiate with a fellow that doesn't *want* to negotiate. He doesn't think he would go out to Phoenix to negotiate much with Mr. Goldwater. . . . They've been winning." . . .

BUNDY: Uh-huh. We'll do it.

LBJ: And let Hubert attend your meeting. . . . Any other news from out there that's worthy?

BUNDY: It's quiet. The actual body count in the last couple of days is favorable. The VC[4] have not done anything violent. Khanh[5] is in a great hurry to go bombing. We had to hold him off today. He wanted to bomb a bridge that Ho Chi Minh[6] is supposed to be dedicating tomorrow. . . . There is some disadvantage in going to the UN. U Thant[7] himself has recommended to Stevenson[8] against the Security Council as the place for us to make our case because he says that'll just make the Russians act as lawyers for the defense. I'm going to try to get Stevenson to say so.

LBJ: That's right. And [Stevenson should] quit going around here saying, "I thought all along we ought to be negotiating."[9]

BUNDY: I know it, Mr. President. Did you see my memo on Lippmann?[10]

LBJ: Yeah . . . If they came across the line from the other side and fired at our compound, he would want us to say, "Thank you."

BUNDY: . . . He hates force. . . . He said, . . . "This is not Korea. These people

1. Regimes in Saigon.
2. Senator Wayne Morse, Democrat of Oregon.
3. In other words, that Johnson will cut them off.
4. Vietcong.
5. Nguyen Khanh, now chairman of the South Vietnamese armed forces council.
6. The North Vietnamese President and patriarch.
7. The United Nations Secretary-General.
8. Adlai Stevenson, LBJ's Ambassador to the UN.
9. Johnson is annoyed at Stevenson's dovishness on Vietnam.
10. The columnist Walter Lippmann, whom Bundy had been courting on behalf of LBJ's Vietnam policy.

have not come across the line." And I said, . . . "That's just the problem—that they *have* come across the line."

LBJ: I'd show him the staging area and show him the camp. Say they hit our barracks.

BUNDY: He admits that that happened, but he thinks that the South has no support and the government has no strength. . . . Rusk makes a statement over the weekend.

LBJ: I think our [statements] a great deal of the time hem us in[1] and—

BUNDY: Can be dangerous.

LBJ: —tie us down. . . . Every newspaperman wants you to say anything you'll say because the more you talk, the more he's got. . . . Look at McNamara's statements about we are bringing back the security guards.[2] . . .

BUNDY: And then we send out our battalion. We get in trouble.

LBJ: And that we are going to be out of there in '65.[3] . . . Some of my statements may look just as bad. . . . We ought to make available to the press everything that we can in the national interest that doesn't injure Taylor and Westmoreland and conduct of the war.[4] I don't think it necessarily has to be done by the President. . . . It ought to be done by McNamara and Rusk. They're all expendable. I think that when your President goes down to the brink, everybody goes down. I don't agree that we've got to let Doug Kiker or Rowland Evans[5] direct our activities. I'm a little afraid of their judgments in these things. . . . I hope that you keep those minutes.[6] I'm not quite sure what Mansfield's position finally was.[7] . . . He said, "Mr. President, I feel that this is a very dangerous and undesirable adventure. But in light of what everybody said here tonight, I will support it." . . .

BUNDY: Let me check my notes.

LBJ: But I think it's pretty important to view the Stevensons and the dissents—the McCones,[8] anybody that might get offboard later—very carefully so we don't get a government that's divided. That's the great danger we face here. Yesterday we had three or four Senators speaking against us. . . . Symington[9] was worried and Church was worried and McGovern was worried. . . . Dirksen calls up and he

---

1. LBJ shows his prejudice in favor of saying as little as possible about the escalation in Vietnam.

2. General Westmoreland was requesting two Marine battalions for Danang—U.S. ground troops to protect airfields from which Rolling Thunder would be launched.

3. Johnson here concedes his and McNamara's public misstatements about Vietnam.

4. To Johnson's mind, public information that does not injure conduct of the war may not be a large amount.

5. The *New York Herald Tribune* reporter and the syndicated columnist, respectively.

6. Of meetings with congressional leaders. LBJ wants to protect himself from later criticism, which is also one of the reasons he secretly tapes conversations like this one.

7. Mansfield attended White House meetings on Vietnam on February 6 and 7. The next day he wrote LBJ to urge against expanding the war. (See letter in LBJL, February 8, 1965.)

8. CIA Director John McCone.

9. Democratic Senator Stuart Symington of Missouri.

loves that. He's siccing them to attack us.[1] . . . So he can do what I did with Eisenhower.[2]

BUNDY: Good tactics.

LBJ: And he's my leader like I was Eisenhower's.[3] . . . He's taking advantage of Burton Wheeler's[4] influence on Mike, and he's using it for all it's worth. He called me last night. He's very pleased. . . . I would point . . . out to these boys . . . that Burt Wheeler and Gerald Nye[5] and a few of them had their own views on World War II. And that we have some of that influence still hanging on now, and Dirksen is making the most of it. Although Dirksen has flipped 180 degrees. He used to be the biggest isolationist. He's like Vandenberg.[6]

DEAN RUSK

Thursday, February 18, 1965, Probably 11:46 A.M.[7]

> Johnson's Secretary of State suggests a UN gambit that might keep the Soviets from siding firmly with the North Vietnamese and Chinese against the South.

RUSK: What would you think of my having a word with David Harlech[8] about the British saying to the Russians, "Why don't we as cochairmen[9] find out from all the governments involved what they think about this Southeast Asia situation?" . . . It might just possibly . . . keep the Russians in the position of a middleman, rather than as an advocate of Hanoi and Peiping. . . .

LBJ: . . . Would the others be so substantial a majority to make us look bad?

RUSK: No, I don't think so. . . . We'd have the British, we'd have ourselves, we'd have . . . some help from the Canadians. . . .

LBJ: . . . I don't believe the Canadians help us any, but you can try it.

---

1. See Dirksen conversation, February 17, 1965, above.
2. LBJ thinks that the Machiavellian Dirksen is provoking Church, McGovern, and other Democratic Senators to attack Johnson so that Dirksen can rise above them as a bipartisan figure, just as LBJ did as Majority Leader in the 1950s.
3. LBJ refers to his across-the-aisle support of most of Eisenhower's foreign policy.
4. Mansfield's fellow Montanan, the late pre–World War II isolationist Senator Burton Wheeler.
5. North Dakota Republican Senator Gerald Nye was a leader of the pre–World War II isolationists.
6. The late Michigan Republican Senator Arthur Vandenberg, whose transformation into an internationalist helped to form Truman's bipartisan post–World War II foreign policy.
7. LBJ Library records do not establish the time of this call for certain.
8. Lord Harlech, British Ambassador to the United States.
9. Of the UN Security Council.

ABE FEINBERG

Chairman, Kayser-Roth Corporation, and Democratic Fund-raiser
Saturday, February 20, 1965, 11:00 A.M.

> Like the Israeli Prime Minister, Levi Eshkol, Feinberg, a large New York donor to the Democratic party and Israeli causes, is upset by Johnson's plans to send planes and tanks to Jordan. LBJ warns him that cutting military aid to Jordan will jeopardize aid to Israel—and he does not wish to take the blame.

FEINBERG: The way [for you to hear the Israeli] voice loud and clear is for you to see someone whom the Prime Minister would send over. I would imagine it would be Golda.[1] . . .

LBJ: . . . That would be about the worst thing that could happen. We would excite the whole world. . . . I can't imagine her getting in to see the President . . . without it circularizing. . . . If the Israel friends in this country want to substitute their judgment about the consequences of Soviet planes[2] [for mine] . . . I'll be perfectly willing. I don't [enjoy being] a munitions maker. . . . I think Ben-Gurion attacking Eshkol on this German tank deal is just an awful thing for everybody. . . . We did unquestionably ask this poor man[3] to send those tanks. We kind of forced him to do it. And . . . his government is going to fall because of a fight they got in among themselves over there. . . . Now . . . I'm friendly to [the Israelis] and I want to help them. . . . If they really . . . feel that we oughtn't to sell these planes to Jordan . . . we won't do it. . . . I'm telling Harriman[4] to tell the Prime Minister that. . . .

FEINBERG: You mean the Prime Minister of Israel?

LBJ: Yeah. Now . . . our judgment is we oughtn't to let this little King[5] go down the river. He's got a million and a half people, and he only controls a third of them. Two-thirds are against him. But he is the only voice that will stand up [against the Soviets] there. If you want to . . . have a complete Soviet bloc, why we'll just *have* to. . . . We'll have to get out of supplying Jordan with money. . . . When that story comes out, it will be on the whole hundred million that goes to Jordan and Israel, too.[6] . . . But I'm not prepared to take on the *New York Times* and Mike Feldman.[7]

---

1. Israeli Foreign Minister Golda Meir.

2. Namely, that the Jordanians will get their planes from Moscow if not from Washington.

3. Johnson refers to former Israeli Prime Minister David Ben Gurion. At LBJ's insistence, West German Chancellor Ludwig Erhard had authorized the sale of U.S.-made tanks to Israel, as part of the American effort to ensure the Arab-Israeli balance of power and—covertly—prevent Israel from developing nuclear weapons. (See *Foreign Relations of the United States, 1964–1968: Arab-Israeli Dispute,* vol. 18, U.S. Government Printing Office, 2001.)

4. Under Secretary of State for Political Affairs Averell Harriman.

5. King Hussein of Jordan.

6. LBJ subtly threatens that aid to Israel will also come under scrutiny.

7. LBJ refers to the *New York Times* editorial page, which he presumes to be pro-Israeli, and his former White House counsel Myer Feldman, a Kennedy holdover who was staunchly pro-Israel.

FEINBERG: [laughs]

LBJ: . . . If we get out, then we've just got to say that . . . we are not going to supply arms to one side or the other. . . . Only reason I'm helping Jordan is on account of Israel. Now if Israel considers them their enemy and not of help, then we just wasted six hundred million.[1]

*   *   *

LBJ: My judgment is . . . that this little King has some value to us, and that we ought to keep him as far away from the Soviet [Union] and Nasser[2] as we can. . . . If [the Israelis] don't, we'll just pull out. We won't sell him a damn thing. But we want it to be clear it's their decision, and we want to be clear we are doing it so that we can *satisfy* the Jews and not *irritate* them. . . . Therefore, if you want to underwrite that, why . . . we'll tell the Congress next week that we can just delete the money for Jordan. . . . We think down the line Israel will be coming back and saying, "Now, wait a minute, we've played hell."

*   *   *

LBJ: We're going to let you write the decision, but we want your name signed on it, and we want your people signed on it. [I] don't want it laid onto a man from Johnson City.[3] . . . If anybody is [pro-Israel], I am. . . . When [the Israelis] were in *real* problems [during the Suez War] and they were getting ready to impose sanctions . . . I stopped it. But . . . I'm not going to . . . have one of them leak it on me that I want to join up with the Arabs.

FEINBERG: I gather that . . . you think that Golda's visit here would be—

LBJ: . . . I think that the Arabs would say, "Good God, what's Johnson doing here?" . . . The Jews would all start sending telegrams. Jim Novy[4] would have me on the phone from Austin in five minutes. . . . What I want is I want Eshkol to tell me what he wants to do, and I don't want him to just tell me. I want him to tell the people over here what he wants to do. . . . Now I cannot imagine any Jew in America getting mad at me for saying, "Mr. Prime Minister, you write the ticket."

*   *   *

LBJ: [changing subject:] Whatever happened . . . on our New York matter that you were going to talk to the Senator about?[5]

FEINBERG: . . . He said he has no feeling of feud. Has . . . no ill feeling. And it was, I would say, an attempt to be as friendly as he can be. It's very tough for him

---

1. Dollars in American aid to Jordan.

2. The pro-Soviet Egyptian President, Gamal Abdel Nasser.

3. Johnson wants the blame placed on American Jews, not him, as a man from an American region with few conspicuous historic sympathies for Israel or Jews.

4. An old Jewish supporter of Johnson's in Austin.

5. LBJ had asked Feinberg to pass Robert Kennedy a confidential message saying that he wanted to patch up their differences.

to be friendly . . . with anybody. . . . I think he would like to make peace, but he finds it hard in his craw to make any overtures.

SITUATION ROOM

Monday, February 22, 1965, 7:41 A.M.

> Johnson calls for information on new turmoil within the Saigon government. The CIA has cabled from Saigon that General Khanh has been "resisting his ouster" as Commander-in-Chief, that his military supporters have seized the Tonsonhut air base, and that it is "far from certain how much actual support Khanh might secure in a showdown."[1]

LBJ: What do you have this morning on Khanh?
DUTY OFFICER: . . . Khanh has evidently given up on any hope of maintaining any power within the government. Everything else seems to be quiet in Saigon. There have been no incidents last evening which involved any U.S. personnel, any injuries, or any damage to any of our installations over there, sir.
LBJ: Okay, thank you.[2]

ROBERT McNAMARA

Monday, February 22, 1965, 8:48 A.M.

> Before going up to Capitol Hill to defend their Vietnam policy, the Secretary of Defense asks LBJ to execute the start of systematic air attacks against North Vietnam. Johnson shows his belief that the Gulf of Tonkin Resolution, passed in August 1964, provides him with almost open-ended authority to make war in Indochina.

McNAMARA: I wanted to check on the advantages and disadvantages of a strike on [February] twenty-third, Saigon time. . . . Dean [Rusk] tells me that the Soviets are considering the British proposal[3] and have not given an answer yet. . . . Max[4] [proposes] . . . we plan it for the twenty-fourth, and that would be my recommendation. If it's agreeable with you, we'll go ahead on that. . . .
LBJ: What about the Soviets moving these antiaircraft stuff in?
McNAMARA: . . . I don't believe the capability will develop quickly . . . unless they send their own people to man it. . . .
LBJ: . . . What'll we do, just ride the day and do nothing?
McNAMARA: I'd ride the day, Mr. President. There will be time tomorrow

---

1. CIA to White House, February 21, 1965, in *FRUS*, vol. 2, pp. 345–46.
2. On February 23, Ambassador Taylor cabled Washington that "Khanh, the troublemaker," was "removed from the scene." (Taylor to State Department, in *FRUS*, vol. 2, pp. 349–50.)
3. Mentioned in the LBJ-Rusk conversation above.
4. Ambassador Maxwell Taylor in Saigon.

morning for you to decide to go ahead on the twenty-fourth, Saigon time, if you choose to do so.

LBJ: All right. [Will] you run into a lot of questions on the Hill?

McNAMARA: I don't think so. I spent all morning . . . Friday . . . on Vietnam. . . .

LBJ: Bob, I think if you do run into any questions, you ought to say when we went into Korea, there was some question about the Congress not expressing themselves. . . . And for that reason, last summer . . . we asked the Congress for a resolution.[1] . . . The strong word in it is "approve" deterring the aggressor and fighting the aggressor . . . on any attempts that he makes on our armed services or on South Vietnam.[2] And they passed it 502 to 2. Now, if anybody wants to see what our policy is, as expressed by the Congress . . . here it is. . . . And here's the statement[3] that transmitted it.

McNAMARA: You used that so effectively Thursday night[4] that . . . I'm going to carry it with me to all the hearings hereafter. . . .

LBJ: I read it last night again . . . and all the statements [we made] at the time. We all said, "We are not trying to seek any wider war, but here is what the Congress says." Now, anytime anybody asks me . . . I would say, now, the Commander-in-Chief has certain inherent powers as Commander-in-Chief, but it so happens in this instance that Congress has expressed theirself very definitely. And here's what it has *said. Period.*

DEAN RUSK

Thursday, February 25, 1965, 9:28 A.M.

The Secretary of State reports that his UN efforts have failed.

RUSK: I finally reached U Thant. . . . He evaded and . . . didn't give very much. . . . He seemed to go back to the business of back last summer that Hanoi was prepared to talk to us. . . . I thought that I would ask Charlie Yost[5] to . . . make the following points. . . . We don't see any . . . indication that Hanoi or Peiping is interested in discussing a peaceful settlement in Vietnam on a realistic basis. There

---

1. The Gulf of Tonkin Resolution.

2. The resolution actually said that Congress "approves and supports" the President's determination to "take all necessary measures to repel any armed attack" against American forces, to "prevent further aggression," and to assist Southeast Asian states linked to the United States by defense treaty.

3. LBJ's August 5, 1964, statement to Congress asking for the resolution.

4. At a National Security Council meeting, at which LBJ said his one objective was "to save South Vietnam" (February 18, 1965, in *FRUS*, vol. 2, pp. 325–27).

5. Stevenson's deputy at the United Nations.

is no possibility of negotiations . . . that would leave South Vietnam the victim of aggression. . . . There has to be some indication that there's a reasonable possibility of success before any negotiation is worthwhile. . . . We are not looking for . . . a face-saver to cover a dignified withdrawal. We are looking for the safety of more than one hundred smaller countries that shouldn't be left to the mercy of big neighbors. . . .

LBJ: . . . I think it ought to be more affirmative. . . . Just start out by saying that many times during the recent years . . . the Presidents [of the United States] had repeatedly stated that if they would leave their neighbors alone, we would be out of there the next morning. . . . That you do think it's a mistake to mislead the world and to get people's hopes up . . . only to have the balloon pop in their face, and then to go to evils we know not of.

BROMLEY SMITH

Executive Secretary, National Security Council
Thursday, February 25, 1965, Time uncertain

> Johnson starts his recording device in midconversation as Smith makes final arrangements for the sustained bombing campaign against North Vietnam.

SMITH: —give you the final sign-off from his side on Rolling Thunder?
LBJ: Yeah, we said we would go ahead. . . . They're sending out the order.
SMITH: Very good. I'll tell Ambassador Taylor then that it's all right for him to talk to the [South] Vietnamese about it.
LBJ: Yeah.

DEAN RUSK

Thursday, February 25, 1965, 10:25 A.M.

> The previous day, the U.S. Embassy in Saigon revealed that for the first time B-57 and F-100 jet bombers have been used against the Vietcong. Johnson is worried that this news will alarm the American public.

LBJ: I want to be very careful that we don't show that we are desperate and dramatic and we are changing our policy. All of TV now is trying to say that this is a [large] escalation, and that the B-57s yesterday are an entirely new policy. I've made clear to the people I've talked to . . . that [there is a] congressional resolution.[1] . . . It says that we will reply to any attacks and we will deter any aggression. . . .

RUSK: Right.

LBJ: Now, when we could deter it with helicopters, we did. When we could deter it with shots from the Vietnamese troops, we do it. When we could prevent aggression with Pathfinders and sending one of our planes in to lead their planes with their Air Force, we did. . . . As [the Vietcong] stepped up and . . . tied down our Ranger companies, we did not change our policy. We changed our equipment. Because they escalated. They brought in the ships with all the guns, and they brought in a lot more people. The infiltration increased, and they had their staging areas, and we had Ranger companies tied down there, and it's going to cost hundreds of thousands of Vietnamese lives.

RUSK: Right.

LBJ: So, at the request of the South Vietnamese government, we busted them up and released those people and saved their lives with the B-57s. Now, it is true that this is probably the first time that B-57s have been used in South Vietnam. But the Congress authorized and directed us to prevent aggression. We have not changed our policy. . . . That resolution is our policy. That is our authority. And until it's repealed . . . that's the policy of this government. And we're within it. . . .

RUSK: Right.

LBJ: . . . What they're going to try to put in our lap is that we're the warmongers and that . . . we've really got no policy at all. . . . Now that's the commentators' line. I think this is the answer to it. And I would keep those 502 Congressmen right chained to me all the time with that resolution. . . . Our policy . . . [is], namely, keep our agreements. Which they have not done. They've abandoned all of theirs. . . . Help these people help themselves. . . . And . . . if they will leave their neighbors alone, we'll come home tomorrow offering peace.

ROBERT McNAMARA

Friday, February 26, 1965, 9:10 A.M.

> While informing LBJ that he is trying to launch Rolling Thunder, the Defense Secretary endorses General Westmoreland's plea to bring U.S. ground forces to South Vietnam to protect the lives of Americans at the Danang air base.

McNAMARA: We have rescheduled the strike for tonight. The weather outlook is still bad. Whether it will come off or not, we don't know. The commanders from

---

1. The Gulf of Tonkin Resolution.

the field are in with unanimous recommendations that we move a portion of a Marine Expeditionary Brigade into Danang to provide protection there. The build-up of Vietcong forces in the surrounding area is fairly substantial. They're fearful that the huge number of aircraft we have in Danang and the personnel are subject to attack. This is a recommendation that I would be very reluctant to accept. But frankly I doubt we have any alternative. . . .

LBJ: . . . Maybe you ought to bring [in] some of your military people. . . . I'm afraid they are going to feel left out.

McNAMARA: I don't think they feel that yet, Mr. President. I'm sure that Bus[1] feels completely integrated in the discussions—and the other [Joint] Chiefs as well. . . .

LBJ: I would just bring them all. . . . Just tell Marvin Watson[2] whatever time is convenient. . . . I think that we ought to try to figure out what we can do. Now we're off to bombing these people. We're over that hurdle. I don't think anything is going to be as bad as losing, and I don't see any way of winning. But I would sure want to feel that every person that had an idea—that his suggestion was fully explored. And I do think that this bombing in South Vietnam has added something. . . . I don't guess there's any way, Bob, that through your small planes or helicopters . . . you could spot these people and then radio back and let the planes come in and bomb the hell out of them.

McNAMARA: This is what we are trying to do, but it's very difficult when they're under the trees. . . . The problem is to spot them and find them. In certain instances, our jets are of no use whatsoever on small, open targets. But on large concentrations and under foliage or something of that kind, the jets are extremely helpful.

LBJ: Are we watching that coastline? Shouldn't we have every damn admiral that we've got that wants some practice, and all these commanders on destroyers, see if we can't find some more of these ships every hundred yards?

McNAMARA: . . . If necessary, we'll use U.S. destroyers.

LBJ: I'd just give enough of these boys . . . ribbons to put all these damn destroyers you've got all over the world out there where you could see them. . . .

McNAMARA: The problem that the Navy is struggling with is whether the destroyer could get in close enough in those shallow waters to stop a ship of this kind, if it's camouflaged and just going down in the bays very close to land. The probability is the Navy couldn't handle it that way, and we have to depend upon this junk fleet that's been set up there. But in any case, we all agree we're going to have to try to tighten up the shore patrol.

LBJ: Maybe we ought to put more helicopters in and patrol them regularly.

---

1. General Earle Wheeler, Chairman of the Joint Chiefs.
2. Special Assistant to the President.

Maybe we ought to put some more PT boats of our own in. . . . And try to figure out any way you can to get some of your people to think of the things we're not doing. We know what we're doing and we see the results. The game now is in the fourth quarter, and it's about seventy-eight to nothing. We've got to try to rescue something. . . . I believe last night was the best meeting we had.[1] . . . It may be that these congressional-senatorial meetings are the only thing that's saving us up on the Hill.

McNAMARA: I think they are. I thought again you were terrific, Mr. President. You really laid it out to them in a way that they felt you were forthcoming and made the problem clear to them. . . .

LBJ: Now, you tell Bus Wheeler to get his Chiefs in. And get somebody to come up with what we can actually do to keep them[2] from splitting up the country. . . . I'm scared to death of putting ground forces in, but I'm *more* frightened about losing a bunch of planes from lack of security.

ROBERT McNAMARA

Monday, March 1, 1965, 10:46 A.M.

> Johnson gives his Defense Secretary the final command to launch Operation Rolling Thunder, which will begin the next day. More than a hundred U.S. aircraft will strike a North Vietnamese ammunitions depot and naval base. Rolling Thunder will roar on for three years, dropping more bombs on the North than were dropped on all of Europe in World War II.[3] To Johnson's outrage, the *New York Times* has reported this morning that the "highest" U.S. officials in Saigon are saying LBJ "has decided to open a continuing, limited air war" in Vietnam.

McNAMARA: Mr. President, I talked to Dean [Rusk] this morning and Bus Wheeler about this strike. . . . My recommendation and Dean's is that we authorize them to go ahead tonight, if they can hit the primary targets. . . .

LBJ: . . . Will that stir up the doves?[4]

McNAMARA: Dean was inclined to think . . . it would be unwise to go on [March] first. That would stir up the Russians and push them closer to the Chinese. But Dean believed it would be wise to go before the end of their meeting.[5] . . .

---

1. LBJ had briefed about fifty members of Congress on Vietnam, noting that he was following the Gulf of Tonkin Resolution "carefully." (President's Daily Diary, October 25, 1965, LBJL.)

2. The North Vietnamese.

3. McNamara, *In Retrospect,* p. 174.

4. LBJ has begun using the term that throughout the war in Indochina would mean those opposed to massive escalation.

5. On March 1, a meeting of about twenty Communist parties was starting in Moscow.

We're getting a little pressure from the field, indicating lack of understanding of why we're doing what we're doing.[1]

LBJ: Are you putting any pressure out there [to prevent] stories like the *Times* story this morning?

McNAMARA: Yeah, we sure are. I don't know how in the world that came out. . . . I thought that was a very bad story.

LBJ: Am I wrong in saying that this appears to be almost traitorous? They're talking about plans that we have agreed upon and what we are going to do.

McNAMARA: I wouldn't call it traitorous, but it's a very irresponsible action. . . .

LBJ: . . . Somebody ought to be removed, Bob. You just can't exist with this kind of thing.

McNAMARA: No, it's terrible.

LBJ: I'd go to Taylor[2] and say that . . . we want some heads to fall. . . . We just can't run a government this way. I don't want to be nuts on the subject. Everybody says I am. But I just see it every morning. I *know* it's not good to say we're going to ship in the Marines before we decide to. I *know* it's not good to say that we've got a plan to bomb this specific area before we're *bombing* it. Because *Christ,* I guess every antiaircraft and everything they can get is alerted.

---

1. Meaning why the delays in starting Rolling Thunder.
2. Ambassador Maxwell Taylor in Saigon.

Chapter Six

"IT MAY LOOK LIKE I'M STIRRING UP THESE MARCHES"

This damn world is shifting and changing so fast. I got 38 percent of these young Nigro boys out on the streets. . . . You take an old hard-peckered boy that sits around and got no school and got no job and got no work and got no discipline. His daddy's probably on relief, and his mama's probably taking mor-phine. Why, he ain't got nothing hurt if he gets shot, I mean, he's better off dead. . . . Selma is nothing. . . . You just wait till the rats get going in Harlem and Chicago.

LBJ *to* JOHN MCCLELLAN, *March 23, 1965*

ADAM CLAYTON POWELL, JR.

Congressman from New York and Chairman, House Labor and Education Committee
Monday, March 1, 1965, 9:32 P.M.

Johnson considers federal aid to education one of the cornerstones of his Great Society. But when the bill was due before Powell's committee on February 8, the chairman had fled to Puerto Rico, dodging a House investigation for abuse of expense funds. Now, though, the Harlem Congressman is back at work. An old ally of LBJ's—he endorsed Johnson over Northern liberals for President in 1960—he wants the President to help reverse a House order reducing his staff expenses. Powell also claims that a clause in LBJ's bill to help white, poor Appalachia is "anti-Negro." With Lady Bird sitting nearby, the President calls Powell from the tiny room off the Oval Office he calls the "little lounge" and turns up the heat.

LBJ: Adam, what the hell has been happening to your committee? I thought you told me two months ago that you were going to pass a bill for me.
POWELL: . . . All hell has broken loose because—

197

LBJ: What the hell are you blackmailing me on a—

POWELL: Let me—

LBJ: The hell you didn't! You wanted a $400,000 appropriation for you. We couldn't pass $1.2 billion for the schoolkids. . . . You damn near defeated the best education bill I've got! I hope you're going to be proud of it!

POWELL: No, no, you know, in your Appalachian bill, that there is—

LBJ: Appalachia ain't got a damn thing to do with you! . . .

POWELL: Yes, but there's a clause in there, Mr. President.

LBJ: There's a clause been in there all the time. If you are going to let Ayers and Edith Green[1] lead you off the reservation, well, then I ran for nothing last year with 15 million votes. . . . If you defeat this . . . why, we can't pass anything! . . .

POWELL: Mr. President, don't you think I was entitled to the money?

LBJ: No, I don't think you're entitled to a damn thing! . . . You looked me straight in the eye and said, "I'll report this bill and I'll get it on the floor." . . .

POWELL: By March first, I told you.

LBJ: Oh, *hell no!* You didn't say March first. You told me you were going to *do* it. Then you ran off for three weeks and they couldn't even locate you. I asked the Speaker to call you and tell you that this was serious.[2] This is bad. This is the thing we ran on all over the country. Your people are being damn well taken care of in it.

POWELL: Now what about the clause in the Appalachia—

LBJ: . . . I never heard of it! . . . Appalachia bill is Kennedy's bill. . . . We're trying to do the best we can with it.

POWELL: All right.

LBJ: But for Christ's sake, don't let somebody put a pistol at your head, Adam! . . . Don't you go *doing* me this way! You let these goddamned outlaws that start these— Bill Ayers is laughing. . . . He said he's stirring up all this trouble.

POWELL: Really?

LBJ: And he's got Miz Green and she has a-l-l-ways been stirring up trouble.

POWELL: That's my problem child.

LBJ: . . . For Christ's sake . . . listen to me. If you can't trust me on Appalachia, you damn sure can't trust an amendment. . . . If there's anything going to happen to Appalachia that's anti-Negro, I won't let it happen. Period.

POWELL: I'm not talking about Negro. I'm talking about . . . the education bill.

LBJ: . . . For *God's* sake, don't get sucked into it. They *used* you for three weeks and murdered me! They got *thirty-two* amendments written while you were gone. They got the *hell* raised in the Senate. They got the NAM.[3] You got the Chamber

---

1. Committee members William Ayers, an Ohio Republican, and Edith Green, an Oregon Democrat, were attacking the bill.
2. Powell had refused to return John McCormack's calls.
3. The conservative National Association of Manufacturers.

of Commerce. You got every fascist organization in the country working, while *you* are trying to get $400,000. . . . I want that bill reported out tomorrow morning . . . and what you want me to do, I'll try to do.[1]

LADY BIRD JOHNSON

Monday, March 1, 1965, Tape-recorded Diary

LADY BIRD: It was really a virtuoso performance. He gave [Powell] all the reasons why he ought to get that bill out of his committee in words that were dazzling, homey, and unanswerable. If I had been on the other end of the line, I would have ended by saying yes without waiting to quite decide why.

WHITE HOUSE SITUATION ROOM

Tuesday, March 2, 1965, 12:47 P.M.

> Operation Rolling Thunder has begun. With no formal public announcement, 104 American B-57s, F-100s, and F-105s and 19 South Vietnamese Skyraiders— the largest number of planes heretofore used in one day against North Vietnam— have been sent against an ammunitions depot and naval base. Johnson minutely supervised such attacks and ordered his staff to awaken him during the night for reports. "They can't hit an outhouse without my permission," he once said.[2]

DUTY OFFICER: Their time over target was to be about seven minutes ago, sir. . . .
LBJ: . . . How long before you should hear something?
DUTY OFFICER: . . . It'll probably be about five or five-thirty . . . before we know how many got back safely, sir.
LBJ: Call me.

WHITE HOUSE SITUATION ROOM

Tuesday, March 2, 1965, Early morning, time uncertain

DUTY OFFICER: We believe . . . there are two U.S. planes missing. . . .
LBJ: . . . What's it look like? Our two pilots lost?

---

1. The elementary and secondary education bill was reported out of Powell's committee by one vote.
2. Quoted in Helen Thomas, *Dateline* (Macmillan, 1975), p. 291.

DUTY OFFICER: . . . Rescue is under way for them at this time, sir.
LBJ: Okay, thank you.[1]

LEONARD GOLDENSON

President, American Broadcasting Company
Wednesday, March 3, 1965, 10:10 A.M.

> President Kennedy's sister Jean Kennedy Smith has asked LBJ to hold a White House fund-raiser for the John F. Kennedy Center for the Performing Arts, under construction on the Potomac. Johnson will not do it. He tells Goldenson, who is helping raise money for the Kennedy Center, that asking for money at the White House from people with business pending before the federal government—even for a charity—would compromise the President.

LBJ: Leonard, I told my lovely friend Jean Kennedy that I would call you. . . . She said you and someone had suggested that we might have a dinner here at the White House and bring in some movie producers and exhibitors to solicit some money for the [Kennedy] Center. I told her that we had decided when we came in that we better not have any meetings of that kind. The Kennedys could . . . get by with it, but if I touched something, why, it's pretty bad business. . . . I didn't want to start raising funds at the White House—even for the Red Cross or United Fund . . . because one person . . . in the room could be having a truck permit somewhere, or have something pending in Congress, and they'd say that he was buying his way into the White House.
GOLDENSON: Right.
LBJ: . . . I don't ever get out much, but if something did develop where you did have a dinner . . . I'd try to send a message to it or . . . drop in.
GOLDENSON: . . . When I started contacting the smaller theaters—particularly all through the South—because it was called the Kennedy Cultural Center, they reacted against it. . . . Then . . . Mary Lasker[2] said, "Maybe these smaller exhibitors could be invited down to the White House. . . ."
LBJ: Mary's a lovely girl, but she'd have a Chautauqua[3] here every hour if it were up to her. And we've got a rule. I never was at but one meeting that was a fund-raising thing here—well, it was two meetings. We had one lunch and we had

---

1. In the first Rolling Thunder mission, six American aircraft were downed, but five of the pilots were recovered.
2. Johnson's friend, the New York philanthropist.
3. The Chautauqua Institution of New York, famous for its long annual summer encampment featuring public speeches.

one reception. And I was sick at my stomach at both of them—and I'm not an unduly sensitive person. But we had every person in the world in with special interests to raise funds for the Democratic party at a luncheon the President gave and the Attorney General. . . . We had all the whiskey people and all the beer people and all the Las Vegas. . . . I thought that if any press man had been unfriendly, that would destroy us. And I have a good many that I *know* are unfriendly. . . . I have tried as religiously as I could to avoid bringing pressure of any kind on anyone since I was here, because I think you've got to realize that the office is more than just the individual. My best friends I've got in the world—I could call up and ask them to do things . . . two years ago that I wouldn't ask now.

*   *   *

GOLDENSON: May I ask you something else, Mr. President?

LBJ: Yes, sir.

GOLDENSON: I'm going down to see Liz Carpenter[1] tomorrow with Jim.[2] We would like to do something since Lady Bird is interested in the cultural development—from a beauty standpoint—of the city of Washington.[3] We wanted to . . . take the city of Washington during the different seasons. She would take the people through . . . the cherry blossom time and then . . . the summer and . . . fall . . . to help stimulate the beautification of other cities in the United States . . . on the same basis that Mrs. Kennedy did for the interior of the White House.[4] We want to put on this type of program in color. . . .

LBJ: I would think anything you all worked out would be happy with me. I don't mess in her business. I'm kind of like Mr. Roosevelt.[5] I let her do what she wants to. She's interested in this field. I'm very happy that she is. . . . I have been almost shocked . . . at the amount of response that we had to our natural beauty message[6] . . . from the taxicab drivers' wives, and the mother of the boy in Vietnam who says she looked through the Capitol to see what he's fighting [for]. . . . And the mail has just been out of this world on it. . . . So if . . . your people that know audiences thought it was good . . . I think it would be a good thing for the country. . . . The natural beauty theme has caught on.

---

1. Lady Bird's aide.
2. James Hagerty, president of ABC News.
3. Mrs. Johnson had started her campaign to "beautify" America.
4. Jacqueline Kennedy had taken CBS television viewers through the newly restored White House in 1962.
5. Franklin Roosevelt's attitude toward his wife, Eleanor.
6. On February 8, encouraged by Lady Bird, LBJ sent Congress a special message on "conservation and restoration of natural beauty," urging laws to create new parks and clean up highways, air, and water.

LADY BIRD JOHNSON

Thursday, March 4, 1965, Tape-recorded Diary

> Goldenson has sold the First Lady on being the centerpiece of an hour-long ABC documentary on the capital's changing seasons called "A Visit to Washington with Mrs. Lyndon B. Johnson on Behalf of a More Beautiful America," which will air on Thanksgiving 1965.

LADY BIRD: It would be filmed over four or five months. . . . I am timid at the thought of that much exposure. I am no authority, just an interested, enthusiastic citizen. I recognize I do have a sort of tool in my hands, by this title I carry, and I want to use it, but I quake at the thought of putting myself forward as a sort of city planner, landscape architect, pedagogue. I think in my shoes there should be someone of exquisite self-assurance who could put other people to work and who, in the most ladylike fashion, is a real salesman.

NICHOLAS KATZENBACH

Thursday, March 4, 1965, 11:39 A.M.

> As the Senate Rules Committee bears down on the Bobby Baker scandal, LBJ's nemesis Don Reynolds has charged that the State Department gave Johnson a considerable amount in counterpart funds for his own use during a vice presidential visit to Hong Kong in May 1961. Johnson wants J. Edgar Hoover to defend him before the Senate.

LBJ: Hoover ought to be asked to testify on what he did . . . so again I wouldn't be made the goat for something I hadn't done. . . . I see . . . the [*New York*] *Times* has got an editorial.[1] And the Senators are obviously putting this out. I think it would be a good thing if you and Hoover would talk to Dirksen and say . . . we think he ought to know the facts about this person.[2] . . . Each day they make charges against me and others that are untrue. The Hong Kong thing. . . . I never had any counterpart funds in my life. Anytime. I never handled any of the funds of the trip. . . .
KATZENBACH: Yeah.
LBJ: . . . I did buy forty shirts at three-and-a-half apiece—which they played up a great deal—and gave them to the people traveling with us. I thought it was a lit-

---

1. Criticizing release of the FBI report on Reynolds's allegations against LBJ (see Chapter 4) as an "extraordinary" Democratic attempt to close down the hearings.
2. Reynolds.

tle memento that a fellow would have, like a tie clasp like a Kennedy PT boat.[1] . . .
I made a mistake because they all played it up as a very lavish display of great
wealth because I bought $120 worth of little things and passed them out to . . . the
crew on the plane and to the reporters and the secretaries and the workers. . . .
Now, have we . . . doctored that report in any way?

KATZENBACH: Not one bit, sir.

LBJ: Well, don't. . . . I know that Curtis and Williams[2] are not going to be fair
with me. . . . But I believe Dirksen will, and I think Cooper would, and I think
Scott would, if they knew the facts.[3]

*   *   *

LBJ: I think . . . you ought to tell the [Washington] Star, . . . "If you want to go on
and try to destroy the presidency, that's all right, but here are the facts." . . . I'd be
happy for you to go into the grand jury with each one of these things. Call anybody. Call the Hong Kong Assistant Secretary of State, the consular office back
here. It's a pure, prefabricated story. Just as much as if they said you raped my wife
last night. Now, I don't know what you do about that in a free country, and if it can
happen to the President, God *knows* what happens to a truck driver!

KATZENBACH: . . . If they wanted testimony . . . it's just my reluctance to get
Hoover as a witness. He's never been a witness in this kind of a situation.

LBJ: Hell, I thought they called him up there on every old topic that came along.

KATZENBACH: . . . To my recollection, Mr. President, he has never testified
with respect to the integrity of an investigation. . . .

LBJ: I'll tell you, when Martin Luther King questioned his integrity, he goddamn
sure responded pretty effectively![4] . . . Just say . . . the President has not a thing in
the world to hide. . . . We paid Reynolds a hundred thousand in the period since
'55—nine years—and he bought twelve hundred dollars worth of advertising.[5] . . .
I never spent one minute with him. . . . He's just a bum here in town that's got us involved. But *I* don't want history to say these things. *I* don't want to be a *Harding!*

LADY BIRD JOHNSON

Thursday, March 4, 1965, Tape-recorded Diary

LADY BIRD: The press is having quite a vendetta with Lyndon, on the subject
of his alleged suppression of news, with Joe Alsop wielding a very sharp rapier

---

1. JFK gave out *PT-109* tie clasps.
2. Senators Carl Curtis and John Williams, Republicans on the Rules Committee.
3. Senators John Sherman Cooper of Kentucky and Hugh Scott of Pennsylvania are also Republicans on the committee.
4. In November 1964, after King complained about Hoover's lack of interest in pursuing Southern
civil rights violations, Hoover called him the "most notorious liar" in the United States.
5. From the Johnsons' Austin station, which Reynolds claimed was a kickback.

and [Rowland] Evans and [his partner Robert] Novak leading the pack. The question is how to combat, or *whether* to combat it. . . . How much can they tear us down . . . and what effect might it have on the way we appear in history?

McGEORGE BUNDY

Friday, March 5, 1965, 10:30 A.M.

> Johnson complains about an NBC report by Robert Goralski that the new bombings of North Vietnam are mainly a device to force the North Vietnamese to the bargaining table. LBJ fears that such reports will defeat the purpose of Operation Rolling Thunder.

LBJ: Anything from out of Vietnam today?

BUNDY: Very irritating Goralski story. . . .

LBJ: I saw it flashed on television. . . .

BUNDY: Couldn't be worse. . . . Goralski is a very naïve reporter and runs awful hard for a headline. It's certainly true that you can find people in the government who will say, "Look, the whole object of these bombings is to bring these boys to the bargaining table." . . . But he's got it all turned around.

LBJ: Why don't you talk to Bob Kintner[1] about that?

BUNDY: You think it's worth it?

LBJ: Yes, I think I would say this—that we don't want to complain, and this is entirely a matter for them, but . . . that we're trying our best to go far enough[2] without going too far. In the last incident, Ron Nelson[3] spent all of his time talking about the big black Cadillacs coming up here and the "great day of crisis"—when there hadn't been a meeting all day. . . . Goralski was following the same practice last night. Special report, flashes "it has been heard that somebody might feel" that may belong to the Cabinet that this could happen. . . . If NBC wants to become that irresponsible, why they can, but he ought to know it. . . . Tell him these two children need a little supervision. The Chancellors[4] don't do anything like that, and this boy that used to be here at the White House. Black-headed boy. He didn't do it that way. What's his name?

BUNDY: Abel?

LBJ: No. Abel split, too. But this boy Sandy Vanocur and this Ray Scherer[5]—

---

1. President of NBC News.
2. In Vietnam.
3. As usual mangling the name of someone he dislikes, LBJ refers to Ron Nessen of NBC.
4. John Chancellor of NBC.
5. Elie Abel, Vanocur, and Scherer are all NBC newsmen.

they're all good. Particularly Chancellor. . . . [But] I wake up and this damn little fellow Nelson had got in the Fish Room and got the flag and got the seal and got in front of it and said [*Johnson mimics reporter's voice:*] "The greatest crisis that ever faced Washington is now coming about. The big, black limousines are dashing in the . . . southeast gate. The delivery chauffeurs are laying out the floor mats for the Cabinet officers. The Cabinet officers with their homburgs are moving in, and we are facing a *gra-a-ve* crisis." And I had been asleep for two hours!

BUNDY: [*chuckles*]

LBJ: I woke up and wondered what the hell happened. I called over . . . and I said, "Go in there and get him out from that flag and that seal. Looks like my office." Reedy said, "It's raining outside and I let him come in out of the *rain*." . . . Goralski is very much the same way. . . . These kids are trying to break through. I would just tell [Kintner] to watch this stuff because it creates all kinds of problems when the Senators see it. They think we are going under . . . and there is just not anything to this. . . . Chancellor doesn't like to pick up this stuff. He's kind of reserved and he sits back and reads Pla-to.

BUNDY: Bright young men do this. That's the trouble. . . . It's like Reston[1] with his pipe, while all his young leopards roam the town.

LBJ: That's right. This Reston's got a trick. I've caught him now. . . . I like him very much, but he'll come over and talk to you and he'll talk to me, and he'll talk to Bob McNamara. Then he'll call over and get Tad Szulc and Max Frankel to write the story. See, he doesn't write them. . . . So we've just got to be awfully cautious. We talk to Scotty as a statesman, instead of a reporter.

BUNDY: That's right. . . .

LBJ: . . . Now, the Marines—I haven't made that decision.[2] I'm still worried about it. I don't know what—34,000 they want to go?

BUNDY: Thirty-five hundred. Two battalions. How far do you want us to go? Bob [McNamara] is talking to the senior Armed Services people,[3] and I said I would check back to see how far you want to go.

LBJ: I wouldn't tell them you want to do it. I'd ask them what they thought about it.

BUNDY: He didn't want to give them that much leeway. . . . He didn't want to get you a lot of advice *not* to do it.

LBJ: Well . . . they're going to say not to do it later.[4]

---

1. James Reston of the *New York Times*.
2. On General Westmoreland's request to send Marine battalions to protect American airmen and airfields in South Vietnam.
3. House and Senate Armed Services Committee leaders.
4. LBJ was prescient.

LADY BIRD JOHNSON

Friday, March 5, 1965, Tape-recorded Diary

LADY BIRD: This was another late night for Lyndon. It was ten-thirty when he ate dinner. By now Zephyr[1] has started leaving it for us for someone to serve and going home—a relief to my state of mind and no inconvenience to us. Lyndon phones during and after these late dinners, so they are hardly separate from his working day. . . . He said, . . . "The only man you can find at seven-thirty in the morning at his desk is Bob McNamara." He worries about him too, almost as though he were a member of his family, and has been saying lately that he looked tired and ill.

HUBERT HUMPHREY

Saturday, March 6, 1965, 11:25 A.M.

> Humphrey has been suffering from renewed press reports that Johnson is ignoring him. From the White House family quarters, LBJ gives him a morale-raising telephone call outlining, in an increasingly shrill voice, what he expects from Congress.

LBJ: Some of the reporters have been asking me assignments that you have. You have more than any man ever had, except Garner.[2] . . . The only Vice President that I've ever looked at that had any influence was Garner. I had none because Kennedy wouldn't *give* me any. . . . Now, I want to make it clear here and now . . . [that] even if it made a break between us . . . your number-one responsibility in my administration comes even ahead of McCormack, Mansfield[3]—anybody else. I expect you to be my liaison with both of them. . . . I think the Vice President is peculiarly equipped because . . . he has the legislative training, he has the contacts, he has the power to make a speech for them, he's on the ticket, he's only one of two elected. He's there with them. The President can't go see them. Hell, I'd love to! I don't even go to a dedication of a gymnasium. . . . But I want to go eat with Allen Ellender.[4] . . . I want to go to the Texas delegation. That's where I want to be. Every day.

HUMPHREY: Yes, sir.

LBJ: I don't want to be sitting down here receiving the Ambassador from Ghana and spending all day down here. . . . Now some Presidents get jealous of the Vice

---

1. Zephyr Wright, the Johnsons' cook.
2. John Nance Garner of Texas was FDR's first Vice President. As a young congressional aide and Congressman from Texas, Johnson had been much in Garner's presence.
3. The House Speaker and Senate Majority Leader.
4. Democratic Senator from Louisiana.

President participating in these acts. I think that education bill is 51 percent yours. I think that Appalachian bill next Tuesday is 49 percent yours. It's Johnson-Humphrey. . . . Half and half. Just as much as you and Muriel[1] own that home.

HUMPHREY: Yes, sir.

LBJ: I want them to understand it and I want *you* to understand it. . . . You just get you a chart. Get those 104 bills[2] and you just watch them like a hawk, because if you're successful . . . you will be a successful Vice President. . . . Garner could run the Senate. . . . He could talk to Rayburn[3] and run the House. And he did. And Roosevelt passed all of his stuff.[4] . . . You've never heard of Old Man Garner, but I stood here and watched him *every damn day,* and that's what I want you to *do.* Now Kennedy felt if I did it, then . . . they'd say I was the master craftsman. . . . He told the Catholics—Mike and them[5] to pay no attention to me and come down here. Now, they don't have to do that. You can negotiate with Mike, you can negotiate with Russell Long,[6] you can negotiate with McCormack. . . . Now let them know that you are speaking for the President. . . . This is a dual operation. . . .

HUMPHREY: Yes, sir.

LBJ: What is our program? Have we got a farm bill? Have we got Appalachia? Have we got a school bill? Have we got a health bill? Is medical care out? . . . We've got to pass it. Now, that's number one.

HUMPHREY: That's right.

LBJ: That's your wife. Then you can get down to your aunts and your cousins later. Second thing you can do is all this Travel USA.[7] . . . I want to have it running out of your damned ears. But the first thing I want is legislative. . . . I want you to be walking down the halls . . . and talking to them, having the administrative assistants telling you what's happening and getting the gossip.[8] . . . You've got Old Lady Green.[9] . . . I've had her down here. I've bragged on her. But she is just a mean woman, and she's going to whup you. When she does, I'm going to put you in the five-cent cigar business like Marshall.[10] . . . We just cain't! We're smarter than they are. We've got more energy. We can work faster. We've got all the machinery of the government. . . .

---

1. Mrs. Humphrey.

2. LBJ's 1965 Great Society legislative demands.

3. Johnson's mentor, House Speaker Sam Rayburn of Texas.

4. LBJ exaggerates FDR's legislative success.

5. LBJ refers to Mansfield and McCormack as "the Catholics."

6. Democratic Senator from Louisiana.

7. To improve America's balance of payments, Johnson had started a program, with Humphrey as chairman, called See the USA, urging Americans to travel domestically.

8. Just as Johnson had done as a young congressional secretary in the early 1930s.

9. Edith Green, Democrat from Oregon, LBJ's antagonist on his education bill.

10. Woodrow Wilson's number two, Thomas Marshall, who had said, "What this country needs is a good five-cent cigar," was considered the epitome of a do-nothing Vice President.

HUMPHREY: Mr. President, I'll go right up there and be right on them all afternoon.

LBJ: Well, you just be on them the next four years. You just say that you are the first Vice President in the country that had responsibility. . . . We've just got to get this legislative program through. . . . If we get Appalachia now, if we get education now, if we get medical care now, then we've got the running gears and we can elect these boys.[1]

HUMPHREY: Yes, sir.

LBJ: But if we don't, they'll say, "His farm program was a flop." . . . What we want to do is take care of this unemployment where it's really distressed, and that's Appalachia—we'll do it. The next thing we want to do is get these people that can't read and write—we want to educate them and make taxpayers out of them instead of tax eaters. . . . The next thing is health. Now, that's basic. That's what I'm after, Humphrey. . . . Don't ever argue with me. I'll go a hundred million or a billion on health or education. I don't argue about that any more than I argue about Lady Bird buying flour. You got to have flour and coffee in your house. Education and health. I'll spend the goddamned money. I may cut back some tanks. But not on health. . . . Education is about to be *defeated* . . . by this old woman[2] unless she meets some opposition. . . .

HUMPHREY: Yes, sir.

LBJ: Every place you go, when you mention education, that's the most popular thing. I'd just propagandize the *hell* out of it, and I'd tell my *staff*, I'd tell my *friends,* and I'd tell my *family* that you are not exactly emulating Garner, but the last time a great program was put on the books in this country,[3] he put it on. . . . Dick Nixon tried to make out like he had something, but . . . Eisenhower cut his guts out and didn't want Nixon to have *any* power. And although Nixon bragged about how he ran everything, if you'll look at these confidential records down here, they treated Nixon just like he wasn't *here*. Eisenhower said he'd take two weeks and then he'd tell them what he did.[4] . . . So I came along and they[5] didn't want me to touch a legislative thing. Foreign aid—they asked me one time to switch Tom Dodd.[6] Which I did.

HUMPHREY: Yes, sir.

---

1. Elect Democrats in 1966.

2. Edith Green.

3. FDR's New Deal, against which LBJ is always privately measuring his own Great Society.

4. Asked by reporters on August 24, 1960, what "major idea" of Vice President Nixon's he had adopted, Eisenhower said, "If you give me a week, I might think of one." (*New York Times,* August 25, 1960.)

5. John Kennedy's entourage.

6. Democratic Senator from Connecticut.

LBJ; Outside of that, that's all. Now the sky's the limit for you. There're 104 bills. They're all yours and mine. . . . That's what we ran on. That's our platform . . . You're half of it. . . . When you go out speaking, you can say we passed education, we passed Appalachia, we passed medical care. And . . . I'll have a majority two years from now.

HUMPHREY: Yes, sir.

LBJ: I'm just dying to go home. But I don't dare go home with the education bill like it is. I want to go this weekend. But I'm just scared to *death* that that woman's going to beat me. . . . We've just got to get *these things passed.* . . . I've got flour and coffee and sugar. That's three things you've got to have.

HUMPHREY: Yes, sir.

LBJ: One of them's education. One of them's medical care. And one of them is Appalachia. Now, I've got Appalachia, and you'll get education next week. . . . And I think the medical care will go through like a dose of salt through a widow woman.[1] . . . I told Martin Luther King, "Hell, *I'm* for voting, and we're going to get voting.[2] *That's* not your problem. . . . The big thing, Dr. King, with you, is $1.2 billion for *Negroes only,* because who the hell do you think *makes* less than two thousand a year?"[3]

HUMPHREY: Uh-huh.

LBJ: "It's the Negroes. Now, by God, they can't work in a filling station and put water in a *radiator* unless they can *read* and *write.* Because they've got to go and punch their cash register, and they don't know which one to *punch.* They've got to take a check, and they don't know which one to *cash.* They've got to take a *credit card,* and they can't pull the *numbers.* . . . Now that's what *you* damn fellows better be working on. If these Republicans want to be for the Nigras—and I hope they do, I want a two-party system—I hope some Nigras vote for Republicans. But you make them go vote for *education!*" And I think you ought to find out this group that's meeting with Miz Green, and as Vice President of the United States, you ought to ask two of them to come to your home on Sunday afternoon. You ought to have two of them at breakfast with you on Monday morning. You ought to have two of them in your office in the afternoon and give them a card to the gallery and give them a picture of you and your wife, and give them one of the President. Then tell them that this is the greatest thing, and their names are going to be written in fire on every schoolhouse in the country. . . . And that the Pope don't get a damn thing out of this but a *pencil.*[4] And . . . that you're Protestant and that this is the

---

1. LBJ refers to the use of epsom salt as a laxative.
2. A bill to ensure African American voting rights.
3. See January 15, 1965, conversation with King, above.
4. Edith Green and others were charging that the help to parochial schools offered by LBJ's education bill was unconstitutional.

best thing that you've ever seen. Because if you can't do more than Old Lady Green, I'm in a hell of a shape! I ought to have had *her!* [1]

HUMPHREY: [*chuckles*] Yes sir, Mr. President.

LBJ: And if she had been a little younger, I might have *picked* her! Goodbye!

RICHARD RUSSELL

Saturday, March 6, 1965, 12:05 P.M.

> Johnson's sixty-seven-year-old mentor is recovering from an emergency tracheotomy to fight emphysema and bronchitis. LBJ consults him about the next big step in Vietnam—sending Marine battalions to defend American airmen.

LBJ: Good God, I'd rather hear your voice than hear Jesus this morning! How are you feeling?

RUSSELL: Well, I'm up to where I can walk a little bit. . . . I'm going down to Puerto Rico for a few days.

LBJ: Oh-h-h, it's wet and damp and you'll get sick down there, all my doctors tell me. I thought you was going out to sit around with Eisenhower in Palm Springs. I'll get you a nice house out there and let you take somebody, and send you out there to look at something.[2] It's dry. . . . God damn! I told those doctors not to send you to Florida. You took pneumonia every time you went. I did too. Puerto Rico's wet too. . . .

RUSSELL: . . . I just want to tell you I never will forget your thoughtfulness.[3]

LBJ: I don't want you to remember my thoughtfulness. . . .

RUSSELL: . . . After you got done talking to one of these nurses, by God, they were scared to get within a foot and a half of my door.

LBJ: Haven't got anybody left like you. You're all I got since my mama and papa and brothers and sisters got away from me. . . . I just couldn't take any chances. I said more prayers about you than I have said since Lady Bird threatened to divorce me two years after we were married.[4]

RUSSELL: [*laughs*]

LBJ: And I'm so glad you come through. I just think you've just got to take it easy. And if you're going to Puerto Rico, fine, and we'll—

---

1. As Vice President.

2. In other words, make it an inspection trip so that the government will foot the bill.

3. LBJ had made arrangements for Russell to be treated at Walter Reed Army Hospital in Washington.

4. This may refer to Johnson's decision to run for Congress in February 1937. Before their marriage in November 1934, she wrote him, "I would hate for you to go into politics." (Jan Jarboe Russell, *Lady Bird,* Scribner, 1999, p. 111). Or it may refer to LBJ's romance with Alice Glass, paramour and later wife of the owner of the *Austin American-Statesman.* (See Caro, *The Path to Power,* pp. 476–92, and Beschloss, *Taking Charge,* p. 251.)

RUSSELL: My doctors don't seem to be too—

LBJ: . . . It rains every afternoon. . . . Maybe they know better than I do. . . . The only thing I care about is your getting well. Now, somebody told me that poor little Bobby[1] was up here. . . . Why didn't he let me know? . . .

RUSSELL: He don't like to bother the President of the United States.

LBJ: You're not bothering me. I yearn for it. . . . All I get is the people I don't want to see. . . . He's got problems?

RUSSELL: . . . They sent him up here to this National Institutes of—

LBJ: Health.

RUSSELL: —Health, you know. . . . Such a socialistic institution out there that they wouldn't even let him buy an aspirin tablet![2] [laughs]

LBJ: Maybe. If that's not any good, I've got the best [doctors] in the United States at Houston. . . . Just tell him we've got a brand-new plane[3] . . . with a bed that holds seven people, that flies 250 miles an hour, that's parked in our barn up there at the ranch that will pick him up . . . and take him to Houston . . . if he'll just let me. . . .

RUSSELL: That's mighty fine and sweet of you, Mr. President.

LBJ: . . . Tell him that it's . . . no expense at all, because we don't ride it. They won't let me anymore because it's connected with the radio station. . . . It just sits there. . . .

RUSSELL: Well, I know it's—

LBJ: It's a brand-new one, though, and it's a honey and got a wonderful pilot. . . . Fly thirty thousand feet high. It'll go above all the clouds and everything. Now, let me ask you one or two other things. We're going to send the Marines in to protect the Hawk battalion, the Hawk outfit at Danang, because they're trying to come in and destroy them there, and they're afraid the security provided by Vietnamese are not enough. All the military and all the Joint Chiefs, and all the everybody including McNamara and Rusk—I told them to clear it with everybody. . . . Has anybody talked to you about it? I'm sure they haven't because you've been sick.

RUSSELL: No, nothing.

LBJ: I guess we've got no choice, but it scares the death out of me. I think everybody's going to think, "We're landing the Marines. We're off to battle." . . . Of course, if they come up there, they're going to get them in a fight. Just sure as hell. They're not going to run. Then you're tied down.[4] If they don't, though, and they ruin those airplanes, everybody is going to give me hell for not securing them, just like they did the last time they made a raid.

---

1. Russell's beloved forty-year-old nephew, a judge on the Georgia Court of Appeals, who was mortally ill with cancer.

2. Russell says this to the President who is now fighting for Medicare!

3. The Johnson family plane.

4. Johnson knew exactly what was going to happen.

RUSSELL: Yeah.

LBJ: So, it's a choice, and it's a hard one, but Westmoreland and Taylor come in every day saying, *"Ple-e-ease* send them on." And Joint Chiefs say, *"Ple-e-ease* send them on." And McNamara and Rusk say, "Send them on." So I told them yesterday to go and clear it with the Congressmen. . . . What do you think?

RUSSELL: . . . We've gone so damn far, Mr. President, it scares the life out of me. But I don't know how to back up now. It looks to me like we just got in this thing, and there's no way out. We're just getting pushed forward and forward and forward and forward and forward.

LBJ: . . . That is exactly right. . . . And we're losing more every day. . . . We're getting in worse.

RUSSELL: These Marines—they'll be killing a whole lot of friendly Vietnamese. They're going to shoot at everything that comes around those airplanes. . . .

LBJ: Airplanes ain't worth a *damn,* Dick! . . . They just scare the countries, they just scare their prime ministers. . . . Bombing anything. They did it in the Ruhr.[1] And I guess they can do it in an industrial city. I guess they can do it in New York. But they can't do it in the barracks. Hell, I had 160 of them over at a barracks, and twenty-seven buildings, and they set two on fire.

RUSSELL: That's right.

LBJ: That's the damnedest thing I ever saw. The biggest fraud. Don't you get your hopes up that the Air Force is going to defend this.

RUSSELL: I haven't at all. I know they're not.

*   *   *

LBJ: The Navy is having to lower its standards, and I don't want to screw anybody, but I think I'll just order them to lower [those of the other services]. . . . It seems to me that you're paying a mighty big price on an Anglo-Saxon white man to make his boy go and fight in Vietnam. But none of the others can because . . . they don't have the exact IQ. . . .

RUSSELL: I held up the whole thing for years, when they tried to cut it back. . . . Smart boys, black and white—you're killing them, and the damn dumb bunnies escape!

LBJ: Well. . . . I think we can improve them. . . . The Navy has said that all this talk about the draft—Goldwater is going to repeal it and all that kind of stuff[2]— has ruined their program. They can't get people for it now. So, they're going to have to lower their physical and mental standards to get them. . . . If they do that, then we'll have to lower them for the others. . . . But just the borderline. In other words, if you say I can't come in to your committee and testify unless I've got a B

---

1. In World War II, the Allies bombed the Ruhr industrial region of Germany.
2. See Chapter 1.

average, I would modify it to D-minus, that's all. I wouldn't drop it to D or F. I wouldn't take a second-grader, but I would just gradually do a little. And you don't have to move it much to pick up ten thousand.

RUSSELL: One thing is clear, we ain't going to do away with the draft. . . . You've got the authority to lower it, if you want to.

LBJ: . . . I don't know, Dick. . . . The great trouble I'm under— A man can fight if he can see daylight down the road somewhere. But there ain't no daylight in Vietnam. There's not a bit.

RUSSELL: There's no end to the road. There's just nothing.

LBJ: The more bombs you drop, the more nations you scare, the more people you make mad, the more embassies you get—

RUSSELL: We're going to wind up with the people mad as hell with us that we are saving by being in there. It's just awful. The Australians and everybody else is going to be madder than hell. It's the biggest—it's the worst mess I ever saw in my life. You couldn't have inherited a worse mess.

LBJ: Well, if they'd say I *inherited*, I'll be lucky. But they'll all say I *created* it! . . . You go get well and come back, and I've got a big bed for you here, and I want to see you. And I've got three women want to see you.

ROBERT McNAMARA

Saturday, March 6, 1965, 2:32 P.M.

> Johnson has been agonizing over the decision to send two Marine battalions to Vietnam. He fears that this will signal Americans that a vast and tragic war may be in their future.

LBJ: The alternative is to risk the loss of the personnel and the planes at Danang or move Marines in?

McNAMARA: Yes, sir, that's the alternative. . . . They[1] were forty miles away today—southwest of Danang . . . giving a hell of a fight to the South Vietnamese forces. . . . The last cable that came in at mid-morning said the fight had not yet broken off. So that came pretty close. They've been infiltrating in the hills behind Danang in large numbers over the past several months. . . .

LBJ: Now, here's what depresses me. [*Reads from McGeorge Bundy memo:*] ". . . Dean and Bob[2] both feel that to hold some of our allies, we may need to be less rigid about talks than we have in the last ten days. . . . Dean's backgrounder yesterday went a little way in this direction. We would all be helped by knowing your reaction to the resulting stories." Well, *my* reaction is, ain't a *damn* bit of *use*

---

1. The Vietcong.
2. Rusk and McNamara.

[in] going out and bombing all *morning* and telling them all *af*-ternoon you didn't mean it and you want to talk at a conference table.

McNAMARA: Couldn't agree with you more, Mr. President. . . . We're drifting from day to day here, and we ought to have inside the government some thought as to what we're going to say tomorrow and the next day and next week, and so we don't get backgrounders like that of yesterday, which as you say[1]—

LBJ: Well, I called them and they say that there is nothing in that at all, and it's just not correct. That this is a pure *New York Times* deal to bring us to the conference table. That Rusk didn't say a thing in the world, and that the *New York Times* and Chalmers's *Post* just got together—Chalmers Roberts—and played it that way, as a kind of a propaganda move. Now, I don't know. Rusk is out of town, Ball's[2] there, and they've got no notes of it.

McNAMARA: I don't know either.

LBJ: Ball said he heard it though, and . . . Rusk said exactly what he'd said all the time for the last two years—that when they left the neighbors alone, there'd be no problem, but until that there's no use, they have nothing to talk about.

McNAMARA: Yeah.

LBJ: . . . I told [Bundy] I don't know how to stop this Wilson,[3] but if he thinks *I'm* going to . . . let Wilson use my platform to talk about my consulting with him about where to have a *conference,* he's crazy as *hell!* If I have to go hide and hole up at Johnson *City,* I'm not going to do it. And he better *tell* him that! And I told Ball that, too.[4] Now, on the Marines, the answer is: Yes, if there's no other alternative. . . . I think that the dangers are maybe sixty-forty against our getting involved in a big war with them, and the Marines fighting with the Vietcong and really starting a land war. I don't think that that necessarily follows our sending them there to guard these things. Might prevent it. But the psychological impact of the Marines are coming is going to be a *bad* one. And I know enough to know that. And I know that every mother is going to say, *"Uh-oh, this is it!"*

McNAMARA: Yeah.

LBJ: And I know that what we've done with these B-57s is just going to be Sunday school stuff, compared to the Marines. And all they're going to do is be a policeman. Damned if I don't know why we can't find some kind of policemen besides the *Marines,* because a Marine is a guy that's got a *dagger* in his hand. And that's going to put the *flag* up. An Army boy is not so much, and a Navy boy is not

---

1. An unofficial background briefing has provoked *New York Times* and *Washington Post* stories saying that the bombing of North Vietnam is mainly a ploy to force Hanoi to negotiate.

2. Rusk's deputy George Ball.

3. The dovish British Prime Minister Harold Wilson, who wants to help broker some kind of peace in Vietnam.

4. Ball was the chief skeptic in LBJ's circle about escalation in Vietnam.

so much. But when George Reedy said, "The Marines are coming into Mississippi," I damned near had to evacuate the White House.[1]

McNAMARA: I know it.

LBJ: When I said the boy with the white jersey is coming in, there's a hell of a lot
of difference. We straightened it out in twenty-four hours. . . . I don't dodge the
question. . . . We ought to be able to find some way besides the Marine uniform,
but . . . if I had to do it—and this is the only way the Joint Chiefs can figure it
out—I'd certainly say that this is . . . a security group somewhere, or a policeman
group. Whatever you call these fellows—

McNAMARA: Police battalion.

LBJ: . . . What group did you take out of there, a thousand one time?[2]

McNAMARA: Security battalion.

LBJ: That wasn't what you called them. What did you call them?

McNAMARA: We called them MP battalions.

LBJ: That's right, MP's.

McNAMARA: Well, these aren't MP's. We can't call them that, but we can call
them security battalions.

LBJ: Well, can't you call them security battalions similar to MP's that preserve
security?[3]

McNAMARA: No, sir, we can't really say that, but we can say security. . . .
They're quite different from the MP's and all the press knows it. We'd just be accused of falsifying the story.

LBJ: All right. We'll just go with it. We know what we're walking into. And
rather than have it said, "We wanted protection for our planes—you wouldn't give
it to us," my answer is yes. But my judgment is no.[4]

McNAMARA: I agree with you. And I told the Members of Congress I talked to,
Mr. President, that was exactly the problem. I didn't say to them we'd decided to
do it. Mansfield told me, "Well, you've decided to do it and I appreciate being informed." I said, "No, we haven't decided to do it, Mike. I'm calling to get your
opinion." I said, "I'm cold as hell to this myself. I'm just telling you that the field
commanders recommend it and can't think of any other solution. And I'd like to
know what you think. I hate to see this done." What I was trying to do was push

1. Actually, Johnson had sent two hundred unarmed Navy personnel in June 1964 to help find three
civil rights workers who were missing and later found murdered. (See Beschloss, *Taking Charge*, pp.
425–26, 438–40.)

2. In October 1963, President Kennedy had ordered a thousand U.S. military personnel withdrawn
by the end of the year as a public advertisement of how well the Americans were training the South
Vietnamese to defend themselves.

3. LBJ is toying with ways to disguise the dispatch of the Marines.

4. Johnson knows what trouble this decision will make for him.

him around to reluctantly agreeing, and I got him sort of half-agreed. But he'll fall off if anybody attacks him. I'm sure of that. All right, we'll take care of it, Mr. President.

LBJ: When are you going to issue the order?

McNAMARA: We should do it this afternoon. I'm just so scared that something will happen out there.

LBJ: When are you going to announce it?

McNAMARA: We'll make it late today so it will miss some of the morning editions, and then there's no afternoon edition on Sunday. I'll handle it in a way that will minimize the announcement. But there's going to be a lot of headlines on it when it comes out.

LBJ: [*chuckles darkly*] You're telling me! [1]

LADY BIRD JOHNSON

Sunday, March 7, 1965, Tape-recorded Diary

LADY BIRD: In talking about the Vietnam situation [during dinner], Lyndon summed it up quite simply—"I can't get out, and I can't finish it with what I have got. And I don't know what the hell to do!"

NICHOLAS KATZENBACH

Monday, March 8, 1965, 8:10 A.M.

In February, after meeting with LBJ at the White House, Martin Luther King, Jr., had told reporters that the President would send a voting rights bill to Congress "very soon."[2] A month later came "Bloody Sunday." On Sunday, March 7, civil rights marchers, hoping in part to build pressure on Johnson to propose a bill now, started from Selma toward Montgomery, Alabama. The segregationist Governor, George Wallace, had banned the march as a danger to public safety. Marchers were stopped at the Edmund Pettus Bridge by state troopers and deputies of Sheriff Jim Clark, who fired tear gas, knocked them to the ground, and beat their heads with nightsticks. Dr. King, who was absent because of a death threat, exhorted the marchers to try again on Tuesday morning.

---

1. The *New York Times*, March 7, 1965: "3,500 MARINES GOING TO VIETNAM TO BOLSTER BASE— 2 Battalions for Danang Are First Land Combat Troops Committed by Washington." The next day the battalions landed. Four days later a third arrived, along with a helicopter unit.

2. *Washington Post*, February 10, 1965.

LBJ: Was it the sheriff or the state troopers that stopped the march?

KATZENBACH: The state troopers stopped it, Mr. President. But most of the brutality was done by the sheriff's deputies. They're the fellows on horses.

LBJ: Uh-huh.

KATZENBACH: King said he was going into court this morning to do something. . . . Might be an alternative to [marching] tomorrow. . . .

LBJ: What would the three judges enjoin the sheriffs from doing?

KATZENBACH: They would enjoin the sheriffs from interfering with the voting . . . and . . . permit Negroes to proceed to the courthouse in Selma there, and to march in an orderly way. . . . It would prevent Sheriff Clark from doing what happened yesterday. . . . That's when they started beating up on them.

LBJ: They weren't injured then. Just when the state troopers stopped them. [*blows nose*]

KATZENBACH: No, no. The state troopers used the gas, and apparently somebody got a few tear gas burns. The injuries were, by and large, when they panicked, started running back into town, and then these deputies chased them on horses. . . . I don't know that anybody was seriously hurt. . . . I had a Bureau[1] agent hurt.

LBJ: What happened to him?

KATZENBACH: He got beat up by two of them. . . . I didn't give the arrests any publicity last night because the two arrested were the ones that beat up the FBI agent. That didn't look right to me from a [publicity] viewpoint. All the Negroes beat up and the only people we arrest are the people who beat up the FBI agents. . . .

LBJ: . . . Did we take every precaution we could have? . . .

KATZENBACH: I think so, Mr. President. . . . Yesterday morning I heard they were going to use tear gas. We told the Negro leaders that. . . . I don't know there's much else the federal government can do . . . short of taking the situation over and sending the Army in.

LBJ: I see they're calling for that.

KATZENBACH: Sure. They always have. . . . If there's a way of communicating with George Wallace . . . that would be what would make a difference. There's no reason . . . why circumstances, terms, and conditions of these people marching couldn't be worked out. . . . But I guess Wallace is determined not to. I don't know what he's heading for.

---

1. FBI.

BUFORD ELLINGTON

Director, Office of Emergency Planning
Monday, March 8, 1965, 8:29 A.M.

> Seizing Katzenbach's idea, LBJ asks the former Tennessee Governor to act as a
> go-between with his Alabama counterpart.

LBJ: The biggest problem we have in the Alabama situation is communicating
with George Wallace. He apparently has his own very strongly held . . . views on
just how this thing ought to be handled. . . . They're going to have another march
tomorrow. As we see it, it's going to go from bad to worse. . . . It would improve
the situation a good deal if we could speak freely with him. . . . Do you think that
you have that much standing with him?
ELLINGTON: Mr. President, . . . my relationship with George has been very
good, but you can't trust him. You talk to him—you don't know what he's going to
say that you said. . . . I can talk to him anytime, but there's an element of danger
there in talking with George.
LBJ: You think he'd believe *you?*
ELLINGTON: He'll trust me, yes, sir.
LBJ: I think what I'd do then is to call the Attorney General. . . . I would explore
it cautiously. . . . It seems to me that . . . you could say, "Governor, . . . they're
wanting us to send troops in, and they say if we can send them into Vietnam, we
can send them in to protect Americans who are, a hundred of them, being beat up
here. Of course, you know our feeling about sending troops. . . . We're not very
anxious to get into that business. But there are three judges down there that might
give an injunction today to stop the sheriff from interfering with the registration.
. . . He's pretty brutal with them."
ELLINGTON: . . . I can talk to [Wallace] on a friendly basis, but he's the kind of
person . . . that—I would like to have somebody sitting with me.
LBJ: . . . You could do it with the Attorney General. I'd take[1] my conversation
with him. The Attorney General will arrange that. . . . There might be three or four
things that you could explore. . . . One of them would be permitting them to march
a part of the way. Two would be seeing if they couldn't get some local citizens to
. . . see if they couldn't get some kind of agreement that they'd carry out the court
order. . . . You might call Wallace and just say, . . . "I'd like to explore some things
I thought of and see, George, what you think about it . . . and it's awfully important that it not get out." We could talk to the other side, too. . . . We sure don't want
to get in a position where we have to send in troops and make it worse.

---

1. "Take" is a word that LBJ uses to mean "tape."

LISTER HILL

Democratic Senator from Alabama
Monday, March 8, 1965, 4:24 P.M.

After an inconclusive call between Ellington and Governor Wallace, the weary LBJ subtly prods his old Senate friend to support a court order that will help avert another conflagration in Selma. With his talent for making each side feel that he is latently one of them, while talking to the white Alabaman, Johnson refers to Martin Luther King, Jr., and his "goddamn march" in a way that suggests distance.

LBJ: This is just between you and me.

HILL: Understood.

LBJ: Don't want it to go any further—I know it won't. . . . I just want some good advice. This fellow sent out wires all over the United States—King has—asking everybody to come in there for the march tomorrow. Asked fifty Protestant ministers from Washington, D.C., for instance. Chartered an airplane. . . . They're flying in and coming by bus . . . from all over the country. We had Buford Ellington talk to George Wallace. Our basic difficulty is . . . we don't know how to talk to him. I think he feels kind of, you know, left out. . . . We're not close enough to talk.

HILL: May I say something very confidentially?

LBJ: Yeah, yeah.

HILL: . . . You remember what he did there at the University of Alabama?[1] . . . He had a court order to admit one [student]. . . . He went there and stood in the doorway and wouldn't let anybody come in until the federal troops [arrived]. . . . He wanted to show the people of Alabama he fought to the bitter end. . . . That's what you're up against down there.

LBJ: Yeah. Now, Buford talked to him, and it looks like he wants a way out because this is getting pretty bad from their standpoint. Looks like King wants a way out. . . . He's concerned about safety and everything. It is a dangerous thing. . . . The Attorney General . . . will join King as a friend of the court and ask one of the Alabama judges to enjoin the state from interfering with a peaceful march. . . . A single march, maybe for a mile or two, and riding buses the rest of the way . . . King has filed a suit at two o'clock.

HILL: Oh, he did?

LBJ: Yeah. . . . He wants the Attorney General to come down there with Governor Collins[2] to try to . . . have some kind of agreement on getting the sheriff to quit

---

1. In June 1963.
2. Former Florida Governor LeRoy Collins was the federal official authorized by the 1964 Civil Rights Act to mediate such local disputes.

interfering and molesting them. . . . He told the *Washington Post* that he . . . told me about the problems of this march and I just sat there passively and showed no interest.[1] Now, that's not correct. He didn't talk to me about the march. But, of course, I'm concerned about it. Both sides and I . . . have . . . a deep interest in nobody getting hurt. . . . The Attorney General and Governor Ellington and Bill Moyers think we ought to . . . send Ramsey Clark[2] instead. . . . Both of them being Southerners, and . . . quiet, careful men. . . . I told them that I had a little doubt about joining as a friend of the court because it would look like I might be advocating the goddamn march, and I don't want to do that.

HILL: That's the trouble there.

LBJ: . . . It may look like I'm stirring up these marches.[3] [But] they say, . . . "If you don't do it, you get a lot of killings." . . .

HILL: . . . Stay out of that court, if you can. . . . It would [look] like . . . you really were encouraging it.

LBJ: . . . But suppose I get down . . . to where I have no alternative. . . .

HILL: Then you've got a hell of a dilemma.

LBJ: . . . I have them like that all day here. All day long. I had one—send the Marines in—yesterday. They said, "If you *don't* send them in, they're going to destroy all your airplanes. You'll have no security for your boys. If you *do* send them in, they'll say the Marines are *coming*." [*laughs darkly*] That's in Vietnam.

HILL: . . . This damned little Wallace! . . . That's a hell of a decision to have to make, because when you move in there, the people down home are going to think, My God, he[4] just moved in there and took *over* for this King!

LBJ: Well, I don't know. . . . Buford . . . suggested . . . that the thing to do is let them march a mile or two and get in a bus and go on over. But I think the Governor thought that would show that he was weak. . . .

HILL: Well, it looks like he put you in a fix then, where you've got to have some kind of court order. Is that it?

LBJ: Well, it is now. . . . And they're all coming in there, and the trouble is you get the Dean Sayres[5] and these preachers in there, you see. Then you get the Bull Connors[6] and they go to throwing those billy clubs. Then they say, "Where was the President? Why didn't he do something?"

---

1. King had met with LBJ at the White House on Friday.
2. Of Texas, Katzenbach's deputy.
3. LBJ shows how he talks to a Southerner with orthodox views on race.
4. LBJ.
5. Francis Sayre, Jr., was dean of the Washington Cathedral, grandson of Woodrow Wilson, and a noted liberal who had infuriated LBJ by criticizing his moral character in the 1964 campaign.
6. Birmingham Commissioner of Public Safety until 1963, infamous for using vicious dogs and fire hoses against civil rights demonstrators.

HILL: To prevent this horrible thing. . . . The trouble is . . . your Governor down there . . . just wants [people] to say, "Oh, God, he died for the cause—he stayed back for the bitter end." . . .

LBJ: . . . I guess the right thing is to try to keep down the disturbance at almost any cost.

HILL: . . . A lot of folks . . . might get killed down there.

LBJ: . . . This thing gets out of hand awfully easy on this subject.

HILL: . . . Sure does. They get awfully excited down there. *Awfully* excited. If you had that court order, why, that would be something to stand on.

LBJ: Yeah, I think that's what I'll do. Thank you, my friend.

HILL: Sorry I can't help you.

LBJ: All right.

EDWARD KENNEDY

Monday, March 8, 1965, 9:10 P.M.

> The Massachusetts Senator has called LBJ to ask for some help for New England. Johnson uses the opportunity to nurture his surprisingly good relationship with the youngest Kennedy brother—knowing that he may need it as his conflict with Robert Kennedy heats up.

LBJ: There's not a member of the Senate that I'll go as far to meet as I will you, because I just think that you've been fair and decent and fine as anybody. . . . You can just count me in. And if you quote me a little bit too far, I'll stand up and say, "Yes, sir."

KENNEDY: . . . Well, that's awfully kind, and, listen, I'm sorry to bother you.

LBJ: This business about my being at crossways with the Kennedys is just a pure lot of crap. I started out here to keep faith[1] and I'm going to do it. . . . I think you know something about how I feel about you. And I have no antagonisms and no antipathy and no wars to settle with anybody else. And I just don't want you to let the damn press do that. There's not anything else I want. I've got more than I can take care of right now. All I want to do is do what's right. . . . You just go on and make your speech, and write your ticket, and I'll do my damnedest to make good on it.

KENNEDY: I appreciate it, Mr. President. . . . I'm sorry to bother you.

LBJ: No, you don't bother. Don't you ever—I've told you you can call me anytime you want to because I want to be true to the trust that's placed in me.

---

1. With President Kennedy.

KENNEDY: We've had some good hearings on the immigration [bill].[1]

LBJ: Yes, you have. And I heard Bobby made a hell of a good statement the other day and it looks like it might be a possibility to get it out of both Houses. Do you think so?

KENNEDY: I think in the Senate we're in better shape than the House. . . .

LBJ: How's my girlfriend, my blonde?[2] Is she still living with you?

KENNEDY: Yeah, she sure is! Keeping her out of trouble. . . .

LBJ: Give her my love.

KENNEDY: I certainly shall.

LBJ: Tell her that I'm sorry that I wasn't looking at you in the picture when I went to visit you in the hospital because I had my eyes—[3] [*laughs*]

KENNEDY: Well, she's forgiven you. . . . You're awfully kind, Mr. President, and I . . . really appreciate—

LBJ: Don't you ever, don't you ever feel the slightest reluctance, my friend, to call me, and I'll try to do whatever I can that will be helpful. . . . Give your mama and daddy my love.

BILL MOYERS

Monday, March 8, 1965, 11:25 P.M.

Moyers reports on Selma to a sleepy Johnson, who is in bed.

MOYERS: I just talked to Katzenbach. The Negroes are still meeting in the church at Selma with Martin Luther King. We have no word back on what their intentions are. . . . Wallace called Buford Ellington a few minutes ago and said that he thought he ought to call out 350 of the National Guard to deal with the situation tomorrow because they could get along better than the local authorities, who were hostile toward the Negroes. Katzenbach's feeling, shared by everyone, was that he should be told . . . not to do anything until we knew more of what the Negroes' intentions were. . . . Do you want to be informed when King calls back?

LBJ: Yeah, yeah, but I would take a much tougher line than we're going to with them. I think that it's absolutely disgraceful that they would get in the Justice Department building and have to be hauled out of there.[4] And I don't care if we never

---

1. Revising the notorious National Origins Act of 1924, Johnson's immigration reform bill, born under JFK, would scrap the existing ethnic quota system.
2. Kennedy's then-wife, Joan.
3. During the 1964 campaign, while visiting Kennedy in the Boston hospital where he was recovering after his plane crash, LBJ had been photographed looking away from the patient and gazing fondly on Joan.
4. Civil rights demonstrators had staged a sit-in at the Justice Department.

serve another hour. They're going to respect the law while they do. I think that if King did in fact call up here and say that he would like to work this thing out on the basis of the friend of the court and the presence of Doar and Collins,[1] that then he ought to be told that we're going to do that, and we're not going to listen to the Javites[2] and the rest of them that are hollering around here. Listen, he better go to behaving himself, or all of them are going to get put in jail. I think that we really ought to be firm on it myself. I just think it's outrageous what's on TV. I've been watching it here, and looks like that man's in charge of the country and taking it over. I just don't think we can afford to have that kind of character running. And I'd remind him what he had said and take a very firm line with him.

BILL MOYERS

Tuesday, March 9, 1965, 7:33 A.M.

Now the aide talks to the President from his home in Southeast Washington, with the cries of the Moyers children in the background.

LBJ: Bill, what happened with Martin Luther King?

MOYERS: I didn't call you back because it was four o'clock by the time he finally called back. But the whole arrangement is this—they will march to the same point they were, they'll sing and pray for less than an hour, and then disperse peacefully. Wallace . . . is talking about calling up the National Guard, which we don't want him to do. The way we suggested to Ellington that he handle that is to say that . . . telegrams have been following into Washington urging the President to do something and that if Wallace calls up the National Guard to halt the march, it will only increase the pressure on Justice to use the National Guard to protect the marchers. So Ellington is at this very moment talking to Wallace. And that's where it stands. Very tenuous, but that's it.

LBJ: Why wouldn't they go with what they agreed on earlier? Join the court and send the—

MOYERS: Collins down?

LBJ: Yeah.

MOYERS: . . . King says his left-wingers would not let the day go by without some symbol of a march with all these people pouring in there. . . . The pressure is too much, he claims, from that side. . . . Katzenbach told me about seven that he talked to him again, and he was very fearful for his life, that he really wanted out of it, but he couldn't get out of at least a token march around Selma. . . . The best

---

1. John Doar of the Justice Department and the federal mediator LeRoy Collins.
2. Republican Senator Jacob Javits of New York, LBJ's image of a mouthy Northern liberal.

we can do now is just hope that Wallace will be true to his word and that King will break them up peacefully after thirty-five or forty minutes of singing and praying.

NICHOLAS KATZENBACH
Wednesday, March 10, 1965, 9:00 A.M.

On Tuesday, Federal Judge Frank Johnson, Jr., had issued a ruling against any march from Selma to Montgomery until Thursday.

LBJ: Where are we this morning?

KATZENBACH: . . . I talked with [King] last night, and he's going to wait and go on into court tomorrow morning.[1] We'll be filing papers in court today. . . .

LBJ: What will you be asking them to do? To protect the marchers, or to allow them to march under—

KATZENBACH: Under restricted conditions, yes. That's what the judge is going to do. . . . He's going to probably restrict the numbers. He's going to tell them they can't interfere with traffic on the highway. . . .

LBJ: All right. . . . Now, what do we do about our pickets at Justice and across [from] the White House?[2]

KATZENBACH: . . . I'm only letting people in here with official business today. It got out of hand. . . . They were starting to wander all over the building, and that's the reason I had to put them out. . . . Those kids need a bath as much as they need anything.

LBJ: Uh-huh. Who is leading them, the SNCC[3] group?

KATZENBACH: Yeah. . . . They're really just kids.

LBJ: . . . McCulloch[4] says that we could have prevented this thing if we'd have acted right. . . . Does McCulloch believe in sending troops?

KATZENBACH: No, I think McCulloch believes in criticizing Democrats. . . .

LBJ: . . . Have we got any legal right to go in with troops to stop a deputy sheriff from hitting a citizen over the head?

KATZENBACH: No, Mr. President. . . . If Sunday's incidents were repeated on a broad scale and a lot more people got hit . . . I think you could do it, but . . . I just think it's disastrous when you get troops in, frankly. . . . You just have to hold as long as you can, even though you can catch it with a lot of criticism. . . .

LBJ: Do you think it might be wise for us to try to get . . . Doar [or] maybe Burke

---

1. King wanted an order protecting the marchers and allowing them to go forward.
2. Referring to civil rights picketers.
3. The Student Non-Violent Coordinating Committee.
4. William McCulloch of Ohio, a Republican on the House Judiciary Committee, was a co-sponsor of the 1964 Civil Rights Act.

Marshall[1] . . . to meet with a lawyer from each one of the groups like Wilkins[2] and like King, and the SNCC crowd and give them our view of the . . . danger of troops . . . and what real dedicated and determined efforts we are making to get the bill that will give them the action they want? We think that's what's important instead of walking fifty miles. The walking just holds up the bill. . . . It divides your time. . . .

KATZENBACH: . . . We've been over that business on troops with them a hundred times. . . .

LBJ: . . . You can also point out that you were not unsuccessful yesterday in the light of an injunction.They still marched and they handled themselves properly, and looked good, and you did keep Wallace behaving. . . . What they have to say to their people is that sometimes the power to use force is better than using it. . . . We had the power to use it with Wallace and didn't, and got him to do everything and more than we could have if we'd sent troops in. . . . Now, what's Bobby [Kennedy] demanding this morning? . . . He's got on television all over. He's saying we've got to have more action from the federal government. . . . Check it. Be sure we've got no conflicts there.[3]

NICHOLAS KATZENBACH

Wednesday, March 10, 1965, Probably 9:32 P.M.

> On Tuesday evening in Selma, James Reeb, a white minister from Boston who was among the marchers, was beaten in the head.

LBJ: This minister's going to die, isn't he?

KATZENBACH: Yes, sir.

LBJ: Is he already dead?

KATZENBACH: No, sir. Well, he is, for all intents and purposes. I think they're just trying to keep him alive in a technical kind of way . . . so that he doesn't die in a time that'll flare things up.

LBJ: What time do you think he'll die?

KATZENBACH: They tell me that he could stay alive for another twenty-four or thirty-six hours under these mechanical things, but I think he'll probably die early tomorrow morning.

LBJ: Do you think you'll have your court order in the morning?[4]

---

1. Assistant Attorney General.

2. Roy Wilkins of the National Association for the Advancement of Colored People.

3. Under a compromise worked out by LBJ's mediator, King led two thousand marchers across the Pettus Bridge. Stopped by troopers, they sang "We Shall Overcome," knelt in prayer, and returned to Selma.

4. Allowing the march to proceed unthreatened.

KATZENBACH: Yeah. . . . He's[1] not going to embarrass King on this. He's not going to find that King was in violation of any law. We're working out . . . that march on pretty satisfactory terms. . . . King has accepted the idea that if this minister dies, the Selma-Montgomery march . . . is going to be in his honor. . . . We'll give a funereal quality to it. . . . Be like going to church. And that'll keep the rowdies down.[2] . . .

LBJ: I think . . . you and Lee White[3] and Bill [Moyers] ought to invite some of them[4] in in the morning to take this heat off and to explain to them what's behind our reasoning and our thinking. . . . Any way that you can to get me out of the line of fire as much as we can. . . . Now . . . they say [that] leaders of the white segregationist forces, including Al Lingo,[5] [should] be arrested for encouraging the officers and troops to violate the civil rights of others.

KATZENBACH: We may have a case against Lingo. We may arrest him. . . .

LBJ: Sheriff Clark?[6]

KATZENBACH: . . . Hell, we've got three cases against Sheriff Clark now. I don't mind arresting him. . . . I'm a little more reluctant with Lingo because it touches the Governor[7] more. . . .

LBJ: I think you ought to say . . . it's not something that the President does. He doesn't go after white segregationists or white integrationists. . . . And [about] withdrawing federal financial assistance from certain principal areas of Alabama,[8] we have no right to do that because somebody says you can or can't march, do we?

KATZENBACH: I don't see why.

LBJ: . . . They want to meet with the President. . . . If it gives them any satisfaction, be glad to do it. . . . What I'm anxious to do is not to have the image that . . . you're following a Southern President over here who is afraid of Lingo. . . . I think that you ought to point out to them that we are doing everything that we can in their interest, including drafting the message.[9] Now, what's the status of that?

KATZENBACH: I got a draft over there tonight at the White House, which I don't like much, Mr. President. I'm going to work some more tonight on it. . . . It just doesn't sing yet.

LBJ: . . . Is Dirksen planning to pull out on us?

KATZENBACH: No, sir.

---

1. The judge.
2. Reeb lingered until Thursday evening.
3. Special Counsel to the President.
4. Ministers and other civil rights leaders who complained that Johnson was not doing enough.
5. Chief of the Alabama state troopers, who stopped the marchers at the Edmund Pettus Bridge in Selma.
6. Sheriff Jim Clark, another determined enemy of the march.
7. George Wallace.
8. Another demand of the civil rights leaders.
9. LBJ's forthcoming address to Congress, asking for a voting rights bill.

LBJ: This is just politics on the television tonight where they say that they may have to go it alone and go the Fifteenth Amendment route.[1] . . .
KATZENBACH: . . . I think he's trying to get in the act, Mr. President, that's all. Dirksen told me that he . . . wanted you to recommend a bill, and he wanted to jointly sponsor it with Mike [Mansfield]. That's the best possible situation.
LBJ: . . . Do you find any agitation against Johnson the Southerner not acting?
KATZENBACH: Not a bit, not a bit, Mr. President.

LADY BIRD JOHNSON

Saturday, March 13, 1965, Tape-recorded Diary

> To Lady Bird's relief, LBJ's longtime private doctors and friends, Dr. Willis Hurst of Emory University, and Dr. James Cain of the Mayo Clinic, have quietly come to the White House to assess the President's health. Hurst was the cardiologist who had received Johnson at Bethesda in 1955, when he suffered his massive heart attack. Cain was the son-in-law of Alvin Wirtz, who served with Johnson's father in the Texas Senate.

LADY BIRD: My dear friends Jim Cain and Willis Hurst are houseguests, and this morning, they completed the purpose of their visit—an examination of Lyndon. Essentially everything is fine—all the basic organs and the functioning thereof. But there is this heavy load of tension and this fog of depression. If you're enjoying what you do, you don't get tired, no matter how hard you work. And if it's frustrating and full of uncertainties, you use up energies struggling against what you have to do. In a nutshell, their prescription is exercise, diet, and a break—to get off to sunshine and rest for a couple of days every two weeks . . . But Lyndon feels chained right here, and it's having an erosive effect on his personality.

LADY BIRD JOHNSON

Sunday, March 14, 1965, Tape-recorded Diary

LADY BIRD: Lyndon . . . was supposed to come home for a nap. But . . . there was a meeting of the leadership of the House and Senate, during which they asked him to come and address them on the subject of the turmoil in the nation. . . . And so, with only twenty-four hours' notice, there will be a major speech Monday

---

1. Relying on the Fifteenth Amendment to battle voting rights violations.

night at nine o'clock! It's like deciding to climb Mount Everest while you are sitting around at a cozy family picnic. . . . I am glad that he is launched, that he is being intensely active. It is the milieu for him. It is his life. He is loosed from the bonds of depression.

RICHARD J. DALEY

Tuesday, March 16, 1965, 10:03 A.M.

On Monday night, in the best speech of his life, written largely by Richard Goodwin, the President told Congress that he would submit a voting rights bill: "It is wrong—deadly wrong—to deny any of your fellow Americans the right to vote in this country. . . . And we shall overcome!" Watching on television, Martin Luther King, Jr., heard the white Southern President uttering his credo, and wept.[1] The Mayor of Chicago calls with congratulations.

DALEY: It was terrific, magnificent, and impressive. Your humility, determination, and your courage manifested through that performance. . . . You were really at your best, Mr. President. . . .
LBJ: Bless your heart, Dick. You don't know how much comfort I get from it. . . . We did what we thought was right. Now, we'll have to see where we go.
DALEY: You handled it magnificently. . . .
LBJ: . . . We had 93 million. Largest audience anybody ever had, they claim. . . . Dick, you're wonderful. I'm so glad I got you as a friend.

EVERETT DIRKSEN

Tuesday, March 16, 1965, 12:55 P.M.

Johnson wants his old friend Donald Cook to succeed Douglas Dillon as Treasury Secretary, but first he wants to feel out Dirksen about a problem—Cook's connection to Bobby Baker.

LBJ: Are you at a wired phone or is this line all right?
DIRKSEN: I think so.
LBJ: This is between me and you and God. I don't want anybody else to know it. Can I talk to you on that basis?
DIRKSEN: Yeah.

---

1. See Garrow, *Bearing the Cross*, pp. 408–9. When Senator Richard Russell heard it, he dismissed his old pupil as a "turncoat." (Dallek, *Flawed Giant*, p. 221.)

LBJ: I've got four men I'm considering for Secretary of Treasury. The bankers and the businessmen and the Dillons and the prudent men want Don Cook, who's president of American Power and Light. He is by far the best and most qualified. . . . He wants to come. . . . He's a great expert and my man. . . . McNamara said he's the smartest man in the country. . . . Sometime during [the early 1950s] Bobby Baker called him up. . . . Asked him to see the president of this MAGIC.[1]

DIRKSEN: Yeah?

LBJ: He saw him, and he said there was a Jew over at SEC[2] that was being unfair to them, and Cook had been former head of SEC. The MAGIC man dropped in on him in New York. . . . He saw him, and he said, "Well, next time I'm in Washington, I'll drop into SEC and see what's wrong." He dropped in, and he found out this little Jewish boy was giving him hell and harassing them, and he talked to Cohen,[3] who's the commissioner, about it, and said what the man needs is a lawyer. . . . He told him who to hire. Jewish lawyer named Friedman. . . . So, he went over and hired him and filed his registration statement, and it was approved. . . . He didn't need any influence. Cook didn't exercise any. A month or two later . . . he bought a thousand shares of MAGIC. He paid, I think, forty for it, and he sold them for thirty-eight. . . . He made no money. . . . Cook is a good, fair man, and he's a man that . . . you could do business with every hour of the day. . . .

DIRKSEN: Don't do it.

LBJ: And if— Huh?

DIRKSEN: Don't do it. If he's got the MAGIC touch on him, you're going to catch hell just as sure as shootin'. . . . There's no use of you bleeding for a goddamn situation of that kind. . . . You will bleed. . . . Outfits like the *Chicago Tribune* are going to *murder* you, and it isn't *worth* it! Find somebody else. . . . Let Cook alone. . . . We can defend him and, I'm sure, get him confirmed, but . . . you know damn well someone will say, . . . "That son of a bitch was in MAGIC up to his ears." And you can't live it down, no matter how long he serves. So good as he is, I wouldn't do it.

LBJ: Uh-huh.

DIRKSEN: Life's too short.

LBJ: All right.

---

1. Mortgage Guaranty Insurance Company of Milwaukee. The Senate was investigating whether Baker had peddled influence for the firm.

2. Securities and Exchange Commission.

3. Manuel Cohen of the SEC, who became chairman in 1965.

THOMAS WATSON, JR.

President, International Business Machines
Tuesday, March 16, 1965, 4:19 P.M.

> Watson discreetly lobbies for his friend David Rockefeller as Secretary of the Treasury.

WATSON: Terrific speech you made last night, sir. I think that thrilled the whole nation.

LBJ: I don't know. I did the best I could.

WATSON: As a matter of fact, I think it was the best speech of that type I ever heard.

LBJ: . . . Thank you, thank you. Got a good reaction in the country, but I don't know how long it'll last.

*   *   *

WATSON: Mary Rockefeller[1] just left here a few minutes ago. . . . As she left, I said, "Mary, what's the story on David and going to work in Washington?" . . . She said, . . . "He said . . . if he were ever really called on to do it, he would have to give it serious consideration." Now, earlier in the game, he had . . . asked me what I thought of that job in connection with your administration. I told him I thought it would be the greatest thing in the world. Maybe somebody had made an overture to him. . . .

LBJ: No, nobody has.

WATSON: He asked me whether I thought he could work with you. I said that I thought . . . he would work with you in a beautiful way. . . .

LBJ: . . . Very confidentially . . . I didn't know how he felt about our money policy. I'm very fearful that some of our New York banks are gonna jump my interest rates. If we don't have a tight money policy . . . we could slow down our economy some. I have enough problems with Martin.[2] Keeping him loosened up. . . . They're always wanting to tighten up. . . . The average banker, and I've been one[3]—thank God I haven't got any advertisement that way—we're the first ones to get our raise. Before the labor unions and before you mark up your machine and before anybody else, the banks always increase their interest. . . . I've got a big problem with my Federal Reserve, making them keeping that money out to keep this interest rate down. And any excuse they find, they raise the hell out of it.

---

1. Wife of Laurence Rockefeller.
2. William McChesney Martin, Chairman of the Federal Reserve Board.
3. Johnson had bought interests in Texas banks, including the Citizens National Bank of Austin.

They're just as dumb as they can be. . . . The second question I raised was the problem with Nelson.[1]

WATSON: Well, I guess that is a problem.

LBJ: Nelson's ambitious, and Nelson wants to be nominated, and Nelson wants to run. And a man's got to be loyal to his brother. . . . What would he do, sitting in my Cabinet, when we're planning how to cut his brother's throat?

GEORGE WALLACE

Governor of Alabama

NICHOLAS KATZENBACH
BUFORD ELLINGTON

Thursday, March 18, 1965, 4:33 P.M.

To avert more violence in Alabama, LBJ took the risk of asking Governor Wallace to the Oval Office on Saturday, March 13. When Johnson pressed him to speed black registration and desegregate schools, Wallace claimed that he had no such power. The President spat out, "Don't you shit me, George Wallace!" During a three-hour performance, he told Wallace that he must choose between a marble monument—"George Wallace, He Built"—or a "little piece of scrawny pine board"—"George Wallace, He Hated."[2] Now Judge Johnson has cleared the way for King and his marchers to walk from Selma to Montgomery on March 21. At Ellington's suggestion, Wallace calls LBJ to ask for help. Johnson speaks slowly and deliberately, knowing that Wallace might be taping his call and that, in any case, Wallace might use his words against him. Despite LBJ's careful handling, after this conversation, just as the President suspects, Wallace will double-cross him.

LBJ: Governor? . . . Glad to hear you.

WALLACE: . . . The court, as you know, has ordered this march. . . . You know, we have very limited amounts of state policemen, and they are off the roads. We've had drunken drivers running into people and killing them the last eight weeks as a result of us not having adequate protection on the highways. These people are pouring in from all over the country. The hotels of all the cities are full. . . . Some of the motels have gone up double on their prices. . . . They're flying in nuns and priests. We've got hundreds of bearded beatniks in front of my Capitol now. . . . We hope that you might use your influence to at least make them have an orderly march. . . . The group coming here, with the language they're using! . . .

---

1. New York Governor Nelson Rockefeller, unsuccessful candidate for the Republican presidential nomination in 1964.

2. Wallace later confessed that LBJ was so persuasive that had he stayed much longer, Johnson would have had him coming out for civil rights. (Merle Miller, *Lyndon,* Putnam, 1980, pp. 524–25). See also Dan T. Carter, *The Politics of Rage* (Simon & Schuster, 1995), pp. 251–54.

Two days ago . . . James Forman[1] suggested in front of all the nuns and priests that if anybody went in a café and they wouldn't serve 'em, they'd "kick the fuckin' legs of the tables off." . . . It inflames people. . . . I'm asking people . . . to stay away from this highway, to "use your superior discipline." . . . But . . . quite frankly . . . they've been stirred up by a lot of things. Of course, I know you don't want anything to happen that looks like a revolution. But if these people keep pouring in here, conducting themselves in the manner they are, why, it's going to take . . . everybody in the country to stop something. . . .

LBJ: Governor, the court has acted now. Obviously, the longer the march is postponed . . . the longer the people from outside are going to stay in Alabama, the more problem you're going to have, and the more problem *I'm* going to have. . . . If you can . . . get that request for a stay[2] out of the way so we don't have to sit here and wait days and days and days . . . while this stuff builds up and blows the cork out, why, it would be good. . . . If you say your patrolmen got to go on back to watch the highways and you call up your own [National] Guard into the service of the state . . . I would . . . assure you that proper contingents of men would be stationed at Craig and Maxwell.[3] . . . If the situation were to deteriorate . . . maybe we'd have to federalize them. . . . I would be glad to take those steps if you felt that the orderly needs of the situation there justified it. . . . Maybe by all of us saying to them, "Let's have the march. Let's get it over as soon as we can." . . . When you talk about revolution, that really upsets us all. . . .

WALLACE: . . . Mr. President, . . . I *do* have some revolutionaries down here.

LBJ: I know that. I understand that.

WALLACE: . . . I don't want anybody to get hurt. But . . . I don't want to be in the position of intimating that I'm asking for federal troops. . . . We have . . . ministers down here that walk up and scratch the patrolmen on their hands. . . . A Negro priest yesterday asked all the patrolmen what their *wives* were doing, whether some of their friends could have dates with their *wives*. You know, trying to provoke them . . . These fifty thousand people . . . jammed in this place are going to be here the next day, and the next day and the next day. They're going to *bankrupt* our state. . . . Of course . . . if these revolutionaries . . . want the federal government to take a state over . . . they probably will . . . require that—unless we can use the good influence of your office to say, "You made your march. Now let's don't keep marching." That's what I'm worried about. What *after* the march, Mr. President?

LBJ: Oh, I guess no one can really prophesy what any group will do. . . . I might issue a statement later today saying that I asked people to not go into the state and

---

1. Of the Student Non-Violent Coordinating Committee (SNCC).
2. Preventing the march.
3. Air Force bases, both in Alabama.

that we're going to jointly try to protect the march. . . . I think it'd be better if *you* called up the Guard, in the service of the state . . . rather than *our* doing it. . . . If your highway patrolmen are going back to the highways to take care of the drunken drivers . . . and you've got this group coming, and the highways moving and the tourist courts filling up, if you call up your Guard, I'll put the best people we've got to work right with them. . . . And I think I just ought to say that I'm asking people in the country not to let this thing get out of hand. We don't need any more marching down there. They've got enough to march.

WALLACE: Well, I think that would be excellent. . . . What I'm going to do is this. . . . I'm going to do whatever we consider necessary to maintain law and order. We're going to use the patrolmen we have available. . . . If necessary, we call the Guard. . . . I appreciate the fact that you may make an appeal that there's enough people in the state to march without other folks coming in.

LBJ: I would seriously consider doing that. . . . I want *you* to take the action . . . with your Guard. . . .

WALLACE: . . . We can handle it through the march, but then after the march, if they are just going to stay in this state eight weeks and congregate fifty thousand strong a *day,* then we're going to have a *revolution.* . . . It's hard to control people. . . .

LBJ: Don't you think we ought to act before it gets beyond where we *can?*

WALLACE: It's not in any such condition as that now.

LBJ: I thought you felt like that we ought to have some Guard called up.

WALLACE: . . . Let's see about when the march takes place. . . . It'll be hard to keep our patrolmen away another two or three or four weeks. . . . That's when it might get unmanageable.

LBJ: . . . They're going to stay there until they take action, Governor . . .

WALLACE: What do you mean? Action on the voter business?

KATZENBACH: I think if that march goes . . . smoothly and they are protected and there's no incidents, that's the best chance of their not staying on and on.

WALLACE: . . . I'm going on statewide television tonight and tell people that . . . "I'm asking you to stay away, and use your restraint." . . . If you say that will help us keep them from staying on and on, that's what we're going to do.

LBJ: Buford, do you want to say anything?

ELLINGTON: George, . . . I think . . . the wisest move you can make is to put your men back out on the highways and call your Guard. . . . That way, I think we get it all over with at once. . . .

WALLACE: I'll consider it. . . .

ELLINGTON: . . . If they know you're going to call out the Guard, then this wild element is not going to come to Alabama. . . . That's the thing that I'm afraid of. I'm not afraid of the good people on either side.

WALLACE: Of course, I hate to call out the Guard. You-all federalize them each time I call them out.[1]

ELLINGTON: . . . You can take my word, I'm not worried about that. And I'm standing in front of all these people while we talk.

WALLACE: . . . We're going to take what action is necessary to protect. Now . . . you know, the President of our nation was slain with all the protection he had over in Texas.[2] . . . If they can't protect our President from being brutally slain, why, it's sometimes hard to keep somebody from getting hit with a rock.

LBJ: Governor, that's sure right. . . . If we . . . had any idea something like this might have happened, why, we might have had our [Texas National] Guard out. We know we got trouble ahead here. . . . Let the march start before people can get there from these other states, and you call up your Guard. . . . And we wouldn't federalize any Guard unless it just got to the point where that was all that was left.

WALLACE: Yes, sir.

LBJ: But we want to take this through you before it gets all out of proportion. . . .

ELLINGTON: George, . . . I haven't even discussed this with the President, but here's what I've had in the back of my mind all the time. This radical element is Lingo[3] and some of the boys. . . . You know that.

WALLACE: Yes, sir.

ELLINGTON: I think completely removing them from the scene . . . and bringing in new faces is the only way we are going to solve this now.

WALLACE: . . . We're not going to have the general out front. We're going to have the corporals and sergeants out front. . . .

ELLINGTON: . . . The more strength you show right here . . . [will bring] the quickest solution. . . . Of course, what you want and what we want is to get them out of there.

WALLACE: I'll show strength insofar as protecting the people on the march, but I would like for you-all to help *me* after they've made that point. Now you say they're going to stay here until the problem's *solved*. . . . They'll be here from now on. . . .

ELLINGTON: I don't think you get what we mean there. . . . Once the march is over and they are successful under the Guard sponsorship, then they would move on.

WALLACE: Yes, well, now, that's fine. That's all right. That sounds good.

LBJ: . . . Governor, I want to do whatever I can . . . to get this thing as peaceful as

---

1. Wallace is thinking of the confrontation over integrating the University of Alabama in June 1963.

2. Referring, of course, to John Kennedy.

3. Colonel Al Lingo, who commanded state troopers, was a close confederate of Wallace and Bull Connor.

I can. I thought Governor Ellington and you-all kind of had a meeting of the minds on it. . . . What do you want to do? . . .

WALLACE: . . . I'm just as concerned as you are about nothing happening. . . . If it takes ten thousand Guardsmen, we'll *have* them. I'll just do whatever is *necessary*. . . .

LBJ: That's okay. That's good. You . . . keep in touch with Buford. . . . I'll be in constant touch with the situation, and you call us anytime.

BUFORD ELLINGTON

Thursday, March 18, 1965, 9:13 P.M.

> Johnson had ended his afternoon conversation thinking that Wallace would let the Alabama National Guard help protect the marchers. But unwilling to look like the lackey of a liberal President and federal authority, the Governor has just told the Alabama legislature, in a televised speech, that his state cannot afford to activate the Guard. Placing the onus on Johnson, he has demanded that the President send federal civil authorities to Alabama instead. LBJ is furious.

LBJ: You're dealing with a very treacherous guy. You-all must not come in even quoting him anymore. Because he's a no-good son of a *bitch!* . . . Wallace said, . . . "We must now submit to mob rule." . . . He said tonight that he would "ask Johnson to provide protection for Negroes marching from Selma to Montgomery." . . . Son of a *bitch!* He is absolutely *treacherous!*

ELLINGTON: . . . I told Burke and Lee[1] all the way through that I didn't trust him. So I'm just not going to answer any calls from him or talk to him.

LBJ: I'd answer one and just tell him, "Now, listen, George, I . . . told the President that I'd talk to you and you wanted help."

ELLINGTON: Yeah.

LBJ: "He called you and offered to give it to you. You ran like a goddamned *rabbit!* Then you ran down to the television and told them that we had created [this situation]. . . . Now, why in the hell didn't you stand up like a man and say what you were going to do to begin with?"

ELLINGTON: . . . If he keeps calling me, I'll waiting till in the morning where I can record it. . . .

LBJ: Come over here. You can record it anytime.[2] . . . I think you might answer him tonight and just say, "Now, let me tell you, George. I just want this for the

---

1. Burke Marshall of the Justice Department and LBJ's aide Lee White.
2. Although generally determined to conceal his White House recording system, LBJ here makes a rare oblique reference to his secret facility.

record. You called me up, asked for *help*. I offered to give it to you. . . . Then you went publicly and you said *this*. Now I want to know whether you mean it. . . . If you do, why, you come out there and put it on the *record*. Because I've got a record, and I'm not going to be double-crossed this way."

ELLINGTON: I will do.

LBJ: I'm going to issue a statement here that kind of burns his tail.

NICHOLAS KATZENBACH

Thursday, March 18, 1965, 10:00 P.M.

LBJ: Here's a wire from Wallace. . . . [*reads aloud*][1] He assured us that he would [deploy substantial numbers of Alabama state troopers and National Guardsmen]. Now he's not doing that, you see.

KATZENBACH: Yeah, yeah.

LBJ: He's welshing on that. You don't think we ought to call him and ask him if he's welshing on what he said to us earlier today? . . .

KATZENBACH: . . . I suppose he's going to say no, he just wants to do it with civil authority. . . . Of course, his figures are perfectly ridiculous.

LBJ: My problem is I've got a reporter been sitting here since seven o'clock and I just got ready to call him in and in comes this goddamned wire. We're getting every bad break we can get.

KATZENBACH: . . . I would answer that by saying, . . . "Obviously the United States did not have some five thousand civil personnel, as Governor Wallace knows perfectly well. But he does have over ten thousand members of the Guard unit trained and equipped to serve this purpose."

LBJ: And if he won't call them out, we *will*.

KATZENBACH: And if he's unable to maintain law, then we will.

LBJ: All right, now. Put the girl on and take that sentence and let's take that down now. [*dictates statement*] . . . Okay, Marie,[2] type it up right quick![3]

---

1. "For the so-called march from Selma, Alabama, to Montgomery, the Department of Public Safety of the State of Alabama advises me that the following personnel will be required in order to provide maximum security. . . . 6171 men, 489 vehicles, 15 buses. . . . The State of Alabama has available 300 state troopers and approximately 150 officers of the Department of Conservation and Alcoholic Beverage Control Department. . . . I respectfully request that the United States provide sufficient federal civil . . . officers to provide for the safety and welfare . . . of the marchers."

2. LBJ's secretary Marie Fehmer.

3. At 10:25 P.M., LBJ read the statement to the press. On Saturday, March 20, he federalized 1,800 Alabama National Guardsmen and appointed Ramsey Clark to coordinate the march to Montgomery.

JOHN McCLELLAN

Democratic Senator from Arkansas
Tuesday, March 23, 1965, 10:05 A.M.

On the triple-screen television in the Oval Office, LBJ has just watched John Young and Virgil Grissom launched on America's first two-man Gemini space flight, a five-hour mission that will be the first of Johnson's presidency.

LBJ: We hope it works out all right. We got a long ways to go. These boys[1] are kind of running rings around us, but we don't get hot until we get real behind and then we start looking for somebody to make a scapegoat out of. . . . But . . . we think that we got a fair chance to keep up with these people by '70.[2]

McCLELLAN: We should keep up.

LBJ: Oh, this research is the most important thing we can do. . . . John, 75 percent of the things we will be making twenty-five years from now we have never heard of now. That's how fast this world changes. And in the year 2000, we're going to have 80 percent of our people, over 300 million, living in the cities of the country. This damn world is shifting and changing so fast. I got 38 percent of these young Nigro boys out on the streets. They've got no school to go to and no job. And by God, I'm just *scared to death* what's going to happen in June and July.[3] You know when you get an old hard-peckered boy—

McCLELLAN: They've got them inflamed.

LBJ: You know when you were seventeen, eighteen— I ran off to California. Didn't think my daddy had any sense, from Texas, when I was a boy sixteen.[4] But you take an old hard-peckered boy that sits around and got no *school* and got no *job* and got no *work* and got no *discipline*. His daddy's probably on relief, and his mama's probably taking mor-*phine*. Why, he ain't got nothing hurt if he gets shot. I mean, he's better off dead than he is where he is.

McCLELLAN: . . . His life isn't worth a damn anyhow.

LBJ: That's right. And they're 38 percent of those unemployed, and they just fill these cities. What you've seen in Selma is nothing. We're handling things reasonably well there . . . but you just wait till the rats get going in Harlem and Chicago. Dick Daley[5] called me the other morning.

---

1. The Soviets.
2. In the effort to fulfill JFK's pledge to land a man on the moon before the 1960s were out.
3. Johnson was worried about a larger reprise of the city riots of the summer of 1964.
4. In retirement LBJ told his aide and friend Doris Kearns, "I always hated cops when I was a kid. . . . I dropped out of school and took off for California. I'm not some conformist middle-class personality." (Kearns, *Lyndon Johnson and the American Dream*, Harper, 1976, pp. 333–34.)
5. Mayor of Chicago.

McCLELLAN: They're going to have it worse up there.
LBJ: Oh, ten times as bad!

DREW PEARSON

Tuesday, March 23, 1965, 11:35 A.M.

> The muckraking columnist, who had supported LBJ for President in 1960, later recalled that when Johnson was in the White House, "I used to argue with him about Vietnam, not very effectively. . . . He was a better talker than a listener."[1] Here is an illustration.

LBJ: I don't believe I can walk out. . . . If I did, they'd take Thailand. . . . They'd take Cambodia. . . . They'd take Burma. . . . They'd take Indonesia. . . . They'd take India. . . . They'd come right back and take the Philippines. . . . I'd be another Chamberlain and . . . we'd have another Munich.[2] The aggressors feed on blood. . . . I'm *not* coming *home! They* may get another President, but I'm not going to pull out. Now, the second thing is negotiation. . . . I've said in forty different speeches I'll go anywhere, I'll do anything . . . in an honorable way to promote peace at any time. . . . Okay. Now let's see whether I need to go to Hanoi or not. Let's see whether I need to go to Peiping or not. My last intelligence from Peiping sums it up pretty well. . . . "Mao Tse-tung says that Emperor Johnson must know that he cannot win at the conference table what he has lost on the battlefield." Now, so far that's pretty strong for China.
PEARSON: It sure is.
LBJ: They denounced Russia yesterday morning for . . . not coming in and raising more hell themselves. So Hanoi—I got a most recent report that says they think that the South is crumbling. They will not talk negotiation . . . until we pull back to San Francisco. Until we get out. Until they take over South Vietnam. Then they'll be glad to talk. . . .

  So the third thing is the LeMay viewpoint.[3] I can take my bombs, and I can take my nuclear weapons, as Barry [Goldwater] says. I can defoliate, and I can clear out that brush where I can see anybody coming down that line, and I can wipe out Hanoi, and I can wipe out Peiping. . . . But I think that would start World War III. . . . I'd have seven, eight hundred million, and I'd have a land war in Asia. I think I'd have to send three or four hundred thousand men there.[4] . . . I haven't bombed

---

  1. Drew Pearson oral history, LBJL.
  2. Referring to the prewar British Prime Minister Neville Chamberlain's appeasement of Hitler.
  3. Referring to General Curtis LeMay, the ultra-hard-line just-retired Air Force Chief of Staff.
  4. To LBJ, this figure is still fanciful in early 1965. But by 1968, over half a million Americans were in Vietnam.

any cities.[1] I haven't killed any women and children. I have said I would be "appropriate and fitting and measured." . . .

The people of South Vietnam forces do have some tear gas and nausea bombs.[2]. . . Every police chief in the United States has them. . . . Rather than shooting people, you give them something that will upset their stomach or make their eyes blink. Hell, they used them in Selma a week ago. . . . All this big propaganda they are making about gas? It's not poison gas. . . . It's the same kind of gas Chief Murray's[3] got right here if the Negroes started moving into the White House and they told them to stop. And it's the same kind used by . . . military police everyplace. Matter of fact, we got them down there right now in case the state troopers and the rest of them take us on in Alabama. . . .

PEARSON: Yeah.

LBJ: . . . When Kennedy didn't have it in Mississippi, they just raised unshirted hell, and he had to . . . fly them in, day and night, so they could protect our people.[4] . . . When the mob gets in action, a hundred thousand people coming at you, turn it loose. . . . These boys—the propagandists and the Communists—are working pretty full string. They keep us, all the time, fighting with our own people, trying to explain that we are not warmongers. Trying to explain to the Goldwaters and to the Nixons[5]—and even to the Lodges and to Rockefeller[6]—why we are not dropping bombs up there. . . . And I have to explain to them. . . . Let's do like I do with my daughter Luci. Let's try to reason with them. Let's be patient. . . . I'll make any sacrifice to keep people from being killed. Just like I didn't want to go into Montgomery and Selma.[7] I did everything a human could to *avoid* it. . . . [Governor Wallace] came up here. I spent three hours with him. . . . He said that he would do it. Then he wouldn't do it because he "didn't have money." So I was left with no choice.

*   *   *

LBJ: How did you like that speech before the Congress?[8]

PEARSON: Which one?

LBJ: Before the Congress in joint session on civil rights?

PEARSON: Oh, that was terrific.

LBJ: Thank you. Bye!

---

1. Not yet.
2. There has been press criticism about use of such weapons.
3. Chief Robert Murray of the Washington, D.C., police.
4. During the struggle to integrate the University of Mississippi at Oxford in 1962, Federal marshals used tear gas against angry white demonstrators.
5. Republican hard-liners on Vietnam.
6. Republican moderates on Vietnam.
7. Meaning sending in the National Guard.
8. Johnson's voting rights address.

WILBUR MILLS

Democratic Congressman from Arkansas and Chairman,
House Ways and Means Committee

WILBUR COHEN

Under Secretary of Health, Education, and Welfare
Tuesday, March 23, 1965, 4:54 P.M.

> Johnson wants to know when Mills's committee will take up Medicare, his plan for government-sponsored hospital insurance for Americans over sixty-five. LBJ considers the bill, which will be introduced in the House at noon tomorrow, "just top of the list" of his Great Society programs. Support from the conservative Mills is essential. Mills fears that Medicare costs might swell the federal deficit but knows that Johnson's huge 1964 majority makes some kind of bill inevitable. He has collaborated with LBJ on how to make the bill unassailable from Republican attack.

LBJ: When are you going to take it up?

MILLS: I've got to go to the Rules Committee next week.

LBJ: You always get your rules pretty quick, though, don't you?

MILLS: Yeah, that's right.

LBJ: . . . For God's sakes, let's get it before Easter! . . . They make a poll every Easter. . . . You know it. On what has Congress accomplished up till then. Then the rest of the year they use that record to write editorials about. So anything that we can grind through before Easter will be twice as important as after Easter.

*   *   *

COHEN: Sir, I think you've got not only everything that you wanted, but we got a lot more on this thing. It's a real comprehensive bill.

LBJ: How much did it cost my budget over what we estimated?

COHEN: Well, I think it would be around, I'd say, $450 million more than what you estimated for the net cost of this supplementary program.[1]

LBJ: . . . Explain that to me again . . . the supplementary you stole from Byrnes.

COHEN: Yes. Well, generally speaking, it's physician services.

LBJ: Physician? . . . Now my doctor . . . pumps my stomach out to see if I've got any ulcers—is that physician?

COHEN: That's right.

---

1. To preempt an opposing bill called Eldercare, proposed by John Byrnes, the senior Republican on Ways and Means, the Johnson administration added insurance for doctors' bills onto Medicare.

LDJ: Any medical services or M.D. services.... Does he charge what he wants to?

COHEN: No, he can't quite charge what he wants to. . . . What the Secretary of HEW would have to do is make some kind of an agreement with somebody like Blue Shield, let's say, and it would be their responsibility . . . [to] regulate the fees . . . of the doctor. . . . What he tried to do is be sure the government wasn't regulating the fees directly, that you deal with the individual doctor.[1] . . . This intermediary, the Blue Shield, would have to do all the policing so that the government wouldn't have its long hand—

LBJ: All right, that's good. Now what does it do for you, the patient, on doctors? It says that you can have doctor's bills paid up to what extent? . . . Any limit?

COHEN: The individual patient has to pay the first fifty dollars deductible. Then he's got to pay 20 percent—

LBJ: —of everything after that. . . . That keeps your hypochondriacs out.

COHEN: . . . For most of the people, it would provide the overwhelming proportion of their physicians' costs.

LBJ: Yes, sir. And it's something that nearly everybody could endure. They could borrow that much, or their folks could get them that much to pay their part . . . even if they didn't have any money. Now what does it get you on hospital and nurses' home? . . .

COHEN: You get the first sixty days of your hospital care with a forty-dollar deductible. Finally compromised on forty, Mr. President.

LBJ: That's good, that's good. . . . All right, now, what do the insurance companies— Are they still raising hell and mad?

COHEN: Yes, I think they're going to go over to the Senate and raise hell on the thing because, quite frankly, there's no longer any role for the private insurance companies to sell insurance policies for people over sixty-five when you take the combination of hospital care and the physician service.

LBJ: . . . That's wonderful. Now, remember this. Nine out of ten things that I get in trouble on is because they lay around. And tell the Speaker and Wilbur to *please* get a rule just the moment they can.

COHEN: They want to bring it up next week, Mr. President.

LBJ: Yeah, but you just tell them not to let it lay around. *Do* that! They want to, but they might not. Then that gets the *doctors* organized. Then they get the *others* organized. And I damn near *killed* my education bill, letting it lay *around!*[2]

---

1. In order to thwart conservative opposition.
2. See Adam Clayton Powell, Jr., conversation, March 1, 1965, above.

COHEN: Yeah.

LBJ: It stinks. It's just like a dead cat on the door. When a committee reports it, you better either bury that cat or get it some *life* in it. . . . [*to Mills, who is back on line:*] For God's sakes! "Don't let dead cats stand on your porch," Mr. Rayburn[1] used to say. They stunk and they stunk and they stunk. When you get one out of that committee, you call that son of a bitch up before they[2] can get their letters written.

NICHOLAS KATZENBACH

Thursday, March 25, 1965, 9:35 A.M.

> In Montgomery this morning, Martin Luther King is speaking to 25,000 triumphant marchers in front of the state capitol: "We are on the move now! . . . How long will it take? . . . Not long!"[3] Relieved that the five-day march has been peaceful, LBJ and Katzenbach now discuss how to pass a voting rights bill. The President is worried that passage might be obstructed by Senate forces who want it to include a ban on the local poll taxes that keep many blacks from voting (Katzenbach thinks that would be unconstitutional) and extension of the vote to eighteen-year-olds.

LBJ: Now, these civil rights groups. . . . What are they going to do when they get through marching? . . .

KATZENBACH: . . . I think King would like to take a little rest. He's got some sore feet. [*chuckles*] I can't say that some of these SNCC[4] kids aren't going to continue to raise a little bit of hell. . . . We'll just try to keep it under control. I want to get the military out of there just as quick as we damn well can. . . .

LBJ: You're reasonably sure we can defend this bill from the poll tax boys and the eighteen-year-olds?

KATZENBACH: Yes . . . Dirksen is staying very solid with us. They're going to have over eighty votes in the Senate for that bill.

LBJ: . . . I would just say, "The President . . . [has] an interest in lowering the age limit, [but] I told him . . . it would bog the bill down." . . . It's disgraceful. . . . [The Negro voter] just forgets to go pay his dollar seventy-five cents the first of the year. . . . I damn near forget it every year myself! . . . O'Daniel was running for governor . . . and he couldn't vote for himself. He ridiculed [the poll tax] so damn

---

1. Johnson's old patron, House Speaker Sam Rayburn.
2. Medicare's opponents.
3. Quoted in Garrow, *Bearing the Cross*, p. 413.
4. Student Non-Violent Coordinating Committee.

much that that might have been one reason he was elected—because the people didn't like it.[1]

JACQUELINE BOUVIER KENNEDY

Thursday, March 25, 1965, 4:56 P.M.

The British people are to dedicate a memorial to President Kennedy at Runnymede, where Magna Carta was signed. LBJ wants to offer Jacqueline a presidential Boeing 707 on which to make the trip. Jackie has just arrived in Hobe Sound, Florida. In contrast to their emotional conversations after John Kennedy's murder, LBJ's deepening feud with her beloved brother-in-law Robert and her new life in New York have created a noticeable distance between the two chief survivors of Dallas.

LBJ: Are you getting any sunshine down there?

JACQUELINE: Oh, it's wonderful. How are you?

LBJ: Oh, I'm harassed to death. I don't know whether I'm going to survive or not, but I may go till the weekend anyway.

JACQUELINE: Well, everything has been just wonderful. Your [voting rights] speech [to Congress] was beyond *belief!*

LBJ: Thank you, dear. I just heard that you were going to probably go to the memorial to the President. . . . I wanted to suggest that if you cared to, that you and your party take one of the 707s. And I think that I might ask Bobby and Teddy if they wanted to go to represent me, along with the Secretary of State and Chief Justice. . . . You just let me know and I'll have it all set up for you. . . .

JACQUELINE: Oh, that's so nice, but that's wasting taxpayers' *money!*

LBJ: No, no, it's not at all. It's very important to us, and very important to the country. . . .

JACQUELINE: Oh, listen, I just don't know what to say!

LBJ: You don't say anything.

JACQUELINE: That's the nicest thing I ever *heard* of!

LBJ: Just quit being so elusive. It's been too long since I saw you. There was that horrible night, you know—Walter Jenkins—when I was trying to think of all the terrible things there.[2] *[chuckles]*

JACQUELINE: Oh, when I *think* of it, I don't see how you *controlled* yourself! . . .

---

1. W. Lee "Pappy" O'Daniel was elected Texas Governor in 1938 on a platform of abolishing the poll tax, which he refused to pay himself.

2. When LBJ called on Jackie in Manhattan just after learning about Walter Jenkins's arrest. (See Chapter 2.)

LBJ: I was sitting there with one of the sweet, beautiful creatures of my life, and all the time my mind was down here about who was going to jail that night.

JACQUELINE: Ah, good God! Well—

LBJ: But maybe our paths will cross before long, and whenever, wherever I can do anything, you know I'm as close as the phone, dear.

JACQUELINE: I know. Thank you, Mr. President. Listen, that's the nicest thing I ever heard of. . . . I really am touched.

LBJ: You just let us know. Anything, dear. Give my love to your children.[1]

NICHOLAS KATZENBACH

Thursday, March 25, 1965, 11:25 P.M.

Johnson is rousted from bed to take a call from Katzenbach, reporting that Viola Gregg Liuzzo, a feisty, red-haired, thirty-nine-year-old white woman from Detroit who was ferrying marchers between Selma and Montgomery, has been shot. Outraged by watching Bloody Sunday on television, Mrs. Liuzzo had told her five children that she was driving immediately to Alabama. Her daughter Penny said she feared she would "never see her again." Liuzzo lustily retorted that she would live to "pee" on Penny's grave.[2] Earlier this evening, Liuzzo was driving a nineteen-year-old black man, Leroy Moton, to Montgomery when four Ku Klux Klan "missionaries" drove up beside them and fired revolvers. Moton survived by pretending to be dead. Shot in the head, Liuzzo was killed instantly, the only white woman ever to die in the civil rights movement.

KATZENBACH: The woman was injured and perhaps killed. . . . The other person with her notified the highway patrol and the highway patrol notified the Bureau.[3] . . .

LBJ: . . . Flat ambushed them or something?

KATZENBACH: Yes. Came by in another car and shot at them. . . . And the car went off the road.

LBJ: Was she driving?

KATZENBACH: . . . Yes.

---

1. Jackie wrote LBJ that with tortured memories of her flight from Dallas to Washington with her husband's coffin on *Air Force One,* "I did not know if I could steel myself to go on one of those planes again." To honor President Kennedy, she would accept: "But please do not let it be Air Force One. And please, let it be the 707 that looks least like Air Force One inside" (March 28, 1965, LBJL). Mrs. Kennedy and her children, along with Robert and Edward Kennedy, flew to London aboard another presidential plane.

2. *Sacramento Bee,* November 29, 1998.

3. FBI.

LBJ: . . . Wonder if we ought to have LeRoy Collins[1] down there. . . . He ought to be . . . saying to the Governor,[2] . . . "Let's try to work this thing out together." . . . It's worth a damn . . . to [avoid] military intervention.

KATZENBACH: Yeah.

LBJ: I'm ready to move out [whatever troops] you think ought to be moved out tomorrow. I guess it's a good thing we're not moving them tonight after this happened because we might have been credited for triggering it. These damn Republicans are being mean on TV. . . . Ford[3] is just raising hell on *Huntley-Brinkley,* and on CBS, too. . . . They say they got themselves all the voters' rights bill and they're going to cover all these states that we don't cover. . . . But we touched up Mr. Ford a little bit. . . . We said that . . . when critical meetings were held, he was out making political speeches and was unavailable. . . . And the real trouble was that . . . the new Republican leadership[4] . . . was very inept and inexperienced. . . .

KATZENBACH: . . . Charlie Halleck . . . said to me last night, "If you need any help, I'm available!"[5]

LBJ: [*laughs*] Well . . . I think it's a pretty good thing to get Ford in line. . . . Let him know that [since] he put some fire in our front yard, we ought to put one in his.

J. EDGAR HOOVER

Friday, March 26, 1965, 8:10 A.M.

> Hoover is worried that he and the FBI might be blamed for Liuzzo's murder. One of the Klan suspects in the case is Gary Thomas Rowe, a paid secret FBI informer. Rowe's inside information has allowed the FBI to arrest Rowe and three other suspects within twelve hours of the crime. To shield the FBI from charges of complicity in the murder or for shoddy protection of civil rights workers, Hoover has started a campaign to defame Liuzzo. FBI files have been sent to LBJ claiming that the dead woman was a manic-depressive who abandoned her family and injected herself with drugs, and whose husband, a Teamster official, was allied with organized crime in Detroit. "She was sitting very, very close to the Negro in the car," Hoover informed Johnson. "It had the appearance of a necking party."[6]

---

1. The federal civil rights mediator.
2. Wallace.
3. The new House Minority Leader, Gerald Ford.
4. Meaning Ford.
5. Congressman Halleck, whom Ford had defeated as House Minority Leader, is happy to retaliate against the man who beat him.
6. Quoted in Curt Gentry, *J. Edgar Hoover* (Norton, 1991), pp. 585–86.

HOOVER: [We had] one of our men in the car. Fortunately, he, of course, had no gun and did no shooting. But he has identified the two men who had guns and who fired guns. I think there were about ten or twelve shots fired into the car in which this woman was.

LBJ: Six-shooter or shotgun?

HOOVER: I think they're revolvers. . . . They discussed that after it was over, if the woman died, they were going to throw the guns into the blast furnace where they worked in those steel mills down there. That's what we are laying for now— to head off these individuals when they come to work this morning and shake them down. If we are lucky enough to find a gun on them, that will be the big break in the case. . . .

LBJ: Thank you so much, Edgar. As usual, you're right on top of it. . . . I just heard a little a while ago about this fellow[1] calling me. . . . I think I'll call him. You see no reason why I shouldn't?

HOOVER: I see no reason why you shouldn't. The radio said he was very angry because they wouldn't put him through to you last night. I don't see any reason why he should have been expected to be put through. . . . I talked with . . . the inspector in charge down there, to immediately move in and take hold of this case. . . . We've got the informant[2] in the office and we're talking to him because he's scared to death—naturally, because he fears for his life.

LBJ: What is an infiltrator and an informant? You hire someone and they join the Klan?

HOOVER: No, we go to someone who is in the Klan and persuade him to work for the government. We pay him for it. Sometimes they demand a pretty high price. . . . For instance, in those three bodies they found in Mississippi, we had to pay thirty thousand dollars for that.[3] . . . Now, this man that we have now, this informant, he's not a regular agent of the Bureau. But he's one of these people that we put in, just like we do into the Communist party, so they'll keep us informed. And fortunately, he happened to be in on this thing last night. Otherwise we would be looking for a needle in a haystack.

LBJ: That's wonderful, Edgar. Thank you so much.

---

1. Liuzzo's husband, Anthony, depicted as angry and weeping on television, had called Johnson.
2. Gary Thomas Rowe.
3. The FBI paid a local informant to learn the location of the remains of three civil rights workers in Mississippi in August 1964. (See Beschloss, *Taking Charge,* pp. 501–2.)

NICHOLAS KATZENBACH

Friday, March 26, 1965, 8:20 A.M.

Johnson asks Katzenbach whether he should personally return the call from Liuzzo's husband. Reporters are already demanding to know why LBJ has not expressed condolences.

LBJ: He just called back. Should I have Lee White[1] talk to the man? Should I talk to him myself?

KATZENBACH: I think I'd have Lee White talk to him, just to get some measure of what kind of fellow he is, Mr. President, so you don't get embarrassed by it. Then have you talk to him and send condolences and say we're doing everything we can. . . .

LBJ: All right. . . . It's my thought from what he sounds like from radio and television that he's not too restrained and was rather ugly. . . . Looks like we ought to give some thought [to how we can] really move in on that Klan more effectively. They've done a lot of that stuff through the South. . . . Is there anything that we can do in the way of legislation on that? . . . It would be rather dramatic if we could—it would be rather helpful too—if we could move some way on this Klan. Pretty well outlawing them.

KATZENBACH: Yeah, I agree with that.

LBJ: And if we could some way get the list of all the members and expose it some way or other.

KATZENBACH: We've got some people in Congress that've been anxious to do that, too. . . .

LBJ: . . . Maybe when we make a statement about arresting them, make a statement simultaneously asking the Congress to immediately begin hearings to outlaw them or to increase the penalties on this kind of stuff. Or make it a federal crime.

LEE WHITE

Associate Counsel to the President
Friday, March 26, 1965, 8:40 A.M.

After calling Anthony Liuzzo in Detroit, White reports back.

WHITE: He's very much in control of himself. . . . Very relaxed and sounded like a pretty fine fellow. . . . Wanted to know . . . "are we going to continue to have

---

1. Associate Counsel to the President.

to give lives to this cause? Will this ever stop?" He had a few unkind things to say about Wallace. . . . He spoke about his own five children. . . . My judgment, sir, is that if you did call him, he's [not] going to be . . . uncontrollable or wild. . . . I read in the paper this morning where he's a Teamster.

LBJ: . . . Maybe I'll just talk to Hoover again myself. . . . I'm going to be in the bathroom shaving, because I've been working on this since seven. I was up till after two. I think that you better write out as much baloney[1] as you can think of about your calling him and what happened and how you expressed sympathy. The President asked you to do it. . . . Give it to George[2] because they're hounding him to death.

J. EDGAR HOOVER

Friday, March 26, 1965, 9:36 A.M.

> When LBJ asks Hoover again whether he should call Liuzzo, Hoover is happy to exploit the opportunity to slander the dead woman and her husband.

LBJ: Before I talk to him, I wanted to . . . be sure that you don't have any reason why I shouldn't, because in your file he's a Teamster man.

HOOVER: Yes, he is a Teamster man. . . . He's had a—I wouldn't say a bad character, but he's well known out there as being one of the Teamsters' strong-arm men. And this woman, his wife—we found on her body numerous needle points indicating that she may have been taking dope. I can't say that definitely because she's dead. But I would be somewhat inclined, if it could be done, to have somebody like White . . . rather than you talk to him.

LBJ: White's already talked to him.

HOOVER: Oh, he has. . . . As soon as I finish talking to you . . . we're going to try to get warrants out right away to arrest the other three men who were in the car with our informant. . . . I'll let you know.

LBJ: Please do, because they're running me crazy over here.

HOOVER: . . . I'm going to talk to Alabama right away. If Doar[3] agrees to the serving of the warrants . . . I'll have them served at once. . . . You can make the statement from the White House there.

LBJ: Maybe you and Attorney General come over and just walk in. . . . When you got some information from Doar, give me a chance to show what good work

---

1. The term LBJ uses to mean fodder for the press.
2. Press Secretary George Reedy.
3. Assistant Attorney General John Doar.

the FBI has done. . . . In just twenty-four hours, you've produced results. I think it might make it a little dramatic.

HOOVER: I think it would be.

LBJ: You give me a call, and the two of you ride over and let the television cover you as you come in.

ANTHONY LIUZZO

Husband of Viola Liuzzo
Friday, March 26, 1965, 2:55 P.M.

> At 12:40 P.M. television viewers saw a grim LBJ, with Hoover and Katzenbach at his side, announcing that four Klansmen suspected in Liuzzo's murder had been arrested—"due to the very fast and always efficient work of the special agents of the FBI." (He did not reveal that one suspect was a paid FBI informant.) Johnson pledged legislation to control the Klan, saying, "We will not be intimidated by the terrorists of the Ku Klux Klan any more than . . . the terrorists in North Vietnam." Martin Luther King, Jr., unaware of Hoover's campaign to disgrace Mrs. Liuzzo, wired congratulations to the FBI Director. Back in the Oval Office, Johnson now calls Mrs. Liuzzo's husband in Detroit.

LIUZZO: Being of Italian extraction . . . being pushed around and kicked around. . . . That people like you push our legislation—I just want to say thank you.

LBJ: I was up most of the night, and I'm glad that we've had some results. . . . I'm glad that we were able to move as fastly and effectively as we could. You know how grieved we are. . . . Miz Johnson and I. . . . I'm glad of this chance to tell you how I know you must feel, and how I want you to be brave, and how anxious I am to correct it, and to see that your dear wife did not die in vain. And that others will, for years to come, have their lot improved in this country because of the sacrifice that she made.

LIUZZO: Thank you, Mr. President. . . . I don't think that she did die in vain. It's going to be a battle all out, as far as we're concerned here in Detroit, in my organization. . . .

LBJ: . . . I'm grateful to you, and thank you so much.[1]

---

1. The three Klansmen charged with Liuzzo's murder were cleared by an all-white Alabama jury. Later they served six years each after a federal conviction for violating Liuzzo's civil rights. After testifying against the other men in the car, Gary Thomas Rowe went into the federal witness protection program. In 1975 he told the Senate that, with the encouragement of the FBI, he had beaten Freedom Riders, killed a black man, and sowed dissent within the Klan by sleeping with Klansmen's wives. In 1983, Liuzzo's children unsuccessfully sued the FBI for negligence in controlling Rowe that led to their mother's murder. (*Chicago Tribune,* October 5, 1998.)

LADY BIRD JOHNSON

Saturday, March 27, 1965, Tape-recorded Diary

> In retirement LBJ recalled, in an unpublished draft of his presidential memoirs, that he felt kinship with "another Southerner named Johnson" who had "tried to hold the country together" after his predecessor's murder and was broken by the national divide over race.[1]

LADY BIRD: Lyndon said, "I've got to read a book on Andrew Johnson." I didn't even know whether there was a good one. I think perhaps he felt himself in many ways in the same situation as Andrew Johnson—even after a hundred healing years.

---

1. Unpublished draft of *The Vantage Point*, LBJL.

Chapter Seven

"THE KIDS ARE LED BY COMMUNIST GROUPS"

We could solve the Vietnam thing if the North Vietnamese and the Chinese really felt that we were there to stay. But our own people are creating doubts, and they're questioning our policies. So the kids are running up and down parading, and most of them are led by Communist groups. . . . They make the North Vietnamese and the Chinese believe that we're about ready to move out. . . . And that's a great disservice to America and it's a great disservice to our fighting men.

LBJ to Robert Spivack, April 29, 1965

NICHOLAS KATZENBACH

Monday, March 29, 1965, 6:24 P.M.

Johnson is angry that his erstwhile friend Joseph Alsop, the columnist, has been complaining to friends that LBJ has ordered his telephone line tapped. Johnson is especially piqued because one of the hidden weapons he believes he has against his enemy Robert Kennedy is knowledge that RFK in 1963 ordered the FBI to wiretap Martin Luther King, Jr., and, as Attorney General, otherwise trampled the civil liberties of personal and political adversaries.

In an unpublished version of his presidential memoirs, Johnson said, "After I became President, I discovered that [Robert Kennedy's] Justice Department had been and still was tapping wires. I had to spell out my orders very specifically so that there would be no wiretapping in the Johnson administration." [1] In the same draft he recalled that RFK ordered "midnight visits of FBI agents to reporters who had covered a stockholders meeting" during President Kennedy's confrontation with steel magnates in 1962, using "Gestapo tactics." LBJ now knows that he can someday exploit Kennedy's wiretapping secrets against him only if his own record on the subject appears unblemished.

---

1. Unpublished draft of *The Vantage Point,* LBJL.

LBJ: Nick, have I ever asked you or suggested to you that you tap a line?

KATZENBACH: No, Mr. President.

LBJ: Don't you have to authorize every one to be tapped?

KATZENBACH: I authorize every one that the FBI taps, Mr. President. I do not authorize taps if they're made by other agencies. I think it would be a good idea if I did. . . .

LBJ: . . . All right. Who else taps them?

KATZENBACH: Defense taps them, and IRS[1] occasionally taps.

LBJ: Well, I want them brought to an irreducible *minimum*. And only in the gravest cases. I want you to authorize them, and then, by God, I want to know about them. I'm against wiretapping, period. And I think you ought to get you up the strongest letter you can to them, and say that none of them [is] to be tapped, except by signature of the Attorney General.

KATZENBACH: To the other agencies?

LBJ: Yeah. For me to sign.

KATZENBACH: All right.

LBJ: . . . You just say the President just called you at 6:24 and said this. . . . I don't know of a human's wire that has ever been tapped. I assume that in one of our friend's cases, from what I have seen, that that must be where the evidence comes from. I mean, on [his] Hawaii jaunts and . . . California, and with some of the women.[2] . . . You know who I'm talking about?

KATZENBACH: Yes.

LBJ: . . . Nobody's ever told me that's where it comes from.[3] And I don't want to know.

KATZENBACH: Right.

LBJ: Joe Alsop is having a change of life. I've gone through a change of life with three or four of my friends. He's just short of the asylum now. He's had two or three breakdowns. But he's going around all over town saying we've got his wire tapped. That doesn't amount to much because most people know he's crazy. But . . . I'm his friend, and I saved him from McCarthy when McCarthy had ahold of this other stuff back there on Joe.[4] But today— [*to Bill Moyers, in room:*] When

---

1. Internal Revenue Service.

2. This refers to Martin Luther King, Jr. When King visited Honolulu in February 1964, his lodgings were thrown under microphone surveillance so that the Bureau could use evidence of his "moral weakness" to ensure that he be "completely discredited." (David Garrow, *The FBI and Martin Luther King, Jr.,* Norton, 1981, pp. 107–8.)

3. In other words, LBJ is provided with information on King's private life, but he is not specifically told how it was acquired.

4. In the 1950s, Senator Joseph McCarthy responded to an Alsop attack by making a thinly veiled reference to Alsop's secret homosexuality. (See Robert Merry, *Taking on the World,* Viking, 1996, pp. 215–16.)

was it, today? Get on the phone over here. . . . [*to Katzenbach.*] Saturday this happened. I'll let Bill tell you.

MOYERS: . . . Scotty Reston called me and said that he would like to come see me in a matter he considered of great importance. He brought with him Joe Alsop. . . . [Joe] said that a number of officials, whom he could name if he felt free to do so, had been intimidated over the possibility of their leaking. . . . People would not go to lunch with him. . . . He had conclusive evidence that his line was being tapped. . . . That certain people were using against him . . . scurrilously collected . . . information about his own personal life.[1] That those contents were being made known to different people around town. . . . And that the use of such material, even if it were accurate, was a gross violation of propriety and decency. . . .

Reston was somewhat humiliated at the whole conversation. But nonetheless . . . he said that he had been approached at the Gridiron Club by an official at the Pentagon, who told him, "Scotty, I think you should know that your son, Dick Reston, is being shadowed by the FBI because of information that he obtained from a confidential source at the Pentagon . . . on the use of foreign aid funds in Thailand." And that this . . . had been ordered as a result of the President's desire to crack down on . . . leaks within the government.[2] Both of the men then jointly concluded by saying that this kind of thing is going to be disastrous to . . . the President and it should be called to a halt immediately. . . .

LBJ: . . . I never heard of Scotty's little boy. . . .

KATZENBACH: The FBI has not been doing anything of that kind, I'm confident.

LBJ: Well, just find out about it. . . . Look at all your wiretaps again. . . . You have to know what they're tapping, don't you?

KATZENBACH: . . . I am confident, Mr. President, that the FBI does not tap a wire without informing me. . . . Now . . . until recently, when I talked to Mr. Hoover about it . . . the Bureau has, under authority which neither I nor my predecessor[3] knew until, oh, in the last couple or three months, there was authority for them occasionally to make a trespassing bug, which they have used in some organized crime matters. . . .

LBJ: . . . I'm a red-hot one-million-two percent civil liberties man, and I'm just *against* them. I guess you've got to have them in treason or something, but I just

---

1. Referring to Alsop's secret homosexuality.
2. This report was wrong. Actually, the FBI was investigating General Accounting Office charges that the United States was mismanaging aid to Thailand. (LBJ-McNamara recorded conversation, March 30, 1965, LBJL.)
3. Robert Kennedy.

sure don't want to trust anybody on that field. . . . Now, I saw the Alsop file.[1] . . . And I saw a file on our Deputy Secretary of Defense.[2] After I saw them, I ordered them put in a safe where nobody else could see them.[3] . . . I resent this so deeply that what I think you better do is just say, . . . "The President . . . has never made a request of any kind on any individual case. . . . He's never *talked* about wiretapping. Never given me any instructions. And I'm the only one that can approve them." . . . I think you ought to talk to Bob McNamara about this—I'm going to as soon as I hang up—about . . . following his boy.[4] Just say now you're willing for the FBI to make a very thorough investigation of any evidence they give you. Anybody, including the President. You'd investigate *him!* . . . [*chuckles*]

MOYERS: Reston said . . . *if* it were happening, government by document is one of the most deplorable of all kinds of government. But he left himself out by saying *if* it were happening.

LBJ: Conversely, government by intimidation is terrible, too, and we're not going to be intimidated by some columnist that doesn't get what you want. . . . Now *my* position with my Cabinet has been that . . . nobody else is authorized to speak for their department, except the President. . . . If you[5] and I can't work together, I'll ask for your resignation and get it in one minute. Until then, you're going to run that department. . . . I make that clear to you, don't I?

KATZENBACH: Yes, Mr. President. You always have, and I hope I've made it clear to you that I was here just as long as you wanted me, and no longer.

LBJ: That's right. . . . It seems to me when the *New York Times* and when Alsop, with his readership, would come into the White House and level these charges and talk about writing [about it]— *I* don't give a damn about his writing about it, because I'm as innocent of it as I am of murdering your wife.

KATZENBACH: Yeah.

LBJ: . . . But I *have* said to my people, . . . "Any newspaperman who wants to come, you talk to him. If I were you, I wouldn't make it a practice of going to their homes during the lunch hour and during the dinner hour and during breakfast, and being a conduit for special information to them. I do detest that. . . . If I were you, I'd stay away from the Metropolitan Clubs and the downtown clubs." Because I just wish they'd stay in the *White House* during lunch. That's when I'm working.

---

1. Brimming with revelations about Alsop's sex life on several continents (see Joseph Alsop file, FBI). According to Alsop's file, one of his lovers was Arthur Vandenberg, Jr., son of the late Michigan Senator, whose private life stopped him from being Eisenhower's appointments secretary in 1953 and whose case LBJ cited to defend himself during the Walter Jenkins scandal. (See Chapter 2.)

2. Probably referring to Roswell Gilpatric, Deputy Secretary of Defense when LBJ took office, who was known for his womanizing.

3. This may refer to the safe that originally belonged to Walter Jenkins, about which LBJ was so worried in October. (See Chapter 2.)

4. Meaning Reston's son.

5. Referring to Katzenbach.

LBJ exuberantly opens his drive to win the presidency by a landslide against Barry Goldwater with a rally in Detroit, September 7, 1964.

Johnson says goodbye to Jacqueline Kennedy after a visit to her new Fifth Avenue apartment, New York, October 14, 1964 (Robert Kennedy in background). After John Kennedy's assassination, Johnson called her, pleaded with her to visit him at the White House, and asked her to tell young Caroline and John Kennedy that "I'd like to be their daddy!"

Walter Jenkins, LBJ's closest aide, arrested less than a month before the 1964 election for sexual relations with another man in a Washington YMCA. Informed of the news by his lawyer-confidant Abe Fortas, LBJ wailed, "I just can't *believe* this!" and asked, "Was a fee involved?" He is certain that Jenkins was framed by Republicans.

In Brooklyn, while campaigning with Senate candidate Robert Kennedy, LBJ agonizes over the Jenkins scandal. Lady Bird wants him to give Jenkins a job with the Johnson family company. LBJ tells her, "Don't create any more problems than I've got! . . . You just can't do that to the presidency, honey!" (Aide Jack Valenti at right)

Lady Bird and LBJ and Luci and Lynda in Austin the day before the 1964 election. On Election Day, Johnson suffers an emotional and physical letdown. "I've been in bed all day," he says. "I just kind of came off the mountain, you know. I've been kind of keyed up and I'm just kind of feeling punch-drunk."

LBJ on election night. Although elected by the largest presidential landslide in modern times, he cannot shake his anxieties. He excoriates television anchors who are saying he was elected as the lesser of two evils—and warns friends that Robert Kennedy will try to enmesh him in scandal: "They're going to make a Warren Harding out of us!"

7

Senator Barry Goldwater conceding his defeat in Phoenix the morning after the election. An angry LBJ insists that the "damn son of a bitch" refused to concede on election night in order to spoil the Johnson victory.

8

LBJ attends a barbecue near the LBJ Ranch the day after his landslide. He is already plotting how to push his Great Society program through Congress.

Inaugural morning, January 20, 1965. LBJ and Lady Bird in the President's White House bedroom.

9

At the inaugural ceremonies, East Front of the U.S. Capitol.

Reviewing the inaugural parade (Lady Bird at right).

12

LBJ in the White House family quarters on Inauguration Day. Despite what should be one of the happiest moments of his life, he cannot shake his forebodings about Vietnam, possible scandal, and Robert Kennedy's arrival in the Senate. Two days later, he collapses with a severe respiratory infection. In her tape-recorded diary, Lady Bird worries about his emotional depression.

February 1965: LBJ orders Operation Rolling Thunder, the repeated bombing of North Vietnam. On the tapes, he says, "Now we're off to bombing these people. We're over that hurdle. I don't think anything is going to be as bad as losing, and I don't see any way of winning."

13

14

The protest against the Vietnam War begins. White House police remove a demonstrator, April 1965. LBJ tells himself that the antiwar rallies are Communist-inspired: "The kids are running up and down parading, and most of them are led by Communist groups. . . . They make the North Vietnamese and the Chinese believe that we're about ready to move out."

Martin Luther King *(below, center)* on the Selma-to-Montgomery march, March 21, 1965. LBJ conferred with King and haggled with the race-baiting Alabama Governor George Wallace *(right)* to hold down violence: "Don't you shit me, George Wallace!"

LBJ and FBI Director J. Edgar Hoover, March 1965. Johnson is using Hoover's FBI both to protect the civil rights marchers and to keep Johnson's own political enemies under control.

Anthony Liuzzo, husband of Viola Liuzzo, Detroit civil rights worker murdered by Ku Klux Klansmen during the Selma march. LBJ consoles him by telephone, March 26, 1965: "I want [to tell] you to be brave, and how anxious I am to correct [injustice] and to see that your dear wife did not die in vain."

LBJ with Abe Fortas in the White House Situation Room, while sending almost thirty thousand American troops to the Dominican Republic, May 1965: "It looks to me like I'm in a hell of a shape. . . . They're going to eat us up if I let another Cuba come in there. They'll say, 'Why did you sit on your big fat tail?' "

American troops in Santo Domingo, May 1965.

Nguyen Cao Ky, installed by military coup as leader of South Vietnam, June 1965. Of the new Saigon leader, LBJ's old Senate mentor, Richard Russell, tells him, "That little old mustached fellow . . . said *we* ought to fight the war and *his* troops ought to pacify the villages in the rear. God, that scared the hell out of me! If they're going to try to fight *that* kind of war, I'm in favor of getting out of there."

July 1965: LBJ makes his most perilous decision of the war—to dramatically increase American ground forces in Vietnam. Here U.S. Marines arrive at Da Nang. Privately he tells McNamara, "I'm very depressed about it. . . . I don't believe [the North Vietnamese are] *ever* going to quit." Two presidential aides are so worried about Johnson's mood swings and rants against hidden enemies all around him that they secretly consult psychiatrists.

While having a bust of himself made, LBJ gestures and argues with Senate Foreign Relations Committee Chairman J. William Fulbright (not pictured) about Vietnam.

LBJ signs the bill creating Medicare with former President Harry Truman at his side. Truman Library, Independence, Missouri, July 30, 1965. In background (left to right) are congressional liaison Lawrence O'Brien, Lady Bird, Vice President Hubert Humphrey, and Bess Truman.

LBJ persuades Arthur Goldberg to leave the Supreme Court to become Ambassador to the United Nations and help him bring peace to Vietnam. Later an angry Goldberg says it was "the biggest mistake of my life."

Having opened a vacancy, LBJ forces his friend Abe Fortas against his will onto the Supreme Court. In 1969, Fortas will resign after charges of taking illicit payments and having been too chummy with Johnson.

LBJ before signing the Voting Rights Act, August 6, 1965, with Lincoln over his shoulder in the Capitol Rotunda.

Johnson hands a signing pen to Robert Kennedy, who by now has publicly criticized him on Vietnam, the Dominican Republic, arms control, and excessive caution on civil rights.

30 Riots in Watts, Los Angeles, August 13, 1965 *(above and facing page below)*. LBJ had earlier told a Southern Senator, "You take an old hard-peckered boy that sits around and got no
school and got no *job* and got no *work* and got no *discipline*. . . . He ain't got nothing hurt if
he gets shot. . . . You just wait till . . . the rats get going in Harlem and Chicago."

LBJ grimly forecasts that Watts and other
riots will lead to a backlash against his
achievements in civil rights and his entire
Great Society. He predicts that two Republicans who will benefit most will be
Richard Nixon and Ronald Reagan.

On LBJ's fifty-seventh birthday, August 27, 1965, Lady Bird points out symbols for Great Society bills on the birthday cake she has designed for him. Although not intended to, the inscription ("you can have your cake and eat it too") goes to the heart of Johnson's problems. He is trying to build his Great Society at the same time as he escalates a costly war in Vietnam.

Like hell. And I can't *find* any of them. I called Moyers today and he was off for a couple of hours chasing around over at some *hotel*. I know the hotel food is not as good as the Mess.[1] I called Harry McPherson.[2] Needed him, and he was at the [Federal] City Club. So, I just got a bunch of damn *society* fellows that are running around here eating off somebody else. And they'll have to pay for it in a *column* someday.[3] I'd rather buy them a hamburger over here and get the columnists obligated to *us!*

KATZENBACH: Yeah. Let me—

LBJ: Wait just a minute! [*talks inaudibly to Moyers, then:*] Shriver[4] says that his line has been tapped, according to Bill, and he doesn't think by the FBI because it's too amateurish a job. Now, we all think our lines are tapped all the time. Every time I hear a click, this operator up here comes in to see if I'm still talking. . . . I thought always my line's tapped. But that's something you might want to look into.

KATZENBACH: Joe Alsop mentioned . . . to me . . . that the FBI was tapping his wire. . . .

LBJ: . . . These people do that. I have a friend in Texas who is about my age and Joe's age, and they go through it, like a woman sometimes. Did you know that?

KATZENBACH: Yeah.

LBJ: It's a menopause, and they have the same problem. [My friend] has told me I've got the CIA after him and the FBI after him, and they're all following him. And he gets his guns at night, sometimes, set up. . . . Took him three years to go through this thing and his wife just had hell. . . . I'll check with Shriver and get any dope he's got on his lines being tapped. Tell him Bill told you. So he won't think that *we're* tapping him. [*chuckles*] I would imagine somebody's promoting this around town. . . . I'm going to check with McNamara. . . . Now, who else— would the CIA ever tap anything?

KATZENBACH: I don't think they ever tap in this country, Mr. President. But I can't say that absolutely authoritatively.[5] . . . My information here is that the worst offender on indiscriminate taps is the Pentagon. I have that only— [*click heard on line*]

LBJ: You hear this click keep coming in there?

KATZENBACH: [*laughs*] I'll check on it right away. My wife says her line's tapped. Bob McNamara says his line's tapped.

---

1. White House Mess, the in-house staff dining room.
2. Johnson's special assistant, counsel, and increasingly close aide, who had also served on his Senate staff.
3. Meaning that in exchange for lunch they will be required to leak secrets to a columnist.
4. Peace Corps and War on Poverty Director Sargent Shriver, also a Kennedy brother-in-law.
5. Katzenbach was right to qualify his answer. As publicly confirmed by the Rockefeller Commission in 1975, the CIA wiretapped or physically surveilled American newsmen between 1959 and 1972 to learn how they were unearthing classified information.

LBJ: [*laughs*] He says he caught them tapping his. Now they may be!

KATZENBACH: . . . I can understand a foreign government doing this with a big person like McNamara, even possibly with me. . . .

MOYERS: Shriver's little girl[1] found a headpiece in his bushes attached to his line, which makes him think it's just somebody doing it outside the government, because it was too amateurish.

KATZENBACH: Well, you know, taps are much more sophisticated than that today. . . . We can tap your line, Bill, in Southeast Washington. Won't have to come any closer to your home than that. We can go further than that and tap it in the way that hears every conversation in your room, too. Just to show you what the state of the art is.

LBJ: That's why it's so damn dangerous. You just go back to being a professor[2] when you get on this wiretapping, because I've been brought up *that* way. . . . By gosh, I don't want any wiretapping around. I'm just *against* it. . . .

KATZENBACH: . . . The ones I've approved, Mr. President, have been only taps for genuine intelligence purposes. The furthest out one is the one that you referred to, which my predecessor authorized, and which I've been ambivalent about taking off. That was done because of the, you know, the existence of those two fellows.[3] . . .

LBJ: . . . Well . . . I'm not a lawyer, and I don't understand what evidence you've got to have. . . . All I know [is] I want you to have as few of them as you can possibly have and only something involving the safety of this country. And no other reason. Goldwater couldn't ever get mean enough for me to want you to even repeat what he told you at dinner.[4]

LADY BIRD JOHNSON

Monday, March 29, 1965, Tape-recorded Diary

The Vietcong have bombed the U.S. Embassy in Saigon, using plastic explosives stuffed into a sedan, killing twenty-two people. During a state dinner for the President of Upper Volta, a White House butler handed LBJ a folded piece of paper, which was his first report of the incident.

---

1. Maria Shriver, much later an NBC correspondent.

2. Johnson means returning to one's basic values.

3. King's associates Stanley Levison and Jack O'Dell, whom the FBI suspected of Communist links.

4. Meaning that no matter how angry he became at Goldwater, he would never want to repeat Goldwater's private conversations by dint of wiretapping. In June 1965, LBJ issued an order prohibiting wiretapping or eavesdropping for reasons other than national security. (See Ramsey Clark oral history, LBJL.)

LADY BIRD: The President opened it, and I am sure every eye there was trying to read in his face its contents. . . . Several Americans and a good many more Vietnamese were killed or seriously wounded. . . . Talks with Rusk. The Situation Room. A late night, I went to bed and it was three o'clock when Lyndon came into my room and wearily pulled up the cover.

WHITE HOUSE SITUATION ROOM

Tuesday, March 30, 1965, 8:10 A.M.

Johnson calls from the family quarters with television news blaring in the background.

LBJ: What have you got on our Saigon development?
DUTY OFFICER: We have a . . . total of two U.S. killed and—
LBJ: Know who they are? Soldiers, women, or what?
DUTY OFFICER: We have women listed so far. Two women.
LBJ: . . . Both American?
DUTY OFFICER: Both American, yes, sir.
LBJ: How many Vietnamese were killed?
DUTY OFFICER: . . . Fifteen Vietnamese killed, with possibly forty injured.
LBJ: They on the streets or in the buildings?
DUTY OFFICER: On the streets and in adjacent buildings also. . . . The only other news, sir, is the South Vietnamese Air Force conducted a strike on an airfield. All the planes have returned safely. The pilots estimate 90 percent damage.
LBJ: What kind of airfield? Jet airfield?
DUTY OFFICER: Yes, sir. . . . A jet airfield in North Vietnam, just over the seventeenth parallel.
LBJ: Must have been right on the demarcation line, huh?
DUTY OFFICER: Just north of it, sir.
LBJ: . . . Okay. Much obliged.

ROBERT McNAMARA

Tuesday, March 30, 1965, 8:14 A.M.

LBJ: Bob, looks like we had a bad night.
McNAMARA: Yeah, we did.

* * *

McNAMARA: Your friend Walter Lippmann sure stuck it in me this morning.[1] [*laughs*]

LBJ: He's going to do it with everyone. . . . And he hasn't got much policy, . . . either. Looks bad, though. It's not a very good day to come up with a new policy out there after they bombed the embassy.

McNAMARA: But it does look good that you pulled the dependents out.

LBJ: Yes, yes. Well, what do you think we do today? . . .

McNAMARA: . . . At lunchtime, Dean [Rusk] and Mac [Bundy] and I can present to you . . . what program we believe we should follow with respect to the North for the next week or so, which, in my opinion, should not be changed as a result of this incident of last night. . . . On the issue of additional combat troops in South Vietnam, I think we can carry water on both shoulders here for a while. . . .

LBJ: All right. Good.

McNAMARA: I want to emphasize—Max[2] himself does not recommend any rush movement of large numbers of U.S. combat troops.

LBJ: Why do they always come quoting embassy sources as saying he's coming here to ask for fifty thousand extra men? . . . Do some junior people put that out?

McNAMARA: I think there may be. . . . But actually . . . he leans toward ultimately putting in, let's say, a division and a half. But he thinks there are pros and cons and many uncertainties associated with it, among them being the reception of the Vietnamese. Quat, as you know, says he doesn't need any U.S. combat troops in there.[3] . . . Max believes that U.S. troops would have great difficulty operating in South Vietnam—particularly in a counterguerrilla role, where they'd be operating by themselves in the countryside. They'd have difficulty in distinguishing Vietcong from Vietnamese, be attacking South Vietnamese villages, make mistakes and kill loyal South Vietnamese people. He says that our troops . . . are poorly trained as counterguerrillas. . . . On the other hand, General Westmoreland has a strong recommendation in for that, and the Chiefs themselves strongly favor it. But I think what we can do here is move very slowly and very gradually and finesse both programs—Westmoreland's *and* the Chiefs'.

*   *   *

LBJ: This civil rights thing's pretty hot. . . . This King really got screwed up Sunday with economic boycotts and all that.[4]

---

1. Lippmann said that two months of bombing North Vietnam had not affected the course of the war and that Johnson should "abandon the halfbaked notion" that the war would be decisive in the Cold War. (*Washington Post,* March 30, 1965.)

2. Maxwell Taylor, Ambassador in Saigon.

3. The South Vietnamese leader feared that his people would resent being engulfed by so many Americans. (George Kahin, *Intervention,* Knopf, 1986, p. 317.)

4. On NBC's *Meet the Press,* King said he might call for an economic boycott of Alabama products to force Governor Wallace to stop his "reign of terror" (transcript, March 28, 1965). Under a hailstorm of criticism, he soon dropped the idea.

McNAMARA: Oh, yeah, absolutely, but I think that the newspapers are taking him down a peg on that.

           *   *   *

LBJ: Congo looks a lot better off. This African president last night told me that.[1] By the way, I need some brownies for not making *you* come! . . .

McNAMARA: [*laughs*] I know. I appreciate that. . . . I said to Margaret,[2] I enjoyed the evening at home twice as much last night because I knew where I *wasn't!* [*laughs*]

LBJ: We had about a 280-pound woman that I was dancing with about one o'clock, and I thought of Bob McNamara. And I thought, "By God, if He didn't reward me in heaven!"

McGEORGE BUNDY

Tuesday, March 30, 1965, 9:12 A.M.

BUNDY: The consensus both from the field and in Defense is that we won't want to do anything very startling and striking. . . . There are, as you know . . . two American dead. . . .

LBJ: I don't know what procedures we've got for notifying their families, but . . . you ought to prepare a letter from me to both of these. . . . Now . . . my own feeling is in the year I've been in here, we've had too much business as usual. . . . I think we've got to get more of an attitude of emergency in our equipping of our staff in these operations. . . . The planes have to be sent back to Cessna to get a special type of refitting and reworking to be adaptable out there. It's going to take till August to get them out. . . . I just *wish* that there was some way that we could go on and get some more planes. . . . The goddamned war is liable to be over before they ever get their stuff![3] . . . We ought to ask, "Is there some way, without being critical of . . . the Army . . . that we can expedite these things?" . . . If your boy was out there sinking for the third time, wouldn't you be in a bigger hurry? There must be somebody out there that's got enough brains to figure out *some* way that we can find some special targets in North Vietnam to hit on.

BUNDY: Yeah, I've already raised that point.

LBJ: . . . They don't know a damn thing about where they can find anybody. But I read every day where this battalion and that battalion— And they've doubled the air strength in this area, and they can't find it. . . . Whether they can or can't, then

---

1. The President of Upper Volta at a state dinner.

2. Mrs. McNamara.

3. LBJ here sounds (allowing for differences in language) like the frustrated Lincoln at the start of the Civil War.

I would sure look at some of these targets in the North, close to the seventeenth parallel, and I'd find if there's not anything that's untouched. . . . If there is something that hadn't been completely wrecked . . . I would sure go at it. And go at it quick. And go at it today, so they don't think that we're just going to do what we've done for fifteen months.[1]

BUNDY: Uh-huh.

LBJ: . . . We ought to get some historian or some professor to study the World War I and World War II and other governments' policies on announcements. I think we've got hydrophobia[2] in the government. . . . I would like to be guided by only one standard—anything that can be told to the American public without in any way injuring . . . our effort ought to be told. . . . My own feeling is that we have put out more information in the last year than any administration in [history]. . . . Now the thing that I think that we're very vulnerable in—I think we have clerks putting out administration policy before it's administration policy. . . .

An example of it in the civilian field is the . . . Tom Wicker story—exactly what I'm going to do about the Klan.[3] Down below they got a paragraph that Bobby [Kennedy] is opposing the outlawing of the Klan. . . . Now, I don't know what I'm going to do about the Klan. We had this very difficult issue in our state . . . thirty-five years ago. And we had to pass a special act but we had difficulties with the Constitution.[4] We can't do it just for the Klan. We have to do it with anyone that concerts and conspires with a group of citizens to take the law into their own hands. It could mean . . . the Baptist young people's organization, or a group of nuns, if they conspire together to violate the law. . . . But Tom Wicker's got all of my thoughts . . . and I've never . . . had any discussion with anybody. What he's got is three little Justice Department lawyers—maybe aided and abetted by the Attorney General.[5]

* * *

LBJ: Joe Alsop, in my judgment, must be going crazy. . . . He . . . says everybody is tapping his wire. . . .

BUNDY: . . . I told him to shut up about it.

LBJ: . . . So I called Nick and asked him if there was any wiretapping going on of any reporter anywhere. And he said no. That there were only fifty-nine wiretapping cases. He had to approve every one. I asked him if I'd ever discussed any one with him, and he said no. Nobody else had except the Bureau.[6] That most of them

---

1. Meaning the stalemate since LBJ took office.
2. Literally fear of water, but LBJ means diarrhea of the mouth.
3. In this morning's *New York Times,* Wicker reports that LBJ will fight the Klan by proposing stronger penalties for civil rights violations.
4. Passing a law that would prohibit or gravely restrict the Ku Klux Klan.
5. With this sentence, LBJ shows that he does not entirely trust Katzenbach.
6. FBI.

had been authorized before he took over, and were left there. That nobody'd ever suggested that they tap a wire for any purpose except the greatest purpose of national interest, treason, or gambling. . . . You never heard of any wiretapping, have you?

BUNDY: No, sir. . . .

LBJ: I went in my office one o'clock this morning. They had found a number of wires under my rug.

BUNDY: Exactly. Just what we all worry about.

LBJ: They were all cut up—old wires that had not been removed. . . . But they had a sweep . . . at one o'clock this morning, when I went by there after this Saigon thing. They were working, about a dozen of them.

BUNDY: Yep.

LBJ: But you better find out if CIA is doing any domestic wiretapping. If so, how many cases. I don't want to know who. I want to know though for what purpose.[1]

JOHN CHANCELLOR

Correspondent, NBC News
Wednesday, March 31, 1965, 11:16 A.M.

> Johnson complains to NBC's John Chancellor about a Robert Goralski report claiming that Maxwell Taylor is quitting as Ambassador to Saigon, to be succeeded by his deputy, the diplomat U. Alexis Johnson, and that Taylor's supposed resignation heralds a change in Johnson's Vietnam policy.

LBJ: This is . . . irresponsible. . . . I don't think it could be worse if the Vietcong were making our announcements. . . . I have received no word, oral or written, from Taylor that he's resigning at any time. . . .

CHANCELLOR: I see. . . . They called me just a few minutes before the newscast to alert me to this, and I left a message for Jack.[2]

LBJ: . . . I called you and they said you couldn't be reached. I guess you were on the air . . .

---

1. In December 1966, Hoover's FBI released documents showing that Attorney General Robert Kennedy had authorized the Bureau to plant illegal eavesdropping devices on suspected criminals. Edward Long of Missouri proposed a Senate investigation of illegal eavesdropping. Bill Moyers told Richard Goodwin, "He is out to get Bobby. Johnson is egging him on." In his 1967 State of the Union, LBJ proposed a bill against all bugging and wiretapping, except in cases of national security. A tight-lipped Kennedy, in the audience, refused to clap. In May 1968, when it looked as if Kennedy might win the Democratic presidential nomination, Drew Pearson, perhaps at Johnson's behest (LBJ presumably hoped to alienate blacks from Kennedy), revealed that RFK had sicced the FBI on Dr. King. (See Arthur Schlesinger, Jr., *Robert Kennedy and His Times,* Houghton Mifflin, 1978, pp. 759–60; and Evan Thomas, *Robert Kennedy,* Simon & Schuster, 2000, pp. 328–30, 378–80.)

2. Johnson's special assistant Jack Valenti.

CHANCELLOR: ... May I say, sir, that sources very high in the White House—

LBJ: Yes, sir. That's right. ... I consider it as big a disservice as [the Vietcong] could figure out. You don't lose the lives that you do when they bomb an embassy. But it's almost as bad because you create a lot of frustration all over the world. It looks like that we have jumped our man. ... I think that NBC has got a wonderful news organization, and I want to help them. But the first thing they better do is get a little maturity.

CHANCELLOR: All right, sir.

LBJ: [*growing more irritated:*] ... You ought to be at least seventeen before you start reporting. Now, this is the second or third Gronouski[1] thing, and I told you about some of Ron's stuff.[2] These boys—they're good for high school annuals and stuff like that. But ... I learned in my high school journalism that you've got to have "who, what, when, why, and where." And they oughtn't be nominating these men to be war commanders without any knowledge at all. And I think I would have some knowledge, because I *select* them. I have no pets, but if I do have ... you would be one of them.[3] ... I'll even interrupt a meeting of the President to answer you if you've got something urgent. We don't need to have this irresponsibility. Bob Kintner,[4] who was a old-time reporter, ... knows better than this. ... And if you don't tell him, I will. ... Taylor ... has stayed much longer than he wanted to stay. ... But he'll probably stay a little longer now on account of this announcement. [*chuckles*] Because we will have to pick up a lot of pieces that you've created. ...

CHANCELLOR: I appreciate that, sir. ...

LBJ: I like Ray Scherer, but I was *really* humiliated beyond *compare* when he says, "Flash! I just want to tell you that the President has just named David Kennedy, Chicago banker, Secretary of the Treasury. ... Now, I'll be back in just a moment with the news." Then they came on and said, "We want to sell you a little Crisco, right quick." And they gave me a minute of Crisco. And he came back on and his face was red even without color television. He said, "I hate to tell you, but it's just been announced that Mr. Fowler is the one."[5]

---

1. LBJ means Goralski. Once again he is mispronouncing the name of someone at whom he is angry.
2. Stories by Ron Nessen to which LBJ has objected.
3. LBJ proved this by appointing Chancellor to head the Voice of America in July 1965.
4. NBC president.
5. Scherer had broadcast a false report that David Kennedy (who ultimately was chosen for the job by President Richard Nixon) would replace Douglas Dillon as LBJ's Treasury Secretary; the actual choice was Henry Fowler.

ROBERT McNAMARA

Wednesday, March 31, 1965, 3:46 P.M.

Johnson complains about news reports that he is intimidating Rusk, McNamara, and other subordinates into following his dictates on Vietnam. He complains of a *Washington Star* report about a secret meeting on Vietnam he held with only three other people, perhaps leaked to the *Star* by one of the men's aides.

LBJ: Have I had any differences with you and Rusk on these matters where my way has prevailed?

McNAMARA: No.

LBJ: Haven't we always agreed before it was over?

McNAMARA: Oh, yes, absolutely, Mr. President. I think that there's more unity . . . on Vietnam policy in the last few months than there has been at any time in the last several years. . . .

LBJ: Where did this story come from that's headlined today? Big banner. "Embassy retaliation ruled out / Johnson bars direct reprisal for bombing." . . . The [*Washington*] *Star* today. . . . Bernard Ga-wertzman.[1] . . . I don't think we ought to be ruling in or out. We oughtn't to be telling people what we're doing. . . . There was four of us there.[2]

McNAMARA: . . . The only person over here that's been involved in it at all is Bus Wheeler. He developed this suggestion of [bombing] Haiphong.[3] . . .

LBJ: . . . Did you tell him you busted up the meeting before I got to accepting his recommendation?[4] [*laughs*]

McNAMARA: No, but I did tell him I recommended against it because I thought it unwise at this stage to reintroduce a tit-for-tat policy. . . . He didn't know a damn thing about the conversation until about roughly noontime today, so I'm sure it didn't come from him. But we've just got a leaky government, I guess, try as we will to tighten up.

WAYNE HAYS

Democratic Congressman from Ohio
Wednesday, March 31, 1965, 5:27 P.M.

Johnson makes sure that an old ally and influential member of the House Foreign Affairs Committee has been briefed on the embassy bombing.

---

1. LBJ irritably mispronounces the name of Bernard Gwerzman.
2. At the meeting in which Johnson discussed possible retaliation.
3. Major North Vietnamese port.
4. Meaning that McNamara dissuaded LBJ from accepting Wheeler's aggressive recommendation.

LBJ: Average Congressman I've observed in thirty years . . . if you don't kiss their ass, then they'll *kick* it. Isn't that right?

HAYS: You don't have to kiss mine.

LBJ: . . . So I called Rooney[1] and I called you, and I called the Senate boys, and I said, "We've had an embassy blown up. . . . It oughtn't to be downtown. It ought to be out in the edge somewhere where we can protect it."

HAYS: I agree with you a hundred percent.

LBJ: Now, I'm going to make a statement that we're going to rebuild it. But before I do, I don't want to be presumptuous enough not to have you-all[2] as my partners. . . . Of the ten men in the United States that were for me[3] back before '60, about three of them were on this list.[4] One of them was John Rooney, who . . . got his little ass kicked all over town. One of them was you in Ohio. . . . My own judgment is . . . they ought to . . . get out of that downtown [Saigon] area, put one up somewhere and put a big stone wall around it . . . as quickly as they can, instead of a big marble palace there.

HAYS: That's exactly what I told them today. . . .

LBJ: All right. Well, you and I were born on the same farm. . . .

HAYS: . . . Incidentally, I had the prettiest little Tennessee walking filly born last week you ever saw.

LBJ: [*laughs*] I'll take a look at it. We'll have to match horses. Thank you, Wayne. Take care.

HAYS: Anything you want—

LBJ: I know, I know.

BILL MOYERS

Thursday, April 1, 1965, 9:05 A.M.

> Johnson asks Moyers to persuade Democrats Jennings Randolph of West Virginia and Lister Hill of Alabama not to let the Senate Subcommittee on Education amend his education bill.

LBJ: You've got to keep Randolph, and you've got to keep Hill any way that you can bribe him. I imagine he's upset, in Alabama. I imagine he's afraid of us. I imagine that they're giving him hell, poor man.[5]

---

1. New York Democratic Congressman John Rooney.
2. Congressional leaders with influence on foreign and military affairs.
3. For President.
4. Of Senators and Congressmen whom LBJ was asked to call.
5. Meaning that Hill is under attack from fellow Alabamians after LBJ has federalized the state's National Guard.

MOYERS. He's cutting off his nose on this one, though, because Alabama comes out very well [in this bill].

LBJ: . . . Do you know Randolph at all?

MOYERS: Oh, sure. . . . I got his son in the Peace Corps three years ago after he'd been turned down. Then I got another son . . . a part-time job while he was doing graduate work. . . .

LBJ: I'd call him and tell him I want to come see him right away on an important matter to West Virginia. . . . Say to him that we want him to take the leadership, because if we get this bill amended, we may be out in the cold. Say . . . I'll go make a speech for him on Appalachia sometime, and help him . . . and I'm his friend. Of course, this thing yesterday damn near ruined him, and he may raise hell about that.[1] He may be so mad this morning. I think I'd try to do that, right quick.'

NICHOLAS KATZENBACH

Friday, April 2, 1965, 8:45 A.M.

> While watching NBC's *Today* program in the mansion, Johnson tells his Attorney General how to deal with an anti–Vietnam War protest planned for Easter at the gates of the LBJ Ranch.

LBJ: I notice [that] a bunch of Communists and Communist fronts and young Communist leagues in Texas is going to picket my ranch.

KATZENBACH: . . . I thought before we decided how to cope with it, we ought to get a little firmer intelligence on it. Just how many people. . . . I would be inclined to use . . . the Governor's people on that, rather than a lot of federal people.[3]

LBJ: Oh, sure. . . . I believe I'd just let them come in to the ranch road right in front of the river there, after you get off the main highway. . . . Maybe let them meet there in the church grounds, across from our graveyard and across from our birthplace house. And if they want to bring me a petition, let them bring it!

*   *   *

LBJ: I got to see ADA[4] today. . . . They want to talk about problems. I'll say there are two—Vietnam and civil rights. And they're going to want to do more on the civil rights fight here at home and less fight overseas. [*laughs*]

---

1. LBJ had refused Randolph's request for accelerated federal aid to depressed West Virginia. (See *New York Times,* April 1, 1965.)

2. The subcommittee approved the bill unanimously, without amendment.

3. In the background as Katzenbach speaks, a child's voice in a television commercial sings, "Mommy put a Curad bandage on!"

4. The liberal Americans for Democratic Action.

KATZENBACH: Which place do they want to use gas?[1] [*laughs*]

LBJ: . . . What about Martin Luther King's economic boycott?[2]

KATZENBACH: It's a terrible idea, Mr. President. But I think that the way you played it yesterday[3] is right because I think he's[4] helping us a little bit to get off the demonstrations down there—cool that off a little bit. I think this economic boycott . . . will . . . fizzle. At the appropriate time . . . we can . . . say rather mildly why it isn't too good an idea. A lot of other people'll say that for you . . . so you don't have to take him on hard. It is helpful not to have a lot of people marching down there.

LBJ: Yeah. What'll be happening to our troops down there? . . .

KATZENBACH: They're all out now, Mr. President. I still have . . . a lot of Bureau[5] [people] and a few marshals down there.

LBJ: Have you got any great man that you know that would agree to be head of the CIA? What about Burke Marshall?[6]

KATZENBACH: He'd be great, Mr. President. . . .

LBJ: Is he mean enough to mix up that hamburger and that pepper?[7] . . . He seems to me like an awful sweet man.

KATZENBACH: He is a sweet man, but he's also hard.

LBJ: . . . You know what some of these guys[8] do, don't you? [*laughs*]

KATZENBACH: Yeah.

LBJ: . . . I don't know about Burke. . . . I don't know whether he would stay awake until two o'clock in the night and take the dirt out behind the brakes and let them run off of it. . . . What I want is a careful man and an analytical man, and a good man, but one that can light the fuse if it's just got to be done to save his country. And when you go strike that match and setting off dynamite, a lot of them hesitate. A fellow like Dave Bell[9] would like to do it, but he just doesn't like to blow up a home.[10]

---

1. Another reference to the use of tear gas in both Alabama and Vietnam.
2. King's proposed boycott of Alabama products.
3. At a press conference LBJ had warned that they "must be very careful to see that we do not punish the innocent"—Alabamians who did not oppose the civil rights revolution.
4. King.
5. FBI.
6. Assistant Attorney General and close associate of Robert Kennedy's.
7. LBJ's way of describing the sometimes violent business of the CIA.
8. In the CIA.
9. Director, Agency for International Development.
10. As Johnson announced on April 11, the CIA job went to a Texan, retired Vice Admiral William "Red" Raborn, former Deputy Chief of Naval Operations, known for championing the Polaris weapons program.

LADY BIRD JOHNSON

Friday, April 2, 1965, Tape-recorded Diary

LADY BIRD: One of my memories in the White House will always be of convocations in the bedroom, Lyndon propped up in the great canopied bed, five newspapers stacked beside him, and a bale of night reading, making imperative-sounding telephone calls.

LADY BIRD JOHNSON

Saturday, April 3, 1965, Tape-recorded Diary

LADY BIRD: Lyndon . . . called the Episcopal Church "that Brooks Brothers Church."[1] They have been giving him a hard time lately for not being active enough in the civil rights movement. Each meal here at Camp David is as though we never expected to eat again, and the crème brûlée was a Roman feast. . . . Before midnight [I] curled up in bed by Lyndon for what I hoped would be a long night. What with Selma and Vietnam, long nights have been hard to come by this spring.

EVERETT DIRKSEN

Monday, April 5, 1965, 12:34 P.M.

The Senate Republican leader has collaborated with Johnson's Attorney General to arm the voting rights bill with a measure against state and local taxes that will not be struck down as unconstitutional.[2] Now Dirksen warns LBJ to ease up his pressure to get the bill through Congress fast.

LBJ: How are you? . . .
DIRKSEN: I'm bushed. This goddamned voting rights bill! . . . Don't make any statements about driving that damn thing through before Easter! We think now we've got a good bill. . . . Mike[3] said if you can get about three or four days of debate on it before Easter, that would be all that was necessary. Then we could leave our Easter recess intact. . . . There's going to be grousing to beat hell up there.

---

1. Meaning the church of upper-class Republicans.
2. Federal courts would be empowered to suspend the poll taxes if they were clearly being used to keep blacks from voting.
3. Majority Leader Mike Mansfield.

They've all made plans [for Easter]. . . . Couple of weeks, and I think we got it made. . . .

LBJ: I never made a statement in my life I was going to drive anything through.[1] . . . *You-all* said that. *I* haven't said anything like that. . . .

DIRKSEN: . . . We've modified this rather substantially to make damn sure that we'll be on good constitutional ground. . . . They're going to have to have a little time to look it over and peck around. I think . . . it's going to save us time in the end.

LBJ: It is, if we don't get into another situation in Selma while we're waiting. That's the damn danger. . . . I sure don't want to have to go through a Selma, because we got through it . . . pretty good. If it hadn't been for that woman the last night,[2] we'd have had a perfect record. But if [the civil rights leaders] think we're dillydallying and off for Easter, why it creates a hell of a lot of problems.

*   *   *

LBJ: Get that education bill passed this week, Everett![3]

DIRKSEN: Oh, we'll get that done.

LBJ: If you don't, you go back over to the House, you put a lot of amendments on it . . . and we'll have to wait another two or three weeks and cause us to be here till November.

CYRUS VANCE

Tuesday, April 6, 1965, 3:45 P.M.

Johnson questions his Deputy Defense Secretary on the latest American bombing of North Vietnam.

VANCE: The U.S. has struck seventeen primary targets. . . . Two Army supply depots, three ammunition depots, two Army barracks areas, eight radar sites, two highway railroad bridges. . . .

LBJ: We haven't done much damage, have we? Have we killed anybody?

VANCE: . . . We can only measure the damage to the installations. The damage has been . . . about medium. . . .

LBJ: Does it look like we really need to have some training of our boys out there?

VANCE: I think they're learning as they go along, Mr. President.

---

1. LBJ's tongue must be sticking through his cheek.
2. The murder of the white civil rights worker Viola Liuzzo.
3. Johnson's $1.3 billion elementary and secondary education bill was passed by the House on March 26.

NICHOLAS KATZENBACH

Wednesday, April 7, 1965, 9:17 A.M.

> Liberals are complaining that LBJ's voting rights bill is not strong enough. The President is especially annoyed by critics who say that he should have included a measure banning local poll taxes, which he thinks would be unconstitutional.

LBJ: Looks like to me they're just really *murdering* us on this publicity on this bill. They're having to redo the bill to protect the country from Texas.[1] . . . Now the Republicans won't get anywhere in the House bill, will they?

KATZENBACH: No, no, Mr. President. . . . The only thing they're likely to do in the House is try to abolish all poll tax by statute.[2] . . .

LBJ: . . . Why don't we get somebody up there to offer a constitutional amendment resolution? . . . I would sure put them on the spot. . . . Nick, you know, they're going to screw you to death on delay. . . . Dirksen is calling up and saying he wants to put off and put off and put off. They're not going to consider this thing now before Easter.

KATZENBACH: . . . And the steam goes out of it. That's the problem. . . .

LBJ: They're making it look like that they're taking it over. Dirksen every day says it's a Dirksen bill. And next day, when they find something wrong, it's a *Johnson* bill!

*   *   *

LBJ: I gave in and just agreed to get raped by your crowd in Wisconsin, so I'm going to put in your man—Governor Whatever-His-Name-Is, this ex-politician.[3] I don't want you and Ramsey[4] ever talking to me about standards anymore, though. . . .

KATZENBACH: Mr. President, they have very high standards [in Wisconsin].

LBJ: The hell they have! This defeated politician, rejected by the people, who's gutting at me all the time. What's his name, Governor—

KATZENBACH: Reynolds.

LBJ: Reynolds. *That's* not very high standards. I can give you a *bunch* of ex-Congressmen, if you want them. Ex-Governors. . . . I'll just feed them to you boys, if you and Ramsey like 'em. [*chuckles*] . . . Have you done any more work on our tax man?[5]

---

1. Meaning a Southern President.
2. The Twenty-fourth Amendment, ratified in 1964, had banned the poll tax as a prerequisite for voting in federal elections but not in others.
3. Former Wisconsin Governor John Reynolds is to become a federal judge.
4. Deputy Attorney General Ramsey Clark.
5. LBJ is inquiring about a new appointment as Assistant Attorney General for Antitrust.

KATZENBACH: Yeah, I got . . . Don Turner from Harvard, who's probably the outstanding younger man in the country. . . .

LBJ: Can't you get me somebody in the Midwest or South or West, besides all these Harvard men? Do you know honestly that nine men out of ten that I name are Harvard men?

KATZENBACH: No, I didn't know that.

LBJ: They are. Just everybody that Macy [1] sends me. I cut about six of them back yesterday, just one right after the other. Now, I know it's a hell of a good school, and I'm for it and I don't mind them having 30 percent. But I want California. They're just raising hell. . . . They've got their feelings hurt. They're mad. They thought we sent Pierre out there to run against them, and they thought that lost them the seat [2] and screwed things up, and I suspect it did. . . . They say if we don't want those forty [electoral] votes in California, the hell with [us]. . . . We're in the same shape in Texas. They're getting mad at us. . . . Ramsey Clark's [3] the only guy. They got nobody in the Cabinet. . . . Dick Daley [4] doesn't get much. . . . There are two states that get everything—Wisconsin and this goddamned Harvard. And, I guess, because Wisconsin's got good public schools. [5] I'm going to start my Library, [6] and I'm going to take a hundred people a year . . . and give them four-year scholarships. Just about got all they can eat and wear during that four years. Make them be straight A's, and then turn them out of Texas every year. That's what I'm going to do when I get out of here. Just go back there and teach, and make the University of Texas finance it. They've already agreed to put in $18, $20 million.

*   *   *

LBJ: I believe 90 percent of this stuff is image . . . I've got more Phi Beta Kappas than anybody in the country, but we . . . [have] an image of wheeler-dealer-political thing. I think you ought to help turn that. Show that you've brought young, practical lawyers that can try lawsuits, who at the same time are up at the top of their class. Here's Ramsey Clark from the University of Chicago, but he tried them day in and day out for the Texas sheriffs—the roughest of them all. Build him up as a rough lawyer. But he's meek and mild as a mouse . . . Just get it where you've got excellence written over every brow in that [Justice] Department. . . . The one thing we want is excellence, equality, equity. . . . This is the Three-E Department. . . . I would just make them start leaking right quick that this Katzenbach is a modest, shy guy, but he won his spurs with Johnson himself. There's

---

1. John Macy, Chairman, Civil Service Commission.
2. Referring to Pierre Salinger's loss of the California Senate seat to Republican George Murphy.
3. Katzenbach's deputy.
4. Chicago Mayor Richard Daley, Johnson's staunch ally.
5. Despite this rant, Turner ultimately got the job.
6. The Johnson Presidential Library, which LBJ has already begun planning.

never been a President and Attorney General more closer, unless it was the Kennedy brothers.[1] Johnson supports him in any damn thing he wants to do, and here's what he's done. . . . In twelve hours, he had the men arrested in this woman's killing[2] and in twelve days he had an indictment. . . . I'd get that little Rosenberg or whatever his name is[3] and just get him about three assistants just working on these damn columnists. . . . We don't play any politics. . . . We don't harass people. We always welcome both sides. But we're right down the middle, and if you're innocent, you sure want to be tried by Katzenbach. If you're guilty, you better get you another court.

KATZENBACH: All right.

LBJ: . . . Let's get some of this political image off of us . . . We're not running for any office. You don't ever have to be elected to *nothing*. You already made it. . . . But during this next three years, let's just show them that . . . there's never been a better Justice Department anywhere. Now, on this [voting rights] bill up there . . . I want fifty-fifty. Tell Dirksen we're willing to go with him. That . . . you don't mind driving the horse with him, but I damn sure don't want to be in the second car in the caravan.

KATZENBACH: All right.

LBJ: . . . I want an antitrust man that is a symbol of what I want in antitrust. . . . I'm not a Gore crusader on antitrust.[4] . . . We oughtn't just go around indicting and harassing and raising hell. We ought to make them comply with it. Then if they don't, then I think we ought to give them the works. . . .

KATZENBACH: Yes, Mr. President.

LBJ: . . . You want to get a man that's got the jib of you and Ramsey—with a big, long jaw, that's quiet and that's not a fellow with my personality. We want a fellow that's not a persecutor. . . . You can sit down with a guy and get a lot more done, and keep from scaring him, with a soft voice. . . . Then if they have to lower the boom, we'll lower it.

ARTHUR "TEX" GOLDSCHMIDT

Director, Technical Assistance, Special Fund Operations, United Nations
Thursday, April 8, 1965, 10:27 A.M.

The previous evening, at Johns Hopkins University in Baltimore, LBJ gave a nationally televised speech pledging that if Hanoi guaranteed South Vietnamese in-

---

1. A large exaggeration, given LBJ's private suspicious about Katzenbach's loyalty to him.
2. Viola Liuzzo.
3. Jack Rosenthal was Katzenbach's spokesman.
4. Senator Albert Gore, Sr., of Tennessee, father of the future Vice President, wanted strong antitrust laws.

dependence, the United States would invest a billion dollars in a Mekong River Delta Project to develop Southeast Asia. He explained why America was in Vietnam and promised that he would "never be second in the search" for a "peaceful settlement." House Minority Leader Gerald Ford complained that "peace with security cannot be purchased with a million American tax dollars." For advice on the project, Johnson has turned to this old Texas friend, who, from the Interior Department in the late 1930s, helped Congressman Lyndon Johnson bring rural electrification to his district.

LBJ: I got a bunch of mean wires who are raising hell. . . . From all over the country. I thought [we] did pretty good on [our] *New York Times,* though.[1]
GOLDSCHMIDT: Well, I think you did.

*   *   *

LBJ: U Thant[2] is supposed to come out with something today and say it's wonderful. . . . The South Vietnamese didn't like it. . . . I'm such a damn fool. I can't understand why they wouldn't want it. . . .
GOLDSCHMIDT: . . . But I've had just terrific reactions here from just, you know, the guys . . . that I talk to in the elevator.
LBJ: Let me show you what they're saying. Atlanta, Georgia: "People are sick and tired of your lies about Vietnam. Bring these troops home." Lubbock, Texas: "We'll back down in Vietnam, as we have everywhere else under your position." . . . "Volunteer blackmail payments cannot purchase loyalty." That's from Pittsford, New York. . . . "Pious nonsense. International bribery." . . . "[Andrew] Johnson was almost impeached [after] Lincoln. You ought to be impeached." . . . "Your speech made me sick. Why bomb? Negotiate!" "Your Vietnam backdown is [an] insult to U.S. men who died in the cause."
GOLDSCHMIDT: You're getting it from both sides.
LBJ: . . . "You've chosen to ignore pleas of most countries of the world for negotiation." Well, I don't know how they figure I ignored them! . . . "Stop the killing of American soldiers." . . . "Good Texans prefer that you stop bombing first, then start spending the billions." California: ". . . Do you really believe that peace can be purchased for a billion?" . . . "Get out of Vietnam. U.S. is the aggressor. Not fooled by your . . . speech." California: . . . "A weak-kneed buyout scheme." . . . "Stop inhuman napalm chemicals." . . . "A billion-dollar appeasement. . . . As Neville Chamberlain was to England, you are to the United States."[3] . . . They're just stacked in here by the dozens.

---

1. A *Times* editorial said that "the country can take pride" in LBJ's speech: "A serious peace offer has been made."
2. UN Secretary-General.
3. Another reference to the century's most famous appeaser.

GOLDSCHMIDT: . . . It was a terrific audience last night. They said 60 million.

LBJ: Yeah. . . . There were more listening percentagewise than there have been to any, although more people listened in March to civil rights.[1] . . . In television, March is a bigger month because it's colder.[2] . . .

GOLDSCHMIDT: Most of these are just crackpot stuff . . . from left and right. . . .

LBJ: . . . I haven't got a damn wire from anybody I know. Isn't that odd?

GOLDSCHMIDT: Really?

LBJ: Not a one! I'll bet you there's five hundred here, but they're all just raising hell. . . . They say we're giving away this foreign aid, you see. Maybe we made a mistake with the billion-dollar figure. I thought we ought to have said that . . . we're going to take the money we're spending on bullets and bombs and spend it on food and medicine, if they'll just quit fighting.[3]

DWIGHT D. EISENHOWER

Thursday, April 8, 1965, 5:58 P.M.

> The former President told LBJ in February that America must prevail in Vietnam,[4] but here he presciently warns Johnson that the South Vietnamese would feel compelled to fight to save their country. As Eisenhower speaks, the term "hearts and minds," one of the Vietnam War's most chilling refrains, makes an early appearance.

EISENHOWER: I listened to your talk last night.

LBJ: I'm complimented.

EISENHOWER: I thought that it was a very fine exposition on what have been America's purposes. . . . No country can be saved by an outsider unless its own heart is in the right place. . . . This poor little devil down there that's trying to make a living on an acre of ground or rice, why . . . he's the fellow we're trying to get at now. . . . These people, as they're trying to figure out what economic betterment could be brought about, why, they also have to take the mental side and the spiritual side of the human and try to better him the same way.

LBJ: Yes . . . there are two places that we have been very deficient. One is in that respect. The other is getting a government that . . . can see this thing through. . . . Of course, their morale's bad. . . . I've got to strengthen it. . . .

EISENHOWER: That's right. . . . We never can keep a government up there just

1. LBJ's voting rights speech to Congress.
2. Spoken like the co-owner of the Texas Broadcasting Company.
3. Ho Chi Minh refused Johnson's offer, but the speech strengthened support among the American people for LBJ's conduct of the war.
4. See Chapter 5.

with bayonets. It's got to be with the consent and desires of the people. That is the problem. . . . If we're going to save a nation, we've got to go after their minds and hearts as well as we do at their stomach. . . .

LBJ: . . . I don't think you could be more right.

CYRUS VANCE
GENERAL FOGEL

Defense Department Command Center
Friday, April 9, 1965, 12:05 A.M.

> Chinese MiG jets have attacked four American planes patrolling the South China Sea, off China's Hainan Island, before a scheduled U.S. bombing raid on three North Vietnamese bridges. One American plane is missing.

LBJ: What do you have on that aircraft loss? . . .

VANCE: . . . The pilot is missing still. His fuel has run out, so he presumably is down. The others are saved. . . .

LBJ: . . . Anybody ever see this plane to know whether it's hit or anything about it?

FOGEL: Sir, he reported over the radio . . . that he had fired his last missile and was . . . returning to the [aircraft] carrier. We have nothing to indicate that he was hit or on fire. . . .

LBJ: I guess it would indicate, though, he was hit, wouldn't it? . . . Do you think after he was out of ammunition that the MiG took him on and brought him down?

FOGEL: That could be it, Mr. President. . . .

LBJ: . . . Okay. You call me when you get anything else. Doesn't make any difference what time it is. I'm up, in and out, all night.

GENERAL COX

Defense Department Command Center
Friday, April 9, 1965, 3:55 A.M.

LBJ: This is President Johnson. What's happened tonight?

COX: . . . We still haven't heard anything from the aircraft that is missing. . . . He was just about over [Hainan] Island, sir, and they don't know . . . whether he got off the island or not. . . .

LBJ: What was he doing over the island?

COX: ... We feel that, probably in the business of fighting off the attack, he strayed over the island. ...

LBJ: Where were the others engaged?

COX: ... Off the coast.

LBJ: Did they all wind up getting over the island?

COX: It sounds that they did.

*   *   *

LBJ: Any other reports on the other missions?[1]

COX: The [U.S.] airplanes all went out and returned safely. ...

LBJ: ... Were they patrolling some roads or something?

COX: They were actually striking a particular target, sir.

LBJ: Did they hit it?

COX: Yes, sir, they did. ...

LBJ: How many planes?

COX: ... Roughly ninety-nine. ...

LBJ: And what was the target? Bridge?

COX: Yes, sir. ... There were forty-eight aircraft that were strictly on the strike. ... And they're all back on the ground now.

LBJ: ... Okay. Thank you, General. If you have anything more, whenever you have it, call me.

JAMES SHANNON, M.D.

Director, National Institutes of Health
Friday, April 9, 1965, 8:38 A.M.

> Judge Robert Russell, the cherished nephew of LBJ's close friend Senator Richard Russell of Georgia, has been undergoing chemotherapy for cancer. His prognosis is grim.

LBJ: Do you reckon I could take him up to Camp David with me for a day over the weekend, or does he have to have a nurse around?

SHANNON: ... I would think that if it didn't involve too much in the way of exercise, if this was a relaxed day, he could take it. ...

LBJ: ... I'd just have a car drive him down here, and then a helicopter ride up there—twenty-five minutes—and he could just go in the living room and sit around the fireplace with us over the weekend. ... Don't tell him, though. I'm not sure. I may go to Texas. But if I decide to go up to [Camp David] on Saturday ...

---

1. To bomb North Vietnam.

it might be a little outing for him and he might feel a little better. Feel like somebody loved him, anyway.[1]

GEORGE BALL

Under Secretary of State
Friday, April 9, 1965, 9:30 A.M.

> In this talk with his Under Secretary of State, Johnson worries that news of the aerial dogfight with the Chinese will interfere with today's scheduled passage of his education bill by deflecting Senate doves onto a new floor discussion of Vietnam.

BALL: There's . . . a question as to whether we engaged in hot pursuit over Hainan, and . . . as to who jumped whom. . . . We want to make clear to the Chinese . . . that this was not the beginning of a closing in on them. . . . The British could pass that word along. . . .

LBJ: . . . I was going home about one, two o'clock today. I rather doubt the advisability of that.[2]

BALL: I think I'd reserve that decision, Mr. President.[3] . . .

LBJ: All right. I sure hope we don't get too much information too quick up at that Senate before they pass that education bill. . . . If we can just get by, I imagine, till twelve or one o'clock, we'll have our bill passed. Unless these Joe Clarks[4] get up and start speaking again on their knowledge of Vietnam.

LAWRENCE O'BRIEN

Friday, April 9, 1965, 10:42 A.M.

> Johnson's congressional liaison reports a crucial victory on his education bill, one day after Medicare passed the House. Here LBJ shows how strenuously he is trying to compete with the legislative triumph of the first Hundred Days of his hero Franklin Roosevelt in 1933.

O'BRIEN: Amendment defeated, 53 to 32.

LBJ: Oh, that's wonderful! Now, you do anything in the world you can to shove

---

1. As it happened, LBJ did go to Texas for the weekend. Russell died in June 1965.
2. Because of the Chinese engagement, LBJ doubts that he should go home to the ranch this afternoon.
3. That evening the Johnsons did fly to Texas.
4. Senate doves, named by Johnson after the Pennsylvania Democrat who turned early against the war.

them the third reading and get that sent to me. . . . We may have a lot of discussion because we've had an unfortunate incident or two. That's why I want to get that one wrapped up. We had a little plane battle last night. Might have a hundred [Senators] out there talking about it. So don't let them stop the education bill. Because you're right inside the Promised Land. I bragged on you yesterday to the Cabinet. Told them what a fine job you've done. Now, you've got to . . . jerk out every damn little bill you can and get them down here by the 12th.[1]

O'BRIEN: All right.

LBJ: . . . What I want you to do is— Roosevelt's got eleven. . . . They were not major bills at all. But you'll have one major one really with education. Now, Appalachia's a supermajor one, and then the others are about like Roosevelt. But on the 12th, you'll have the best Hundred Days. Better than he did!

O'BRIEN: Right.

LBJ: And that gives your boys [in Congress] something to run on if you'll just put out that propaganda. . . . That they've done more than they did in Roosevelt's Hundred Days. Because the guys we want to reelect are those that helped you pass your medical care yesterday. . . . Larry, take a clipping in your pocket and just put out to one or two of your friends—the Evanses, the Mary McGrorys[2] or somebody you talk to in confidence. . . . Put out to them . . . that every guy that votes for Medicare and education, that his grandchildren are going to say, "My grandpa was in the Congress that enacted these two."

O'BRIEN: Yeah, yeah. That's good.

LBJ: . . . Take a list of what you might jam through—even if it's the saline thing.[3] Or something that you can add to your eleven to get to the White House. The trouble is medical care [and] voting rights won't get here.[4] . . . [laughs] Now, what I want is twenty bills!

LADY BIRD JOHNSON

Friday, April 9, 1965, Tape-recorded Diary

LADY BIRD: We arrived home—the ranch—about 10:45 [P.M.] on the Jetstar. On the way, Lyndon talked of the last week. He said, "Never has there been such a Hundred Days." And what a week this has been! Thursday, the House passed Medicare. . . . The committee reported out the [voting] rights bill, and then the success of the education bill. This was a week to put a golden circle around. So let us remember it, because there will be many ringed in black. But this is the heady

---

1. April 12 is the twentieth anniversary of FDR's death.
2. Columnists Rowland Evans and Mary McGrory.
3. Saline Water Conversion Act.
4. These bills will not make it to LBJ's desk for signature before the Hundred Days are over.

wine of success. I looked at handsome, charming Sargent Shriver and bright, sharp Eunice,[1] who must have so many memories, and wondered what they were thinking. To me, they are the easiest of the Kennedys to be around. I think their involvement with the [Johnson] program is enough that they look beyond their brother who is not there. . . . Sometimes she seems a little caustic. He would be a success in any field.

LADY BIRD JOHNSON

Saturday, April 10, 1965, Tape-recorded Diary

LADY BIRD: We lay on top of the deck of the boat and Lyndon said, "If you want to know what my idea of heaven is, this is it." He talked about retiring. He wanted to have a class—maybe two—at the University of Texas and then maybe one at San Marcos.[2] . . . For the first time, I am beginning to feel that he could retire happily, to ranching, teaching, watching the building of the library.[3] Vistas opened up. Perhaps there would be a book or two and visitors would beat a path to our door, and trips and a little banking and TV on the side. Well, a boat is a good place to dream. Marianne[4] is sort of soft and cheerful and pretty. I believe those are the chief qualities Lyndon wants in a woman. . . . We had catfish for dinner and then a trip down to see Cousin Oreole[5] for everybody but me, and I luxuriated in *Gunsmoke*.[6]

J. EDGAR HOOVER

Tuesday, April 13, 1965, 4:55 P.M.

The FBI Director and Johnson have both been criticized by the press for seeming to have passed judgment on the four Ku Klux Klan members accused of Viola Liuzzo's murder in Alabama when they announced at the White House on March 26 that the men had been arrested and would be immediately arraigned. LBJ uses this as another opportunity to butter up Hoover.

---

1. The Peace Corps and War on Poverty Director and his wife, JFK's sister, were visiting the LBJ ranch.
2. LBJ's alma mater, Southwest Texas State Teachers College at San Marcos.
3. LBJ Library.
4. LBJ's friend Marianne Means of the Hearst newspaper chain.
5. Oreole Bailey, who lived in a small house on the LBJ Ranch.
6. Lady Bird's favorite television program.

LBJ: Sure am proud of what you've done in this civil rights thing, and I think history will so show it. I've said so every chance I get.

HOOVER: . . . A number of editorials I've seen . . . try to make it appear as if you had prejudiced these people against a fair trial. Of course, your statement was very carefully worded, I thought.[1]

LBJ: . . . I made the Attorney General sit down and go over every word of it. I didn't say these men's guilty. I said the *Klan* is guilty. And I said you'd arrested these and charged them. I didn't say you'd *convicted* them. . . . You'll be proud of what history will say about what you've done here. Anybody that could have a man in that car—that's the most unthinkable thing I ever heard of![2] It makes me scared, by God, to even talk back to my wife! [*laughs*] Afraid you'll have somebody there arresting *me*!

PHILIP POTTER

Washington Bureau Chief, Baltimore Sun
Saturday, April 17, 1965, 9:01 A.M.

> Today Johnson will issue a statement rejecting pleas for a bombing halt in North Vietnam by figures such as Democratic Senator Frank Church, Indian Prime Minister Lal Bahadur Shastri, and Canadian Prime Minister Lester Pearson, who infuriated LBJ by making such a demand in public on April 2, the day before he was to visit Johnson at Camp David. To buttress his position, the President pleads his case by telephone with a friendly reporter and pretends to be more optimistic about Vietnam that he really is.

LBJ: [This] Asian situation . . . is the number-one problem on my desk. I'm trying, with everything I've got, day and night. A good many people don't know and can't know all the things that we're trying to do. Because it would considerably weaken us. But I can assure you that the Churches and the Indians don't want peace as much as I do.

POTTER: I'm sure of that.

LBJ: . . . Pearson comes out with his suggestion that we have a cease-fire. . . . He says, "Don't bomb three or four days, and see if you can't work out . . . some kind of an agreement." And I said, . . . "[If we] just did nothing, can you, Mr. Russia, indicate to me that they would quit? . . . Could you indicate, Mr. British, that they would quit? Could you indicate, Mr. France, that they would quit? . . . That I

---

1. On March 26, announcing arrests in the Viola Liuzzo case. (See Chapter 6.)
2. Gary Thomas Rowe, the FBI informant in the Klansmen's car, who, it was later revealed, earned between $200 and $300 a month from the FBI. (*New York Times,* October 4, 1998.)

wouldn't lose everything I'd done?" No! No! None of them can give you any-thing!

POTTER: I understand.

LBJ: . . . They wouldn't quit. They would really move in then and try to take our planes out of Danang. Or they would hit our Pleiku compound. . . . We think we have made phenomenal progress. The report I got from out there yesterday was just unbelievable. Looks like almost a new day, although I . . . don't want to be too much optimistic, because I always get thrown for a loss when I do.

POTTER: Yes, sir.

LBJ: . . . [The Senate] Foreign Relations [Committee] really has no great strong leadership. . . . Fulbright philosophizes. He's a great liberal, but he's against wage-and-hour.[1] And he's a gre-e-eat man, but he wants Armed Services to take over all the military assistance.[2] He just doesn't want to take on anything that's real tough.[3]

LADY BIRD JOHNSON

Sunday, April 18, 1965, Tape-recorded Diary

LADY BIRD: We talked about the short nights Lyndon has been having for sev-eral months. He asked to be waked up whenever there was an operation going out.[4] He won't leave it alone. He said, "I want to be called every time somebody dies." He can't separate himself from it. Actually, I don't want him to, no matter how painful. In Washington, he seldom gets to sleep until about two.

HARRY TRUMAN

Monday, April 19, 1965, 11:42 A.M.

Johnson once again leans on the 33rd President, who had suffered through his own Asian land war—in Korea—for fatherly consolation.

LBJ: Mr. President, how're you feeling?

TRUMAN: Well, I'm all right, and how are you?

---

1. Legislation to ensure fair wages and hours for workers.
2. Johnson suggests that Fulbright wants to dodge the tough issue of military aid to other countries.
3. LBJ's bitterness against the dovish Foreign Relations Committee Chairman is growing.
4. In Vietnam.

LBJ: Oh, I've just got all kinds of hell all day and all night, from Vietnam to the Berlin Wall to—

TRUMAN: Well, you're doing a hell of a good job.

*   *   *

LBJ: The State Department is made up of all these career people, and they've got this damn fool Fulbright that fights me on everything. He wants [to run] foreign relations, and he's in with Chou En-lai[1] and the Russians this morning on wanting me to stop bombing out there. He doesn't want them to stop bombing *Americans* and killing people.

TRUMAN: Make sure you're the President and you make the policy!

LBJ: And he doesn't want them to stop killing secretaries in the American Embassy, but he wants us to stop knocking out *bridges!*

*   *   *

LBJ: I'll be damned. He gave out an interview this morning. . . . Can you imagine putting handcuffs on American bombers and saying, "We ought to let them shoot at you, but you can't shoot back."

TRUMAN: That's the whole story! That's the whole story!

LBJ: God bless you.

LEE WHITE

Tuesday, April 20, 1965, 7:54 A.M.

> While watching a Vietnam report on NBC's *Today* program in the family quarters, Johnson tells his civil rights adviser of his anxiety that since the Selma march, leaders of the movement have not been in contact with him.

LBJ: What have you heard from them? Looks to me like they've been pretty cool since Alabama. . . . Do you think that we made some mistake with the troops or something . . . that's kept us from hearing from King or Wilkins[2] or any of them telling us what a good job we did? Normally they are telling you that you're either playing hell or you're doing a good job. We just haven't heard anything.

WHITE: . . . Farmer[3] has . . . made it clear that he was really happy. . . . You got [a letter] from him expressing great appreciation for having sent that copy of the [voting rights] speech. . . .

---

1. Chou En-lai, the Chinese Premier.
2. Roy Wilkins of the NAACP.
3. James Farmer, chief of the Congress of Racial Equality (CORE).

LBJ: You just send him about a dozen copies, and tell him he might want to send it to some of his friends.

ROBERT McNAMARA

Tuesday, April 20, 1965, 7:15 P.M.

> Johnson's Secretary of Defense reports from Honolulu, where he has just met with General William Westmoreland and Ambassador Maxwell Taylor on Vietnam. They have agreed that bombing cannot "do the job alone" in Vietnam. In a fateful recommendation, they will ask LBJ to send nine American battalions between now and the end of the summer. This would increase the American presence in Vietnam from 33,000 to 82,000 men. They have also concluded that "it might be necessary" to further increase the number to 123,000.[1]

McNAMARA: I think we can avoid any recommendations for substantial acceleration or expansion of the bombing program in the North. I think we can all be in agreement that we've got to do more to win in the South. I think the introduction of U.S. troops that will be involved will be agreed upon by the various parties. And I think Max will go back [to Saigon] feeling in good humor. . . .

LBJ: . . . That's wonderful. . . . *New York Times* has got a story that we're out there planning a new strategy and a lot of extra commitments. . . . What do they think about all these statements about the Chinese coming in?

McNAMARA: They think . . . that's unlikely to develop in the near future.

LBJ: Are they carrying on kind of a propaganda campaign now with Fulbright and Company, all of them trying to lower the boom on us propagandawise?

McNAMARA: I'm not entirely sure. But none of us feel that the Chinese are likely to come in, in the near term. They are reasonably optimistic that over the next three to six months, with additional U.S. combat troops in there—and there's still a little disagreement as to how many there should be ultimately, but no disagreement as to how many there should be in the next ninety or a hundred and twenty days—they feel that they can sufficiently stiffen the South Vietnamese and strengthen their forces to show Hanoi that Hanoi cannot win in the South. It won't be that the South Vietnamese can win. But it will be clear to Hanoi that Hanoi can't win. And this is one of the objectives we're driving for. There is general agreement we reached this morning that it would be unwise anytime in the near future . . . to bomb Hanoi, Haiphong, or any of that area.

LBJ: Are they pretty encouraged by what's happened in the last few weeks out there in South Vietnam?

---

1. Diary of Maxwell Taylor, April 20, 1965, quoted in *FRUS*, vol. 2, pp. 572–74.

McNAMARA: I wouldn't say very encouraged, but it's a change from a sharp downward trend to a bottoming out or a leveling off, with potential for some slight upward movement.[1]

LBJ: Uh-huh. Looks like they killed a good many. They claim they killed a couple hundred today.

McNAMARA: Yes. Last week, the VC kill was relatively low, however. Although the previous two weeks have been very high. . . . Despite some of these favorable signs, there is . . . this very large Vietcong buildup over the last several months and the concentration of Vietcong strength in the center of the country, which could break out at any time and cause serious trouble to us. And they're very much afraid of some catastrophic loss at Bienhoa or Danang or one of these areas. And it's to protect against that that they now agree that there should be some U.S. combat troops introduced. . . . I mean, in the next ninety to a hundred and twenty days. Beyond that, there is some disagreement as to how much eventual U.S. troop involvement would be required in South Vietnam.

LBJ: They feel pretty good about the stability of the government?

McNAMARA: They feel much better about it, yes. They feel that Quat[2] hasn't been fully tested as yet, but that he's behaving himself very well and is gradually gathering more support. The generals still are a rather unruly group . . . but they haven't united enough to cause Quat any trouble. Quat is very much aware of the potential for trouble there and seeking to hold them down.

LBJ: Are we taking every precaution we ought to take against any unforeseen catastrophic—

McNAMARA: I think so. This is one of the subjects we've discussed at great length today. To avoid possible catastrophe at Bienhoa, where we have a huge concentration of equipment and U.S. forces, and also at Danang, I think we would all recommend to you . . . introduction of a brigade at Bienhoa and several additional battalions at enclaves along the coast. This [is] both to protect us against catastrophe and also to relieve some of the South Vietnamese and . . . allow some of our units to participate in counterinsurgency operations. And as a result of all this, to show the North Vietnamese that they can't win in the South.

LBJ: Was Max as exercised as his cables indicate?

McNAMARA: I don't think so. In any case, by the time we leave today . . . I'm confident we'll all be in harmony again.

LBJ: Okay, Bob, that's wonderful.[3]

---

1. Compare this comment to LBJ's April 17, 1965, blarney with Potter about the "phenomenal" progress in Vietnam.

2. The South Vietnamese leader since February 16, Prime Minister Phan Huy Quat.

3. When LBJ discussed the recommendation to escalate the next day with his advisers, George Ball opposed it, warning, "This transforms our whole relation to the war" (*FRUS*, vol. 2, pp. 578–81).

THOMAS MANN

Under Secretary of State for Economic Affairs
Saturday, April 24, 1965, 9:35 A.M.

At the same moment LBJ stands at a crossroads on Vietnam, there is an unexpected new crisis. Army officers in the Dominican Republic, led by Colonel Francisco Caamaño Deno, have overthrown Donald Reid Cabral, head of the country's civilian junta, on whom the United States has lavished $100 million since he ousted the leftist, non-Communist Juan Bosch in September 1963. Most of the rebels demand Bosch's return to power from exile in Puerto Rico. Fighting has broken out in Santo Domingo, the Dominican capital.

MANN: It isn't good this morning. . . . A large part of the army that's in Santo Domingo . . . is supporting the rebel government. The loyalties of the troops outside the capital are still uncertain. . . . Looting is going on in the city and a lot of chaos. They've got about fourteen hundred [U.S.] Marines onboard the ship standing offshore.[1]

*   *   *

LBJ: What's our Ambassador—he's cut off, huh?[2]
MANN: He was asked to come up on consultation by the Bureau,[3] who were worried about the deteriorating situation. They didn't expect it to come so soon.
LBJ: I'm getting worried. . . . I just wonder if we shouldn't . . . find some way to throw a few bones to Panama.[4] . . . What I want to do is do any bribing I can now, because it's relatively inexpensive, compared to what we're doing in Vietnam. And I just don't think we can take much troubles now. . . . I sure think we ought to give thought to getting kind of a preelection barbecue at Laredo[5] . . . and serving them some beer. . . . Why don't you leak that to your girl from Scripps-Howard, Virginia Pruitt,[6] that the feeling is here in Washington that this will happen? . . .
MANN: All right, I can do that.
LBJ: She's real good to you, and I'd cultivate the hell out of her. . . . I'd just say to her that you talked to the President, and the President's very anxious to get on with the negotiations. . . . I might leak it to some of the guys who've been giving

---

1. LBJ had ordered the USS *Boxer,* an aircraft carrier, to patrol off Santo Domingo.
2. Ambassador William Tapley Bennett had returned the previous day to visit his family in Georgia.
3. State Department's Bureau of Inter-American Affairs.
4. Recalling the Panama crisis of January 1964 (see Beschloss, *Taking Charge,* pp. 155–57, 161–62), LBJ wishes to sweeten the pot in negotiations now under way with the Panamanians to make sure that arena does not blow up again.
5. Meaning a social gathering at which to make nice with the press. As Johnson knew, Mann was born in Laredo.
6. Scripps-Howard diplomatic reporter.

you hell on the [*Washington*] *Post*. . . . We're going to have to really set up that government down there[1] and run it and stabilize it some way or other. This Bosch is no good. I was down there.[2]

MANN: He's no good at all. And the tragedy behind all this is the price of sugar. . . . You can't . . . raise the price of sugar without putting Castro firmly in the saddle. They're both sugar economies. . . . And if we don't get a decent government in there, Mr. President, we get another Bosch. It's just going to be another sinkhole.

LBJ: . . . So that's your problem. You better figure it out.

MANN: I think we'll know in the next six or eight hours how this fighting's going. If Wessin[3] comes out on top, the man to get back, I think, is Balaguer.[4] . . .

LBJ: . . . I see where they claimed last night that we were in on the shooting of the palace and . . . we were resisting Bosch.[5] . . . ABC was putting it out. We ought to correct that. . . . Why don't you call in the AP . . . and point out this is not in the interest of our government to be saying these things? . . . We're not supporting one [side] against the other.

DEAN RUSK

Monday, April 26, 1965, 8:45 P.M.

> Johnson wants to give a job to Patricia Roberts Harris, an African American law professor at Howard University.

LBJ: Why don't we make her Ambassador to Luxembourg? . . . These women— I want to move them up. Women and Nigroes.

RUSK: . . . If she were our deputy legal adviser, she'd do a lot more work and be more help to us than . . . as Ambassador to Luxembourg.

LBJ: Yes, but it wouldn't have the honor and the standing and the status and the glory that all the Nigroes want—and the women. . . . I don't want to send her to Jamaica, but I want to send her to some Scandinavian country or Luxembourg, or something like that.[6]

---

1. In Santo Domingo.
2. JFK had sent LBJ as his representative to Bosch's inauguration in February 1963.
3. Dominican Air Force Commander Elias Wessin led right-wing forces against the rebels.
4. Former President Joaquin Balaguer was defeated for reelection by Bosch in 1962.
5. Anti-Bosch forces had strafed the national palace in Santo Domingo. LBJ is anxious that no one think the United States is taking sides.
6. Harris indeed went to Luxembourg as America's first black woman Ambassador.

THOMAS MANN

Tuesday, April 27, 1965, 7:17 A.M.

> Mann reports on the Dominican crisis. On April 25, the "loyalist" right-wing forces under General Wessin launched air attacks against the rebels. In San Juan, former President Bosch announced that he would accept the rebels' invitation to resume power. Fighting increased between the two sides. Johnson plans to hold a press conference this afternoon.

MANN: Early this morning, [we've] assembled some four hundred or more Americans, mostly tourists, in the Hotel Ambassador.[1] They're ready for evacuation. We didn't want to try to get them out at night because with all these Commies[2] running around, we thought it was too dangerous. Early this morning, we hear reports that the [Dominican] navy, which has gone back with the Wessin air force group, is threatening to . . . bombard [Santo Domingo]. . . . What I think we should do, if you agree, is to tell our Navy to come into the port of Haina.[3] . . . [Announce] that we insist on a cease-fire until we can get these Americans out. . . . Then use this time to try to get a junta set up of some kind, which will stabilize the situation.

LBJ: All right. . . . Why would they want to be bombarding the city until we got our people out, after they had agreed it was all right to take them?[4]

MANN: Well, I think they're kind of desperate. The navy and the air force and Wessin's forces are cut off from the city. . . . About all they can do is strafe and bomb. . . .

LBJ: It's awful, isn't it?

MANN: Yes, it is.

LBJ: How much did we know about all this, Tom?[5]

MANN: Well, we knew that it's a graft-ridden place. This guy Reid,[6] I think, has done a very courageous job in . . . doing all these unpopular things, [like] collecting taxes from the rich. . . . It pinches everybody's toes who are used to all these unusual privileges. The price of sugar dropped. . . . That's why Bennett was up here[7]—to tell us we had about two or three weeks to do something about it. We put in a good deal of money, but money doesn't do everything we hope it will some-

---

1. In Santo Domingo.
2. Mann already refers to the rebels as Commies, although, as events will show, this is mainly unjustified.
3. About seven miles from the center of Santo Domingo.
4. Both sides had issued statements the previous evening promising to permit an orderly U.S. evacuation.
5. Johnson wants to know what kind of advance warning he was given about the civil war.
6. Donald Reid Cabral.
7. The U.S. Ambassador was back in the United States when the coup erupted.

times. They had thirty years of a very strong rule,[1] and they just don't know how to manage their own affairs now that they have the responsibility themselves. . . .

LBJ: Does it mean, you think, that this[2] is another Castro government?

MANN: Not yet, no. Hard to tell what comes out of one of these messes, who comes out on top. We don't think that this fellow Bosch understands that the Communists are dangerous. We don't think that he is a Communist. What we are afraid of is that if he gets back in, he'll have so many of them around him—and they're so much smarter than he is—that before you know it, they would begin to take over.

LBJ: What is it that they see in him? Why does he have this following?

MANN: Bosch . . . writes books. He's the most impractical fellow in the world. Sort of an idealist. Floating around on cloud nine type. He's a handsome man and a good orator, and the people just don't have the maturity to distinguish between words and deeds. . . .

LBJ: What should I say about it in this press conference?

MANN: That the situation is fluid. That we are evacuating Americans. . . . And we're in touch with both sides, hoping to do what we can to stop bloodshed.

᛭   ᛭   ᛭

LBJ: Is it likely that we might just start moving our people out and they start shooting?

MANN: There's a certain risk . . . that somebody will shoot. As long as you have all of these Commies and everything else around, and the chance of misunderstanding. . . . Certainly with these threats of bombardment—

LBJ: Where do you get those threats? . . . Gossip?

MANN: No, no. . . . I suspect it's just a radio threat. . . . I think the sooner we get started this morning, the better off—

LBJ: How long does it take us to get ours out?

MANN: . . . It would take several hours. . . .

LBJ: . . . I'd get them out of there as quick as I could.

JACK HOOD VAUGHN

Assistant Secretary of State for Inter-American Affairs
Tuesday, April 27, 1965, 3:40 P.M.

Vaughn reports that the U.S. Navy has evacuated a thousand Americans from Santo Domingo.

---

1. Under Rafael Trujillo, assassinated in 1961.
2. The rebel provisional government that had ousted Reid.

VAUGHN: Bennett thinks casualties have been heavy, in the range of four to five hundred people. . . . Wessin's troops have crossed the bridge, supported by infantry, and the rebels are scattering in all directions. . . . We may have order established by nightfall.

LBJ: Have we had anything to do with this?[1]

VAUGHN: No, we haven't. And the involvement, sir, of the Communist elements is becoming clearer and clearer.

LBJ: I sure hope we say something like that in this [news conference]. I guess we don't— No, too early to say it, I guess.

DEAN RUSK

Tuesday, April 27, 1965, 5:41 P.M.

> During his news conference, at 4:00 P.M., Johnson said he hoped that order would be restored in the Dominican Republic. He was not asked a single question on the crisis.

RUSK: I hope you'll slip away and relax a few minutes and have that drink that Virginia[2] prescribes for me. You did a fine job.

LBJ: Well, thank you.

RUSK: That was really first class. . . . It was calm, but it was very clear, and you handled the tough questions with great skill and I think it made a tremendous impression on everybody. Delighted. Thank you very much.

LBJ: Hope it didn't get you in any trouble.

RUSK: None at all. Thank you a lot.

WHITE HOUSE SITUATION ROOM

Wednesday, April 28, 1965, 3:30 A.M.

LBJ: Have we got any more planes out in South Vietnam and North Vietnam?

DUTY OFFICER: Yes, sir. There are two more armed reconnaissance missions scheduled over target at this time. . . .

LBJ: What are they looking for? Trucks, or have they got some specific targets?

DUTY OFFICER: One has a span of a bridge to knock out. The other ones are just . . . looking for targets—trucks and rolling stock.

LBJ: Much obliged.

---

1. LBJ is asking whether the United States can be accused of having acted on behalf of the Wessin forces.

2. Mrs. Rusk.

ABE FORTAS

Wednesday, April 28, 1965, 10:20 P.M.

Today, the Dominican rebels seemed to be surging toward victory. Ambassador Bennett cabled Washington at 1:43 P.M. that it was now a fight "between Castro-type elements and those who oppose." At 5:14 P.M. he sent a top-urgent "CRITIC" cable warning that the situation was "deteriorating rapidly." The loyalists were about to collapse. Bennett recommended "immediate landings" of U.S. Marines. These, he said, could be explained as essential to protect the evacuation of more Americans.

To Johnson, Bennett's cable meant that if he tarried, he might wake up to find that Santo Domingo had become the second Communist capital in the Caribbean. Seventy-six minutes after he read it, he ordered four hundred U.S. Marines to be landed in the Dominican Republic. This would be the first such American landing in Latin America in thirty-seven years. At 8:40 P.M., on live television, LBJ announced the action—"to protect American lives" that were "in danger."

Now, as his confidant Fortas calls, Johnson has stepped out of a formal White House dinner to watch his speech replayed on television. Fortas volunteers to act as a back channel to Juan Bosch through Jaime Benitez, chancellor of the University of Puerto Rico, a mutual close friend of Bosch and Fortas.

LBJ: Wait just a minute. [*LBJ watches remainder of his remarks*] Go ahead.
FORTAS: . . . Bosch is right there in the chancellor's summer house. So we have got that means of communication, if it's useful. . . .
LBJ: Good. . . . We notified the OAS.[1] . . . [But] I didn't think I could wait twenty seconds for the OAS to call that group together . . . when I had two wires from the Ambassador[2] within the hour—when he's a very calm, sober, judicious career man—to just not act on. I had Adlai in and Fulbright[3] and all of them, and we went over it, and I put in a strong statement on OAS and cut out anything that might be interpreted as alignment [of the rebels] with the Communists.[4] Which our people tell us they are. They don't think Bosch is. They think he's just a stooge in the deal. But nobody thought Castro was either.

---

1. Organization of American States.
2. Bennett.
3. UN Ambassador Adlai Stevenson and Senate Foreign Relations Committee Chairman J. William Fulbright, during a meeting with the congressional leadership. LBJ here refers to bell-wethers of liberal opinion.
4. LBJ had refused advice to explain the Marine intervention as necessary to prevent the rebels from establishing a Castro-Communist government.

McGEORGE BUNDY

Thursday, April 29, 1965, 9:48 A.M.

> Bundy reports on the Marine landing to Johnson, who is still in the White House family quarters.

LBJ: Mac, how are you doing this morning?

BUNDY: Just fine, Mr. President.

LBJ: [*chuckles*] I didn't know we were in that good a shape!

BUNDY: [*laughs*] Why, as for people with two wars they don't want, we're in as good shape as you can expect. . . . The rebels have dug in down in [Santo Domingo] with in-town guerrilla techniques of bazookas and mortars. There's going to be a very tough fight, unless they're starved out. . . . Bennett doesn't want more than the four hundred [Marines] he's got. . . . We've got another thousand men right offshore[1] when we want them. . . . If there is this kind of violence by Castro types in the city, I think we can expect very good support in the OAS because it is just what about two-thirds of those governments[2] are afraid of. The Castro people have taken out after us very hard on the radio, and the Soviets are beginning to do so. . . . My guess is that we now have a sufficient force on the ground so that we will . . . see if the Dominicans can't handle it for themselves with this moral support. But we'll have to keep a sharp eye to be ready to take stronger action if it looks as if the Communists[3] are beginning to win. . . .

LBJ: Do the rebels have much strength? . . .

BUNDY: . . . If the rebels extend their holding in the city, you could have yourself a very tough cleaning-up operation. It would not be a happy decision to have to ask the Marines to do that.

LBJ: No. . . . We want to be very, very careful not to sit here and let [the rebels] augment their forces. Where are these Castroites coming from? Inside?

BUNDY: Oh, this is all inside, as I understand it so far, Mr. President. . . . I will be very surprised if the Cubans try anything in the way of an invasion. . . .

LBJ: I sure don't want to wake up . . . and find out Castro is in charge. . . . Now, who are we depending on to avoid that? Bennett?[4]

BUNDY: . . . Bennett and the Agency.[5] . . . The Agency was extremely slow in informing us yesterday,[6] and we climbed up and down their backs. It's not

---

1. On the USS *Boxer*, which had landed the original four hundred Marines.
2. In Latin America.
3. Bundy is now referring to the rebels as Communists.
4. Ambassador Bennett.
5. Central Intelligence Agency.
6. Of the rebel surge.

Raborn's[1] fault. But some of his technical people were protecting their goddamn code words, and it took one of their important messages five hours to get here. Bennett, fortunately, was not interrupted. It was very, very good work by Bromley Smith,[2] who was feeding [Bennett's cables] in to us yesterday afternoon that allowed us to [send] the troops . . . in before nightfall. It would have been damned hard to put them in if we hadn't done it that fast. . . .

LBJ: Now, they tell me that . . . the CIA has been [warning] us about [this crisis] every day [until it happened]. Is that true?

BUNDY: . . . There was nothing . . . that gave me any sense of alarm. . . . First I knew of it was when Bennett came up here.[3]

LBJ: They're already saying, "I told you so."

BUNDY: You can count on it! There's always some bastard who wants to play that game. . . . I'm supposed to be in New York today. . . . If you would feel more comfortable, I can cancel the New York thing. I don't, myself, think it's that kind of a crisis, but I'm more concerned that you should feel your machine is working.

LBJ: . . . Well, go on. We'll—

BUNDY: Might as well get out of the way and not be a fall [guy] for this war? [laughs]

LBJ: No, no, no, no. But I would imagine that there are going to be some decisions today that are pretty important. . . .

BUNDY: . . . I think we did the right thing yesterday.[4] . . . We'll never be sure they[5] wouldn't have won without us. We only know that we couldn't take that chance. . . .

LBJ: Well . . . I think where we're going to be wrong is when we—

BUNDY: Don't do enough.

LBJ: When we don't do enough or when we go in and do too much. We haven't done anything now but evacuate.

BUNDY: That's right.

LBJ: But if we, if we became a party to this action[6]—

BUNDY: . . . Bennett, incidentally, does not want [U.S.] airplanes to buzz, and we've held that up. . . . There ought to be plenty on the scene—and visible, so that the morale effect will be decisive.[7] . . .

---

1. Admiral William "Red" Raborn, just sworn in yesterday as LBJ's Director of Central Intelligence.
2. Executive Secretary of the National Security Council.
3. Returned to America just before the crisis began.
4. Landing the Marines.
5. The rebels.
6. A belligerent.
7. In thwarting the rebels.

LBJ: . . . I can well understand why he wouldn't want them buzzing around. . . . [But] I don't see why you keep [the thousand additional Marines] on a carrier, where they can't [be seen]. . . .

BUNDY: The politics of four hundred and the politics of fifteen hundred are identical. . . . So you might as well get them ashore.

LBJ: . . . You might get some of them killed. That's the only thing.

ROBERT SPIVACK

Columnist, New York Herald Tribune
Thursday, April 29, 1965, 12:43 P.M.

> The national storm against Johnson's involvement in Vietnam is gathering. On April 17, in one of the first large antiwar demonstrations, sponsored by Students for a Democratic Society, Women Strike for Peace, and other organizations, six-teen thousand men and women marched to the Washington Monument and lis-tened to Democratic Senator Ernest Gruening of Alaska, the leftist editor I. F. Stone, and other speakers denounce American involvement in the war and de-mand "immediate cessation" of the bombing. Judy Collins and Joan Baez sang. On Easter, outside the LBJ Ranch, an antiwar group carried protest signs for eleven hours and demanded to present the President a petition. LBJ circumvented the crowd by taking a dirt road to church in Blanco and had a low-level aide accept the document. On April 20, seventeen young antiwar demonstrators sat down in the driveway of the White House.
>
> Furious, LBJ sees the growing antiwar movement as a serious threat to two of his main purposes: keeping the American people and Congress from being aroused about Vietnam in a way that might endanger passage of the Great Society legislation—and forcing the North Vietnamese to sue for peace out of fear that a united American people will do whatever it takes to win the war. To discredit the protesters, LBJ, armed with FBI reports from J. Edgar Hoover, claims that they are inspired by Communists.[1]

LBJ: Really one of the good stories that ought to be written is "Americans Be-ware!" Our CIA reports show from all the capitals of the world that we could solve the Vietnam thing if the North Vietnamese and the Chinese really felt that we were there to stay. But our own people are creating doubts, and they're questioning our policies. So the kids are running up and down parading, and most of them are led by Communist groups. This Du Bois Club.[2] Hoover spent an hour here yesterday.

1. Richard Helms, who served Johnson as Deputy Director (1965–1966) and then Director of Cen-tral Intelligence, told the author in 1987 that LBJ incessantly pressured the CIA to provide proof that the antiwar movement was directed by Moscow or Peking and was frustrated when Helms could not.

2. In 1965, starting on the West Coast, Du Bois Clubs, named after the late black Marxist scholar W. E. B. Du Bois and known for their young, multiracial membership, began forming. The Justice De-partment considered them to be aligned with the Young Communist League.

You can say most of them are led by beatniks and these left-wing groups, and the few Senators that are joining and going to the campus to stir them up. Then they drop leaflets next day, and they make the North Vietnamese and the Chinese believe that we're about ready to move out. . . . And that's a great disservice to America and it's a great disservice to our fighting men. . . . Even the good liberal Senators know that we're being sucked in. Nobody is really on that side except Morse and Gruening.[1]

SPIVACK: I don't know what the hell's the matter with Morse. . . . He's got to be a real fanatic on this damn thing. . . . This is almost demagogic, the way he's playing it. I haven't seen Gruening . . . but my God, the performance! . . . Even if one disagrees, I mean, this stuff that he was pulling the other day about Johnson's war and McNamara's war, and where your place will be in history. . . . Is something else eating him?

LBJ: No, no, he just feels very strongly. But he's bought their line, and that's that.

ROBERT McNAMARA

Thursday, April 29, 1965, 1.04 P.M.

> Today, for the first time, American forces in Santo Domingo have come under rebel fire, from snipers who attacked a seventy-man Marine force protecting the U.S. Embassy. As LBJ suggested to Bundy earlier in the day, he wants to land additional Marines. But he wants Ambassador Bennett to bear the onus by calling for them first.

McNAMARA: My suggestion, Mr. President, is that we go ahead and order five hundred additional Marines in there immediately. . . . In the meantime, take an hour or two and try to get from the Ambassador a recommendation as to what he thinks ought to be done.

LBJ: Is there no way of instantaneously talking to him? Even if the damn wire is open, why wouldn't we say, "We have a report . . . that this danger to our people [the rebel action] is very great, and therefore we are doing this." Then let him yell, if he wants to, bloody murder, and we can evaluate it.

McNAMARA: Let me just see if I can't get that done.

LBJ: . . . Failing in that, I'd just go on and order [the Marines] in. . . . You talk to him. . . . Just say that I'm distressed at this message[2] and that we are proceeding to take action. Then listen for him to cough right loud.[3] And if he doesn't, why, let's move!

---

1. The Democrats from Oregon and Alaska were the only Senators to oppose Johnson's Gulf of Tonkin Resolution.
2. About danger to Americans.
3. To show some objection.

GEORGE BALL
THOMAS MANN

Thursday, April 29, 1965, 2:22 P.M.

> Johnson has ordered a thousand additional Marines landed in the Dominican Republic. Ambassador Bennett says that there is no immediate need for the United States to get more involved in order to prevent a rebel victory.

BALL: On the whole, I would say that [he] is reasonably optimistic. . . . The junta[1] still seems to be engaged in a cleanup operation. . . . [He doesn't] at the moment foresee the need for any direct American intervention. . . .

MANN: . . . [The loyalists have] knocked out two rebel tanks in the last few hours. . . . Tapley [Bennett] sounded less apprehensive than—while it's far from being over—than at any time since he's gotten back [to Santo Domingo].

LBJ: Well, he wasn't very apprehensive at all up to yesterday afternoon, when he thought we had to charge. . . .

MANN: . . . Both sides are hungry and tired. . . .

LBJ: Did you tell him extra Marines were coming to shore?

BALL: Yes. . . . I think they'll have up to fourteen hundred. . . .

LBJ: Whatever we do, let's try to keep control through backgrounders[2]— George, you and Tom—of our good intentions in this thing. So we don't just . . . let a few critics run us over.

BROMLEY SMITH

Thursday, April 29, 1965, 4:26 P.M.

> Now Bundy's aide reports to LBJ that Ambassador Bennett and the U.S. mission in Santo Domingo are under rebel attack.

SMITH: Tap Bennett [and other embassy officials are] under fire from snipers. . . . The Marines have been ordered to fire back, and they are firing back. . . . The rebels are becoming more aggressive. . . . In response to your instruction, [we] have put ashore five hundred more Marines. . . .

LBJ: I *sure* think that they ought to bring this to the attention of the Latin American [embassy] people about how they're firing upon us, as soon as they can.

SMITH: Ambassador Bennett had a meeting with the Latin American ambassa-

---

1. Anti-Bosch junta.
2. Quiet official guidance to reporters.

dors down there. They were all almost pleading with him.[1] The only protection they really had were our Marines.

LBJ: Well, they ought to be telling their *country* that. Tell Bennett to be sure that they get this message to their country. . . . This is going to be bad in our country.

GALE McGEE

Democratic Senator from Wyoming
Thursday, April 29, 1965, 4:29 P.M.

> In the midst of the Dominican crisis, LBJ thanks the hawkish young Senator for his support on Vietnam and shares his conviction that Communists are behind the young Americans protesting the war.

LBJ: Gale, I just saw some nice things you said . . . on the Vietnam thing. . . . French newspaperman was here yesterday, and told us, "If you really are going to stay, as you say you are, then you'll win. But I've been with the Vietcong the last two months, and they all think you're going to throw in the towel." . . . Every facility that the Communist world has at its disposal is being used to divide us. One of the boys in this Du Bois movement, this youth organization—

McGEE: Yes, sir?

LBJ: His mother really is one of the leaders in the Communist party in this country. They got schedules every week, all over the country. They got a bunch of them coming up to Texas next week. Edgar Hoover was very upset about it. Brought [the files] over last night. They're going into the colleges and the faculties and the student bodies, and trying to get them to send . . . wires . . . that come right out of Communist headquarters. . . . Said he was going to talk to Tom Dodd[2] and try to get him to expose it. Because he's been a former FBI agent. But a lot of our good, well-intentioned friends don't know how much these folks are urging that we have a cease-fire or stop our bombing. If we did, they'd raise so much hell we could never start it [again]. . . . Their principal play is to—abroad—to bring pressure on us here to throw in the towel. And that's what they're asking the students to do. That's this fifteen-thousand meeting the other day.[3] Now Hoover's got most of these groups infiltrated.[4] And his people go right with them and hear all their discussions.

McGEE: . . . It does deeply disturb me. . . .

---

1. For protection by the United States.
2. The fiercely anti-Communist Democratic Senator from Connecticut.
3. The aforementioned Washington Monument demonstration.
4. Hoover has infiltrated left-wing groups.

LBJ: I think I'll get some CIA messages, showing where the reports come from, and some FBI messages, and ask some of them to come talk to you.

McGEE: Oh, that would be very helpful.

LBJ: You don't necessarily have to identify the country and you don't have to smear anyone. . . . But we do want to show what they're doing, so that our people don't become nitwits.

McGEE: Well, you think that ours would learn sometime.

LBJ: You would. But I remember when I was a young man in Congress, I hated war so much that I signed a congressional petition to discharge a bill from a committee that would have required us to vote on going to war.[1] I look back and wonder how I could have been that crazy. But I loved peace so much that I thought that if we could debate it and vote on it, that it would be the thing to do. Of course, that was the day before the nuclear bomb, but it was crazy even then because *I* had no information to vote on it.

McGEE: . . . I just think that we can mobilize a far different front there on those campuses. It's just that the good guys don't sound off. . . .

LBJ: That's right. . . . Well, I'll have [someone] contact you. . . . It'll probably be Deke DeLoach of the FBI.

J. EDGAR HOOVER

Thursday, April 29, 1965, 5:45 P.M.

> At LBJ's behest, Hoover has agreed to show FBI files to Senators Everett Dirksen and Thomas Dodd which suggest that Communists lurk behind the growing demonstrations against American involvement in Vietnam. Three days hence, drawing on his FBI briefing, Dodd will charge on NBC's *Meet the Press* that there is a Communist "central outpost" stirring up troubles in Vietnam and the Dominican Republic.[2]

HOOVER: We are going tomorrow . . . to talk with Senator Dirksen and Senator Dodd. . . .

LBJ: Excellent.

HOOVER: . . . And we have the material we have prepared for each one of them—an outline of material which they can use. . . .

LBJ: That's good, that's good. Couldn't be better. . . . I'll be back in touch with you. Maybe next week we can have lunch.

---

1. The Ludlow Amendment would have required a national referendum to go to war.
2. *New York Times,* May 3, 1965.

Chapter Eight

"DO WE LET CASTRO TAKE OVER?"

The Castro forces are really gaining control. . . . We begged the [Organiza-
tion of American States] to send somebody in last night. . . . They're just the
damnedest fraud I ever saw. . . . These international organizations ain't
worth a damn, except window dressing. . . . It looks to me like I'm in a hell
of a shape. . . . They're going to eat us up if I let another Cuba come in
there. They'll say, "Why did you sit on your big fat tail?"

LBJ *to* MIKE MANSFIELD, *April 30, 1965*

ABE FORTAS

Friday, April 30, 1965, 10:50 A.M.

Johnson worries that new rebel victories in the Dominican Republic will usher in
a Communist regime. This morning, Bundy is urging Johnson to steel American
public opinion by declaring that "Castro Communists are in control" in Santo
Domingo, even though the evidence for such a claim is weak.[1]

LBJ: They're killing our people. . . . They've captured tanks now and they've
taken over the police, and they're marching them down the street, and they've got
a hundred of them as hostages, and they're saying they're going to shoot them if
they don't take over. Now, our CIA says this is a completely led, operated, domi-
nated—they've got men on the inside of it—Castro operation. That it started out
as a Bosch operation, but he's been moved completely out of the picture . . . and
their people took over.
FORTAS: Mr. President, that may very well be true—
LBJ: They *say* it is! Their people on the inside *tell* us.[2] . . .
FORTAS: I don't doubt that. I don't know one way or the other. I have a very sim-

---

1. See Dallek, *Flawed Giant*, p. 264.
2. The CIA.

ple point. . . . The first thing we've got to do is to show that this is a Castro Communist operation, and the most dramatic way to do that is to let Bosch call for a cease-fire and let those damn guys continue fighting. . . .

LBJ: . . . But if they've got the tanks and if the people are capitulating, and if they've got all the police, will there be anybody left to fight? . . . They'll just take charge, start running the government. . . .

FORTAS: I don't see how they can, with our military troops down there.

LBJ: We're not stopping them running the government. . . . Since last Saturday, Bosch lasted for a few hours. Then Castro started operating. They got forty-five more in there last night—Castro-trained, Castro-operated people. . . . They[1] . . . came in here last night and said to me, . . . "We've got nine hundred men, the most elite [police] force . . . in Santo Domingo holed up here in this prison." . . . I said, "Well, let's protect them." [They said,] "No, we can't do that because that would be partiality." I said, "Then let's evacuate them and get them to another part of the island." "We can't do that because that would be sending our Navy in, and the Ambassador says that would be showing partiality." I said, "Then get the Dominican navy to evacuate them from the Communists." They said, "All right, we'll do that." Well . . . they called me and said . . . the Dominican navy didn't want to have anything to do with it.

So, I got up this morning. . . . They've added nine hundred to their strength of nineteen hundred. And they're marching them down the streets of Santo Domingo with their guns on their backs, and they're taking a hundred of them and saying, "We're going to kill you unless these people[2] quit and give up." They haven't eaten in three days, and they're about ready to give up. The question is, What does the United States do? We've done this now for a week—done *nothing* because we don't want to be *partial*.

FORTAS: Uh-huh.

LBJ: But they're firing consistently, every hour, *on our embassy*. . . . When we can locate a sniper . . . we shoot at him and he hides for a little while and we kill four or five. But the OAS . . . spent all night denouncing us. We finally got a cease-fire out of them.[3] . . . I think we ought to get the CIA, who have men right in these operations—just like Hoover had one in that car down in Alabama[4]—that know what's happening. And there ain't no doubt about this being Castro now.[5] We

---

1. CIA Director Raborn and other national security advisers.
2. The anti-Bosch forces.
3. Delegates to the Organization of American States were indignant about Johnson's unilateral action in sending the Marines. They approved an American call for a cease-fire and a neutral zone around foreign embassies in Santo Domingo for refugees.
4. Gary Thomas Rowe, the FBI informer on the Ku Klux Klan.
5. Meaning that the rebels are aligned with Castro's Cuba.

haven't said that [1]   *We* know it's Communist. So I think we ought to get [the CIA] to give us name, address, chapter and verse . . . and say, "This is a case of Cuba doing this job." That's number one. I think, number two, we ought to have our military forces in sufficient quantity . . . to take that island. And if we can get any other forces to join us, well and good. . . . [They should be] ready to do whatever job they may be called upon, without taking any overt action at this moment toward the invasion. . . . But if all that *fails,* I'm not going to *sit* here and say, . . . "I can work it out after the Communist government is set up and start issuing orders."

*   *   *

LBJ: I think that we've got to give serious thought to saying to the American people pretty soon that—in a speech—that the Communists have captured this revolution, they're taking it over, the extraneous forces have invaded the island, that we're not going to allow another Cuba to develop, and that we want all the people in the hemisphere to join with us, but if they don't, why, we're going to move *anyway.*

ABE FORTAS

Friday, April 30, 1965, 11:30 A.M.

LBJ: They are moving other places in the hemisphere. It may be a part of a whole Communistic pattern tied in with Vietnam. . . . The intelligence reports show that the Communist countries have felt that we were pulling out of Vietnam. . . . During the election period and November and December . . . I didn't respond to the . . . Saigon air base attack.[2] . . . We didn't because we didn't know it was North Vietnamese. . . . We thought it might be a local outfit. Like we thought [the Dominican coup] might be a local uprising and not Communist. . . . Our softheaded people, Abe, spent the first three days saying, "This is just a civil war—just local stuff." That [Bosch] is just a benevolent operator. . . . Hanoi, Peking, Moscow, the Eastern European countries have taken the position that if you can just hold out a little while longer, there'll be so much division and fighting in the United States, the pressure will be so great. We've got Lippmann and we've got the *New York Times.* We've got the *Washington Post,* and we've got McGovern and Morse, Church and Fulbright.[3] Now, the last three weeks, really since Baltimore, when I

---

1. In public.
2. The Bienhoa attack of November 1964.
3. Antiwar Senators.

offered to talk,[1] they felt . . . we weren't going to be so brittle and easy and we might stay. So they've been a little discouraged. A French newspaperman was in, day before yesterday. Been with the Vietcong the last two months, and he says there's been a radical change, and they think now that we may *win,* so they're defecting and coming over to our side.

*   *   *

LBJ: I don't think that God Almighty is going to excuse me for sitting with adequate forces and letting them murder human beings. . . . They've been doing that for three days and we've done nothing. I just feel terrible about it. . . . I don't believe we ought to let Castro set up his government, when he announces victory. . . . Do you?

MIKE MANSFIELD

Friday, April 30, 1965, 11:51 A.M.

> LBJ implores the Senate Majority Leader to support him on the Dominican Republic.

LBJ: The Castro forces are really gaining control. . . . They're marching [nine hundred police] down the streets as hostages. . . . They're going to set up a Castro government. . . . We begged the OAS[2] to send somebody in last night. They won't move. They're just phantoms. They're just the damnedest fraud I ever saw, Mike. . . . They just talk. These international organizations ain't worth a damn, except window dressing. . . . The big question is, Do we let Castro take over and us move out? . . . The OAS called for a cease-fire last night, but they went home and went to sleep. . . . I'm trying to get them back today. And I suppose they don't [meet] today? Do I let them take over? It looks to me like I'm in a hell of a shape either way. . . . I'm putting the heat on, but how would you respond to this call for help of the nine hundred police? If I let them fall, you know what the Dirksens[3] are going to do to us.

MANSFIELD: That's right.

LBJ: They're going to eat us up if I let another Cuba come in there. They'll say, "Why did you sit on your big fat tail?" I'm afraid to talk to them, Mike, because they go out and talk. . . . I'm really afraid to talk to anybody. I'm afraid if I talk to Fulbright . . . he'll tell the *New York Times.* . . . You just can't talk to Fulbright or Dirksen. They just talk.

---

1. Offered to negotiate with North Vietnam in his April Johns Hopkins University speech.
2. Organization of American States.
3. Hawkish Republicans.

ABE FORTAS

Friday, April 30, 1965, 12:17 P.M.

FORTAS: Have you gotten the report on Bosch's press conference?
LBJ: No.
FORTAS: . . . This damn, lousy American press! . . . One of our great, loyal press men[1] said, "What will do you if the American Marines join with Wessin?"[2] Bosch said, "I don't believe they will, but if they do, we will, of course, repel aggression." . . . [Bosch] said, "These soldiers and fighters are Dominican democratic heroes. Please don't try to convert them to Communist heroes. . . . What you are doing is giving the Communists credit that they don't deserve." . . .
LBJ: God, I think it's worse than before we *started*.
FORTAS: Why?
LBJ: Well, because it *is* Communist! And he's *misleading* them! He's just *fronting*. . . . You know damn well . . . our choice is whether we're going to have Castro or intervention. . . . I think that the worst domestic political disaster we could suffer would be for Castro to take over.

ROBERT McNAMARA

Friday, April 30, 1965, 12:52 P.M.

LBJ: It seems that the biggest move now we can make is to really try to get Wessin to . . . say that he'll withhold his forces temporarily and agree to a cease-fire.
McNAMARA: I fully agree with you. . . .
LBJ: Get him to say, "We'll agree to a cease-fire, for a limited amount of time, if the OAS will act to prevent bloodshed." But I'm not going to sit here and let the streets run red with human blood while they sit on their ditty box.

McGEORGE BUNDY

Friday, April 30, 1965, 5:00 P.M.

In Santo Domingo, a U.S. Marine has been killed by rebels while trying to establish an "international safety zone," as requested by the Organization of American

---

1. Fortas's voice drips with sarcasm.
2. The right-wing leader.

States, to protect foreign nationals from the fighting. Overnight 2,500 U.S. Army paratroops have arrived to support the 1,700 Marines on the island.

BUNDY: Did you get the ticker on the Marine?
LBJ: No.
BUNDY: [*reading from AP story:*] "One U.S. Marine was killed and at least six others wounded today as American troops fought beside Dominican troops against a ragtag army of young civilians and soldiers. . . . Marine casualties came after leathernecks moved out of their staging area at the Ambassador Hotel." . . .
LBJ: I walked with the press,[1] and they are getting awfully Joe Clarkish.[2] I just wished I could say something to them.
BUNDY: You've got that statement.[3]
LBJ: I do, yeah, but you kind of *vetoed* it.
BUNDY: Well, Mr. President, I'm not sure you're ready to call it Commies, that's all.
LBJ: Figure out something else. Let's figure out what we can say. . . . The clock is ticking. The hour is right now. . . . Get me a statement.

ROBERT McNAMARA

Friday, April 30, 1965, 5:05 P.M.

Johnson has arranged to speak on live television about the Dominican Republic two hours from now. McNamara warns him that there is not enough evidence to claim that Castro Communists are in charge of the rebels.

LBJ: Why don't you think I should say that . . . powers outside the republic are trying to gain control? We all know they are. . . .
McNAMARA: I think you've got a pretty tough job to prove that, Mr. President. . . . You'd have a hard time proving to any group that Castro's done more than train these people. . . . It, I think, puts your own status and prestige too much on the line. . . .
LBJ: You don't think CIA can document it?
McNAMARA: I don't think so, Mr. President. . . . They haven't shown any evidence that I've seen that Castro has been directing this or has had any control over those people once they got back there.

---

1. Johnson liked to give impromptu press conferences while strolling on the White House grounds.
2. Dovish, in reference to the Democratic Senator from Pennsylvania.
3. A draft presidential statement telling the public that Castro Communists are controlling the rebellion.

LBJ: Well, should we modify the statement by saying that people trained outside the Dominican Republic are seeking to gain control over the rebel movement?

McNAMARA: . . . That's much more appropriate for you, as President, to say.

LBJ: . . . "There is significant disturbing signs that revolutionary aims are being perverted." You'd cut that out?

McNAMARA: No, that's all right.

ROBERT McNAMARA
BILL MOYERS

Friday, April 30, 1965, 5:40 P.M.

Both Moyers and McNamara are trying to keep Johnson from accusing the rebel movement of being inspired by pro-Castro Communists.

LBJ: Bill Moyers has a feeling that . . . if we talk about the people trained outside seeking to gain control, we might drive [the rebels] together. I have this feeling, Bob, if we don't take over that island within the next twenty-four hours . . . we never will. . . .

McNAMARA: Well, I don't think those sentences are critical to your speech . . . and they may cause a lot of controversy, which you could avoid by having some of the rest of us put those out. . . .

LBJ: What, would it antagonize liberals, you think?

McNAMARA: I think so. I think you're getting more of the Clarks and the Pells, and the Churches, and the Fulbrights and that crew[1] excited if you leave those sentences in.

MOYERS: The CIA Cuban man tells me Havana is still taken off balance by this. . . . Their hope is that we don't give some push to Cuba to try to get in there in a way they're not in there right now.

McNAMARA: . . . I think Cuba's got all the incentive it needs to do everything it can, and no matter what you say, they're going to push to the utmost.

LBJ: . . . You haven't [gotten the facts] about the Marine yet?[2]

McNAMARA: No.

LBJ: Well, you jerk up that admiral and tell him we don't want to have to read about it in . . . [the newspapers] first.

---

1. Senate liberals, including Democratic Senator Claiborne Pell of Rhode Island.
2. The Marine who was killed, mentioned in the 5:00 P.M. Bundy conversation above.

McGEORGE BUNDY

Friday, April 30, 1965, 6:00 P.M.

> Suffering from a cold, Johnson sounds rattled and shrill. In a voice that rises to an angry wail, he reproaches himself for being too slow to intervene in the Dominican Republic.

LBJ: While we were talking yesterday, we ought to have been acting. . . . I think they're[1] going to have that island in another twenty-four hours. . . . I think this statement is a predicate. Kind of "put your hand up [her] dress." Morse[2] . . . says our only basis for action is to keep the Communists from taking over. We won't even admit that there's . . . any conspiracy. We've run under the table, and we've hid. . . . When we go all day in a hot situation like this without saying anything, and then we wait until late in the evening until they act, I know that we're going to look like we are just a bunch of *interven-ors* and we're not peacemakers at *all!*

*   *   *

BUNDY: The thing the [State] Department is saying is if you put heat through the ticker tapes [on] the OAS in session, you may get a backfire.
LBJ: [*furious, shouting:*] *All right, let's see if we can satisfy that bunch of damn sissies over there on that question! Let's cut it out and let's just call them then and say that they're[3] "great statesmen!"*

ROBERT McNAMARA

Friday, April 30, 1965, 6:25 P.M.

> Somewhat calmer now, LBJ insists on saying that outside forces are influencing the Dominican rebel movement.

LBJ: Every one of the citizens of this country knows that there're disturbing signs there, and there're people that are trained outside in there. And I think that if I don't say so, then it looks like I'm concealing it and trying to cover up.
McNAMARA: I don't think it's bad to leave that in, Mr. President. . . .
LBJ: State thinks that by saying that, we are . . . taking on the liberals and the Communists. . . . Do you think that we [can] justify our not mentioning this if we put out a statement? . . . Every press man asks, . . . "Mr. President, are you going to sit here and not be concerned at all?"

---

1. The rebels.
2. The Vietnam dove Democrat Wayne Morse of Oregon, in a Senate floor speech.
3. The rebels whom LBJ wants to brand as Communists.

McNAMARA: Well, they're baiting you.

LBJ: Yes, sure. . . . But I think that reflects the opinion of the American people. They are concerned, and they expect their leader to tell them what the facts are, if he's going to talk. . . . And I've delayed talking two days.

ABE FORTAS

Friday, April 30, 1965, 7:20 P.M.

> Delivering his statement on live television, Johnson has just told Americans that "people trained outside the Dominican Republic are seeking to gain control" in Santo Domingo. He has called on the OAS to help enforce a cease-fire.

FORTAS: I thought it was absolutely wonderful. I'm so pleased.

LBJ: [*irritated:*] Well, they had a light [that was too bright]. I couldn't see. I had a TelePrompTer that was ten feet away. I begged George Reedy to go [fix] it, [but] he is the *laziest,* no-good son of a *bitch!*

McGEORGE BUNDY

Friday, April 30, 1965, 7:31 P.M.

> Standing in his office, LBJ is watching a television report on his speech when the weekly Western *Rawhide* appears. The program's opening theme music ("Rolling, rolling, rolling, Raw-*hide!*") can be heard in the background.

BUNDY: Have you got a minute?

LBJ: Yeah, let me cut this TV off. [*turns off sound*]

BUNDY: One of our aircraft has dropped bombs on a Cambodian village. . . . The operational question is whether we admit it to the Cambodians, who are now accusing us on it. . . . This is a flat violation of standing target rules. They gave a target that was nearer the border than we normally allow. Then the fellow bombed the wrong village and it was in the wrong country. . . . It's occurred to us that since Cambodia initially and mistakenly identified the aircraft as GVN,[1] we could perhaps ask the GVN to accept responsibility for the incident. . . . Dean Rusk feels it would be terrible to try to off-load the responsibility on any other country. We could, of course, pretend it never happened. . . .

LBJ: I'll wait till the board[2] comes in.

---

1. Belonging to the government of South Vietnam.
2. Of officers appointed by General Westmoreland to fix responsibility for the incident.

McGEORGE BUNDY

Saturday, May 1, 1965, 2:21 P.M.

Responding to an invitation from four hundred members of the University of
Michigan faculty, Bundy has agreed to debate Professor George Kahin of Cornell,
an antiwar scholar, at one of the first "teach-ins" on Vietnam, to be held in Washington on May 15. Johnson does not say so to Bundy, but he is indignant that
Bundy made the commitment without consulting him. If Bundy goes through with
the debate, LBJ wants him to tell the students that the antiwar movement is
Communist-inspired and aiding the enemy. Johnson knows that his request will be
distasteful to Bundy. At a moment when he is growing suspicious of his aide's motives, this is almost certainly a test of Bundy's loyalty to the President.

LBJ: I think that you ought to quietly say, "Johnson will not permit any
McCarthyism, but we must . . . tell you that we read that Hanoi and even Moscow
and Peking, Eastern Europe, and others say . . . the people . . . are divided and
they can't hold out much longer, because all the students are doing this and all the
Congress is doing this."
BUNDY: [*tight-voiced:*] Uh-huh.
LBJ: . . . "Now . . . I'm seeing the pattern. And I just can't be silent because . . .
thirty-one people called on Johnson to parade.[1] Twenty-one of them had good
records. Some of them's mamas were on the board of directors of the Communist
party. And what they're doing in La Paz, Bolivia, what they're doing in Mexico
City, and what they're doing in Vietnam, and what they're doing in the Dominican
Republic, is not totally unrelated. And you people ought to know that."

GEORGE REEDY

Sunday, May 2, 1965, 9:01 P.M.

Fighting in Santo Domingo has not stopped. There is constant firing on the American Embassy. More American military forces have arrived to prevent the original
battalion of Marines from being overwhelmed. Congressional leaders were called
to the White House. LBJ told them he was "not supporting *either* side" but "trying
to stop murder." When Senator Fulbright asked him whether Bosch was a Communist, Johnson replied, "It doesn't make any difference. His own people got
sidetracked."[2]

---

1. Referring to the Easter antiwar protesters who presented a petition at the LBJ ranch.
2. Dallek, *Flawed Giant*, p. 265.

Now the President is to deliver another speech from the White House on the Dominican crisis, his third in four days. None of the three television networks has consented to broadcast this address live. Only ABC and NBC have agreed to carry the speech on radio. As Jack Gould reported in the *New York Times*, the television networks "have become increasingly sensitive over Mr. Johnson's tendency to take to the air on short notice."[1] Under stress, LBJ is suffering from a cold and his voice is hoarse.

REEDY: ABC, NBC, and CBS are planning to tape it for television and then carry either excerpts or possibly the whole thing later on. . . .
LBJ: . . . They don't want to carry it? . . . I'd tell the [network executives] . . . "When the President meets two hours with the [congressional] leaders on Sunday afternoon and a soap opera is more important, then I don't want to ever hear from you boys on televised press conferences or equal time."[2] Not threatening them. No ultimatum. . . . Let 'em get *that* to their boss!
REEDY: Okay, sir. If they [decided] to carry it live, they'd require about a half hour to clear channels.
LBJ: [*angry:*] Why the hell haven't they [done] it *already?*
REEDY: Well . . . the decision has been to tape, sir.
LBJ: Well, they ought to have a flash.[3] . . . [*disgusted:*] Okay, I won't bother. I've got to run this thing *myself.*

FRANK STANTON

President, Columbia Broadcasting Company
Sunday, May 2, 1965, 9:15 P.M.

Johnson persuades his old friend to carry his speech live on CBS television, preempting *Candid Camera.*

LBJ: A three-year-old boy would know that a President wouldn't be meeting with the Joint Chiefs and all the [congressional] leaders unless it was of some significance. I don't think there's any question about whether you got a soap opera or this. I don't care *personally.* . . . What we're doing is we're authorizing two additional battalions and sending in forty-five [hundred] men extra tonight. . . . We have got three thousand [foreign nationals] evacuated, and we're trying to pull

---

1. *New York Times,* May 3, 1965.
2. Network news presidents had badgered Johnson to hold more televised press conferences and to suspend the equal time provision so that Barry Goldwater could debate him on television in 1964. (LBJ had blocked the suspension in Congress so he could dodge a debate.)
3. A special report interrupting normal programming.

five thousand of them more out. . . . George Reedy says they want to get excerpts from it and tape it, and I said, "I know Jesse Kellam[1] usually does that, but this is a different operation."

STANTON: No, absolutely. . . . We've got to move at nine-thirty, if you want to move at nine-thirty.

LBJ: Well, I'm just trying to get it out of the typewriter, if I can. . . . Boy, I got a bad cold.

STANTON: Boy, you sure sound like it.

LBJ: I've been working all night.

EUGENE ALLEN

White House Butler
Sunday, May 2, 1965, 9:22 P.M.

> Scheduled now to speak at ten o'clock, with only CBS covering him live on television, Johnson is exhausted, tense, and agitated. He needs to change clothes and is searching for one of his valets.

LBJ: Allen, have Ken and Paul[2] gone home?

ALLEN: I think so, Mr. President. . . .

LBJ: Well, go in there and find a blue tie for me and a blue shirt right quick[3]— well, never mind. I'll do it. Never mind.[4]

LADY BIRD JOHNSON

Sunday, May 2, 1965, Tape-recorded Diary

> In his television speech, Johnson announced that he is sending 6,500 more Americans to the Dominican Republic. It was a bad performance. He read two paragraphs from the TelePrompTer twice. Exceeding the evidence, he insisted that a "popular democratic revolution" had been hijacked by "a band of Communist conspirators." He would not "permit the establishment of another Communist government in the Western Hemisphere." The speech "damaged Johnson," wrote

---

1. General manager of the Johnson television station in Austin, KTBC.

2. Air Force Sergeants Kenneth Gaddis and Paul Glynn were LBJ's valets.

3. Politicians of the mid-1960s favored blue shirts for television, because the cameras of the time caused white shirts to glare.

4. As with Reedy, the harried LBJ is feeling that all his aides are incompetent and that he has to do everything himself.

Rowland Evans and Robert Novak, "for the simple reason that he was so obviously running scared."[1]

LADY BIRD: I saw a twenty-minute news clip of it. He had a cold. He was obviously very tired. The TelePrompTer didn't work. . . . But with great earnestness, quite clearly and quite solemnly, he explained why we were there. . . . I felt a wave of sympathy. What the last two or three days must have cost him in terms of sheer physical endurance!

HUBERT HUMPHREY

Tuesday, May 4, 1965, 12:20 P.M.

Unwilling to provoke more controversy while he is sending Marines into the Dominican Republic and trying to enact the Great Society, LBJ fears calling attention to his major increase in U.S. ground troops in Vietnam—to 82,000 by mid-June. But he wants to be free to claim that he has consulted the House and Senate before moving. And he wants to show the North Vietnamese that Congress is behind him.

Johnson has therefore submitted a $700 million military appropriation request to Congress "to meet mounting military requirements in Vietnam." He added a message to the bill stating that it was not "routine": "Each member of Congress who supports this request is also voting to persist in our effort to halt Communist aggression in South Vietnam."[2] With Americans already in harm's way in Vietnam, LBJ knows full well that Congress is unlikely to vote against such language.

HUMPHREY: Mike [Mansfield] and I met with Morse and Ellender.[3] All is well.
LBJ: It will be right on up then?
HUMPHREY: . . . If it comes up today, they can act in the House tomorrow, and we'll act on it on Thursday. . . .
LBJ: . . . Wonderful job. . . . That'll make a great President and a great emperor out of you if you'll just be here [in Congress] and do those things. That just shows you what you can do. . . .
HUMPHREY: Yes, sir.
LBJ: So, let's watch anybody else that might cause trouble. . . . To deny or to delay this request means you're not giving a man ammunition he needs for his gun. You're not giving him gas he needs for his helicopter. You got him standing out nekkid and letting people shoot at him. And we don't want to do that.

---

1. Rowland Evans and Robert Novak, *Lyndon B. Johnson: The Exercise of Power* (New American Library, 1966), p. 523.
2. Quoted in McNamara, *In Retrospect,* pp. 183–84.
3. Wayne Morse and Allen Ellender, Democratic Senators from Oregon and Louisiana, respectively.

JOHN STENNIS

Democratic Senator from Mississippi
Tuesday, May 4, 1965, 1:05 P.M.

> Lobbying Stennis, a member of the Armed Services and Appropriations Commit-
> tees, for his Vietnam spending bill, Johnson resorts again to colossal overstate-
> ment, this time suggesting that passage of the bill will force the North Vietnamese
> to cave in.

LBJ: [The North Vietnamese] say if they can hold out two or three weeks longer,
we're liable to quit. And we want to show them that we got the money and that the
Congress is behind us.

*   *   *

LBJ: I want you to know that this is worth more to me than a division psychologically.
STENNIS: I think you're right.
LBJ: . . . If we can just let them know in forty-eight hours that we're in this thing
to stay, I think they'll fold.[1]

HUBERT HUMPHREY

Tuesday, May 4, 1965, 5:10 P.M.

> By now, there are nearly 20,000 American troops in Santo Domingo.[2] Crying
> "gunboat diplomacy," critics are castigating LBJ for his May 2 television speech
> warning of a Communist threat. In a Senate speech Robert Kennedy criticized
> Johnson for failure to consult the Organization of American States in advance.
> Provoked by the Dominican crisis, not Vietnam, critics now begin warning that
> Johnson is prone to exaggeration and deception to justify using military force.
> LBJ complained to an AFL-CIO audience that he had become "the most de-
> nounced man in the world."
>
>   Later this month the *New York Herald Tribune*, using the phrase for probably
> the first time, will describe LBJ's problem as a "credibility gap."[3] When the State
> Department issues a list of fifty-four "Communist and Castroist" rebels in the Do-
> minican Republic, liberals howl "McCarthyism." A little more than three months
> into Johnson's term, a chasm is already opening between American liberals and

---

1. Johnson's appropriation bill was approved in the House on May 6 by 408 to 7, and the Senate by
88 to 3.
2. As of May 5, there were 12,439 Army troops and 6,924 Marines.
3. *New York Herald Tribune,* May 23, 1965.

the architect of the most progressive domestic program of the twentieth century LBJ wants his Vice President to respond to charges from his fellow liberals.

LBJ: You better watch these liberals around town [complaining] about "gunboat diplomacy," because we've got a fairly good story here. . . . Wednesday afternoon at 5:16, the roof fell in[1] and we had to decide whether we were going to endanger eight thousand people[2] or act. . . . Now we've got some pretty rough names suggested to lead the government.[3] I told them, . . . "We don't want this. Go back and get us some good progressive, liberal people that would have the respect of folks, but be sure they're not dictators." . . . Up till now, God's been with us. We haven't killed a single civilian and we've got an extra three or four hundred[4] out again today.
HUMPHREY: Wonderful.

GEORGE MAHON

Democratic Congressman from Texas and Chairman,
House Appropriations Committee
Wednesday, May 5, 1965, 11:55 A.M.

> Johnson claims that the Gulf of Tonkin Resolution of August 1964 is all he really needs to prosecute the war in Vietnam, and that his new Vietnam appropriation bill is merely evidence of his willingness to go the extra mile in consulting Congress.

LBJ: I've [already] got a vote of confidence. Five hundred and two to two on the August thing,[5] which says, "Prevent any aggression anywhere and protect armed troops anywhere." I thought, though, this would be a masterstroke with the Congress to show them I was frank and candid, and when I needed something, I would put it right in their belly, and if they didn't want to give it to me, they'd say so. . . . And if they gave it to me, why, they'd say, "We can trust the guy. Although he's got authority, he didn't write his check. He let us in on it."
MAHON: Yes. . . .
LBJ: . . . If I hadn't have been there thirty years on the Hill, I would have just signed the document that came to me transferring funds. . . . So I laid my cards on

---

1. Referring to Ambassador Bennett's April 28 cable demanding that the Marines be landed.
2. Foreign nationals in Santo Domingo.
3. Both sides have agreed to a truce, brokered by Ambassador Bennett and the OAS, and there are discussions of an interim Dominican government.
4. Foreign nationals.
5. Gulf of Tonkin Resolution.

the table. If they want those helicopters to fly, if they want that fuel in them, if they want ammunition in their guns, they can pass that bill.

*   *   *

LBJ: Since I became President . . . we've killed 26,000 Vietcong. But they've infiltrated enough where we estimate they've got 40,000 now. . . . Practically everyone we killed is in South Vietnam, where they've invaded. . . . They've come across this line, and we are having to use a good deal more helicopters . . . planes . . . fuel . . . [and] maintenance. And unless we want to pull out, why, we've got to have the funds to do it with. . . . If you don't want us to do it, we can just quit. . . . We'll see whether they believe in the Executive being frank and candid and open with them.

CHARLES MOHR

Correspondent, New York Times
Thursday, May 6, 1965, 7:36 P.M.

> Johnson defends himself on the Dominican Republic with a reporter from the paper whose coverage of the crisis has angered him most of all.

LBJ: This was not a fight between a great literary, fine, sweet poet and mean old Wessin. It was a fight between two goddamn *thugs!*[1] . . . By the time the Marines had really landed, there was a good deal of evidence that the Bosch people . . . had been turned from what everybody conceived at the moment to be a pro-Bosch revolt to one that was led by the extremists.
MOHR: Right, right.

*   *   *

LBJ: A fourth-grade Dominican just doesn't know how to hack it. These people[2] are specialists. . . . This thing is going through the hemisphere and they're working at it. And we've got to be aware of it, without being a McCarthy or a McCarran.[3]

---

1. Johnson is saying that Bosch and the right-wing leader are both thugs.
2. Castro Communist revolutionaries.
3. Johnson shows how the "McCarthyite" charges have stung him. Democratic Senator Pat McCarran of Nevada was another zealous 1950s Communist hunter.

BIRCH BAYH

Democratic Senator from Indiana
Friday, May 7, 1965, 4:45 P.M.

> Senator Edward Kennedy, backed by his brother Robert, has proposed an amendment to LBJ's voting rights bill that would ban the poll tax as a prerequisite for voting in nonfederal elections. Johnson and Attorney General Katzenbach believe such a ban would be declared unconstitutional and might sink the entire bill. Already nettled by RFK's speech against his handling of the Dominican crisis, LBJ suspects that the Kennedy brothers' actual purpose is to show that they are stronger on civil rights than the Southern President is. Bayh tries to mollify Johnson by explaining why he is siding with the Kennedys.

BAYH: I'm motivated because of a philosophical conviction and because I'm staring down the gun barrel of a sizable percentage of Negro voters in two of our largest metropolitan areas.[1] . . .

LBJ: . . . I told the Attorney General I was going to say at a press conference that I was against the poll tax.[2] . . . And I had instructed him to go as far as he could within his constitutional limits. . . . Now, he feels that this is going to mess up the bill. . . . I'd hate to have the public interpret that we were a bunch of kids fighting among ourselves. I'm willing to move as far as a human being can. . . . I think I'm doing more for those Negro groups than anybody has ever done for them.

BAYH: No question about that.

LBJ: . . . You ought to try to pull them into some unified action, or else we'll be like the Dominican Republic. We'll have a party that's split half and half, and really no leader. They pay no attention to their President. They don't follow their Attorney General. . . . Now this man's[3] been Bobby's lawyer, he's been Teddy's lawyer, and he's been my lawyer. They asked me to keep him and I have kept him, and I'm following what he says. . . . One of the Senators was told this morning, "Oh, you better watch out, there's going to be a Kennedy President here." . . . That's not good. . . . I don't believe that we ought to have a brilliant young Senator that we want to make our future out of,[4] and a brilliant young Attorney General, and we can't get together. . . .

BAYH: You've done more than any other to see that these differences have been pulled together.

---

1. Gary and Hammond, Indiana.
2. At an April 27 press conference, LBJ stated his position.
3. Katzenbach.
4. LBJ knows that Bayh is friendly with the Kennedys.

LBJ: I can't get Jim Eastland.[1] But there's no reason why I can't get you and McCarthy[2] together because basically Teddy and Mondale[3] and those people believe the same things. And Katzenbach is the champion of you *all*. He's not [a] Johnson man that came up from Texas to be Attorney General. [*sounding rueful:*] Every President's entitled to his lawyer. . . . But I took [the Kennedys'] lawyer, because I foresaw . . . that I would be charged with not being quite strong enough on civil rights. And I initiated . . . the voting rights [bill] myself. Nobody else did. No Negro leaders. I did that at the ranch in November. And I came up with that bill. . . . You and Teddy and me—we're all going to be off asleep somewhere, speaking at some barbecue. This guy [Katzenbach] is going to have to be [administering this bill]. And [there's] no reason why the Kennedys can't get along with Nick Katzenbach. . . . He lo-v-ves them, and he's loyal to them, and he's devoted to them. And I'm devoted to him, and he has no orders or instructions from me except "do what's right."

BAYH: The most unfortunate thing about this is that apparently there are people . . . trying to put some of us who feel very strongly about this whole issue in a very untenable position. . . .

LBJ: . . . I have no time to fight with any Democrat. And particularly you're the last one I want to. . . . You represent what I want in my party and the future of my party. You're going to be doing just what I've been doing all through the years as I'm laid aside. And I'm pretty well crippled up anyway now with all these problems I've got. But I do know that there're times when you don't like what your younger sister thinks or what your older brother says. But in the interest of your mother, you-all ought to get in a room and try to find some area [of agreement]. You just ought to do it. Because all of you're for the Negroes.[4]

McGEORGE BUNDY

Friday, May 7, 1965, 7:40 P.M.

Johnson complains about television coverage of the Dominican crisis.

LBJ: Our side never really gets over. . . . I see *Life* magazine has . . . huge pictures showing our distribution of food and they're wonderful. . . . But I just watched the TV shows tonight, and the CBS reporter from [Santo Domingo] just

---

1. The segregationist Democratic Senator from Mississippi.
2. Democratic Senator Eugene McCarthy of Minnesota.
3. Edward Kennedy and Democratic Senator Walter Mondale of Minnesota.
4. Assisted by Mansfield and Dirksen, LBJ managed to quash Edward Kennedy's amendment on May 11 by a vote of 49 to 45. Martin Luther King, Jr., called the amendment's rejection "an insult and blasphemy."

says we run wild through the rebel zone and just invite people to shoot us and just try to stir up trouble. We're just mean sons of bitches and outlaws, and they're nice, virtuous maidens.

LADY BIRD JOHNSON

Saturday, May 8, 1965, Tape-recorded Diary

LADY BIRD: A little after six, I went into Lyndon's office, hoping to hear that there would be some rest, some fun this weekend. Sure enough, without any prompting from me, he said, "Who would you like to take with you to Camp David?" . . . I persuaded Lynda to go with us, with promises of bowling and bridge. . . . And a little past eight, we were all in the chopper, headed in a very gay spirit for Camp David. The first thing when we got there, we charged up to the bowling alley. . . . It's the funniest thing to watch Lyndon when he gets a strike. He turns around to look at everybody and all but takes a bow. . . . We had a late, happy, congenial dinner and I watched *Gunsmoke*. And Lyndon did the most desirable thing of all. He got into bed and went to sleep a little past eleven.

ADLAI STEVENSON

Ambassador to the United Nations
Wednesday, May 12, 1965, 10:57 A.M.

> UN Secretary-General U Thant has been criticizing LBJ's growing involvement in Vietnam and demanding negotiations, saying, "Frankly, most Americans don't know the true facts behind the war in Vietnam." Johnson blames Stevenson for failing to lobby Thant effectively enough. In fact, Stevenson privately shares Thant's doubts about Johnson's war.[1] Around this time he has told his friend Arthur Schlesinger that when he considers what Johnson did in the Dominican crisis, "I begin to wonder if we know what we are doing in Vietnam."[2] Now LBJ asks him to inform Thant secretly that, without public announcement, he will briefly halt the bombing of North Vietnam in honor of Buddha's birthday, in the hope that the North Vietnamese will reciprocate. As Johnson concedes to Stevenson, he is almost certain they won't.

---

1. In June 1965 prominent liberals who had worked for Stevenson's presidential campaigns demanded that he resign in protest over Vietnam and the Dominican Republic and become a "spokesman again for that which is humane in the traditions and people of the United States." (See Jean H. Baker, *The Stevensons*, Norton, 1996, pp. 430–33.)

2. Schlesinger, *Robert Kennedy and His Times*, pp. 691–92.

LBJ: I just cannot afford to be murdered on it. . . . I'm going to notify our friends in Hanoi . . . that . . . we're going to stay out of the north part of their country for a while. . . . If they take steps that endanger our security, why, we'll have to reconsider. . . .

STEVENSON: This refers to the Vietcong.

LBJ: Yeah, yeah, yeah. . . . We're going to take the initiative . . . and see what, if any, reaction they have. We don't think they'll have any. We think . . . the negotiation thing is poppycock. But the Russians have been saying, . . . "If you'd only negotiate." Then we say at Baltimore we'd negotiate. Then they say, "Well, if you'd only stop your bombing." So, we're going to stop it. . . .

STEVENSON: . . . There will be press speculation about it, won't there?

LBJ: I hope not, but I'm sure there will. I think the first thing they'll do is go to the colonels in Danang and say, "Why didn't you bomb North Vietnam Tuesday night?"

STEVENSON: Yeah. Then Hanoi may leak it too, won't they? . . .

LBJ: Perhaps. . . . If . . . they definitely identify this as what it is, we will be stopped on several grounds. First, Quat[1] . . . can't survive it. And . . . I don't know what we could do in the Congress. The liberals are not going to be with us anyway.[2] They're going to be raising hell around all over the lot, and the only other support we've got is very much against this kind of a move. . . . Hell, we can't even let our generals know it here! We'd almost have a walkout. Because they think it's a very tragic thing to do. . . .

STEVENSON: But you don't expect they're[3] going to call off the Vietcong.

LBJ: We don't think they're going to call off anything. . . .

STEVENSON: . . . Then you would resume again. . . .

LBJ: . . . My judgment is we'd resume again pretty strong. . . . We're just hoping and praying that this will have some appeal to them and they'll stop a few of their ferries for a few days. If so, we can pull in a little further and they can pull in a little further, work ourselves out of it, like we did [in] Cuba.[4]

ROBERT McNAMARA

Wednesday, May 12, 1965, 11:20 A.M.

In Santo Domingo, despite the OAS-sponsored cease-fire, rebel snipers are still firing on American forces. Opposing the rebels is a five-man junta backed by General Wessin and headed by General Antonio Imbert Barreras.

---

1. Phan Huy Quat, Premier of South Vietnam since February 16.
2. In other words, the liberals oppose LBJ's Vietnam policy.
3. The North Vietnamese.
4. LBJ refers to how the Americans and Soviets deescalated the Cuban Missile Crisis.

LBJ: Are we considering every possible thing that might occur, and what we do about it?

McNAMARA: . . . The problem is that every one of them is bloody—and very bloody. For us and the Dominicans.

LBJ: I think the time's going to come before very long when we have to kind of make up our choice to either let Castro have it or take [the island by force]. . . .

McNAMARA: . . . We're prepared militarily, Mr. President, in every way I believe we can be.

LBJ: . . . I . . . think . . . you're going to have some extensive grilling on what warnings you had from the services and from CIA [about the crisis].[1] . . . They're after the CIA, and they want to kind of make a goat out of it, like they did with the Bay of Pigs thing.

*   *   *

McNAMARA: We just have got to get a political [settlement] here.

LBJ: Well, if [the rebels] are controlled by the Castroites, they're not going to *give* it to you.

McNAMARA: I don't think they are. How the hell can fifty-eight people control them when they've got several hundred?[2] I just don't believe the story that Bosch and Caamaño[3] are controlled by the Castroites. . . . I don't believe that fifty-eight people—or two hundred people, for that matter—can . . . physically control this other bunch.

LBJ: I don't think so, but they can sure have a hell of an influence. The *New York Times* is having an awful influence in this country right now,[4] and it's just one. . . .

McNAMARA: I know it, but you know damn well the *New York Times* doesn't control the country at the moment.

---

1. Having lived through bruising postmortems on why Presidents Roosevelt and Kennedy were not better prepared for Pearl Harbor, the Bay of Pigs invasion, and the Cuban Missile Crisis, Johnson is bracing for his own ordeal.

2. Even LBJ's Defense Secretary refuses to go along with Johnson's public claim that the Castroites and Communists listed by the State Department on May 4 are "controlling" the revolution.

3. Colonel Francisco Caamaño Deno, the rebel leader, was sworn in on May 4 as president of a provisional pro-Bosch regime, insisting that the revolution was not Communist-controlled. The three-man military junta remained, giving the island two rival governments.

4. A May 9 *New York Times* editorial, for example, scored Johnson for circumventing Congress in the Dominican crisis and Vietnam. It said that his $700 million appropriation bill was a "caricature" of consulting the House and Senate.

EVERETT DIRKSEN

Wednesday, May 12, 1965, 4:45 P.M.

> Johnson tries to buy some support for his Dominican policy from the Senate Republican leader by noting CIA evidence that Communists are exporting revolution throughout the Americas.

LBJ: I think that we've got a hell of a problem with our folks up there[1] on Vietnam and the Dominican Republic. . . . Everett—very confidentially, and not coming from me—but the intelligence reports on all of Latin America are constantly bad.

DIRKSEN: Oh, I think so.

LBJ: Every day, every morning, they say Bolivia or Guatemala or Uruguay—all of them—are provoking trouble. And Colombia. Six [Latin American governments] fell under Kennedy in three years. . . . I think our handling has been reasonably good in Brazil . . . and in Chile and in Guatemala and in the problems we've had in Panama. We have not just been pushed around.[2] . . . Now, it's true that the sob sisters and . . . some of the extreme liberals are thinking that we are throwing our weight around, but I don't believe you ought to wait and have a Cuba[3] and then try to do something about it.

DIRKSEN: Yeah.

LBJ: But there's not any leadership on that island that's not really bad leadership. . . . It could be awfully bloody in the Dominican Republic.

DIRKSEN: Yeah, well, we haven't failed you?

LBJ: No, and I think we generally see things pretty nearly [the same] way, but a lot of the folks are going to be squealing that we oughtn't to be sending our boys in. . . .

DIRKSEN: That's always happened.

LBJ: I keep you pretty well informed. They laugh. They say that I always call the Congress, but I think it's better to *tell* them than to have them *read* about it.[4]

---

1. On Capitol Hill.

2. LBJ knows Dirksen will be impressed by the claim that Johnson is tougher than Kennedy was.

3. Another Communist-backed revolution in Latin America.

4. LBJ here claims that, if anything, he is guilty of consulting Congress too much about foreign policy—his defense against complaints that he is waging a war in Vietnam on the flimsy basis of the Gulf of Tonkin Resolution, and that he is withholding from Congress key information about the progress of the fighting.

ROBERT McNAMARA

Wednesday, May 12, 1965, 5:50 P.M.

> The day before his unannounced Vietnam bombing pause is to start, LBJ asks his
> Defense Secretary about the progress of the war.

LBJ: Is our position improved in Vietnam over ninety days ago?

McNAMARA: In terms of the stability of the [Saigon] government and the
morale of the civilians and military forces, *definitely* so. In terms of our own ability to protect . . . key installations at Danang, Bien Hoa, and other areas, definitely
so because of the introduction of the ten Marine combat battalions. . . . In terms of
the control of territory or control of the numbers of people, there's been very little
change in that ninety-day period.

LBJ: . . . Is our equipment capture rate increasing and our defector rate decreas-
ing? And vice versa for the enemy? . . .

McNAMARA: There's been an increase in the defectors, a very substantial increase. . . . The weapon and fatality rate, ratios are, oh, slightly improved. I
wouldn't put too much weight on that, Mr. President.

CARL SANDERS

Democratic Governor of Georgia
Thursday, May 13, 1965, 8:35 P.M.

> When Governor Sanders complains that the Johnson administration is pushing
> him too hard to desegregate Georgia schools, LBJ shows his visceral understand-
> ing of the dilemmas of a Southern racial moderate.

SANDERS: You know and I know that I couldn't do that with a shotgun if I had
to in most areas of the state right now. . . .

LBJ: . . . I know what you've got to do, and God, my heart bleeds for you. . . .
Wanting to do what's right and doing what's right's two different things. Sometimes
it's a long hill to climb in between. And we've got to be understanding. We can't go
through another Reconstruction. We've taken a hundred years to live that down.[1]

*   *   *

LBJ: Speaker came out against us [on the poll tax] today, and the House wrote it
in the bill.[2] They just got no sense about these things. . . . Katzenbach said if they

---

1. Once again LBJ cites the first President Johnson and the failure of Reconstruction.
2. McCormack came out against Katzenbach's position and endorsed a flat ban on state poll taxes.

say you can't have a poll tax, they can say you can't have a gas tax or a cigarette tax. . . . Federal government is telling the states, pretty tough, what their business is. Now, you can say that they can't discriminate, but I've got to prove that it discriminates, and I can't prove it in Texas. There's more Nigras voting there than there are white folks—and more of them [paying] poll taxes now than white folks. . . . Just, by God, anybody that can get up and pay a dollar and six bits can vote. And so let me do it the right way. If Alabama won't let a Nigra vote because of the poll tax and I can . . . prove it, . . . I'll go right direct to the Supreme Court. But that's not good enough for them. . . . Majority of my party went against me in the Senate, and they make me look like, by God, that I'm trying to go back to Bilbo. They want to make a Bilbo out of me.[1]

SANDERS: Right.

LBJ: . . . We know these poor people that live in those states. We know that they're good people. And they're God-fearing people. And we know if we ever want to go up Mount Suribachi[2] or put that goddamn flag on top of a hill, we know who's going to *be* there with it. It's going to be some old boy from Alabama, Mississippi, Georgia, Texas.[3] . . . The rest of them are going to be, some of them, 4-F's.[4] I just don't want to make them so damn mad that they just can't, in self-respect, hold their head up. . . . That's *my* problem, and it's *hell* for me.

BILL MOYERS

Thursday, May 13, 1965, 9:15 P.M.

McGeorge Bundy's debate at the Washington teach-in on Vietnam is two days ahead. LBJ is even more incensed than before that his aide didn't clear the appearance with him. He has been informed that the event is to be broadcast nationally and piped by telephone lines to college campuses across the country, no doubt provoking more demonstrations against the war. Exhausted and feeling beleaguered by liberal criticism on Vietnam and the Dominican Republic, Johnson is in a suspicious mood. He wonders why Bundy has allowed himself to be used by Johnson's enemies and whether Bundy's first loyalties lie not with him but with his academic friends and the Kennedys.[5]

Bundy does not know it yet, but his decision to debate at the teach-in, even

---

1. Theodore Bilbo, Democratic Senator from Mississippi from 1934 to 1947, was an infamous and outspoken white supremacist. Earlier LBJ said repeatedly that his enemies wanted to make "a Harding out of me."

2. Where the American flag was raised during the Battle of Iwo Jima in 1945.

3. LBJ conveys his view that, when called to defend their country, Southerners are the most reliable.

4. Those young men classified 4-F were deferred from the draft for medical reasons.

5. See Kai Bird, *The Color of Truth* (Simon & Schuster, 1998), pp. 318–23.

though he will be defending the administration, has broken Johnson's confidence in him. Only three months earlier, Lady Bird was confiding in her diary that she wished Lynda Bird could find "a twenty-five-year-old McGeorge Bundy" to marry."[1] But from now on, Bundy's relationship with LBJ will never be the same.

LBJ: I think it's awful, Bill, for Mac Bundy to be debating. . . . Doesn't that bother the hell out of you?

MOYERS: Yes, sir, it does. . . . I just hate for the President's representative to be debating with that bunch of— A lot of them would be kooks, a lot of them just misguided zealots. It just sort of demeans our position. I don't think the White House ever has to debate. . . . You don't make decisions by debating. You make the decisions and then history will justify them. . . . There's reports that they're going to be picketed over there. And the Communists will try to get in and raise a little hell. TV live cameras will be there. Of course, it's gone so far he can't back out. . . .

LBJ: . . . I don't know who'd care if he backed out. He's not a *debater*. . . . We didn't *hire* him to come down here and debate with a bunch of kooks. . . . Has he ever talked to you about it?

MOYERS: Not a word.

LBJ: Hadn't me either. . . .

MOYERS: I thought maybe you'd approved it.

LBJ: No. Hell, no! Never heard of it.

MOYERS: It gives the other side a real platform.

LBJ: Leaves the impression in the world that we're divided.

LADY BIRD JOHNSON

Thursday, May 13, 1965, Tape-recorded Diary

LADY BIRD: Suddenly the phone rang and Lyndon asked me to come over. I sat quietly in his office while he phoned for about an hour and a half,[2] reading *Newsweek*, getting in a word when I could. His small office[3] looks very handsome—green velvet, traditional furniture. Elegant but cold. I look at the ticker and the three wide TV sets[4] in the big office, and I thought it looked like we'd gone into the white goods business—the cold meat counter itself. Oh, well, maybe we can get it changed. . . . We had dinner at ten-thirty. Just the two of us. Then I got

---

1. See Chapter 4.
2. Including the preceding conversations with Sanders and Moyers.
3. The room off the Oval Office that LBJ used for intimate meetings and naps and called the "little lounge."
4. LBJ had installed a wire service machine and television sets tuned to all three networks. They were in white cabinets.

back to my exercises, neglected of late. . . . Lyndon gave his up in September of last year, and we haven't been able to get him started since. I haven't the heart to really keep after him. His days are so full of troubles.

McGEORGE BUNDY

Friday, May 14, 1965, 4:06 P.M.

> Reacting to a request from Vice President Humphrey to meet with him, LBJ complains that Humphrey leaks too much to the press. Johnson shows his efforts to keep his number-two man's hands tied.

LBJ: He's the biggest sieve in town. . . . He *says* his staff's all right, but I know better.
BUNDY: Yeah.
LBJ: . . . You better tell him if he can come without *any* of his staff knowing it, you would like for him to drop over to visit the President on a meeting, but we do not want anybody else to know it because he sees more reporters a day than he sees Congressmen. . . .
BUNDY: While we're on that topic, a letter came in from Prime Minister Quat today inviting the Vice President to visit Saigon. They've very properly asked what our judgment is.
LBJ: Our judgment is absolutely *no*. *Period*. Beyond the three-mile limit of our *boundaries!*[1]
BUNDY: [*guffaws*] I hear you!
LBJ: I've made it clear to Rusk *forty* times, and you *twenty-one*.
BUNDY: I know it. I'm just passing on—
LBJ: [*laughs*] You don't need to do that anymore.
BUNDY: All right.
LBJ: You just say there's nobody going to be going *anywhere*. To funerals or anything else. . . . When we want . . . the Vice President . . . to go, we'll notify him.
BUNDY: [*laughs*] I heard.
LBJ: And you can tell anybody else that's asking in that general area so that we don't get any promotion stunts. Because it's very irritable[2] to me.

---

1. In other words, LBJ does not want Humphrey to go out of the country, where he might make mischief.
2. Johnson means "irritating."

WALTER REUTHER

President, United Automobile Workers
Friday, May 14, 1965, 4:19 P.M.

Referring to his narrow success in defeating Edward Kennedy's poll tax amendment to his voting rights bill, LBJ complains that only when a measure is in jeopardy is it named after him.[1]

LBJ: When it's going good and it's high and mighty, it's a bill that's drafted by the Kennedy boys' Attorney General and Mansfield and Dirksen. But when the son of a bitch gets in trouble, it becomes the *Johnson* bill! Well, it's not mine. I just told [Katzenbach], . . . "I'm not going to be President *long*, but while I *am* President, brother, I'm going to take care of voting in this country. *Everybody's* going to be able to vote. . . . I would like to do it at eighteen. I'd like to do it free. I don't give a damn *how* ignorant they are. They got enough instinct to know how to vote because they've been voting for *me* all these years. A *lot* of ignorant people.
REUTHER: If you only got Ph.D. degrees, you'd never have made it, would you?
LBJ: [*laughs*] Never would. No, *sir!* My Mexicans,[2] most of them can't read and write. . . . They're just like my beagle. . . . My beagle runs up and he smells my ankles, and he knows that this is the *man,* right here!

NICHOLAS KATZENBACH

Friday, May 14, 1965, 7:25 P.M.

Eager to put his friend Abe Fortas on the Supreme Court, LBJ has asked his Attorney General how soon he can expect to fill his first vacancy. Katzenbach believes that Justice John Marshall Harlan is likely to leave the Court in the summer of 1965.

KATZENBACH: Harlan is conservative. . . . I think probably . . . Harlan will resign after the end of this term.[3]
LBJ: How does it line up now? . . . I don't even know that.
KATZENBACH: . . . If the average fellow was lining them up, he would line five clearly on the liberal side of the Court. That would be the Chief Justice [Earl

---

1. In 1966 the Supreme Court banned the poll tax as a violation of the Fourteenth Amendment's equal protection clause.
2. Mexican American voters who supported LBJ in Texas.
3. An Eisenhower appointee, Harlan actually stayed on the Court until 1971.

Warren] and [Hugo] Black and [William O.] Douglas and [William] Brennan and [Arthur] Goldberg. And he would line up on the conservative side—this is crude—but . . . [Potter] Stewart, [Tom] Clark, [Byron] White, Harlan. So you're taking one from . . . the conservative side.

LBJ: What is [Harlan]? What party?

KATZENBACH: He's a Republican.

LBJ: Much obliged.

ABE FORTAS

Friday, May 14, 1965, 7:29 P.M.

> Johnson has sent his confidant and friend on a secret mission to San Juan, where Fortas has been negotiating with Juan Bosch in an effort to form a Dominican coalition government. "Abe disappeared suddenly and no one knew where he had gone," his wife later recalled. "I was quite uncomfortable."[1] Operating under a code name (Mr. Davidson), Fortas reports that he has hit pay dirt.

FORTAS: Okay, boss, we've got a deal.

LBJ: All right.

FORTAS: Now, my suggestion is this—that you send a professional . . . McGeorge [Bundy] or somebody . . . here to San Juan. . . . This fellow who has agreed to be the number-one man[2] will be coming in here . . . to talk with J.B.[3] I think that we ought to arrange for the man whom you select[4] to talk with him at the same time. . . . Then for your man to go over and talk to the five-man committee[5] and say, "This is it, and this is the way for you guys to write your names high in history."

LBJ: . . . What does my man do down where you are? Hell, you've been as good a man as I got![6]

FORTAS: . . . I think he ought to . . . talk to the future number-one man and just sort of do a belly-to-belly job[7] on him. . . . Set the scene for the future. . . . I'd be glad to do it, but it just seems to me that somebody who is going to continue the relationship ought to do it.

---

1. Quoted in Kalman, *Fortas*, p. 237.
2. Silvestre Guzmán Fernández, who has been Bosch's secretary of agriculture.
3. Bosch.
4. As Johnson's special envoy.
5. An anti-Bosch junta led by General Antonio Imbert Barreras, previously preferred by the Americans.
6. With Johnson's current animus toward Bundy, he does not want to give him such an important task.
7. A Johnson phrase for intense two-man negotiation.

LBJ: . . . I don't know anybody that I think could do it better than you can, and I'm not going to accept your resignation! . . .

FORTAS: I've got to. I've done my job! [*laughs*]

LBJ: No. Here's our problem. . . . My right wing . . . won't give me forty cents if I'm not careful. . . . I've got my Ambassador and I've got my general and I've got my CIA people and I got my Navy admiral, and they're just about to *revolt* on me.[1] . . .

FORTAS: Well, the events today almost knocked this thing out. . . . I have shed gallons of tears—enough to damn well put on rubber boots—because of that one goddamned baby that was killed in the attack on the radio station.[2]

LBJ: Well. . . . the baby's . . . life's not worth any more than that Marine that they got, you know. . . . This same crowd, you see, they were bombing us, too. We didn't know any more about that bombing than you did.

FORTAS: I know that, but you know what kind of people I'm dealing with.

LBJ: Sure I do, but you have to make them see that every time they lose a baby, I lose a Marine, and that this damned airplane was coming right over us and our people were shooting it, and got one of them, brought one plane down.

FORTAS: What I would do, if I may say so—I would button this whole damn thing up in thirty-six hours.

LBJ: All right, that's what we want to do. If he's going to be there in the morning, you just button it up with him.[3]

ABE FORTAS

Friday, May 14, 1965, 8:45 P.M.

> During another intense telephone conversation between LBJ and Fortas comes a moment more fitting for Abbott and Costello. A White House switchboard operator accidentally patches in a call between Walter Messner and his brother Cecil, a retired White House operator now living in Denver, and several other friends, including one named Jim.[4]

LBJ: They're just sending in real tough cables here saying, "We must be allowed to defend ourselves and protect our people." . . . It's just not too good. [*Telephone lines are crossed.*] *Hello?*

---

1. LBJ worries that the truculent Ambassador Bennett and other advisers will denounce him as soft for accepting this compromise.

2. When fighter pilots loyal to the Imbert junta strafed the radio station controlled by the Caamaño forces on May 13, a five-year-old boy was killed. Fortas is not too deeply sentimental about the death.

3. Bundy indeed arrived in San Juan the next day, to meet in secret with Fortas and Bosch.

4. This happened because White House staff members sometimes patched calls through the mansion switchboard to avoid paying long-distance charges.

JIM: . . . When are you leaving now for Mexico?

WOMAN: A week from tomorrow.

FORTAS: *Hello!*

WOMAN: . . . Walter wanted to say hello to you again. . . .

FORTAS: [*furious:*] *Hello! Hello!*

WALTER: Hi, Jim.

JIM: Hi, Walt. How're you doing?

WALTER: . . . What's this? Aren't you feeling too well?

JIM: No, I'm back in bed.

WALTER: Aw, for land's sakes! . . .

FORTAS: *Hello! Get off the goddamned line! Hello!*

JIM: . . . Who was that?

WALTER: I don't know who it was. . . .

FORTAS: [*shouts:*] *He-l-l-o-o-o!*

LBJ: [*amiably:*] You go ahead and finish your conversation. The lines have evidently crossed, Walter and Jim. You-all go on and finish.

WALTER: . . . Thanks, Jim, and want you to know that we look forward to you coming out someday. . . .

LBJ: Hello. Operator, can we finish? You put another call right in here. . . . Operator, who are you?

WOMAN: This is Denver.

LBJ: *Denver?*

WOMAN: Yeah, where are you calling from?

LBJ: This is Washington.

FORTAS: [*shouts:*] . . . *Get the hell off the line!*

LBJ: Please let us finish, operator.

FORTAS: . . . *This is an urgent conversation. Please get off the line. Please!*

WOMAN: . . . Are you in Washington?[1]

LBJ: Yes.

WOMAN: Well, I wonder where the other party is.

LBJ: I don't know, but would you just hang up and let us talk? He can hear me and I can hear him, if you'll just get out of our way, honey. Huh? Is that all right?

WOMAN: Yes, it is. All right. I'll put my call in again.

LBJ: Oh, I thought you were an operator.

WOMAN: Oh, no, I was calling from Denver.

LBJ: Who are you calling?

WOMAN: Well, what number are you on?

LBJ: I'm on 408. Who is it that you want? And I'll see if I can help you.

---

1. The woman has no idea she is talking to the President.

WOMAN: Well, I'll have to call back. Thank you.
FORTAS: Oh, my!

LADY BIRD JOHNSON

Friday, May 14, 1965, Tape-recorded Diary

LADY BIRD: I awoke to a darkened room. Had no idea what time it might be. Turned restlessly. Couldn't go back to sleep, but cherished the steady breathing, the quietness of Lyndon. For a long, long time, after what seemed hours, I tiptoed quietly out, headed for my room, only to have him say when I stepped on a creaking board, "Where are you going?" Then I couldn't persuade him to go back to sleep. He turned on the light and, sure enough, it was 10:30 A.M.[1] What a blissful, wonderful event! . . . It was nearly ten when Lyndon came over for dinner. . . . Dinner itself was full of telephone calls and plans being made. They are concerned with the Dominican Republic. I do not wish to know too much about them. . . . It's odd to hear people like Adlai Stevenson and many, many columnists say that the President, alas, is not as interested in— does not give as much time to foreign affairs as he does to domestic affairs. Foreign affairs devour his days and nights. It's just that the problems are harder to solve than domestic affairs. True, he takes less joy in them, but whatever bad happens in them, it's not for lack of trying. . . . I went to bed a little past eleven, not even reacting to the excitement in the air and soggy with the willingness to sleep, and happy that Lyndon had at least had his one late morning.

GEORGE BALL

Saturday, May 15, 1965, 10:32 A.M.

> Johnson bellows against liberal complaints about Ambassador Bennett and Under Secretary of State Thomas Mann as reactionaries in the Dominican crisis. Note how, in his harassed and angry mood, LBJ refers to liberals.

LBJ: I'm not going to let . . . a bunch of little yellow pinkos run them out of the government. . . . They're loyal and they work hard. They're not going to get rid of *me* for four years, and they're not going to get rid of *them*. So they just might as well find out we play on the same team. . . . You're as loyal as my wife. I admire that and I appreciate it. But I just think it's terrible that little fellows down the line

---

1. Friday.

would take a crack at the Secretary or the Under Secretary. . . . They do it to me. That's what drives me so damn close to all of you.

LADY BIRD JOHNSON

Sunday, May 16, 1965, Tape-recorded Diary

> Despite his initial misgivings, LBJ has ordered Bundy to fly secretly to San Juan to see Fortas and Bosch. Then Bundy will go to Santo Domingo, along with Thomas Mann, Cyrus Vance, and Assistant Secretary of State Jack Hood Vaughn. This arrangement has forced Bundy to withdraw from the Vietnam teach-in without explanation, just three hours before he was to debate Professor Kahin, opening him to charges of cowardice or presidential pressure.
>
> At the teach-in, held at the Sheraton Park Hotel in Washington, Arthur Schlesinger, Jr., the historian and Kennedy White House alumnus, criticized the Dominican intervention and Vietnam bombing but praised LBJ's purposes in Southeast Asia. Other academics, such as Hans Morgenthau and William Appleman Williams, denounced Johnson without restraint. Embarrassed by his sudden forced absence, Bundy later concluded that LBJ had sent him to Puerto Rico partially to "keep me away from all those wild men" at the teach-in.[1]

LADY BIRD: The papers are full of carpings and recriminations about McGeorge Bundy not showing up for the teach-in Saturday afternoon and speculations as to where he might be. I watched part of the program on TV, and it was almost enough to shake your faith in the intellectuals. One wonders if there is a necessary relationship between intellectual attainment and good judgment and experience. I watched Arthur Schlesinger awhile on Saturday and was quite favorably impressed with him, although I understand he took some swipes at us before I tuned in. But I must weigh that against the continuing efforts of friend and foe to say, "Sic 'em, sic 'em," at all the Johnson adherents and all the Bobby Kennedy adherents.

ROBERT ANDERSON

Former Secretary of the Treasury, Eisenhower Administration
Monday, May 17, 1965, 9:07 A.M.

> With an eye to keeping Eisenhower aboard on the Dominican crisis, LBJ talks to the ex-President's close friend and adviser, who was one of the men who sold the

---

1. Quoted in Bird, *The Color of Truth,* pp. 319–20.

Austin radio station KTBC to the Johnsons. Anderson is also negotiating revisions in the Panama Canal treaties on behalf of the Johnson administration.

ANDERSON: Ninety percent or more of this country is solidly behind you in Vietnam. You're going to have these intellectuals. We've had them all of our lives.

* * *

LBJ: We've got a hell of a problem down in Dominican. We almost had an agreement worked up, when goddamned *New York Times* jumps up our negotiators and got it all out now, and got them all divided.[1] . . . Every issue of the *Times* gives me another crisis.

ANDERSON: Let me tell you one thing to remember about the *Times,* Mr. President. They are a trust. They're not in there to make money. . . . They're not responsible to a board of directors. And to me this is not a good thing. . . .

LBJ: . . . Tad Szulc[2] and them. . . . They're awful. But we can't say anything about it. Just got to take it in our stride. . . . Our great problem— Here's what we're really faced with. We think that we can get a good mediocre, non-Communist president.[3] But the rebels do not want it. They want complete victory. . . . The same thing is true of the Imbert crowd.[4] . . .

ANDERSON: Well, I hope you can do the . . . former.

LBJ: That's what I thought. . . . I've had him checked out carefully. . . . Bosch likes him. . . . He'll give us a pledge against Communism . . . and he'll work with our people. . . . The other choice is to let this Caamaño get [together] with this Imbert, neither of whom have any principles . . . and say, "To hell with the Yankees!" . . . The only thing I can be guided by now is my own CIA and FBI, and they have suspicions of everybody. . . . But I've got a man who is not a strong man. That's the damn difficulty. The strong ones become extremists. He's a moderate, fair, good, honest man. And our basic choice is either taking him . . . or just sitting there and letting them fight it out, deteriorating.

J. EDGAR HOOVER

Monday, May 17, 1965, 3:02 P.M.

Johnson wants the FBI Director to check out possible members of a new Dominican coalition government.

---

1. Perhaps agitated by a *New York Times* report on the secret talks, Imbert has dug in his heels.
2. *New York Times* reporter.
3. Silvestre Guzmán Fernández.
4. General Antonio Imbert Barrera, chief of the five-man anti-Bosch junta.

LBJ: We're trying to get this Guzmán, who was a rich farmer and Cabinet officer, and if wc can, we're down now to where we've just got to get this chief of staff. If we can get this Army man that's not a Communist, we're all right.

HOOVER: We'll have a report on him, certainly by not later than the morning. . . .

LBJ: Thank you.

LADY BIRD JOHNSON

Monday, May 17, 1965, Tape-recorded Diary

LADY BIRD: I got a call from Lyndon—a request to come swim with him. I have been trying to get him back to the pool, back into exercises, ever since last September. This was victory! When I arrived there, I found, however, he had Jack Valenti and Bill [Moyers] and Abe [Fortas], and they were talking business while they swam. But just as well. We took Abe upstairs with us for lunch. He leaned over while Lyndon was on the phone and said to me, holding his thumb and finger close together, "We are this close to a settlement." He meant the Dominican Republic. I do not know, try not to know much that's going on. What I don't know I can't talk about unknowingly and in front of the wrong people. The names of Mr. G and Davidson[1] . . . go back and forward. Sometimes I wonder if such people exist.

McGEORGE BUNDY
THOMAS MANN
JOHN BARTLOW MARTIN

Former Ambassador to the Dominican Republic
Tuesday, May 18, 1965, 12:01 A.M.

> Along with colleagues, Bundy reports from Santo Domingo that they are nearing a tentative deal for a coalition government, although Imbert is continuing to squawk.

BUNDY: By the use of very strenuous verbal measures with the loyalist military, we have a bargain. . . . I propose to say to Mr. G within the next half hour . . . he can expect you to move in the two directions which Mr. Davidson discussed with you this afternoon, with respect to troops and assistance. . . . We expect to press

---

1. Code names for Guzmán and Fortas.

for OAS participation in the announcement, and we are considering now at what time to turn around the chicken-livered lazybones who went home this afternoon because they wouldn't believe us.[1] We hope to wake them up at the hour that's most inconvenient for them!

LBJ: [*laughs*]

* * *

LBJ: Now we're not getting into any position where . . . people can . . . say that we sold out and turned it over to the Commies?

MANN: No, no, they can't say that truthfully. . . .

LBJ: . . . How are you going to get Mr. I [2] to quit making these inflammatory statements? . . .

MANN: I think we may get some more.

LBJ: . . . You know us right-wingers are supposed to hang together, Tom![3] [*laughs*]

* * *

MANN: It's the lesser of many evils. There is no approved solution to this, Mr. President.

LBJ: It doesn't look like to me that there is any evil in this—if we get reasonably honest people, if they're anti-Communists, if we're going to have a popular referendum in two months on the basics of the machinery—the constitution. . . . Now, I don't know what else you could do. We could pick a dictator and just say, "To hell with the constitution!" . . . Looks to me like we're being about as democratic as you can be. . . . I don't know what else we could do if we stayed there a million years.

* * *

LBJ: Do you have anybody representing the United States that's violently disagreeing with us?

MARTIN: No, I think not.

LBJ: Okay, John, don't you overwork yourself! I've been afraid that you've been overdoing it because, you know, you're not big and fat and paunchy, as I am.

* * *

LBJ: All right, I guess we've talked long enough. . . . I think you . . . better go out there and put on your Sunday-go-to-meeting clothes, and take this Imbert and give him the best you've got.

---

1. Referring to OAS officials, Bundy sounds as if he is pandering to his boss by using LBJ's language and mimicking his views on the Organization of American States.

2. Imbert.

3. LBJ is lampooning the right-wing label that liberal critics have now pasted on him over his handling of the Dominican crisis.

ABE FORTAS

Wednesday, May 19, 1965, 10:57 A.M.

> Johnson is eager to ensure that none of the men in the recommended government turns out to be a Communist.

LBJ: First thing's going to happen is they're going to go tell Tom Dodd . . . that I didn't check it, and I've got a notorious Communist as secretary of the [Dominican] army. . . . And I'll be destroyed.
FORTAS: . . . With your permission, I'll get Deke.[1]
LBJ: Please. . . . Tell Raborn[2] we thought it'd been checked out. We want both [the FBI and CIA] to give us a letter[3] because I'm not going to have them running *up* and saying, "Johnson didn't check and he turned it over to a bunch of Communists."

ABE FORTAS

Wednesday, May 19, 1965, 11:40 A.M.

> Negotiations are stalling. Johnson's closest advisers are divided. As Dean Rusk recalled, he and Mann wanted categorical assurances that there would be no Communist participation in the new Dominican regime. Fortas, Bundy, and Vance did not demand such a pledge.[4] Despite their close friendship, Johnson makes it clear to Fortas that, especially after the liberal firestorm against his Dominican policies, he sides with Rusk and Mann.

LBJ: Now Mann takes the position that we ought to support Imbert?
FORTAS: Yes, sir. Now, you see, there's a direct conflict. There always has been in terms of fundamental viewpoint between Mann . . . and Mac Bundy. . . . I share Mac Bundy's view. That's the plan we've been working on right along. . . . There's going to have to be a decision. . . .
LBJ: Well now, really honestly, I have more confidence in Mann's judgment than I do in Bundy's. Just like I have more confidence in your judgment than I do Paul Porter's.[5] They're about alike. One of them's quick and brilliant and fast and so

---

1. DeLoach of the FBI.
2. Director of Central Intelligence William Raborn.
3. Clearing the man of Communist sympathies.
4. Dean Rusk, *As I Saw It* (Norton, 1990), p. 375.
5. Fortas's partner at Arnold, Fortas and Porter.

forth, but is absolutely screwball on a good many things.[1] And I look at it the next week and find it out. I never have found Mann wrong.

* * *

LBJ: I have high regard for Mann's courage, for his ability, and for his knowledge, and I think he knows more about Latin America than any person we've ever had. . . . Now he is a whipping boy, and he has incurred the displeasure of the Bundys and the Schlesingers[2] and the rest of them, because he doesn't agree with each theoretical thing.

J. EDGAR HOOVER

Wednesday, May 19, 1965, 12:00 P.M.

> Johnson wants the FBI Director to check out the recommended members of the new Dominican government, but he also wants to ensure that Hoover will not cast quiet aspersions on a settlement. Characteristically, LBJ makes a particular attempt to speak to Hoover in his own language.

LBJ: All right now, Edgar, here is the play. . . . Our State Department, as far as I can tell—and I wouldn't say this to anybody but you—is not worth a damn.
HOOVER: Yeah.
LBJ: They're a bunch of sissy fellows. They never come up with any solution . . . except just sit there. I've sat there—with thirty thousand people now[3]—for nearly a month, and we've done nothing. Now, Fortas . . . is as close to me as you are. . . . He is of the progressive type, but no Communism in him. Now, his position is, and it's my position . . . that Imbert and Wessin and the military people that started this thing . . . just made a farce of it, and are no goddamned good, and they can't have any following either there or in Latin America. . . . There's nobody that will support them. They're about like Bilbo in this country—or about like Strom Thurmond, as far as being elected President's concerned.[4] You just can't sell Strom Thurmond as President.
HOOVER: No, you can't.

---

1. LBJ had not thrown such gibes against Bundy before his willingness to join the Vietnam teach-in without asking the President.

2. Now Johnson lumps Bundy with Arthur Schlesinger, Jr., whom he considers a liberal foe.

3. The current size of the American military force on the island.

4. LBJ again refers to Theodore Bilbo, the Mississippi racist. South Carolina Senator Strom Thurmond was a segregationist who walked out of the 1948 Democratic convention over civil rights, staged a third-party "Dixiecrat" presidential campaign that fall, and became a Republican in 1964.

LBJ: Now, maybe you oughtn't have Bobby Kennedy. But you might be able to get a Johnson that's progressive that's still not going to be sold out to [the Communists]. . . . So that is what I have asked done. . . . We want a democracy. . . . But we can't just boss everything. We can't run things any more than you can run the state of Alabama. But we want a man that's cooperative. . . . So, let's get an anti-Communist government. . . . We might have a liberal like Stew Udall[1] in it, but not somebody that's going to turn it over to them. . . . Guzmán is such a man. . . . He's got lots of money. He doesn't want to lose it. . . . He's not anti-American. Most people *are* anti-American because we've acted such damn fools, throwing our weight around.

HOOVER: Yes, we have.

LBJ: And so, now, we are trying to get a Cabinet. . . . What we have done is take a big bunch of names from Bosch, who we do not believe is a Communist, but who we think is subject to Communist influences, and from some of these progressives and liberals on the island. . . . Now, a good many of them Imbert has been willing to buy. . . . So we really want to take one or two of the Strom Thurmond–Dick Russell[2] men in the Cabinet. We want to take three or four of the Johnson men in the Cabinet. We want to take one of the Edgar Hoover men in the Cabinet. And we'll have to take a Stew Udall or two.[3] . . . But we don't want any that are card carriers[4] because we don't want them taking orders from higher up. Now, Fortas has been trying to get the CIA and the State Department and others to get him that list, and I have told him to tell Deke [DeLoach] and to tell Raborn that I've got to decide today . . . whether these men are acceptable or not. . . . I'm not going to decide on anybody that either you or Raborn . . . doesn't tell me that they believe that they're not Communists.

HOOVER: Yes. I understand that.

LBJ: . . . They all laugh when I say, "I've got to get Hoover to act on this thing." They say, "That's not the State Department." Well . . . I'm a Johnson City boy. . . . I'm not infallible. Hell, I've made mistakes in my life!

HOOVER: We all do.[5]

LBJ: . . . So you get the best men you've got to check these names. . . . I don't want to work a month and make a deal and send in thirty thousand soldiers and then piss it off to the Communists.

HOOVER: That's right.

---

1. The Interior Secretary, Stewart Udall.
2. Referring to the Republican Senator from South Carolina and the Democrat from Georgia, both conservatives whom Hoover admires.
3. LBJ is playing to Hoover's antiliberal tendencies.
4. Communists.
5. An amazing admission from the self-righteous Hoover.

LBJ: And you're the man I'm depending on to keep me from pissing it *off!* Now, that's ugly language, but that's expressive, and you know what I want.

HOOVER: We won't let you down.

BILL MOYERS

Wednesday, May 19, 1965, 12:30 P.M.

LBJ: The State Department never comes up with anything. But Tom Mann is coming in with a report which . . . favors Imbert. . . . My own judgment is that Imbert . . . will never have mass support. But that's the way they've pictured Johnson through the years. And that wasn't true last November![1] And I know the Kennedys[2] are more dramatic. . . . But it doesn't look like to me Guzmán has got anything except liberals behind him. . . . Mansfield and Fulbright and them are very critical [of Imbert], and Congress is going to be very critical, although I think the people are 90 percent behind us now. Not behind *New York Times* and the liberals. . . . Now, Abe [Fortas] is of the opinion . . . we ought to . . . put Guzmán in. . . .

I have more confidence in Tom [Mann] on Latin America than I do Abe. I don't believe that Tom is the reactionary and the hater that they say he is. I think they have pictured him—just like they picture you—as a young, impractical fellow, or that you were a political beneficiary when you became Deputy Director of the Peace Corps.[3] I think they're just as unjust to him as they were to you. . . . First days around here, they had you as a homosexual.[4] So if we don't stand up to them, why, we don't get them. We've got to be sure they're right. And so I want you to watch it as a judge and not as an advocate. . . . My own judgment is that there'd be more of a mass behind the liberal government, the Guzmán, than there ever would behind Imbert.

HUBERT HUMPHREY

Wednesday, May 19, 1965, 12:45 P.M.

Resisting Humphrey's effort to lobby him for a jobs program, Johnson tells him to make his case by memorandum.

---

1. When LBJ was elected by a landslide.

2. Meaning the Kennedy-like Dominican progressives.

3. When Moyers got the job under President Kennedy, some said it was a political favor to his mentor LBJ.

4. Referring to untrue accusations against Moyers when he became a White House aide at the start of Johnson's presidency.

HUMPHREY: This youth opportunity program on employment that we talked about with you at the Cabinet meeting—I talked with Willard [Wirtz][1] this morning, and he feels that it's terribly important that we move ahead on it, and we wanted to just get your concurrence. . . .

LBJ: Put what you-all want to do on a piece of paper. Put "approve or disapprove" down at the corner. Explain it, and have whoever's recommending it put it on there. I'm with Bill Douglas[2] in a little meeting. We're [listing] the liberals in the government. Beginning with the Vice President.

HUMPHREY: Well, I'm glad to hear that, Mr. President.

LBJ: . . . We might give them some Calomel.[3] That's what Sam Rayburn used to take. Or we might get you drunk!

HUMPHREY: [*laughs*] Well, I'll take a little of both!

LBJ: Little of both, huh?

*　　*　　*

LBJ: What are you doing this afternoon?

HUMPHREY: . . . I've got a meeting . . . at 3:30 . . . over in Bill Moyers's office.

LBJ: . . . You might come to a meeting at 2:45 that I'm going to have—get a report from the Dominican. . . . It'll be in my mansion. Second floor. . . . I wouldn't let my office staff know I was coming. I don't want anybody to know.[4]

WHITE HOUSE SITUATION ROOM

Thursday, May 20, 1965, 2:00 A.M.

> Sleepless, Johnson inquires about the murder by gunfire of the pro-Bosch Colonel Rafael Fernández Dominguez, in Santo Domingo. Bosch had sent him to tell Caamaño to step aside and let Guzmán be provisional Dominican president. In Vietnam, it has been another night of Rolling Thunder.

LBJ: What's the story on this colonel that got killed?

DUTY OFFICER: . . . We have . . . an FBI report that says that he was shot by Americans. Accidentally. Shot in the back. . . .

LBJ: . . . What about our planes—any of them back—in Vietnam?

DUTY OFFICER: None back yet, sir. No word.

LBJ: I'm sure anxious on those that are going up there close to Hanoi. . . . You let me know if we lose any. Whatever time of night it is.

---

1. Secretary of Labor.
2. Supreme Court Justice William O. Douglas, a New Deal liberal and (usually) LBJ friend.
3. A country remedy for fevers. Johnson sometimes refers to liberals as "red hots."
4. LBJ is always worried about the tendency of Humphrey and his staff to leak.

GEORGE REEDY

Thursday, May 20, 1965, 11:25 A.M.

> Johnson advises his press secretary to deflect embarrassing questions about the shooting of the Dominican police minister. Angry rebels are certain that an American soldier pulled the trigger.

REEDY: Abe Fortas tells me that . . . Guzmán is breaking off discussions because of the death of Fernández. . . .

LBJ: What is the question, George? Hurry!

REEDY: . . . The question is I wanted to be sure that my instructions were proper. . . . What McNamara suggested I say is, "The President has said from the beginning that it is essential that we maintain . . . impartiality between junta and rebel forces." And then refer all of the questions to the Defense Department.

LBJ: What I would say is this. Take this down. . . . "The President's instructions to the troops were to fire only when fired upon and . . . to maintain strict neutrality. . . . I have no evidence of any deviation from these instructions." . . . Then I'd just stonewall it. . . . I don't want you denying something that may be true.

REEDY: . . . But I would like to get you in a position . . . where you're making very strong inquiries [about the charge].

LBJ: No, no! God, no! The last thing I want to do is "I've heard that my wife is a whore, and I'm looking into it and I've got a board set up to study it." I wouldn't do that. That gives some *vent* to it!

LADY BIRD JOHNSON

Thursday, May 20, 1965, Tape-recorded Diary

LADY BIRD: Sometime in the middle of the night, Lyndon came and crawled into bed with me. This morning, haggard and worn, he looked at me and said, "The most awful thing has happened!" . . . He said Bosch's friends, five of them, were returning to Santo Domingo. The one who was the key to the situation was shot in street fighting and killed. . . . Lyndon said he had only slept two hours Monday night and very little last night. How I wish I could reach him, ease him! Actually the only thing I *can* do is not impose upon him any questions, decisions, troubles. Fortunately my own life has been smooth and free of these, these last few months.

ABE FORTAS

Sunday, May 23, 1965, 5:10 P.M.

> Johnson worries that members of Fortas's proposed Dominican regime are vulnerable to charges of softness on Communism. LBJ is angry about liberal complaints that he is using military force to impose an American junta on the Dominicans. In this almost Shakespearean soliloquy with his intimate friend, LBJ now, amazingly, tortures himself with the notion that he should never have sent American troops into the Dominican Republic. Because of what he now sees as his own missteps in the crisis, he agonizes that he has destroyed himself with liberals in his party. He blames himself, but he also complains that advisers "misled" him.

LBJ: Abe, . . . I can't sell [this proposal] to Russell and to Dirksen and to Ford and to the George Mahons[1] for one dollar. I just can't! I can't stand the pressure if we have a government that's soft or sympathetic or even kind in dealing with the Communists. . . . I'm not ever going to get Schlesinger's[2] support or the liberals' support. . . . If the agreement is [to let the Communists] be in the back room and go underground when we have a Sunday church meeting but to come out and run it all the rest of the week, I don't think [we can] seriously consider it. . . . It's really got to be anti-Communist *and* pro-liberal.

*   *   *

LBJ: To [have people think] that we've lost a lot of prestige and we went [into the Dominican Republic] for the purpose of setting up a satellite state . . . would be a tragic mistake. God knows I don't want my brand *on* this satellite state. Because I don't know a one of them. I never heard of one of them. I doubt all of them. . . . I don't want . . . to be putting the LBJ brand on every country in the Western Hemisphere. . . . They're already demanding an investigation. Arthur Schlesinger's ADA[3] yesterday wants a full investigation, and they're going to get one.

*   *   *

LBJ: Bosch's group has damn near destroyed us in Europe and abroad with the liberals . . . and the articles out of here that this is a unilateral operation. . . . They take the position now that this man Johnson is another Führer. . . . I don't want [a new Dominican government] to come out with the LBJ brand, with the LBJ name, saying, "This is what the Führer put to them." Because I think Bobby Kennedy will be pointing this out and Arthur Schlesinger will be pointing this out. And while I'm taking them on on the left. . . . then the right—the Russells and the

---

1. Leading congressional foreign policy conservatives.
2. Arthur Schlesinger, Jr.
3. Americans for Democratic Action, a liberal organization.

Rivers[1] that control the [Armed Services] committees—will say, "You sent [the Marines] in there, and you marched them up the hill and then marched them down again."

* * *

LBJ: I don't really, as you know, go all the way with Bundy. It wasn't my idea that Bundy go down there. You remember, he grabbed the phone every time you called me and you always started off by saying, "We want Bundy." And we wound up with Bundy. And if we get him back without wrecking him—and me too—I'll say a good prayer to my dear Lord. Because I think he's a brilliant man and I'm attached to him, and he's indispensable to me, but I think he's pretty positive and pretty precise and pretty inflexible.

FORTAS: He's learned a lot from these negotiations.

LBJ: I tried to talk to him two days after the Bay of Pigs, and President Kennedy said, "Please, stay away from him. Don't mention anything to him. He's awfully upset. He's just so *nervous*." He gets pretty nervous in these things. We're going to have to live with him a long time, and I'm prepared to do it.[2] I have nothing in the world I want, except to do what I believe to be right. I don't always know what's right. Sometimes I take other people's judgments, and I get misled. Like sending troops in there to Santo Domingo. But the man that misled me was Lyndon *Johnson*. Nobody else! I did that! I can't blame a damn human. And I don't want any of them to take credit for it. . . . And I'll ride it out. . . . I know how it looks. It looks just the opposite of the way I want to look. I don't *want* to be an intervener. But I think Mr. Castro's done intervened pretty good when he kicked old Reid out.[3] And honestly, of all the people I saw, I thought Reid was the least dictatorial—and the most genuine and honest of any of that crowd I met.[4]

FORTAS: Well, this didn't have anything to do with Reid.

LBJ: I think it did. I think Reid was trying to clean up these goddamned generals and trying to get a government that would work and an economy that could sustain itself. And these crackpots overthrew him while he was doing it. Incidentally, I think that's what's happening to *me*. I may be the Reid of North America. Because I try to get my system going that can support this thing with jobs and money and economy, and while I'm doing it, I've got these experts in the London *Times* and the Kurzmans[5] and the Szulcs and the Schlesingers all giving

---

1. Armed Services Committee Chairman Mendel Rivers of South Carolina.
2. Not the warmest praise for one of his two chief advisers.
3. LBJ affirms that Castro was behind the April coup against Dominican President Reid.
4. When Johnson went to Santo Domingo in 1963.
5. Referring to Dan Kurzman of the *Washington Post*.

me the works. So I may be in the same place as Reid. Just holler, "Move *over* next week!"[1]

DEAN RUSK

Tuesday, May 25, 1965, 1:44 P.M.

> Chester Bowles, Ambassador to New Delhi, cabled the Secretary of State, asking for his old friend Vice President Humphrey to tour Southeast Asia. Humphrey's staff, eager to find a role for their boss, has circulated the message, ostensibly to pressure LBJ into sending him. Johnson is not happy.

LBJ: I thought I had made it abundantly clear to you my view some time ago on the Vice President's going out of the United States. . . . I would tell Bowles that if he feels that he's inadequate to his assignment, well, we can get another man. But the President doesn't desire to make available the Vice President right now.
RUSK: Right, right.
LBJ: And I don't like the tone of his wire anyway, and I'd just tell him . . . not to be sending these wires. Now Humphrey's boys got them, and you're going to have some more flak. . . . You tell whoever gets those cables to send them to you and then put a stop to it.

BILL MOYERS

Wednesday, May 26, 1965, 3:35 P.M.

> Bundy has returned from Santo Domingo. Reedy has infuriated the President by suggesting in Bundy's presence that the national security adviser hold a press conference defending American actions in the Dominican Republic. LBJ shows that he is still angry at Bundy for consenting to speak at the Vietnam teach-in.

LBJ: I told George to quit talking and embarrassing me in front of Bundy about what [Bundy] ought to do. Now, I don't think he ought to have a public press conference. . . . I don't agree with his going out and getting in sit-ins.[2] . . . I don't think a White House staff member ought to be doing these things, except the press secretary.

---

1. While the Dominican crisis opened an irreparable schism between LBJ and many American liberals and created abiding doubts about Johnson's trustworthiness, his Ambassador to the OAS, Ellsworth Bunker, finally helped to establish a satisfactory provisional Dominican government in September 1965. Nine months later, in a free presidential election, the moderate rightist ex-President Joaquin Balaguer defeated Bosch in a landslide, followed by surprising political stability.
2. Johnson means teach-ins.

MOYERS: No, it ought to be a principal.

LBJ: That's right. . . . If he does it with a press conference, he has to do it on television. If he does it with television, they're going to go ahead and invite him to come right down to the Foreign Relations Committee and Armed Services when this investigation[1] starts. And I don't want the President's employees to be subject to committees—in particular, a man that's sitting in that spot. Just like Roosevelt had to keep Harry Hopkins from going down,[2] I've just got to keep Bundy from going down. Blut he wants the limelight.

VANCE HARTKE

Democratic Senator from Indiana
Thursday, May 27, 1965, 6:30 P.M.

> Johnson has nominated former Air Force Vice Chief of Staff William "Bozo" McKee as head of the Federal Aviation Administration. LBJ is especially ardent for the appointment because the new FAA chief will be responsible for building an American supersonic transport plane that can compete with those being developed by the British and French. Senator Hartke has angered the President with a minority report refusing to exempt McKee from a law requiring a civilian to hold the job. As Majority Leader, LBJ treated Hartke as a protégé after his first election in 1958. He now barks at Hartke as if he were still a freshman Senator.

LBJ: Now, I know there's a bunch of chickenshit little pilots around here[3] that didn't understand it. . . . But . . . I have problems if the strongest administration men I've got and the best friends I got are up, by God, chasing around after him and saying it oughtn't be done. . . .

HARTKE: Mr. President, they've got eighty-nine [military] people . . . right now in the payroll in FAA, contrary to what the concept was.

LBJ: I don't give a *shit* about the concept! . . . Why in the hell don't you want me to *have* the best people? . . . I want you to have the best damn human you can get. . . . I just haven't got a civil service clerk that can do it, or a big, fat businessman from Texas. . . . They just don't know the business. . . . And I'll have another TFX. They'll just be testifying all day long.[4]

HARTKE: . . . I don't mean you any trouble. . . .

---

1. Of LBJ's handling of the Dominican crisis.
2. To testify before Congress, when Hopkins was a member of FDR's White House staff.
3. The Aircraft Owners and Pilots Association opposed McKee's appointment.
4. Always worried that a scandal will be pinned on him, LBJ thinks that development of the supersonic transport might lead to charges that he improperly used his influence to tip the contract to one firm over another, as with the TFX contract in 1963. (See Chapter 4.)

LBJ: I know that. You help me, or I wouldn't call you. I don't call my *enemies.* Hell, I let them go to hell. Just chuck them out. But . . . you don't want to be defending *me* when they impeach me. . . . Don't you go after him. You just tear up that damn thing and put it in your ass pocket. . . . Tear it up and tell Martha[1] that, by God, you want to kiss her and spend some time with her and a little less on that minority report because I've got to have this man handling hundreds of millions. . . .

HARTKE: . . . I wouldn't know him from Adam's apple. . . . I mean, he's probably a great guy. . . . But this is not just an ordinary situation. . . .

LBJ: . . . I've got a brother-in-law that I'd like to bring up here from Texas and put in that job, if I was appointing them like Bobby Kennedy.[2] But this man's got the wisdom and the judgment. You take that home and you use it for some toilet paper, that report. . . . Go on now. Tear that up! And don't you cause me any trouble! I've got enough trouble. I've got trouble in Vietnam and Dominican Republic and every other damn thing in the world. If you'd see what some of the Joint Chiefs are recommending here to me,[3] you'd drop the phone and go see your grandchild.[4]

---

1. Mrs. Hartke.
2. A dig at President Kennedy's appointments of his brother and two brothers-in-law to his administration. LBJ does have a brother-in-law, Birge Alexander, who works for the FAA in Fort Worth.
3. Expanding the war in Vietnam.
4. McKee was narrowly confirmed on June 29, after a special bill was passed exempting him from the civilian requirement. Hartke opposed the bill.

Chapter Nine

"I DON'T BELIEVE THEY'RE *EVER* GOING TO QUIT"

It's going to be difficult for us to . . . prosecute . . . a war that far away from home with the divisions we have here. . . . I'm very depressed about it. Because I see no program from either Defense or State that gives me much hope of doing anything, except just praying and gasping to hold on . . . and hope they'll quit. I don't believe they're ever going to quit. And I don't see . . . any . . . plan for a victory—militarily or diplomatically.

LBJ *to* ROBERT McNAMARA, *June 21, 1965*

ROBERT McNAMARA

Saturday, June 5, 1965, 4:50 P.M.

Johnson faces brutal, fundamental decisions on Vietnam. Today Ambassador Taylor has cabled Washington that the Saigon government is in crisis. Soon, after a military coup, the new Prime Minister will be General Nguyen Cao Ky, who favors a zippered flying suit adorned with twin pearl-handled revolvers and who will opine, "We need four or five Hitlers in Vietnam."[1] Assistant Secretary of State William Bundy considers Ky and the new chief of state, General Nguyen Van Thieu, "absolutely the bottom of the barrel."[2]

With Saigon's army collapsing, the Vietcong have launched a new offensive to exploit the monsoon season, which will make it harder for the United States and South Vietnam to defend ground forces from the the air. In his cable Taylor said, "It will probably be necessary to commit U.S. ground forces to action."[3] As

---

1. General Ky said this to a British reporter soon after his elevation (*Sunday Mirror,* London, July 4, 1965).
2. William Bundy oral history, LBJL.
3. Taylor to Rusk, June 5, 1965, in *FRUS,* vol. 2, pp. 719–24.

McNamara later recalled, the President read Taylor's telegram "with growing anxiety."[1]

McNAMARA: It seems to me we're in a very dangerous situation out there. . . .

LBJ: On account of the change in government?

McNAMARA: Yes, yes.

LBJ: What's happening in the fighting?

McNAMARA: We've had a very unhappy week. The losses have been extremely high. . . . In terms of killed, wounded, and missing in action, the total will be [over] a thousand.[2] We've had several serious setbacks, including an attack . . . by a Vietcong battalion-size force only ten miles from Saigon. We're beginning to see the use of that Vietcong reserve that we've all known was there. . . .

LBJ: Are you scheduled to get any more people in there anytime?

McNAMARA: Three more combat battalions are scheduled to go in mid-July. You've already approved that. That will make a total of thirteen combat battalions. There are ten there now, three to go in within the next . . . forty-five days. . . . The total today is [about] fifty thousand. . . . There'll be roughly seventy thousand there . . . at the end of August. . . . At some point, you and Dean [Rusk] and Mac [Bundy] and I should meet privately [on] how you'd like us to proceed—particularly with this bombing on the North. Under no circumstances would I recommend to you . . . in the near future that we bomb the IL-28s.[3] . . . On the other hand, I do think that it's absolutely essential that we keep the bombing on the North militarily effective. That means, I think, that we must go north of the twentieth parallel.[4]

MIKE MANSFIELD

Tuesday, June 8, 1965, 5:05 P.M.

When LBJ met with congressional leaders on June 3, the Senate Majority Leader had found him "very pessimistic about Vietnam." Johnson said that the Joint Chiefs and other advisers were insisting that the United States bomb Hanoi and that he had "stalled them off for a week" because he feared the Chinese would respond by entering the war. Senator Russell Long said, "We may have to face up to the sixty-four-thousand-dollar question and bomb China."[5] Aghast, the dovish

---

1. McNamara, *In Retrospect*, p. 187.

2. The *New York Times* reported on June 4 that the South Vietnamese had lost a thousand men that week.

3. The Soviets had moved a small number of IL-28 bombers into North Vietnam. McNamara worried that attacking them might trigger a dangerous Soviet response. (McNamara to LBJ, June 2, 1965, in *FRUS*, vol. 2, pp. 706–7.)

4. Above that parallel were Hanoi and Haiphong, although McNamara wished for now to avoid striking those cities.

5. Mansfield memo, June 3, 1965, in *FRUS*, vol. 2, p. 709.

Mansfield wrote the President a memo imploring him not to bomb the North Vietnamese capital.[1] Now, in an effort to keep his Majority Leader onboard, LBJ pretends to be going behind his advisers' backs to consult Mansfield on Vietnam.

LBJ: I don't see exactly the medium for pulling out [of Vietnam]. . . . [But] I want to talk to you. . . . Rusk doesn't know that I'm thinking this. McNamara doesn't know I'm thinking this. Bundy doesn't. I haven't talked to a human. I'm over here in bed. I just tried to take a nap and get going with my second day, and I couldn't. I just decided I'd call you. But I think I'll say to the Congress that General Eisenhower thought we ought to go in there and do here what we . . . did in Greece and Turkey, and . . . President Kennedy thought we ought to do this. . . . But all of my military people tell me . . . that we cannot do this [with] the commitment [of American forces] we have now. It's got to be materially increased. And the outcome is not really predictable at the moment. . . . I would say . . . that . . . our seventy-five thousand men are going to be in great danger unless they have seventy-five thousand more. . . .

I'm no military man at all. But . . . if they get a hundred and fifty [thousand Americans], they'll have to have another hundred and fifty. And then they'll have to have *another* hundred and fifty. So, the big question then is: What does the Congress want to do about it? . . . I know what the military wants to do. I really know what Rusk and McNamara want to do. . . . And I think I know what the country wants to do *now*. But I'm not sure that they want to do that *six months* from now.[2] I want you to give me your best thinking on it. See how we ought to handle it, if we handle it at all. . . . We have . . . some very bad news on the government [in Saigon]. . . . Westmoreland says that the offensive that he has anticipated, that he's been fearful of, is now on. And he wants people as quickly as he can get them.

*   *   *

MANSFIELD: [Fulbright] is tremendously disturbed about the situation in Vietnam.

LBJ: Well, we *all* are.[3]

MANSFIELD: I know, but I mean, *really*. . . . He just feels it's too little and too late.[4] . . .

LBJ: . . . Unless you can guard what you're doing, you can't do anything. We

---

1. Mansfield to LBJ, June 5, 1965, in ibid., pp. 725–27.

2. In other words, Americans might turn against the war.

3. Mansfield warns Johnson about the man, once LBJ's close ally, who will become his chief Senate antagonist on the Vietnam War. The President is not taking his warning seriously enough.

4. Referring to LBJ's request to Congress on June 1 for $89 million for new electric power and other development projects in Southeast Asia—in part a response to Fulbright's suggestions that the way to win the war was not militarily but by improving the daily life and morale of the South Vietnamese.

can't build an *airport,* by God, much less build an REA[1] line. And it takes more people to *guard* us in building an airport than it does to *build* the airport. . . . That's why we had to limit it to just three or four REA projects, and one little dam. . . .

MANSFIELD: Yeah, but some people seem to think that we're just building it for the Vietcong to take over.

LBJ: It could very well be.[2] But I have the feeling from the way Bill Fulbright talked[3] . . . that the feeling on the Hill was that we ought to be doing more of that, and that might be a better answer than the bombs.

MANSFIELD: . . . There's a feeling of apprehension and suspense up here that's pretty hard to define. . . .

LBJ: Well, we have it *here.* . . . Do you have any thoughts about the approach that we might make to the Congress[4]—whether one is wise, and if so, how?

MANSFIELD: If you make another approach to the Congress,[5] I think really the roof will blow off this time, because people who have remained quiet will no longer remain silent. . . . I think you'd be in for some trouble. The debate would spread right out.

LBJ: I think you might near *got* to have the debate, though, hadn't you?[6]

MANSFIELD: Yes, sir.

LBJ: Do you think that we ought to send all these troops without a debate?

MANSFIELD: No, sir. I think that we've got too many in there now. And we've been bombing the North without any appreciable results. . . .

LBJ: What do we do about [Westmoreland's] request for more men? . . . If it assumes the proportions that I can see it assuming, shouldn't we say to the Congress, "What do you want to do about it?"

MANSFIELD: I would hate to be the one to say it because, as you said earlier, it's seventy-five thousand, then it's a hundred and fifty thousand, then it's three hundred thousand. Where do you stop?

LBJ: You don't. . . . To me, it's shaping up like this, Mike—you either get out or you get *in.* . . . We've tried all the neutral things. And we think they[7] are winning. Now, if *we* think they're winning, you can imagine what *they* think.

MANSFIELD: They *know* they're winning.

LBJ: And if they know that, you can see that they're not anxious to find any an-

---

1. The Rural Electrification Administration. LBJ had helped bring electric power to his rural Texas district in the 1930s.

2. LBJ here shows how uncertain he is, even in June 1965, that the South can win the war.

3. When LBJ met with congressional leaders.

4. Consulting Congress about Westmoreland's request.

5. After having appealed to it for the Gulf of Tonkin Resolution and the $700 million appropriation for Vietnam.

6. Having ordered this call taped, LBJ may be deliberately putting himself on record as suggesting a congressional debate even though he does not actually want one.

7. North Vietnam.

swer to it. . . . We seem to have tried everything that we know to do. I stayed here for over a year when they were urging us to bomb before I'd go beyond the line. I have stayed away from [bombing] their industrial targets and their civilian population, although they[1] urge you to do it.

MANSFIELD: Yeah, but Hanoi and Haiphong are spit clean, and have been for months.[2] You bomb them, you get nothing. You just build up more hatred. You get these people tied more closely together because they are tied by blood, whether from the North or the South.

LBJ: I think that's true. I think that you've done nearly everything that you can do, except make it a complete white man's war.

MANSFIELD: If you do that, then you might as well say goodbye to all of Asia and to most of the world.

LBJ: That's probably . . . right. Therefore, where do you go?

MANSFIELD: You don't go ahead. . . . You don't pull out. You try to do something to consolidate your position in South Vietnam. And that may take more troops. It certainly will take more [South] Vietnamese [soldiers].

LBJ: They're getting more of them in, Mike, but . . . they're deserting just like flies!

MANSFIELD: When McNamara speaks about three hundred thousand American troops against Giap's[3] thirty-one divisions in North Vietnam, that's the absolute minimum.

LBJ: Yes, he knows that.

MANSFIELD: When he speaks about a hundred and sixty thousand being increased, with respect to the [South] Vietnamese army, he knows he isn't telling the truth. Because they're not coming. . . .

LBJ: . . . He thinks he's telling the truth, because the [Saigon] government assures him they'll stop them. But they can't do it. . . . That's what Taylor[4] told us this morning. I don't know quite how to approach this, Mike, so far as the Congress is concerned, before we make up our mind. When we take it much further than you and McCormack,[5] you know what I get into—discussions[6] and so forth. . . . Do you have any feeling whether it would be better to let [Taylor] go up before Foreign Relations and Armed Services, or would it be better to just have some of the representative ones of them here? . . .

MANSFIELD: . . . If you start picking out a selected few, you're asking for trou-

1. LBJ refers to the Joint Chiefs.
2. The North Vietnamese had prepared for possible U.S. bombing of the two prize targets.
3. Vo Nguyen Giap, the legendary North Vietnamese Defense Minister.
4. Ambassador Maxwell Taylor.
5. Speaker of the House John McCormack.
6. Leaks.

ble, because others will feel they've been left out and they'll get grumpy. To put it mildly.

LBJ: Would your thought then be that it would be best to ask Russell and Fulbright[1] to have a joint hearing with him, and do the same on the House side? We'll have this all in the papers then.

MANSFIELD: If you see a few, it's going to get in the papers. I mean, how could you pick out three or four or five and not expect it to leak?

LBJ: . . . Do you have any feeling about Taylor coming out?[2] . . .

MANSFIELD: . . . I have more feeling about Lodge going in, to tell you the truth. . . . Lodge is not well loved on the Hill, and he was tied in somewhere with Diem.[3] That was the big mistake.

LBJ: [*defensive:*] They like [Lodge] better out there than anybody we've had. . . . And . . . my people tell me that he is less likely to get us in an Asian war than Taylor. . . . He'd like to talk it out, rather than fight it out. And that's pretty appealing these days. [*chuckles*] He's experienced, and he has the language . . . and he gets along pretty well with the Catholics [and] the Buddhists. To start all over with a new man is pretty rough.

MANSFIELD: That's true. It has to be done, I guess.

LBJ: No, it doesn't. We can do anything that looks better. We've had Rusk and McNamara and Bobby Kennedy and all of them offer to go[4]—and Mac Bundy. But I don't believe any of them are in either Lodge's or Taylor's class. . . . Lodge . . . goes [for] this economic stuff that Bill [Fulbright] is talking [about] all the time. . . . Fulbright kept shoving Lodge [on me] the other night . . . and demanding we do it, and I kind of indicated, "All right, we'll try some of this, if you want us to."

ROBERT McNAMARA

Thursday, June 10, 1965, 6:40 P.M.

Three days before this conversation, McNamara received what he called a "bombshell." General Westmoreland had cabled from Saigon that he needed 41,000 more combat troops in Vietnam immediately and 52,000 more later. These addi-

---

1. Chairmen of the Senate Armed Services and Foreign Relations Committees.

2. Taylor is leaving his post, to be replaced by Henry Cabot Lodge, former Republican Senator from Massachusetts and Eisenhower's UN Ambassador. Lodge had preceded Taylor in Saigon; LBJ is reappointing him largely to maintain Republican support for his actions in Vietnam.

3. Mansfield thinks that Ambassador Lodge was too close to South Vietnamese President Ngo Dinh Diem, whose excesses, he believes, provoked his assassination in November 1963 and began the parade of coups that have decimated the Saigon government.

4. As Ambassador to Saigon.

tions would increase American strength to 175,000 troops. Instead of a "defensive posture," he wishes to "take the war to the enemy," for which "even greater forces" may be required. McNamara wrote in 1995 that Westmoreland's cable was the most disturbing he ever received as Secretary of Defense: "We were forced to make a decision. We could no longer postpone a choice about what path to take." After reading the cable, McNamara told colleagues, "We're in a hell of a mess."[1]

McNAMARA: The Chiefs met for two hours this afternoon. . . . They discussed two plans—essentially the Westmoreland plan and the . . . Taylor-McNamara plan.[2] And they came out unanimously in favor of the Westmoreland plan. . . . At tomorrow's meeting, you might simply want to hear the pros and cons of the matter and just leave it undecided. Then, after it appears you've given it ample thought, send your decision down.

LBJ: All right. Had you given any thought to letting Goodpaster[3] present these things to Eisenhower too and get his ideas? . . . I don't see that he's overeager. . . . He's emphasizing the economic and the morale . . . pretty strongly, and looks to me like they're playing on him pretty strong on the television.[4] Do you watch television?

McNAMARA: I see it sometimes. . . .

LBJ: I'm going to make them get you one of these sets in your office where you can turn them all three [networks] on. . . .

McNAMARA: There's a little danger here, Mr. President. Eisenhower's a great one to simply support . . . the commander's recommendations.[5] . . .

LBJ: . . . Has anyone [assessed] the disadvantages of the division's location and the danger of entrapment?

McNAMARA: Yes, and therefore they've modified the plan. . . . They [will] keep it down on the coast. . . .

LBJ: Then it gets down to a question of numbers. You're talking about one division. . . . Are we talking about an eighteen-thousand-man division?

McNAMARA: . . . Westmoreland recommended ten additional battalions over and above the thirteen you've already authorized, which would have a strength of something [like] forty-five thousand men. I would recommend five battalions with the strength of about twenty-five thousand men. So, we're talking about . . . the difference of twenty thousand people. But they're all combat people. And it's

---

1. McNamara, *In Retrospect,* pp. 187–88.

2. McNamara had proposed limiting additional deployments to 95,000. (See McNamara, *In Retrospect,* p. 192.)

3. General Andrew Goodpaster, who had served as Eisenhower's close White House aide.

4. Television reporters were soliciting Ike's views on Vietnam.

5. McNamara was right. When LBJ sent Goodpaster to brief Eisenhower on Westmoreland's request, Ike flatly approved it, saying, "We have got to win." (Quoted in McNamara, *In Retrospect,* p. 190.)

quite a difference in risk. . . . Really this is the difference. And this is a hard one to argue out with the Chiefs, because in the back of my mind, I have a very definite limitation on commitment [on U.S. ground troops] in mind. I don't think the Chiefs do. In fact, I *know* they don't.

LBJ: Do you think that this is just the next step with them up the ladder?

McNAMARA: Yes. They hope they don't have to go any further. But Westmoreland outlines in his cable the step beyond it. And he doesn't say that's the last.

LBJ: I don't guess anybody knows.

McNAMARA: I don't think anybody knows. . . . But I'm inclined to think that unless we're really willing to go to a full potential land war, we've got to slow down here and try to halt, at some point, the ground troop commitment.

*   *   *

LBJ: I've got to see Reston[1] in the morning. He is very concerned about the "narrowing of the basic decisions of government." Now, our old friends [Robert Kennedy and his clique] are feeding [him] some stuff [saying] it's too concentrated. In a matter of a decision like this this morning, Mac [Bundy] says that the decisions and recommendations are made by these same people [that made them under Kennedy]—the field people, the Joint Chiefs, the McNamaras and the Vances, and the Rusks, and the Balls, the Bill Bundys and the Mac Bundys and the President. . . . Do you have any people in your outfit that . . . feel that they made decisions [under Kennedy] that they're not in on now?

McNAMARA: No. . . .

LBJ: . . . The only one I know that might not be is the Attorney General. And he's not my brother![2] [*laughs*]

*   *   *

LBJ: Is Taylor going up to see the committee[3] in the morning?

McNAMARA: Yes. . . .

LBJ: . . . I think that the line he ought to take is . . . that there has been a constant [Vietcong] buildup, and the buildup came really before the bombing. . . . We may have made it more difficult. But they keep coming [into South Vietnam]. And . . . you've got to do something about it. . . . They're going to keep putting their stack in, and moving new chips into the pot. We've either got to do one of two things. We've got to tuck tail and run, or we've got to have somebody . . . tell us that "the Indians are coming" and protect us. . . . That puts [Congress] in the position of either tucking tail and running or giving us what we need. . . .

I would just say, "I know the President is troubled [about] this. . . . But . . . they've got a pistol at our temple, and we've got to react. And the only way we can

1. The *New York Times* columnist James Reston.
2. A swipe at Robert Kennedy, who was JFK's dominant foreign affairs and military adviser.
3. Senate Foreign Relations Committee.

react is to put a pistol at *their* temple. Now   we know that with two pistols at temples, one of them's liable to go off. But it doesn't seem that we're ready to tuck tail and run. . . . We waited as long to bomb as a human could. . . . We made every diplomatic initiative and overture that we know to make. . . . And a good many that we didn't believe in. . . . [Now] they've got to go through this monsoon season. We don't believe that we ought to . . . leave these fifty thousand boys there without some help. . . .

[The Senators] just got the living hell scared out of them. . . . [Mansfield] came down with two memos in an hour [saying,] "Oh, my God, don't send any resolution[1] up here!" They don't want to *vote* against doing it. They just want to talk and *whine* about it. . . . I just chucked it back to him. I said, . . . "I don't want to do anything that doesn't represent the reasonable unanimity of this country. We ought to have these things settled at the water's edge. Then . . . we ought to be one nation united. I'm willing to let you write the ticket.[2] If you'll write it. I thought you wrote it with the SEATO treaty.[3] I thought you wrote it when you approved the . . . appropriation[4] and the [Tonkin Gulf] action. But if you . . . want to tuck tail and run . . . you can just pass a joint resolution." . . . That jarred him, but it hasn't jarred him enough . . . to keep him from whining. He ran to Aiken.[5] . . . They had breakfast, and Aiken comes out . . . and says that Johnson is going to put us on the spot and get off the hook himself.[6] Did you read that?

McNAMARA: Oh, sure I did.

LBJ: [*laughs*] Of course I would like to do that. But . . . in submitting it, I think I'm just making more trouble for myself. . . . Did you notice how quick Russell got away from us?[7]

McNAMARA: Yeah, sure did.

LBJ: . . . I think Taylor's got to say, . . . "Here's the [Gulf of Tonkin] Resolution, which says 'to deter aggression.' . . . In order to do that, I've got to have these men. If there's anyone who thinks we oughtn't to, he ought to introduce a resolution repealing it." . . . I think it would be disastrous to the country. I'd object to it as a citizen. But the Congress is the policy-making branch of the government, and they've got a right to pass on it. . . . Now, tell me . . . the position . . . that our

---

1. To escalate the war.
2. Make the decision on Vietnam.
3. The American commitment to defend South Vietnam.
4. The $700 million military appropriation.
5. Vermont Republican Senator George Aiken.
6. On the Senator floor on June 9, Aiken said that LBJ was seeking a war declaration to take himself "off the hook."
7. At a meeting with the President, Rusk, and McNamara that morning, Senator Russell had said he would like to find a way out of Vietnam but didn't see how without losing face. (McGeorge Bundy notes, June 10, 1965, in *FRUS*, vol. 2, pp. 745–49.)

friend [Robert Kennedy] took on what happened to our [bombing] pause. Did we do it wrong? Didn't do it the right day?[1]

McNAMARA: No, he didn't rake that over.

LBJ: Did he show any . . . appreciation of the fact that we had heeded the suggestion and tried it?

McNAMARA: Yeah. . . . I think that he would say that . . . it didn't work, but it was wise to have done it. But now the line [he takes] is . . . we have an unlimited liability here that we're accepting: "Advancing toward world war. . . . We haven't told the people why. . . . Sleight of hand constantly." . . . So I said to him, "Do you think we ought to go to Congress with a resolution . . . [and] debate [it]?" [He said,] "Yeah, I probably would. . . . The President ought to go on TV and explain what it is we're doing, how far we're going to go."

LBJ: I can't do that, can I?

McNAMARA: No, no, you can't.

LBJ: Do you know how far we're going to go?

McNAMARA: No.

LBJ: Or do the Joint Chiefs know? *What human being knows?* I would imagine if they wiped out a thousand boys tomorrow, we might go a hell of a lot further than we'd do if they just wiped out four.

McNAMARA: Sure. . . . There's going to be uncertainty here. It *is* risky. That's the nature of the problem. I do think there can be more said about how many troops . . . we've decided to have, and what their role would be. This could be explained . . . much the way you're talking about Max [Taylor] explaining tomorrow that there's been this continued Vietcong buildup and we have to respond to it. . . .

LBJ: Well, I wouldn't say that we *have* to respond. I'd say there's been this constant buildup, and we must *protect* ourselves as best we *can*. . . . Now, this is not a warlord here. This is Mr. Johnson and Mr. Taylor . . . and General Westmoreland, who has been out there a good long time and hasn't tried to invade the North. And *they* think that in the light of the developments, this is essential to protect our people. Now, we don't say that putting these people in is going to win [the war], but we say if you *don't* put them in, you're going to lose substantially what you have. . . . This is . . . a holding action. . . . We're trying to be prudent. . . . Now, not a damn human thinks that fifty thousand or a hundred thousand or a hundred and fifty thousand are going to end that war.

McNAMARA: That's right.

LBJ: And we're not getting out. But we're trying to hold what we *got*. And . . .

---

1. Johnson is being sarcastic. RFK had called on him in April to suggest a bombing pause.

we're losing, at the rate we're going. . . . He could say we've tried to be as peaceful as we can, and we've had our bombings limited. . . . But the cold hard facts are that . . . they're taking extra territory. They killed six hundred last week, compared to a normal hundred. . . . We want to come in there and do everything we can [so] that the [South] Vietnamese . . . will have enough people to resist it. When they can't resist it and they're overrun, why, we got to carry in men to help them.

LADY BIRD JOHNSON

Thursday, June 10, 1965, Tape-recorded Diary

LADY BIRD: It was a late night for Lyndon. . . . Eleven o'clock when he came home to dinner. . . . Sometimes it makes me almost angry because he's spending himself so. But I don't know a better thing in the world to spend himself for. . . . From my small viewpoint, it just looks like the problems of the world are so much more insoluble than those of these United States. We can work on these here and make a dent—a rather wonderful dent.

LADY BIRD JOHNSON

Friday, June 11, 1965, Tape-recorded Diary

The Johnsons spend the weekend at the LBJ Ranch.

LADY BIRD: Lyndon, like a man of thirst in the Sahara, was rushing us all to get on the chopper for the boats. . . . For a while, we watched Lyndon in the little boat with the demonstrating water-skiiers. . . . A truly wonderful day to be alive. And so Luci must have thought too because she had asked her daddy in her very sweet way if she could use a car to go and "see a friend." Her daddy . . . smiled . . . and said, "You just use any one you want." So when we woke up the next morning and found that Luci had chosen the best Lincoln and had departed to see the friend, I felt a good deal of a louse for not telling Lyndon that the friend lived in Lubbock— almost clear across the state of Texas, eight hours' drive away.

ROBERT McNAMARA

Sunday, June 13, 1965, 2:45 A.M.

South Vietnamese troops are losing a three-day battle for Dong Xoai, sixty miles northeast of Saigon. The Vietcong have also raided a nearby U.S. Special Forces camp.

McNAMARA: I'm sorry to wake you, Mr. President, but Westmoreland . . . says the [South] Vietnamese have suffered a serious defeat. They've had their troops . . . chewed up.[1] The Vietcong are apparently going to occupy a rubber plantation and certain other areas . . . from which they will probably launch further attacks upon us. He considered it essential that they be defeated. The [South] Vietnamese aren't capable of doing so. He's inclined to favor committing the 173rd Airborne Brigade to that battle, therefore. He believes he has authority to do so. . . . There is still time for us to stop him, however, if we wish. . . . Dean Rusk . . . agrees with me . . . that we should not stop them. . . .

LBJ: . . . I think that's exactly correct.

LADY BIRD JOHNSON

Sunday, June 13, 1965, Tape-recorded Diary

LADY BIRD: Lyndon [looked] at a new ranch that is for sale. Almost an addiction with him. . . . We choppered to Haywood[2] for a late lunch, hungry and eager, and out in the boat. I am a coward. I do not like to go fast as the wind in that new boat, the front up high and our hair streaming. Lyndon loves it. A new ranch, a fast boat are to him perfect release from Vietnam and the Dominican Republic, any array of troubles. . . . Luci, bless her, arrived back at the ranch . . . from her cross-country trip to Lubbock. . . . Her daddy had prepared to be very stern with her, was completely undone by her smile and her teasing. . . . Much as I dislike the expression, she's learned how to "handle him."

BIRCH BAYH

Tuesday, June 15, 1965, 1:20 P.M.

> With old Senate allies like William Fulbright differing with him on Vietnam, LBJ is trying to build up young Senators like Bayh of Indiana, elected in 1962, who support the war.

LBJ: None of us want to do what the Joint Chiefs of Staff say you ought to do to win—and that's "go in and bomb the hell out of them." I'm . . . refusing to do that. On the other hand, if we walked out of [Vietnam], we would bust every treaty we got. Forty-four nations would say that United States couldn't be depended on for anything. Whether it's Tokyo or Berlin or NATO or any of the rest of them—

---

1. Some South Vietnamese officers fled out of fright. (See Stanley Karnow, *Vietnam: A History,* rev. ed., Penguin, 1991, p. 437).

2. Another ranch LBJ had purchased years before.

SEATO, CENTO.[1] So we can't walk out—and we can't walk in . . . with heavy bombs and atomic weapons. . . . We're trying to deter them and wear them out, without losing a lot of people. Now, we've lost four hundred,[2] but we've lost a hundred and sixty thousand casualties since World War II. . . .

I held off as long and long and long as I could [on the bombing] because I knew the [American] people would raise hell. I knew it didn't look good. It didn't have a peace image. But it has done what we thought it ought to do.[3] . . . It's hard as hell for them to get any more men down [into South Vietnam]. . . . They get to a bridge and the damn bridge is out. So then they've got to . . . get a ferry and . . . unload their truck . . . and take it by pieces [to] the other side. Then they . . . go four miles . . . to another bridge that's out. . . .

[The bombing] has got them all scared to death. They . . . hide and get in their caves. . . . We hope that by that war of nerves, over . . . several months, they'll finally say, "Let's talk." As it is now, they spit in our face. When I gave them the [bombing] pause and told them I wouldn't do anything for a week if they talk, they just spit in our face. They wouldn't even open the letter telling them that. They're arrogant as hell. I don't blame them. I defeated Goldwater [by] 15 million [votes]. Now why would I want to give Goldwater half my Cabinet? They're winning. Why would they want to talk? All the talk would do is get them to give up something they're going to win.

BAYH: . . . The thing that gripes me . . . is that these so-called intellectuals, the people that are supposed to have all the brains, are . . . clear out in left field. They just can't conceive of what you have to do there.

LBJ: That's right. I said . . . yesterday [to] a group of intellectuals,[4] "What would you have me do that I'm not doing?" . . . They said, "Stop your bombing." I said, . . . "The only way you can get a political solution . . . is to have some pressure on them. The only pressure I've got is the bombing. I don't instigate any incidents. They go and kill us. They're gone before we can even get waked up to bury our dead." . . . They said, "Maybe you ought to . . . [go to] the United Nations." . . . [But the United Nations] ordered the North Vietnamese to come in there last August, up to the Security Council.[5] And the North Vietnamese said, *"Fuck you!"*

---

1. Referring to America's commitment to defend Tokyo and West Berlin and its other treaty obligations.

2. It is a poignant fact that of the nearly sixty thousand Americans who would die in Vietnam, only about four hundred had been killed as of this date.

3. LBJ knows this is not true. He had hoped that the bombing would erode the enemy's will to fight and stiffen the Saigon government.

4. The previous day LBJ spoke to a group of foreign correspondents and to 400 participants in the White House Festival of the Arts. During the festival John Hersey read from *Hiroshima,* darkly alluding to the bombing of North Vietnam. Dwight Macdonald circulated a petition against LBJ's foreign policy.

5. During the Gulf of Tonkin incident.

* * *

LBJ: Eighty-five percent of the people in this country are for what we're doing in the Dominican Republic and Vietnam. And the polls so show it. . . . Eight or ten are against it. But they're the ones that are raising hell. Now, we read the Communist bulletins. Their orders go out to do it. This Du Bois youth thing. It's doing all these colleges. They've got a sit-in tomorrow.[1] They're all led by Communist people. Hoover's[2] got people after them all the time. But if I get out and go talking about the Communists, they say, "Oh, he's a McCarthy!"[3] . . . But . . . they're stirring up this agitation. . . . The Chinese got their folks working. The Russians got their folks working. This Russian Ambassador—hell, he's talking to all of our Senators![4] After he has lunch with one of our Senators, it takes me *two weeks* to get the fellow to where he doesn't think I'm a warmonger again!

BAYH: . . . They're using the propaganda from our own Senators against us.

LBJ: Oh, yeah. . . . They get one speech by Morse[5] . . . and print it in leaflets. Drop it out to all of our people. Then they come back and say that the country is so divided. . . . This morning some article . . . said 85 percent of the Senators in the United States Senate were really undercover against Johnson's position. I believe 85 percent of them are *for* it.

BAYH: That's right.

LBJ: But the alternatives! Do I want to go [with] LeMay[6] and bomb Peking? If I do, I'll get thirty-five, forty divisions the next morning. . . . Do I want to get out like Morse? No! Do I want to just sit there and get hit like I did for several months? I don't think I ought to ask an American boy to get shot at and not shoot back. So . . . I tell them to defend themselves. . . . We've got to put men in there. Because they're . . . going to . . . build up their forces and try to run us out during the monsoon season. . . . So it's going to be real rough for the next ninety days. We hope at the end of that period, we'll wear them down some. . . . They hope they can wear *us* out. And I really believe they'll last longer than we do. One of their boys gets down in a rut and he stays there for two days without water, food, or anything and never moves. Waiting to ambush somebody. Now an American, he stays there about twenty minutes and, God damn, he's got to get him a cigarette![7]

---

1. Demonstrators led by the Committee for Nonviolent Action, including the radical Du Bois Clubs, roamed through the Pentagon on June 16, handing out pamphlets.

2. FBI Director J. Edgar Hoover.

3. Referring to Senator Joseph McCarthy's 1950s war against domestic Communists.

4. LBJ read FBI reports on the wide American social contacts of Soviet Ambassador Anatoly Dobrynin.

5. Oregon Democrat Wayne Morse.

6. Former Air Force Chief of Staff Curtis LeMay, who would later become famous for his suggestion that North Vietnam be bombed "into the Stone Age."

7. LBJ was taking a risk by throwing such a barb, even while talking to a friendly Senator, at an American soldier. But his point was that, unlike the Vietcong, American troops were not fanatics.

GEORGE MEANY

President, American Federation of Labor and Congress of Industrial Organizations
Tuesday, June 15, 1965, 2:07 P.M.

Johnson draws some comfort from the hard-boiled, hawkish old labor leader.

LBJ: George, I'm real worried about what these Commies are doing. I read these reports every night. What they're doing in the Dominican Republic, what they're doing all over the world. . . .
MEANY: What they're doing right here in this country! . . . I went over a copy of the *Sunday Worker*.[1] . . . You know who their fair-haired boy is? . . . Wayne Morse! . . .
LBJ: It's just unbelievable.
MEANY: And of course, they're in these colleges, you know. We're trying to see what we can do to get some of [what] I call the *American* kids to counteract this.
LBJ: [*laughs*] . . . God bless you! I'm awful grateful I've got a man like you.

LADY BIRD JOHNSON

Tuesday, June 15, 1965, Tape-recorded Diary

LADY BIRD: To my pleasure, Lyndon said, "I think I'll go to bed. I don't believe I'll have any night reading tonight." . . . A little later, I went in and found . . . Lyndon . . . stretched out on the massage table, absorbing his night reading with the TV turned on, to which he was utterly oblivious. If something comes on that he wants to hear, some extra nerve alerts him. He stops reading, turns it up, and watches it. Otherwise the noise doesn't seem to bother him in the least. Me, it drives mad! It was, however, one of the earliest nights in a long time for him. By midnight we were both in bed.

ROBERT McNAMARA

Wednesday, June 16, 1965, 12:55 P.M.

Before a Pentagon press conference, McNamara tells Johnson that he will announce that the United States is sending six more battalions to Vietnam, achieving a total strength of seventy or seventy-five thousand.

---

1. American Communist newspaper.

LBJ: Then how are you going to say you'll do in the future what's necessary?

McNAMARA: I'm not going to say a thing beyond this. And then the questions will come. . . . "Aren't you going to send some more? Aren't you considering it?" And I'm going to say that . . . the President has said we will do what's necessary to assist the South Vietnamese . . . to preserve their independence, and will not do anything more than is absolutely necessary to achieve that objective.

LBJ: . . . When will they be in there? About the 15th of July?

McNAMARA: Yeah, between the 15th and 25th.

ROBERT McNAMARA

Thursday, June 17, 1965, 3:25 P.M.

> Before his own press conference, Johnson reads from a UPI story about congressional Republican complaints that the administration is sending more troops to Vietnam but not asking for more money to finance them.

LBJ: What do I say about that when I'm asked?

McNAMARA: . . . I don't think, Mr. President, any defense bill in recent years has ever gone through the Appropriations Committee with as little change.[1] It's absolutely fantastic. . . .

LBJ: Yeah, but they say that you ought to have more.

McNAMARA: The answer is we don't need more.

LBJ: They say you got more men going out.

McNAMARA: . . . The number of men we have is the number of men we planned for in the budget. We have to feed the men, house them, equip them . . . whether they are in the United States or in South Vietnam. . . .

LBJ: Well, in light of the President's decision to escalate the war—

McNAMARA: I don't know that you *made* any decision to escalate the war. In any case, this question . . . frequently comes up—do we need more in the budget for '66? And the answer is, "Not now." We may later, depending upon what happens in the next thirteen months. . . .

LBJ: Now, McGovern[2] says that "the war is taking a very dangerous new turn with a commitment of large land forces to a combat mission. These guerrillas have lived twenty years off the countryside. . . . Their strength is they are part of the people and the terrain in which they fight, and how long will it take for some people to realize that bombing Hanoi or Peking will have little or no effect on the guerrilla forces fighting a thousand miles away in the jungle?"

---

1. Today the House Appropriations Committee approved LBJ's $45 billion annual defense bill.
2. Senator George McGovern, Democrat of South Dakota.

McNAMARA: If bombing won't have any effect and the added men are undesirable, what in the hell do we do? Get out? . . .

LBJ: The Senator said instead of continuing bombing, we [should] have taken advantage of the forthcoming Afro-Asian conference[1] . . . to encourage discussion with the Vietcong leaders.

McNAMARA: Now, this is the new tack. First, you didn't say what the objective was. Then we wouldn't tell them what the strategy was. Then we should have stopped bombing, and had the pause. Then we should have been ready for negotiation. Now the theme is . . . we haven't talked to the Vietcong. This is becoming more and more the dominant theme and criticism. And I think we're going to have to answer that.

LBJ: And how are we?

McNAMARA: . . . The answer is that they are a creature of the North Vietnamese, and the North Vietnamese . . . are the ones that we're trying to deal with. . . .

LBJ: Would you say it's just like asking the Vietcong and Vietnam to negotiate with Mississippi? [*laughs*]

McNAMARA: Yeah, I think so. . . . I just wanted to tell you, unless you see some reason not to, I'm planning to have dinner with Jackie [Kennedy] tonight in New York. I can do something on that front, if I can't on Bobby.[2] I confess to failure on the latter, but I have been able to do a little on the other.

LBJ: I sure hope so. . . . Confidentially . . . after your second drink, when you think that you can have some influence, I would sure urge her to keep Dick Goodwin down here to help us. I think [he's] getting some encouragement to move . . . away.[3]

WILLIAM FULBRIGHT

Thursday, June 17, 1965, 7:45 P.M.

> Johnson is still trying to blunt the Senate Foreign Relations Committee Chairman's opposition on Vietnam.

LBJ: We've got thirty B-52s that have just unloaded their bombs on a square mile in South Vietnam [where] there's . . . a concentration of Vietcong that has been

---

1. A sixty-nation Afro-Asian conference was scheduled to open in Algiers on June 29. It was later canceled.

2. LBJ had urged McNamara to try to dampen RFK's hostility toward him. He is also still trying to improve his relationship with Jackie.

3. Johnson means encouragement from RFK. Goodwin was friendly with both the late President's brother and his widow. He had written Johnson that he planned to leave his position as a presidential speechwriter in the fall. (Richard Goodwin, *Remembering America,* Little, Brown, 1988, p. 420.)

giving us all this trouble.[1] . . . I didn't want you hearing about it on the radio and think that I had started a new war. . . . They asked me in my press conference today . . . about . . . your friend Joe Clark[2]—your protégé: "Joe Clark says that you'll never get anywhere unless you negotiate with the Vietcong." I said Senator Clark's a very able Senator. He wanted to get on [the] Foreign Relations [Committee] a long time, all the time I was leader, and I've observed he's recently become a member of the Committee. [*laughs*] I wanted it known he'd become a member after I left.[3] But it's right and it's his duty to give his thought.

*   *   *

LBJ: If you will look at my press conference and find anything good to observe, I'd like to have [you say so], because I'm tired of reading these AP dispatches about "Fulbright, the voice of Johnson in the Congress, differed with him." . . . [Even] if you don't find anything except a little reference down there to the state of Arkansas,[4] say, "I embrace it."

GERALD FORD

Thursday, June 17, 1965, 7:50 P.M.

> Johnson consults the House Republican leader. Ford will be President of the United States ten years later, when the Vietnam War ends with an American defeat. LBJ plays down the importance of sending new ground forces.

LBJ: Sorry about your boy.
FORD: His sister slammed the car door on his finger. . . . It's pretty badly cut up.
LBJ: Sounds like he's got a Democratic sister!
FORD: [*laughs*] I hope not.
LBJ: I'm sitting here with Tom Dewey.[5] He's listening to us talk. . . . We sent thirty B-52s over a square mile area in . . . South Vietnam . . . [against a] concentration of Vietcong. . . . There will be some excitement on the television and radio. . . . But . . . that's the only way we could get them. . . . I sent Goodpaster up . . . to go over it with General Eisenhower.[6] He thought that it ought to be done. He also

---

1. In the first use of B-52s of the Vietnam War, the twenty-seven heavy jet bombers struck the Vietcong thirty miles north of Saigon and then returned to their base in Guam.
2. Dovish Democratic Senator from Pennsylvania.
3. In other words, that as Majority Leader LBJ had refused Clark the appointment, implying both that he did not think Clark was qualified for the committee and that Clark might be making trouble for Johnson now in revenge.
4. Fulbright's home state.
5. The two-time Republican presidential nominee was there to discuss crime in Washington, D.C., with Johnson, but LBJ is happy to exploit him to show Ford how bipartisan he is.
6. LBJ waves another Republican talisman in front of Ford.

felt we ought to approve Westmoreland's request for these troops . . . to protect his bases.[1] . . .

FORD: . . . The one question that I hoped we could sit down and talk about before we go any further is: How much are we going to use the ground forces? . . .

LBJ: Only when and if and as necessary to protect our national interest. Presently we have . . . about . . . thirteen thousand of combat on the ground. We'll move those up . . . to seventy to seventy-five. Out of that, I would guess we'll get another eight or ten thousand combat. Now, [when] those combats . . . go out, we'll try to keep them [at a] distance where they can't lob their mortars in for three miles. We'll constantly be on patrol. . . . When [the South Vietnamese] get in trouble . . . they'll call us. We'll come to their rescue. They did that last week. Westmoreland said, . . . "I'm going to authorize it. You want to cancel it?" . . . I said, "Hell no, I'm not going to cancel it." I just hate to see twelve hundred American boys involved. But this is no Sunday school picnic. . . . I can't tell a commander on the ground that he's got to let his people get wiped out or let his allies get wiped out. That's why we're out there. . . .

FORD: I fully agree. . . . The only thing [is] if we're going to do more offensively on the ground, then I think we all ought to sit down and talk about it.

LBJ: I'll be glad to do that. If I can stay out of the papers. I don't want to tell either the North Vietnamese or . . . China. And I haven't been to a meeting yet that they don't get something out about what happened. . . . You don't send a general out and a bunch of damn troops and tell him that "you got to get them killed." . . .

FORD: I agree with you a thousand percent.

LBJ: . . . Westmoreland went out there from West Point because he's the best general we had. . . . They ask this damn fool McCloskey,[2] . . . "Has Westmoreland got authority to keep our American boys from getting killed?" Answer is yes. "When did Johnson give him that authority?" This damn fool says, "I don't know, but I'm sure he got it." . . . So then the headline read, JOHNSON ENTERS NEW PHASE / COMBAT WAR IN VIETNAM. When I looked at the damn paper, I called up and said, "Who's smoking *marijuana* around here?" . . . I [told Reedy],[3] "Here's a statement. I want you to put it in your eleven o'clock briefing. 'No order has been issued. There's no change in the situation.' " . . . Then they wrote the story: . . . "The government's right hand doesn't know what the left hand's doing. And Johnson is a dictator."

FORD: . . . Don't worry about that kind of thing.

LBJ: I'm not worrying. I'm explaining to you so that you're on this team. It's

---

1. Johnson knows that Westmoreland wanted the troops to do more than simply "protect his bases."
2. State Department spokesman Robert McCloskey.
3. Johnson's press secretary.

your country. And a good many of these boys, I'm told, are *Republicans*.[1] I don't think they use good judgment in their party. But . . . they're out there fighting, and I think you ought to know the facts.

*   *   *

FORD: I agree exactly with what you did with the B-52s. . . . As I have done in the past, you know, I sit shoulder to shoulder with you.

LBJ: I know that. I'm proud of you, and your country's proud of you. The only thing I regret is that you're going to pick up some Republican seats [in Congress in 1966] as a result of that kind of a forward-looking policy.[2] I won't be happy [about] that, unless they're like you. . . . But I think you ought to get a muzzle on Laird and make him quit telling me that I can't have ground troops I need to protect my own airplanes.[3] Because I can't bomb like he wants to if the goddamned Vietcong are destroying my airplanes on the ground. . . . Would you consider letting me trade Morse[4] to you for Laird?

FORD: [*laughs*]

LBJ: Take care of your boy, and I'm sorry to bother you, Jerry.

JAMES WEBB

Administrator, National Aeronautics and Space Administration
Thursday, June 17, 1965, 8:10 P.M.

> Webb is at a State Department reception for the Gemini 4 astronauts, James McDivitt and Edward White, the first American to walk in outer space. The two men had set an endurance record, orbiting the earth sixty-two times during the first week of June. With his almost childlike penchant for surprises, LBJ wants to send them, along with Vice President Humphrey, on a presidential plane at 4:00 A.M. tomorrow to the International Air Show in Paris. Webb is Johnson's old friend and fellow Texan, but he balks.

LBJ: Jim, why can't these astronauts go to the Paris show?

WEBB: . . . We've not wanted to build up a show that de Gaulle[5] is trying to make . . . really big for him.

LBJ: . . . We don't give a damn. I just want to make something big for the United

---

1. LBJ is crude in reminding Ford that many American soldiers in harm's way are Republicans.

2. LBJ foresees that an unpopular war may cost him congressional strength in the next election.

3. Wisconsin Congressman Melvin Laird, one of Ford's rivals, declared on June 15 that bombing should be expanded and that if Johnson's objective was a "negotiated settlement," there should be no "needless sacrifice of American lives."

4. The antiwar Senator Morse.

5. French President Charles de Gaulle, who is causing LBJ problems over NATO and the U.S. role in Vietnam, which he has just called a "dirty affair."

States. They're standing in line [for] blocks to see our boys. . . . We're in such bad shape in the world, we ought to [use] everything we can. I'm getting them killed in Vietnam by the dozens. . . .

WEBB: . . . We've got a certain amount of debriefing we need these boys for. They're awful tired right now. And . . . the Russians have upstaged us on almost everything . . .

LBJ: They'll *keep* upstaging us if we just put on a buffet supper in our own State Department, Jim. . . . I've got three or four fat Congressmen over at the air show, and a B-58 blowing up.[1] I want them to . . . see what America's doing in the world. . . . You've got the Asia-Africa conference [coming up], and they're denouncing the hell out of us. And the UN is trying to screw us up. . . . I got beds on the plane. The whole damn outfit can go to sleep. . . . I'd just tell my wife, get her a gown, put on some perfume, and let you get in the President's bed. Then let these astronauts stretch out and we'll make a bed for them. Take all their goddamn kids and everybody they want to and go to the fair. . . .

WEBB: You sweep me off my feet. You know how much I love you. . . . But I do have to think about what's going to happen to you next week and the week after that. . . .

LBJ: What's going to happen to me? . . . What's wrong with the astronauts going to the air show? . . . God damn it, quit debating with me! . . . I'll be over there in a minute.[2]

LADY BIRD JOHNSON

Friday, June 18, 1965, Tape-recorded Diary

LADY BIRD: Luci's new car had arrived—a green [Corvette] Sting Ray, a combination graduation and birthday present. Lyndon is the sort of man who absolutely cannot keep from opening a gift, . . . nor can he wait until the exact birthday[3] to give his little daughter her present. . . . Luci came out [of the White House] and she looked at it and she squealed and ran and she hugged him. The look in her eyes was just like when she was about four years old and Lyndon had brought her a big box from a trip down into Virginia. . . . She looked down and

---

1. At the air show on June 15, two hours after the Soviets unveiled their new AN-22, the world's largest plane, an American B-58 jet bomber crashed, killing the pilot.

2. LBJ went immediately to the State Department. In what Lady Bird called the "shocker of the evening," he issued his invitation to the astronauts and their wives, who "sat openmouthed." She lent clothes from her own wardrobe for the wives to wear on the sudden trip. After a few hours' sleep at the White House, the astronauts and their wives, along with Humphrey, flew to Paris. (Lady Bird Johnson Diary, June 17, 1965, LBJL.)

3. Luci's birthday was July 2.

there she saw a little beagle. . . . And when she raised her eyes to her daddy's face, not all the angels in heaven ever had a sweeter expression or one more full of joy.

ROBERT McNAMARA

Monday, June 21, 1965, 12:15 P.M.

Now Robert Kennedy is turning against Johnson on Vietnam. In January, LBJ had considered RFK so hawkish that he worried the Senator might accuse him of betraying President Kennedy's commitment to Saigon.[1] But, unsettled by Rolling Thunder, in April RFK privately (and successfully) asked Johnson to consider a bombing halt. When the President asked for $700 million for Vietnam as a vote of confidence in his policies, a furious Kennedy thought Johnson was manipulating Congress. RFK voted for the bill but warned during a May 6 Senate speech[2] that his vote was no "blank check" for a wider war: Escalation in Vietnam would risk sending "hundreds of thousands of American troops" and "might easily lead to nuclear warfare."[3]

Johnson sees Kennedy's rising criticism as proof of his old anxiety that RFK will search for some pretext on which to break with him and challenge his leadership. Especially now, therefore, he worries about RFK's continuing friendships with McNamara, Bundy, Katzenbach, Goodwin, and other Kennedy holdovers in his administration. Years later Johnson said he wished he had cleaned house after the 1964 election and appointed people who owed him total loyalty.[4] As this conversation shows, LBJ resents McNamara's friendship with RFK, but he wants to exploit that friendship in an effort to keep Kennedy under control.

LBJ: I think that you ought to spend some time with your friend Mr. Kennedy. I don't want this repeated to him.[5] But . . . I think that he's functioning in this Vietnam field and Dominican field a little bit overtime. With he and some of his stooges very much against us. . . . His general feeling is that we should not have asked for the $700 million appropriation. . . . He wanted to demonstrate his independence. And while he wouldn't vote against it, he [made] the speech he did.[6] . . .

Certain Senators tell me that they talk to him in the cloakroom, and that they

---

1. See LBJ-McNamara conversation, January 13, 1965.

2. The same one in which he criticized LBJ's Dominican policies. (See headnote to LBJ-Humphrey conversation, May 4, 1965.)

3. See Schlesinger, *Robert Kennedy and His Times,* pp. 729–30.

4. Johnson confided this regret, for example, in 1970 to Vernon Jordan, then the new chief of the National Urban League, who related their conversation in 1997 to the author.

5. That LBJ considers it necessary to ask McNamara not to reveal a President's confidential conversation to his chief political enemy shows how much the friendship between RFK and McNamara, whom he otherwise trusts, unnerves him.

6. On May 6.

hear little snide remarks about the situation.[1] . . . Bobby's going to be in the background, because he operates . . . that way. But they're going to be asking for a new congressional debate [on Vietnam]. . . . Tell him that . . . we don't think it would be wise, but that we have asked Fulbright if he thinks we ought to have a new resolution [of support]. And we've asked Mansfield, . . . Dirksen, and . . . Russell. They are the men in this field in the Senate.[2] . . . I think you [also] ought to talk to him about the new [bombing] pause that's being proposed.[3] . . . We're afraid that if we do pause, we [get] hell knocked out of us. . . .

McNAMARA: Oh, I don't think now is the time.

LBJ: I just think that we ought to talk to him about it, because this is where most of our real trouble's coming from. . . . The real flare-up came on this statement[4] on this $700 million. . . . We don't object to McGovern and Church.[5] . . . We have never asked one Senator not to speak. And we haven't asked him. We put on a pause.[6] Let's see what else he thinks ought to be done. [But] I think that it's very potentially dangerous to our general cause on Vietnam.

In time, it's going to be like the Yale professors said.[7] It's going to be difficult for us to very long prosecute effectively a war that far away from home with the divisions we have here—and particularly the potential divisions. That's really had me concerned for a month. I'm very depressed about it. Because I see no program from either Defense or State that gives me much hope of doing anything, except just praying and gasping to hold on during monsoon and hope they'll quit.

I don't believe they're *ever* going to quit. And I don't see . . . that we have any . . . plan for a victory—militarily or diplomatically. . . . You and Dean [Rusk] have got to sit down and try to see if there's any people that we have in those departments that can give us any program or plan or hope. If not, we got to . . . have you . . . go out there and take one good look at it and say to these new people,[8] "Now you changed the government about the last time. And this is it. Call the Buddhists and the Catholics and the generals and everybody together and say we're going to do our best. And be sure they're willing to let new troops come in. Be sure they're not going to resent them. If not, why, you-all can run over us and have a government of your own choosing. But we just can't take these changes all the time."

---

1. Meaning LBJ's policies in Vietnam.
2. LBJ means that these Senators, unlike RFK, have commanding reputations on foreign policy.
3. McGeorge Bundy is proposing another pause, as is the *New York Times* in an editorial.
4. By Kennedy on May 6.
5. Senators George McGovern of South Dakota and Frank Church of Idaho, both Democratic critics on Vietnam.
6. As Kennedy had requested.
7. LBJ refers to Staughton Lynd, William Sloane Coffin, and other Yale professors who have come out against the war.
8. Generals Ky and Thieu, the new leaders in Saigon.

That's the Russell plan. Russell thinks we ought to take one of these changes [of government] to get out of there.[1] I don't think we can get out of there with our [SEATO] treaty like it is and with what all we've said. I think it would just lose us face in the world. I just shudder to think what [other countries] would say. . . . You . . . better talk to your military people. . . . Say . . . the President wants some kind of plan that gives us some hope of victory.

*   *   *

LBJ: [The North Vietnamese] just laugh at us. Ho Chi Minh and Chou En-lai both have made statements on this [Harold] Wilson mission, telling him to go to hell.[2]

McNAMARA: No indication they want to talk now. That's clear.

LBJ: I think Wilson will just screw up things more when he comes over here. . . . Couldn't we say, . . . "We're very anxious to work on this thing if you have any chance of seeing them at all. But if you don't, don't . . . just make a big speech dividing our country." . . .

McNAMARA: I don't think you can keep him out of here. . . . It would be awfully difficult for you to say, "You can't come here, unless you're going to be accepted in Hanoi and Peking."[3]

EDWIN WEISL

Monday, June 21, 1965, 12:39 P.M.

Johnson is having this well-connected lawyer and close friend track Robert Kennedy's every move. Weisl dislikes RFK even more than Johnson does. Johnson has put him in charge of all federal appointments in New York—a privilege that should normally have gone to Kennedy as the state's senior Democrat.[4] Now the President carps that Kennedy is spreading a false story that "key White House aides" are boosting Assistant Secretary of Labor Daniel Patrick Moynihan for Mayor of New York.[5] Johnson views Moynihan as a Kennedy man and is annoyed at the excessive public credit Moynihan had received for helping draft a major civil rights speech LBJ gave at Howard University in early June.[6] With his knack for mispronouncing the names of people at whom he is fuming, Johnson calls him "Monn-ihan."

---

1. Russell has been privately saying this to Johnson since May 1964, when he advised him to "get some fellow in there that said he wished to hell we would get out." (Beschloss, *Taking Charge,* p. 363.)

2. On June 17, at a British Commonwealth meeting, British Prime Minister Harold Wilson and three Commonwealth colleagues were authorized to contact the leaders of North and South Vietnam, China, the Soviet Union, and the United States in an effort to broker a Vietnam peace.

3. On June 22, Washington and Saigon publicly pretended to welcome a Wilson mission. But the gambit was rejected by Hanoi, Peking, and Moscow, which killed it.

4. See Schlesinger, *Robert Kennedy and His Times,* pp. 685–86.

5. *New York Times,* June 18, 1965. Moynihan was ultimately elected in 1976 to the late Robert Kennedy's New York Senate seat.

6. See Godfrey Hodgson, *The Gentleman from New York* (Houghton Mifflin, 2000), pp. 108–9.

LBJ: A little mean story this morning. . . . I think it's released by Bobby Kennedy. . . . Saying the White House is doing this and . . . doing that. I haven't . . . talked to one human. . . . I haven't talked to Bobby. . . . What about . . . this man Monn-ihan that Bobby is running?

WEISL: Nobody ever heard of him.

LBJ: . . . Arthur Schlesinger had a big dinner . . . last week, in which . . . Bobby Kennedy and Dick Goodwin . . . and the Averell Harrimans[1] . . . all agreed that this Monn-ihan was quite a fellow.[2] [They told] Mary McGrory, who is Irish Catholic like he is, . . . and she wrote a big story.[3] . . . We called [a reporter] and told him that . . . nobody over here [in the White House] is supporting him. . . . How's Bobby's standing up there?

WEISL: It's on the downslide.

GEORGE BALL

Tuesday, June 22, 1965, 10:15 A.M.

> With his increasing doubts about the loyalty of those around him, LBJ asks his number-two man at the State Department about what he considers a hostile comment made by his speechwriter Richard Goodwin.

LBJ: Dean [Rusk] distressed me some yesterday by telling me that Dick Goodwin had [told] you . . . about our Dominican policy, . . . "You made a fine argument for a very poor objective." . . .

BALL: I didn't mean that he should repeat that, Mr. President. It was said more or less in jest. . . .

LBJ: What I wanted to do is just find out. I don't even intend to mention it to him. But . . . I don't want anybody in the White House speaking up, taking issue, or arguing with my Cabinet officers. . . . I have some reservation about boys over here not always agreeing with our policy. If they don't, I'd like to know it. . . .

BALL: The subject came up . . . at Kay Graham's[4] house [over] dinner. . . . This was a kind of half-humorous remark. . . .

LBJ: Said it in front of . . . other people? . . .

---

1. Harriman was a former New York Governor and an RFK friend.

2. By Moynihan's memory, the dinner was actually at Harriman's house. (Hodgson, *Gentleman from New York,* p. 105.)

3. In the *Washington Star,* June 20, 1965.

4. President of the Washington Post Company and widow of Johnson's close friend Philip Graham, Katharine Graham has exasperated LBJ with *Washington Post* coverage that he considers more hostile than it would have been were her husband still alive. He increasingly sees her as the doyenne of the Georgetown-Kennedy crowd that makes him so anxious and angry. (See Graham, *Personal History,* pp. 398–402.)

BALL: I guess there were other people that overheard it. . . . I didn't want to [get him] in trouble, and I'm sorry.

LBJ: Oh, you're not getting him in trouble. He's leaving [after] the summer.

McGEORGE BUNDY

Wednesday, June 23, 1965, 10:58 A.M.

> Today Robert Kennedy is making his first major speech in the Senate—on the spread of nuclear weapons. At LBJ's behest, Bundy and his staff have scrutinized the advance text to discover whether it exploits classified information on nuclear proliferation that might have been leaked to RFK by Johnson officials. With his increasing suspicions of his people who socialize with RFK, Johnson wonders whether they are handing him government secrets for use against their boss.

BUNDY: You got the analysis of the Kennedy speech . . . I sent last night. . . . There are one or two things that ought not to have been out of the Executive circle that aren't terribly big but that were in secret memos to you and . . . were really in-house stuff. . . .

LBJ: . . . We were told by a newspaperman about a week ago that the Senator had the Gilpatric report[1] and was going to . . . make a speech on it. That he wanted to establish an independent posture. That he'd like to find something that he could disagree [with me] on. [As] "a matter of principle." . . . I didn't say anything about it because I didn't care. . . . I did not see anything in it that hurt us. I believe that if it were a Communist agent or editor or Alsop[2] or an enemy—incidentally, I hope you'll see what Alsop's writing and write it down, because that's your old friend.[3] . . . I don't know what criteria you use for those friendships, but he's my old friend too. I never heard of the stuff that he's talking about as B-52.[4] . . . I think it's blackmail. . . . Pure blackmail. I think he wants some secrets that he's not getting. And . . . Johnson does not feel that the war plans ought to be turned over to the Alsops. . . . As long as you're associated with me, what you say to him oughtn't to be anything, except what I think ought to be said to him. . . .

BUNDY: . . . There have been periods when I wouldn't see Joe for that reason. . . .

LBJ: These people that really destroy us, I would say my people spend half the

---

1. Drafted by a top-secret panel on the spread of nuclear weapons appointed by LBJ in November 1964 and chaired by former Deputy Secretary of Defense Roswell Gilpatric.
2. The columnist Joseph Alsop.
3. Bundy had followed Alsop to Groton and Yale.
4. This morning, Alsop had called the first use of B-52s in Vietnam, on June 17, a "public relations stunt" and said that under LBJ "informing the American public has become a high crime." (*Washington Post,* June 23, 1965.)

days with them. . . . The other day . . . the *New York Times* spent four hours and twenty-five minutes . . . with my people.[1] Preparing to castrate me. . . . I issued instructions to nobody in my office to ever talk to Teddy White because he was not a man that would tell the truth. . . . Yet they all sat around and talked to him.[2]

McGEORGE BUNDY

Thursday, June 24, 1965, 10:00 A.M.

Johnson had planned to include dramatic proposals to reduce nuclear proliferation, based on the secret Gilpatric report, in a speech for the twentieth anniversary of the United Nations in San Francisco. Worried that he will seem to be aping Robert Kennedy, he orders all such references removed from his address. He also shows the dread of newspaper leaks and hidden foes in his midst that will cause him to narrow his circle of advice.

LBJ: I do not want to get into proliferation in any way so it looks like I'm copying . . . Bobby. . . .
BUNDY: . . . The damned nuisance about it is that . . . people will play it as if this was something he prodded us into.

*   *   *

LBJ: The newspaper boys have been trying to make something of a fight out of the Dominican Republic.[3] . . . That's Bobby's line. . . . One of the New York reporters tells me that . . . [Bobby] wants to do a little needling. . . . Brings him a little recognition. . . . And that he wants to develop a little independent stance in these things. I think . . . we ought to . . . let the peace lovers get onboard with Bobby. . . . Now . . . the one thing that I would like to have in the speech . . . if it didn't knock off or throw overboard the South Vietnamese, if it didn't harden things up . . . with Russia, I would like to . . . ask the United Nations to call in all parties and try to find a resolution to this thing. . . . I'd go just as far as we conceivably could with demagoguery.[4] Assuming that they're not going to do any of it. But if they did—
BUNDY: We could live with it.
LBJ: We could live with it. . . . If they say I'm a hypocrite, well . . . that's the

---

1. LBJ tried to monitor how much time people on his staff spent with which reporters.
2. The previous day, the *New York Times* reported that White's new book, *The Making of the President: 1964* (Atheneum, 1965), revealed that, during the talk in which LBJ told him he would not be Vice President, RFK had been "restrained" because he suspected the conversation was being secretly taped—and that Johnson leaked the private conversation, complete with insulting impersonation of Kennedy, to reporters. (See Beschloss, *Taking Charge,* pp. 476–88).
3. RFK's barbs at Johnson's performance in the Dominican crisis.
4. "Demagoguery" is Johnson's word for rhetoric offered mainly for public consumption.

word I hate more than any other word. If you ever want to call me something, just say I'm a hypocrite, and that'll ruin me. But I'd say the same thing about the unconditional discussions . . . [and] the [bombing] pause.

*   *   *

LBJ: Now we've got another leak. . . . Cy Vance[1] was . . . real disturbed . . . when the story Saturday morning [said] that the State Department had said that this [B-52] raid was a farce.[2] . . . I asked Bill Bundy . . . [to] look into it. He and Vance talked further during the day. But now that one conversation with Bill Bundy is known to Rowland Evans.[3]

BUNDY: Oh, God!

LBJ: Now, that means I can't talk to Rusk and . . . I can't talk to Bill Bundy. I don't think I can talk to George Ball because I told him that Dick Goodwin was resigning and an hour later Carroll Kirkpatrick[4] called Dick Goodwin and asked him. . . . So that narrows me down in my State Department. . . . So we just have to just, I guess, act without it. It's a hell of a note that you have to [circumvent the State Department]. . . . Don't repeat it to anybody, but that's how dangerous our State Department thing is now.

CYRUS VANCE

Thursday, June 24, 1965, 10:20 A.M.

> Inflamed by the hostile stories about the B-52 raid, Johnson orders his Deputy Secretary of Defense to take drastic action against leakers on Vietnam.

LBJ: I think no President ever encouraged your saying more to the press. But so far as a guy promoting himself by talking to some columnist and buying some insurance and leaking something . . . I have utter contempt. I'd rather have resignations in a bloc from all the Joint Chiefs and Secretaries concerned than have one of them give one figure to Marquis Childs[5] that's not available to other people. . . . We've got the best bunch of leakers you ever saw over here. I've got them in surplus. If I need anything leaked, *I'll* leak it. But I sure as hell don't want my Joint Chiefs leaking it!. . . .

VANCE: Right, sir.

LBJ: . . . You and Bob [McNamara] ought to study [what] is the smart, wise, tough

---

1. Deputy Secretary of Defense.
2. On June 19 the *New York Times* reported that State Department officials felt that the B-52 raid had been a "humiliating failure."
3. The columnist.
4. Carroll Kilpatrick was a *Washington Post* reporter. Once again LBJ mangles the name of someone on his bad list.
5. A columnist and Washington correspondent for the *St. Louis Post-Dispatch*.

way to handle this. . . . Do just whatever you're willing to do to put these leaks at a minimum. And that means Marguerite Higgins and that means Peter Lisagor.[1] That means Rowland Evans, and that *particularly* means Joe Alsop and Scotty Reston. . . . That doesn't mean that everybody shouldn't see them. . . . See them. Tell them nothing. Smile. . . . That's what I do when Reston comes to see me. . . . He can't get mad because I didn't tell him something. I have seen him. But I don't allow myself to arm the man who is going to shoot me with the pistol and with the cartridges. . . . And if *I* go down, why, it's not going to look very good on you-all's part.

VANCE: Absolutely, sir.

LBJ: . . . I'm going to start [with the] State Department, if I have to fire everybody. I told Rusk that yesterday. . . . I'd rather have a one-eyed farmer as Secretary of State than, by God, a fellow that I can't write a memo to without having it in the front page of the [*New York*] *Times*.

GERALD GRIFFIN

Editorial Page Editor, Baltimore Sun
Thursday, June 24, 1965, 4:55 P.M.

> The *Baltimore Sun* has reported that LBJ's speech for the UN's twentieth anniversary in San Francisco will include proposals to reduce nuclear proliferation. Johnson calls to deny it, falsely claiming that there never was such a plan.

LBJ: My favorite paper this morning says that I'm making a major speech that . . . will involve a lot of new and dramatic proposals. I have no such thing in mind. Never have. It's off the top of somebody's head. My guess is that some of the boys in . . . [the] UN or some of the former Kennedy lobbyists . . . wanted to get ideas [into the speech] . . . Now they're going to say I'm a flop. I'm not doing any of it. I don't think that a birthday party[2] . . . is any place for me to announce what [our] program is going to be in the year 2000. . . . I've got a good many proposals [already] on the table . . . which Bobby Kennedy copied yesterday in his speech. . . .

---

1. The longtime *New York Herald Tribune* correspondent and the *Chicago Daily News* Washington bureau chief. On June 4, LBJ had complained to J. Edgar Hoover about a Lisagor story of the previous day revealing that the Soviets had put IL-28 jet bombers into North Vietnam, prompting the "most serious discussion within the administration on what the Soviet action portends and how it should be met." Johnson said that the IL-28s were known only to Rusk, McNamara, Thomas Mann, and the Joint Chiefs. He wanted the FBI to investigate. The FBI reported back that Lisagor had gotten the information from Higgins, whose "reputation is spotty" and whom colleagues, it said, called "mattress-back Maggie." She had "probably" obtained the information from her husband, retired Lieutenant General William Hall, who had "high-ranking connections . . . among the Joint Chiefs of Staff," and given it to Lisagor, to whom she was "very close." (C. D. DeLoach to John Mohr, June 4, 1965, Lyndon Johnson file, FBI.)
2. Referring to the anniversary celebration.

GRIFFIN: I thought they looked familiar.

LBJ: . . . I make such a fetish of never being inaccurate with you-all that I wanted you to know the facts. I don't want anybody, though, to say I'm calling an editor. . . . I don't care if you want to run an ad saying, "We predict Johnson will pull off his britches and walk down the Cow Palace." But I just tell you I'm not going to. . . . I don't want the *Baltimore Sun* to . . . make a big prediction that I'm going to walk down the street nekkid. . . . What I'm really afraid of [is] that Scotty [Reston] and maybe Walter Lippmann [1] will come out with a column saying, "We are looking [at] Johnson [to] see what kind of leadership he gives us." . . . Then when I just say, "Happy Birthday," they'll say, "God, he was disappointing, wasn't he!" . . . When somebody plants something with you, you-all are being used. Just like a twenty-one-year-old girl somebody wants to sleep with.

WILLARD WIRTZ

Thursday, June 24, 1965, 5:30 P.M.

> Johnson complains to his Secretary of Labor about criticism from Robert Kennedy and Arthur Schlesinger, Jr., including the charge that the President is increasingly refusing to consult people who disagree with him.

LBJ: Arthur . . . clips us all the time on foreign policy, and I don't know why. . . . I'm trying to carry out what I found here the best I can. . . . The same people are making decisions [as did under President Kennedy]. Same ones working faithfully and killing themselves. And he and Bobby both clip us. I don't know how to stop it. . . . I don't want to fight with them. I don't want the Democratic party divided in two camps. I'm not a Goldwater, but they try to picture us that way.

WIRTZ: That would not be Arthur's view. . . . He would think he's rather an ambassador to the intellectuals. . . .

LBJ: . . . I see him talking to the Senators who are clipping us and cutting us all the time, and I think he's the fountainhead of some of it. . . . Why don't you some night sit down— Don't tell him you've talked to me, but just try to find out . . . where he thinks we are in error. . . . I don't know of a goddamned President in the history of Arthur Schlesinger's lifetime that's done as much in the domestic front as we have.

---

1. Columnists.

MIKE MANSFIELD

Saturday, June 26, 1965, 7:38 A.M.

Johnson had agreed to UN Ambassador Adlai Stevenson's request to announce a new American position on UN financing, suggested by Stevenson, in his San Francisco speech.[1] Then he reneged after someone—he suspected a Stevenson aide—leaked the news to the *New York Times*. One of Stevenson's friends recalled that the Ambassador felt "betrayed." Porter McKeever, a Stevenson biographer, wrote, "Adlai's humiliation was apparent to all."[2]

After complaining about Stevenson, Johnson exaggerates to Senator Mansfield his hopes that the Vietnam problem can be solved by a negotiated settlement. Dealing with Mansfield is among LBJ's many lamentations about his lot in life. "Why do I have to have a saint for Majority Leader?" he once asked. "Why can't I have a politician?"[3]

LBJ: They were very anxious, Stevenson and Cleveland,[4] for me to make a proposal . . . that we would . . . not require the Russians and the French to kick in their share. . . . I told them it wasn't a matter to be debated at an anniversary party. . . . Stevenson is demanding overnight[5] that he be permitted to do it, and I turned him down.

* * *

LBJ: Now what about Vietnam? . . .

MANSFIELD: . . . It appears to me that this fellow Ky . . . is starting off on the wrong foot with those executions in the public square and cutting down on the newspapers. He's starting out on the right foot in trying to root out profiteers.[6]

LBJ: And was wrong in canceling recognition of France, wasn't he?[7] . . . We begged him not to.

MANSFIELD: . . . It's a sign of instability on his part. For us it's going to be nothing but trouble.

---

1. Worried that the UN General Assembly would grind to a halt, Stevenson had asked LBJ not to insist on the literal application of Article 19 of the UN Charter, which would deprive the Soviet Union, France, and much of the Eastern European bloc of their votes in the General Assembly because their dues had not been fully paid. The dispute was threatening to break up the United Nations.

2. See Porter McKeever, *Adlai Stevenson* (Morrow, 1989), p. 557; and John Bartlow Martin, *Adlai Stevenson and the World* (Doubleday, 1977), pp. 854–55.

3. Quoted in Califano, *The Triumph and Tragedy of Lyndon Johnson,* p. 44.

4. Harlan Cleveland, Assistant Secretary of State for International Organizations.

5. In a cable to Johnson.

6. On June 16 the Ky-Thieu regime announced that suspected corrupt officials and black marketers would be shot to death in the central Saigon marketplace. Vietnamese-language newspapers in the city were shut down.

7. On June 24 the Saigon government broke diplomatic relations with France, charging that President Charles de Gaulle had abetted its enemies.

LBJ: We're afraid of that.

MANSFIELD: I'm afraid, Mr. President, that eventually some government in Saigon is going to have to enter into negotiations with the Vietcong.

LBJ: Would that be the worst thing that could happen to us?

MANSFIELD: No, sir.

LBJ: Looks to me like that if they just keep on and keep on and keep on, and we can't get a government that we can support, and we can't get a strategy that'll win, and we can't get enough people to protect it, looks like ultimately that might be forced upon us. . . . We're anxious to talk to anybody. [But] we don't want to make this [South Vietnamese] government fall again. . . . Frankly, this is between us, but U Thant[1] . . . thinks that . . . he may be able to shove and push . . . to make Hanoi talk to somebody. Not Ho Chi Minh himself, but somebody lower. . . . I told him Averell Harriman[2] was sitting in an airplane and would talk to anybody anytime. . . . [U Thant] thinks that the Chinese won't give an inch. He thinks the Russians really want to be friends and sign up with us on this, but they, in the public eye, haven't got to that point. . . . He thinks if we would be a little bit reasonable with our demands, and could work out something with Hanoi, that Hanoi would rather go to Russia, and Russia would rather go with us and isolate China.

ABE FORTAS

Monday, June 28, 1965, 3:00 P.M.

> Johnson renews his objections to government wiretapping and complains that Robert Kennedy is orchestrating left-wing critics and JFK holdovers at State and Justice to cause him trouble.

LBJ: Senator Long[3] tells me he's going to carry a series of hearings around the country about the Internal Revenue [Service] tapping people's wires. . . . I've told them every time I seen them that if I ever caught them doing that, it'd be too bad. I'm just wondering if you wouldn't, [in] the next day or two, just say [to the Internal Revenue people], "Confirming our many previous conversations, I want you to know once and for all that I want anybody fired that even proposes a wiretap." . . . They had microphones in Senators' hotel rooms and stuff like that out in Las Vegas. . . . I don't want a wiretap anywhere.

*   *   *

LBJ: I know you don't believe this much, [but there is a] real left-wing group that [is] not overly worked up about our flag or soldiers. . . . The Lippmann type that's

---

1. UN Secretary-General.
2. Ambassador-at-Large.
3. Russell Long of Louisiana.

been associated with every [leftist] organization there was in his days.[1] Teddy White . . . is a very bad actor. It got so damn bad that Luce had to let him go.[2] They are being used by this fellow[3] very effectively and not a thing we can do about it. . . . I'm getting a little uncomfortable about some of the people around us. Particularly the State Department, where I see it every day. A little bit in the Justice Department. . . . They slipped over a letter for me to sign, asking Archibald Cox to stay on as Solicitor [General], saying he's the best one they've ever had.[4] . . . He was just Kennedy's clerk from Massachusetts. . . . I worked with him up in the Senate. . . . I didn't think he was too damn effective. . . . I see no reason why we got to keep the top man with a law job in the country for one of Kennedy's professors.[5]

* * *

LBJ: The [people in the State Department] just screw me to death. . . . Harlan Cleveland [is] not my friend. He's really against me. He cuts me all day long. . . . As soon as he writes a memorandum, he calls in Scotty Reston. He and Stevenson both give all kinds of backgrounders of what I'm going to say . . . and I've never heard of it, and then I don't say it and they say, Well, they're all disappointed. . . . Both of them just cut me to pieces.[6] . . . Stevenson, I'm sure, is going to quit.

DEAN RUSK

Tuesday, June 29, 1965, 4:32 P.M.

> Stevenson has reproached LBJ for cutting his ideas about UN financing, nuclear proliferation, and Vietnam out of his address at the UN's twentieth-anniversary celebration in San Francisco.

LBJ: How much static are you getting from Adlai these days about [my] not saying what he wanted to? . . . He spent about an hour with me trying to get me to go on and say that we had retreated from our position, and I just wouldn't give an inch.

---

1. Johnson exaggerates the columnist's progressive youth.
2. Theodore White left Henry Luce's Time-Life organization over their disagreements about Communist China.
3. Robert Kennedy.
4. Cox, as a Harvard Law professor, had coordinated academic advice to JFK during the 1960 campaign. (In 1973 he was fired by President Richard Nixon as special Watergate prosecutor.)
5. LBJ has Judge Thurgood Marshall in mind for Cox's job. Marshall would be the first black Solicitor General. See July 7, 1965, below.
6. Johnson refers to his suspicions that Stevenson's colleagues had leaked to the *New York Times* what he would say in San Francisco and the UN Ambassador's irritation when, as a result, LBJ took those passages out of his speech.

RUSK: There are some differences between Adlai and me on this. We've had a tussle on this for some time.

LBJ: I know it. And he makes that clear every time I see him. . . .

RUSK: . . . Adlai is usually ready to throw in the deck of cards right away . . . [when] everybody wants us to move [and] the Soviets won't move.

HALE BOGGS

Congressman from Louisiana and Majority Whip, House of Representatives
Wednesday, June 30, 1965, 6:55 P.M.

> Johnson has narrowly escaped a House defeat of his bill to provide rent subsidies for certain needy families, which Republicans denounced as a "socialistic" attempt to "change the social and living patterns of America." To LBJ, the near-defeat is an early warning sign of the backlash he has anticipated from members of Congress he has shoved and pressured to pass his Great Society and civil rights laws.

LBJ: Good job!

BOGGS: God bless you. It was a miracle. . . .

LBJ: . . . It was pretty close, wasn't it?

BOGGS: Mr. President, this was the roughest one we've had this year.

ROBERT McNAMARA

Wednesday, June 30, 1965, 7:35 P.M.

> Johnson asks his Defense Secretary to intervene with his friend Robert Kennedy and other Senate critics on Vietnam.

LBJ: You've got to sit down and talk to Bobby. He's getting ready to tour Latin America. And you've got to sell the liberal bloc [in the Senate] on "You cannot run out [of] there [in Vietnam] and you can't stay there without [more] people. You've got to back these men." So that he doesn't get off on a tangent again.

McNAMARA: . . . I'll get ahold of him tonight.

LBJ: You just got to have a serious talk with him. Go over the figures and . . . facts. Tell him that . . . you presented [the situation in Vietnam] . . . to Eisen-hower[1] . . . and that you just can't find anybody who thinks we ought to leave

---

1. Over luncheon in the mansion that day, along with General Earle Wheeler and Senator Dirksen.

these boys out there and do nothing. And we can't give up. I don't see anything to do except give them what they need, Bob. Do you?

McNAMARA: Mr. President, I'm very much of that frame of mind. I must tell you I don't think others in your government are. . . . But Cy [Vance] and I feel very strongly on that point. We want you to be sure that you see the full risk of this. It is a very heavy risk. But that's my vote.

LBJ: I don't believe it is as big a risk as walking out.

McNAMARA: Neither do we.

LBJ: Now, what are the alternatives?

McNAMARA: . . . The alternative is to go in in a half-assed way.

LBJ: I think we'll get wrecked doing that.

McNAMARA: I went through the Bay of Pigs, and I'm responsible in part for that.[1] And we were wrong not because we did what we did. We were wrong because we failed.

LBJ: That's right.

LADY BIRD JOHNSON

Wednesday, June 30, 1965, Tape-recorded Diary

> While LBJ and McNamara discussed their options in Vietnam with Dwight Eisenhower over lunch in the White House family quarters, Mrs. Johnson encountered Bethine Church, wife of the antiwar Democratic Senator Frank Church of Idaho, at a White House reception honoring LBJ's new program for the early education of poor children, Project Head Start. Lady Bird knows that her husband is approaching a crossroads in Vietnam.

LADY BIRD: I am always happy to see her. But the shadow of Frank's strong dissent on Lyndon's position on Vietnam does fall between us.[2] . . . Lyndon was upstairs, having a very small lunch with General Eisenhower. He's been mighty helpful to him. . . . I know the grist for their mill. It could only be serious and bad.

---

1. As Defense Secretary, McNamara was involved in the humiliating failure of JFK's effort to use CIA-backed Cuban exiles to retake Cuba in April 1961.

2. Four days earlier Senator Church had denounced the Vietnam War as a struggle between "rotten dictatorships" in Hanoi and Saigon.

Chapter Ten

"WE KNOW IT'S GOING TO BE BAD"

We know ourselves, in our own conscience, that when we asked for this [Gulf of Tonkin] resolution, we had no intention of committing this many ground troops. We're doing so now, and we know it's going to be bad. And the question is, Do we just want to do it out on a limb by ourselves? I don't know whether those [Pentagon] men have ever [calculated] whether we can win with the kind of training we have, the kind of power, and ... whether we can have a united support at home.

LBJ *to* ROBERT McNAMARA, *July 2, 1965*

BILL MOYERS

Thursday, July 1, 1965, 9:55 A.M.

By July, Bill Moyers was worried about what he considered the President's psychological and emotional deterioration. He recalled that, even during the best of times, LBJ had been prone to paranoid outbursts and depression. But "it was never more pronounced than in 1965, when he was leading up to the decision about the buildup in Vietnam." Years later Moyers told the historian Robert Dallek that Johnson's depression came from "the realization, about which he was clearer than anyone, that this was a road from which there was no turning back."

As Moyers recalled, LBJ knew that his decision to send large numbers of ground troops to Vietnam would likely mean "the end of his Presidency. . . . It was a pronounced, prolonged depression. He would just go within himself, just disappear—morose, self-pitying, angry. . . . He was a tormented man." One day, lying in bed with the covers almost over his head, Johnson told Moyers that he felt as if he was in a Louisiana swamp "that's pulling me down."

Moyers recalled that he was so troubled by the President's "paranoia," which made him "irascible" and "suspicious," that he even went to see Lady Bird: "I came away from it knowing that she herself was more concerned, because she was more routinely and regularly exposed to it." Moyers got calls from "Cabinet officers and others" who were "deeply concerned about his behavior." He noted that

378

one day the President would be in severe depression. Then, "twenty-four hours later, no one who had seen him this way would ever have suspected it." LBJ would convince himself that he could win the war. Or the passage of a bill would "be an antidote." But when Johnson returned to the problems in Vietnam, the "cloud in his eyes" and the "predictably unpredictable behavior" would reappear.[1]

Both Moyers and Richard Goodwin independently confided their worries about LBJ's mood swings to psychiatrists. As Goodwin recalled, one doctor told him that the President's "disintegration could continue . . . or recede, depending on the strength of Johnson's resistance and, more significantly, on the direction of . . . the war, the crumbling public support, whose pressures were dissolving Johnson's confidence in his ability to control events."[2]

Stung by ridicule for ducking out of the Vietnam teach-in of May, McGeorge Bundy arranged to debate Professor Hans Morgenthau on television in late June. Once again he was defying the President's wishes. A furious LBJ told Moyers, "Bill, I want you to go to Bundy and tell him the President would be pleased, mighty pleased, to accept his resignation." Startled, Moyers did not reply. "That's the trouble with all you fellows," Johnson carped. "You're in bed with the Kennedys."[3] Moyers lunched with Bundy to convey the President's annoyance with his debate and other speeches Bundy planned to deliver. Now he reports back to Johnson, who tells him that the real problem is that Bundy has been co-opted by the Kennedys.

MOYERS: He knew that he had . . . gone against the President's . . . wishes on these speeches. But he reiterated to me . . . "my honest understanding of the President's desire, stated three or four months ago, to make some speeches in the right way." . . . He . . . felt it was good to take some of the . . . criticism from the liberal community . . . away from the President and attach it to him. . . . As best I could tell, Bundy was trying to say to me, "Look, if the President has any idea that anything's wrong with me . . . there's not. . . . I'm very happy in my job." . . .

LBJ: You see, they [Robert Kennedy and his circle] would naturally talk to Bundy, and to Larry, and to Dick.[4] . . . That's where they would start. Then they'd take on . . . people . . . like Cater. Maybe Harry.[5] They're kind of liberal and on the fringe, and not known as tied too closely [with me]. And then move in. I would imagine, though, that this started with Bundy. Because he's had to be sat down a time or two. . . . The other day . . . he insisted on bringing up the Javits resolu-

---

1. See Dallek, *Flawed Giant*, pp. 281–84.

2. Goodwin, *Remembering America*, p. 403. One of those consulted was Dr. Joseph English, chief psychiatrist of the Peace Corps, who recalled telling Goodwin and another Johnson aide that it would be "an ethical violation" for a psychiatrist to give an opinion in the absence of "a full clinical evaluation." (Quoted in James Toole and Robert Joynt, eds., *Presidential Disability*, University of Rochester, 2001, pp. 292–3.)

3. See Bird, *The Color of Truth*, pp. 320–23; and Goodwin, *Remembering America*, p. 400.

4. The congressional liaison Lawrence O'Brien and the speechwriter Richard Goodwin, because they and Bundy were Kennedy men who maintained friendships with RFK.

5. Johnson's aides Douglass Cater and Harry McPherson.

tion.[1] I said, "No, I'll think about that." He said, "We've got to decide it." . . . I just had to finally just really embarrass him and say, . . . "I told you two or three times, quit that! Let's go on to the agenda." . . . It was rather rough. . . . You can see the crowd that's doing this. Bobby's going to Latin America now.[2] He's got Gilpatric working for him. You saw the Gilpatric story in the *New York Times* this morning.[3] That's not accidental.

MOYERS: I saw that. Of course, I think there's a lot can be done with just more candidness. I think that's our basic problem, as I have mentioned to you before. Our image is due . . . primarily to their interpretation of our being overly secretive. I just think more candid and sincere discussion—

LBJ: And I just think you ought to say that—on Jack's speech[4]—that you know that it's amusing to some of them that a man should have this affection for another man. But . . . if they will look at anyone who has been with me twenty-five years . . . John Connally . . . Walter Jenkins . . . all of them have this feeling. And that you have it. And that as far as this business of saying somebody's a "messenger boy," you just have never heard that. You have always given your honest opinion, and a good many times you've been vetoed. But . . . at thirty years old, you have made more big decisions that have been approved by the President than would have been approved if you had been working for AT&T.

MOYERS: Which is true.

LBJ: . . . Just say, "Now I know I'm not supposed to be a Sorensen,[5] but Sorensen went much stronger than Jack [Valenti] did. He said that Kennedy[6] was Christ." Compared him to Christ! But . . . they had a better feeling for Kennedy than they do [us]. And they've never liked Jack because they feel Jack is a personal servant of mine. And he is wonderful for me. He is not irritating to me. He's pleasant. He's soft. I think Buz is good for me. I think Harry is awfully good for me. I don't have men that clash with me? Marvin just says every day, "Mr. President, I don't think we ought to do this." But he does it in a nice, kind way.[7]

---

1. New York Republican Senator Jacob Javits had said that the Gulf of Tonkin Resolution was "outdated," not enough of a mandate for a possible major conflict: "Neither is a Gallup Poll." He wanted Congress to debate a new resolution, to answer "nagging and worrisome" questions before any serious escalation began in Vietnam. (*New York Times,* June 25, 1965.)

2. In November. LBJ took this as an effort by RFK to improve his foreign policy credentials to run for President.

3. Noting that RFK but not Johnson had promoted the recommendations of the report on nuclear proliferation by Roswell Gilpatric, who as JFK's Deputy Secretary of Defense had been close to both John and Jacqueline Kennedy (whom, after she was a widow, Gilpatric dated).

4. In a Boston speech Jack Valenti had called LBJ a "sensitive" and "cultivated" man, adding, "I sleep each night a little better because Lyndon Johnson is my President," thereby eliciting criticism that LBJ was surrounded with "yes-men" and "messenger boys."

5. JFK's aide and speechwriter Theodore Sorensen.

6. President Kennedy.

7. LBJ refers to his aides Horace Busby, Harry McPherson, and Marvin Watson. He need not mention that all are Johnson men, not Kennedy holdovers.

ROBERT McNAMARA

Friday, July 2, 1965, 8:41 A.M.

> Johnson must now decide among three main proposals for the American future in Vietnam. McNamara wants a serious escalation. George Ball wants to negotiate withdrawal. William Bundy is for "holding on" at present force levels but using American troops for more aggressive "search and destroy" missions, which, if successful, could lead to more U.S. ground troops. McGeorge Bundy wrote LBJ on July 1, "My hunch is that you will want to listen hard to George Ball and then reject his proposal. Discussion could then move to the narrow choice between my brother's choice and McNamara's. The decision between them should be made in about ten days."[1]

LBJ: I'm pretty depressed reading all these proposals. They're tough, aren't they?

McNAMARA: They are. . . . But we're at a point of a fairly tough decision, Mr. President. . . . We purposely made no effort to compromise any of our views. . . .

LBJ: Two or three things that I want you to explore. First, assuming we do everything we can, to the extent of our resources, can we really have any assurance that we win? I mean, assuming we have all the big bombers and all the powerful payloads and everything else, can the Vietcong come in and tear us up and continue this thing indefinitely, and never really bring it to an end? . . . Second, . . . can we really, without getting any further authority from the Congress, have . . . sufficient, overwhelming [domestic] support to . . . fight successfully? . . . You know the friend you talked to about the pause [Robert Kennedy].[2] You know the Mansfields. You know the Clarks.[3] And those men carry a good deal of weight. And this fellow we talked to the other day here at lunch has a good deal of weight. . . . He's got cancer, in my judgment. I've never told anybody, but I saw him yesterday coughing several times.[4]

McNAMARA: He doesn't look good.

LBJ: He went home that very day and he hasn't been back since. Had a stomach upset. He can't carry on much for us. We have to rely on the younger crowd. . . . The McGoverns and the Clarks and the other folks. . . . If you don't ask them, I think you'd have a long debate about not having asked them, with this kind of a

---

1. See *FRUS*, vol. 3, pp. 117–18.
2. In April, RFK had helped persuade LBJ to try a bombing pause in Vietnam.
3. Senate doves.
4. Johnson is probably talking about Senator Everett Dirksen, who lunched with LBJ, McNamara, and Eisenhower on June 30. When Dirksen, a chain smoker, died in 1969, he was indeed suffering from emphysema and probable lung cancer. (Byron Hulsey, *Everett Dirksen and His Presidents*, University Press of Kansas, 2000, p. 272.)

commitment. Even though there's some record behind us, we know ourselves, in our own conscience, that when we asked for this resolution,[1] we had no intention of committing this many ground troops. We're doing so now, and we know it's going to be bad. And the question is, Do we just want to do it out on a limb by ourselves? I don't know whether those [Pentagon] men have ever [calculated] whether we can win with the kind of training we have, the kind of power, and . . . whether we can have a united support at home.

McNAMARA: . . . If we do go as far as my paper suggested, sending numbers of men out there, we ought to call up Reserves. You have authority to do that without additional legislation. But . . . almost surely, if we called up Reserves, you would want to go to the Congress to get additional authority. . . . Yes, it also might lead to an extended debate and divisive statements. I think we could avoid that. I really think if we were to go to the Clarks and the McGoverns and the Churches and say to them, "Now, this is our situation. We cannot win with our existing commitment. We must increase it if we're going to win, and [with] this limited term that we define [and] limited way we define 'win,' it requires additional troops. Along with that approach, we are . . . continuing this political initiative to probe for a willingness to negotiate a reasonable settlement here. And we ask your support." . . . I think you'd get it. . . . And that's a vehicle by which you both get the authority to call up the Reserves and also tie them into the whole program.

LBJ: That makes sense.

McNAMARA: I don't know that you want to go that far. I'm not pressing you to. It's my judgment you should, but my judgment may be in error here. . . .

LBJ: Does Rusk generally agree with you?

McNAMARA: . . . He very definitely does. He's a hard-liner on this, in the sense that he doesn't want to give up South Vietnam under any circumstances. Even if it means going to general war.[2] Now, he doesn't think we ought to go to general war. He thinks we ought to try to avoid it. But if that's what's required to hold South Vietnam, he would go to general war. He would say, as a footnote, "Military commanders always ask for all they need. For God's sakes, don't take what they request as an absolute, ironclad requirement." I don't disagree with that point . . . I do think . . . that this request[3] for thirty-four U.S. battalions and ten non-U.S., a total of forty-four battalions, comes pretty close to the minimum requirement. . . .

LBJ: When you put these people in and you really do go all out [and] you call up your Reserves and everything else, can you do anything to restore your communication and your railroads and your roads?[4] . . .

---

1. Gulf of Tonkin Resolution of August 1964.
2. Meaning World War III.
3. By General Westmoreland.
4. In South Vietnam.

McNAMARA: Yes, I think so. . . . By the end of the year, we ought to have that railroad[1] . . . and . . . the major highways opened. . . . The problem is you can't send an engineering company into an area . . . unless you send combat troops with them. And we just don't have the combat troops to do that. . . .

LBJ: What has happened out there in the last forty-eight hours? Looks like we killed six or seven hundred of them.[2]

McNAMARA: Yeah, we killed a large number, I'd say, over the last three or four days. . . . At least five hundred.

LBJ: . . . Can they continue losses like that?

McNAMARA: . . . Of the numbers that are killed by [U.S.] Air Force actions, and a great bulk of these people are killed that way, I would think that 75 percent are probably not from what we call the . . . guerrilla force.[3]

DWIGHT EISENHOWER

Friday, July 2, 1965, 11:02 A.M.

LBJ: I'm having a meeting this morning with my top people. . . . McNamara recommends really what Westmoreland and Wheeler[4] do—a quite expanded operation, and one that's really going to kick up some folks like Ford.[5] He says that he doesn't want to use ground troops. He thinks we ought to do it by bombing. We can't even protect our bases without the ground troops, according to Westmoreland. And we've got all the Bobby Kennedys and the Mansfields and the Morses against it. But [Westmoreland] recommends an all-out operation. We don't know whether we can beat them with that or not. The State Department comes in and recommends a rather modified one through the monsoon season, to see how effective we are with our B-52 strikes and with our other strikes. . . . Westmoreland has urged . . . about double what we've got there now. But if we do that, we've got to call up the Reserves and get authority from Congress. . . . That will really serve notice that we're in a land operation over there. Now, I guess it's your view that we ought to do that. You don't think that we can just have a holding operation, from a military standpoint, do you?

EISENHOWER: . . . You've got to go along with your military advisers, because otherwise you are just going to continue to have these casualties indefi-

---

1. Along the Vietnamese coast.
2. Meaning the enemy.
3. McNamara shows how difficult it is going to be to fight this war against Vietcong hiding in the jungle.
4. General Westmoreland, commander in South Vietnam, and Army Chief of Staff Earle Wheeler.
5. House Minority Leader Gerald Ford.

nitely. . . . My advice is, do what you have to do. I'm sorry that you have to go to the Congress . . . but I guess you would be calling up the Reserves.

LBJ: Yes, sir. We're out of them, you see. . . . And if they[1] move on other fronts, we'll have to increase our strength, too. . . . [The State Department says] we ought to avoid bombing Hanoi until we can see through the monsoon season whether, with these forces there, we can make any progress . . . before we go out and execute everything. Of course, McNamara's people recommend taking all the harbors. . . . Mining and blowing the hell out of it. . . . They go all out. State Department people say they're taking too much chance on bringing China in and Russia in. . . . They [want] to try . . . during the monsoon season to hold what [we've] got, and to really try to convince Russia that if she doesn't bring about some kind of understanding, we're going to have to give them the works. But they believe that she doesn't really want an all-out war.

EISENHOWER: . . . [For them to] agree to some kind of negotiation . . . [you must say,] "Hell, we're going to end this and win this thing. . . . We don't intend to fail." . . .

LBJ: You think that we can really beat the Vietcong out there?

EISENHOWER: . . . This is the hardest thing [to decide,] because we can't finally find out how many of these Vietcong have been imported down there and how many of them are just rebels.

LBJ: We killed twenty-six thousand [Vietcong] this year. . . . Three hundred yesterday. . . . Two hundred and fifty of them the day before. But they just keep coming in from North Vietnam. . . . How many they're going to pour in from China, I don't know. . . .

EISENHOWER: . . . I would go ahead and . . . do it as quickly as I could.

LBJ: . . . You're the best chief of staff I've got. . . . I've got to rely on you on this one.[2]

LADY BIRD JOHNSON

Saturday, July 3, 1965, Tape-recorded Diary

The family spent the long Independence Day weekend at the LBJ Ranch.

---

1. The enemy.
2. LBJ is trying hard to implicate Eisenhower in escalating the war. At the 11:35 A.M. meeting with Rusk, McNamara, McGeorge Bundy, and Ball, Johnson said he would hold off a final decision on Westmoreland's request until the end of the month, when Congress was expected to vote on the Medicare and voting rights bills. He asked McNamara to visit Saigon. Averell Harriman should fly to Moscow and ask the Russians to reconvene the old Geneva conference on Vietnam. Ball should look for quiet chances to make contact with the North Vietnamese and Vietcong. (See Dallek, *Flawed Giant*, p. 272.)

LADY BIRD: We helicoptered to the Coca-Cola Cove, where the big boat met us. . . . Marianne [Means][1] put on a good demonstration of waterskiing . . . while I sunned and read. . . . When the fast boat whirled past us, Lyndon had exactly the expression of a little boy aged two and a half sitting in the ice cream parlor chair—a mischievous, happy, the-world-is-mine look.

LADY BIRD JOHNSON

Monday, July 5, 1965, Tape-recorded Diary

LADY BIRD: Lyndon . . . is as proud of the new fast boat as Luci is of her green Sting Ray—Took all of the pretty girls he could gather . . . for a ride. . . . I [talked] to George Reedy about something serious and sad that worries me. He's having trouble with his feet. He will have to leave to have an operation. . . . It has been excruciatingly painful for months. . . . I flinched to think of George as a very old and kindly-natured bull in a pen, the daily object of the sharp darts of a host of rather brutal picadors. . . . He feels like he's at his rope's end and will leave for this operation just as soon as Lyndon gives the go signal on [a new] press secretary. Lyndon had spoken about Bill Moyers. . . . I think I do not remember three successive days at the ranch with such a minimum of calls from McNamara and McGeorge Bundy and Dean Rusk. . . . Briefly the world has stopped to take a breath.

THURGOOD MARSHALL

Judge, U.S. Court of Appeals
Wednesday, July 7, 1965, 1:30 P.M.

> Johnson offers the job of Solicitor General to Judge Marshall, who famously championed school desegregation before the Supreme Court in the landmark 1954 case *Brown v. Board of Education* and succeeded in twenty-eight other cases before the Court. Without saying so flat-out, LBJ makes it clear that he intends one day to appoint Marshall as the first black Justice on the Supreme Court. (This he ultimately did in June 1966. When an aide later suggested another black judge, Leon Higginbotham, for the Court, Johnson glared and said, "The only two people who ever heard of Judge Higginbotham are you and his mama. When I appoint a nigger to the bench, I want everyone to know he's a nigger."[2])

LBJ: I want you to be my Solicitor General.
MARSHALL: Wow!

---

1. The Hearst reporter and Johnson family friend.
2. Quoted in Dallek, *Flawed Giant,* p. 441.

LBJ: Now, you lose a lot. You lose security, and you lose the freedom that you like, and you lose the philosophizing that you can do [on the Court of Appeals]. . . . I want you to do it for two or three reasons. One, I want the top lawyer . . . representing me before the Supreme Court to be a Negro, and to be a damn good lawyer that's done it before. . . . Number two, I think it will do a lot for our image abroad and at home. . . . Number three, I want you to . . . be in the picture. . . . I don't want to make any other commitments. I don't want to imply or bribe or mislead you, but I want you to have the training and experience of being there [at the Supreme Court] day after day. . . . I think you ought to do it for the people of the world. . . . And after you do it awhile, if there's not something better, which I would hope there would be, . . . there'll be security for you. Because I'm going to be here for quite a while.[1]

MARSHALL: That's right, that's right.

LBJ: But I want to do this job that Lincoln started, and I want to do it the right way. . . . I think you can see what I'm looking at. I want to be the first President that really goes all the way.[2]

MARSHALL: I think it would be wonderful.

LBJ: . . . I want to do it on merit. . . . Without regard to politics. . . . I'm not looking for votes. . . . I had [a margin of] 15 million. All I want to do is serve my term and do it well. But I also want . . . to leave my mark, and . . . see that justice is done. And you can be a symbol there that you can't ever be where you are.

MARSHALL: The answer is yes.

LBJ: Well, it's got to be!

*   *   *

LBJ: I've thought about it for weeks.

MARSHALL: I'm so appreciative to be able to help.

LBJ: Well, you can. Because you live such a life, and they've gone over you with a fine-tooth comb, and they could never use anything about you to thwart us, and we're on our way now.

MARSHALL: Wonderful!

LBJ: And we're going to move!

---

1. In other words, if a Court vacancy does not appear, LBJ will give Marshall another administration job.
2. To the Supreme Court.

MARTIN LUTHER KING, JR.

Wednesday, July 7, 1965, 8:05 P.M.

With a House vote on the voting rights bill just ahead, Dr. King is concerned about a substitute proposed by Republican Congressman William McCulloch of Ohio that, he fears, will dilute its effect. McCulloch's substitute would not enforce voting rights automatically. Federal action would require a complaint by twenty-five or more citizens in a voting district, possibly opening the way to local intimidation to keep blacks from voting. LBJ uses this opportunity to complain to King about his recent public criticism of Johnson's Vietnam policies.

KING: This McCulloch [proposal] . . . would stand in the way of everything we are trying to get in the voting bill. . . .

LBJ: . . . We're confronted with the . . . problem that we've faced all through the years—a combination of the South and the Republicans. . . . How do we avoid this combination? . . . I've done the best I could. But they're hitting me on different sides, and the press is. . . . [on] Vietnam or the Dominican Republic. Some mistake here or some mistake there. I'm getting kind of cut up a little bit. And Wilkins[1] is having a national convention. And you're somewhere else. I called Meany[2] to ask him to help and he'd gone to Europe. . . . I called Joe Rauh[3] and said, "For God's sakes, you try to get in here before it's too late." . . . They got a wire sent from Roy to all the Republicans. But the Republicans are . . . going to quit the Negroes. They will not let the Negro vote for them. Every time they get a chance to help out a little, they'll blow it. . . . They could elect some good men in suburban districts and in cities. But they haven't got that much sense. That's why they are disintegrating as a party. . . .

Now, when I went up with my message,[4] I could have probably passed it by seventy-five. But [our situation in Congress] is deteriorating. The other day, they almost beat my rent subsidy, which is very important to . . . the poor people.[5] . . . Smith comes out and says my bill has had a lot of venom in it.[6] I have a "great hatred for the South," and I'm like a "rattlesnake." I'm trying to "punish" them. . . . So, he gets the Congressmen from the thirteen old Confederate states, and he [adds] a hundred [of them] with a hundred and fifty Republicans. That gives him two hundred and fifty. . . . A good majority. . . .

Unless we can pull some of the Republicans away, we're in trouble. . . . Now

---

1. The NAACP chief, Roy Wilkins.
2. The AFL-CIO chief, George Meany.
3. The Washington lawyer and civil rights activist.
4. To Congress in March on behalf of voting rights.
5. Johnson here means black people.
6. Howard Smith, the segregationist Virginian, Chairman of the House Rules Committee, will hold up the bill for five weeks.

the smart thing to do . . . would be to get some language that [will] . . . get this bill passed and start registering our people and get them ready to vote next year.[1] . . . You-all are either going to have confidence in me and in Katzenbach, or you ought to pick some leader you do [trust] and then follow [him]. I started out on this voting bill last November, right after the election. . . . I called you down here and told you what I was going to do. I went before the Congress, made the speech, and asked them to work every weekend. . . . They're getting tired of the heat from me. They don't like for me to be asking for rent one day and poverty the next day, and education the next day, and voting rights the next day. They know I can't defeat them out there in their district in Michigan and some other place.

So I'm just fighting the battle the best I can. I think I'll win it. But it's going to be close, and it's going to be dangerous. . . . I cannot influence the Republicans. The people that can influence the Republicans are men like the local chapters of CORE[2] or NAACP, or your group in New York . . . and these states where you've got a good many Negro voters. You've got to say to them, "We're not Democrats. We're going to vote for the man that gives us freedom. We don't give a damn whether it's Abraham Lincoln or Lyndon Johnson. . . . We're smart enough to know, and we're here watching you. Now, we want to see how you . . . answer on that roll call."

*   *   *

LBJ: You ought to find out who you can trust. . . . If you can't trust [me], why, trust Teddy Kennedy or whoever you want to trust. . . . The trouble is, that fire's gone out. We've got to put some cedar back on it, and put a little coal oil on it. . . . My recommendation would be that you . . . come in here and follow my political judgment and see if we can't get a bill passed.

KING: All right. . . . Now there's one other point that I wanted to mention to you, because it has begun to concern me a great deal. . . . In the last few days . . . I made a statement concerning the Vietnam situation.[3] . . . This in no way is an attempt to engage in a criticism of [your] policies. . . . The press, unfortunately, lifted it out of context. . . . I know the terrible burden and awesome responsibilities and decisions that you have to make. . . .

LBJ: . . . I did see it. I was distressed. . . . I'd welcome a chance to review with you my problems and our alternatives there. I not only know you have a right, I think you have a duty, as a minister and as a leader of millions of people, to give them a sense of purpose and direction. . . . I've lost about 264 lives up to now[4]

---

1. In time for the 1966 congressional elections.
2. Congress of Racial Equality.
3. On July 2, King told a Virginia rally, "I'm not going to sit by and see war escalated without saying anything about it." The Vietnam War "must be stopped. . . . We must even negotiate with the Vietcong." (*New York Times,* July 3, 1965.)
4. The actual figure was 446. (See *New York Times,* July 2, 1965.)

And I could lose 265,000 mighty easy. I'm trying to keep those zeros down, and at the same time not trigger a conflagration that would be worse if we pulled out.

I can't stay there and do nothing. Unless I bomb, they'll run me out right quick. . . . The only pressure we can put on is to try to hold them back as much as we can by taking their bridges out . . . [and] their ammunition dumps . . . [and] their radar stations. . . . A good many people, including the military, think that's not near enough. . . . I don't want to pull down the flag and come home running with my tail between my legs. . . . On the other hand, I don't want to get us in a war with China and Russia. So, I've got a pretty tough problem. And I'm not all wise. I pray every night to get direction and judgment and leadership that permit me to do what's right. . . .

KING: I certainly appreciate . . . your concern. It's true leadership and true greatness. . . . I don't think I've had the chance to thank you for what I considered the greatest speech that any President has made on the question of civil rights.[1] . . .

LBJ: I'm having some new copies printed. I'll send you some of them. . . . And I hope that you do talk to Roy [about the voting rights bill]. You-all see what can be done quick, because . . . this thing will be decided Thursday and Friday.[2]

LADY BIRD JOHNSON

Wednesday, July 7, 1965, Tape-recorded Diary

> Lady Bird is spending most of the summer at the ranch while her husband stays in Washington. LBJ told one aide, "I don't like to sleep alone, ever since my heart attack." He feared that he would suffer another coronary and no one would be there to help. When Lady Bird was away, Johnson would ask friends, like his secretary Vicky McCammon and her husband, to stay the night in the First Lady's dressing room: "The only deal is you've got to leave your door open a crack so that if I holler, someone will hear me."[3]

LADY BIRD: [Lynda] said something that brought a pang to my heart. She had been talking to her daddy. He sounded lonesome. She said, "You know, Mother, he's never the same without you." . . . She had called Jack Valenti . . . and asked about Lyndon. And he felt too that he was tense and lonesome. I feel selfish, as though I was insulating myself from pain and troubles down here. But I do know I need it.

---

1. In his June 4 speech at Howard University, LBJ demanded "not just equality as a right and a theory but . . . as a fact and . . . result."
2. Johnson prevailed.
3. Califano, *The Triumph and Tragedy of Lyndon Johnson*, pp. 29–30.

LADY BIRD JOHNSON

Thursday, July 8, 1965, Tape-recorded Diary

At St. Matthew's Cathedral in Washington, eighteen-year-old Luci Johnson has converted to Catholicism. Her parents and sister attended, but Lynda left the church in tears. Lady Bird "could not help but think we went in four and came out three."[1] LBJ is indignant at Father James Montgomery, who gave Luci a "conditional" baptism, implying that her Episcopal baptism as an infant was invalid. He is also angry at Episcopalians like Bishop James Pike and Dean Francis Sayre of the Washington Cathedral, who have called Luci's decision an "insult" to their church.[2] Leaving her husband at the White House, Lady Bird later flew back to the ranch.

LADY BIRD: He's hurt and angry at the Catholic Church. He thinks they've let her down. And he is hurt and angry too at the Episcopalians. . . . No one is surprised Bishop Sayre took the occasion to preach a sermon. . . . The gist was that she had done wrong. . . . Anybody that hurts his little girl wounds Lyndon deeply. . . . I called Luci, and I found, from her standpoint, that she had been consoling *him.* She said, "But you know, that bad man didn't come home until twelve o'clock for dinner last night. But I was the best daughter I could be, and I tried to help him." . . .

Luci's self-confidence is shaken. She is almost hurt and frightened that she should have caused a rift, a disturbance, trouble for her parents . . . between any churches. Perhaps in part this will have a sobering effect on her, [and show her] that she can always trust her own judgment. . . . She was also blissfully wide-eyed, happy, that she had had a message . . . from the Holy Father himself, welcoming her: "To *me,* Mama, *Luci*—just a little girl!" . . . Bishop Hannan[3] . . . talked to Lyndon. . . . [He will] issue a statement that the Church . . . [intended] no reflection on her previous baptism. . . . Well, one can only go forward. . . . So I tried to console and love.

I wish I could have been more use to Lyndon. He said, "Things are not going well here. . . . Vietnam is getting worse every day. I have the choice to go in with great casualty lists or to get out with disgrace. It's like being in an airplane and I have to choose between crashing the plane or jumping out. I do not have a parachute." . . . When he is pierced, I bleed. It's a bad time all around.

---

1. Lady Bird Johnson Diary, July 2, 1965, LBJL.

2. Sayre had criticized Johnson's ethics in 1964.

3. Philip Hannan, Auxiliary Bishop of the Archdiocese of Washington, had presided over President Kennedy's funeral.

LADY BIRD JOHNSON

Saturday, July 10, 1965, Tape-recorded Diary

Johnson joins his wife at the ranch for the weekend.

LADY BIRD: About every ten minutes, Lyndon picked up the talking machine [in his car] to give Dale Malechek[1] a job to do—hinge off a gate here, a cow has got a cancer eye, put in a cattle guard there. Dale needs a stenographer's pad in his pocket when we are at home! . . . Lyndon . . . has every reason to feel fulfilled and proud this weekend. Last week the voting rights bill passed [the Senate] and the Medicare bill [passed the House]—that impossible bill.

LADY BIRD JOHNSON

Sunday, July 11, 1965, Tape-recorded Diary

LADY BIRD: Lyndon talked to [Luci by telephone]. Then he handed the phone to me, saying, "I'll let your mother talk. She's like an old cow when her calf gets out. She just moos and bawls and looks around for her." If Lyndon has lost a certain something by the lack of the most polished Eastern education, he has the compensation at least of the earthy expressions, some so amusing, that really say what he thinks in a clear way. . . . [I] said goodbye to Lyndon in his city clothes. I almost look upon them as fighting uniforms these days. And it is a little sad to say goodbye to him heading back to the city of troubles.[2]

DEAN RUSK

Thursday, July 15, 1965, 9:12 A.M.

The previous day at noon, after a telephone call, LBJ walked into the office of his secretary Juanita Roberts and said, "Well, Adlai Stevenson just died."[3] On a London street the UN Ambassador had suffered a heart attack, fallen backward, struck his skull on the sidewalk, and died. When Lady Bird heard the news at the ranch, she knew "how heavily this blow must fall on Lyndon . . . coupled with Lyndon's own heart attack." She said, "I want to be right by Lyndon's side when he goes to

---

1. Ranch foreman.
2. Washington, D.C.
3. President's Daily Diary, July 14, 1965, LBJL.

any service for Adlai."[1] "That Stevenson!" Johnson said, later in the week. "Why did he have to die right now? He was always off in his timing.[2] Who am I going to get to take his place?"[3] Eager to fill the vacancy quickly, LBJ consults his Secretary of State.

LBJ: What thought are you giving to the Stevenson successor?

RUSK: . . . I would wonder whether Frank Church is worth considering. But he's got a Republican governor.[4]

*   *   *

LBJ: Mansfield wouldn't be interested, would he?

RUSK: . . . He might be. . . .

LBJ: Fulbright wouldn't be. . . . Would he be insulted if he'd be asked?[5] . . . I think the man we need is somebody [with] a genuine, deep interest in the poor part of the world. Particularly the Africa-Asia group. . . . I don't know whether Fulbright could do that with Africa.[6] . . .

RUSK: You know, Bill is not really into great liberal tradition. He's a sort of a maverick.

LBJ: . . . Do you think George Ball would consider it upgrading?

RUSK: Oh, I think so. After all, no one steps down to occupy a post that Adlai Stevenson occupied.

LBJ: . . . I've felt that Ball was a good man, and I believe that he's been loyal to me.[7] . . . I rather like his willingness to be a little independent [on Vietnam] and say to me, "Now wait a minute, I want to give you the devil's side of it." I also have a feeling he might be a little bull in the china shop and run over them a little bit if he needed to. Would be a little autocratic. I don't like those qualities in anybody. Including myself. And I have them.[8]

RUSK: . . . I think we could come to a point later in the fall on Vietnam[9] where George's own views on the matter would make him rather uncomfortable. This hasn't been just the devil's advocate's point of view. . . .

LBJ: . . . I'm not going to tell Lady Bird. . . . I don't want you to tell a human. . . . But my preference would be to have, if I had to decide it in the next minute, . . . Ball

---

1. Lady Bird Johnson Diary, July 14 and 15, 1965, LBJL.
2. A reference to Stevenson's two campaigns against the wildly popular Eisenhower.
3. Quoted in John Kenneth Galbraith, *A Life in Our Times* (Houghton Mifflin, 1981), p. 456.
4. Who would appoint a Republican as Senator from Idaho if Church resigned.
5. By suggesting Church, Mansfield, and Fulbright, LBJ sounds as if he wants to use the Stevenson vacancy to reduce the number of doves in the Senate.
6. Political realities in Arkansas compelled Fulbright to be backward on race.
7. LBJ shows his mercurial opinions of those around him. See his June 24, 1965, conversation with Bundy for castigation of Ball as an undependable leaker.
8. Johnson here reveals a flash of self-knowledge.
9. Meaning a dramatic escalation.

succeed Stevenson for whatever time that he would give us . . . and at least get us over this sad day and this period . . . and Clifford[1] take his place [as Under Secretary of State]. . . . I just think Clifford would just be a hell of a good witness [in Congress] when you're out and he's got to appear. He just appears right and you don't have to hold his hand. . . . He's not throwing his weight and he's not a bulldog.

BILL MOYERS

Press Secretary to the President
Thursday, July 15, 1965, 9:35 A.M.

Impatient with the shambling, long-winded George Reedy and disgruntled by growing animosity from the press, Johnson has installed Moyers as press secretary, using Reedy's foot surgery as the excuse. (As a consolation prize, LBJ gave Reedy one of his old white Lincoln Continentals and helped him find a job in business.) Now Moyers asks LBJ for guidance on a question from Charles Bailey of the *Minneapolis Tribune* about whether Johnson has recently purchased land near the LBJ Ranch, which would suggest that he is circumventing his blind trust.

LBJ: Just tell him you don't know anything about what he's talking about. . . . That . . . I have acquired no land of any kind that I know of in the last twelve months.[2] . . . We have some leases. The Hightower place, immediately across from the ranch, is twenty or thirty acres. We were afraid they're going to build a beer joint [there]. . . . I don't believe that the company[3] has bought a thing in twelve months, although we have nothing to do with it . . . and they don't discuss it with us. . . . [Tell Bailey] you have nothing to do with these financial things. That . . . the Kennedys have very comparable things. [Bailey should] spend a lot of time with them getting all the dope on their gas and oil holdings. . . . He doesn't realize how trivial ours is. . . . The company's completely in the hands of trustees. . . .

We don't know [of] any obligation to discuss the acres of land we have anyway, if it's got no government subsidy. . . . Any more than we have a right to check on how many times he screwed his wife last night. . . . We have the greatest [blind] trust agreement that anybody's ever written. . . . I don't know what kind of trust agreement Bobby Kennedy's got. He's got $10 million invested in oil and gas in Texas, and he's up there voting. [Bailey doesn't] have the slightest interest to do a goddamn thing but harassing us. . . . He [wants to get] a big *Wall Street Journal*

---

1. LBJ's private adviser, the lawyer Clark Clifford.
2. Although Lady Bird has said in her June 13, 1965 diary, above, that buying nearby ranchland is "almost an addiction" with LBJ.
3. The LBJ Company.

story going again.[1] . . . He don't pay us for a damn thing.[2] He's never done anything for us. I haven't seen one friendly story he's written.

LADY BIRD JOHNSON

Friday, July 16, 1965, Tape-recorded Diary

> Lady Bird returned from the ranch to attend Adlai Stevenson's memorial service at the Washington Cathedral with her husband. In her White House closet was a black dress, which she would wear should LBJ suddenly die in office. Although the public was encouraged to believe that the President was as healthy as anyone, Lady Bird never passed a day without remembering that he was a heart patient and that Johnson men usually died before the age of sixty-five.[3]

LADY BIRD: I . . . put on the black silk dress I had bought in February[4] and never yet worn, having, in the back of my mind when I bought it, the grim, unacknowledged thought that I might need a black dress for a funeral. . . . [That evening] Lyndon asked Abe [Fortas] to come [into his bedroom] and talk while he started his massage. But it was not long until Abe emerged, saying that [Lyndon] had gone to sleep, which often happens—a great armor for him. So we said good night with a sense of an emotionally and physically exhausting day.

RICHARD RUSSELL

Monday, July 19, 1965, 6:07 P.M.

> During the first hymn at Stevenson's memorial service, Arthur Schlesinger or Edward Kennedy or both let John Kenneth Galbraith, the Harvard economist who had served JFK as Ambassador to India, know that LBJ was considering him to replace Stevenson at the UN.[5] Galbraith did not want the job but knew he had better have an alternative or Johnson might force him to take it. He told LBJ that Arthur Goldberg was restless on the Supreme Court.[6] Johnson liked Goldberg, who had been appointed to the Court by Kennedy after serving as Secretary of Labor. LBJ had called the Justice for advice on his first evening as President in November 1963.[7]

---

1. In 1964 the *Wall Street Journal* had infuriated LBJ with an exposé on his finances. (See Beschloss, *Taking Charge*, pp. 290, 298.)
2. Johnson's way of saying that reporters should give favors to get favors.
3. She also remembered that this month was exactly ten years after LBJ's near-fatal heart attack.
4. After LBJ came down with semipneumonia.
5. Galbraith heard his puckish friend(s) sing, "Oh God, our help in ages past / Our hope for years to come / You are the first on Lyndon's list / In our eternal home." (Galbraith, *A Life in Our Times*, p. 455.)
6. Ibid., pp. 456–77.
7. See Beschloss, *Taking Charge*, pp. 20–21.

As usual, there was another layer to Johnson's machinations. Having begun to lay the foundations of the Great Society, he presumably feared that, as with his hero Franklin Roosevelt's New Deal, the Supreme Court might repeal some of the programs as unconstitutional. He wanted to appoint Abe Fortas to the Court. Fortas not only would be a reliable pro Great Society vote but from Johnson's point of view, he could keep the President confidentially informed of what the Justices were doing and warn him if there were trouble in the offing.[1] With this in mind, Johnson had asked his Attorney General in May when the next Court vacancy might occur.[2] He had tried to entice Goldberg to leave the Court to be Secretary of Health, Education, and Welfare but failed.[3]

If Goldberg would accept the UN post, Johnson would win both a prestigious Ambassador and the chance to appoint Fortas to the Court. Invited to the White House the day after Stevenson's Washington service, Goldberg was asked by Jack Valenti if he might reconsider the HEW offer. By Goldberg's recollection, he said, "I'm walking out. I'm not interested in HEW." Johnson called him into the Oval Office and said he was actually offering the UN, with "a key role in the Vietnam situation."[4] LBJ turned up the heat on Goldberg on July 19, while flying with him on *Air Force One* to the Stevenson burial in Illinois.

During their conversations, with minimal sincerity, LBJ told Goldberg that his next UN Ambassador had the chance to make peace in Vietnam. With that under his belt, Goldberg might be in line to become the first Jewish Vice President: "You never know what can happen, Arthur. . . . You can't get to the Vice Presidency from the Court."[5] Goldberg wanted to think about it. He would recall in 1983 that he had the "egotistical feeling" that he could keep LBJ from getting "overly involved" in Vietnam.[6]

Johnson was so certain he had Goldberg in the bag that, while flying back from Illinois, he called Fortas from *Air Force One:* "I am arriving, and I am going to announce your appointment to the Supreme Court." "God Almighty, Mr. President, you can't do that," said Fortas. "I have got to talk to you about it." Now LBJ asks Richard Russell how he would like Goldberg at the UN.

LBJ: What do you think I ought to do with Stevenson's successor?
RUSSELL: I'd appoint either Ball or Gruenther.[7] . . .

---

1. See Dallek, *Flawed Giant,* p. 233.

2. See Chapter 8.

3. On May 10, showing his intentions, LBJ asked the FBI for background checks on both Fortas and Goldberg. (Dallek, *Flawed Giant,* p. 234.)

4. Arthur Goldberg oral history, LBJL.

5. President's Daily Diary, July 19, 1965, LBJL; and Bruce Allen Murphy, *Fortas* (Morrow, 1988), p. 171.

6. Arthur Goldberg oral history, LBJL. Certainly Goldberg also had political ambitions. In 1970 he ran for Governor of New York and lost.

7. Retired General Alfred Gruenther had helped plan the invasions of North Africa, Sicily, and Salerno during World War II and later served as Supreme Commander of NATO.

LBJ: Gruenther's sick, and nearly everybody I talked to said I ought to keep Ball where he is because he knows so damn much about what he's doing. . . . I was pretty strong for Ball . . . but the more I've talked to folks, the more problems I see it would create here. The Vietnam thing is important. . . . Arthur Goldberg's been suggested. He is the best one. He's very— He can speak at the drop of a hat, and he's a Johnson man. He's pretty understanding of our country, he's a product of our system, he's tolerant of everybody. . . .

RUSSELL: But he's a man that I'd hate to get taken off the Court. . . .

LBJ: . . . What would it do to the Arabs, Dick? Rusk said it wouldn't do anything, except show that in our system that we didn't discriminate against people. . . . I was afraid that . . . they'd say Johnson didn't even know the Arabs were [UN] members. . . . Goldberg would be able to answer the Russians . . . very effectively. . . . He's pretty abrasive. . . . He's got a bulldog face on him, and I think this Jew thing would take the *New York Times*—all this crowd that gives me hell all the time—and disarm them.[1] And [I'd] still have a Johnson man. I've always thought that Goldberg was the ablest man in Kennedy's Cabinet, and he was the best man to us. . . . He has a better understanding of us than most Jews have. I guess the lawyers would cuss me for taking him off the Court.

RUSSELL: Have you considered who you'd put in there? . . .

LBJ: . . . [I'd like] to put Abe Fortas on. . . . Abe Fortas is one of the great lawyers in this country, and one of [my] great friends.[2] . . . Goldberg sold bananas, you know. . . . He's kind of like I am. He's shined some shoes in his day and he sold newspapers, and he has had to slug it out. He's like a Georgian.[3] It just wasn't all inherited.

*   *   *

LBJ: Want to work the hell out of you when McNamara gets back here. Just quietly down here, asking questions. . . . So you just better . . . get rested. . . . Did you see where Chou En-lai just announced . . . that, by God, he's going to send . . . a good deal of equipment . . . to North Vietnam? Russia answered, . . . "We're sending a hell of a lot." The last thing I want to do is . . . say, "I want $3 billion or $4 billion [for Vietnam] right now." I want to get through this monsoon season . . . in the hope that maybe . . . I don't think there's much hope, about 5 percent hope [that] . . . maybe they'll be willing to have some kind of a Laos treaty.[4] . . . I've

---

1. Johnson naively expected to gain points for Goldberg's nomination because the family that owns the *New York Times* was Jewish.
2. LBJ had already tried to sell Russell on Fortas as Attorney General in January. (See LBJ-Fortas conversation, January 22, 1965.)
3. Only LBJ while trying to lobby Russell could claim that Goldberg was "like a Georgian."
4. An agreement to neutralize Vietnam.

got $700 million and $89 million in economic [aid]. . . . I don't want to put enough in where [Russia and China] will unload [money into] North Vietnam.[1]

ARTHUR GOLDBERG

Associate Justice, U.S. Supreme Court
Monday, July 19, 1965, 8:28 P.M.

Johnson has grown ever more intent on sending Goldberg to the UN. Not only will this create an opening for Fortas on the Supreme Court but just as he is about to escalate the war, LBJ knows he can show off Ambassador Goldberg, a skeptic about the war, as walking, talking proof of his eagerness to negotiate peace. (It is not by accident that Johnson's other candidates for the UN job are doves such as Ball, Fulbright, Mansfield, and Church.) Now LBJ tries to close the sale by serenading Goldberg with the glowing reviews he has gleaned on his character and ability. But the Justice wants more time. The President pressures him for a final decision. Otherwise Goldberg's name will leak to the newspapers, where it might arouse opposition. Johnson also wants to surprise the world with his appointment.

LBJ: I've got some very interesting reports. Fulbright says he considers you the best man in the United States. . . . Bundy . . . says you're the best. . . . Russell said . . . the first thing you know, you'll be leading the Arabs, you're so goddamned much smarter than they are.[2] . . . It's a difficult job, the most important we could have. [The UN] is going under. . . . I can't help it if they think you're smart and . . . patriotic and . . . able. And so we've gone too far now [to turn back]. [Except that] Abe Fortas says he won't take the Supreme Court Justice seat. . . .
GOLDBERG: I'll tell you what. Let's do it tomorrow morning.
LBJ: No, I'm afraid it'll be in the papers by eleven o'clock. Fulbright told me that Senators are already being asked about it by the reporters. Let me read you Abe's letter.[3] . . . We'll just have to start working on him tomorrow.

---

1. Yes but, as he told Vance on July 16, Johnson also feared that if he asked Congress for more than $300 or $400 million in extra money for Vietnam before January, it would "kill" his domestic program. (See Dallek, *Flawed Giant*, p. 274.)

2. If Russell said this, he said it in part of their conversation that was not recorded.

3. Refusing Johnson's Court offer: "After painful searching, I've decided to decline—with a heart full of gratitude." (Fortas to LBJ, handwritten, July 19, 1965, LBJL.) Fortas's letter claimed that his wife, Carol Agger, wished him to accept, but actually she thought he was too young to join the Court and worried about the lost income and disruption to their lives. (Kalman, *Abe Fortas*, pp. 241–43.)

DEAN RUSK

Monday, July 19, 1965, 8:45 P.M.

> Johnson consults his Secretary of State about problems a Jewish envoy might have
> with Arab delegates at the UN.

RUSK: We have to expect some Arab reaction. . . . I just don't think there's ever
been a man in that position of the Jewish faith, so you've got to . . . brace for
that. . . .

LBJ: Oh, I'm braced for anything. . . . I want [you] to be comfortable with [him]
first, because I am as devoted to you as I am to my wife. . . . This man has . . . ability and . . . loyalty, I believe, to the Johnson administration. . . .

RUSK: . . . I didn't want to run the risk of surfacing the name, [so] I haven't been
able to find out how active he's been in the Zionist groups, . . . Israel Bond drives,
and things like that.

LBJ: I don't think much. But . . . I told Goldberg . . . what Russell said. I said,
"He said, 'You'll have to quit being a Zionist and . . . quit leading the Jews and
start leading the Arabs!' And he said that you'd be smart enough to do that." He
just laughed.

*   *   *

LBJ: After Goldberg, if something happened to him, you would like McCarthy?[1]
. . . McCarthy is more discreet than Humphrey. And Humphrey is just a big damn
fool. He put out the damnedest statement today about how he was . . . furnishing
Congressmen tickets to go home.[2] He was just bribing them. Just the damnedest
fool statement you ever saw. To show that he's active. You know, a Vice President
feels that everybody thinks he's inactive. And he is. And he tries to blow it up. But
he just made a hell of a statement today. Just real embarrassing to me. I leaned very
closely toward McCarthy [for Vice President in 1964] for that reason.[3] But every
human I talked to just said he's just lazy as hell. He won't come to [Senate] committee meetings. . . . He goes off and they [can't] locate him. Now, if he did that up
at the United Nations, we'd be in a hell of a shape.

RUSK: . . . It's a sixteen- or eighteen-hour-a-day job up there.

LBJ: I like him. . . . I thought he made the best speech in nominating Adlai that I

---

1. Eugene McCarthy, Democratic Senator from Minnesota. McCarthy would ultimately declare an
antiwar candidacy against LBJ in 1968. In December 1968 he was offered the UN post by President-
elect Richard Nixon.

2. Humphrey made this joking offer to encourage members of Congress to get Johnson's program
passed quickly so they could return home.

3. Not really. (See Beschloss, *Taking Charge,* pp. 469, 471.) LBJ is just very annoyed with
Humphrey at the moment.

nearly ever heard.[1] . . . His wife's good. . . . Lady Bird and I are very strong for them. We'll consider him if something happens here. Maybe we'll just have to tell him everybody says he's just too damn lazy and then see if he'll do anything about it.

ARTHUR GOLDBERG

Monday, July 19, 1965, 9:00 P.M.

> Goldberg assures Johnson that he will take the UN job, while assuring himself that the President is comfortable with his Judaism and commitment to Israel.

GOLDBERG: You know me. I am a very proud Jew. . . . I will never be anything less than a proud Jew. . . . I am what I am. I can't change that. I didn't know anybody would be that interested in what I was. . . . The main thing is I want to do what's best in the service of my country. . . . So you have my commitment that I am going to serve. . . . However, I don't think that [we should announce] this late at night. . . . We ought to do this in a dignified way in the morning. . . . I would like to . . . notify my children and bring Dorothy[2] with me. . . .

LBJ: . . . Whoever you talk to tonight . . . for God's sakes . . . let's don't get it out in the paper. . . .

GOLDBERG: You heard what I said about the Jewish question. Does that cause any problems for you?

LBJ: . . . All I know is . . . I've always been proud of America because I have believed that we had equality. . . . One of the reasons I would like you to take it is to show the world that I don't want to be the President that says a Jew can't be my top ambassador any more than I want to say a Negro can't sit on the Supreme Court.[3]

GOLDBERG: . . . I believe profoundly that people who deny their origin do not warrant respect. . . .

LBJ: I do too.

GOLDBERG: . . . I have said[4] that I am a Zionist. I was brought up as a boy to believe the Messianic expectation that Jews should be brought back to their ancient homeland. I was taught that in the Old Testament. I said I was a Zionist in the

---

1. "Do not reject this man who made us all proud to be Democrats," said McCarthy in an eloquent address nominating Stevenson for President at the 1960 Democratic convention. LBJ liked it because he hoped that McCarthy and Stevenson would steal enough votes from JFK to let Johnson be nominated.
2. Mrs. Goldberg.
3. Nominating Thurgood Marshall for the Court is much on LBJ's mind.
4. In a statement he had sent to Johnson.

sense that Winston Churchill was a Zionist. . . . I, as a member of my government, would be working towards peace in the Middle East. . . .

LBJ: I don't see a damned thing wrong with that.

GOLDBERG: . . . You got that piece of paper with some of the words?

LBJ: Oh, yes, yes. I will [read] it tonight.

JOHN KENNETH GALBRAITH

Professor of Economics, Harvard University
Tuesday, July 20, 1965, 12:06 P.M.

In the White House Rose Garden, LBJ has announced Goldberg's appointment. Already there are stories that the appointment demonstrates that the President is earnest about seeking a peaceful way out of Vietnam. If Johnson weren't serious about peace, why else would Goldberg give up a seat on the Supreme Court? To LBJ's delight, the choice has surprised the press. He is exhilarated by his coup and, at least for this moment, sounds as if he feels he has once again become the master of events. He calls Galbraith to thank him for suggesting Goldberg at the UN and confides that he will one day appoint Thurgood Marshall to the Court. As LBJ calls, his Oval Office television set is blaring out an insect extermination commercial featuring "Otto the Orkin Man."

LBJ: Well, you got your man named. . . .

GALBRAITH: Who?

LBJ: Arthur Goldberg!

GALBRAITH: Oh, my gosh! . . .

LBJ: . . . I checked it out with a good many people. . . . They had some concern about the Arabs, but . . . I didn't think that we ought to take the position that we couldn't have a Negro on the Court, or we couldn't have a Jew in the United Nations. That's not very much in line with the kind of government I thought we had. . . . While he likes the Court . . . he loves peace more, and he thinks he has a better chance to do something about it here.

*　　*　　*

LBJ: And I'm going to appoint Thurgood Marshall to the Court. Not to succeed [Goldberg]. But after he's Solicitor [General] for a year or two. The first vacancy I have. I haven't told anybody that. And I don't want you to. . . . At the end of a year or two, no one can say he's not one of the best-qualified men that was ever appointed. . . . We'll break through there like we're breaking through on so many of these things.

LADY BIRD JOHNSON

Tuesday, July 20, 1965, Tape-recorded Diary

Lady Bird has returned to Washington for a brief visit.

LADY BIRD: Lyndon . . . asked, "What about dinner on the boat?" That's always a treat, though sometimes I resent anything that takes me away from work when I'm so far behind. . . . The answer's simple. After a day of Vietnam, anything that is solace, nirvana for him, makes sense. Mostly he makes up the [guest] list. . . . Tonight it [included] the Bill Fulbrights and *dear* Senator Russell. . . . The evening was superb, the views a balm to the spirit (but the river full of floating debris), and the talk good. There was a big comfortable chair at the very end of the *Honey Fitz* [1]—that's Lyndon's favorite of the boats—and Lyndon ensconces himself there and gets some pretty ladies clustered around him and spends his evening. Sometimes he even goes to sleep. . . . We had dinner on trays. One of the nicest things about the boat is that you have the feeling that every guest is glad that he got included.

ABE FORTAS

Wednesday, July 21, 1965, 4:31 P.M.

Despite Fortas's note declining the Supreme Court, Johnson has not given up. As Lady Bird recalled, LBJ "didn't believe that Abe Fortas did not want to be on the Supreme Court." [2] Now he hopes to soften Fortas up by asking for other names, perhaps to show Fortas that there is no other candidate as qualified as he.

LBJ: I got your letter, and I'm mighty sorry. . . . It was a sweet, gracious, lovely letter that only you could write. And I regretted it. But we'll debate it a little later. What I called you about now— I wish you would think of every human you could that we ought to give thought to [for the Court], so we have the best appointee anybody you could ever conceive of. And I want to get away from Harvard and the professors up there.

*   *   *

LBJ: I would really like to have, if I could, everything else being equal . . . a lawyer that was . . . a little left of the center. About what I think I am. I would like to

---

1. The presidential yacht named by JFK for his grandfather, Boston Mayor John "Honey Fitz" Fitzgerald.
2. Quoted in Dallek, *Flawed Giant*, pp. 234–35.

have one fifty years old . . . that everybody in the United States had heard of. . . . A good lawyer that was a man of compassion. . . . Somewhat of a Warren's[1] general stature, temperament, disposition, and philosophy. . . . I wouldn't care if he's Republican. I would really like it if he were a Republican. Incidentally, I got a new FBI [report] on you. . . . I'll talk to you about it some of these days. . . . There wasn't a critical word. Not a black mark on it. Just a perfect report.

LADY BIRD JOHNSON

Wednesday, July 21, 1965, Tape-recorded Diary

> During an all-day meeting, McNamara, back from his tour of South Vietnam, urged Johnson to increase American troops in Vietnam to between 175,000 and 200,000 as well as call up 255,000 Reserves. Ball doubted that an "army of Westerners" could fight "Orientals" in an "Asian jungle." He wished to let South Vietnam and its government "fall apart" if necessary, and be taken over by Communists. Then the United States could move on to defense of Thailand. McNamara replied that no one could predict how the Vietcong would behave "when confronted by 175,000 Americans." LBJ said that withdrawal would be a "disaster." Harsher bombing could bring in the Russians and Chinese. He had decided to "put in his stack."[2]

LADY BIRD: Lyndon had . . . a meeting at eleven with McNamara, just back from Vietnam, and Dean Rusk and McGeorge Bundy. And their cars were still there when I got back from the beauty parlor at five. So it had been a sheer hell of a day for him. . . . Bill Moyers is riding a wave of euphoria of compliments from all sides. . . . Every one's deserved. And yet every one is a pang or thrust toward George [Reedy]. I wish we could avoid comparisons in all fields. He gave us years of wisdom, work, and loyalty. He simply isn't a bullfighter. I know that the pluses for Bill carry with them also for Lyndon a weight of sadness.

LADY BIRD JOHNSON

Thursday, July 22, 1965, Tape-recorded Diary

> This afternoon, LBJ told McNamara and the Joint Chiefs, "We are in a new war. This is going off the diving board."[3] Years later he recalled that he knew the day

---

1. Chief Justice Earl Warren.
2. See Meeting Notes, July 20, 1965, in *FRUS*, vol. 3, pp. 189–204.
3. See *FRUS*, vol. 3, pp. 209–20; Dallek, *Flawed Giant*, pp. 275–76; Clifford, *Counsel to the President*, p. 414.

Congress exploded "into a major debate on the war, that day would be the beginning of the end of the Great Society."[1] He is searching for a way to announce his Vietnam decision that will not provoke Congress or the American people.

LADY BIRD: I woke about five-thirty to hear Lyndon say, almost as if he were in the middle of a sentence but . . . had been interrupted, "I don't want to get in a war and I don't see any way out of it. I've got to call up 600,000 boys, make them leave their homes and their families."[2] It was as though he were talking out loud, not especially to me. I hope the refrain hadn't been in his mind all night long. Feeling like the boy that leaves the burning deck, I went to my own room to try to get another hour or two of sleep—fitful and unsatisfactory.

DWIGHT D. EISENHOWER

Friday, July 23, 1965, 11:45 A.M.

> Eisenhower warns Johnson that, with monumental decisions on Vietnam about to be made, Republican congressional leaders feel he is not consulting them enough.

EISENHOWER: Mr. President, I had a call yesterday from . . . the Republican leadership. Both the Senate and the House. . . . They said, "Look, we have been supportive. . . . But [there] are rumors that the Reserves are going to be called up and great strength needed in the armed forces, and a lot of troops going to move in." They'd really like to be informed. . . .
LBJ: . . . Here's our problem. General Westmoreland has made some recommendations. . . . To hold the bases that he has, and to release the South Vietnamese who are now guarding them, he wants a hundred thousand people in there between now and the first of the year. Or as soon as he can get them. He thinks he may need that many more at that time. But he wants to see what effect the monsoon has. . . .

We have been a little bit fearful that we were driving [the Chinese and Russians] closer together because of Vietnam. . . . Every time we announce that we are going to do something in South Vietnam, Ho Chi Minh runs to . . . Mao Tse-tung and says, . . . "The Americans are . . . going to send a hundred thousand and 3 billion or 10 billion. . . . You do the same for us." . . . They go to the Russians and . . . do the same thing. Both of them read . . . some speeches that folks have made, including Wayne Morse. The intelligence indicates that . . . many of them . . . think we almost got a Civil War Congress again, with all of them telling every day

---

1. Kearns, *Lyndon Johnson and the American Dream*, pp. 282–83.
2. LBJ will have to call up Reserves to achieve 600,000 additional men by mid-1966. (See *FRUS*, vol. 3, p. 191.)

what ought to be done.[1] . . . And a good many [in Congress] are sympathetic with the Communists. They think they're not, but . . . Ho Chi Minh said he'd fight on for twenty years, if he needed to, because he had the support of the world. Including a good many Americans. . . .

Now, I just finished an hour and a half with Everett Dirksen . . . and Mansfield. . . . We have reached no conclusions on what action to take on Westmoreland's recommendations.[2] Although the odds are ninety-nine to one you know what they'd be without my telling you. But I called in the Joint Chiefs because I wanted each one of them to evaluate Westmoreland's recommendations. . . . They all supported [them] unanimously. . . . They charge McNamara has computerized the [Defense] Department, and that he is the . . . quiz kid, whiz kid . . . and that I'm downgrading the military. . . . So . . . this morning, I got the [civilian] secretaries in. . . . When we . . . decide what we ought to recommend . . . I will call in the leaders. The moment I call them in, though, it's going to be in the papers . . .

EISENHOWER: Now, I wonder if you could just . . . call Everett [Dirksen] . . . and ask [him] to calm Ford down.[3] . . . Just say I have talked to you, and that I do know that you are trying to get all your ducks in a row with all the military. . . .

LBJ: . . . As long as they're calling you, why, they're not going to be too erratic. . . . Now we've got authority to call up the Reserves, but Ford got into a political thing yesterday. He said, "You called up the Reserves in the Cuban Missile Crisis. You called up the Reserves after Khrushchev's meeting [with Kennedy] in Vienna.[4] . . . [But] we [Republicans] never had to call up the Reserves in eight years of Eisenhower. So I think Johnson ought to come down here and . . . be questioned why." . . . I'll tell Dirksen to . . . tell . . . Mel Laird[5] and Jerry [Ford] just not to get excited. . . . I have had more meetings with the [congressional] leadership in the first six months of this year than any President has had with any leadership in history. . . . [Of] the hundred thousand [troops], I may put in forty at one time, and forty at another, and twenty at another so that it doesn't scare the British and scare hell out of everybody else that we're going into a world war.[6] . . . We are going in with . . . what the . . . commander says we need to hold what we've got, so that they can launch some offensives. . . .

EISENHOWER: . . . That's . . . all you can do. I just wanted to calm these people down by telling them I talked to you.

LBJ: . . . You tell them . . . that, of course, I'm going to talk to all of them before

---

1. Members of Congress tried to hamstring Lincoln's conduct of the war.
2. Johnson does not want leaks, even from Eisenhower.
3. On July 22, Gerald Ford warned LBJ to seek a congressional endorsement before calling up Reserves for Vietnam.
4. In June 1961, when the Soviet leader threatened to march against Berlin.
5. Wisconsin Congressman and Chairman, House Republican Conference.
6. And ruin Johnson's domestic program in Congress.

we do anything. That they're going to know every bit of it. . . . I don't want to keep any secrets. I want all of them in on it with me.

LADY BIRD JOHNSON

Friday, July 23, 1965, Tape-recorded Diary

> The Johnsons are spending the weekend at Camp David with houseguests including the McNamaras, the Clark Cliffords, the Arthur Goldbergs, and the John Connallys. During the next few weeks LBJ will have Goldberg at his side at Camp David, the LBJ Ranch, and official events, brandishing him as public evidence of his desire for peace in Vietnam.

LADY BIRD: When we reached Camp David, I wanted only to get into slacks, seek the solace of a drink, curl up on the sofa, and listen. . . . I could only feel that I had made Lyndon's time more difficult by not really understanding his plans for the weekend, so that I was tense and on edge. . . . After midnight, when I couldn't go to sleep, I . . . found *Brownstone Front* by Louis Auchincloss, and . . . read until two-thirty. The light wakened Lyndon. He put his head in the door. Said, "Can't my darling sleep? I'm so sorry." So I put a blanket across the crack between the doors, read a little, and then turned it out.

It was a short night. I waked at five-thirty, with the birds chirping the dawn. For an extraordinarily healthy, tough, reasonably happy person, sleeping is becoming the hardest thing for me to do, particularly when I feel that I have not played my role well, that I have been a hindrance and not a help. For Lyndon, the day had been a constant diet of Vietnam. . . . The fact the poverty bill had passed . . . had not prevented Vietnam from dominating the news.[1] . . .

At dinner we discussed . . . one of the favorite subjects of conversation around Washington these days—Schlesinger's book, LBJ versus RFK, the story of who said what on the fateful day [in 1960] the decision was made about who should be Vice President.[2] And the nasty little thing that [David] Schoenbrun claimed Stevenson had told him.[3] Goldberg said, "We are all gripers, to an extent. You come home and gripe to Lady Bird. I go home and gripe to Dorothy. We've got to blow off steam somewhere. Stevenson was tired. He was frustrated. But don't for

---

1. The previous day the House had passed Johnson's $2 billion antipoverty bill.

2. *Life* was serializing *A Thousand Days,* Arthur Schlesinger's forthcoming memoir of the Kennedy administration. The book suggested that JFK had made LBJ only a pro forma offer of the Vice Presidency, which he expected Johnson to reject.

3. The CBS reporter had publicly revealed that over dinner five days before his death, Stevenson had complained of defending Johnson's policies on Vietnam and the Dominican Republic, which he called "a massive blunder." (Martin, *Adlai Stevenson and the World,* pp. 860–61.)

one moment ever believe that he thought or said a moment's disloyalty to . . . the President."

Lyndon told . . . about how Stevenson had come to him [in the spring of 1964] and told him he was thinking of running for the Senate in New York. . . . Lyndon said, "I think it will be awful. You were made for this [UN] role you're in. I just don't want to think of anybody else in it." Stevenson, somewhat taken aback, said, "Is that what you really want me to keep on doing?" Pitilessly Lyndon said, "Yes, I do." And Stevenson never cast a backward glance to the Senate. He went right on to a job in which he was, in theater terms, perfectly cast.

LADY BIRD JOHNSON

Saturday, July 24, 1965, Tape-recorded Diary

LADY BIRD: I simply abdicated my command post and curled up and went to sleep, hoping that everybody found a place they liked to talk privately, or exercise violently, or just sit and look at the trees. I slept two blissful hours, and when I woke up, I found that John [Connally] and all the Texas folks were gone. I said I wished they had stayed for lunch, and Lyndon said rather plaintively, "I wanted them to, but I didn't know whether I could ask them. It might be too many." He really needs a tougher wife—or a better executive, because I failed to touch that base of telling him to ask them.

LADY BIRD JOHNSON

Sunday, July 25, 1965, Tape-recorded Diary

In Aspen Lodge, late on Sunday afternoon, LBJ sat down, drinking a glass of Fresca, with Goldberg, McNamara, and Clifford to talk about Vietnam. When the Defense Secretary suggested calling up Reserves and putting the nation on a war footing, Goldberg told Johnson, "You do that and you don't get my letter of resignation!"[1]

When Goldberg described his wish to take Vietnam to the UN, Clifford dismissed it, warning that the risks outweighed the potential gains. Clifford said he doubted that America could win the war. Until January 1966, they should "underplay Vietnam" in public, with "no talking about where and why we are there." Then, after the monsoon season, they should find a way "to get out." McNamara briskly replied that without a rapid military buildup, Saigon would fall. LBJ abruptly said that no one wanted peace more than he did. Then the man who so

---

1. From the Supreme Court. (Arthur Goldberg oral history, LBJL)

craved having people around him spent two hours driving and walking the grounds of Camp David alone.[1]

LADY BIRD: I'm determined to get a portrait [of Lyndon]. And every time I pass [that of] President Wilson, my determination hardens.[2] We had a late lunch on the porch. . . . Lyndon is in his element with a sizable crowd. He bores in and . . . concentrates on whatever set of individuals he needs to learn from . . . at that time. . . . I can see him getting the business of the weekend done. At one point, he walked away with Arthur Goldberg . . . for about an hour on the golf course. . . . Both earnest. Lyndon frequently with his hands in his pockets. Walking, stopping, gesturing, listening intently to each other. . . . Goldberg is a daring . . . choice [for the UN]. So far there have not been screams from the Arabs. . . .

When I woke up, I found Lyndon stretched out on a chaise longue on the terrace, talking to John Chancellor.[3] I curled up quietly beside him. He said, . . . "If this [war] winds up bad, and we get in a land war [in] Asia, there's only one address they will look for. . . . Mine." . . . Lyndon went on to say that there had been twenty-four major advances [in Congress] last week and not one got a quarter of an inch [in the newspapers]. Vietnam got all the space. . . . Lyndon spoke of sending McNamara out to Vietnam [earlier in July], and how frightened Lyndon was every time he went. He said, "I have kept him away from there almost a year now, and I lie awake until he gets back." . . . Flying in [from Camp David by helicopter,] Clark Clifford . . . said, "It's been a good weekend for us all. It's been a good weekend for the country."[4] . . . His tone was so weighted that I felt some pretty important decisions had been arrived at.

RICHARD RUSSELL

Monday, July 26, 1965, 5:46 P.M.

The Joint Chiefs are recommending that the United States bomb the new surface-to-air missile (SAM) sites in North Vietnam. Since they are probably Russian-operated, an attack that killed Russians may risk bringing the Soviet Union into the war. Johnson had told the Chiefs, "This is a war, and the stakes are high."[5] Russell once again shows the President his grave misgivings about escalating the

---

1. See *FRUS*, vol. 3, pp. 238–39; and Clifford, *Counsel to the President*, pp. 418–21.
2. Lady Bird felt that every President should have his portrait painted early in his term, before the traumas of the job ravaged his looks.
3. Chancellor, another guest at Camp David, would soon resign as NBC White House correspondent to direct the Voice of America.
4. Clifford's comment came from either politesse toward the First Lady or a hope that LBJ had listened to his warning about Vietnam.
5. See Meeting Notes, July 26, 1965, in *FRUS*, vol. 3, pp. 240–45.

war.[1] But LBJ is no longer listening. With his big decision made, all he wants from Russell is tactical advice.

LBJ: Westmoreland says that we ought to take out everything simultaneously. He's just really a firefighter. He's an old South Carolina boy, and I guess he's been out there messing with them long enough, and he's getting fed up with it. . . . Wheeler and the Joint Chiefs are real tough on taking out Six and Seven[2] immediately. They'd be glad to take out everything in the whole of Southeast Asia. But they *really* want to take these out. . . . McNamara thinks you've got to take them out, and the quicker the better. If you don't, you'll send a false signal to Russia that she can do this with impunity . . . and pretty soon we'll have no planes in the air . . . because they'll knock them out. . . . Notwithstanding what people think . . . [McNamara] holds down the military a good deal. . . . Most [people] think he's a hawk and that he's always raising hell to go to war.

RUSSELL: . . . I think he's got the military to where they're somewhat circumscribed from expressing themselves freely.

LBJ: . . . I've had [the military] over here for hours.[3] . . . Some of them are awfully irresponsible. They'll just scare you. They're ready to put a million men in right quick. . . . Rusk thinks that we ought to go . . . and take these sites out. Ball and Goldberg and Humphrey kind of wobbled on both sides. . . . We think that the Russians are manning [the sites]. . . . We don't want anybody to know that. . . .

RUSSELL: No, I'd say they were manned by North Vietnamese. . . . I think the Russians have got people there showing them how to shoot them. But I would never mention that.

LBJ: We don't want to put them behind the wall where they got to fight back. . . . That's why I'm trying to hold down this play. . . . We told [the Russians] what our defense budget was. We said, "Ours is $2 billion lower. You lower yours." And they did. When we cut out this nuclear production . . . last year, you wondered why it hadn't been cut out before. It was running out of our ears when I first came in as President. They cut down theirs.[4] Now . . . I don't want to . . . say, "I'm just going to have a hell of a lot of billions of dollars." Because . . . [North] Vietnam is trying to pull [China and Russia] back together.[5] . . . Any big, dramatic announcement on my part will throw them together. . . . So five minutes from now, they're coming in here to decide what to do about the SAM site. The weight of opinion is pretty solidly on taking out Six and Seven tonight. . . .

---

1. See Beschloss, *Taking Charge,* pp. 363–70, 400–3, and LBJ-Russell conversation, March 6, 1965, above.
2. The Pentagon had numbered the sites.
3. In a meeting that afternoon.
4. In 1964, when LBJ cut production of enriched uranium by 25 percent, the Russians reciprocated.
5. Reversing earlier policy, Mao was opening Chinese railroads to shipment of Soviet weapons to Hanoi. (See A. J. Langguth, *Our Vietnam,* Simon & Schuster, 2000, p. 351.)

RUSSELL: I'd take . . . every one out. . . . And I'd at least take out one other that I knew exactly where it was.

LBJ: If you do, that gets you in the Hanoi area. That gets you in civilians. That gets . . . the world upset. I just can't do that on these others. They're not bothering me and my targets. . . . [Six and Seven] are right in line with all the targets I've got that's worth a damn. I can't send my boys up there without knocking them down. The Hanoi ones don't bother me too much. . . . If [you hit those other sites], you're going to hit the goddamn capital. You'll have [Russia and China] in the war in fifteen minutes . . . when you go to bombing Hanoi. I think [the North Vietnamese] are trying to trap us into doing that.

RUSSELL: Our CIA thinks they moved a lot of the government out of Hanoi.

LBJ: . . . We'll debate that later. This one is right up now.

RUSSELL: I'd say yes, get them tonight, if I could. But I'd hate like hell to try to get them and miss them.

LBJ: We think we're likely to miss them. . . . They may just have strips of ground that look like a landing strip and have mobile ones that they move in just like a trailer and move out.[1] . . . Now . . . on this other thing,[2] I think I'm going to work out a deal where I give Westmoreland what he needs in about three increments.[3] Thirty or forty thousand each. Send a division right away from down at your Fort Benning. . . . Give [us] . . . that division right quick, and then do it in two or three increments between now and the first of December.

RUSSELL: You have one damn good soldier out there named Walter Brown Russell, Jr.[4] . . .

LBJ: Is he in that crowd?

RUSSELL: Yes, sir. . . .

LBJ: He knows he's going, does he?

RUSSELL: Oh, yeah. They all know it. They're just sitting there waiting for it. . . .

LBJ: We don't think we'll ask for much money [from Congress] because we don't want to blow this thing up.

RUSSELL: I'm with you on that. . . . I didn't see a bit of need of pressing so damn hard.

LBJ: We don't think we'll need any legislation. We'll tell them to get the Reserve plans ready . . . if next year we do. Then I'm going to do everything I can with this

---

1. That night the United States attacked sites Six and Seven, but evidently Six was a dummy site and there was no equipment at Seven. (See *FRUS,* vol. 3, p. 257.)

2. Westmoreland's request for a major escalation in ground troops.

3. Johnson presumes that sending men to Vietnam in smaller increments will arouse less public attention.

4. Lieutenant Colonel Russell was the Senator's nephew, stationed at Fort Benning. Later in 1965, he went with the First Air Cavalry to Vietnam, where he was shot, almost killed, and paralyzed for a time.

Jew up at the United Nations,[1] and everywhere in the world, to find a way to get out without saying so. But if I can't do that, January I'll have to decide on the Reserves. But I don't think I'll call them up now. I think it's too dramatic. I think it commits me where I can't get out. And it puts me out there further than I want to get right at the moment. Now, does that make sense to you?

RUSSELL: Yes. Except it adds to old Ho Chi Minh's argument that we ain't going to stay in there. That we're going to pull out. It may ease the pressure that we . . . hoped Russia would put on to get him out.

LBJ: What do you think?

RUSSELL: Call up the Reserves. They understand that language. They understood it in Berlin.[2] . . .

LBJ: If I extend the enlistments, if I put a hundred thousand out there, they'll understand it. I'm afraid they'll understand it too much. I don't have to have the Reserves to do that. And I'm going to step up my draft calls. Double them.

RUSSELL: You shouldn't send many more than a hundred thousand over there, Mr. President.

LBJ: No, I'm not. I'm not going to try to send more. . . . I'm just going to send a little less, maybe.

RUSSELL: You've been living with it every minute. I just live with it at night.

LBJ: I never worked on anything as hard in my life. I've had every human—

RUSSELL: It's just nearly driven me mad. I guess it's the only thing I've ever hit in my life I didn't have some quick answer to. But I haven't got one to this. . . .

LBJ: . . . I want to [brief] . . . the [congressional] leaders first. Then the Foreign Relations and Foreign Affairs and Armed Services [Committees]. . . . Do you think I ought to send a message to Congress or just make a statement? I'm not going to need any appropriation or any legislation . . . [for] my decision out there. Couldn't I just give a statement and say, "I'm going to send thirty thousand within the next few days and thirty thousand more, and it will be a total of a hundred thousand additionally that will be added. And if I do need anything, I'll call you back." . . . I don't want to dramatize it and throw Russia—

RUSSELL: . . . If that's the way you're going to play it, I'd play it down.

LBJ: You wouldn't have a Joint Session [of Congress]?

RUSSELL: I wouldn't cut down on the actual fighting, because those people over there are playing for keeps.

LBJ: Oh, I'm putting a *hundred* thousand in there. *Gosh,* I've moved a hundred and fifty thousand in the last ninety *days!*

RUSSELL: Has all the First Division got there yet?

---

1. Goldberg.
2. When Kennedy called up the Reserves during the Berlin Crisis of 1961.

LBJ: I don't know. All I know is I've got eighty thousand there, and I've got a hundred thousand that I'm going to authorize.

RUSSELL: I don't know. It has a mighty good psychological effect to call up some Reserves. . . .

LBJ: Yeah, but it upsets the hell out of [the North Vietnamese]. They'll immediately go to . . . pressing . . . for commitments now that they are not getting from Russia. I don't want to force them.

RUSSELL: . . . God knows, . . . and the thing that scares me worse is that these damn [South] Vietnamese are going to say, "Here is your war. Go ahead and take it!" And they'll quit fighting. That's what I've been looking for them to do. That little old mustached fellow [General Ky] was on the television. He indicated that *we* ought to fight the war and *his* troops ought to pacify the villages in the rear. God, that scared the hell out of me! If they're going to try to fight *that* kind of war, I'm in favor of getting *out* of there. If they're not going to really fight. The Koreans fought every inch of the way. . . . Even when they were taking staggering losses, they were increasing their units. . . . These people are letting theirs run *down*. They're not making any real effort over there now.

LBJ: . . . You don't think that I ought to have a Joint Session, do you?

RUSSELL: No, if I wasn't going to call up any Reserves . . . I wouldn't. . . . I think I'd just do it on television.

MIKE MANSFIELD

Tuesday, July 27, 1965, 2:43 P.M.

> Johnson has refused suggestions to ask Congress for large sums of money for Vietnam, call up the Reserves, put the country on a war footing, and declare a state of emergency with a dramatic address to a Joint Session. Instead he will play down his decision to escalate the war. He will merely announce at a routine press conference that troop commitments will rise from 75,000 to 125,000, with more forces sent later as required. Although LBJ has made his decision, Mansfield asks him to listen one more time to a group of Senators with expertise in foreign and military affairs.

MANSFIELD: Bill Fulbright came to me and suggested that it might be a good idea for him, Dick Russell, John Sherman Cooper, George Aiken, and John Sparkman[1] to come down and see you . . . on the present Vietnamese situation.

LBJ: . . . I've talked to practically all of them. All I think would come out of it

---

1. Cooper is a Republican from Kentucky, Sparkman a Democrat from Alabama.

would be a story in the paper about the worrying and the mess and the difficulty and their whining. I've been out on the boat with Bill [Fulbright].[1] I've had him down for breakfast. . . . We're going to see them all tomorrow morning in great detail.[2] The fact is, there is no easy way. . . . Bill's never going to be much of a leader. He's going to find things to worry him and concern him. His stuff he puts out of his meetings on Dominican Republic hurt us down there. [*sarcastically:*] He's really worried about things in Vietnam. I sit down with him and he agrees with me when I get through, and I think he will in the morning, when we get through. . . .

I'm going to tell you everything that I know this afternoon.[3] . . . I'm taking the soft line of the deal. A good many of my Cabinet, and a good many other people, think that [since] Kennedy called up the Reserve in '61 [and] in the Cuban Missile Crisis, we ought to go all the way. . . . I'm not doing that. I'm following more or less your memorandum.[4] I'm saying to them that I want Rusk and Goldberg and you and Clark Clifford and Abe Fortas, all the folks who really don't want to be in a land war there . . . to do all they can, around the clock. For Rusk to just lock himself up with the greatest experts he can—the Kissingers, the Bohlens,[5] anybody that he can think of . . . and try to find a way to get out. . . . I would tell [Fulbright] that we don't want to move into Hanoi, where either Russia or China will have to do more than she's doing now, if we can avoid it. . . .

Number two, we don't see how we can run out [of Vietnam]. . . . Number three, we don't think that we can leave these boys there inadequately protected at these bases. . . . Now . . . we're . . . giving [the military], in our own way, what they say they have to have. But we're not [letting] them . . . go with any new adventures. And we're hoping . . . to get through the monsoon season. . . . Hoping that maybe the other thing[6] will work. If it doesn't, then by January, you may have to appropriate and appropriate and appropriate. And you may have to do other things. But I'm doing my best to hold this thing in balance just as long as I can.

I can't run out. I'm not going to run in. I can't just sit there and let them be murdered. So I've got to put enough there to hold them and protect them. And . . . if we don't heat it up ourselves, and we don't dramatize it, we don't play it up and

---

1. See Lady Bird Johnson Diary, July 20, 1965, above.
2. To brief them on his announcement.
3. At a White House meeting of congressional leaders.
4. This is a whopper. As Johnson well knew, in his June 9 memorandum to the President and in other conversations, Mansfield asked for a negotiated settlement, not escalation. (See *FRUS*, vol. 2, pp. 741–44.)
5. Henry Kissinger of Harvard, who had served JFK as a foreign policy consultant, and Ambassador to France Charles Bohlen, who, drawing on his time as Ambassador to Moscow in the 1950s, advised Eisenhower and Kennedy on the Soviet Union.
6. The negotiation track.

say we're appropriating billions and we're sending millions and all [those] men, I
don't think that you [will] get the Russians . . . or the Chinese worked up about it.
That's what we are hoping.

MANSFIELD: Fine. . . .

LBJ: . . . I think that Bill has a responsibility as leader, just as you do. . . . I've
asked George Ball and Rusk to be available every Tuesday morning or any morning that Bill says—Bill and whoever he wants on that committee, any of them—to
go there regularly and keep right up with the constant surveillance of this thing.
But kind of have a responsibility for it. Not just to bellyache outside. . . . I'd just
give anything if he'll assume a little of the responsibility for it.

ABE FORTAS

Wednesday, July 28, 1965, 11:48 A.M.

> After twisting Fortas's arm for days, Johnson has now concluded that the only way
> to get his friend onto the Supreme Court is to shove him into the swimming pool.
> At 12:30 P.M. he is scheduled to have a press conference at which he will declare
> that fifty thousand new troops will go to Vietnam. He has also decided to an-
> nounce, whether Fortas consents or not, that his old friend is going to the Court.[1]
> LBJ calls Fortas at his law office to ask him to attend his press conference. Having
> known Johnson since the 1930s, Fortas suspects what he is up to.

LBJ: Are you going to watch my press conference today?

FORTAS: Yes, sir. Absolutely. I just left a meeting to do it.

LBJ: How's your blood pressure?

FORTAS: A little worried of what you may do. [*chuckles nervously*]

LBJ: [*chuckles*] Well, anything I do will be all right, won't it? Why don't you
come over here and watch the press conference? . . . Come on over and go down
with Bird or Marvin or Jack[2] or some of them at 12:25.

FORTAS: Okay.

LBJ: I don't know what will happen or what questions or anything I'll get. But
don't be surprised!

---

1. Such pressure tactics were standard weapons in LBJ's arsenal. In November 1963, knowing that
Russell would refuse, he announced that the Georgia Senator would go on the Warren Commission before asking him to serve. In February 1964 he browbeat Sargent Shriver into becoming chief of the
War on Poverty program before Shriver had a chance to say no. (See Beschloss, *Taking Charge*, pp.
66–68, 202–5, 208–10.)

2. Lady Bird, Marvin Watson, and Jack Valenti.

ARTHUR GOLDBERG

Wednesday, July 28, 1965, 7:20 P.M.

When Fortas arrived in the Oval Office, LBJ told him he was going to announce that fifty thousand men would go to Vietnam—and that Fortas would join the Supreme Court. If those young men could sacrifice for their country, so could Fortas. Johnson added that since it was his appointment being announced, Fortas should go along with him. At first, the stunned Fortas was silent. Then he said, "I'll accompany you."[1] Fortas later recalled, "To the best of my knowledge and belief, I never said yes."[2]

In the East Room, Johnson told reporters that "our fighting strength" in Vietnam would rise "to 125,000 men, almost immediately. Additional forces will be needed later, and they will be sent as required." He would double the monthly draft call and "step up our campaign for voluntary enlistments," but he would not call up the Reserves. Sending "the flower of our youth" into battle, he said, was the "most agonizing" duty of "your President." But "we will stand in Vietnam." Then the President announced that he was sending Abe Fortas to the Court. Fortas had not wanted to be a Justice, he said, but "in this instance, the job has sought the man."[3]

Johnson also told the reporters that today in New York his newly sworn UN Ambassador, Arthur Goldberg, would present Secretary-General U Thant "with a letter from me, requesting that all the resources, energy, and immense prestige of the United Nations be employed to find ways to halt aggression and to bring peace in Vietnam." Privately Johnson looks on this action as window-dressing but as he shows in this conversation, he is working hard to give Goldberg the illusion that he is at the center of decision making.

GOLDBERG: I want to congratulate you on your speech.

LBJ: Thank you, my friend.

GOLDBERG: . . . And I want to congratulate you on the appointment to the Court.

LBJ: God bless you. . . . I just followed both your recommendations. Now, you wanted a peace initiative. So I turned it over to you. . . . Ask every one of the 114 [delegates] personally. . . . Just say to each one, . . . "The President asked me to ask you to give any suggestion you can."

GOLDBERG: . . . The Secretary-General was very flattered that you sent him a letter. . . . He said he would [explore] with the Russians . . . whether or not there are any hopes. . . .

---

1. Lyndon Johnson, *The Vantage Point* (Holt, 1971), p. 545.
2. Abe Fortas oral history, LBJL.
3. Later Johnson told Fortas's law partner, Paul Porter, "Look, this was the only way I could do it, and I'll take complete responsibility for it." (Paul Porter oral history, LBJL.)

LBJ: I didn't get much hope out of Averell [Harriman's message], but we'll try it.[1]

GOLDBERG: Averell made a lot of Kosygin's statement that . . . he regarded the Vietnamese thing to be a small thing. . . . The Secretary-General said that his recent soundings to the Russians haven't indicated that. . . . He talked a little bit about his favorite proposal of putting the cease-fire in first. But I said, "Hold that up. This isn't a good time for you to come out with any cease-fire proposal."

*   *   *

LBJ: I got our [Medicare] passed today.[2]

GOLDBERG: Good, good. . . . What's been the reaction? . . .

LBJ: Oh, we got a few gripers, but by and large, it was wonderful. I've got all the governors coming in tomorrow.[3] . . . Would you like to fly down here and meet with them?

GOLDBERG: . . . If you would like me to, I would.

LBJ: . . . . Come on down here and just show them that you kind of got an open door here. . . . You can shake hands around and meet some of your old friends.

NICHOLAS KATZENBACH

Thursday, July 29, 1965, 9:20 P.M.

> Republican operatives are trying to scuttle the Fortas nomination with charges that Fortas had peddled influence with the Johnson administration to help legal clients. Telegrams from ultraright groups are pouring into Washington denouncing Fortas as a Jew, a left-winger, and a Communist. LBJ asks his Attorney General to take charge of the situation.

LBJ: We got a lot of static on the Fortas thing. We got a bunch of Republicans from the National Committee that's trying to organize a big fight on some oil thing in Puerto Rico. Fortas never had anything to do with it. He represents the Commonwealth of Puerto Rico. Some lawyer in his office handled the technical detail. . . . Secretary [of the Interior] decided it. . . . You better locate Udall[4] and get a complete record of just what Fortas had to do with it, if anything. . . . The second thing is Walter Jenkins. [Fortas] talked to the [*Washington*] *Star* people.[5] . . . He

---

1. From Moscow, Harriman had conveyed a private comment to him by Soviet Premier Alexei Kosygin that Vietnam should not obstruct American-Soviet relations and suggested enlisting the Russians to help solve the problem. (See *FRUS*, vol. 3, pp. 147–52.)

2. By a Senate vote of 70 to 24.

3. LBJ was to brief forty-nine governors in the State Dining Room on Vietnam.

4. Interior Secretary Stewart Udall.

5. Asking those at the *Star* and other editors to suppress the story of Walter Jenkins's arrest when the scandal broke in October 1964. (See LBJ-Fortas conversation, October 14, 1965.)

did this without my knowledge. . . . Third is that he was Bobby Baker's lawyer. . . . I don't think he ever took any fee from Bobby. Don't think he ever appeared for him. I think he just listened.[1] . . .

Now the big mistake was . . . he wanted to go off and have a vacation [with] Carol.[2] She was upset. She didn't want him to go on the Court. . . . They set the hearing [on his nomination] for August the 5th, at my request. . . . Then the damn fool wanted to change it. . . . It just [lets] every Hunt organization in America [make] trouble.[3] . . . Get it as soon as you can, so the Hunts and all the play can get over with. . . .

KATZENBACH: I was in Hruska's[4] office this morning . . . and he showed me about forty telegrams he had against Abe Fortas. . . . "Don't appoint this liberal . . . this Communist." . . . Hruska . . . said, . . . "You know all the people who wrote them? . . . They're all John Birch."[5]

LBJ: . . . I've got a good many saying that certain races[6] are taking over the [government].[7] And "they don't own it," and "they haven't got a title to it," and "he's a Communist." . . . I just don't want to get it built up where it goes too far.

* * *

LBJ: You got your poll tax stuff wound up, didn't you?[8]

KATZENBACH: Yeah. Walking on eggs all the way. . . . They're going to [submit the compromise version of the voting rights bill] in the House for a vote Tuesday.

LBJ: Okay. God bless you.

McGEORGE BUNDY

Friday, July 30, 1965, 9:35 A.M.

This afternoon LBJ is to fly to Missouri and sign the Medicare bill at the Harry Truman Presidential Library, alongside the ailing thirty-third President, who had

---

1. Fortas defended Baker until LBJ became President, when he resigned the case to avoid conflict of interest with his new role as an outside presidential adviser.

2. Mrs. Fortas.

3. LBJ refers to H. L. Hunt and other ultraright leaders who disdain Fortas. He worries that the later the hearings, the more chance they will have to make trouble.

4. Republican Senator Roman Hruska of Nebraska, of the Judiciary Committee.

5. The ultraconservative John Birch Society.

6. The Jews.

7. With Goldberg and Fortas appointed to key positions within the same month.

8. Thanks to LBJ's July 9 call to Martin Luther King, Jr., above, and administration pressure on other civil rights leaders, a compromise version of the voting rights bill omitted a flat ban on poll taxes.

once tried and failed to expand public health care. He complains to Bundy about new State Department leaks about Vietnam.

LBJ: I want you to try to get some loyalty in the State Department. . . . Work on Bill [Bundy] to use his personal influence with the Assistant Secretaries . . . over there to be loyal to Johnson and quit slicing us and saying we don't know about foreign affairs. These underlings doing it—find out who they are and get rid of them.

MIKE MANSFIELD

Friday, July 30, 1965, 10:00 A.M.

Johnson asks his Senate Majority Leader to move the Fortas hearings up to August 5th, to forestall opposition. But this date will require Fortas to cancel the vacation hastily arranged to calm his wife's fury at him for surrendering to the President's "dirty trick." When LBJ called to mollify her, she accused him of trying to "destroy Abe" and barked, "You don't treat friends that way!" Johnson told an aide, "Oh boy, Carol was furious with me!"[1]

LBJ: Ramsey[2] very foolishly . . . said they'd like to have [the hearings on August] 12th, because Abe would like to spend some days with his wife. . . . She said her life had been ruined.[3] I don't know—these women! Their lives get ruined mighty easy! . . . Abe is going to be here, after she got through crying one night. He's not going to have to take her off and stay with her a week. . . . So it ought to be on the 5th. . . .
MANSFIELD: Okay. I'll call him . . . right away.
LBJ: . . . Put the blame on me or Ramsey. . . . Don't talk about the wife.[4]

---

1. Kalman, *Abe Fortas*, p. 245; Murphy, *Fortas*, pp. 181–85.
2. Ramsey Clark, Deputy Attorney General.
3. This is exactly what Walter Jenkins's wife had said during his scandal in October 1964. (See Chapter 2.)
4. Fortas was unanimously approved by the Senate Judiciary Committee and confirmed by the Senate on August 11 by voice vote.

Epilogue

RIDING ON A CREST

*Whatever the strains and tensions and distresses of the day in Washington
had been, they were not noticeable in Lyndon's manner. He was like a man
riding on a crest of achievement and success.*

LADY BIRD JOHNSON, *August 27, 1965*

To finish the story of Lyndon Johnson's pivotal year as President, this epilogue
uses excerpts from the tape-recorded daily diary kept by Lady Bird. Always more
conscious than anyone else of her husband's highs and lows, she records his pride
in his monumental accomplishments in Congress interwoven with his increasing
dread about Vietnam and the backlash he anticipates against the Great Society and
his successes in civil rights.[1]

LADY BIRD JOHNSON

Sunday, August 1, 1965, Tape-recorded Diary

Standing in the LBJ Ranch swimming pool at the start of August, Johnson tells his
new domestic adviser, Joseph Califano, that he has laid the foundations of the
Great Society—Medicare, education, voting rights. But he wants more from Congress: "There are too many damn agencies fiddling with transportation. I want to
put them . . . in one Cabinet department. . . . I want to rebuild American cities. . . .
I want a bill that makes it possible for anybody to buy a house anywhere they can
afford to."[2] Califano is startled that, "in spite of his decision to step up the war,"
Johnson refuses to concede any limits to his future domestic program.[3] LBJ and

---

1. The relatively few tapes that LBJ made himself in August 1965 have not yet been released by the
LBJ Library.
2. Johnson got all three wishes. Congress established the Department of Transportation and Model
Cities program in 1966. The Fair Housing Act was passed in 1968.
3. Califano, *The Triumph and Tragedy of Lyndon Johnson*, pp. 51–52.

Lady Bird take Califano and his wife, along with Arthur and Dorothy Goldberg and their son, to the First Christian Church of Johnson City.

LADY BIRD: How can the summer have flown so swiftly? . . . We got off in a great flurry for church, nine of us in the station wagon. . . . I could hardly keep from giggling—at least three Jews and two Catholics. . . . Father Akin's [1] helpers, pausing in front of everybody, with the bread and the wine, would simply shove it a little close, for a moment, until they understood the gentle shake of the head. . . . Lyndon has certainly shaken things up around Johnson City, indeed around much of this nation.

LADY BIRD JOHNSON

Tuesday, August 10, 1965, Tape-recorded Diary

On Friday, August 6, an exuberant Johnson had gone to Capitol Hill to sign the Voting Rights Act of 1965. With a bust of Lincoln over his shoulder in the Rotunda, LBJ declared "to every Negro in this country: You must register. You must vote. . . . Your future and your children's future depend on it." Building on his audacious June speech at Howard University demanding equality "not as a theory" but "as a fact and a result," he considers the Civil Rights and Voting Rights Acts only the start of what he plans to achieve in civil rights. With his terror about leaks concerning Vietnam, LBJ hauls the entire House and Senate, in groups, to the White House to brief them on the war. After one such briefing, he asks Lady Bird to join him for a cruise down the Potomac on the presidential yacht *Sequoia*.

LADY BIRD: I got a call from Lyndon: "How would you like to go out on the boat with a bunch of Texas folks?" Dull, sleepy, in a bad humor, I started to say, "No, I want to go to bed." And then I thought of *his* program today: Senate leadership meeting, House briefing, and an hour and a half of the hardest thinking and exchange. This has been a week in which he has tried to tell the whole Congress, the House and Senate—he and General Taylor and McNamara and Secretary Rusk—bring them up to date on Vietnam. . . . And I thought, "If a trip on the boat after a day like that would rest him, let's have it."

---

1. Ray Akin, lay minister of the First Christian Church of Johnson City.

LADY BIRD JOHNSON

Sunday, August 15, 1965, Tape-recorded Diary

Exactly five days after Johnson signed the Voting Rights Act, the backlash he has feared is about to begin.[1] In the Watts section of Los Angeles, after a twenty-one-year-old unemployed black man is arrested for suspected drunk driving, hundreds of blacks throw rocks at the police. Five thousand rioters break windows, loot stores, and burn them. Four people are killed, more than a hundred injured. The Los Angeles police chief, William Parker, taunts LBJ by saying that violence is inevitable "when you keep telling people they are unfairly treated and teach them disrespect for the law."[2]

Hearing about Watts from the ranch, Johnson is disconsolate. California Governor Pat Brown and other officials beg the White House for federal help, but the President will not return Califano's telephone calls.[3] Instead he grimly cuts himself off from the bad news, boating on Lake Lyndon B. Johnson and riding around the ranch in his white Lincoln. Forced to exceed his authority, Califano personally gives "presidential approval" for the U.S. Army to help maintain order in Watts.

Johnson has Bill Moyers announce that the President finds the riots "tragic and shocking." By Saturday night more than twenty people are dead, six hundred injured, fourteen hundred arrested. In his gloom, LBJ tells Califano that Watts and other riots are going to kill the chances for more progress on civil rights. Just as during Reconstruction, Negroes are going to "end up pissing in the aisles of the Senate" and make "fools" of themselves out of "frustration, impatience, and anger." He orders an investigation of whether the Watts rioters have been incited by a "Communist conspiracy."[4]

With his gift for seeing around corners, Johnson predicts that one of the riot's beneficiaries will be Ronald Reagan, an almost certain Republican candidate for Governor in 1966, who opposed the Civil Rights Act.[5] A week before the election of 1964, Reagan delivered a television address for Barry Goldwater called "A Time for Choosing"; the speech launched his career in national politics. It will become a manifesto for the countermovement against Johnson's Great Society that, by 1980, will propel Reagan into the presidency.

LADY BIRD: Lyndon has spent a sizable part of yesterday and this morning on the phone about Los Angeles. He issued a strong denunciation of the Los Angeles

---

1. In March, LBJ had told John McClellan that he was "scared to death" of what would happen when the "Nigro boys on the streets" got going in the cities that summer. (See March 23, 1965, conversation, above.)
2. Quoted in Califano, *The Triumph and Tragedy of Lyndon Johnson,* p. 59.
3. The only time this ever happened during his four years with Johnson, he later wrote. (Ibid.)
4. Ibid., pp. 59–63.
5. Lou Cannon, *Reagan* (Putnam, 1982), p. 107.

rioters [and] arranged to give [California Governor Pat Brown] all the help the federal government could—trucks, jeeps, rations, anything for the California National Guard. . . . I hope a lot of people heard him, because he's going to get the blame for letting [blacks] go too far, too fast. I think he's tough enough to stand up to both sides, but he sure is the one in the middle. . . .

After dinner we walked down to [Cousin] Oreole's,[1] Lynda and I together. . . . Oreole welcomed us with delight. And then, when Aunt Ellen came in with Jesse,[2] I introduced her and said, "This is my aunt from Alabama." Oreole said, "Oh, yes. That's where the niggers are cutting up all the jacks, and that's what caused everything that's going on in Los Angeles."[3] What a condensation of history. . . . And I'm afraid it's exactly what millions of people are thinking.

LADY BIRD JOHNSON

Wednesday, August 18, 1965, Tape-recorded Diary

> Back at the White House, Johnson's spirits lift as he basks in acclaim for his successes in Congress. At Lady Bird's behest a bust and a portrait of him are being made.[4] Liberal scholars are invited to interview the President about his achievements on Capitol Hill. The historian William Leuchtenburg tells him that this Congress has arguably been the most significant ever. "No, it isn't," LBJ replies. "It isn't arguable."[5] He is not kidding.

LADY BIRD: At ten o'clock I called Lyndon and asked him when we could expect him to come join us for dinner. He gave me the rejoinder that he was over having fun with an office full of beautiful women and did I want to come over and see him. I did. [When I arrived] there was Larry O'Brien, Jack [Valenti], and Lee White.[6] He was telling Lee White that he didn't want him to leave the government, that he'd send him to Vietnam if he didn't like what he was doing now. Jokingly, of course, but earnest too. . . . I extracted Lyndon. . . . We went home for dinner. . . . Lyndon was gay and ebullient, riding the high tide of work that was yielding some achievements. . . . Nobody can spread delight, express pleasure in a more sparkling way than Lyndon, when he feels it.

---

1. Oreole Bailey, LBJ's elderly cousin who lived on the ranch.

2. Ellen Cooper Taylor, wife of Lady Bird's father's brother, and Jesse Kellam, general manager of the Johnson broadcasting enterprise.

3. Cousin Oreole was referring to Selma. By "jacks" she probably meant the common people. (*Oxford English Dictionary,* Oxford, 1971.)

4. The portrait, by Peter Hurd, provoked Johnson's famous reaction, "That's the ugliest thing I ever saw." (See *New York Times,* July 10, 1984.)

5. Quoted in William Leuchtenburg, "A Visit with LBJ," *American Heritage,* May–June 1990.

6. All Johnson staff members. White, LBJ's counsel, had told him he wanted to leave the White House.

LADY BIRD JOHNSON

Sunday, August 22, 1965, Tape-recorded Diary

Spending a weekend in Washington, LBJ and Lady Bird attend National City Christian Church.

LADY BIRD: Lyndon said he liked to go down to the coffee hour. He said, "One reason why I like to go to church is to see the people. In this life I lead now, I don't have much chance just to get out and mix with folks, and it makes me want to get more education for them, and better health care, and more of the things they need." It is a sort of shot of adrenaline to him.

LADY BIRD JOHNSON

Monday, August 23, 1965, Tape-recorded Diary

Hypersensitive to the danger that his name will be tarnished by scandal, and under attack for the costs of the Great Society, LBJ has a fight with Lady Bird over her expenses.

LADY BIRD: [The day] began with a blowup. I was in Lyndon's bedroom with Marvin [Watson] and Jake [Jacobson] and Jack [Valenti][1] coming and going, discussing with Lyndon . . . approval of travel for the girls . . . who advance trips like mine to the Grand Teton. . . . Lyndon, ever fearful of raising expenses and arousing any just criticism, was looking at it with a hard eye. I took the position that my few speeches, my few trips for Head Start,[2] beautification, and so forth had to be advanced and ought to be paid for. My own personal ticket I would buy. And then I walked out, angry and hurt, after what must have been a very flabby presentation of the case. . . .

When I returned from the beauty parlor, I had a message that the President would like to see me in his office. I went with a certain amount of trepidation, because the last thing I need to bring to him, along with Vietnam and the steel strike,[3] is personal problems. He was so sweet. He knew I had been worrying about money to run the White House with when my separation pay from KTBC[4] comes

---

1. White House aides.
2. LBJ's program to aid preschool education.
3. LBJ was trying to broker an agreement between labor and the steel industry over wage demands. He succeeded on September 3.
4. Under the Johnson blind trust, Lady Bird's relationship with the family's Austin station was suspended until the end of Johnson's presidency.

to an end this month, and for Luci's foolishly expensive car[1] and clothes to live up to the life we lead. He put his arms around me and said, "You don't have to worry about anything. You ought not to worry about money. I'll get you whatever you need." And then he said, "One of the Jetstars[2] has to go to Fort Worth to be worked on. . . . It will be ready whenever you are ready."

I was speechless and closer to tears than I had been in four or five years. I hugged him and walked out, not trusting myself to talk. Poor man, trying to walk the tightrope between loving and wanting to please his family and make them comfortable, and wanting to live up to the ethics, a sort of thrift, for the private actions that could face public scrutiny. Toughness must be one of the qualifications for this job, both public and private. . . . It had been a tense and exhausting day. Emotions—angry, sad, or happy—are exhausting to me.

LADY BIRD JOHNSON

Thursday, August 26, 1965, Tape-recorded Diary

> Feeling beleaguered by Vietnam, a looming steel strike, and the white and black anger over Watts, Johnson has called the ranch and told Lady Bird that he might not fly home to Texas for his fifty-seventh birthday tomorrow.

LADY BIRD: I talked to Lyndon several times. He sounded hurried, distraught, concerned about the steel strike. Not sure he was coming, which I completely discounted. Concerned also about the children's using Camp David. . . . He is divided between two attitudes on our life in the White House, the luxuries thereof—the use of the boat, of Camp David, the planes and helicopters—for me, for the children, in some ways for himself. He swings between the poles of severe austerity—to leave the boats in dry dock, don't go to Camp David, thinking of economy. . . . The other pole is the happiness it gives him to give us something, to make us happy. I am caught in between, with understanding and compassion for both sides, but with the conviction that we ought to give the job all we've got, all four of us, and happily accept the luxuries that come with it.

---

1. The Corvette Sting Ray.
2. In the presidential fleet.

LADY BIRD JOHNSON
Friday, August 27, 1965, Tape-recorded Diary

> The President is scheduled to speak in Johnson City this afternoon, presenting his
> newly restored boyhood home to the National Park Service. But his rapidly chang-
> ing moods make his birthday turbulent.

LADY BIRD: Lyndon's fifty-seventh birthday was oddly divided between a
quiet morning (I actually lay in bed and did some recording) and hours of riding
the knife edge of tension. Sometime during the morning, I got a call from Lyndon—a hesitant, uncertain sort of call. What would I think if he didn't come at all?
Things were in turmoil. The steel strike was pressing on him. I quickly marshaled
my thoughts and said if he didn't, I would go through with the park presentation,
rush it up, if possible, and then catch the quickest commercial [flight] or anything
back to Washington to be with him, even if it was midnight of his birthday. He said
all right, he'd let me know.

And then . . . a call from Bill Moyers, which disturbed me. He said something
had happened that he wouldn't go into—it was all his fault. . . . "It may have hurt
my relations with the President permanently." . . . The President might not come
[to Texas], and if he didn't, Bill realized it would upset my plans very much for the
park dedication and for the birthday party, and he wanted me to know he was
sorry. There was something about his tone that worried me far more than either the
presentation or party. He said he took the full blame, that it was all his fault. And
what it is, I have no idea. Bill contributes a certain quality of brilliance, of wit, and
a mixture of aloofness from us, with yet enough devotion to us, that Lyndon needs.
. . . I could not bear to lose him, and his words . . . fell like a stone on my heart. . . .
There's nothing to do with uncertainty but to live through it and keep on with the
business at hand. . . .

It was one-thirty, our time, [when] we got the word that [Lyndon] was actually
in the air [to Texas]. . . . Helicopter Number One settled on the ground, and Lyndon emerged like a whirlwind. . . . He got [into the car] with us and we drove to
the park. It was a sight to see! Our platform was the base of a float, decked with
paper rosebuds. A band was playing in one corner, a motley crowd, half of whom
I recognized as Johnson City folks. . . . The usual quota of towheaded, barefooted
boys. And I was suddenly struck with thinking, "How must this look to sophisticated city people from New York?"[1] Pretty hopeless, with . . . the worn-out re-
frigerators behind the hardware store. . . . I had [not been sure] Lyndon was going
to say anything. He has a certain reluctance about this whole thing. Could he think

---

1. A delegation was present from *Life* magazine, which was running an article on the boyhood
home under Lady Bird's byline.

... people are laughing at his little hometown? He made an amusing, bucolic, reminiscent sort of little speech about some of his memories of Johnson City. ...

It was the end of a tense day. I was utterly ready for the top deck of the big boat, a pillow, a drink, good companions, the sunset and the new moon. ... John and Nellie [Connally] were on the big boat coming back with us. He and Lyndon were talking about plans for John for the future. John said he was not going to run again [for Governor of Texas]. ... Lyndon said, "You're crazy! Think what you can do for the state. And then maybe you could be Vice President or President of this country." I wondered what sort of a forecast that meant for me and my plans for '68.[1] I agree so wholeheartedly about John. He looks like Texas. He's the best of Texas, though too conservative sometimes for me and Lyndon. ... Nellie was happy, pretty, lively, flirting just a little bit with all the men, and everybody naturally gravitating to her. ...

Then inside for birthday cake. ... A really wonderful cake, produced by ... the White House kitchen's artistry and some of my suggestions. On the top of it, "You can have your cake and eat it too." ... And a hypodermic needle [representing the Medicare act] ... some tiny modern houses [the housing act], and a roadway building [the Appalachia act]. "Major achievements" all over the cake. ... It was after 12:30 A.M. when we got home, and probably 2:00 before we went to sleep.

But whatever the strains and tensions and distresses of the day in Washington had been, they were not noticeable in Lyndon's manner. He was like a man riding on a crest of achievement and success. He was also a happy and relaxed man. I shall remember his fifty-seventh birthday with happiness.

*   *   *

For removing shackles from black Americans and attacking poverty, disease, ignorance, and injustice, Lyndon Johnson had dreamt that history might rank him alongside Abraham Lincoln and Franklin Roosevelt. On his fifty-seventh birthday, as LBJ rode on the crest of the wave, his "dream must have seemed so close that he could hardly fail to grasp it," as F. Scott Fitzgerald wrote of his most famous hero.

But on that birthday night Johnson knew that the dream was likely to elude him, tied to the deadweight of an Asian land war. He had told Lady Bird that summer that he felt like the pilot of an airplane going down in flames.[2]

After the victory of 1964, the old master had warned his staff that, despite the huge Democratic margin on Capitol Hill, they would have only six months or so before exhausted, resentful members of the House and Senate began to rebel against the lash of the White House. After enacting the most important legislative program since FDR's First New Deal, LBJ suffered his initial major repudiation—

---

1. Meaning her insistence that LBJ retire in 1968.
2. Quoted in Lady Bird Johnson Diary, July 8, 1965, above.

on home rule for the District of Columbia—in September 1965. "It only takes one for them to see they can cut us and make us bleed," he told his aides. "Then they'll bleed us to death on our other legislation."[1] About Congress he was rarely wrong. The bleeding had begun.

Once again LBJ showed his propensity for physical breakdown under political stress. On Election Day 1964 he had taken to bed. In January 1965, immediately after the inauguration, he came down with a serious respiratory infection and the depression that so worried Lady Bird. As the summer of 1965 turned to fall, after the pressures of Selma, the Dominican Republic, the escalation in Vietnam, the herculean effort to shove the Great Society through Congress, Johnson was hospitalized with an excruciating attack of kidney stones and had his gallbladder removed.

His recovery took longer than expected. By the end of 1965 he looked gaunt and chastened. Joseph Califano was startled to learn that the President had stopped drinking. LBJ wanted to be certain that, at any hour of the day or night, his mind would be clear in case he had to make a sudden decision about "my boys" in Vietnam.[2]

By 1966, as Johnson had predicted, the backlash against the Great Society, civil rights, and a stalemate in Vietnam was in full snap. In the midterm elections Republicans gained forty-seven seats in the House, three seats in the Senate, and eight new Governors, including Ronald Reagan in California. Richard Nixon chortled to friends, "We've beaten hell out of them, and we're going to kill them in '68!"[3]

"The first year or two in the White House was wine and roses," Lady Bird told the author of this book in 1998. "But by the end, it was *pure hell.*" In 1967 there were riots in Newark and Detroit. Students were so inflamed by the war in Vietnam that the Secret Service told LBJ he should no longer speak on campuses. The armed truce with Robert Kennedy was over. Johnson was sure that RFK would run for President.

By then McGeorge Bundy, Jack Valenti, and Bill Moyers were gone from the White House.[4] "I was fond of the old bastard," said Bundy in 1994. "He was a marvelous guy, except that he's such a bitch."[5] LBJ's admiration for Robert McNamara crumbled when the exhausted, tormented Secretary of Defense privately concluded that the war had been a mistake. Many years after McNamara left the Pentagon, he said, "I don't know whether I resigned or was fired."[6] Johnson told friends he had

---

1. Quoted in Califano, *The Triumph and Tragedy of Lyndon Johnson,* p. 230. See also LBJ to King on his deterioration in Congress, July 7, 1965, above.
2. Ibid., p. 121.
3. Quoted in Stephen Ambrose, *Nixon,* vol. 2 (Simon & Schuster, 1989), p. 100.
4. Bundy became president of the Ford Foundation. Valenti became president of the Motion Picture Association of America. Moyers became publisher of *Newsday.*
5. Quoted in Bird, *Color of Truth,* p. 323.
6. He said this to the author in 1996.

let McNamara go because "we just can't afford another Forrestal," referring to James Forrestal, the first Secretary of Defense, who had killed himself.[1]

Arthur Goldberg bitterly concluded that leaving the Supreme Court was "the biggest mistake of my life."[2] Goldberg carped that Johnson had asked him to "try to extricate our country" from Vietnam. Instead the President had "used" him to distract the public while he escalated the war. Goldberg recalled a small White House meeting where Johnson, asked why America was in Vietnam, "unzipped his fly, drew out his substantial organ, and declared, 'This is why!' "[3] In 1971, when LBJ's memoirs said that Goldberg had left the Court because he was restless, the irate Goldberg called the former President in Texas and sputtered, "I loved the Supreme Court. I did it as a national duty." He demanded that Johnson return a painting Dorothy Goldberg had given him: "I don't want that in your house."[4]

As for Johnson's first nominee to the Supreme Court, the passage of time would show why Fortas had dragged his feet on LBJ's offer. Fortas had no doubt suspected that it would be dangerous for him as a Justice, in light of the constitutional separation of powers, to continue giving LBJ the service he expected—writing speeches and offering confidential advice, even about the inner workings of the Court. He was right to be worried. In 1968 Fortas's enemies used his intimacy with the President to kill his nomination as Chief Justice.

Another reason Fortas had not wished to join the Court was that he felt he couldn't afford it.[5] He was right to be worried about that too. So strapped did Fortas feel that he made secret arrangements for cash payments from a businessman, which, when revealed in 1969, required him to quit the Court in disgrace.[6] By then it was too late for Johnson to learn that when people refused a job offer, it might be wiser not to force them.[7] "I made him take the Justiceship," the former President lamented. "In that way, I ruined his life."[8]

The third volume of *The Secret Johnson White House Tapes* will show Lyndon Johnson coping with domestic antiwar insurrection, the burning of the cities, a

---

1. Quoted in Deborah Shapley, *Promise and Power* (Little, Brown, 1993), p. 427.
2. He told this to the author in 1981.
3. See Dallek, *Flawed Giant,* p. 491.
4. Arthur Goldberg oral history, LBJL.
5. Although he and his wife had earned large salaries for years and had no children to support, they never stopped feeling financially overwhelmed. (See Kalman, *Abe Fortas,* pp. 242–43.)
6. See Ibid., pp. 372–76.
7. As he had also done with Richard Russell, Sargent Shriver, and others. (See footnote to LBJ-Fortas conversation, July 28, 1965.)
8. Johnson said this to Harry Middleton, Director of the LBJ Library. (See Murphy, *Fortas,* p. 1.) By saying that he had ruined Fortas's life, LBJ unwittingly chose the same phrase used by Walter Jenkins's wife in October 1964 (see LBJ-Lady Bird conversation, October 15, 1965) and Fortas's wife in July 1965 (see LBJ-Mansfield conversation, July 30, 1965).

six-day conflict in the Middle East, and a rebellious Congress; tempted to break his pledge to Lady Bird and run again in 1968; brooding over the murders of Martin Luther King, Jr., and Robert Kennedy; struggling to end the war in Vietnam; furious at what he considered to be candidate Hubert Humphrey's disloyalty about the war; and then finally turning the presidency over to Richard Nixon.

EDITOR'S NOTE

Taking Charge and *Reaching for Glory,* the first two volumes of this trilogy, cover about two-thirds of the roughly 642 hours and 9,500 private conversations that Lyndon Johnson secretly taped between November 1963 and January 1969.[1] As his presidency rolled on, LBJ taped less and less.[2]

During the year portrayed in this volume, Johnson made many of the most important decisions of his five years in the White House—to escalate the war in Vietnam; to fight for voting rights, Medicare, a War on Poverty, education, and other bills that constituted perhaps the most substantial legislative year of any President in history. By September 1965 the contours of the rest of Johnson's term were in place—the deepening chasm in Southeast Asia, campus and street demonstrations at home, riots in major American cities, Johnson's diminishing clout in Congress, his growing clash with Robert Kennedy.

I have conceived this trilogy in the style of an edited and annotated anthology of private letters written by a public figure in the days when leaders did business on paper, revealing their private purposes, methods, and obsessions. The conversations thus appear in chronological order, suggesting the variety of issues and people with which a President has to deal almost simultaneously, how he obtains information and reacts to it, the pressures on him, the flow of his hourly decision making. My chief standard in selecting which conversations or parts thereof to include is whether they add something of historical importance to what we knew be-

---

1. This Editor's Note includes some language adapted from the Editor's Note in *Taking Charge.* That version should be consulted for a more comprehensive description of the provenance of Johnson's taping. As in that version, I use the word "tapes" to refer to both Dictabelts and reel-to-reel recordings made by Johnson. The alert reader may note that I have added the word "secret" to the subtitle of *Reaching for Glory.* This is to distinguish the extraordinary secretly recorded tapes of Presidents Kennedy, Johnson, and Nixon (and the much smaller number made by FDR and Eisenhower) from the more innocuous recordings that later Presidents have made of, for example, media interviews, after ensuring that all parties know they are being taped.

2. The 642 hours do not include a separate collection of more formal meetings recorded by LBJ late in his presidency.

fore, and whether they show us a heretofore unseen facet of Lyndon Johnson and the people with whom he dealt.

Most of the conversations in this volume and its predecessor took place on the telephone. A few were personal encounters, captured by the hands-free "squawk box" on LBJ's Oval Office desk, which was tied in to his hidden recording system.[1] The time offered for each conversation is local time.

The mandate for a historian writing a book of his own prose is to draw on all sources available—tapes, letters, memos, cables, memoirs, oral histories, and other material—and strive to make lasting judgments. The editor of a volume of new primary source material, like this one, has a different responsibility—not to drown out the subject's voice with his own or pretend that definitive judgments can be based solely on a single category of source material, however rich. His pre-eminent task is instead to explain what the new material means and what it tells us beyond what we know already.

Like any fresh primary source, secret White House tapes must be analyzed with skepticism. As Richard Nixon showed us while trying to maneuver his counsel, John Dean, into taking the blame for Watergate, a President who knows he is tap-ing a conversation can manipulate or entrap an interlocutor who does not. He can also try to present the best face for later historians.

The tapes thus far opened reveal surprisingly few obvious efforts by Johnson to preen on them for history. Not only were many of the recordings made for another purpose—to give him a record that could be useful in his daily business—but, be-leaguered as he felt even at the best of times, LBJ was unlikely to impair an effort to work his will over someone in order to impress some distant future historian. And during many of these conversations Johnson had forgotten or was otherwise unaware that the hidden recorder was still running.[2] I have nonetheless indicated several cases where LBJ may have been playing to the microphone.[3]

Any historian must always question whether a collection like this has been san-itized, with embarrassing tapes altered or destroyed. Neither Mildred Stegall, the White House aide to whom LBJ entrusted the tapes for safekeeping, nor Harry Middleton, the Director of the Johnson Library, who took custody of them after LBJ's death, knows of any effort by Johnson or anyone else to tamper with them—with one exception.[4] The President's Daily Diary for November 24, 1966, notes

---

1. For example, LBJ's conversation with Robert Kennedy of September 3, 1964.

2. Unlike in the voice-activated Nixon system, LBJ had a conversation recorded by telling a secre-tary, "Take this" or "Get it down." If he was in the midst of an exchange going unrecorded and wanted it preserved, he might "mash a button" (Johnson's phrase) to summon a secretary and then twirl his finger in the air. Often, after the exchange that Johnson wished to record was over, the recorder ground on, capturing other conversations that LBJ almost certainly did not intend to preserve either for daily business or to burnish his historical reputation.

3. See, for example, his conversation with Mike Mansfield of June 8, 1965, in this volume.

4. Stegall and Middleton interviews with the author, 1997.

that the Dictabelt of a conversation between Johnson and his continuing confidant, Justice Abe Fortas, was "destroyed on President's instruction." The absence of an effort to sanitize the Johnson tapes is almost impossible to prove, but it is given credence by other records and the frankness of much of the material in the collection.[1]

In no case have I shown the transcript of any of these conversations to a participant in it in an effort to discover what he or she or the President "really" meant. Even the most self-restrained human beings would find it hard to resist the temptation to "spin" what they and the President said long ago, in order to present themselves or LBJ in the most favorable historical light.[2] If I offered one such person the privilege to "revise and extend" private long-ago remarks, I would feel compelled, in fairness, to offer the same opportunity to the hundreds of other people who appear in this book (or perhaps their surviving relatives). At that point the actual conversations from 1964 and 1965 would be overwhelmed by strident accounts of what people "really" said or "meant" to say—or what "must" have been on the President's mind.

In creating this book I have listened to virtually every Johnson tape for the period from September 1, 1964, to July 31, 1965—often many times. Some of the tapes I have transcribed from scratch. For others I have started with rough transcripts created by LBJ's secretaries[3] or by a professional transcriber and listened repeatedly to the tapes, making substantial corrections, adding emphasis, punctuation, and transliteration of some words.

None of the tapes is easy to decipher. The Dictaphone of the 1960s was designed not for historiography but to record an executive's dictation. Sound quality is often flat and scratchy.[4] Many of the people on these tapes—not least LBJ himself, especially when he is tired—speak with accents that are difficult for the outsider to un-

---

1. Like all government holdings, the tapes are subject to official declassification rules, which allow the National Archives and the LBJ Library to close portions of the tapes to preserve national security or honor the donor's deed of gift, usually to prevent damaging living persons or releasing sensitive family, medical, or financial information. Roughly less than 4 percent has been withheld.

2. I imagined being told, "I may have seemed to assure the President that we could win in Vietnam by the end of 1965, but what I really meant was that the war would take ten years and we'd lose." In a few cases, as the reader will note from my footnotes, I have used insights from interviews I did with key figures for other projects to illuminate what is said on the tapes.

3. They transcribed some of the tapes at the time, for Johnson's use in doing business, others after his presidency, for use in his memoirs. The real-time transcripts are full of inaccuracies because the tired secretaries were working under pressure. The classic example is November 29, 1963, where the secretary has LBJ telling John McCormack that he has a "pack them bastards" waiting for him. Close listening to the tape and examination of Johnson's records show that he actually said "the Pakistan Ambassador." (See Beschloss, *Taking Charge*, p. 551.)

4. Especially for the tapes of October 1964, when LBJ was off campaigning, and July 1965, when LBJ's aides briefly tried out an inferior new recording system. I hired sound engineers accustomed to working with historical recordings to improve the quality of the tapes that were the most difficult to hear.

derstand. Some of the Oval Office recordings feature the President talking while beverage glasses are rattling, papers are being shuffled, commercials are blaring out of a television set, and aides are chattering in the background. Thus the only way to make these tapes a reliable source is for a historian to be steeped in the daily history of LBJ's presidency, armed with names, issues, and context, and to listen hard to every syllable—sometimes twenty times or more.

Readers should remember that transcription of any historical recording—especially from tapes whose quality is often poor—will be, at least to some extent, subjective. Nor can the historian always divine exactly what was in the speaker's mind as he or she spoke. In *Taking Charge,* for example, I had LBJ telling Hubert Humphrey that he didn't want the "farmers" saying he had changed his position on civil rights.[1] Rereading that passage long after the book's publication, I realized that LBJ was actually talking about the "Farmers"—civil rights leaders who shared the views of James Farmer, chief of the Congress of Racial Equality.[2]

As a source revealing a historical moment, the tape of a conversation usually has a towering advantage over a memorandum of the same exchange. Meaning is conveyed through not just language but tone, intensity, pronunciation, pauses, and other aspects of sound. In transforming the conversations from taped sounds into the words that appear in this book, I have tried to render these elements as faithfully as possible.

One obvious issue is dialect. It would be easy to condescendingly render LBJ, with his Hill Country accent (more noticeable when he was in Texas or talking to other Southerners) as some kind of Grand Ole Opry character. Instead, what I have done in the case of Johnson and others who speak with distinctive accents, stresses, or pronunciations is to use italics or show the words phonetically only when these instances are conspicuous or when the more literal rendering adds significant color or meaning. For instance, in this book, only rarely is a "g" dropped from a Johnson participle. As I suggest, to some he says "Negro," to others "Nigro." On rare occasion, he uses the word "nigger." Johnson consistently says "you-all"—not the Alabaman's "y'all" or the Northerner's "you all."

I show in brackets where Johnson and his interlocutors laugh or chuckle. Bracketed adjectives are used to convey the tone of some of the statements heard. Where Johnson or someone else uses incorrect grammar or pronunciation, I usually render it as heard, without adding the interjection "[sic]." If a statement, standing alone, might confuse the reader, I have sometimes included a bracketed word to clarify. I have edited each conversation to exclude extraneous words and repeti-

1. Beschloss, *Taking Charge,* p. 337.
2. If any reader of this book discovers an instance where the transcription falls short, I would be grateful to be contacted about it in care of my publisher, whose address appears at the front of this volume, so that I may correct it in future printings.

tion, but not where they might change the meaning.[1] Ellipses appear where shorter parts of conversations have been pared; a larger break is used for longer deletions.

This book, like *Taking Charge,* also includes excerpts from heretofore unpublished notes and portions of the recordings that Lady Bird Johnson made almost every day of her husband's presidency in order to create a White House diary.[2] As with my first volume, since Mrs. Johnson's tapes have not yet been processed by the Johnson Library, the excerpts from her dictation that appear here come from transcripts created by her staff. I have also drawn in a few cases from heretofore unpublished early drafts of Lyndon Johnson's White House memoirs, *The Vantage Point,* which provide some sidelights on the years 1964 and 1965. As an Appendix, I offer excerpts from a heretofore-unavailable transcript of a tape recording of LBJ, while writing those memoirs, privately reminiscing in August 1969 about his life and career.

1. Words eliminated without indication are usually interjections like "uh," "well," "kind of," but only where the deletion does not change meaning.
2. A fraction of the diary was published as Lady Bird Johnson, *A White House Diary* (Holt, 1971). All diary excerpts appearing in *Reaching for Glory* have never before been published.

CAST OF CHARACTERS

Here are key figures who appear in *Reaching for Glory,* identified by the principal title(s) they held during the period covered in this volume.

Joseph Alsop (1910–1989). Columnist, *Washington Post.*

Clinton Anderson (1895–1975). Democratic Senator from New Mexico.

Robert Anderson (1910–1989). Former Secretary of the Treasury.

Bobby Baker (1928–). Former Secretary to the Majority, U.S. Senate.

George Ball (1909–1994). Under Secretary of State.

Birch Bayh (1928–). Democratic Senator from Indiana.

W. Tapley Bennett (1917–1994). Ambassador to the Dominican Republic.

Hale Boggs (1914–1973). House Majority Whip and Democrat of Louisiana.

Juan Bosch (1909–). Former President of the Dominican Republic.

McGeorge Bundy (1919–1996). Special Assistant to the President for National
    Security Affairs.

William Bundy (1917–2000). Assistant Secretary of State for Far Eastern
    Affairs.

Joseph Califano (1931–). Special Assistant to the President (from July 1965).

Francisco Caamaño Deno (1933–). Dominican rebel leader.

Liz Carpenter (1920–). Press Secretary and Staff Director to the First Lady.

Fidel Castro (1926–). Premier of Cuba.

John Chancellor (1927–1996). Correspondent, NBC News; Director, Voice of
    America (from September 1965).

Frank Church (1924–1984). Democratic Senator from Idaho.

Clark Clifford (1906–1998). Partner, Clifford & Miller, Washington, D.C.

Wilbur Cohen (1913–1987). Under Secretary of Health, Education and
    Welfare.

John Connally (1919–1993). Democratic Governor of Texas.

Thomas Corcoran (1900–1981). Partner, Corcoran, Youngman & Rowe, Washington, D.C.

Richard J. Daley (1902–1976). Democratic Mayor of Chicago.

Charles de Gaulle (1890–1969). President of France.

Cartha "Deke" DeLoach (1920–). Assistant Director, Federal Bureau of Investigation.

Everett Dirksen (1896–1969). Senate Minority Leader, Republican of Illinois.

Anatoly Dobrynin (1919–). Soviet Ambassador to the United States.

James Eastland (1904–1986). Chairman, Senate Judiciary Committee, Democrat of Mississippi.

Dwight D. Eisenhower (1890–1969). Thirty-fourth President of the United States.

Buford Ellington (1907–1972). Director, Office of Emergency Planning.

Billy Sol Estes (1925–). Financier.

Rowland Evans (1921–2001). Syndicated columnist.

Abe Feinberg (1908–). Businessman and Democratic fund-raiser.

Gerald Ford (1913–). House Minority Leader, Republican of Michigan.

Abe Fortas (1910–1982). Partner, Arnold, Fortas & Porter, Washington, D.C.; Associate Justice, U.S. Supreme Court (from October 1965).

J. William Fulbright (1905–1995). Chairman, Senate Foreign Relations Committee, Democrat of Arkansas.

John Kenneth Galbraith (1908–). Professor of Economics, Harvard University.

Arthur Goldberg (1908–1990). Associate Justice, U.S. Supreme Court; Ambassador to the United Nations (from July 1965).

Leonard Goldenson (1905–1999). President, American Broadcasting Companies.

Arthur "Tex" Goldschmidt (1919–2000). Director, Technical Assistance, Special Fund Operations, United Nations.

Barry Goldwater (1909–1998). Republican nominee for President, 1964; Senator from Arizona (until January 1965).

Richard Goodwin (1931–). Presidential speechwriter.

Billy Graham (1918–). Evangelist.

Katharine Graham (1917–2001). President, Washington Post Company.

Ernest Gruening (1887–1974). Democratic Senator from Alaska.

W. Averell Harriman (1891–1986). Under Secretary of State for Political Affairs; Ambassador-at-Large (from March 1965).

Vance Hartke (1919–). Democratic Senator from Indiana.

Wayne Hays (1911–1989). Chairman, House Administration Committee, Democrat of Ohio.

Lister Hill (1894–1984). Democratic Senator from Alabama.

Ho Chi Minh (1890–1969). President, Democratic Republic of Vietnam.

J. Edgar Hoover (1895–1972). Director, Federal Bureau of Investigation.

Hubert Humphrey (1911–1978). Senate Majority Whip; Vice President of the United States (from January 1965).

Walter Jenkins (1918–1985). Special Assistant to the President (until October 1964).

Lady Bird Johnson (1912–). First Lady.

Luci Baines Johnson (1947–). Daughter of Lyndon Johnson.

Lynda Bird Johnson (1944–). Daughter of Lyndon Johnson.

Lyndon Baines Johnson (1908–1973). Thirty-sixth President of the United States.

Nicholas Katzenbach (1922–). Attorney General.

Philip Kazen (1907–1985). Lawyer and Laredo, Texas, Democratic leader.

Edward Kennedy (1932–). Democratic Senator from Massachusetts.

Jacqueline Bouvier Kennedy (1929–1994). Widow of John F. Kennedy.

Robert Kennedy (1925–1968) Democratic Senator from New York (from January 1965).

Nguyen Khanh (1927–). Leader, South Vietnam (until February 1965).

Nikita Khrushchev (1894–1971). Chairman, Council of Ministers, Soviet Union (until October 1964).

Martin Luther King, Jr. (1929–1968). President, Southern Christian Leadership Conference.

Alexei Kosygin (1904–1980). Chairman, Council of Ministers, Soviet Union (from October 1964).

Nguyen Cao Ky (1930–). Premier, South Vietnam (from June 1965).

Mary Lasker (1900–1994). Philanthropist.

Walter Lippmann (1889–1974). Columnist.

Viola Liuzzo (1925–1965). Civil rights worker.

Henry Cabot Lodge, Jr. (1902–1985). Ambassador to South Vietnam (from August 1965).

Russell Long (1918–). Democratic Senator from Louisiana.

John McClellan (1896–1977). Democratic Senator from Arkansas.

John McCone (1902–1991). Director of Central Intelligence Agency (until April 1965).

John McCormack (1891–1980). Speaker of the House, Democrat of Massachusetts.

Gale McGee (1915–1992). Democratic Senator from Wyoming.

George McGovern (1922–). Democratic Senator from South Dakota.

Robert McNamara (1916–). Secretary of Defense.

Richard Maguire (1917–1983). Treasurer, Democratic National Committee.

George Mahon (1900–1985). Democratic Congressman from Texas.

Thomas Mann (1912–). Assistant Secretary of State for Inter-American Affairs; Under Secretary of State for Economic Affairs (from March 1965).

Mike Mansfield (1903–). Senate Majority Leader, Democrat of Montana.

John Bartlow Martin (1915–1987). Former Ambassador to the Dominican Republic.

Marianne Means (1934–). Columnist, Hearst Newspapers.

George Meany (1894–1980). President, AFL-CIO.

William Miller (1914–1983). Republican nominee for Vice President, 1964; Congressman from New York (until January 1965).

Wilbur Mills (1909–1992). Chairman, House Ways and Means Committee, Democrat of Arkansas.

Duong Van "Big" Minh (1916–). Chief of State, South Vietnam (until October 1964).

Thurgood Marshall (1908–1993). Judge, U.S. Court of Appeals; Solicitor General (from August 1965).

Charles Mohr (1929–1989). Correspondent, *New York Times*.

Wayne Morse (1900–1974). Democratic Senator from Oregon.

Bill Moyers (1919–). Special Assistant to the President; Press Secretary to the President (from July 1965).

Richard Nixon (1913–1994). Former Vice President of the United States and Partner, Nixon, Mudge, Rose, Guthrie & Alexander, New York.

Robert Novak (1931–). Syndicated columnist.

Lawrence O'Brien (1917–1990). Special Assistant to the President.

Kenneth O'Donnell (1924–1977). Special Assistant to the President.

Drew Pearson (1897–1969). Columnist.

Lester Pearson (1897–1972). Prime Minister, Canada.

Philip Potter (1907–1988). Washington Bureau Chief, *Baltimore Sun*.

Adam Clayton Powell, Jr. (1908–1972). Chairman, House, Education and Labor Committee, Democrat of New York.

Phan Huy Quat (1909–1979). Premier, South Vietnam (February to June 1965).

William "Red" Raborn (1905–1990). Director of Central Intelligence Agency (from April 1965).

Ronald Reagan (1911–). Actor.

George Reedy (1917--). Press Secretary to the President (until July 1965).

Donald Reid Cabral (1923–). Provisional President, Dominican Republic (until April 1965).

James Reston (1909–1995). Associate Editor and Columnist, *New York Times*.

Walter Reuther (1907–1970). President, United Automobile Workers of America.

Juanita Roberts (1913–1983). Personal Secretary to the President.

Dean Rusk (1909–1994). Secretary of State.

Richard Russell (1897–1971). Chairman, Senate Armed Services Committee and Democrat of Georgia.

Carl Sanders (1925–). Democratic Governor of Georgia.

Arthur Schlesinger, Jr. (1917–). Historian, former Special Assistant to President Kennedy.

Sargent Shriver (1915–). Director, Peace Corps and Office of Economic Opportunity.

Bromley Smith (1911–1987). Executive Secretary, National Security Council.

Robert Spivack (1915–). Columnist, *New York Herald Tribune*.

Frank Stanton (1908–). President, Columbia Broadcasting Company.

Mildred Stegall (1908–). Assistant to Walter Jenkins.

John Stennis (1901–1995). Democratic Senator from Mississippi.

Adlai Stevenson (1900–1965). Democratic nominee for President, 1952 and 1956; Ambassador to the United Nations.

Maxwell Taylor (1901–1987). Ambassador to South Vietnam (until July 1965).

Nguyen Van Thieu (1923–). Chief of State, South Vietnam (from June 1965).

Harry Truman (1884–1972). Thirty-third President of the United States.

Jack Valenti (1921–). Special Assistant to the President.

Cyrus Vance (1917–). Deputy Secretary of Defense.

Jack Hood Vaughn (1920–). Assistant Secretary of State for Inter-American Affairs (from March 1965).

George Wallace (1919–1998). Democratic Governor of Alabama.

Thomas Watson, Jr. (1914–1993). President, International Business Machines.

James Webb (1906–1992). Administrator, National Aeronautics and Space Administration.

Edwin Weisl, Sr. (1896–1972). Partner, Simpson, Thacher & Bartlett, New York.

Elias Wessin y Wessin (1924–). Dominican counterrevolutionary leader.

William Westmoreland (1914–). Commander, U.S. Military Assistance Command, Vietnam.

Earle Wheeler (1908–1975). Chairman, Joint Chiefs of Staff.

Lee White (1923–). Associate Counsel to the President.

William S. White (1905–1994). Syndicated columnist.

Roy Wilkins (1901–1981). Executive Secretary, National Association for the Advancement of Colored People.

Harold Wilson (1916–1995). Prime Minister, Great Britain.

Willard Wirtz (1912–). Secretary of Labor.

Douglas Wynn (1932–). Lawyer and Greenville, Mississippi, Delegate to 1964 Democratic National Convention.

Ralph Yarborough (1903–1996). Democratic Senator from Texas.

APPENDIX

While starting to assemble his White House memoir, *The Vantage Point,* on August 19, 1969, LBJ taped himself during a rambling conversation in his Austin post–presidential office about his life and career with his aides Harry Middleton and Robert Hardesty, who were helping to write the book. When Middleton and Hardesty tried later to tape Johnson, hoping to capture the flavor of his language for the book, he would say, "Turn that thing off." Here are excerpts from the one recorded conversation: [1]

On JFK as presidential campaigner in 1960

Kennedy was pathetic as a Congressman and as a Senator. He didn't know how to address the chair.[2] Kennedy had the squealers who followed him. . . . All of us have had squealers after us—the girls who giggle and the people who are just happy to be with you. But Kennedy was the only one the press saw fit to report on.

On JFK's invitation for LBJ to be Vice President in 1960

I thought it was unthinkable that Kennedy would want me—or that I would want to be on the ticket. . . . I didn't want to be Vice President. . . . I told Kennedy, "If I hadn't given you a good run, they'd say the Catholics put you in."[3] . . . I told Kennedy, "Rayburn is against it and my state will say I ran out on them."[4] Kennedy

---

1. Courtesy of the LBJ Foundation, as are other quotations from the materials used to prepare LBJ's memoirs that appear earlier in this book. According to Harry Middleton, he only rediscovered the transcript, made by him, in the summer of 2001. As of this writing, the tape itself has not been found.

2. Speak on the Senate floor.

3. Meaning that if LBJ had not challenged JFK for the nomination, Kennedy would have been lampooned as the product of Catholic city bosses.

4. LBJ is saying that his mentor, House Speaker Sam Rayburn, opposes his joining the ticket and that Texans would scorn his running with a liberal.

said, "Well, think it over and let's talk about it again." . . . Pretty soon Bobby came in. He said Jack wanted me but wanted me to know that "the liberals will raise hell. . . . Mennen Williams[1] will raise hell." I thought I was dealing with a child. I never did understand Bobby. I never did understand how the press built him into the great figure that he was. He came into public life as McCarthy's counsel and then he was McClellan's counsel[2] and then he tapped Martin Luther King's telephone wire. I said, "Piss on Mennen Williams! . . . The only question is—is it good for the country and good for the Democratic party?" . . . The Vice President is generally like a Texas steer. He's lost his social standing. . . . He's like a stuck pig in a screwing match. Kennedy talked Rayburn into it. . . .He asked him, "Do you want Nixon to be President? He called you a traitor." . . . Rayburn came in . . . and said, "You ought to do it. . . . Nixon will ruin this country in eight years."

On his own Vice Presidency

The Vice President's relationship to a President is like the wife to the husband. You don't tell him off in public. . . . I think Kennedy thought I was autocratic, bossy, self-centered.

Bobby elbowed me out. . . . Many times [President Kennedy] talked to me about the most intimate things one man can discuss with another. He asked me to do things, I'm sure, Bobby didn't approve. . . . On civil rights, I recommended to the President that no savings and loan association or no [federally chartered] bank could continue if they did not make loans for open housing. Bobby called and said, "What are you trying to do? Defeat the President?" We didn't get it in any executive order from Kennedy. But . . . as President, I told civil rights leaders . . . I would try to get Congress to pass it in a bill. And we passed that bill. . . . But the media was so charmed. It was like a rattlesnake charming a rabbit. But I believe men will look back on this era fifteen years or so from now . . . and say, "Okay, how did we do it?"[3]

On the Kennedy-Johnson trip to Texas, November 1963

Yarborough rode with Thomas part of the way, not with us.[4] I didn't care, but the newspaper boys went wild. It was the biggest [story] ever since de Gaulle farted.

---

1. Liberal Michigan Governor.

2. Referring to RFK's onetime service as Senate counsel to the red-baiting Joseph McCarthy and the segregationist John McClellan.

3. In other words, how did civil rights really happen.

4. LBJ refers to his nemesis Texas Senator Ralph Yarborough's refusal to ride in his car the day before the assassination, riding instead with Houston Congressman Albert Thomas.

There were headlines the next morning. . . . I got up early . . . for breakfast.[1] Mrs. Kennedy didn't want to go to that breakfast. Her stomach was just not conditioned to raucous Texans so early in the morning.

Kennedy was . . . in his shorts.[2] . . . He was putting on his shirt, walking around and talking. . . . That was the way he always dressed. He would put on his shorts, and then put on his shirt. . . . I would always dress the other way—put on my shorts, then put on my trousers. I had been raised to cover up that part of me first. . . . He said, "How did you like that about us not taking any time to get ready?"[3] He was looking for a compliment or a laugh about his little witticism. Presidents always look for that kind of thing and people always give it to them.

I was very impressed and very pleased with the crowds [in Dallas]. Then we heard shots. It never occurred to me that it was an assassination or a killing. I just thought it was firecrackers or a car backfiring. . . . The first time I knew that there was anything unusual was when the car lunged. . . . It zoomed. . . . This great big old boy [Rufus Youngblood] from Georgia[4] said, "Down!" And he got on top of me. . . . Youngblood was tougher and better and more intelligent than them all. Not all the Secret Service are sharp. It's always worried me that they weren't. They are the most dedicated and among the most courageous men we've got. But they don't always match that in brains. But the problem is, you pay a man four or five hundred dollars a month and you get just what you pay for. This fellow Kellerman[5] . . . he was about as loyal a man as you could find. But he was about as dumb as an ox. Youngblood put his body on me. . . . When I got . . . out of that car, I had been crushed.

On assuming the Presidency

The greatest bigots in the world are the Democrats on the East Side of New York. Eastland[6] is charitable compared to an eastern bigot. . . . I told Scotty Reston[7] I'd have to do it all in six or eight months: "The eastern media will have the wells so poisoned by that time that that's all the time I have. They'll have us peeing on the fire. . . . I don't think any man from Johnson City, Texas, can survive very long."

---

1. With the Fort Worth Chamber of Commerce.
2. LBJ describes his last private talk with JFK, in Kennedy's suite at the Hotel Texas.
3. During his speech in the hotel parking lot Kennedy had joked that Jacqueline Kennedy took longer to dress than himself and LBJ because she looked "better than we do when she does it."
4. LBJ's Secret Service agent.
5. Roy Kellerman, the agent in JFK's car.
6. Segregationist Mississippi Senator James Eastland.
7. The *New York Times* columnist.

On Vietnam

We started the day after we got back to Washington after Dallas to try to bring peace to Vietnam. We avoided the course this thing took and continued to avoid it until July 1965. At Tonkin Gulf, we got authority from the Congress. Anything we think "necessary." We took that approval from one August to the next August. One year, trying to avoid using it. . . . The enemy is already in Laos. . . . Indonesia might stand, but I doubt it. Ten years from now, we'll be back in the Philippines.[1] And we'll wonder then—didn't we learn anything? People say there's nothing worse than Vietnam. Well, I think there are lots of things worse than Vietnam. World War III would be much worse. The good Lord got me through it without destroying any Russian ships, or Chinese. . . . China and Russia are like two brothers-in-law who don't like each other. One misstep could have kicked off World War III.

They were ruthless people, sure. Ho Chi Minh was. But . . . it was ruthless of the United States government, with our boasted list of freedoms, to condone assassination because you don't approve of a political philosophy.[2] I don't believe that Martin Luther King or Stokely Carmichael[3] should ever be assassinated because somebody disagrees with them. . . . I don't think a proud nation ought to furnish the guns to knock off anybody. That's what our government was party to.[4] . . . Ky[5] gave stability. He had courage. We don't underwrite all the practices of any country. Thieu and Ky emerged as leaders. We brought them about as fast as we dared.[6] . . . I have no reluctance about those two men. When Madame Chennault told them they would get a better deal out of Nixon, they broke faith with me and held back the peace a little while, I think.[7] But I can understand why they did it. They thought this [was] what they would have to live with.

In 1968 . . . I have not the slightest doubt that, if I'd wanted to, I could have been reelected. . . . I would have won over Nixon by a substantial margin. Humphrey started out as the leader of the Green Bay Packers and then he turned around and went in the opposite direction.[8] . . . Chicago[9] hurt. Of course it did.

---

1. Meaning that America would have retreated to the Philippines.
2. LBJ refers to the Kennedy Administration's complicity in the murder of South Vietnamese leader Ngo Dinh Diem in November 1963.
3. Radical champion of black power.
4. LBJ may be alluding to the Kennedy Administration's involvement in assassination plots against Castro.
5. Nguyen Cao Ky, who took power in Saigon in June 1965.
6. LBJ means that he pushed Ky and his partner, Nguyen Van Thieu, toward reform as fast as he felt he could.
7. Just before the 1968 election, acting on Nixon's behalf, Anna Chennault quietly helped to persuade Ky and Thieu to obstruct LBJ's efforts to use a bombing halt to bring peace to Vietnam in hopes of getting a better deal if Nixon were elected.
8. By suggesting at Salt Lake City that he would be more dovish than LBJ on Vietnam.
9. The bloody turmoil over antiwar protesters at the 1968 Democratic convention.

Humphrey believed in everything I believed—until I announced I wouldn't run. . . . He's a wonderful human being, but you can't be all things to all people. Humphrey doesn't like to face cold decisions. Well, neither do I. Neither does anyone. . . . Until July 1965, I tried to keep from going into Vietnam. Nearly 85 percent of the people in the Congress said, "We're not for your poverty program, but we're sure behind you on Vietnam." If I'm the only man left in this country to say, "Aggression must not succeed anywhere in the world," I'll say it. I believe Dulles was right on SEATO.[1] When any outlaw breaks the law, the police ought to come in. Kennedy and Harriman[2] were playing a soft policy in Laos in 1961. The enemy said, "Oh-oh." Diem stood up to them and they killed him. Nixon is buying time. If we get out, it's going to be tragic for this country. . . . If we let them take Asia, they're going to try to take us. . . . I think we ought to have stopped Castro in Cuba. Ike sat on his fanny and let them take it by force. . . . If you let a bully come in and chase you out of your front yard, tomorrow he'll be on your porch, and the next day, he'll rape your wife in your own bed.

On his own mortality

I've never been afraid to die. But I always had horrible memories of my grandmother in a wheelchair all my childhood. Every time I addressed the chair in 1959 and 1960, I wondered if this would be the time when I'd fall over. I just never could be sure when I would be going out. . . . No one can ever understand who was not . . . in the valley of death how you are always conscious of that. . . . I would think, "What if I had a stroke like my grandma did?" And she couldn't even move her hands. I would walk out in the Rose Garden and I would think about it. That was constant with me. All the time.

If you really trust people, there are few who don't reciprocate. Nearly every person in the world is good. Those who are not were messed up by someone. Mrs. Kennedy[3] once told me that she wanted her children to grow up with animals. She felt they would understand people more if they did. If you scratch the head of a bull, he'll cut out his meanness.

I watch the people going into my birthplace, out by my ranch. . . . The women all want their sons to grow up to be Presidents. If they knew a little bit more about the job, I'm not sure they'd feel that way.

In Johnson City, the old men sit out in front on the sidewalk and play dominoes all day long. And one of them, after I became President, said, "Old Lyndon sure has moved up in the world, hasn't he?" And the other one said, "Yeah, up the road about a half a mile."

---

1. John Foster Dulles, pledging Saigon's defense under the SEATO treaty.
2. Assistant Secretary of State W. Averell Harriman.
3. Jacqueline Kennedy.

ACKNOWLEDGMENTS

This book is dedicated to James MacGregor Burns, who has been my teacher and friend for twenty-seven years. When I was a senior at Andover, my headmaster, Theodore Sizer, told me that if I really wanted to become a historian of the presidency, I should go to Williams College and study under Jim Burns. Beginning when I was a sophomore, Jim took me on as almost an apprentice. I learned to do historical research while working on his books and benefited from his close guidance while writing my senior honors thesis on the relationship between Franklin Roosevelt and Joseph Kennedy, which became my own first book.

We used to talk a lot about Lyndon Johnson. Although a Massachusetts Kennedy man, Jim had admired LBJ for attacking the congressional provincialism he denounced in his 1963 book *The Deadlock of Democracy*.[1] He was one of the liberal academics whose support Johnson solicited during long conversations at the White House. As my teacher, he predicted that I would someday want to write on LBJ. He said Johnson would be a tantalizing problem for historians my age, as we weighed his performance in Vietnam and his domestic record. That work would require decades of hindsight and illuminating new sources. Neither of us could have known that LBJ had taped almost ten thousand of his private conversations—or that, by the 1990s, these tapes would start to be released.

One piece of advice Jim gave me was a misfire. "If you ever write about LBJ," he said, "you'd better prepare yourself for the fact that this was one of the most boring men who ever lived." Jim felt this way, I realized while working on this trilogy, because the side of his personality that Johnson strained to show him was what he thought a New England professor would like—preacherly, stilted, devoid

---

1. Prentice-Hall, 1963. Unknown to Jim at the time, the new President Johnson cited his book while prodding Republicans to move on his program. By telephone LBJ congratulated Congressman Gerald Ford for staying in Washington for Thanksgiving: "Thank God there's somebody in town! I was getting ready to tell MacGregor Burns he's right about the Congress—they couldn't function." (See Beschloss, *Taking Charge,* pp. 46, 64).

of the bluntness, stories, and imperishable language that bursts out of the Johnson of the tapes.

I first went to the Johnson Library when I was twenty-two and had the pleasure of lunching with its courtly chief, Harry Middleton. Harry is the Joe DiMaggio of presidential library directors. By his account, when he took the job in 1970, LBJ told him, "I suppose you think that if I pick up the paper one day and read about something in these files I don't like, I'll raise hell." Harry admitted that this thought had occurred to him. Johnson said if it ever happened, Harry should tell him, "Mr. President, one of us is full of shit and we've got to decide right now who it is." [1]

Harry often cites that conversation to justify his eagerness to open the record of the Johnson presidency as widely and fast as possible. The best example of this is his decision, with the consent of Lady Bird and others in the Johnson entourage, to process and open LBJ's secret tapes, despite the former President's request just before he died in 1973 that the tapes be sealed for fifty years after his death and, after that, possibly destroyed.[2] As this second volume on those tapes is published, Harry is retiring as director of the library he did so much to build. Happily he will remain at the LBJ Foundation. Part of Harry's legacy is the superb staff of the Johnson Library. I thank Patrick Borders, Tina Houston, Linda Seelke, Claudia Anderson, Regina Greenwell, Philip Scott, and their colleagues for their help on this project.

Lady Bird Johnson kindly gave me permission to read and quote from the unpublished portions of her tape-recorded diary. Tom Johnson and his LBJ Foundation colleagues gave me similar authority to read and quote from unpublished material that former President Johnson created and used while writing his memoirs. In both cases permission was granted without restriction or obligation. As with *Taking Charge,* no portion or version of this book will have been shown to any member of the Johnson family or the Johnson circle before publication.

The indefatigable, shrewd, and diplomatic Michael Hill helped me to research the context of the conversations in this book and aided me in countless other ways. Cherryl Maddox, Rebecca Purdy, and Maryam Mashayekhi provided invaluable research, transcription, and administrative help as I listened to the tapes over and over and over again. My friend and literary agent Esther Newberg was her usual enthusiastic and sagacious self, enhancing the experience of research, writing, and publication. I also thank her colleagues Jack Horner, John DeLaney, Karen Gerwin, Judith Schell, and Liz Farrell.

Reaching for Glory is my second book with Alice Mayhew, who again brought to bear her fierce intelligence and mastery of postwar America. Had Alice taken

---

1. Harry Middleton, *LBJ* (Abrams, 1990), p. 261.
2. See Beschloss, *Taking Charge,* pp. 547, 550–51.

another path in life, she would have been an excellent historian, but she contributes just as much or more to our profession by editing so many history books of quality. Roger Labrie shepherded this book through to publication, as he did its predecessor, with sensitivity and aplomb. I have also benefited from the high expertise and support of Jonathan Newcomb, Jack Romanos, Carolyn Reidy, David Rosenthal, Victoria Meyer, Aileen Boyle, Nancy Inglis, Jeanette Olender, Michael Accordino, Jonathan Jao, and their colleagues at Simon & Schuster, as well as Susan M. S. Brown, who copyedited the manuscript.

I owe much to the scholars, journalists, and memoirists who have written on Lyndon Johnson and his times. Every historian stands on the shoulders of those who have gone before. This may be even more true in the case of a scholar trying to analyze a new collection of primary sources—in this case, tape recordings—and assess how they change what we knew before.

Above all, I thank my wife, Afsaneh Mashayekhi Beschloss, and our two sons, Alexander and Cyrus, who are seven and five this year, for their unstinting support and for putting up with my absorption in an era that the two boys consider as remote as that of the dinosaurs. This necessity was somewhat mitigated by their opportunity to learn about Texas. Lyndon Johnson may be many things to Americans, but to our sons he is bucking broncos, cactus, and armadillos.

Michael Beschloss
Washington, D.C.
August 2001

INDEX

451

PHOTO CREDITS